Language and Literacy in Roman Judaea

THE ANCHOR YALE BIBLE REFERENCE LIBRARY is a project of international and interfaith scope in which Protestant, Catholic, and Jewish scholars from many countries contribute individual volumes. The project is not sponsored by any ecclesiastical organization and is not intended to reflect any particular theological doctrine.

The series is committed to producing volumes in the tradition established half a century ago by the founders of the Anchor Bible, William Foxwell Albright and David Noel Freedman. It aims to present the best contemporary scholarship in a way that is accessible not only to scholars, but also to the educated nonspecialist. It is committed to work of sound philological and historical scholarship, supplemented by insight from modern methods, such as sociological and literary criticism.

John J. Collins
General Editor

THE ANCHOR YALE BIBLE REFERENCE LIBRARY

Language and Literacy in Roman Judaea

A Study of the Bar Kokhba Documents

MICHAEL OWEN WISE

Yale
UNIVERSITY
PRESS

NEW HAVEN
AND
LONDON

Yale University Press books may be purchased in quantity for educational, business, or promotional use. For information, please e-mail sales.press@yale.edu (U.S. office) or sales@yaleup.co.uk (U.K. office).

Printed in the United States of America.

Library of Congress Cataloging-in-Publication Data

Wise, Michael Owen, 1954–
Language and literacy in Roman Judaea : a study of the Bar Kokhba documents / Michael Owen Wise.—1st edition.
pages cm.—(The Anchor Yale Bible reference library)
Includes bibliographical references and index.
ISBN 978-0-300-20453-7 (alk. paper)
1. Literacy—Palestine—History. 2. Language and culture—Palestine. 3. Jews—Palestine—Intellectual life. 4. Judaea, Wilderness of—Antiquities. 5. Bar Kokhba, –135. I. Title.
LC157.P35W57 2015 302.2'244095694—dc23 2014037410

A catalogue record for this book is available from the British Library.

This paper meets the requirements of ANSI/NISO Z39.48–1992 (Permanence of Paper).

10 9 8 7 6 5 4 3 2 1

Dedicated to James Alan Wise†
Little brother, best friend

Accept for now these things, final gifts of an ancient custom given,
sad of duty and wet with a brother's tears.
—Catullus

Contents

Acknowledgments

When I first began graduate study of the ancient Near East at the University of Chicago years ago, wonderful as that opportunity proved, it also meant closing the door to the classics and especially to Greek literature, my first academic love. This was a love born of such as James Allen's *First Year of Greek*, of Plato and Herodotus and Candaules, the man who fell in love with his own wife. I always hoped that one day it would become possible to go back and push that door open again. Some years ago the opportunity did present itself, and I entered a second doctoral program, this time at the University of Minnesota.

There I found a place of academic rigor combined with nurture and unquestionable goodwill directed toward the students. I was taught well by able and distinguished faculty who had invested their lives studying Greek and Latin literature and attendant fields. I found with them and with my fellow students what I sought: not merely the text, but fellowship around the text. It is a pleasure to record my deep gratitude to the department and especially to Doug Olson, Betty Belfiore, Chris Nappa, Phil Sellew, and Nita Krevans, and most particularly to George Sheets, my principal instructor. George taught me much about classical philology and Latin literature and became a good friend as well as my dissertation advisor. The present book grew out of that dissertation and so owes much to George and his mind, which grinds very fine indeed.

Others at my own institution, the University of Northwestern–St. Paul, aided and encouraged this project. Boyd Seevers displayed an unflagging interest in the matters under discussion and offered helpful ideas regarding the geography of the Bar Kokhba finds based on his intimate familiarity with the land in which he lived long himself. Walter Schultz read portions of the manuscript and discussed them with me after passing the pages beneath his philosopher's flaw-magnifying logic. Our statistician Jonathan Zderad read and critiqued the first and final chapters and generously offered his expertise when the needs of the argument outran mine. My department of Biblical & Theological Studies bore without complaint the burden of my absences and the extra committee work it meant for them. The academic administration helped me decidedly with release time and financial support. Thank you all!

Other friends and colleagues in the academy buoyed me with their encouragement and helpful observations. I include Marty Abegg, Jr., Ed Cook, Andrea Berlin, Alex Jassen, and Jim VanderKam here. I also include the anonymous reader of the first portion of Chapter 2, which appeared with his or her improvements as "Murabbaat and the First Revolt" in the Festschrift for my first *Doktorvater*, Norman Golb (*Pesher Nahum: Texts and Studies in Jewish History and Literature from Antiquity Through the Middle Ages Presented to Norman* [*Nahum*] *Golb* [2012]). One of the volume's editors, Michael Wechsler, aided in solving certain technical issues with that submission that proved of enduring worth to this parent project. Norman himself first taught me to read the Bar Kokhba texts with their cursive and exceedingly cursive scripts and brought me into contact with the period of Jewish history that gave them birth. To each one named, a warmly heartfelt thanks.

My sister, Victoria Pryce, who was always supposed to be the writer in the family, read and commented on portions with her exquisite sensitivity to language. My mother, Imogen Wise, the most widely read person of my actual acquaintance, also read and discussed the book with me while she was still with us. My Timothy in this project has been Matt Selby. He has invested countless hours assisting me on everything from the cartography to dealing with recalcitrant fonts never intended to operate with Macs. Over these past years he has matured before my eyes; once a callow student of Greek and Latin, now he works beside me as my research assistant and goes home to Anna and David, with another on the way. He may have read this manuscript more times than I have myself. I would be proud to call him my son. Vicki, Mom, Matt: thanks!

Every scholar is well aware that in almost any area of research we enter as grasshoppers a land formerly (and sometimes presently) indwelt by Anakim. I have profited from the prior insights of crowds of others, and I hope that the depth of my indebtedness will properly be made clear by the copious notes appended to this study. Even so, it seems right that I underscore from the outset that this study would not have been possible without the diverse and magisterial contributions of J. T. Milik, Ada Yardeni, Hannah Cotton, Tal Ilan, and Hanan Eshel. A glance at virtually any page of this book will illustrate the truth of this statement. Perhaps "thank you" is not really the proper expression here, but surely admiration is.

Speaking of admiration, it has been my profound pleasure to work with the professionals at Yale University Press. This has not been an easy manuscript to get into shape, but they have met the challenge. A special shout-out to Jennifer Banks, Susan Laity, Heather Gold, and Jessie Dolch. One of the anonymous readers employed by the press offered concrete suggestions for Chapters 1 and 5 that I was happy to accept. John Collins, the general editor of the series, initially agreed to look at the manuscript simply as a friend. After a bit he encouraged me to submit it for consideration as a part of the Anchor Yale Bible Reference Library. That the book exists as such, I owe to him first of all. Once again, thank you all.

Ever since we first met early in the most glorious Chicago fall in living memory, my work has had special purpose because of my wife, Cathy. Without her, there simply would be no point. Once again she has read and discussed and critiqued and structured, always with a smile and always with a sparkle in her ridiculously big blue eyes. I realize now that I will never figure out what I did to deserve her, but at least I am smart enough to understand this: her presence in my life is proof of the reality of grace.

In most families, my experience suggests, there is one person who stands at the center and attracts and properly orders all the others. Without that person, gravity gives way. In our family that center was James Alan Wise. We called him Jamie. From our childhood we were best friends, and we used to talk about buying land and building a sort of compound where we would live with our wives and children and nieces and nephews and grandchildren and dogs and maybe even a turtle or two. That was supposed to happen when we got old. Alas, it will never be. We do not grieve as those without hope, but we do grieve—and endlessly remember.

I dedicate this book to Jamie.

Abbreviations

Primary and Secondary Sources

Aeg	*Aegyptus*
Ag. Ap.	Josephus, *Against Apion*
A.J.	Josephus, *Antiquitates judaicae*
AJP	*American Journal of Philology*
APF	*Archiv für Papyrusforschung*
BA	*Biblical Archaeologist*
BAR	*Biblical Archaeology Review*
BASOR	*Bulletin of the American Schools of Oriental Research*
BASP	*Bulletin of the American Society of Papyrologists*
BDAG	Bauer, W., F. W. Danker, W. F. Arndt, and F. W. Gingrich. *Greek-English Lexicon of the New Testament and Other Early Christian Literature.* 3rd ed. Chicago: University of Chicago Press, 1999.
Bib	*Biblica*
B.J.	Josephus, *Bellum judaicum*
BJRL	*Bulletin of the John Rylands University Library of Manchester*
BMAP	*Brooklyn Museum Aramaic Papyri*
BO	*Bibliotheca orientalis*
CAP	Cowley, A. E. *Aramaic Papyri of the Fifth Century B.C.* Oxford: Oxford University Press, 1923.
CB	*Cultura biblica*
CBQ	*Catholic Biblical Quarterly*
CD	Damascus Document

CGFP	*Comicorum Graecorum fragmenta in papyris reperta.* Edited by Colinus Austin. Berlin: Walter de Gruyter, 1973.
CHCL 2	*The Cambridge History of Classical Literature 2: Latin Literature.* Edited by E. J. Kenney and William V. Clausen. Cambridge: Cambridge University Press, 1982.
CHJ	*Cambridge History of Judaism.* Edited by W. D. Davies and Louis Finkelstein. Cambridge: Cambridge University Press, 1984–.
ChrEg	*Chronique d'Egypte*
CIIP	Hannah M. Cotton, et al. *Corpus Inscriptionum Iudaeae/Palaestinae: A Multi-lingual Corpus of the Inscriptions from Alexander to Muhammad. Volume I: Jerusalem. Part 1: 1–704.* Berlin: De Gruyter, 2010.
CJ	*Classical Journal*
CP	*Classical Philology*
CPJ	*Corpus papyrorum judaicorum.* Edited by V. Tcherikover. 3 vols. Cambridge, 1957–1964.
CQ	*Classical Quarterly*
CR	*Classical Review*
CRAIBL	*Comptes rendus de l'Académie des Inscriptions et Belles-lettres*
CRINT	Compendia rerum iudaicarum ad Novum Testamentum
CW	*Classical World*
DCH	*Dictionary of Classical Hebrew.* Edited by D. J. A. Clines. Sheffield, 1993–.
DEJ	*The Eerdmans Dictionary of Early Judaism.* Edited by John J. Collins and Daniel C. Harlow. Grand Rapids, Mich.: Eerdmans, 2010.
DISO^2	*Dictionnaire des inscriptions sémitiques de l'ouest.* Edited by Ch. F. Jean and J. Hoftijzer. 2nd ed. Leiden, 1995.
DJD	Discoveries in the Judaean Desert

DSD	*Dead Sea Discoveries*
EDSS	*Encyclopedia of the Dead Sea Scrolls*. Edited by Lawrence H. Schiffman and James C. VanderKam. 2 vols. Oxford: Oxford University Press, 2000.
EHR	*The English Historical Review*
EI	*Eretz Israel*
GR	*Greece and Rome*
GRBS	*Greek, Roman, and Byzantine Studies*
HALOT	Koehler, L., W. Baumgartner, and J. J. Stamm. *The Hebrew and Aramaic Lexicon of the Old Testament.* Translated and edited under the supervision of M. E. J. Richardson. 4 vols. Leiden, 1994–1999.
HibJ	*Hibbert Journal*
HS	*Hebrew Studies*
HTR	*Harvard Theological Review*
HUCA	*Hebrew Union College Annual*
IEJ	*Israel Exploration Journal*
JANES	*Journal of the Ancient Near Eastern Society*
JAOS	*Journal of the American Oriental Society*
JBL	*Journal of Biblical Literature*
JDS	Judean Desert Studies
JEA	*Journal of Egyptian Archaeology*
JEOL	*Jaarbericht van het Vooraziatisch-Egyptisch Gezelschap (Genootschap) Ex oriente lux*
JHS	*Journal of Hellenic Studies*
JJP	*Journal of Juristic Papyrology*
JJS	*Journal of Jewish Studies*
JQR	*Jewish Quarterly Review*
JR	*Journal of Religion*
JRA	*Journal of Roman Archaeology*
JRS	*Journal of Roman Studies*
JSNT	*Journal for the Study of the New Testament*
JSOT	*Journal for the Study of the Old Testament*
JSS	*Journal of Semitic Studies*

JTS	*Journal of Theological Studies*
LASBF	*Liber annuus Studii biblici franciscani*
LCL	Loeb Classical Library
LSJ	Liddell, H. G., R. Scott, H. S. Jones. *A Greek-English Lexicon*. 9th ed. with revised supplement. Oxford, 1996.
Mnemos.	*Mnemosyne*
NT	*Novum Testamentum*
NTS	*New Testament Studies*
NTT	*Norsk Teologisk Tidsskrift*
P&P	*Past and Present*
PEQ	*Palestine Exploration Quarterly*
RB	*Revue biblique*
Rev. Ét. Lat.	*Revue des études latines*
RevQ	*Revue de Qumran*
SBFLA	*Studii biblici Franciscani liber annus*
SBLSP	Society of Biblical Literature Seminar Papers
ScrHier	*Scripta hierosolymitana*
Sem	*Semitica*
STK	*Svensk teologisk kvartalskrift*
VT	*Vetus Testamentum*
VTSup	Supplements to Vetus Testamentum
WZKM	*Weiner Zeitschrift für die Kunde des Morgenlandes*
ZDMG	*Zeitschrift der deutschen morgenländischen Gesellschaft*
ZNW	*Zeitschrift für die neutestamentliche Wissenschaft und die Kunde der älteren Kirche*
ZPE	*Zeitschrift für Papyrologie und Epigraphik*

Additional Abbreviations

ABH	Archaic Biblical Hebrew
BA	Biblical Aramaic
BH	Biblical Hebrew
EBH	Early Biblical Hebrew

LBH	Late Biblical Hebrew
LXX	Septuagint
Mas	Masada
MH	Mishnaic Hebrew
MT	Masoretic Text
Mur	Murabba'at
NEB	New English Bible
PN	Proper name
QA	Qumran Aramaic
QH	Qumran Hebrew
SBH	Standard Biblical Hebrew
SLA	Standard Literary Aramaic

Qumran, rabbinic, and classical literary works are not fully explicated in this list. Abbreviations for these works follow standard scholarly protocols. Qumran and rabbinic works may be found in the Society of Biblical Literature *Handbook of Style*. Classical (Greek and Latin) abbreviations in this book follow the listing found in *The Oxford Classical Dictionary* (3rd ed.).

1 *Status Quaestionum* and the Present Study

A Day in En Gedi During the Second Jewish Revolt

Late in the year 132 C.E., apparently fueled in part by desperation regarding the restoration of the Temple in Jerusalem, lying now in ruins for more than half a century, the Jews of Judaea rose against Rome and the emperor Hadrian. Some time passed before Hadrian realized the seriousness of the challenge, which spread beyond Judaea to regions north and east: Roman control of the eastern empire was at risk. Losses at the outset were enormous and sparked emergency measures. Soldiers were conscripted in the provinces, including Britain and both Eastern and Western Europe, and even—rare for that time—Italy itself.[1] Additional armies were raised in Asia Minor. Military diplomas show that thousands of seamen of the *Classis Misenensis* found themselves transferred to the legions in Judaea in 133–134. As many as twelve or thirteen legions may ultimately have come to be involved, and failures of Roman generalship required that Julius Severus, the most capable general the Romans possessed, be rushed from Britain to rescue the situation.

Ultimately, the Romans prevailed, history tells us, but it was a Pyrrhic victory. Unlike the First Jewish Revolt, no *Judaea capta* victory coins memorialized this affair. True, in 136 the emperor accepted the title of *imperator II* and conferred *ornamenta triumphalia* on three Roman generals: Severus; Poblicius Marcellus, erstwhile governor of Syria; and Haterius Nepos, governor of Arabia in 130–131. But his announcement to the Roman senate of the war's end pointedly omitted the traditional statement: *Si vos liberique vestri valetis, bene est; nos exercitusque nostri valemus* (If you and your children are well, it is good; we and our army are well) (so Cassius Dio). They were not, in fact, well. No one was.

The insurgents evidently exterminated at least one legion, the Legio XXII Deotariana, attested for the last time in 119 C.E. According to Dio, the Jews suffered the razing of 985 settlements and the deaths of 580,000 guerrilla soldiers, with untold additional women, children, and old men lost as well. These numbers are perhaps more accurate than most such ancient tallies, being derived from provincial census figures and Hadrian's report to the senate. It is likely that 70 percent of the Judaean population perished in a veritable genocide. Not a single village or town known to have existed at that time and thus far excavated lacks archaeological evidence of destruction. So devastating was the war to the Jews that the center of their civilization shifted permanently, coming to reside in the near term in the regions of Sepphoris, Tiberias, and the Galilee. The Temple was never rebuilt. Nearly two millennia would pass before Jerusalem again came under Jewish dominion. As for the Romans, no plunder issued from ravaged Judaea to reward the surviving war-weary soldiers. Taxes and other revenues ceased for at least two generations. As a culminating punitive act, Hadrian erased Judaea from memory, renaming the province Syria-Palestina, metaphorically revivifying the dead bones of the archetypal ancient enemies of the Jews, the Philistines.[2]

Thus the bigger picture. Still, in the midst of this horrific drama, Judaean life went on as usual much of the time in various places, until nearly the end. One day in early November of 134, nine men gathered in a scribal shop in En Gedi, a "very large village of Jews" situated on the western shore of the Dead Sea.[3] The participants included some of the leaders of the revolt. Within a year, most would be dead. Yet that day their thoughts were far from war, focused on entirely mundane matters. Precisely that is what makes the occasion interesting.

For on ordinary occasions people do what they usually do. They perform the little tasks. They engage in the quotidian behaviors and everyday human interactions, the "ordinary things" that constitute the warp and woof of life as we experience it. Hence, if we would truly understand the lives of these people, it is the ordinary that we want to examine. Here, we are interested in the more or less ordinary document that they had gathered to compose, known to us as *Papyrus Yadin* 44 (henceforth *P.Yadin* 44).[4]

This was an agreement reapportioning land that two of them, partners, had leased some time earlier from Jonathan b. Mahanaim, a civil administrator (Hebrew, פרנס) of En Gedi.[5] On that day in the scribal shop, the land was to be subdivided between two partnerships comprising four of the men in the room: on the one hand, the original partnership, Eleazar b. Eleazar b. Hita, scion of a prominent En Gedi family, with his partner Eleazar b. Samuel, who would ultimately be responsible for the actions that ensured the lease's survival to our own time; and on the other, two Jews from a Nabataean village, Mahoz Eglatain, located on the southeastern shore of the Dead Sea.[6] Like numerous others of their kinsmen, since the outbreak of the revolt three years earlier these two had relocated to Jewish territory and were now residing in En Gedi. They were Tehinah b. Simon, the scribe of three Greek documents that have come down to us wherein he describes himself as a *librarius,* and his partner Alema b. Judah.

The scribe the partners had engaged for this occasion, Joseph b. Simon, began to compose the contract: "On the 28th of Marheshvan in the third year of Simon b. Kosiba, Premier of Israel, in En Gedi." Departing from centuries of legal custom in the region, he did not inscribe the papyrus in a dialect of Aramaic. Rather, the words flowing from his stylus were an idiomatic Hebrew, of a kind notably different from that of the Jewish scriptures. Moreover, rather than indite the document in a cursive script of the sort characteristic of documentary texts, as he wrote he carefully formed each letter with a gorgeous, calligraphic bookhand, many letters ornamented with the tittles of Matthean fame.

The words that Joseph set down represented a discussion that had already taken place, whether in Hebrew, Aramaic, or perhaps Greek we cannot know, although that is an important question. The document itself was constitutive of the leasing agreement being made. That is, it did not merely describe what had previously been agreed; rather, in itself it was the agreement. For this reason the signatures of principals and witnesses—of all the men gathered—were of the essence.[7]

When he finished composing the contract, Joseph passed the stylus to Eleazar b. Eleazar. Grasping the pen with an evidently uncertain grip, Eleazar began to write: "Eleazar b. Eleazar hereby (witnesses) concerning himself."[8] The letters he drew—and that is the proper verb; he did not so much write as draw—contrasted sharply with the beautiful forms Joseph had set down on the papyrus. Eleazar's were crooked, ungainly, and disproportionate—from a modern perspective, akin to a child's writing. These letters bring to mind the lines from the *Pseudolus: An, opsecro hercle, habent quas gallinae manus? Nam has quidem gallina scripsit* (Or, by Hercules, do hens have hands of some sort? For certainly a hen wrote these letters).[9] (The young man Calidorus has received a letter from his love, the flute-player Phoenicium, written in a very uncertain hand). Eleazar was a "slow writer" (βραδέως γράφων), an expression drawn from much better attested contemporary Egyptian Greek documents.[10] There on occasion the term explicitly attached to a person on the lowest rung of literacy, only just able to inscribe his or her name, in some danger of slipping off that rung back into illiteracy. Eleazar was clearly not accustomed to doing much writing. Nevertheless, he inscribed his agreement in Hebrew, using the proper term for son, *ben,* rather than the Aramaic *bar,* and using proper Hebrew orthography and morphology (על נפשו).

Now it was the turn of Eleazar's partner Eleazar b. Samuel to sign. But he did not. Instead, another man stretched out his hand to receive the reed pen, Masabala b. Simon. Masabala was a man about whom, relatively speaking, we know a considerable amount. One of the current military commanders of En Gedi, Masabala was also the issuing official for the document being prepared. The text stated in line 16 that it was being issued "on my terms" (על אסרי), referring to his presence.[11] A man of perfervid revolutionary spirit, Masabala was co-addressee of numerous letters from the leader of the revolt, Simon b. Kosiba, better known to history as Bar Kokhba. Cached for safekeeping in a cave from which they were never reclaimed, these letters survived to our own time to be discovered by the 1960 expedition to that cave led by Yigael Yadin.[12] They form the basis for much of what we know about Masabala.

Brandishing the pen with sure fingers, Masabala wrote in Hebrew, but not with a calligraphic bookhand as had Joseph. Rather, his rapid strokes produced a fluid documentary hand: "Eleazar b. Samuel hereby (witnesses) concerning himself; Masabala b. Simon wrote at his request" ([מ]רצונו).[13] Masabala was acting as an amanuensis or *hypographeus* (ὑπογραφεύς) for Eleazar b. Samuel. Again, this was a customary term used explicitly in the legal setting of contemporary Egypt,[14] and one convenient for our use as well (although, as we shall see later, it might be argued that the more precise term for Palestine would be *cheirochrestes,* χειροχρήστης). Masabala was almost certainly the brother of Joseph, scribe of the text, and—to judge from both his hand and his actions—a scribe himself. Likely, it was in Masabala's family scribal shop that the men were assembled.

Next the second group of principals, beginning with Tehinah, moved to affix their signatures, though in fact neither actually signed. Both employed *hypographeis.* Initially, it may seem surprising that Tehinah did not sign; after all, was he not formerly employed as an official scribe of Greek documents in Mahoza? Tehinah could have signed in Greek or, presumably, Aramaic. For legal, ideological, or perhaps personal reasons, however, he chose not to sign. He was almost certainly present, not using an agent, for that was expected of the principals to such leases. Moreover, the wording ("at his dictation," מאמרו) strongly implies his physical presence at the signing. Siphon b. Simon, to judge from the patronym and his role, another scribe belonging to the family of Joseph and Masabala, wrote for him: "Tehinah b. Simon hereby (witnesses) concerning himself; Siphon b. Simon wrote at his dictation." As had Joseph, Siphon inscribed his words in a calligraphic bookhand.

As Alema could not sign, the pen next passed to Joseph, the text's scribe, who wrote with smaller but still markedly gorgeous letters in Hebrew, "Alema b. Judah hereby (witnesses) concerning himself; Joseph b. Simon wrote at his dictation." It was not because the text was in Hebrew that Alema did not sign it. He was unable to sign at all. Otherwise, he would have signed in another language that he did know, probably Aramaic, as his brother Eleazar was about to do. Alema was entirely illiterate: no writing, no reading. For as we shall see, if a person in ancient Judaea could not sign his or her name, normally he or she could not read either. On such a legal occasion as he now found himself, Alema was vulnerable to the literates' sense of ethics, having no way of being certain that the contents of the contract as actually written conformed to what he had orally agreed to perform—thus the safeguard of his literate brother's role as witness.

Before Eleazar b. Judah inscribed his name, however, Judah b. Joseph signed as the first witness. His small, perfectly formed letters betrayed a trained scribe used to producing book scrolls. He wrote in Hebrew "Judah b. Joseph hereby witnesses." Presumably, the Joseph of Judah's patronym was the now familiar Joseph, principal scribe. If so, then Judah was the fourth person of the same scribal family to participate in creating this contract.

Now Alema's brother Eleazar signed. His was a documentary cursive hand, experienced but clearly less expert than a scribe's. Unlike all the other signatories, he wrote in Aramaic, not Hebrew: אלעזר בר יהודה שהד, "Eleazar b. Judah hereby witnesses."[15] The stylus then circulated to the third and final witness, one Simon b. Joseph.

With a florid scribal cursive Simon affixed his signature in Hebrew: "Simon b. Joseph hereby witnesses." A much smaller, equally graceful cursive hand (Joseph, departing from his earlier calligraphy?) later added three words alongside Simon's signature. The words are quietly dramatic: "he went up from Bethar" (עלא מן ביתר). Bethar was the village location of the fort where, according to rabbinic tradition, the final battle of the Second Revolt culminated in utter defeat for the Jewish cause, witnessing the deaths or enslavement of Bar Kokhba and all the freedom fighters at his side. For official, business, or personal reasons Simon had traveled from Bethar to En Gedi, where he now found himself drafted to help with the lease. Why was he drafted? We cannot really know, of course, but it is reasonable to suggest that it was because he both knew Hebrew and, as a scribe, wrote easily. As with all the scribal participants, Simon would have received a proportionate fee for his services, and so for him it was a chance to earn a little money. The notation of his alien provenance would make it possible to find him if the contract should ever come under legal challenge and the witnesses were needed to testify.

On completion, *P.Yadin* 44 was ephemeral no less than most other such documents, of real interest to the principals alone. Much more fleetingly would it have engaged the scribes and witnesses, the other six gathered that day. Only two thousand years later—participants long since dust, property erased from memory, everything described impossible to locate—has this lease attracted broader interest. Decency may compel a moment's pause in the face of this irony. These were real people, after all, not just names; learning to know them just a little is undeniably an aspect of the contract's newly garnered interest.

Romance and the human dimension duly noted, attention centers on the contract's presumed typicality, especially on the variety of linguistic behaviors it witnesses as typical—or possibly, study may show, as atypical. Questions are many. Why, for instance, was the lease written in Hebrew, since we "know" that Aramaic was the usual language of written legal discourse? And why was the body composed in a calligraphic bookhand, when we "know" that cursive or extremely cursive documentary hands were usual for such? Why did the witnesses and subscribers behave as they did? More precisely, why did all of the signatories but one, Eleazar b. Judah, sign in Hebrew—merely an arbitrary decision for each? And why did some signatures mirror the body's calligraphic refinement, whereas others used everyday cursive forms? More broadly, what did all of these behaviors signify in the multilingual social milieu that surrounded these men that day? What evidence for issues of ancient Judaean language patterns, for literacy and illiteracy, do the body of the contract, the various subscriptions, and the signatures respectively constitute?

Pursuit of a study that would hope to address these and related questions calls first for a measure of contextual understanding. Thus follows a brief résumé of current consensus on Judaean languages, literacy, and selected collateral issues in late Second Temple times, and how they came to be formed.

Language Patterns in Roman Judaea

Most scholars today would agree that Judaeans in the first century C.E. and the first third of the second century were a trilingual society, using Hebrew, Aramaic, and Greek. Beneath the surface of this apparently straightforward statement, however, lie disputed nuances and contested details, substantial questioning and fractious uncertainty. Moreover, in the past generation or two, opinions have shifted notably.

Before the discoveries between 1945 and 1965 of the Dead Sea Scrolls and documentary materials in the Judaean Desert, scholars had thought the situation well understood. If one were to survey the consensus in say, 1920, something like the following characterization of conditions would emerge. Aramaic was the dominant language for daily life. Hebrew had long since given way before its cognate, and by the time of Jesus—usually the focus for such discussions in older scholarship—only a small minority of the population any longer knew the *sermo patrius,* its use being confined to liturgical and sacral contexts.[16] In the contest of languages, Greek was thought by most to run a poor third, attractive mostly to aristocrats and those rare other individuals with pretensions of membership in the broader Greco-Roman world. The Jews as a whole, it was said, were an insular race, opposed to Hellenistic ways of thinking and doing, obsessed with their ancient Law—which, however, odd as it may seem for a people so obsessed, most could read only in translation.

For Biblical Hebrew was now a learned tongue, possessed by the educated alone, by definition an elite. The situation was roughly analogous to medieval Europe and its use of Latin. Mishnaic or Tannaitic Hebrew, when it was acknowledged at all by scholars of that time, was portrayed as a sort of scholarly construct, a *Mischsprache* compounded of elements taken here from Biblical Hebrew, there from vernacular Aramaic. None but scholars were said to speak this artificial tongue, repairing to it for rabbinic ratiocinations. Indeed, Gustav Dalman, famed Aramaist and one of the most influential scholars in crafting and disseminating this view of matters, regarded the very existence of Mishnaic Hebrew as proof that Aramaic was the Jewish vernacular: "The syntax and the vocabulary of the Hebrew of the Mishna[h] . . . prove themselves to be the creation of Jews who thought in Aramaic."[17]

After expounding the significant evidence that he found for the use of Aramaic in the Palestine of Jesus's day—oral translation of biblical texts into Aramaic in the synagogues, the practice later giving birth to the written Targumim; Aramaic terms for people and central institutions used in the New Testament and the writings of Josephus, and Aramaic forms labeled "Hebrew" (for example, σάββατα and ἀσαρθά) in those same corpora; the existence of old, official writings such as the *Megillat Ta'anit,* composed in Aramaic; legal documents quoted or otherwise portrayed in the Mishnah, their formulae exclusively Aramaic; the alphabet itself a borrowing from Aramaic, Palestinian Jews having forsaken their earlier Hebrew alphabet—Dalman pronounced, "From all these considerations must be drawn the conclusion that Jesus grew up speaking the Aramaic tongue, and that He would be obliged to speak Aramaic to His disciples and to the people in order to be understood."[18]

In arriving at this position Dalman was arguing nothing essentially new. He simply offered additional evidence and reflection to ramify the views of earlier scholars such as Abraham Geiger. Author of an estimable grammar of Mishnaic Hebrew (*Lehr- und Lesebuch zur Sprache der Mischnah,* 1845), Geiger nonetheless minimized Jewish use of that language: "Since the time of the second temple the vernacular of the Jews was Aramaic . . . Hebrew had accordingly ceased to be a living language."[19] In 1909 Theodor Zahn asserted even more strongly, "At the time of Christ Hebrew was the native language of no Jew."[20] Forceful though he was, Zahn was just another link in a concatenation of specialists affirming the judgments of eminent forebears: of Hebraists, such as Wilhelm Gesenius, for whom the last native speaker of ancient Hebrew passed from the earth shortly after the Maccabean Revolt;[21] and of historians, such as Emil Schürer, author of the regnant nineteenth-century history of Second Temple Jewry, who propounded the argument that "the language of the Jewish people of all the districts here mentioned [Judaea, Galilee, and Perea] was, since the last centuries before Christ, no longer Hebrew, but Aramaic."[22]

These judgments of nineteenth- and early-twentieth-century scholarship continued to be echoed right up until 1965. In that year, Masada's excavations yielded hundreds of inscribed ostraca, many—as expected—inscribed in Aramaic; but equally many bore Hebrew and Greek words.[23] Just one year before, the leading Aramaist of his generation, Franz Rosenthal, had written, "Given present understanding of the history of Aramaic, there can be no doubt that the prevailing language in Palestine at the beginning of our era was Aramaic, not Hebrew."[24] Rosenthal's judgment was by no means overturned by the Masada finds, and since 1965 similar sentiments can boast strong adherents, especially and perhaps understandably among the restricted circles of Aramaists.[25]

Yet the discovery—and more so, the incipient digestion—of the Judaean Desert treasures has noticeably eroded this erstwhile consensus. By 1970, James Barr could say regarding the speech of Jesus, "a Hebrew theory is once again in the field—if also, we must add, in some widely differing forms."[26] J. A. Emerton had already observed of Hebrew in 1961, "it is quite possible that it continued to be used by some Jews as late as the second century A.D."[27] A dozen years later he had moved from the possible to the probable: "it [is] probable that Hebrew was still used as a vernacular by some Jews in the first century A.D., and that it continued to be used well into the second century, and perhaps even into the third to a more limited extent."[28]

More than any other single scholar, it was Harris Birkeland with *The Language of Jesus* who began to give scholars second thoughts regarding the status of Hebrew in the Judaea of these years. His Norwegian heritage, with its welter of spoken forms, its *Landsmål* and *Bokmål*, perhaps sensitized him to nuances that heretofore had not entered the debate. To the mostly written evidence that Dalman proffered, Birkeland riposted, "That Aramaic was *written* in Palestine at the time of Jesus is no evidence that it was the popular language, the language of the masses, the proletariate."[29] Birkeland was convinced that vernacular Hebrew survived the exile of the Judahite elite in the time of Nebuchadnezzar, the subsequent return of that elite's then Aramaic-speaking progeny from Babylon to reassume leading roles, and the centuries of Persian dominion during which Aramaic served as the Near Eastern lingua franca: "The language of the common people in Palestine in the time of Jesus was Hebrew. To a great extent M. H. Segal must be right. But, firstly, he also supposes that Aramaic is a language found among the lower classes. Secondly he assumes that Mishnaic Hebrew was a popular language. In these points he does not seem to be right."[30]

For Birkeland, Aramaic in the time of Jesus remained what it had been for centuries, a language of the educated classes and of immigrants: "In any case Aramaic was a language of high reputation. Therefore it was used for religious purposes, in divine sayings, in prayers and in religious speeches."[31]

The consensus represented by Dalman, he argued, mistakenly relied upon Aramaic literary works in formulating its views. Proper evidence would be nonliterary descriptions explicitly declaring Aramaic the spoken tongue, and these, he noted, appeared only with certain rabbinic writings of the third century C.E. and later, the Gemara. As for Mishnaic Hebrew, Birkeland saw it as a developed, literary form of vernacular Hebrew, not as the vernacular itself.

Many scholars questioned specific aspects of Birkeland's thesis while nonetheless entertaining the whole.[32] In particular, he seemed to have overargued his points about the use of Aramaic. Still, the distinctions he drew between written and spoken language, and between the usages of different social classes, elevated the sophistication of scholarly interaction to a new level. Hebrew was once more "on the table," aided in no small measure by the evidence of the Judaean Desert, on-the-ground findings that Birkeland highlighted as such: "[Mishnaic Hebrew] really seems to have been adopted by extreme nationalist circles as a literary language also for non-religious purposes. Thus it was used by the rebel Simon ben Koseba (bar Kokeba). This we know from the texts found in Wadi Murabba'at in 1952."[33]

Birkeland's mention of Moses Segal—the foremost early-twentieth-century proponent of Hebrew as a Roman-period vernacular—signaled his indebtedness to the person from whom he had assumed the prophet's mantle.[34] Until Birkeland wrote, Segal's voice had been virtually inaudible over the hurricane of support for Aramaic as *Jesu Muttersprache.* Now his arguments began to get a new hearing. They had always been impressive.

The first systematically to assemble all the linguistic evidence pertinent to the issues,[35] accomplished over a thirty-year period, Segal labored to define precisely the relationships among Biblical Hebrew, Mishnaic Hebrew, and Aramaic.[36] He argued that an artificial language conjured from Biblical Hebrew and Aramaic would scarcely display so many characteristics derived from neither parent. Mishnaic Hebrew could not be a simple amalgam of the other two:

> In its main characteristics the grammar of MH [Mishnaic Hebrew] is practically identical with the grammar of BH [Biblical Hebrew]. Where it differs from BH grammar, the genesis of the difference can generally be traced back to an older stage in the language, out of which the new forms developed in a natural way. Forms that deviate from the regular type of BH are usually found in BH in isolated cases as grammatical irregularities. It is nearly always possible to trace the connection of a MH form with a BH prototype, at least in later BH literature. If such forms in MH and late BH happen also to be found

> in Aramaic, they are usually also found in other Semitic languages, especially in a late stage of development. They are thus not Aramaisms, but grammatical phenomena common to the whole, or to a portion, of the Semitic family. On the other hand, MH has also a considerable number of forms which are quite unknown in Aram[aic], and which could not have arisen if MH had been the artificial creation of men whose natural language was Aramaic.[37]

The principal differences with Biblical Hebrew, Segal noted, were syntactic: a recasting of the tenses, a different expression of the genitive relation, and different methods for constructing dependent clauses. But these differences were only the sort to be expected between any developed *Kunstprosa* and the patois of ordinary peasant speech. Segal acknowledged that Mishnaic Hebrew shared much vocabulary with Aramaic, and he did not deny that significant borrowing had occurred; yet as a counterpoint he emphasized borrowings in the opposite direction and the fact that the Mishnaic form of Hebrew possessed many words attested neither in Aramaic nor in Biblical Hebrew. A listing revealed three hundred verbs found in rabbinic diction but absent from the biblical corpus. Of these, Segal calculated that only about 8 percent were also Aramaic.[38] As to morphology, Segal pointed to a number of forms that contrasted Mishnaic Hebrew with Biblical and that could not be explained by Aramaic influence: for example, אנו, "we," instead of Biblical אנחנו; ליקח, "to take," instead of לקחת; אלו, "these," instead of אלה; and a new verbal conjugation, *Nitpaal,* replacing in part the biblical *Hitpael.*

He further noted that if the position he was advocating was correct, ex hypothesi Mishnaic Hebrew should preserve some authentic ancient vocabulary that happened not to occur in the limited corpus of the biblical writings. Such could indeed be identified, including חזר, "return"; סמך, "harvest olives"; עצר, "uproot"; צריך, "necessary"; and טחול, "spleen." Full assessment of the nonbiblical lexicon of the Mishnah and other early rabbinic writings, uncovering as it did so many apparent connections to the daily life of peasants, persuaded Segal that the language's invention for use in scholastic discourse was impossible. Why, his argument implied, would *scholars* need or invent terms for "plow" or "dates" that the *farmers* everywhere around them did not use?[39]

Thus Segal's underpinnings, overlaid by Birkeland's more sophisticated approach to the use of Hebrew among the Jews of Jesus's day, eventually helped to recast the old consensus. Arguments favoring Hebrew and derogating Aramaic as the dominant vernacular now began to be made on the basis of additional theoretical approaches.[40] But Birkeland, Segal, and more nuanced theory did not alone suffice to alter the terms of the debate. Reasoned theory and argument, no matter how well done, can seldom persuade like something concrete. Here entered the Judaean Desert discoveries. Even in the early days of research on the Qumran manuscripts, their number in the hundreds was patent. So, too, was the dominance of Hebrew as the language of their composition (today the ratio is known to be approximately five to one, Hebrew over Aramaic). Yet only a few Qumran texts displayed a more vernacular dialect or register; none of these particular scrolls was to be published for many years.[41] The vast majority of the Dead Sea Scrolls seemed to represent more or less successful efforts at writing in Biblical Hebrew, the old literary language. Such works, impressive though their number might be, could attest to Hebrew as vernacular among the Jews only indirectly.

Accordingly, it was the discoveries associated with the later period—the contracts and documents of the Bar Kokhba period—that provided the more direct argument for Hebrew as a vernacular; and it was the letters that advanced this view. For as in the modern world, so also in the ancient: letters were often a substitute for personal presence. Here, if anywhere, ancient Judaeans might be found in intimate mode. The original editors pressed this argument from the very beginning: "The thesis of scholars such as Segal, Ben Yehuda, and Klausner that Hebrew was a language spoken by the population of Judaea in Persian and Greco-Roman times is no longer mere hypothesis: it is an established fact. Numerous writs from Murabbaʿât are written in Mishnaic; they are, however, less numerous than those in Aramaic. But Mishnaic is the only language used in correspondence."[42]

In the years following the era of desert discoveries, perhaps Chaim Rabin made the strongest case for Mishnaic Hebrew as vernacular.[43] With an appreciative nod to Birkeland and Segal, Rabin constructed a detailed case that drew together all of their best points while adding compelling new considerations. Rabin pointed to forms in Mishnaic Hebrew linguistically more archaic than their Biblical counterparts (for example, feminine singular זו for זאת "this," and *tertiae infirmae* third-person feminine singular perfects such as הית for Biblical היתה). He focused on "Mishnaic" influences: on the language of later biblical books, on the lexical understanding of the translators of the LXX, and on the presumed Semitic originals of certain of the Pseudepigrapha. Rabin further adduced the phenomenon of Mishnaic Hebrew loanwords present in Christian Palestinian Aramaic and Samaritan Aramaic. Since these were non-Jewish dialects, such borrowings could scarcely be explained by positing that the speakers were acquainted with rabbinic literature. And, of course, Rabin underscored the significance to the issues of the Bar Kokhba texts and the manuscripts discovered near Qumran. Within the latter, he highlighted involuntary lexical and grammatical Mishnaisms in the writers' attempts at Biblical Hebrew, mistakes betraying the idiom with which they were more familiar.

Today, a broad swath of scholarship agrees that both Aramaic and Hebrew found significant expression among the Jews of late Second Temple Judaea.[44] The Jews spoke both of these languages, as the rabbis would say, בדרך שגורה בפיהם ("words flowed from their mouths"). Certainly not all scholars would concur: consensus is the proper word, not unanimity.[45] Still, a common judgment is that of Robert Gundry: "Proof now exists that *all three languages* in question—Hebrew, Aramaic and Greek—were commonly used by Jews in first century Palestine."[46] Gundry's inclusion of Greek recalls the third linguistic dimension. Was that tongue really widely used in these years, as he asserted, given that Hebrew and Aramaic were both of much longer standing and, evidently, both still very much alive in Roman Palestine?

A significant number of scholars would take issue with Gundry, maintaining tenaciously the early-twentieth-century consensus alluded to above. Greek was not a language of the Jewish peasantry but was—Greek ethnic centers such as the Decapolis aside—largely confined to inhabitants of several Jewish cities: Jerusalem, Jericho, Sepphoris, and Tiberias. Even there, it was mostly a possession of the elite. Thus, for example, the judgment of Lester Grabbe: "The use of Greek seems to have been confined to a particular segment of the population, namely, the educated upper class. To what extent it penetrated into the lives of the bulk of the population is difficult to determine; however, the number of Jews outside the Greek cities who were fluent in Greek seems small."[47] The situation of Greek in Palestine would then essentially mirror that of Phoenicia and Egypt.[48]

Grabbe's view remains common, although in the years since the Judaean Desert finds, especially, a growing cadre of scholars would give a nod to A. W. Argyle's pithy simile. Argyle wrote particularly of Jesus and the Galilee, but his words are often cited as encapsulating the Judaean situation as well: "To suggest that a Jewish boy growing up in Galilee would not know Greek would be rather like suggesting that a Welch boy brought up in Cardiff would not know English."[49] Indeed, a few scholars would sail out somewhat farther on this heading, *preferring Greek* among the linguistic options, at least as regards the usage of a significant plurality of the populace.[50] But they must reckon with a strong headwind. For every A. W. Argyle, a Mark Chancey stands opposed. Chancey argued that we simply cannot know how much Greek was in use in the region. Regarding Galilee, in particular, he questioned scholarly confidence in substantial use, finding it "all the more surprising given that we have no extant first-century texts of proven Galilean provenance." Indeed, he went on to emphasize, the problem was broader than the first century; "we have very, very few Galilean inscriptions from the Early Roman period" at all—essentially, only coins.[51]

Inscriptions have necessarily been the focus regarding Jewish Greek in this period. The earnest advocates for Greek as a literary language among the Jews of Roman Judaea have never managed to assemble a compelling case. The problem has been a lack of clear evidence. While fragments do survive of a dozen or more authors of that time and earlier (figures such as Artapanus, Eupolemus, Theodotus, and Pseudo-Hecataeus), in many cases their Palestinian-Jewish bona fides is suspect.[52] No one is sure where most of them lived. Many of the fragments derive from quotations of a non-Jewish author, Alexander Polyhistor. Accordingly, the case for Judaean use of Greek hinges on assessment of the epigraphic evidence, and attention comes to rest almost exclusively on vernacular or lower register rather than literary usage.[53] Inscriptional evidence in Judaea is noteworthy, though sharply restricted to a few genres. It mainly consists of a small number of public inscriptions and a good many funerary inscriptions, the latter mostly found on ossuaries. The materials for Jerusalem in the Hellenistic and Roman periods through 70 C.E. have recently been collected and published in the first volume of a magnificent new series, *Corpus Inscriptionum Iudaeae/Palaestinae*.[54]

Judaean use of ossuaries developed during the reign of Herod the Great, evidently as an aspect of the significant Romanization that began during that man's rule.[55] Roman custom in those years was to cremate the dead and then deposit their ashes in a small stone container known as a *cinerium*. Judaeans did not cremate the dead, but a corresponding small, casket-shaped urn arose to house the bones of the deceased in secondary burial. Bodies would initially be laid out in a niche (Hebrew, כוך) within a rock-cut tomb. After a year or so the bones were collected and placed in the boxes. Because rock-cut tombs were costly, this custom engaged the well-to-do—although not necessarily only the highest echelon. Today, some three thousand ossuaries are known, almost all of them associated with either Jerusalem or Jericho.[56] Somewhat less than one-third of them bear inscriptions, and *CIIP* presents more than five hundred from Jerusalem.[57] These inscriptions potentially furnish an important window into language usage in Judaea, and many of them are in Greek.

Table 1.1 provides an overview.[58] An initial appraisal of these data would certainly give the impression that at least the upper classes of Jerusalem used a good deal of Greek. If bilingual and trilingual ossuaries—inscribed with Greek and either Semitic tongue (or both)—are taken together with those inscribed in Greek alone, the total is 236 inscriptions. This is 40.2 percent of the total. Straightforwardly, such a robust percentage of Greek inscriptions on ossuaries would seem to reflect knowledge of Greek among a roughly corresponding percentage of the population represented.[59] This intuitive understanding is encouraged by the editors' estimate of the addressees of these inscriptions: "Ossuary inscriptions were essentially labels identifying the deceased for the benefit of the family in their private, sealed cave; there was no wider 'audience.'"[60] According to this view, the inscriptions were normally products of the family itself—written as an expression of grief, perhaps, or as a way of organizing the various ossuaries contained in a tomb. By such reckoning the writings could reasonably be held to mirror language usage in the family.

Doubtless the editors were correct in large measure, and many of the inscriptions were indeed family affairs. But just how many? A variety of considerations tells against facile equation of the ossuary inscriptions with actual language usage by the families concerned. Care must be taken. For one thing, it is clear that the tradesmen who made the boxes often wrote the

Table 1.1. Funerary inscriptions in Jerusalem

Language of inscription	Total no.	% of corpus
Greek	191	32.5
Indistinct Semitic	163	27.8
Aramaic	128	21.8
Hebrew	45	7.7
Greek/indistinct Semitic bilingual	24	4.1
Greek/Hebrew bilingual	13	2.2
Hebrew/Aramaic bilingual	11	1.9
Greek/Aramaic bilingual	7	1.2
Other (Latin, Palmyrene)	4	0.7
Greek/Hebrew/Aramaic trilingual	1	0.2
Total	587	100.1

inscriptions as well.[61] Inscriptions that were proofed and corrected evidence this fact;[62] so do instances where lids and boxes were separately inscribed (being so labeled to facilitate their reuniting later in the work process),[63] and situations where the inscriptions were integrated with the mason's artistic design.[64]

Moreover, contrary to the editors' suggestion, an element of display seems apparent in an appreciable number of the ossuaries. Others besides the family were plainly intended to admire the ossuary and its inscription. The artistic integration of ornamentation and inscription would count here. So, too, would instances of monumental scripts, expertly incised:[65] only rarely would a family be able to produce such an ornate lettering by itself. The money and time spent to produce it argue that people outside the family were the audience. Otherwise, a careless cursive scrawled across the bone-box by a family member would have served equally well. Also telling regarding display are honorary expressions incised on the boxes or nearby walls, and even at times explicit statements of agency—hardly necessary, one supposes, for anyone within the family. As an example of the latter, note the inscription, "This loculus was made for the bones of our parents" (no. 460). Instances of the former include "Simon, builder of the Temple" (no. 54), "Hananiah b. John the Nazirite" (the name in Aramaic, the title in Hebrew, no. 72), "Joseph b. Hananiah the scribe" (again, with only the title in Hebrew, no. 86),[66] and "Menahem, from the sons of Yakim, priest" (no. 183). Especially interesting is no. 98, "The ossuary of Nicanor of Alexandria, who made the gates" (of the Temple). Bearing a name uncommon in Judaea, this Nicanor is known from other sources and was a veritable ancient celebrity. Were the intended readers only the family, anything beyond the name would seem pointless.

Additionally, the display value of the Greek language appears to emerge from the data shown in Table 1.1. Unless Greek really were much better known in Judaea than most scholars have been ready to countenance, it is overrepresented on the ossuaries. The most reasonable explanation of this apparent fact would be that even people who did not themselves know the language chose it so as to associate themselves and their families with Rome and the dominant Mediterranean culture. But once again, if people outside the family never saw the Greek, the attempt at association would fail. As Tessa Rajak has written, "Those who put Greek on their tombs need not be Greek speakers; just as the Latin on English gravestones was not put there by Latin speakers, but adopted because it was associated with worship and study."[67] Given the character of our data, one could imagine that a relatively small number of ossuary factories, employing a limited cadre of workers capable in Greek, might by their products badly skew modern estimates of how much Greek the inhabitants of Jerusalem actually used. Consider: Greek is much more common in the funerary settings than it is on inscribed *instrumenta domestica,* where just 12.8 percent of the sample is Greek and 87.2 percent is Semitic.[68] In sum, then, funerary texts do not reliably put us in contact with the language the entombed used in life. This is the first problem with the ossuaries as evidence for Judaean language patterns.

Another problem with the ossuaries and Greek, in particular, involves the fact already noted: their virtually exclusive association with Jericho and Jerusalem. Even the older consensus acknowledged significant Hellenization in the larger cities, so this association with the two cities arguably comports with either the maximalist or the minimalist view of Greek use among Jews. And then there is the brevity of the inscriptions themselves—most often, merely a name, occasionally augmented with a patronym or other one-word designation of familial standing. This is pretty thin fare from which to draw conclusions on the penetration of Greek language and culture.

Problems similarly attend the oft-cited evidence of the Beth Sheʿarim inscriptions for Judaean Greek. Undertaken between 1936 and 1959, excavations at the site unearthed an enormous complex of funerary chambers hewn from the soft limestone hills.[69] Thirty-one catacombs have emerged, some with more than 400 individual graves, and nearly 300 inscriptions have been uncovered. Their language is heavily weighted toward Greek: nearly 220 are in the tongue of Javan, only about 60 in the tongues of Seth. One of the inscriptions has become famous for its Hellenic cast. Composed in Homeric hexameters, it embodies a Greek fatalism seldom found in Jewish reveries about death outside Qoheleth. A portion reads:

> Having journ[ied to] Hades, Justu[s . . . he]re lies,
> With many of his own, for mighty Fate so wished.
> Take heart, Justus, none is immortal.[70]

The facts are impressive and led one of the excavators, the esteemed epigrapher Nahman Avigad, to conclude: "It emerges that Greek was the tongue spoken by many Palestinian Jews. . . . The Greek inscriptions are not only more numerous, but also generally longer and more heterogeneous in content. . . . The Hebrew inscriptions, on the other hand, were short and meager in content: most of them contained one or two words; only two were longer."[71] Yet, closer examination may raise questions about the confidence with which Avigad made this statement and so give pause concerning the straightforward application of these data to the linguistic situation of late Second Temple times.

The most obvious issue is of course the date. The acme of this necropolis was the era of Rabbi Judah the Prince (who may actually be buried in catacomb 14). Besides the locals, Jews came in their final days or were brought postmortem from Antioch, Tyre, Sidon, Beirut, Byblos, Palmyra, Messene, and even South Arabia to be interred alongside the famous editor of the Mishnah and his rabbinic compatriots. With burial on the Mount of Olives forbidden to the Jews in the wake of the Bar Kokhba revolt, Beth She'arim took its place; apparently the thinking was כל הקבור בארץ ישראל כאילו קבור תחת המזבח (As for everyone buried in the Land of Israel, it is as though he were buried under the altar itself).[72] Based on the numismatic evidence, the site seems to have been destroyed during the abortive Jewish revolt put down by Gallus in 352. Thereafter, few, and only very poor, graves were added.

Thus these materials postdate the watershed of the Second Jewish Revolt. It is likely prima facie that this social cataclysm affected language along with everything else; moreover, scholars acknowledge that Hellenization increased perceptibly between the floruit of Simon b. Kosiba and the third and fourth centuries. To some degree, increased acceptance of the dominant civilization—or, to prefer the flip side of the coin, decreased resistance arising from categories of self-identity—must have followed upon the two disastrous defeats at the hands of Rome.[73] The fight eventually leached out of many people. True, reduced attachment to Judaism presumably infected the Palestinian Jews buried at Beth She'arim very little. Their place of burial speaks for itself. But the seismic social shifts, aftershocks of the revolt, would have had an effect nevertheless. Issues of language usage are always social as much as individual. The general social movement would have shaped everyone simply by virtue of being the milieu of their daily lives. A greater receptiveness to Greek therefore would have characterized even the devout.

Similarly, as more and more time passed under Roman dominion—a dominion that expressed itself in a myriad of ways, but almost always in Greek—more and more people would have adopted that language as a practical matter, as happened likewise in Egypt.[74] So, the social situation at the time of the Beth She'arim inscriptions cannot safely be equated with that of the first and second centuries.[75]

For any who would generalize from these inscriptions to the Palestinian Jewry of an earlier time, another obstacle interposes itself: the graves and their inscriptions scarcely represent a cross-section of society as a whole, even for their own time. They are monuments to an elite, and to the language usages of that elite. Not infrequently the inscriptions provide information about the social standing of the dead: "the interred were people of importance such as rabbis, public officers, merchants, craftsmen, and scribes."[76] Butchers, bakers, and candlestick makers are conspicuously absent. Beth She'arim had in fact been an elite enclave since Herodian times, when the environs were crown properties. This status continued, mutatis mutandis, until Rome ceded the area to Rabbi Judah the Prince. With an occasional rare exception to prove the rule, commoners were not buried there. Indeed, the illegitimacy of generalizing from this site to other times and places in early Roman Palestine comes clearly into focus when attention shifts to the non-Greek inscriptions. Some of the most interesting of these epitaphs are inscribed in Mishnaic Hebrew. Most scholars agree that whatever may have been the case in the first or early second centuries, by the fourth Hebrew was essentially dead. Nevertheless, the rabbinic families of catacombs 14 and 20 seem to have used the tongue idiomatically. As Avigad has noted, their inscriptions are far from formulaic. Were their knowledge of the language merely literary, one would expect instead stereotypical, frozen expressions.[77] These people still spoke the לשון בני אדם ("language of humankind," that is, vernacular Hebrew as the rabbis titled it). Yet no one has urged on that basis that Hebrew was broadly *viva vox*. If one cannot rightly generalize from the Hebrew, should the Greek be any different?

In fact, the inscriptions that probably are truly representative of the language of the ordinary Jew of these times number a mere two. They are rubricated Aramaic curses painted on the walls of certain arcesolia, warnings addressed to grave robbers—surely members of the peasant class.[78] The choice of language is telling. For these several reasons, caution (not counting) would seem to be the prudent approach to the Beth She'arim inscriptions. Broader considerations must frame that caution. In regions such as Judaea that underwent Romanization, special caution is needed when assessing epigraphic evidence. For that process typically brought with it an increase, not just of governmental inscriptions and public display, but also of private inscriptions—including those associated with burials.[79] Further, local languages tend to appear less frequently in the inscriptions than their actual use by the population would have predicted, while Greek and Latin are correspondingly overrepresented.[80]

Argument about the use of Greek by the Jews of late Second Temple times is emblematic of larger disputes concerning their Hellenization. Hellenization involves far more than language, of course; cultural, political, and economic aspects are equally important, to name but a few. Still, it is fair to say that many scholars have felt that they could use language as a kind of barometer. The degree to which Judaeans employed Greek has been thought diagnostic of the presence of less visible expressions of Hellenism that would naturally follow in trail. More than four decades have passed since the massive work by Martin Hengel *Judaism and Hellenism* (1973) famously renewed debate on relations between Athens and Jerusalem.[81] Arguing then for very considerable Hellenization, Hengel yielded no ground in the years leading up to his death in 2009. His opponents likewise have doggedly continued to mount sorties, though perhaps with diminished energy.[82] An accurate measure of the Jewish knowledge of Greek, and of the level of Greek literary culture among Jews, would go far in assessing the larger problem.

That some measure of Aramaic, Hebrew, and Greek was in use among the Jews of late Second Temple Judaea is thus agreed. Any attempt to move a single step beyond that banality, however, and consensus dissipates like fog in the morning sun. The logical next question finds no satisfactory answer. "What is uncertain," Emerton has written, "and is probably impossible to determine, is the precise proportions in which Hebrew and Aramaic—and, indeed, Greek—were used."[83] No approach to the issue of proportionate use has been available. The present study is in part the proposal of just that. It seems that something may be said about "precise proportions." Of course, when it comes to understanding the ancient realities in all their dimly realized complexity, no one should be under the illusion that more is possible than modest progress. Current evidential realities simply allow no more. Still, the linguistic Gordian Knot can perhaps be slipped a bit. Fresh deductions are there to be wrested from the evidence that does survive by taking hold of it in new ways. Distinctions and interaction between spoken and written language are necessarily involved, so implicating the matter of literacy in late Second Temple Judaea. Comment on previous scholarly study of ancient literacy, particularly Jewish literacy, is therefore in order.

Judaean Literacy in Late Second Temple Times

Historical literacy studies are a relatively recent development in scholarship. Though the discipline is now in full flower, the first seeds were sown only in the late 1960s.[84] Its investigations may conveniently be characterized as of two basic sorts, these tending to be pursued by anthropologists and historians, respectively. The first is sometimes called the "fundamentalist" perspective. Such studies explore broad psychological and cultural implications or effects that attach, exponents claim, to the introduction or spread of literacy in a given society. Exemplifying this type of study in the field of classics was Eric Havelock's *The Literate Revolution in Greece and Its Cultural Consequences* (1982).[85] Havelock argued that the alphabet changed the very thought processes of the ancient Greeks, creating, as it were, a new kind of Hellenic mind.[86]

The second sort of investigation into ancient literacy may be termed "relativist" studies. This approach, pursued primarily by historians, is interested in detailed, culturally specific manifestations of literacy in a given setting. It eschews—indeed, often abominates—broad theoretical claims for literacy and its effects (such being cast as "technological determinism"). Mediating approaches have arisen in more recent years, but as a summarizing generalization the portrait of a sharp divide remains valid.[87] For the present study, the historian's approach offers the more immediately relevant perspectives.

In 1989 the field of literacy studies welcomed a new work of this kind. It came to the study of Greco-Roman reading and writing bearing gifts of thoroughness and precision not previously seen. Authored by William Harris, *Ancient Literacy* wielded significant influence, sparking heated debate and launching numerous further investigations.[88] Oddly, perhaps, Harris refused to say precisely what he meant by "literacy," but this indirection was arguably more virtue than fault, since the term defies all efforts at simple definition. Literacy is not one thing, and Harris did not try to make it one. He found its absence easier to define. An illiterate, he suggested, was a person "who cannot with understanding both read and write a short simple statement on his [or her] everyday life."[89] Woven together with this negation were three phrases: "mass literacy," "scribal literacy," and "craftsman's literacy." Mass literacy was for Harris the situation of the West since the late nineteenth century, and he gave it only cursory attention. His focus was rather on the second and third terms:

> By [scribal literacy] I mean the sort of literacy which predominated in ancient Near Eastern cultures and in the Minoan and Mycenaean worlds, literacy restricted to a specialized social group which used it for such purposes as maintaining palace records; and which also predominated in western Europe from late antiquity until at least the twelfth century. By craftsman's literacy I mean not the literacy of an individual craftsman but the condition in which

> the majority, or a near-majority, of skilled craftsmen are literate, while women and unskilled labourers and peasants are mainly not, this being the situation which prevailed in most of the educationally more advanced regions of Europe and North America from the sixteenth century to the eighteenth century.[90]

Essentially, then, Harris was thinking in terms of the social history of Western Europe since late antiquity. *Ancient Literacy* was a "high-level," comparative study—as much a matter of analogy as of archives and archaeology: "Investigation of the volume of literacy in other societies, and in particular of the growth of literacy in early-modern and modern Europe, has shown that writing ceases to be the arcane accomplishment of a small professional or religious or social elite *only* when certain preconditions are fulfilled and *only* when strong positive forces are present to bring the change about."[91] Harris identified three things essential for mass literacy: extensive networks of schools, technology capable of producing and distributing vast quantities of texts at low cost, and a predominantly urban demographic pattern. Since these preconditions were always absent in the Greco-Roman world, literacy always remained the accomplishment of a select few. Only in exceptional times and places was even a craftsman's level of literacy achieved. Working his way through the evidence of archaic, Classical, and Hellenistic Greece and the Greek East, as well as that of the Roman world from archaic times until late antiquity, Harris came to conclusions that he anticipated might cause "severe mental indigestion" in some classicists and prove "highly unpalatable" to others.[92]

Athens in the early fifth century, he argued, could probably boast a literacy rate for the entire population, including women and slaves, little higher than 5 percent. By the time of the Persian Wars the number may possibly have doubled, but greater change was forestalled by the virtually universal illiteracy of Greek women. Much higher rates, bordering on figures known from early modern Europe, were probably achieved at certain places during the Hellenistic period—numbers as high as 30 to 40 percent, for example, at Teos. But literacy did not subsequently advance; rather, rates fell back to earlier levels. Roman citizens, Harris estimated, were no more than 10 percent literate when Cicero and Julius Caesar were born. During the Principate the situation varied greatly according to region, but literacy rates on the whole were always by modern standards exceedingly low. Very few outside the elite living in the major cities could read or write either Latin or Greek. Everywhere women, the poor, small farmers, and ordinary folk were ordinarily illiterate.[93]

Ancient Literacy did not merely confirm the worst fears of the idealists among the guild of classicists: it exposed those fears as insufficiently morbid. Eric Turner had once queried tremulously twenty years earlier, "Are we to accept the depressing conclusion that the ordinary man cared little for literature, even if he could read it?"[94] The answer, it developed, was yes. The ordinary man probably did not care, and almost certainly could not read it. (For the ordinary woman, Harris would say, the sentence also applies, but remove the "almost.")

Harris anticipated that some colleagues would reject his conclusions, and he was right. Negative response did come, though not always for the reasons foreseen. J. David Thomas fulfilled Harris's expectations in remarking, "My own impression, from studying the Greek papyri from Egypt and the Latin tablets from Vindolanda, would be somewhat more optimistic." Harris's numbers were too low. He faulted the Columbia University scholar for insufficient attention paid to the evidence of letter writing, and to literacy in languages besides Latin and Greek.[95] Carol Thomas's immediate reaction was similar. She spoke openly what others, presumably, thought only privately: "A view that literacy was not widespread in ancient Greece and Rome lessens the accomplishment of those cultures in our eyes." Though she made no effort to refute Harris's theses—noting that his work was careful and cautious, hence his conclusions reasonable—her considered response was critical nonetheless: "My only serious question," she concluded, "concerns not the extent of literacy but its importance in the community."[96]

Running in a similar vein was the reaction of another specialist in ancient literacy studies, Rosalind Thomas. She commented: "His argument is essentially a negative one, and his book in a sense the culmination of a certain approach to literacy, which concentrates on its extent. Where one goes from here therefore deserves serious consideration." She questioned, "How much did such low levels of literacy matter?"[97] Essentially, she seemed to say, Harris had done a competent job, but as a sort of waste of time, laboring over a question that held little real interest or importance. A number of other scholars echoed these sentiments, seeming to find his numbers and the process of arriving at them boring. They insisted that Harris should have asked different questions.[98] Yet for social phenomena such as literacy and its place in a given society, numbers and proportional issues are surely fundamental. They are the necessary starting point for other questions.[99] Perhaps Harris's was not the most interesting question that could have been asked about Greco-Roman literacy—perhaps; all the same, no question seems more deserving of being asked first.

The negative reaction of these scholars was, however, a minority viewpoint. The broad reaction was congratulatory. E. J. Kenney, for example, himself the author of respected work on ancient book culture, embraced Harris's study: "Most classical scholars who have expressed an opinion on the subject have taken a somewhat roseate view of the general level of literacy in ancient Greece and Rome. Harris' book attacks and, I think it fair to say, demolishes this position." He concluded, "This sober and informative book is likely to remain the standard treatment of the subject, in English at all events, for some time to come."[100] The *Journal of Roman Archaeology* took Harris so seriously that it devoted an entire supplementary series volume to the evaluation of *Ancient Literacy,* soliciting eight different specialists to provide analysis. The focus was, of course, on the Roman side of Harris's volume.[101]

None directly challenged Harris's main point, that literacy levels in Greco-Roman antiquity were extremely low. But several scholars were diffident, uneasy about the nature of the evidence that survives, noting how much chance is involved in matters of survival, recovery, preservation, and dissemination.[102] Of those who were uneasy, the most dyspeptic response—and easily the most colorful—was that of Nicholas Horsfall. Confessing that he had himself once contemplated writing a volume such as Harris's but had been deterred by lack of funding and conceptual issues, he began: "I had no desire to seem to return to the topic as a grumpy outsider, an extraneous warthog chased from an intended waterhole by a large pedigree carnivore, and left to grub in the undergrowth."[103]

Horsfall's essay exemplifies the sorts of criticisms that the unreceptive brought to bear. He took most trenchant issue with the method of *Ancient Literacy,* concentrating attention on the question of schools. Conceding the absence of widespread institutional schooling in the Roman world, he nevertheless contended that home-taught literacy, only grudgingly acknowledged by Harris, might have raised literacy rates well beyond the book's calculations. Further, he insisted, informal processes must have been operative. Noting Hermeros's phrase *lapidarias litteras scio* from Petronius (Petr. 58.7), Horsfall remarked that he had himself learned to read informally, puzzling things out piecemeal, a method that seemed to work well enough. "Public inscriptions in the Roman world," he observed, "provided a large-scale and abundant reader for any child who learned his letters informally." And Horsfall identified three incentives to informal acquisition of literacy that

Harris had either entirely neglected or given scant attention: the household with literate slaves; the army, with its wealth of bureaucracy and attendant forms; and the stimulus that work conditions might provide: "If the ability to write makes you faster, more useful, better-paid or better-treated at work, then, if you cannot already, you surely learn quickly, somehow, if you possibly can." Literacy improved prospects for livelihood. Why else would the practically minded, upwardly mobile guests at Trimalchio's banquet plan for their younger generation schooling to that end? But these were all "low-level" matters, the on-the-ground data that Harris had intentionally marginalized in favor of his comparative method.[104] Neglect of such evidence irritated Horsfall: "It is truly perplexing that Harris does not discuss the rich documentation of the Magdalensberg, revealing an extraordinarily complex and active commercial life in import, export and local re-sale under the early Julio-Claudians." For Horsfall, Harris's approach was irredeemably flawed, because medieval and early modern Europe were improper *comparanda.* The ancient world simply worked by different rules, so that "Roman states of mind outwit modern statistical methods." By implication, then, though in the nature of things no statistics could be possible, literacy rates were higher than Harris's methods could discover.[105]

James Franklin also suspected that Harris had somehow missed something, although like Horsfall he disclaimed any ability to supply it. Concerning himself with the parietal inscriptions of Pompeii, he conceded all of Harris's institutional arguments and that high levels of literacy might not be expected in his city. Nevertheless, he countered, "The vivacity and sheer mass of the evidence suggests a widely literate population." This intuition, he freely admitted, could not be supported; that would require "a close study of the evidence that has hardly begun." Still, he could identify graffiti written by prostitutes, laborers, passersby, and gladiators. Some of these nonelites even used abbreviations. This sort of case-by-case analysis promised "to allow us to progress beyond the failure of statistics to characterize the evidence."[106]

These criticisms were heartfelt and not without weight. Impervious as they were to numbers, however, they were equally impervious to refutation. As Harris had anticipated some might, these scholars just found *Ancient Literacy* "highly unpalatable." But the other contributors to the volume were in better gustatory humor. Mary Beard assessed: "Harris has given us . . . a history of numbers and levels, learning and schooling, messages and information. His achievement is, on any reckoning, impressive."[107] Alan Bowman opined: "After reading Harris' book, few will feel that there is much to be said for arguing the opposite case. The argument that mass literacy, as it is understood in modern times, cannot have existed in the ancient world because that world lacked the institutions by which it could have been achieved, is coherent and forceful."[108] And Keith Hopkins summarized: "Harris has written an interesting, important and path-breaking book on a large and important subject. . . . His main hypothesis is clear and completely convincing."[109] Hopkins nevertheless went on to write: "In securing his victory, Harris underplays the impact of absolute number and density. For example, if adult male literacy was about 10% across the Roman empire, then there were roughly 2 million adult males who *could* read. . . . In world history, this was an unprecedented number of literates in a single state."[110]

This important observation may be taken as conveying the main sense of these responses to Harris. His book was sophisticated and thorough, setting a new standard; yet withal, it could do little more than glide over the surface of far deeper waters. A great deal more remained to be said than had been said. Gaining a holistic view of literacy in the Greco-Roman world would require considering it as a medium of communication, as a visible symbol, and as an instrument of ideological power. It would be necessary to pay "attention to the substance of the written tradition, differences in reading and writing skills, the levels (commonly different) of facility in them, the uses and functions of literacy, variations in the significance of literacy from one culture to another, and the *complexity of literacy in bilingual and multilingual contexts.*"[111] Soon, studies attempting to address some of these further issues began to appear. One such focused on Palestine and literacy in that multilingual context. This was Catherine Hezser's *Jewish Literacy in Roman Palestine* (2001).[112]

Her study was closely modeled after Harris and was thus, as with his book, a "high-level" survey of the evidence. Only occasionally did Hezser descend into the trenches with literary whiskbroom to sweep time's dust from the primary sources and take a close personal look. But in one very important respect she departed from her methodological mentor and took her cue from his critics. She had no interest in attempting to discover how many ancient Jews could read or write. "The present study," she wrote, "will examine the various forms, levels, and social contexts of reading and writing rather than try to determine ancient Jewish literacy rates."[113] As to the chronological limits of her work, Hezser was specific: "The broad time limits are Pompey's conquest of Jerusalem in 63 B.C.E. and the onset of Islamic rule at the beginning of the seventh century C.E. . . . The focus is on the so-called rabbinic period after the destruction of the Temple and before the expansion of the Jewish use of writing in early Byzantine times."[114] With its center of gravity thus weighted to the years after 200 C.E., *Jewish Literacy* only partially overlapped the focus of the present study.

Part 1, "The Conditions for the Development of Literacy," essentially followed Harris's method but with specific reference to Palestine (seen, notably and properly, as an integral part of the larger Greco-Roman world). Hezser weighed the evidence for widespread public schooling among the Jews and found it wanting. Traditional scholars had long taken at face value sweeping Talmudic assertions about the ubiquity of such schools. Hezser charged those holding such views with "historically uncritical argumentation."[115] She examined the production costs of books and judged them beyond the means of the ordinary Jew. She also argued in this first portion of the volume for an inverse relation between rural living—the situation for most ancient Palestinian Jews—and literacy. In all of these matters Hezser was adopting the procedural steps modeled by Harris. She had now established the Jewish lack of all three of his sine quibus non. This "People of the Book" was not really bookish at all. They could not have enjoyed mass literacy.

Other features of Part 1 included analysis of the ideas of written and oral law, magical writings, and the distribution of languages among the Jews. One of her book's great virtues was that Hezser recognized the need to speak of language and literacy together. Did one learn in the first instance to read and write Hebrew, Aramaic, or Greek (or perhaps, in certain locales, some other tongue)? Oddly, however, Hezser offered no fully explicit conclusions on this issue. She did make known her view that the everyday languages of Palestine were Aramaic and Greek, not Hebrew. The holy tongue was for prayers and Torah reading, not for letters or business notes. No one learned it as a mother tongue. For most people, no particular incentive existed to learn it at all. The most that might accrue to such a person was a modicum of honor or prestige, the occasional opportunity to be a Torah-reader in the synagogue. No other social benefits, not to mention monetary ones, would be forthcoming. At best, therefore, a few Aramaic-speaking students acquired a passive knowledge of Hebrew. Only a tiny number of individuals used Hebrew for writing, and such use was always ideologically charged.[116]

Based largely on her reading of rabbinic texts, Hezser's argument was nevertheless that most people who learned to read, learned Hebrew.[117] Did they then acquire only Biblical Hebrew, or also some form of the rabbinic variety? And if it was not a development from vernacular dialect(s), whence

Mishnaic Hebrew? On these matters, Hezser said nothing. Nor did she ever address whether, and in what venue, the ordinary person learned to read or write Aramaic, the language she clearly held as dominant for speech. Of course, absent concern with this threshold question, she never considered *what form* of Aramaic a villager might learn to read, or just who was the intended readership for the literary dialect(s) evidenced, for example, by some 120 of the Dead Sea Scrolls. Thus it is fair to say that on the Semitic side, Hezser touched upon, but did not really plumb, the linguistic dimensions of Jewish literacy.

As to Greek, she argued that circumstances in Palestine were essentially those of many other parts of the eastern empire. The wealthy elite arranged for tutelage in literature and formal Greek language as part of their children's education, and no one else learned to read it. As noted, however, for Hezser many of these same Jewish illiterates could speak the language. Though never addressing the issue outright,[118] presumably Hezser would say that, except for immigrants, they learned it through everyday interactions with speakers in their cities and villages, encouraged by the social and economic benefits in prospect.

Part 2 of *Jewish Literacy* was devoted to an overview of the surviving material according to types of text: letters, documents such as nametags, contracts and receipts, the epigraphic record, *et alia similia plura.* As to literary materials, Hezser focused on only the rabbinic literature—strikingly maintaining, in fact, that this was essentially all that mainstream Jews ever produced during her period of study (on which, more below). Part 3 then summarized and synthesized all of the evidence from the dual perspectives of "the readers of the texts" and "the writers of the texts." Her global conclusion was that Palestinian Jewry during the years 63 B.C.E. to roughly 600 C.E. was less literate, and less involved with reading, writing, and texts of all kinds, than was Greco-Roman society as a whole.

The book was an impressive achievement, erudite in its methods and comprehensive in its coverage of a vast secondary literature. The discussions and analyses of rabbinic literature, Hezser's strength, were particularly laudable. Reviewers were quick with praise. Tessa Rajak called it "an invaluable guide and companion to scholars of every aspect of Second Temple and rabbinic Palestine and of early Christianity." H. Gregory Snyder expected that "readers will be much obliged to Hezser for the amount of material that she has assembled in this impressive contribution to the study of ancient literacy." And Meir Bar-Ilan concluded his (admittedly more lukewarm) review saying, "There is no doubt that the book under discussion will remain for a long time as a basic sourcebook on Jewish literacy in antiquity."[119]

Nevertheless, the book was not without defects, some potentially debilitating to its principal conclusions. Four problems have special relevance for the years with which the present study is concerned, from Pompey to Hadrian.

The first problem was particularly profound. Hezser conceived her work as examining a Jewish Palestine extending chronologically from Pompey's conquest (63 B.C.E.) to the advent of Islam in roughly 600 C.E. To thus treat as an undifferentiated whole this span of seven centuries seems an almost Talmudic mindset, as though things played out in a timeless, unchanging, and constructed world, not in an actual one. In the actual world, a great deal changed over those years. It is very unlikely prima facie that the realities of Jewish literacy could have stood aloof from those changes. If not, and literate expressions changed, then the framing concept of an undifferentiated whole necessarily crumbles.

As remarked earlier, the Bar Kokhba conflict was a true watershed for Jews and Judaism. Very little was the same afterward. Fergus Millar recently cast the immediate aftermath of the Second Revolt as follows: "Given the massive scale of losses, the creation of a pagan *colonia* as a substitute for Jerusalem, from whose territory Jews were excluded, and the step-by-step creation of a network of Greek cities, whose territories between them came to include almost the whole provincial area, we might be struck rather by the fact that Jewish communal life, Jewish observance and the use of Hebrew survived at all."[120]

The Jews came then to inhabit a pagan Roman province. Hezser's conception of the issues took no account of this radical shift from antebellum realities. Ironically, two important books published in the same year as her study (and so of course unavailable to her) have served to focus attention precisely on those two centuries subsequent to Bar Kokhba. The books are Seth Schwartz's *Imperialism and Jewish Society, 200 B.C.E. to 640 C.E.* and Nicole Belayche's *Iudaea-Palaestina: The Pagan Cults in Roman Palestine (Second to Fourth Century).*[121] These two scholars converged on a striking thesis: in the aftermath of the loss to Rome, so far as surviving evidences permit an understanding, the Jewish population of Palestine lived largely assimilated lives. As Schwartz put it, "The core ideology of Judaism [as known in the Second Temple period] was preserved in profoundly altered but still recognizable form mainly by the rabbis, *but had a weak hold, if any, on the rest of the*

Jews."[122] Later, with the Christianization of Palestine during the period after Constantine, Jews were pressured as never before. Now, rather than enjoying an easy coexistence with paganism, they faced an often-hostile government motivated by a Christianity with no interest in religious compromise. The somewhat surprising result was a renewed and revivified Judaism. Thus, these centuries saw prodigious changes, some of them precisely in those aspects of life most closely tied to Jewish language, literacy, and self-conception. Against this kaleidoscopic backdrop, Hezser's broad generalizations appear problematic, to say the least.

The second problem was Hezser's frequently repeated contention—inspired by statements in rabbinic literature—that the Jews of Palestine were systematically taught only to read. They did not learn to write: "Although some Jewish children may have been instructed in writing by their parents or the one or the other teacher, neither rabbinic nor epigraphic sources support the notion that the writing of Hebrew letters [*litterae,* not *epistulae*] was generally taught in Jewish elementary schools."[123] If true, this statement would make education in Palestine unique in the Greco-Roman *oikoumene,* so far as surviving evidence indicates, in failing to teach writing at the first stage of education. In fact, however, Hezser's denial notwithstanding, documentary evidence from Palestine (indeed, the very materials of the present study) clearly demonstrates that writing was taught—arguably, as in contemporary Egypt, even before students began to learn to read.[124]

Hezser's mistaken conclusion owed to a critical imbalance of evidence. She relied almost exclusively on statements of the rabbis—these mostly made in passing, almost random literary evidence, as opposed to concentrated, intentional description. In particular, rabbinic silence on instruction in writing is less telling than she made it seem. Literary descriptions written elsewhere in the broader world of their time demonstrate such silence to be typical, and it cannot be taken as representing what people actually did in educating their children. As with Greek and Latin writers on literary education, rabbinic descriptions focused on the later stages of education, when the procedures became more interesting to the commentators themselves.

For Greco-Roman Egypt, it is the papyri that, after close study, divulge the actual procedures of ancient education at each of three stages. Literary authors on education such as Libanius, Quintilian, and Plutarch are repeatedly shown to be imprecise. The papyri exemplify instruction in writing even while the literary sources ignore it. Both types of evidence are needed to arrive at a rounded picture, but the documentary correction to its literary counterpart is decisive.[125] So, too, one suspects, for Palestine. Reasonable analogy would privilege the documents over the rabbis, what people did, so far as that can be discovered, over what people wrote in offhand remarks—the reverse of Hezser's method.

Ironically, the third noteworthy problem with *Jewish Literacy* was the opposite of the second: a failure to consider literary sources. Heszer passed over almost without comment the writings of the Second Temple period, which consequently became the missing variable in her literacy equation. "Jewish literary output seems to have been very limited during the entire period of discussion here," Hezser wrote. Elsewhere she repeated, "Extra-biblical literary composition and writing was very limited in Roman Palestine." For any reader who may have missed these statements, she remarked yet again, "The only literary works which can certainly be attributed to Palestinian Jews of the first century C.E. are the writings of Josephus and the no longer extant work of his opponent Justus of Tiberius." Hezser explicitly based these judgments on "the surviving literary works datable to the period under discussion." That is to say, despite the ravages of twenty pitiless centuries of Middle Eastern history, of time, armies, and religious execrations, what survives is, she urged, a proportionate representation of what once was. Hezser recognized that this might seem to some an argument from silence but was undeterred, insisting rather that for Palestine during these years absence of evidence really is evidence of absence: "The limitedness of the evidence for all types of writing cannot be explained away by reference to the general vicissitudes of document survival."[126]

But why not? Hezser offered no argument to substantiate her assertion. To ignore as she did the relatively humid Palestinian climate as compared with that of, say, Egypt, and to label a mere "vicissitude" its detrimental effect on the organic writing materials the Jews preferred (papyrus and animal skins) hardly seems judicious. Is it credible that essentially nothing was produced in the cultural capital, Jerusalem, during all these years and that this fact, rather than the "vicissitudes" Hezser waves away, explains why archaeologists have never discovered there a library or an archive—remembering that hundreds of hard-material remains, seals and bullae produced centuries earlier than our period, have been uncovered?[127] The idea that Second Temple Jerusalemites neither wrote books nor owned them, when such have been so lately discovered in the nearby Judaean Desert in such volume, strikes one as curious.

In fact, it is these very materials that best serve as a touchstone for estimates of Jewish literary production in the late Second Temple period.

Since roughly 1945, the Qumran caves have yielded the following numbers of extrascriptural books:[128] Cave 1, twenty-three different works; Cave 2, eight; Cave 3, six; Cave 5, seven; Cave 6, fourteen; Cave 7, two; Cave 8, one; and Cave 11, ten different works. The "mother lode," Cave 4, alone vouchsafed 289 different extrascriptural books.[129]

This is a total of 360 *different writings* from the later years of the Second Temple. Virtually none of them, it must be appreciated, was known to scholarship before its modern discovery. Apart from the exemplars found on the shores of the Dead Sea, and excepting a half dozen works adopted by Christians or that by paths unknown made their way to the Cairo Genizeh, these Jewish books vanished, evanescent as Jonah's gourd, leaving no trace in historical sources. The survival of these particular materials was fortuitous, owing principally to a single of Hezser's "vicissitudes": they were stored in a sere climate akin to that of Egypt and so had to weather only worms, rats, and soil chemistry to arrive at our own day. That proved possible.

Given the long odds involved in both the survival and the discovery of the Dead Sea Scrolls, by what calculus would the historian go on to extrapolate that the Jews of these years produced almost nothing else? Hezser's insistence on this point puzzles. We simply cannot know what once existed.[130] That it was more than we know, however, emerges from the scrolls themselves.

The physical and scribal characteristics of the scrolls argue that these manuscripts were but the tip of a literary iceberg. Many other books, and many, many additional manuscript copies, surely existed as well. This is not the place for full discussion, but a selection of phenomena pertinent to origins and numbers may briefly be noted. (1) Of the scriptural scrolls found near Qumran, no two demonstrably share an immediate prototype; neither did any manuscript give rise to identifiable daughter copies.[131] Provisionally, the same may be said of the nonscriptural manuscripts, although here the evidence has not yet been fully sorted out. (2) The absence of autographic texts among the Qumran caches is conspicuous. With the possible exception of one or two manuscripts (for example, 4Q175), none of the writings manifests the features diagnostic of ancient authorial originals.[132] Nearly all of the texts are, it seems, copies. (3) Also missing is the signature of a scribal school, those features-in-common normally found among any group of ancient or medieval books produced in a single locale over a few generations. On the contrary: these manuscripts manifest diverse techniques for preparation of skins and ink, correction of errors, orthography, treatment of the *nomen sacrum,* rubrication and *incipita,* paragraphing, etc., using as well five different scripts:

paleo-Hebrew, standard "Jewish," and three different cryptic scripts.[133] (4) A disproportionately high number of individual hands appears among the scrolls. Of roughly 930 manuscripts (some 210 of them scriptural books), no more than 65 or 70 seem to come from the hands of scribes who copied one or more other texts as well.[134] The matter has yet to receive sufficiently detailed analysis, but conservatively estimated, more than five hundred different scribes are represented by the Dead Sea Scrolls. (5) The existence among the caches of numerous apparently nonscribal, personal copies—cheaply produced, sloppily copied, even opisthographic—alongside premier luxury editions such as the *Temple Scroll* (11Q19), together with the entire gamut between these two market extremes, indicates a diverse origin for the manuscripts.[135]

These phenomena ill comport with the hypothesis that these books were wholly the product of a small sect dwelling on the shores of the Dead Sea, *sine ulla femina, omni venere abdicata, sine pecunia, socia palmarum* (without women and renouncing all sex, without money and having only the palm trees for company), as the elder Pliny describes a group of Essenes.[136] The facts seem to require the mass of the scrolls to have originated elsewhere, not at the Qumran site—indeed, possibly in many different towns and villages. If so, the books necessarily constitute a kind of cross-section of what existed, a glimpse into the broader literary culture of late Second Temple Jewry.[137] True, some of the nonscriptural texts are "sectarian" (perhaps 15 to 20 percent), so it remains to be clarified how representative this cross-section may be.[138] On the basis of what can still be read of these fragmentary writings, however, a significant majority evidences no sectarian slant. Most would seem to have been acceptable to all Jews, sectarian or mainstream (however those problematic terms be defined). Proportionately, some 300 of these 360 books are reasonably seen as the products of wider Palestinian Judaism—authored and copied, that is, not merely read by that greater polity outside of Qumran.

If it is true that most nonscriptural manuscripts among the Qumran discoveries originated elsewhere, then cladistic considerations alone would entail thousands of nonscriptural scrolls in the hands of Judaean Jewry in the years between Pompey and Hadrian. Significant literate behavior would, of course, accompany these books, only partially a function of how many people could actually read them. Palestine during these years was evidently far from an impoverished literary culture. This conclusion, arising as it does mostly by examination of the physical and scribal properties of the texts—inherently less controversial, perhaps, than a reading of the texts—is the more compelling for its origin.

This portrait contrasts sharply with that offered by Hezser. How is it, then, that she ignored these writings and the evidence they provide and so arrived at her position?

Her comments on the texts made the answer clear. Hezser held to an obsolete paradigm of Qumran scholarship. "The practice of literary composition and writing amongst the Qumran group," she wrote, "cannot be considered representative of contemporary Palestinian Judaism as a whole."[139] Born with the first relatively meager manuscript discoveries (seven scrolls, to be precise), the theory she espoused portrayed all of the scrolls as the products of an isolated sect living at Qumran, identified as Essenes. Certain elements of the "Essene hypothesis" still predominate, but not overwhelmingly, certainly not as once they did. Many of the verities of the first two generations of Qumran scholarship are now being reexamined and questioned in light of the full publication of the texts, completed in 2002. In particular, one element that no longer enjoys much specialist support evidently remained Hezser's view, although without any justifying counterargument on her part—what one scholar has dubbed the "theory of the small scribbling sect."[140] In failing even to broach the issue, Hezser appeared ill informed.

Unfortunately, her problem with Second Temple literature did not end there but extended well beyond the Dead Sea Scrolls. She similarly made little or no mention of other notable Jewish literature composed, most scholars judge, during the years between the coming of Rome and the Second Revolt. Her analysis left to one side the *Psalms of Solomon,* the *Similitudes of Enoch,* pseudo-Philo's *Book of Biblical Antiquities, Second Baruch, Fourth Ezra,* and the *Assumption of Moses*—to say nothing of the New Testament.[141] Failure to come to terms with the surviving literature of late Second Temple Judaism was the third problem with Hezser's book, and it was, for the early period of her coverage, fundamental.

Her fourth problem concerned the Aramaic language and its place among the Jews. "Aramaic was not an essential component of Jewish identity," she opined, continuing, "Nobody will have been particularly interested in its preservation."[142] She further cited with approval comments by Chaim Rabin that "Aramaic was not a bearer of a culture," at least not for first-century Jews. It is hard to know what to do with such statements. Prima facie they cannot be squared with elementary facts. Aramaic was commonly spoken, perhaps most commonly. Can any spoken language succeed in communicating but somehow avoid bearing culture? Surely people discussed important aspects of culture in this language as in any others. Aramaic was a vehicle for significant works of literature, written, read, or both in the first century; also for biblical translation and commentary, at first oral, then later written in the form of the Targumim. Some of that interpretive activity was already under way in the first century C.E. and even earlier, to judge from the presence among the Dead Sea Scrolls of three Targumim—two of Job and one of (at least a passage of) Leviticus.[143] What is literature if not a bearer of culture?

Perhaps the most important cultural realm over which Aramaic reigned was that of law. The Jews of Palestine in the late Second Temple era composed a great many of their legal documents in one or another dialect of Aramaic. Theirs was a legacy dating back to much earlier Neo-Babylonian practice; formal legal elements from that ancient tradition were now combined with native, Greek, and Roman elements.[144] The idea that any people would possess a centuries-old legal tradition but that the language of that tradition would nevertheless fail to bear culture beggars the imagination. Moreover, if many people learned to write their names in Aramaic precisely so that they could take part in the legal culture, signing documents as needed—and as we shall see, this is what the documents of the present study, and much comparative evidence, suggest—then Hezser's misconceived estimate of the language's role among literate Jews is, once again, fundamental for its potential bearing on her conclusions.

Some years before Hezser wrote, Abraham Wasserstein had penned a programmatic essay in which he considered the role of Aramaic among the ancient Jews. In that essay he wrote:

> In the Near East there had existed for centuries before Hellenism appeared on the scene another supra-national civilisation, that of the various Aramaic-speaking peoples and indeed of others who, though not using Aramaic in their daily speech, had other uses for it such as employing it as the chancery language of multi-national (and hence multi-lingual) empires. . . . This, it is true, was not as all-encompassing and as easily definable as the Hellenistic civilisation. It was more pluralistic than Hellenism and more preservative of existing different local cultures. . . . Its various constitutive elements, linguistic, social, political, administrative, had been formed, acquired, assimilated and retained over many centuries, in a large part of the Near East, the populations of which over the same period succeeded in preserving their own national, regional, religious cultures. . . . Hellenism took its place beside local aramaicised cultures; it did not supplant them.[145]

Ironically, Hezser knew of this essay, for she cited it (though not this passage).[146] That she allowed Wasserstein's words no more formative role in her own thinking about Aramaic and culture was unfortunate.

If the preceding criticisms of Hezser's *Jewish Literacy* are considered fair and convincing, that judgment should not be allowed to detract from the perceived value of her work as a whole, recalling that its real focus was the Talmudic period. But these problems with her analysis do sharply call into question the reliability of her conclusions as they pertain to the years between Pompey and Hadrian. Perhaps the People of the Book were bookish after all? At the least, Hezser's analysis invites cross-checking from a different perspective and set of evidences. Her views of language usage among the Jews, particularly her repudiation of the notion of Hebrew as vernacular, also remind us of how precariously balanced is modern consensus here. The desire actually to know—however naïve we may realize that to be, recognizing how uncertain are the best of our certainties about the ancient world—joins with a tantalizing possibility of real progress in our understanding of both language and literacy. We turn to a new approach.

The Present Study

The present study examines the texts conventionally known as the Bar Kokhba texts for what they can teach us concerning ancient Jewish patterns of language and literacy. These texts derive from caves in the Judaean Desert where refugee owners took them, mostly as they fled the collapsing Second Revolt. Many of these people were captured or died, betrayed or otherwise tracked down by the Romans, sometimes starving to death beneath the grim watch of sentries who stood above the cave entrances, seeking to ensure that none exited alive. Others may have escaped. If so, they never returned for their precious documents.

Discovered sometimes by archaeologists, more often by bedouin, the texts first met modern eyes in the early 1950s. For about a decade the primary discoveries continued in a virtual cascade, although even in the past several years new exempla have emerged in less spectacular fashion, new caves being examined, old caves reexamined using better technology.[147] Thus, depending on the specifics of a particular papyrus or scrap of leather, the Bar Kokhba texts have been known to scholarship for as many as sixty years. Known to exist, that is. For a variety of reasons, publication has often been extraordinarily delayed. Several of the most significant collections of material have become fully available only within the past decade.[148]

For reasons that shall become clear, it is the signature-bearing documents and the letters among these diverse finds that are of primary interest. It is perhaps surprising at first reconnoiter, but these legal and epistolary materials actually span more than 150 years. For while the central time period of the Bar Kokhba finds is naturally closely connected to the events of the revolt, and so focused on the years 132–136 and shortly before, many of the documents are in fact much older, having been archived by individuals or families for decades preceding their flight to the caves. The traceable history of a given piece of property may sometimes be as much as sixty or seventy years, as it changed hands several times, contracts recording each transaction, and the documents were passed down in sequence with the property to new owners, the last of whom took the bundle to a desert refuge.

Sometimes texts significantly older than the time of the Second Revolt have come into association with the Bar Kokhba materials for other reasons. In the case of the Murabbaʿat finds, in particular, it has recently become apparent that there were not one, but two textually represented periods of residence in the caves: one at the time of Bar Kokhba and another much earlier, in the trail of the First Revolt (66–73 C.E.).[149] In yet other cases, documents long believed to derive from Qumran Cave 4 appear instead to have been found in Bar Kokhba caves, subsequently being mixed up or misrepresented by their bedouin vendors. In two such instances, recently recognized textual joins or contextual connections with certainly provenanced Bar Kokhba documents remove all doubt that such has occurred.[150] Two manuscripts once believed to belong to the Qumran caches, 4Q342 and 4Q347, purchased in the same lot as the preceding, postdate the destruction of the Jerusalem Temple according to radiocarbon dating.[151] Most of the remaining "Cave 4" economic documents are suspect by association, being among the same purchase lot as the four falsely identified. Indeed, it is possible that essentially no documentary texts, as opposed to literary ones, actually come from any of the Qumran caves.[152] Each suspect text requires careful examination and individual argument, of course.

Accordingly, the span of time for the documents of this study, all arguably associated with Bar Kokhba caves, begins in the late first century B.C.E. and, after a gap of several decades, continues with reasonably even distribution right through the first century and on to the end of the Second Revolt.

The documents sufficiently preserved as to yield the requisite information number 145: 118 contracts and 27 letters. They are composed in four languages: Hebrew, Jewish Aramaic, Greek, and Nabataean (with bits of Latin and

Arabic also in evidence). Geographically, they cover all of Judaea and beyond. This is not to hazard a guess. One can usually know the provenance not only of a given legal document, wherein the place of writing is typically part of the dating formula, but also of principals and witnesses, including any alien to that locale.[153] As described earlier, scribes would annotate the origin of such alien participants in case they needed to be tracked down later. Thus, no matter where the contract may have been written, we often learn about the literate behavior of adult participants who as children learned to read or write elsewhere. Accordingly, it is possible to affirm that the contracts and their participants represent to us aspects of the linguistic and literate behavior of more than forty separate cities, towns, villages, and even, it seems, latifundia that Jews inhabited.[154]

In the years between the two revolts, the Roman province of Judaea comprised Judaea proper, Galilee, Samaria, and Peraea.[155] It is in this broader sense that the term is generally used in the present study. Judaea proper is exceptionally well represented (see Figure 1.1). People or texts derive from the following known towns and villages, moving roughly from north to south: Galoda, Gophna, Sha'alabbim, Jericho, Tsuba (Zobah), Kislon, Jerusalem, Qumran, Haradona, Bethar, Beth-Bassi, Ha-Horemet, Herodium, Kiryat-'Arbayya, 'Ir Nahash, Tekoa, Murabba'at, Hebron, Kephar-Barucha, Ziph, Yaqim, Beth 'Amar, Aristoboulias, En Gedi, 'Anab, and Masada. Additionally, materials survive representing Peraea: Philadelphia (Rabbat-Ammon), Livias, and Kephar-Baru. Significant documentation originating outside the Jewish polity, in Arabia, including materials from Rabbat-Moab, Mahoza (with its subdivision, Luhit), Mazra'a, Zoar, and Petra, is also a part of the study. Numerous additional thus-far unidentified toponyms attach to contracts, or to people within the contracts. Most of these places were probably in Judaea, but one or two may have lain outside the borders.[156]

Important beyond the representative geographical spread is what might be termed the representative social spread. The majority of the communities known from the documents were rural. Accordingly, the materials of the present study frequently transport us beyond the great centers and their urban elites to a realm far from the world of Philo and Josephus. Here, unmediated by literary rendition, we glimpse directly the lives and mores of that 70 percent or more of Judaeans who dwelled in agricultural settings. For the most part, however, the lowest classes—the day laborers queued for work who inhabit the Gospel parables—lie outside the picture. Judging from the amounts of money changing hands in the contracts, and from the quality of

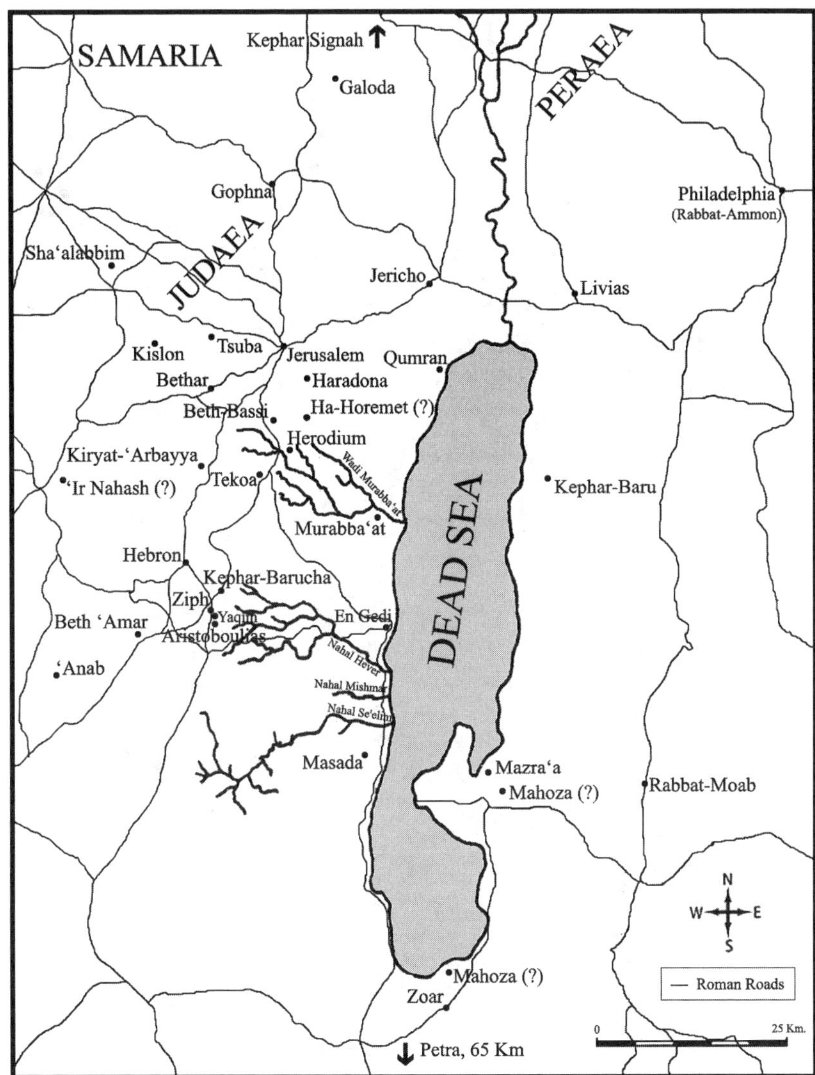

Figure 1.1. *Map of the origins of people and texts in the Bar Kokhba corpus.* (*Map by author.*)

material possessions found in archaeological context with many of the texts, most of the principals and witnesses were village aristocracy and gentry. This fact will affect consideration of literacy more than that of language.

Some four hundred mostly wealthy individuals are in evidence. Prosopographical analysis of these people yields an understanding of their language and literacy habits broader than their personal behavior alone could afford and so helps bring into focus the society as a whole. The population of Palestine in these years was probably about one million;[157] our four hundred, however, are almost entirely drawn from the top quartile of that population.[158] Thus we have an essentially random sample of four hundred individuals from a pool of 250,000. It is reasonable to think that this sample has statistical validity. Moreover, these are precisely the kind of on-the-ground data that may serve as checks to high-level models like Hezser's—the sort of approach Horsfall had in mind as he grubbed extraneously in the undergrowth of Harris's *Ancient Literacy.* As usual with the study of ancient history, we have to make do with snippets, individual frames lifted here and there from within a moving picture. They stand before us isolated and stationary. Yet, if the frames are sufficiently and fortunately distributed, one may hope to recover and extrapolate a fair idea of the plot. Notable gaps will persist, but restrained imagination can accomplish much.

The search for family connections among and beyond these four hundred individuals is central to the prosopography of the present study. But here an apparent problem rears its head. To recognize such connections, usually one must rely on shared identifiers, especially patronyms. Given the Jewish onomasticon in the late Second Temple period, however, assigning family connections on the basis of names may be adjudged tenuous, unreliable. The number of different male names was, by modern Western standards, severely limited, somewhat as with Roman *praenomina.* It can seem that every family had a Simon, a Joseph, a Judah, an Eleazar. In fact, about twenty common male names dominated the onomastic repertoire; the seven Hebrew names of the Hasmoneans were particularly ubiquitous. For women even fewer names were in common use, and virtually any family with daughters would boast a Mariam, a Salome, or a Shelamzion.[159] These are the cautionary facts. They are the reason that scholars by and large have refrained from making the sort of family identifications here adduced.

Yet that reticence, while doubtless laudable on general principle (who does not favor scholarly caution?), has partially closed off a promising analytical tool for the Bar Kokhba texts.[160] Reticence is praiseworthy, after all, only when it is appropriate. Too much caution is only slightly better than too little. Several considerations argue for the approach taken here.

One point is merely to acknowledge ancient pragmatism. In those societies, where many people were illiterate, sooner or later *someone* had to sign or subscribe a document for the person who could not—and for many, none was as trustworthy as a family member. That person could be expected to have one's interests at heart. Further, family members not infrequently had something personal at stake in the legal undertaking. They served as signatories and witnesses in part to keep an eye on such matters, or to reassure others that they were doing so. Mortality rates were high. With the death of a principal, rights and property—or, less happily, fees and obligations—would often pass to someone else in the family. As matters of practical necessity, legal transactions therefore often became family affairs. In Greco-Roman Egypt, where the ancient onomasticon is friendlier, these familial connections are more transparent to modern eyes, and everywhere to be found.

In Egypt the role of family members was especially prominent in situations involving illiterates. Egyptian women were typically analphabetic and therefore in need of help to transact any business requiring signatures or subscriptions. Following Greek custom, this would be done through the agency of a male guardian, the κύριος, for which role a fairly rigid, legally stipulated hierarchy of relatives existed, based on degrees of kinship. If the woman were married, her husband would sign; otherwise, her son, father, grandfather, or brother, in that order. If none of these men were alive, well, or available, the lot fell to a more distant relative, but still a legal συγγενής: a nephew, perhaps, or a cousin, finally, a brother-in-law. Only if the woman were completely without male family would an outsider become her κύριος.[161] Likewise, male illiterates in Egyptian texts turned to family members to write or act as witness for them: usually close relatives, most often sons or brothers.[162] At times the texts of the present study make explicit precisely the same dynamics regarding women and illiterates.[163] In addition to the general considerations, this intersection encourages cautious reasoning from the better known situation, Egypt, to the lesser known, Palestine, and inference of analogous familial involvement.

A second line of evidence suggesting that one should expect to see family involvement in the legal texts of the Bar Kokhba corpus is the fact that early rabbinic literature legislated against (certain types of) such behavior. In particular, apart from stipulated, very specific situations, the early rabbis disallowed family members acting as witnesses to contracts. The reason is obvious. Because the family would see things through the eyes of their principal, they could not legitimately be considered third-party witnesses to the legal facts. A text composed in the light of this general prohibition is *t. Git.* 7:11:[164]

גט שחתמו עליו חמשה עדים נמצאו שלשה הראשונים קרובים או
פסולין תתקיים עדות בשאר עדים

A writ of divorce that five witnesses signed, of which the first three were discovered to be family members or (otherwise) disqualified: (the writ's) testimony stands, on the basis of the remaining witnesses.

That family members were not considered legitimate witnesses is here explicit. The writ stands only because the number of witnesses remaining after the disqualified witnesses are abstracted is still the legal minimum, two. The understanding that the expression "disqualified witness" (עד פסול) included family members then clarifies *m. Ketub.* 2:3: "If witnesses (having signed a marriage contract) said, 'That is our signature, but we were forced to sign'; or, 'We were minors'; or 'We were disqualified witnesses [פסולי עדות]';—they are regarded as truthful." Here, in the judgment of the rabbis, family members were forbidden to witness a marriage contract.

A very specific exception to the general prohibition obtained for a certain type of *Doppelurkunde* (the "double contracts," such as constitute the majority of the Bar Kokhba contracts, the rabbinic מקושר, "knotted writ"). To produce a *Doppelurkunde,* the scribe would write out the text twice: once as an "outer text," which would remain open for consultation, and once as an "inner text." The latter would subsequently be folded over and tied, the witnesses signing beside each of the knots that secured the inner folds. Only in the event of legal challenge would the inner portion be unfolded.[165] Normally, family members were not to sign along the knots. But it might happen that a writ of divorce of this type would lack sufficient witnesses, that is, have fewer witnesses than knots. It was then known as a "bald writ" (גט קרח). In such a situation, according to *t. Git.* 6:9, even relatives were permitted to fill out one of the missing slots (קרובים משלימים עליו)—but no more.[166] The implicit understanding is manifestly that this situation was exceptional. The usual prohibition of family involvement was being waived.

The fact that early rabbinic literature legislated against family members signing as witnesses almost certainly means that it was happening. Moreover, it was probably customary. This deduction arises from the axiom that ancient legislation was virtually never programmatic, but rather, a reaction to what was happening. Hence, if legislating authorities disapproved of a reality, they would legislate against it. If they approved, they legislated to encourage it. Holding up a mirror to the legislation reveals the reality. For common examples one need only think of the Roman sumptuary laws, or the *ius trium liberorum*. If, then, we discover frequent concord or congruence between the patronyms of Judaean principals and those of witnesses, it is unlikely to be mere chance. These people were probably related.

And frequent concord is indeed what we find. The fact constitutes the third consideration in favor of the proposed prosopographic procedure. Even with the comparatively limited Jewish onomasticon, the frequency of concord is too great for coincidence. Examples abound, but consider the following: *Mur* 18, a bill of loan composed in 55 C.E., had as a principal Zechariah b. Yohanan. Signing as witnesses were, among others, Yohanan b. Simon and Joseph b. Yohanan, presumably Zechariah's father and brother, respectively. *Mur* 29, a deed of sale written in 67 in Jerusalem, included Eleazar b. Zechariah as a principal; Simon b. Zechariah signed as a witness. 4Q344, an acknowledgment of debt written, as it seems, between 72 and 127, had as a principal Eleazar b. Joseph. Signing as witness was another b. Joseph whose first name has been lost to damage. *P.Hever* 22, dating to the late first or early second century, is a deed of sale. One principal was a b. Eleazar. Signing as witness was another b. Eleazar (both first names are lost). *P.Jericho* 7, the sale of a date crop composed in 84, included among the principals Joseph b. Yohanan. Signing as witness was Yohanan b. Simon. *P.Yadin* 5, a deposit written in Greek in Mahoza in 110, featured Honi b. Simon as a principal and Simon b. [PN] as a witness. In *P.Yadin* 7 (deed of gift, 120 C.E.), [Simon] b. Menahem was principal, [PN] b. Menahem was witness; in *P.Yadin* 8 (purchase contract, 122 C.E.), those roles belonged to Bar Simon and Eleazar b. Simon, respectively. Lastly, in *Mur* 42, the famous Second Revolt letter of affidavit concerning ownership of a cow, Eleazar b. Joseph was one of those giving affidavit. Witnesses included Joseph b. Joseph and Jacob b. Joseph. Many more might be cited, but presumably these examples suffice to establish the point.[167]

The fourth reason that one should expect to see family involvement in the legal texts of the Bar Kokhba corpus arises from the social demographics of Judaea during these years. Most rural villages comprised large networks of extended families, heavily intermarried, with strong ties of kinship.[168] Accordingly, if (as here) one has to do with legal texts mostly originating in identifiable rural settings, ipso facto one should anticipate a high degree of family participation in those documents.

These four considerations strongly argue that to expect to find—and therefore to seek—family connections in the texts of this study is reasonable and proper. To do so here, where one should expect them to exist, is not incautious, though it doubtless would be in situations with texts of unknown provenance. Here, family connections certainly exist. The results will not be particularly tenuous, although of course occasional mistaken identifications are probably unavoidable. From time to time, despite one's best efforts, the onomasticon will have its way. Nevertheless, the heuristic value to be gained from identifying family members promises to outweigh unrecognizable and unavoidable mistakes of detail that may occur now and again.[169] The potential ability to peer within families, to distinguish among members' linguistic and literate behavior, is simply too valuable to foreswear on the grounds that identifications cannot always be absolutely certain.

The present study proposes, then, to investigate some four hundred individuals and their families as they emerge from the Bar Kokhba letters and legal materials. The proposed royal road to knowledge of their linguistic and literacy patterns is a socially contextualized study of their signatures, subscriptions, and other written representations. It is especially the signatures that promise to disclose much about both aspects of Judaean life, and they have never been studied.

As to language: the signatures tell us about these patterns because of a peculiar fact that seems to have gone unremarked but that insistently intrudes upon the reader of the contracts. *Normally, if possible, people signed a contract in the same language in which the body was composed.* To put it another way, the decision as to which language to use when signing was not, in most circumstances, merely random, a whimsical choice among the tongues one happened to know. A preliminary glance at some numbers will clarify the point (all of these data will receive much fuller discussion later).

As we turn to these numbers, certain distinctions should be borne in mind. For one, the principals to a contract will be a more random grouping of the population than will the witnesses or *hypographeis.* The reason is that, viewed from the historian's perspective, the principals emerge by a roll of the dice. These were just people who happened to want to sell some dates or perhaps buy a house or pay a tax. They may or may not have been literate; it was not of the essence. Nor was their knowledge of the language in which the transactions were to be recorded necessarily a prime concern for anybody. But for the witnesses or *hypographeis* matters were different. On this occasion their entire purpose was to write. Accordingly, they were chosen because they could sign—and ideally, as will become apparent, sign in the language of the contract. They were of course never illiterate altogether. They could sign in some language. Among the principals, illiteracy was common. What one can learn from the two groups is thus somewhat different, but complementary.

As Table 1.2 illustrates, within the corpus of this study forty-six principals were presented with an opportunity to sign an Aramaic document. Of those forty-six, thirty-three could do so, while thirteen could not sign at all. Twenty-nine signed in Aramaic. One principal, bearing a Greek name, signed in Greek. No one signed in Hebrew. Of the witnesses and *hypographeis* to these same legal materials, eighty of eighty-four affixed an Aramaic signature. Two signed in Hebrew, another in Greek, and one in a mixture of Aramaic and Hebrew. For these latter four, as will be shown, reasonable explanations for each behavior exist, mostly emerging from the prosopography.

When faced with a contract composed in Hebrew, as Table 1.3 shows, eight principals were unable to sign at all. Only four of nineteen signed in

Table 1.2. Aramaic text totals

	Judaean principals (46 total)		Judaean witnesses/*hypographeis*/ officials (84 total)	
Language	No.	%*	No.	%*
Sign in Aramaic	29	67.4	80	95.2
Sign in Hebrew	0	0.0	2	2.4
Sign in Greek	1	2.3	1	1.2
Sign in mixed Aramaic/Hebrew	0	0.0	1	1.2
Cannot sign	13	30.2	0	0.0
Other	3	—	0	0.0

*Percentages are calculated with "Other" discounted; see discussion in Chapter 5.

Table 1.3. Hebrew text totals

	Judaean principals (19 total)		Judaean witnesses/*hypographeis*/ officials (42 total)	
Language	No.	%*	No.	%*
Sign in Aramaic	1	6.3	10	25.6
Sign in Hebrew	4	25.0	24	61.5
Sign in Greek	1	6.3	0	0.0
Sign in mixed Aramaic/Hebrew	2	12.5	5	12.8
Cannot sign	8	50.0	0	0.0
Other	3	—	3	—

*Percentages are calculated with "Other" discounted; see discussion in Chapter 5.

Hebrew. One signed in Aramaic, two in mixed Aramaic and Hebrew, and one, bearing a Greek name, signed in Greek. Of forty-two witnesses and *hypographeis,* twenty-four signed in Hebrew, ten in Aramaic, and five in a mixture of Hebrew and Aramaic. None signed in Greek.

Observe in Table 1.4 that nine principals within the corpus of this study had occasion to sign contracts composed in Greek. Most lived in Mahoza, a mixed Jewish and Nabataean community. None signed in Greek; in fact, seven were illiterate. Two signed in Judaean Aramaic. None used Hebrew. Among the Judaeans chosen for their ability to write, the Judaean witnesses and *hypographeis,* just twenty-three of ninety-one signed in Greek. None signed in Hebrew, sixty-eight in Aramaic. Twenty-one Nabataean witnesses set down signatures in that language, and three in Greek.

For the Nabataean materials set out in Table 1.5, one must distinguish between Jewish participants and Nabataean ones, as far as names make that possible. No Jew ever signed in Nabataean: one of five principals wrote in Aramaic (the others being illiterate), and twelve of twelve witnesses and *hypographeis* signed in Aramaic. No Jew signed in Hebrew or Greek. The three Nabataean principals signed in Nabataean, as did all sixteen of the Nabataean witnesses and *hypographeis.*

Certain patterns in these numbers are strongly defined. Overwhelmingly, people signed Aramaic materials in that language if they could write. Grouping principals with witnesses and *hypographeis,* the percentage that

Table 1.4. Greek text totals

	Judaean principals (9 total)		Judaean witnesses/ *hypographeis*/officials (91 total)		Nabataean witnesses/ *hypographeis*/officials (24 total)	
Language	No.	%	No.	%	No.	%
Sign in Aramaic/ Nabataean	2	22.2	68	74.7	21	87.5
Sign in Hebrew	0	0.0	0	0.0	0	0.0
Sign in Greek	0	0.0	23	25.3	3	12.5
Sign in mixed Aramaic/Hebrew	0	0.0	0	0.0	0	0.0
Cannot sign	7	77.8	0	0.0	0	0.0

Table 1.5. Nabataean text totals

	Principals (8 total)		Witnesses/*hypographeis*/ officials (28 total)	
Language	No.	%	No.	%
Sign in Aramaic	1	12.5	12	42.9
Sign in Hebrew	0	0.0	0	0.0
Sign in Greek	0	0.0	0	0.0
Sign in Nabataean	3	37.5	16	57.1
Sign in mixed Aramaic/Hebrew	0	0.0	0	0.0
Cannot sign	4	50.0	0	0.0

did so was 95.6 (109/114). When it came time to sign in Hebrew, a much lower (though still notable) percentage did so: 59.6 (28/47). In this connection it is also interesting that virtually no one signed non-Hebrew contracts in Hebrew. Of a total of 207 literate Judaean signatories faced with the option, only 2 people signed a non-Hebrew contract in Hebrew (1.0 percent). Similar to Hebrew was the situation for Greek. Of the literate Judaean signatories to Greek contracts, 26.9 percent signed in that language (25/93), but just 3 of 174 signed non-Greek contracts in it (1.7 percent). When Jews signed a contract composed in a language other than Aramaic, but did not sign in the language of the body, overwhelmingly they chose to sign in Aramaic: 98.9 percent of 95 signatories (94/95). In the terms of our computer age, Aramaic was plainly the default language, at least for legal situations.

Taken as a whole, these numbers speak clearly and eloquently. The choice of language in which to sign was seldom aleatory. On this point the behavior of the witnesses and *hypographeis* is particularly informative. They were engaged (sometimes hired) specifically to do a given thing that customary law expected in the situation. Accordingly, the pattern of what they actually did spotlights the ideal for which they were striving. If many signed Hebrew contracts in Hebrew, Greek in Greek, etc., the legal expectation is made manifest.

One can examine the matter in terms of formal statistical method and perform a chi-squared test on the data regarding the witnesses in Tables 1.2–1.5.[170] We begin with a standard formulation in terms of statistical hypotheses:

1. Null Hypothesis: No correspondence exists between the language of the contract and the language signed.
2. Alternative Hypothesis: A correspondence exists between the language of the contract and the language signed.
3. Practical Significance: A difference of more than 20 percent from the expected "values" in any of these cells would be practically significant.

Table 1.6 illustrates the expected and observed "values" (in this case, numbers of signatories) relative to the hypotheses. The table shows that for Aramaic contracts—to take one example—the null hypothesis would predict 53.7 signatories in Aramaic. This is the expected or "random" number the method would predict if people simply signed the contracts in any of the four contractual languages without their considering the language of the particular contract. What we actually find is that 80 signatories used Aramaic to sign, far more than a "random" choice among languages would have us imagine. This difference is easily "practically significant." Similarly, for Hebrew contracts a "random" expectation would predict 4.7 signatories using that language to affix their John Hancocks. What we actually get is 29! At the end of the day, the chi-squared value for this test is 259.66, with a p-value less than 0.001. The meaning: this difference in language signed is *extremely statistically significant.* Accordingly, the alternative hypothesis is correct beyond a reasonable doubt, and we may fairly assert that a very strong correspondence exists between the language of the body and the language of the signatures.

So the data of the tables support the conclusion that Judaeans in the years between Pompey and Hadrian ordinarily signed a contract in the language of its body if possible. If they did not, the data suggest that they usually could not. Early rabbinic literature seems to confirm the social portrait sketched by these numbers. For example, consider *t. B. Bat.* 11:8: משנין שטרות מעיברית ליוונית ומיוונית לעיברית ועושין לו קיום (If contracts change

Table 1.6. Expected and observed values for witness signatures

	Language signed (expected/observed)			
Language of the contract	Aramaic	Hebrew	Greek	Nabataean
Aramaic	53.7/80	10.1/3	8.5/1	11.7/0
Hebrew	24.9/10	4.7/29	4.0/0	5.4/0
Greek	73.5/68	13.8/0	11.7/26	16.0/21
Nabataean	17.9/12	3.4/0	2.8/0	3.9/16

from Hebrew letters to Greek, or from Greek letters to Hebrew, they are recognized as legal).[171] Linguistic changeover was very likely conceived as coinciding with the signatures of the witnesses, because the other possible interpretation—that the body of the contract itself might change language—is virtually without example in extant Second Temple materials.[172] If this reasoning is correct, then a useful inference follows. The need to make the given statement in the Tosephta presupposes an ideal or normal situation wherein the language of a contract did not change, namely, the witnesses signed in the language of the body.

Similarly, *m. Git.* 9:8 allowed witnesses to sign in Greek even if the document were written in "Hebrew letters" (or possibly "Aramaic") and vice versa.[173] The reason why explicit permission was required goes unmentioned but was adduced in a later text, *y. Git.* 50c. Here, the famous rabbi Rav argued against the Mishnah just cited. Rav stated, אין העדים חותמין אלא אם כן היו יודעין לקרות (the witnesses do not sign unless they know how to read). Ultimately, despite Rav's logic, the halakhah followed the earlier Mishnah, allowing signatures in a language different from the body, but his point remained. To sign in a language other than the body's normally meant that a witness could not read the contract, or as may be, could not understand it when read aloud. This was hardly a perfect situation, but such were the realities on the ground in Roman Judaea.

Historical witness and logic concur. Only those who could sign in the language of the body could affirm that it said what it was supposed to say. Any who signed in other languages were affirming no more than their understanding that an agreement had been reached. They vouched for a discussion surrounding the document but not for the actual document itself. Hence signatures had different meanings, meanings presumably recognized as different by customary law, differences upheld by the halakhah. The ideal is apparent yet again: stipulations and signatures should all be in the same language.

The difference in legal force that depended on language helps to explain what would otherwise be a puzzling phenomenon. Why did witnesses to Hebrew contracts ever sign in Aramaic? After all, the difference between an Aramaic signature and a Hebrew one was a mere two words: יהוסף בר יהודה שהד, say, as opposed to יהוסף בן יהודה עד. And one of the two Hebrew words, בן ("son"), was surely known to any Judaean, since it was an element of so many personal and place-names regularly read from the scriptures in the synagogue or voiced by Hebrew speakers around them.

Moreover, the scripts for the two languages were identical. Theoretically, if one could inscribe Aramaic, one could inscribe Hebrew. With minimal coaching, any reasonably intelligent person literate in Aramaic would have been able to sign Hebrew contracts in Hebrew. Yet one-fourth of the signatories in this study nevertheless chose to sign in Aramaic. It is now apparent why.

To sign in Hebrew rather than Aramaic meant that one either could read the Hebrew of the contract or, more likely, could affirm the content of the contract when the scribe read it aloud. Accordingly, to sign in Hebrew amounted to a claim to know Hebrew (normally, as will be discussed later, a vernacular rather than the Biblical version). Few people would have been so bold as to attempt a false claim, since signatories normally lived among the other parties to the contract, and inhabitants of agricultural villages would naturally "know everybody's business"—including the linguistic proficiencies of their neighbors. Because signatures had recognized legal force that differed, people were deterred from learning the word or two they might need to sign in Hebrew. Signing was about more than just the words.

If one spoke Hebrew and could write Aramaic, one could also write at least simple Hebrew, such as a witness attestation required. By this reasoning we can arrive at an interesting computation. On the basis of the data in Table 1.3, a rough estimate would be that something like one-half of the Jews of Judaea in these years knew Hebrew.[174] One recalls Emerton's statement already cited: "What is uncertain and is probably impossible to determine, is the precise proportions in which Hebrew and Aramaic—and, indeed, Greek—were used."[175] Perhaps it is not impossible after all.

Of course, the matter is not nearly so simple. This estimate will require much further discussion, justification, and nuancing, and it may need significant revision. Many questions might be raised. For example, a potential objection to the foregoing line of reasoning would be to ask: "Yes, but how many of these signatories may have been scribes? Surely most scribes would learn Hebrew as a matter of course while being trained in the scriptures. So how valid can any deduction based on these contracts claim to be?" This question forces attention back to the signatures themselves. The present study proposes that they hold some measure of the answer to the objection. (Perhaps it is becoming clearer why progress in understanding the language patterns of ancient Judaea cannot easily be pursued apart from issues of literacy.) Our interest must focus specifically on "signature literacy."

Signature literacy is a shorthand expression for the analysis of signatures as an approach to the study of literacy. This was the method by which many Western European countries monitored their own progress toward mass literacy—counting signatures on marriage registers, beginning in the 1820s.[176] As an approach to the investigation of historical literacy, signature analysis can lay claim to an impeccable scholarly lineage. Pioneered by R. S. Schofield, it came to the fore almost with the genesis of historical literacy studies. In a 1968 study of literacy in England in the years leading up to the Industrial Revolution, he pondered what canon of measurement might exist and be effective for that period.[177] Schofield realized that the signatures of men and women in the Anglican marriage registers could serve his needs. By an act of Parliament in 1753, everyone but Jews, Quakers, and members of the royal family had been drawn into a parish system whereby only registered marriages, signed by the parties and two witnesses, were accorded legal status. From this *terminus a quo* almost all married Britons would be evidenced. Schofield saw specific advantages to the method for the purposes of comparing different times and places:

> To enable historical comparisons to be made, any measure of the diffusion of literacy skills that is adopted must meet two conditions. First, it must be applicable . . . to people of a wide range of age and economic and social conditions and over a long period of time. Second, it must also be standard as a measure from one person to the next, from one group to the next, from one region to the next, and from one historical period to the next. . . . There is one test of literary skill which satisfies almost all the requirements of a universal, standard and direct measure, and that is the ability to sign one's name.[178]

David Cressy made this method the underpinning of *Literacy and the Social Order: Reading and Writing in Tudor and Stuart England* (1980).[179] He emphasized with Schofield that signatures were a universal, standard, and direct measure of literacy. He adduced other virtues of value to the historian as well: "The test of alphabetic literacy is a direct, authentic and personal indicator of one particular skill. Faced with an autograph signature or mark on a document we do not have to guess or make inferences about its relationship to literacy."[180] Cressy dealt in convincing fashion with certain objections to using the method. To the common cavil that many people might learn to read but not to write, potentially vitiating the method's effectiveness, he responded by showing that "[beginning with at least the sixteenth century] both the incentive and opportunity to acquire a capacity to sign without other attributes of literacy were extremely slender."[181] As a further response he cited research on the situation in nineteenth-century France that evidenced a very strong statistical correlation between being able to sign and complete literacy. In general, he concluded: “Objections can be raised against every type of indirect evidence, and none of them alone can reveal the dimensions of literacy. Taken together, however, the impressions generated by one body of evidence may reinforce those from another to build a compelling picture. . . . Only through a study of the direct evidence of marks and signatures can [a given] impression be tested, sharpened and substantiated.”[182]

Many other scholars have utilized this approach for studies investigating literate behavior in a wide variety of different times and places. For example, Kenneth Lockridge and Jennifer Monaghan adopted it in separate examinations of literacy in colonial America; Roger Collins and Margaret Mullet in their studies of literacy in medieval Spain; Rab Houston to examine illiteracy in early modern Scotland; D. Vincent to plot changes in literacy rates in England between 1750 and 1914; and Anthony J. Barbieri-Low to investigate writing and literacy in early China.[183] And a variation of signature literacy informed much of the research of M. T. Clanchy in his magisterial study of medieval literacy in England. In those years the ability to write was constrained by the use of parchment and quills, which required a rather technical know-how. But another technology provided the equivalent of a signature: “The possessor of a seal was necessarily a person familiar with documents and entitled to participate in their use. . . . Possession of a seal implied that its owner could read his own name, as well as being prepared to authenticate documents with the impress of his ‘signature.’”[184]

The use of signature literacy is thus well established as a way of taking some measure of the past. Further, it is also a step in the direction of taking the ancient world on its own terms. Greco-Roman testimony indicates that the ability to write one’s name was sometimes considered the boundary between the lettered and the unlettered. A famous example unearthed by Herbert Youtie may illustrate.[185] From 184 to 187 C.E., Petaus son of Petaus was a town clerk in the vicinity of Ptolemais Hormu, Egypt. His record-keeping functions were significant, employing several professional scribes. Yet Petaus was by modern standards an animate oxymoron—an illiterate scribe:

> He practiced his signature from time to time. . . . We have one of his practice sheets. He traced the formula [Πεταῦς κωμογραμματεύς ἐπιδέδωκα] twelve times in a most awkward hand. At line 5 he made a mistake, omitting the first letter of the verb. From there to the end of his exercise he invariably omitted the letter. On the verso of the sheet he wrote the sentence twice from memory, and he made an incredible botch of it. No description would do justice.[186]

On one occasion Petaus dealt with a complaint sent to him for verification. A town clerk in his vicinity, Ischyrion, was being denounced as incompetent to do his job and charged with illiteracy. Petaus investigated and cleared Ischyrion of the charge, offering as explanation his judgment, "He is not illiterate, for he countersigns the documents he submits to his superior, and other writs of the village clerk's position."[187] Youtie wryly summarized the situation: "Petaus and Ischyrion are in precisely the same position—both of them town clerks, both of them illiterate, both of them masters of a single short sentence which they laboriously pen at the bottom of documents."[188] Presumably, Petaus knew that his assessment would satisfy his superiors and settle the matter.[189] Hence we learn a working definition of literacy in Roman Egypt. Unlike most modern definitions of literacy, the ability to write one's name was a touchstone at home in the ancient world.

The study of signatures is therefore contextually appropriate, and it is useful. In fact, to assess practical literacy, the study of signatures is even more useful for the Greco-Roman world than for the medieval and early modern periods of the West. The reason is simple. Unlike the people of later Europe, very few in that earlier world learned to read without also being able to write. On the contrary, their educations in literacy *began* with writing and were expressly designed to give a person the ability to sign his or her name even if literacy progressed no further—as, for many, it did not. Rafaella Cribiore is the scholar whose work cataloging and analyzing school exercises has done most to demonstrate this sequence of writing, then reading, and the focus on learning to sign:

> The school exercises shed light upon another area that is ignored by modern histories of ancient education: the practice of teaching a beginner to write his own name. . . . It appears that in antiquity learning to write one's personal name at a very early stage of education was even more crucial than it is today. Since only a few privileged individuals completed their education, and many of the students who started school remained there for a limited period, it would have been desirable to teach students to write their name at the very beginning. Even though professional scribes and literate friends and neighbors were available for help, innumerable subscriptions display the signatures of slow writers who chose to engage in this painful exercise rather than ask someone else to sign for them.[190]

Cribiore's study of school texts showed definitively that writing and reading were not merely two aspects of a single, undifferentiated and interactive process, especially not at the beginning. Students would start out by copying letters, laboring to produce passable versions of the various letters of the alphabet (semicursive forms),[191] then copy phrases, all the while being ignorant of the meaning of the schoolmaster's copies they were struggling to reproduce. Later they learned to read. This process began with the inscription and pronunciation of nonsense syllables; decipherment of words and phrases followed; then copying and reading of lists, short passages, long passages, *scholia;* and finally composition and paraphrase, in a steady upward progression.[192] Becoming the master of an ungainly hand, working with lists and syllabaries, might occupy three or four years, the entire time many students were able to spend in training for literacy. The foregoing steps completed, entry was now made into the formal study of grammar. At this point the student passed from the realm of the elementary teacher, or γραμματαδιδάσκαλος, to instruction by a "grammarian", or γραμματικός.[193]

This was an intermediate stage, and only a few students possessed the luxury of time and money to pursue it. Egyptian students would now canvass much larger portions of Greek literature. Homer always stood first. In the elementary stage, students had worked with limited portions of his epics; now they read portions they had not encountered before, while studying in greater depth the earlier, familiar passages. Study was made of glossaries to Homeric language, of lists of rare words and obscure realia, and of commentaries. Euripides, Isocrates, Herodotus, and Thucydides now made their entry, as did other authors. Menander was especially popular.[194] As at the first stage of education, the goal was not merely to read, but to memorize, extensively—as David Carr has phrased it, to "write on the tablet of the heart." This second-stage "grammatical" education was the true watershed. Students who completed it possessed what has been called "literary literacy," an ability to pepper their conversations with appropriate quotations from Attic literature, or to allude knowingly to Homer.[195] Only now could they read roughly as we experience that activity today.[196] Now they could perform as Dionysius of Halicarnassus described the goal: "It is only when a considerable lapse of time has implanted firmly in our minds the forms of the words that we execute them with the utmost ease, and we read through any book that is given to us unfalteringly and with incredible confidence and speed."[197] A very few, essentially only the elite, would finally progress to the third stage of education, study of rhetoric under a ῥήτωρ (rhetor) or σοφιστής (sophist). Philosophy, medicine, and other subjects sometimes complemented that study.

The earliest stages of this curriculum may seem clumsy, psychologically barren, and unconcerned with true nurture. Yet in its ancient setting the approach was eminently practical:

> Since most individuals in Greco-Roman Egypt had access to education only for a few years, teaching was structured to make them functional members of the society, once they reached the adult stage. A minimal level of direct involvement in a culture that was thoroughly penetrated by the written word was represented by the ability to sign one's name and reproduce a subscription. . . . Thus basic copying skills and the ability to produce a signature were probably considered more desirable in the first place than the ability to read properly, especially when balanced against the time and effort needed to produce such results.[198]

As students progressed, because they copied what they read, their hands improved correspondingly. For this reason analysis of hands affords a rough idea of how far any given writer has traveled down the road to reading. In other words, for Greco-Roman Egypt *signature literacy is a sensitive index not only of writing, but also of reading ability.*

Cribiore divided student hands into four categories.[199] The first category, what she called the "zero-grade hand," was the hand of the absolute beginner, a person who, in the words of Quintilian, "was at a loss about the shapes of the letters" (*haesit circa formas litterarum*).[200] Since this hand was rapidly outgrown, it is rarely in evidence in the surviving school exercises. The second level she designated the "alphabetic hand," belonging to a person able to write the alphabet properly but without fully developed hand-eye coordination. These first two categories would bracket βραδέως γράφοντες ("slow writers"). Such people, Cribiore noted, "trace each letter separately and often separate the individual characters by large spaces. Slow writers had probably attended school for one or two years, attaining a minimal literacy: they had learned to copy from models, but never proceeded to a stage where they were required to write rapidly. After leaving school . . . they did not go back exactly to the forms learned in school, but regressed to a stage of minimum discomfort and maximum legibility."[201]

The "evolving hand" was Cribiore's third category. This stage characterized a person trained by daily writing over a considerable period of time, but the letters could still look clumsy, uneven, and out of alignment. The evolving hand would persist for years. Being still in development, however, it might grow into the fourth type of student hand, the "rapid hand." By this point the writing was fluent and often possessed personal characteristics. A teacher writing informal notes or a scholar copying out a work of literature for private study would often possess such a hand. It might be difficult to separate a rapid hand from that of a professional scribe. A person owning this fourth hand could read with some ease; owners of the third type, with some difficulty; of the first two types, if at all, perhaps haltingly for a line or two. Literary literacy would attach only to the rapid hand.[202]

Little imagination is required to apprehend that Cribiore's mode of analysis, linking hands to education levels and reading ability, might significantly enhance understanding of the Bar Kokhba writers and signatories—provided moderate confidence that, mutatis mutandis, Judaean methods of education during this period essentially corresponded to those of Greco-Roman Egypt. Cribiore's own study helped to undergird such confidence. As noted by a specialist reviewer: "[Her] picture of education practices derived from Graeco-Egyptian texts is essentially the same as that offered by the ancient literary sources. . . . In this respect, as in many others, Egypt appears no different from the rest of the Greek-speaking East. Thus the book reinforces the idea that there existed, in Hellenistic and Roman times, a Mediterranean *koine* of education."[203] If an educational koine did exist, then one would expect an appropriate Palestinian reflex.

Further foundation for this expectation may be found in the ancient Near Eastern patterns of scribal education to which Judaea during this period was to some degree heir. These age-old patterns did not differ greatly from the general contours of education for literacy in Greco-Roman Egypt, except that they had been the experience of very few other than scribes. Consider the following description of a typical education for cuneiform literacy in Mesopotamia, the region for which most evidence survives:

> In the first phase of the curriculum, students were taught to write; they were to acquire good handwriting and ease in transcribing. . . . They developed writing skills first by copying and memorizing lists—of syllables, words, names, sentences, and proverbs—after which they moved on to excerpts from longer literary texts. Aside from belletristic texts, students had to familiarize themselves with grammar, law, business administration, mathematics, science, music, and historiography. The pedagogy was geared toward the mastery of the technical vocabulary of these various disciplines; the emphasis lay on memorization and scribal skills rather than on the intellectual grasp of the subject matter.[204]

New Kingdom Egyptian education, also comparatively well known by reason of the number of surviving sources, was similar to its Mesopotamian counterpart. Scribal students began by learning to write hieratic, then turned to a compendium (*Kemyt*), where they studied epistolary formulae, model letters, standardized phraseology, and similar practical subject matter. They also spent time on lexicographical lists, acquiring the rarified literary vocabulary never encountered in ordinary speech. After four to five years, they began study of classical (Middle Kingdom) literature, focusing initially on wisdom texts such as the *Satire on the Trades.* Students chanted, memorized, and copied out these writings. Four years of such led to the title of "scribe," although most continued for as many as twelve additional years, acquiring ever more specialized esoterica, mastering hieroglyphs. By age twenty, advanced students would usually have completed all training.[205]

Pedagogical processes in Syria-Palestine and First Temple Israel are far less well attested, but what is known or possible to infer is consonant with procedures in Mesopotamia and Egypt.[206] The Near Eastern heritage of Roman Judaea would have been such that the koine methods best known to us from Egypt would not appear alien. In particular, learning first to write, then to read would have seemed natural. It was the way things had always been.

Additional reason for confidence in the notion of a Jewish reflex to an educational koine comes in the form of artifacts arguably attesting that reflex explicitly. The abecedaries and name lists of Greco-Roman Egypt are echoed by Hebrew abecedaries and name lists, usually inscribed on ostraca but sometimes on leather or papyrus. The Hebrew name lists follow alphabetical order so are identical from site to site. These sorts of material are typically labeled scribal exercises, and such some of them may be; but others are better explained as student exercises. For example, *Mur* 11, an abecedary and possible palimpsest, indited with what Milik described as clumsy ("assez maladroite") lettering, ill fits the profile of a scribal warm-up.[207] Similarly, *Mur* 79 is an alphabet inscribed on an ostracon written by an incompetent hand ("exécuté par une main peu habile").[208] The person responsible for this production inked a portion of the alphabet a second time, attempting to inscribe the letters in order but forgetting *yodh.* Evidently, the alphabet was yet to be written on the tablet of this student's heart. Another half dozen abecedaries from Murabbaʿat, Masada, and Herodium also seem "clearly [to be] educational exercises."[209]

In a similar vein are two *tituli picti* (inked inscriptions) from Masada that have escaped comment in the literature. Both were intended to identify the owners of store jars and so were, presumably, inscribed by those same men. Both inscriptions are Aramaic. Mas514 reads כתבה שמעון, "Simon wrote it," repeated a second time with slightly differing orthography. Mas515 is damaged, the proper name lost, but כתב [ב]ידה, "wrote it with his own hand," is still legible.[210] Notable is that the two men wrote as though signing a contract, using typical witness formulae. Such labels were out of the ordinary, as the other thirty personally inscribed jars discovered at Masada demonstrate. Normally, one would simply write one's name. The most natural explanation for the forensic expression is that the men learned this formulaic way of signing as children, training for pragmatic literacy, being prepared to sign contracts—an early stage in Palestine, it would seem, just as it was in Egypt. Now those grinding childhood drills reasserted themselves. Indeed, over the intervening years the men probably never had occasion to write their names absent these formulae. Signature literacy was evidently as much a concern for the Jews as for Greeks, Romans, and the rest of the Mediterranean *oikoumene.*

In a broadly persuasive culminating chapter of his remarkable book *Writing on the Tablet of the Heart* (2005), David Carr argued that the Jews did indeed create an indigenous reflex to the Mediterranean educational program. It focused on cultural treasures that were specifically, intentionally opposed to the corpus of Greek educational texts: the Hebrew scriptures. Long almost the exclusive property of the hereditary priesthood, these writings were now generalized to become the core curriculum of Palestinian Jews as a whole. This was a move associated with the Hasmoneans, but it was in keeping with the Zeitgeist. Several coeval movements (Pharisees, Essenes, the Qumran group[s], whoever they were) were also implicitly arguing for analogous mechanisms, whereby all Palestinian Jewry would become truly a "nation of priests." Thus Carr proposed,

> Just as elite Hellenic identity appears to have been shaped by education and participation in a culture defined by Greek literature, the Hasmonean period saw the emergence and gradual diffusion of an emergent elite Jewish identity shaped by a sharply defined collection of Hebrew texts. Greek cultural forms were now opposed, balanced, and/or supplemented by a distinctively Jewish, purportedly pre-Hellenistic Hebrew form of *politeia* based—at least for elites—in a Hebrew *paideia.*[211]

"The alphabet," Carr observed, "was the water in which the student swam throughout his education, in both the Greek and Hebrew systems."[212] At a prereading stage, students would learn to write the alphabet, then their names—a fact, it seems, vitalizing the study of signature literacy. As elsewhere, the letterforms they learned were semicursive, not bookhands. Ancient Judaean signatures promise to offer new insight into language knowledge and use in this exceedingly complex milieu. Whether set down in Hebrew, Aramaic, Greek, or even Nabataean, the signatures of several hundred individuals—joined with other materials of the Bar Kokhba corpus, principally the letters—can fairly direct pursuit of those linguistic issues.

Moreover, by virtue of the relative fluency of their execution, these same signatures can also reveal indirectly something about the educational attainments of their authors and therefore about those same authors' capacities to read, to analyze, and to explain the defining literature of Palestinian Jewry in late Second Temple times.[213] In order to extract that information, the present study proposes to adapt Cribiore's categorization of hands.

Four categories are suggested, differing somewhat from Cribiore's because here the writers in view are almost exclusively adults, not students. Her descriptions of the appearance of the hands largely carry over. Figures 1.2–1.5 exemplify each type. Level 1, or the "alphabetic hand," is the habitation

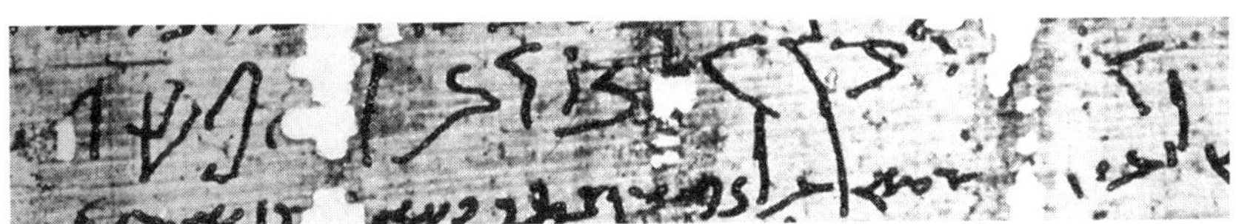

Figure 1.2. *Representative level 1 "alphabetic hand" from* P.Yadin *44. Eleazar b. Eleazar (top). Courtesy the Israel Exploration Society, Jerusalem.*

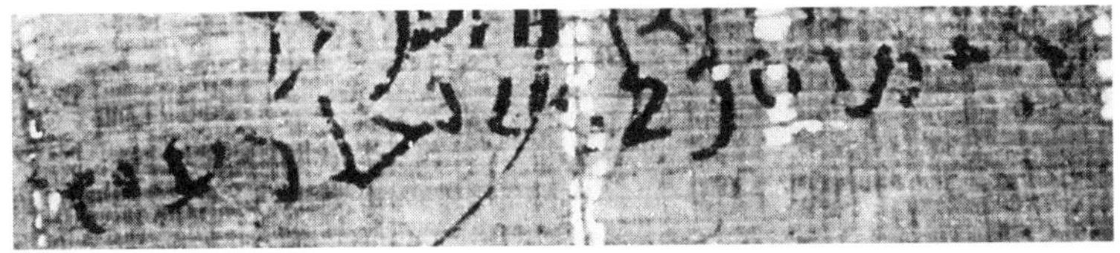

Figure 1.3. *Representative level 2 "unpracticed hand" from* P.Yadin *46; Joseph b. Eleazar (bottom). Courtesy the Israel Exploration Society, Jerusalem.*

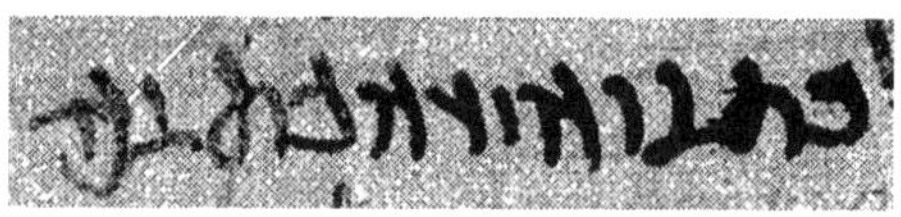

Figure 1.4. *Representative level 3 "practiced hand" from* P.Yadin *15; Judah b. Khthousion. Courtesy the Israel Exploration Society, Jerusalem.*

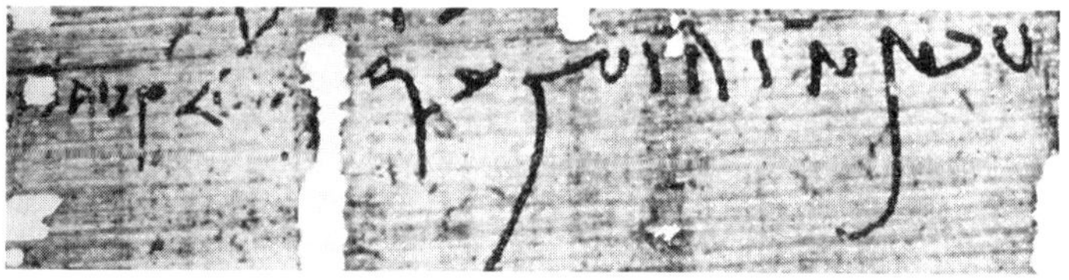

Figure 1.5. *Representative level 4 "scribal hand" from* P.Yadin *44; Simon b. Joseph. Courtesy the Israel Exploration Society, Jerusalem.*

of the slow writer represented by Eleazar b. Eleazar, the first to sign *P.Yadin* 44 on that long-ago day in En Gedi. He could sign his name, but when faced with a sophisticated literary text, his year or two of schooling would leave him essentially helpless. Similarly, people such as Joseph b. Eleazar of *P.Yadin* 46, possessed of an "unpracticed hand," would fare poorly in any serious encounter with a classical Hebrew opus. He exemplifies level 2. Only with the "practiced hand" of people such as Eleazar b. Khthousion, known to us from many texts, including *P.Yadin* 15, do we encounter an individual who, shaped by years of study, memorization, and copying, could read fluently. This is level 3, the literary literate. Professional scribes comprise the final category, level 4, of whom Simon b. Joseph, the final signatory of *P.Yadin* 44, is a parade example. We particularly want to distinguish scribes, it will be recalled, when analyzing Hebrew signatures to contracts.

An obvious element of subjectivity accompanies any such effort at categorization. Somehow, one must slip past Procrustes and evade his fatally inviting bed. Yet, given the generalized use proposed for our results, the problem does recede a bit. We require no finely tuned instrument. Principally what we seek is an estimate of how many people could read and interpret the sacred texts, and so act as the "text brokers."[214] The different levels of literacy need be distinguished only broadly. To know that much about Judaean society in the years between Pompey and Bar Kokhba is nevertheless to know a great deal that we cannot say we know now, with the potential to shape additional questioning and study.

Still, one does want to moderate the subjective element as much as possible. To this end it is critical to consider the circumstances of the signatories. We finally return, then, to the prosopography—but not only that. More generally, the social and historical circumstances surrounding the people and their documents are of the essence. The more that can be known about the individuals in these regards, the better chance one has of seeing their linguistic and literate behaviors contextually, and the better the odds, too, of dodging Procrustes' hospitality. Therefore, the prosopography of the texts must be a major focus if we hope to make our way to Eleusis and gain some genuine knowledge of these ancient mysteries.

The road leads first through the Wadi Murabbaʿat.

2 Jerusalem, Herodium, Jericho, and Environs

Murabba'at: History of the Discoveries

In October 1951 bedouin of the Ta'amireh tribe, the same tribe involved with the discovery of Cave 1 and the initial Dead Sea Scrolls several years earlier, appeared at the Palestine Archaeological Museum in Jerusalem to present the remains of a leather sandal and a fragment from a scroll.[1] They informed Joseph Saad, secretary of the museum, that the objects derived from a new cave, some distance to the south of Cave 1. Saad requested that the men return with those who had actually made the discovery, then waited nervously for several days with no sign of them. His superior, G. Lankester Harding, was away from the city, and Père Roland de Vaux, famed senior archaeologist attached to the École Biblique et Archéologique Française de Jérusalem, was in Europe at the time, so the anxious Saad could not consult them about what to do. He grew increasingly uneasy, convinced that it was critical to act, and act quickly.

Finally, deciding on a course of action, he made his way to the École Biblique, where he showed the scroll fragment to someone and was reassured that the inscribed leather appeared to be both genuine and ancient. Thus confirmed, he turned next to a friend whom he had made during the earlier scroll adventures, a Brigadier Ashton of the British Army. Ashton supplied Saad with a Jeep, some men, and a letter with which he could requisition further military assistance should that prove necessary. Escorted by Ashton's personal bodyguard, Saad drove to Bethlehem, then immediately on to the nearest camp of the Ta'amireh.

Received with typical desert hospitality, Saad shortly began to inquire about the tribe's recent cave explorations. The bedouin were evasive. Why was Saad here? He muttered something about doing some hunting but found no very plausible explanation when it was pointed out that he had brought no gun. Concluding that further questioning would only stiffen the tribe's resistance, Saad desisted and, after spending the night among them, arose early the next morning to drive into the desert with his men. He would seek signs of tribal activity on his own.

It was not long, however, before Saad realized that his makeshift caravan was being followed. This being so, by now his movements would be broadcast throughout the tribe's territory. Even if he did somehow manage to arrive near the critical cave, it would be impossible to identify, because the workers would have halted their labors and gone into hiding. To continue was pointless. Discouraged and uncertain of his next move in the evolving chess match, Saad gave the order to return to Bethlehem.

Shortly after arriving in that city, his next move thrust itself upon him. Meandering down the road toward the Jeep, but clearly oblivious of its occupants, came one of the original group of bedouin who had showed Saad the sandal and the scroll. At sharp orders from the secretary, the vehicle skidded to a halt; questioned, the man refused to answer, whereupon he was summarily pitched into the vehicle. The company did an about-face and headed immediately back into the desert. As they drove, Saad explained to his involuntary guest in pellucid terms that any further refusal to cooperate would have nothing but the gravest consequences. Given what had already transpired, and stealing a glance at the hard faces of the soldiers all around him, the frightened tribesman found such threats easy to believe. He reluctantly agreed to show the way to the cave.

After stopping at an army post to pick up additional soldiers per Ashton's letter, Saad and the party started out on the heading that the bedouin provided. The driving soon became impossible even for an army Jeep; disembarking, they began what would finally become a seven-hour trek on foot. As they headed east, as the Wadi Taʿamireh became the Wadi Murabbaʿat the walking became more and more difficult. Saad and the soldiers gradually found themselves in a deep ravine whose nearly vertical inclines towered 180 meters into the air on either side of them.

Suddenly, upon rounding a turn, they spied clouds of dust wafting from two enormous cave entrances more than sixty meters up the northern face of the cliffs. Simultaneously they were spotted themselves. As shouts of alarm echoed down the canyon, a dozen tribal workers darted from the caves, stumbling over each other, urgently seeking to scale the crags in order to escape. Several warning shots fired into the air over their heads halted their flight, and the soldiers began to herd the dust-covered bedouin together so that they could be questioned.

Although exhausted, Saad and his bodyguard took this opportunity to climb up the cliff and enter the nearer cave. They found themselves standing in an enormous cavern, six meters wide, with the roof three meters above their heads. A boulder-strewn floor stretched back forty-five meters, fading into Stygian darkness. Dust from the illicit digging still hung thick in the air, but it could not disguise the facts. To Saad's experienced eye it was evident that the bedouin had already removed anything lying near the surface. An expert team of archaeologists might find more, but his own immediate prospects were nil. Meanwhile, the soldiers had questioned the workers, always receiving the same reply: yes, magnificent things had indeed been found here, but not by these men, and not today. As Saad pondered his options, he realized that the tribesman who had led them into the desert was his one secure link to the discoveries that had been made. The chances of keeping that man with him would diminish markedly if the group heeded the urgings of their aching muscles and settled for the night at the cave. Almost certainly the man would find some opportunity to slip from their grasp. Therefore, bone-weary though he and all the soldiers were, he gave the order and they turned to trudge the seven-hour return trek, guide in tow.

Saad arrived in Jerusalem just as morning was dawning. On the way he had handed the bedouin over to authorities in Bethlehem. Now back home, he dutifully contacted the local inspector of antiquities and reported all that had happened, turning over as well the sandal and the scroll fragment. Then he fell exhausted into bed, awaking much later in the day to find himself accused of kidnapping and incarcerating their guide. To this charge there was, of course, some truth; but the man himself had been involved in illegal activities. Matters were eventually smoothed over, Saad suffering nothing more serious than a severe reprimand. While this storm was playing itself out, the inspector whom he had contacted, Awni Dajani, made his way to Bethlehem and, led by one of Saad's companions, hiked out to inspect the caves at Murabbaʿat. He was thus able to confirm the secretary's story, and Harding and de Vaux, both having returned to Jerusalem, were informed of all that had transpired.

Yet three months were to pass before the official excavations at Murabbaʿat got under way, on 21 January 1952. Looking back some sixty years later, and knowing what we do today concerning the caves of the Judaean

Desert, such a delay is hard to understand. But the reason for it was simple. Shortly after Saad and Dajani, several members of the American School of Oriental Research visited the cave in which the bedouin had been working. Finding that the tribesmen had already rummaged it, and thinking that the textual material that had so far emerged was unimpressive, they argued that further excavation was pointless.[2]

The intervening months changed that thinking. De Vaux and Harding were approached by various members of the Taʿamireh—seemingly in a kind of competition—offering for sale a variety of materials, all allegedly issuing from Murabbaʿat. On occasion, different groups would present the same materials, as though unaware of the other would-be vendors; presumably, this was merely a tactic to extract the best price. Though a few minor pieces were purchased in November, the spigot opened wide and splashing in the following month. On the ninth of December de Vaux acquired *Mur* 1, a fragment of Exodus inscribed in an elegant bookhand; *Mur* 44, a well-preserved letter of Bar Kokhba; and a portion of *Mur* 115, a contract for remarriage, composed in Greek and dating to the year 124 C.E. Little more than a week later, a second lot was presented for purchase, this one comprising an I.O.U., *Mur* 114; fragments of Aramaic contracts; and *Mur* 24, a Hebrew record of agricultural subleasing by one Hillel b. Garis, done in the name of Simon b. Kosiba. By the end of the year, de Vaux and Harding had managed to bypass the competing groups to enter into direct negotiations with tribal leaders. Many additional portions came to their hands just as excavations were about to start.

Harding and de Vaux were there to direct when the first shovel bit the dirt. Prominent among the difficulties the excavators faced was the issue of supplies. Everything needed to be transported by pack animal the seven-hour distance from Bethlehem, and this was still the rainy season. Arriving at the plateau above the Murabbaʿat caves, the mules and donkeys, balking at attempting the vertiginous, water-slicked final descent, had to be unpacked. Bedouin workers bore the loads down on their own backs at risk to life and limb.

The excavations occupied slightly more than a month, until 1 March.[3] Two caves in addition to the original two evidenced human occupation; as with the Qumran caves, each received a numerical designation. Caves 1 and 2, the original caves, were the only ones to yield the archaeologists written materials. It is believed that all of the documents sold by the bedouin also derived from these caves, mostly from Cave 2. Not quite forty meters to the west of that grotto was Cave 3. About 180 meters in the opposite direction, and at a slightly higher elevation, was Cave 4. A large Roman cistern, lined with plaster and furnished with steps and a small holding tank, had been hewn in front of Cave 1, and most of the habitation in the caves proved likewise to date to the Roman period. A few materials of the Chalcolithic, Bronze, and Iron Ages—as indeed of the Arab period—showed that occasional travelers had used the caves as a caravanserai down through the ages.

Roman-period finds included much pottery, later dated by comparison with the ceramic discoveries even then beginning to be made at Khirbet Qumran, eighteen kilometers to the north. Iron nails, a variety of tools, a heavy, curved iron key, bone dice, combs, buttons, spoons, remnants of sandals (including a child's), and numerous wooden and stone spindles incised with geometric designs yielded themselves to the archaeologist's pick and shovel. One of the biggest surprises was an ancient medical kit. Two coins were also unearthed, and these—added to approximately a dozen other coins that the Ta'amireh later offered for sale—were to be decisive in attempting to draw the difficult distinction between proximate Roman-period habitations.

Written materials proved sparse compared with what already had been, or later would be, purchased from the bedouin.[4] Within Cave 2, sloping down steeply from the entry chamber, two tunnels led to a third, more level underground passageway about forty meters in length. Here, it seemed, was the original mother lode, the vein from which most of the bedouin scroll fragments had been mined. John Allegro, a member of the excavating team (later to become famous for his maverick activities and views as a member of the Dead Sea Scroll editorial team), described the search for remaining inscribed materials as follows. He also described a certain "fertilizer problem" identical to that which Bernard Grenfell and Arthur Hunt found at Oxyrhynchus:[5]

> The written documents came almost entirely from the Second Cave. A few are fairly well preserved, but most had suffered from the depredations of visiting animals, human and otherwise, and particularly in the activities of rats who, with regrettable lack of appreciation of true values, had used the precious leather and papyrus manuscripts as linings for their nests. In fact, the excavation developed into a hunt for rats' nests, since each one was almost sure to produce remnants of a written document or two. Another contributory factor in the denudation of written material was that the later habitation by birds and small animals of the caves over hundreds of years had resulted in

an abundant supply of guano which the bedouin had for years been collecting and selling in Bethlehem. It is not at all improbable, as Father De Vaux points out, that the Jewish orange groves near Bethlehem were fertilized with priceless ancient manuscripts written by their forefathers![6]

In one corner of Cave 2 the bedouin reported having found the scriptural scrolls of Genesis, Exodus, Deuteronomy, and Isaiah. All had been ripped, cut, and otherwise desecrated in antiquity, evidently at Roman hands. The fragment of Genesis chapters 32–35 survived only in a thin strip, violently torn across three columns. But a complete phylactery escaped these ravages. Inscribed on very fine skin, minute semicursive letters spelled out the same four scriptural passages prescribed by the rabbis for such works: Exod 13:1–10, 11–16; Deut 6:1–4; and Deut 11:13–21.

In March of 1955, three years after the official excavations ended, five bedouin shepherds exploring the same region augmented the scriptural findings with a scroll of the Minor Prophets (*Mur* 88). It was discovered inside a cave overlooked in the earlier searches, removed about 270 meters from the original caves, subsequently denominated Cave 5. Here a long tunnel delved deep into the rock, bifurcating after a considerable stretch into separate branches. Just at this intersection, archaeologists following up on the bedouin discovery came upon a pile of human bones and tattered clothing. Near the gruesome find nature had carved out from the cave wall a small niche, sealed since antiquity by a symmetrical stone that the bedouin treasure hunters had pried out. Within this crevice the scroll had been sequestered, perhaps the final act of the ancient insurgent who had borne it for safekeeping to the cavern that became his death trap.

For several more years materials claimed to be from Murabbaʿat continued to filter through bedouin hands to the eager grasp of Western scholars. Prominent among such was *Mur* 43, a letter that evidently preserves the signature of the "messianic" leader of the Second Revolt, Simon b. Kosiba, *propria manu.*[7] Sometimes documents leaked out piecemeal from the tribesmen. An example was *Mur* 30, a Hebrew deed of sale: initial portions were purchased in 1952, remaining portions in September 1958. That date is the latest officially recorded for the Murabbaʿat inscribed finds, attaching also to *Mur* 29, the upper contract of a *Doppelurkunde,* obtained with string and sealing intact.[8]

All told, 174 numbered literary and nonliterary texts comprised the Murabbaʿat discoveries, written on ostraca, papyrus, and leather in Hebrew,

Judaean Aramaic, Greek, Latin, and Arabic.[9] Undoubtedly, the centerpiece was the Bar Kokhba letters, seven of which were clearly recognizable as such. De Vaux assigned the Hebrew and Aramaic materials to J. T. Milik, who masterfully deciphered the cursive and "sténographique" (extremely cursive) scripts; Pierre Benoit adroitly edited the Greek and Latin texts, and A. D. Grohmann the Arabic. De Vaux himself published the archaeological findings. The entirety of their treatments was packed off to Oxford University Press late in 1958, and the *editio princeps* appeared as *Les Grottes de Murabba'ât* in 1961, a decade after Western scholars first learned of Cave 1.[10] Considerable portions had by then appeared in preliminary studies, photographs sometimes included, so that *Les Grottes* profited from an accumulation of lively and learned discussion, gaining thereby more definitive stature.[11] More definitive—but not yet definitive; in 2000, the Israeli paleographer Ada Yardeni put scholars deeply in her debt by publishing the dual volumes of *Textbook of Aramaic, Hebrew and Nabataean Documentary Texts.*[12] In these magisterial tomes she treated all of the Semitic texts from Murabbaʿat in new editions, wresting from the often stubbornly resistant writings many new readings and improved interpretations. Her work amounts to the *editio maior* for these materials and is the point of departure for the present study.

Who Took the Texts to the Caves? First Revolt Texts

For de Vaux, Milik, Benoit, and all subsequent scholars sifting their treatments, the four years of the Second Revolt represented the principal phase of the Murabbaʿat caves during the Roman era. On the basis of what was known when *Les Grottes* was published, this conclusion was eminently sensible. Until recently, little reason existed to question it. But fundamental questions are now in the air and cannot be ignored. At issue is the matter of accurate attribution of the finds. For the present study the matter is clearly critical, since chronology is frequently a variable in language and literacy patterns. Accordingly, the "quest of the historical Murabbaʿat" beckons.

De Vaux acknowledged that some evidence most likely should be associated with the First Revolt. Such included four bronzes spanning the years 42–69, the last a minting of Year Four inscribed לגאלת ציון, "for the redemption of Zion." Certain of the ceramics had parallels with those of Khirbet Qumran period II, which ended with the First Revolt. Of the textual material, Milik assigned to First Revolt habitation *Mur* 18, an I.O.U. explicitly dated to the second year of Nero, and more tentatively (on the basis of paleography) the copies of Deuteronomy and Isaiah (*Mur* 2 and 3), a nonscriptural literary text (*Mur* 6), and a marriage contract (*Mur* 21).[13] Alongside the much more plentiful materials of the Second Revolt, however, these several pieces of evidence were comparatively minor. De Vaux was inclined to associate them with habitation by a single refugee family: "It is therefore possible that at the end of the First Jewish Revolt, or in the aftermath of that war, the caves became a refuge for a Jewish family fleeing the Romans, or for zealots continuing the resistance."[14]

To de Vaux the Second Revolt period seemed to be abundantly documented by dated objects. Numismatic evidence was critical and included city coins dated by the emperors, one of 113/114, one of 119/120, and nine Bar Kokhba issues.[15] The dated or securely datable texts were equally fundamental to de Vaux's conclusions: *Mur* 19, a writ of divorce (understood to date to 111 C.E.); *Mur* 20, a marriage contract (thought to date to 117 C.E.); a deed of sale, *Mur* 22 (131 C.E.); the διάστρωμα of 124 C.E., *Mur* 24; the several Bar Kokhba letters; and finally *Mur* 115, the previously noted Greek contract of remarriage (124 C.E.). The sure lines laid down by these objects guided the archaeologist's thinking regarding the less precise brush strokes of other types of evidence: "The joint witness of the coins and the texts demonstrates the character of this occupation. During the Second Jewish Revolt, Murabbaʿat was the hideout of a group of rebels fighting against the Romans. Some of the items that they left behind—small sandals belonging to children, spindle whorls, combs—show that they had taken refuge here with their families."[16]

The first suggestion that the evidence for Roman-period habitation at Murabbaʿat might need to be reassessed came just a few years after publication of *Les Grottes*. As noted, Milik had dated *Mur* 19, a writ of divorce composed at Masada, to the year 111. The Aramaic document explicitly indicated its date and place of composition twice, in lines 1 and 12: באחד למרחשון שנת שת במצדא, "On the first of Marheshvan, Year Six, at Masada." For Milik, "The era implied is clearly that of the Eparchy (of Provincia Arabia, of Bosra), which began on 22 March 106."[17] He believed that the Romans under L. Flavius Silva, having taken the fortress in 73, gathered a heterogeneous population, including Jews, to raise crops at Masada for the garrison. These people continued to inhabit and cultivate the forbidding rock for years afterward. Their ranks eventually came to include one Joseph b. Naqsan, who divorced his wife Miriam b. John and gave her this writ as required by customary law. How the document came to be deposited for later discovery at Murabbaʿat, Milik did not venture to explain. Of its dating, however, he was confident.

Others were not so sure. Elisabeth Koffmahn was the first to protest. She found Milik's agricultural scenario somewhat bizarre: "One can scarcely imagine that following the conquest by the Romans in 73 C.E. a Jewish writ of divorce was issued there."[18] She noted that the then-recent discovery and publication of materials from Naḥal Ḥever showed that dating by the provincial era of Arabia would be done explicitly, not with a mere mention of "year six." The Greek papyri of Ḥever's Babatha Archive, produced in Mahoza, used such wording as κατὰ τὸν ἀριθμὸν τῆς νέας ἐπαρχίας 'Αραβίας (according to the dating of the new Eparchy of Arabia). The date reference in *Mur* 19 had to mean something else: "This can only have been the 'Era of Freedom' of the Jewish War against the Romans, especially since we know from the Bellum Iudaicum of Flavius Josephus that in Masada a group of unyielding freedom fighters, the so-called Sicarii, maintained themselves for three years after the fall of Jerusalem. Masada was the only site in which a 'Year Six' dating from the liberation or recapture of Jerusalem in 66 C.E. existed."[19] Accordingly, she concluded, the date of *Mur* 19 might well reference a day in October 71 C.E.

Arriving independently at a similar verdict was Yigael Yadin, whose views took on special force since he had just completed directing the excavations at the site of Masada. In the preliminary report on those excavations published in 1965, Yadin observed in a footnote that he had never been persuaded by Milik's analysis. His own discoveries at Naḥal Ḥever had shown him that "whenever Jewish documents were dated by the era of Arabia . . . this fact was expressly mentioned."[20] The Aramaic texts used the expression ועל מנין הפרכיה דא, "and according to the reckoning of this eparchy," which presumably should have appeared in *Mur* 19 if Milik's dating was correct. In his popular work *Bar-Kokhba,* Yadin adduced another telling argument—the coins: "Our excavations at Masada from 1963–5 revealed not one coin of Bar-Kokhba among the five thousand coins discovered there, and from the level of the Roman garrison nothing was found which could be associated with Jewish families. It seems to me, therefore, that the unspecified era on the deed refers to the First Revolt."[21] The inhabitants of Masada had begun the war dating by its era, commencing in 66 and known from the coins of Year One to Year Five. After Jerusalem fell, they simply continued to use that era, thereby refusing to concede Roman victory.

Since Koffmahn and Yadin wrote, a significant number of specialists, amounting it would seem to a consensus, has found their perspectives convincing.[22] *Mur* 19 should be assigned to the Murabbaʿat texts of the

First Revolt. With this reassignment, the first domino tumbled, striking *Mur* 20.

Milik himself had raised questions about *Mur* 20. The first line of the *ketubbah* gives a date in "year eleven" (שנת חדה ע]שרה) but then breaks off. Milik pondered the possibility that the reference might be to a regnal year, but because he believed the lacuna too short to encompass any reasonable possibility, he doubled back to implicit dating by the eparchy of Arabia, essentially reprising his view of *Mur* 19.[23] Koffmahn rejected this reasoning. She saw no reason to doubt that the lacuna could fit an emperor's name, provided it be short, and she opted for Nero.[24] Klaus Beyer adopted her suggestion in 1984, and others have since agreed that a regnal year is entirely possible.[25] In fact, *pace* Milik, we do not know precisely how long the lacuna may be, and no particular option can be ruled out on physical criteria alone. In view of David Goodblatt's thorough demonstration that, as he put it, "Not a single document certainly written in Iudaea bears a date citing the Arabian era," it seems that some ruler's name ought to be supplied.[26] Nero or Claudius are the two most likely options. If the reference was originally to the former, *Mur* 20 dates to 65; if to the latter, to 51. When all is said and done, the totality of the evidence probably favors the dating to Claudius, as will become clear.

Thus, today two of the "certainly dated" manuscripts that framed de Vaux's arguments concerning the central Roman phase of Murabbaʿat have by consensus been removed to the First Revolt column of the ledger. Nor have revisionist suggestions stopped there. The dominoes have continued to topple.

In the mid-1980s Beyer argued for a possible First Revolt setting for two additional documents, *Mur* 23 and *Mur* 32. The date formula partially preserved in the first line of *Mur* 23 allowed a dating of 67: ב10 לשבת שנת חדה לחר]ות, "on the 10th of Shevat, Year One of the free[dom (of Jerusalem)." The Hebrew word for "son," however, that Beyer read in (what seemed to be) the lone surviving signature to the contract persuaded him that the more probable dating was to the Second Revolt (i.e., 133), when he believed the use of Hebrew had been mandated by Simon b. Kosiba. Thus, the First Revolt date was a tentative suggestion at best.[27] *Mur* 32 preserves no date formulae, but Beyer argued that the use of *zayin* to represent the historical phoneme */d/* in the Aramaic text indicated a date in the latter half of the first century B.C.E.[28] This suggestion also proved a false start, however, since the readings in question were extremely uncertain and could equally well be read as *daleth,* the expected reflex for either the first or second centuries C.E. Thus, neither of Beyer's specific suggestions took root in scholarship. Yet the mere fact that questions were being raised about the dating of the Murabbaʿat texts was in itself notable. Arguably, Beyer helped channel a critical undercurrent into the 1990s, when the really fundamental reexamination began.

In 1999 two scholars, working, as it seems, each without knowledge of the other, separately suggested reassigning a notable selection of the manuscripts to the First Revolt. Their selections overlapped but were based on largely different arguments. Hanan Eshel made his suggestions in a paper delivered at a conference jointly hosted by the University of Minnesota and Macalester College 21–23 April 1999.[29] His focus was on the Murabbaʿat texts that mentioned Jerusalem prominently: *Mur* 22, 25, 29, and 30. The first two texts listed used related date formulae, לגאולת ירושלים and לחרות ירושלים, respectively "of the redemption of Jerusalem" and "of the freedom of Jerusalem." The second grouping of texts explicitly specified the place of composition as Jerusalem. For Eshel, Milik's dating of these texts to the Second Revolt initially became problematic because as time had passed, almost no Bar Kokhba coins had ever been discovered in Jerusalem.[30] This phenomenon seemed very difficult to explain on the hypothesis that the rebels under Simon b. Kosiba held Jerusalem for any appreciable time during that uprising. Moreover, Eshel had himself discovered in a refuge cave used by Jews during the Second Revolt two Aelia Capitolina coins, the sort minted by Hadrian.[31] "These finds clearly led to the conclusion," he explained, "that Aelia was founded in 130 C.E. during Hadrian's visit to Judea, and coins were minted in Aelia before 135 C.E. Clearly, the rebels could not have held Jerusalem during 133–5 C.E."[32] In obvious contrast, of course, Jewish rebels did hold Jerusalem from 66 to 70 during the First Revolt.

To gain greater clarity regarding the proper dating of these texts, Eshel had two of them, *Mur* 22 and 29, subjected to carbon-14 analysis. The results: both very probably antedated 78 C.E. The case for attributing all four of these texts to the era of the First Revolt was thus persuasive.

Finally, Eshel suggested that a fifth manuscript, 4Q348, previously thought to originate elsewhere, ought rather to be assigned proximately to Murabbaʿat and ultimately to First Revolt Jerusalem.[33] As noted in Chapter 1, this manuscript was among a group of texts that had been purchased from the bedouin with the understanding that they derived from Qumran Cave 4. When they were officially published, however, Ada Yardeni and Hannah Cotton, the editors, argued that they actually derived from Naḥal Ḥever.[34] Yardeni read the beginning of 4Q348 line 13, where one would expect a date formula, as containing the damaged name of a high priest: ◦◦◦◦וס כוהן גדול[, commenting, "No combination of the [uncertain] letters [before וס] . . . produces the name of a high priest known to us from historical or literary sources."[35] Eshel now proposed to read the letters as *vav, daleth, yodh* and the name in question as קומ]ודיוס, referring it to Joseph b. Camydus, high priest from 46 to 47. Paleographically, this suggestion was possible. Because the fragmentary text also preserved the phrase "Simon of the timber market," referencing a section of Jerusalem that Josephus mentions in passing (*B.J.* 2.530), Eshel logically concluded that it came from Jerusalem (as indeed Yardeni also believed) and more provocatively opined, "I believe that this document was found in the caves of Wadi Murabbaʿat that were used as refuge caves at the end of the First Revolt."[36] Thus it came neither from Qumran nor from Naḥal Ḥever but from yet a third locale—a suggestion that, if true, must shake scholarly confidence concerning document attributions made solely on the basis of bedouin assurances.[37]

Since he accepted the arguments for the early dating of *Mur* 19, and *Mur* 18 is explicitly dated to the reign of Nero, Eshel was now arguing for the assignment of six Murabbaʿat texts to the era of the First Revolt, and including 4Q348, for a total of seven documents having been taken to those caves at the end of that rebellion. In all of these points he seemed likely to be correct. If so, the proportion of the Murabbaʿat materials assigned to each revolt was now markedly changed, which implicitly raised the possibility that de Vaux's understanding of the relative significance of the Roman-period occupations, and equally that of scholarship in his wake, might need a more thorough reanalysis. Hannah Cotton pushed matters still further.

In an article published in that same year of 1999 in the *Zeitschrift für Papyrologie und Epigraphik*,[38] Cotton began by noting the difficulty of dating *Mur* 29 and 30 to the Second Revolt, as Milik had done. For if that dating were adopted, then it would follow that the Jews had control of Jerusalem as late as September/October 135, the date putatively given in *Mur* 30. Such would be highly problematic for the accepted scholarly view (based on rabbinic literature) that the fall of Bethar occurred two or three months earlier, in July of 135. Was one to believe that Jerusalem was still in rebel hands *after* the supposedly climactic defeat at the village to its southwest?

Moreover, Cotton had been informed by Yardeni of the latter's new reading of the date formula in *Mur* 22, "on the 14th of Marheshvan, Year Four of the redemption of Israel,"[39] that is, October/November of 135—yet another month beyond the (seemingly impossibly late) date of *Mur* 30. The chronological and geographical implications now in prospect would overturn much that had been believed about the Second Revolt. Rabbinic literature gave no indication that the Jews ever took Jerusalem at all. Were scholars now to acknowledge not only that Jerusalem had fallen to the Jews, but that imperial forces were continuously repulsed, unable to recapture and hold the city, so that the rebels invested it for at least three years, from August/September of 133 (the date of *Mur* 29) until nearly the end of 135? In that case, why would rabbinic literature fail to record a "Battle of Jerusalem" as the climax to the revolt, rather than making Bethar decisive? Cotton's solution to all these vexations: reassign the Hebrew contracts *Mur* 22, 29, and 30 to the First Revolt.

Supportive of that possibility, she noted, was the archaeological fact that Murabbaʿat had been inhabited at the time of that earlier bid for freedom. Therefore, it was possible that its caves had served as refuge during both revolts. Beyond that, Cotton emphasized the differences between the date formulae of *Mur* 29 and 30 and those preserved in texts certainly composed during the Second Revolt. The latter group, numbering eight texts, (almost) always mentioned the name of Simon b. Kosiba and typically gave him credit for "freeing" or "redeeming" Israel.[40] Of course, neither sort of phrase was found in the texts Cotton proposed to reattribute. In other words, she implied, First Revolt texts could usually be distinguished by the absence of regnal dating.

That observation led her directly to *Mur* 19 and "Year Six" at Masada, and thence to other Aramaic texts from Murabbaʿat. None disputed the dating of *Mur* 18 to 55/56, Nero's second year. *Mur* 20, referring to "Year Eleven" and inscribed, as it said, in Haradona (near Jerusalem), likely could refer to the same emperor. Milik himself had suspected that *Mur* 21 was earlier than the Second Revolt materials. The broken date formula in *Mur* 23 could be read either as Milik had done, שנת חדה ל], "Year One of," or as Yardeni was now suggesting, שנת חמש ל], "Year Five of." For Cotton, the new reading was decisive: "[it] must refer to the first revolt."[41] *Mur* 25 was dated to "Year Three of the freedom of Jerusalem," which by analogy to the Hebrew texts might well refer to the First Revolt. Finally, *Mur* 26, though lacking a preserved date formula, was akin to *Mur* 20 in having participants said to be from Jerusalem or nearby. Thus, Cotton was proposing that a total of ten Murabbaʿat manuscripts should certainly or would better be assigned to the First Revolt.

Her collection included all of Eshel's except for 4Q348, plus *Mur* 20, 21, 23, 25, and 26. Taking the two scholars together, then, eleven texts were now being assigned to the First Revolt and the region of Jerusalem, ten of which had not been among de Vaux's original assessment. Eshel's proposals seemed as sound as such things are likely to be; as for Cotton, a number of her suggestions were entirely convincing, especially where her selection overlapped Eshel's and her reasoning fortified his suggestions by offering new arguments. For texts such as *Mur* 22, 29, and 30 their combined case for a First Revolt dating appeared decisive. Yet arguments for other texts in Cotton's list fell short of that degree of probability, as her own cautious wording recognized.

Regardless of an individual scholar's view of any one of these proposed reassignments, the need for further consideration is surely evident. A different approach, summarized perhaps by a new question, may prove heuristic. Accordingly: Who took the texts to the caves? What can one reconstruct of the human dimension involved? What can prosopography contribute? This promising avenue has never been adequately pursued for Murabbaʿat texts attached to the Second Revolt; for those potentially of the First Revolt, it has never been explored at all.

The place to begin is with the concept of archive—that is, not just documents, but *groups of related documents*.[42] Many of the Murabbaʿat papyri are legal writ of one sort or another. The mere fact that a person fleeing for his or her life took them to the caves speaks for their perceived immense importance. When decisions were being made about what to carry along and what to leave behind, individuals in extremis chose these documents. They evidently hoped to use them to reconstruct their lives, to regain property and reclaim status when life returned to normal. Nor were these arbitrary selections from a communal village archive. They are manifestly writ concerning the legal affairs of individuals.

We know from the archaeology that a relatively small number of individuals—and naturally, fewer families—fled to the caves. In ideal circumstances, therefore, it would be possible to recognize connections between the related texts. One could name names, as it were, for a great portion of what survives. The archives would then lie patent to modern eyes. Unfortunately, fortuitous manuscript survival and uncertain recovery at least jeopardizes, and perhaps dooms, any such effort at intellectual salvage.[43] Certain of the original connections are surely lost; others are now obscured and opaque. Yet, given the potential benefit to historical understanding, the search is worth pursuing. The objective must be to reconstruct one or more "conceptual archives." These are personal archives not found in situ, hence only conceptual, loosely held—but archives nevertheless: archives potentially historical. If possible connections can be discerned and people related among the surviving texts, then the likelihood is good—much better than in a random situation—that the connections are real and that actual archives, not mere imaginary constructs, are in view. If further documents, relationships established, can be dated as groups and attached to the First Revolt, then this archival approach will confirm, and perhaps even expand, earlier suggestions by Eshel, Cotton, and others.

Judging from both rabbinic literature and actual archaeological discoveries, it is plain that many ancient Judaeans did possess personal archives. Tannaitic texts presuppose the fact without explanation. Consider, for example:

> עשרה דלוסקמין מליאין שטרות יש לי בידך
>
> You have ten bags full of my documents. (*t. Shebu.* 5:11)

> מצא בחפיסה או בדלוסקמא תכריך של שטרות או אגודה של שטרות
> הרי זה חזיד
> וכמה אגודה של שטרות? שלשה קשורין זה בזה
>
> If one found within a satchel or a bag a bundle of documents, or a batch of documents, they must be returned. And what is a "batch" of documents? At least three attached to one another. (*m. B. Mesi'a* 1:8)[44]

People had batches, bundles, and bags of documents. Legal writ permeated late Second Temple Judaea. Whereas praxis in Persian times had arguably been largely oral, with the advent and progress of Hellenization, Jewish society began to put markedly greater emphasis upon the written instrument.[45] Many people came to possess personal legal materials, and theoretical scenarios such as those portrayed by the excerpts above were a part of the warp and woof of daily existence. Any propertied individual was likely to have at least a small archive sequestered in some safe place. This archive would, of course, feature the person's own name, along with those of family members, prominently, repeatedly. Family members would appear in such roles as witness and *hypographeus.*

Early rabbinic literature further evidences that personal archives often embraced more than a single individual, family, or generation. Archives were personal but at the same time included documents belonging to the extended family. Not only would it be prudent, even legally necessary, to keep a continuous record of transactions involving property that the person or earlier family had bought or sold, but it was also common to archive the significant documents of earlier generations, retaining them long after such family members had departed to the "house of eternity." Two passages serve to exemplify these points:

לא מצינו בין שמרותיו של אבא ששטר זה פרוע

> We have not found among our father's documents that this I.O.U. was ever repaid. (*m. Shebu.* 7:7)

אמר להם הוציאו לי כתובת אימותיכם הוציאו לו

> (Hillel) said to them, "Bring me your mothers' marriage contracts." They brought them to him. (*t. Ketub.* 4:9)

The people these passages discuss continued to hold their parents' legal documents even though in the first case clearly, and in the second probably, those parents were now dead. Here are multigenerational records, potentially available for use to establish any number of legal points long after the principals ceased to need the documents. Here, too, is reason to believe that, according to legal necessities, Jews in these years might retain the records not only of parents, but also of grandparents, and perhaps of yet earlier ancestors.[46]

The archives discovered in the Cave of Letters at Naḥal Ḥever can further sensitize us to potential patterns among the Murabbaʿat texts. Four archives were evident there. The first, that of Babatha, unearthed was contained in a kind of leather valise and comprised thirty-five documents written in Greek, Judaean Aramaic, and Nabataean. A number of these documents concerned matters other than Babatha's own property and affairs. One such papyrus, *P.Yadin* 7, was a deed of gift that had formerly belonged to her mother. Three others attached to Babatha's stepdaughter, Shelamzion: a marriage contract, a deed of gift, and a renunciation of claims (*P.Yadin* 18, 19, and 20, respectively). Yet another document, *P.Yadin* 8, belonged originally to one of Babatha's brothers, Joseph b. Simon or Bar Simon, both of whom were involved in the sale of a white donkey.[47] Thus, although her own materials predominated, the archive might better be characterized not as Babatha's archive per se, but as that of her immediate family.

A second Naḥal Ḥever archive belonged to Eleazar b. Samuel. His papyri were less personal than Babatha's, consisting entirely of leasing contracts he had signed with farmers in En Gedi. Yet the archive was discovered stuffed into a woman's leather bag. Potentially, this fact could be interpreted to mean that Eleazar had requisitioned an old, unwanted bag for his own purposes. But given that Babatha carried some materials for the men in her life, it is preferable to recognize here an archive carried and sequestered by a female relative of Eleazar's, or a female friend—perhaps Babatha herself (on which, see Chapter 3).

Similar in certain respects to Eleazar's archive was the third collection, that of John b. Baʿyah, one of the commanders of Bar Kokhba's forces in En Gedi. His archive comprised nothing but letters received from Simon b. Kosiba and his lieutenants. Like Eleazar's, John's archive was hidden among the personal belongings of an anonymous woman, wrapped in a bag for wool work. In addition to the fifteen letters in Judaean Aramaic, Hebrew, and Greek, the water skin contained dyed, unspun wool, skeins of wool in various colors, a spindle, a glass jar, and sundry other objects. Evidently, a woman was holding the letters for John.

The fourth archive from the Cave of Letters is a conceptual archive, purchased piecemeal from the bedouin, who claimed in the 1950s that it derived from Naḥal Ṣe'elim. Since archaeologists later discovered additional portions of some of the same documents in the Cave of Letters, however, the actual provenance, Naḥal Ḥever, has become apparent.[48] Hannah Cotton has reconstructed the archive as belonging to a young woman, Salome Komaise, who, like Babatha, lived out most of her tragically short life in Mahoza.[49] Six Greek documents and one Judaean Aramaic document make up the archive: a rent or tax receipt evidently once belonging to her first husband, Shamoa b. Simon; a land declaration from the census of 127 that belonged to Salome's brother (whose name is lost); Shamoa b. Simon's land declaration of that same census; a deed of renunciation between Salome and her mother, Salome Grapte; a deed of gift involving the same two women; a tax or rent receipt that Salome received; and Salome's marriage contract issued by her second husband—Shamoa evidently having died—and dated to August of 131. Thus this archive, as with Babatha's, combined the woman's personal documents with those of family members. In all four cases, then, it seems that women were carrying the archives.[50] If one may safely extrapolate, women often played the role of family archivist in ancient Judaea.

Informed by these roughly coeval archives and rabbinic descriptions, one is alerted when sifting the Murabbaʿat materials to the possibility of multigenerational and multilingual archives. As well, they might be the holdings of entire families, not just of single individuals; and they may often be attached to female archivists.

With these guidelines in mind, and well aware of the necessarily tentative character the evidence assigns to any proposal, three First Revolt families seem to be in view among the Murabbaʿat texts. An archive represents each family. The first archive, including two (possibly three) documents, may conveniently be denominated the Archive of the Family of Eutrapelus. The three texts are *Mur* 26, *Mur* 29, and possibly *Mur* 22. Linking the first two is the patronym of the two principals, Eutrapelus son of Eutrapelus and Cleopas son of Eutrapelus.[51] Of some thirty-five hundred separate, named Judaeans listed in Ilan's *Lexicon of Jewish Names in Late Antiquity,* only one man bore this name apart from the individuals now in question.[52] A Greek name so rare in Judaea is extremely unlikely to have belonged to two separate men, contemporaries at that, both of whom sired sons, both of whose sons were then named among the relatively few texts found in the caves of Murabbaʿat. Further linking *Mur* 26 and *Mur* 29 is the fact that the principals, Eutrapelus and Cleopas, signed them with reasonably practiced hands in Greek, even though *Mur* 26 is an Aramaic deed and *Mur* 29 a Hebrew one. Only one other Judaean principal or witness in the entire corpus of the present study signed a Semitic text in Greek. Everyone else signed in a Semitic tongue—usually, as noted in Chapter 1, in the language of the writ.

Two considerations suggest the provisional placement of *Mur* 22 in the Eutrapelus archive. First, the scribe of *Mur* 29, Simon b. Shabi, is also apparently the scribe of *Mur* 22.[53] This connection could indicate that the Eutrapelus family patronized the same scribal shop, presumably one in their vicinity within Jerusalem, more than once, perhaps regularly for all of their business transactions. Second, both documents mention as neighbors bordering the two properties under transaction "Honi and others." This Honi (a hypocoristic) appears to find mention in other Murabbaʿat First Revolt texts. His full name was Hananiah b. John (on which more immediately below). A reasonable hypothesis would be that he and his family lived within the city and owned fields immediately outside it, doing both in proximity to the home and holdings of the Eutrapelus family.[54] For it is observable in late Second Temple legal materials generally that people who lived as neighbors also frequently owned fields and agricultural plots situated near one another's holdings elsewhere. These considerations are inconclusive in assigning *Mur* 22 to this archive, but they are sufficiently suggestive to warrant its tentative inclusion.

The second proposed archive may be termed the Archive of the Family of Honi b. John, the man alluded to above. Several forms of his name, Hananiah, run throughout the Murabba'at texts. They are especially notable in those texts already proposed as belonging to the First Revolt. One encounters the formal name only in *Mur* 30, where a John b. Hananiah is among those listed as intended witnesses (he does not actually sign). Studying the text to discover possible reasons for John's being a witness, the name of Salome, one of the principals, draws attention: Salome b. Honi b. John. John was presumably her brother and so, as discussed in Chapter 1, a logical candidate to witness the transaction. He had been named John on the principle of papponymy, a common practice among the Jews of the Second Temple. And one of Salome's neighbors is listed as Hanin b. John, quite likely her father, Hananiah. Here, then, the same man is plausibly Hananiah, Honi, and Hanin.

Mur 22 then contributes an additional datum. The inner contract describes as bordering on the property being sold one Hanin b. Honi (חנין בר חוני). The outer contract, however, identifies that neighbor as Hanin b. Hanina (חנין בר חנינא). Thus the same father is alternately Honi or Hanina. Apparently, he was known indifferently by either of these hypocoristic forms—as well, of course, as by the formal name Hananiah, and again by Hanin. His son, Hanin, also would have borne the formal name Hananiah, as his listed name is yet another hypocoristic for that rather common, indeed biblical, Hebrew appellation. Thus one finds as allonyms Hananiah, Honi, Hanina, and Hanin: a confusing, dangerous quadruplet for the historian.

A fair number of the contracts designate men by one of these onomastic options. In normal circumstances it would be rash to conclude that they all involved the same family. But here, given the very restricted population pool represented by the Murabba'at refugees, that danger is greatly diminished. Nevertheless, the proposal to connect these individuals must be understood as surmise, for all that it fairly forces itself upon the reader of the writs. Which of several potential men may be in view, grandfather or father or son, is naturally more tentative by a degree of separation.

The proposed texts for the Archive of the Family of Honi b. John include the following: *Mur* 18, 19, 25, 27, 32, 33, and 38 and 4Q348. The borrower in the I.O.U. *Mur* 18 is one Absalom b. Hanin, said to hail from Kefar Signa, perhaps located in southern Galilee. At the time of the contract, however, he lived in Kislon, where the contract was executed. It may well be, then, that Honi b. John and his family were originally from Kefar Signa and that they came to reside in Jerusalem only a few years before the outbreak of the revolt.[55] *Mur* 19 is the Masada writ of divorce issued to Miriam b. John. Conceivably, she could be Honi's sister, but that option seems unlikely. For if she were, she would have been born in the neighborhood of 10 C.E., the approximate date suggested for him by a genealogical reconstruction (see Figure 2.1). That would make her an old woman at the time of her divorce in 71 and also place her and her erstwhile husband among the rebels at Masada as sexagenarians. This is not impossible, but it is hardly an attractive reconstruction. Hence it seems better to suggest that Miriam was the daughter of that same John who was the potential witness of *Mur* 30 noted above. She then would have been born about 50 and in her early twenties at the time of her divorce. (Women typically married as early as age thirteen or fourteen.) Leaving Masada, she made her way, presumably not alone but under escort, to the caves of Murabbaʿat and her family. The implied connection between freedom fighters who plainly knew each other's location after the fall of Jerusalem should not be overlooked.

Her putative father, John, finds mention in *Mur* 32, which is probably an I.O.U.[56] That text, it will perhaps be recalled, was one over whose paleographic date Milik wavered, tending at times to date it as early as *Mur* 18. Yardeni also favored a first-century date on paleographic grounds, assigning it to the years 66–73.[57]

Mur 25 is a deed of sale involving a house, land, and the accompanying immovables. The vendor is designated simply Hanina. As it was composed in "year three of the freedom of Jerusalem," this is a third text (with *Mur* 18 and 19) potentially dating this archive to the First Revolt. *Mur* 27 is another deed of sale for immovable property, whose principal's patronym survives, the first name lost, as b. Hanina. One of the witnesses to the text, whose name has broken away, came from Hebron, just as did a witness to *Mur* 26—almost certainly a First Revolt text from Jerusalem.[58] That person's name also failed to survive. Here, then, we see a tenuous wartime Jerusalem connection. Conceivably, these contracts involve the same Hanina b. Honi known from *Mur* 22; *Mur* 25 might also be writ belonging to the father, Hanina b. John. Yardeni allowed that both texts could be first-century products on the basis of the paleography.[59]

Mur 33 is an especially interesting text in that it connects two of the suggested First Revolt families. It concerns some money that has changed hands, the amount lost in lacunae, and so is either an I.O.U. or a receipt. Attached to the money is Simon b. Hanin, presumably another son of Honi

b. John. Simon is illiterate; a *hypographeus,* the scribe of the text, signed for him.[60] That a scion of a wealthy Jerusalem family would be incapable of signing his name is not without interest. But the more immediately pertinent datum in the contract is the signature of the only witness: he appears to be the Cleopas son of Eutrapelus known from *Mur* 29. There, as the vendor of a plot of land, perhaps a vineyard, he commissioned a contract written in Hebrew and signed it in Greek. Here, acting as witness—and so, not the man who hired the scribe—he signed an Aramaic document with a Nabataean reflex of his Greek name: [קלובו בר א]וטרפלוס שהד.[61] Why a Nabataean form should have been the choice is a mystery, though such forms were not especially uncommon among the Judaeans of these years.[62] In general, we know that certain Greek/Semitic equivalencies existed in late Second Temple culture as a matter of convention. Thus, קלובו perhaps would have been an ordinary reflex of Κλέοπος, just as Semitic ישוע was of Greek Ἰάσων, or שמעון of Σίμον.[63] *Mur* 33 appears to cement the case that the families of Eutrapelus and Honi b. John knew each other, probably as neighbors in Jerusalem. The signature of Cleopas also confirms the placement of *Mur* 33 among the First Revolt texts.

Mur 38 comprises six fragments whose assignment to the same document relies almost entirely on the quality and appearance of the papyrus.[64] Only one of those fragments, fragment 4, preserves more than a single legible word: seven damaged signatures in Aramaic. Two of those signatures are of the essence. After the two principals signed, the second witness was one חנין ב]ר. חנין was a form of חנניה, here displaying nasalization of the final open syllable, a phenomenon common in late Second Temple texts and affecting both Hebrew and Aramaic.[65] Accordingly, this witness, "Hananiah b. [PN," signed his name the way it sounded. The fourth witness then wrote חוני[, "Honi [b. PN."[66] It seems, then, that we have here Hananiah (Honi) b. John and his son Hanin b. Honi, but because the patronyms of the signatures do not survive, we cannot determine which is which. In any event, both men are βραδέως γράφοντες. Taken with Simon as noted above, therefore, none of the family of Honi for whom we have evidence was sufficiently literate as to read a book.

The last of the eight documents that may belong to Honi's family archive is 4Q348, and this one requires a bit more discussion. Eshel had proposed, it will be recalled, that 4Q348 derived ultimately from Jerusalem and came to be deposited among the Murabbaʿat materials when refugees fled the city after its fall in 70. He also argued for a reading of line 13 as קומ[ודיוס כוהן גדול, referring to Joseph b. Camydus, high priest from 46 to 47. These were significant claims to make and represented a breakthrough in the understanding of this enigmatic document. Intensive study of photographs of the text suggests, however, that these impressive claims are also partially incorrect.

Eshel was correct in connecting 4Q348 to Jerusalem. He did not observe it, but the city's name can be read in just the portion of the contract where form criticism suggests it ought to occur: for the lower text, at the end of line 13.[67] With the provenance now certain, further progress in comprehending this document becomes possible—for Jerusalem's customary law with regard to deeds of sale differed from that observable elsewhere, as for example in the materials from En Gedi or Mahoza.[68] Jerusalem contracts uniquely began by listing, after the particulars of date and place, the witnesses or signatories (Hebrew, חותמים) to the transaction. Thus, for example, *Mur* 30: בעשרים ואחד [*sic*] לתשר שנת ארבע לגאולת ישראל ברשלים חותמים, "On the twenty-first of Tishri, year four of the redemption of Israel, in Jerusalem: witnesses . . ." (four names follow). Similarly, *Mur* 22: בארבעה עשר לאלול שנת שתים ל[גאולת יש[רא]ל בירשלים חותמים, "On the fourteenth of Elul, year two of the [redemption] of Is[rae]l, in Jerusalem: witnesses . . ." (again, four names follow).[69]

These examples demonstrate that the ordinary formulae for a deed of sale in First Revolt Jerusalem were dates (by day, month, year, and era), place, and witnesses. Further, the usual number of signatories, in addition to the principals, would be four. Bearing these form-critical patterns in mind, it becomes possible to make sense of something Yardeni remarked as puzzling in 4Q348: "It appears to be unlike other deeds that have survived from that period. The surviving part of the text consists mainly of names."[70] Knowing that the text should list four witnesses by name, however, one can suggest that lines 13–16 comprise that listing, followed by the principals, who are indeed unusually numerous but just where form criticism would put them. The following reading and reconstruction emerge:

13. [ב(*date*) ל(*month name*) שנת שתים ליהוסף קמ]ודיוס כוהן גדול ביר[ו]ש̇ל̊י̊ם̇
14. [חותמים PN בר PN PN בר י] הוסף מתתיה בר שמעון אלעזר [בר שבי]
15. אמרו PN בר PN PN בר יהו]חנן אלעזר בר שמעון בר חוני כ̇[לם מן]
16. [ירושלים לPN בר PN PN בר PN יהוס]ף̇ ב[ר י]הוחנן יהוסף בר ◦◦◦◦

[13][On the (date) of (month), the second[71] year of Joseph Cam]ydus the High Priest, in Jer[u]salem. [14][Witnesses: PN b. PN, PN b. J]oseph, Matthew b. Simon, Eleazar [b. Shabi]. [15][PN b. PN, PN b. Yo]hanan, Eleazar b. Simon,

(and) Bar Honi, a[ll of them from Jerusalem, said] [16][to PN b. PN, PN b. PN, Jose]ph b. [Y]ohanan, (and) Joseph b. (illegible PN) . . .

It appears, then, that eight men other than the witnesses were involved in the obscure transaction recorded by this contract. Several of the people named beg comment. The first, the witness Eleazar b. Shabi (אלעזר [בר שבי]), probably requires by his mere presence a revised date for the document, placing its composition in the early 60s, some fifteen years later than Eshel had suggested. The reasoning is as follows. The witnesses to 4Q348 signed it in an exceptional manner, rotating the papyrus ninety degrees and inscribing their names perpendicularly between the upper and lower texts, rather than, as is usual with *Doppelurkunden,* signing on the reverse. Traces of three names remain. Only one can be read with any confidence, but this is the name that connects this text with at least two other Murabbaʿat texts likely to derive from First Revolt Jerusalem: [א]לׄעׄזׄרׄ בׄרׄ שבי.[72] Recall that another b. Shabi, Simon b. Shabi, signed *Mur* 29 as a witness and was the probable scribe of *Mur* 22. Note, too, that the name Shabi was exceptionally rare. Apart from its appearance in *Mur* 29 and here in 4Q348, the name is attested on two ossuaries discovered in Isawiyya, near Jerusalem, and published by Eliezer Sukenik in 1930.[73] These ossuaries, evidently related, are thought to antedate the fall of Jerusalem in 70. Otherwise, the name never occurs in Second Temple sources. Accordingly, the two men, Simon b. Shabi and Eleazar b. Shabi, are very likely to be brothers, and both of them scribes as well. If so, given the dating of *Mur* 22 and 29 to the decade of the 60s, when Simon was active, one may most reasonably attribute the activity of the second scribal brother, Eleazar, witness to 4Q348, to the same decade. This probability in turn focuses attention on a second figure in the text, the high priest, Joseph Camydus.

Eshel had identified the high priest of 4Q348 with a figure twice referenced by Josephus (*A.J.* 20.16, 103), bearing a name usually regularized in English as Joseph b. Camydus. In point of fact, however, his patronym is variously spelled in the manuscript tradition of *Antiquities* as Καμεί, Κάμη, Καμυδός, Καμοιδί, Κεμοιδί, Κεμεδί, and Κεμεδή. Most scholars would see this tradition as an increasingly corrupt rendering of Semitic קמחית.[74] This name is attached by the Talmud to an earlier, presumably ancestral high priest, Simon b. Camithus (17–18 C.E.) and may be related to the Aramaic word for "flour," קמחא. But even this connection is problematic, hence probationary. The entire discussion of this name is little more than informed guesswork. We do not know for certain how the name was heard, or whence derived, in either Greek or Semitic. Josephus renders the ancestral Camithus as Κάμιθος, perhaps related, but obviously not identical, to the name Καμῆτις recorded in Egyptian papyri and sometimes suggested as a *comparandum*. A derivation from Latin Commodus has also been proposed.[75] Uncertainty and complexity are the watchwords here. It is entirely possible that none of the proposed Greek, Latin, or Semitic *comparanda* and derivations is correct. Eshel's proposed reading steers well through dangerous waters, but the degree of our ignorance about ancient onomastica and the contingent interplay here between that ignorance, paleography, and history must be frankly acknowledged. If, however, on balance, קמודיוס is the best option for reading 4Q348, and that Semitic spelling does represent a reality hidden as Καμυδός behind Josephus's welter of readings, then another complication intrudes itself. A man with a name similar to Eshel's Joseph Camydus ascended to the high priesthood in 61–62 C.E.

That man bore a name usually rendered as Joseph Cabi b. Simon (*A.J.* 20.196; *B.J.* 6.114). The manuscript tradition for Cabi is comparable to that for Camydus, offering variously Καβί, Δεκαβί, and Κάμης.[76] With the last name we step once more onto the onomastic merry-go-round we have already visited for Joseph Camydus, and scholars therefore typically consider this later figure to be related both to Eshel's man and to the ancestral Camithus.[77] Accordingly, if קמודיוס can reference Joseph Camydus, high priest in 47–48, it can equally well reference Joseph Cabi b. Simon, occupant of the office some fifteen years later. And that later option better accords with the probable floruit of the two sons of Shabi. If this reasoning is accepted, then Eshel's suggestion for the dating of 4Q348 to the earlier man must be modified. This document dates instead to the year 61 or 62, the eve of the First Revolt, the approximate time when Josephus returned from a diplomatic mission to Rome and set foot anew in Palestine: "There I found revolutionary movements already on foot and widespread elation at the prospect of revolt from Rome."[78] The explosive social setting both explains the use of a high-priestly era for the dating of 4Q348 and turns attention to a third figure in the text.

The high-priestly era is highly significant. Eshel somewhat underplayed the sharp political force of the fact when he explained it in terms of halakhic scruple: "If we are correct that the high priest is mentioned in the dating formula of this deed, then this evidently proves that some people dated deeds according to the high priests' service. It can be assumed that these were Jews who were scrupulous in not using the years of the reign of the

Roman emperors when dating their documents."[79] The matter was actually more akin to the Boston Tea Party than to a discussion of the tithing of dill and cumin. First Maccabees provides the lens through which to regard this dating. According to that work, in 141 B.C.E. the Jewish people slipped from beneath the control of the Seleucids to the north and proclaimed that fact by using new dating formulae in their documents: "In the one hundred seventieth year the yoke of the Gentiles was removed from Israel, and the people began to write in their documents and contracts, 'In the first year of Simon the great high priest and commander and leader of the Jews.'"[80] To begin dating by the high priests in the run-up to the First Revolt was a revolutionary act, by intent a repulsion of the Roman yoke, and probably tells us something about each of the participants in this contract. In early-60s Jerusalem, revolution was the topic of the hour among priestly circles, especially younger priestly circles, and it was a matter of parties and factions.[81] This connection spotlights the name of Eleazar b. Simon in line 15 of 4Q348.

The name Eleazar b. Simon is very prominent in Josephus's narratives about the First Revolt.[82] A priest and member of the ruling class, he was the ringleader of a faction that Josephus denominates "Zealots" (not to be confused with the generic term for revolutionary). This faction helped to seize control of the Temple in 66 and force cessation of the sacrifices on behalf of the emperor, an action that precipitated a chain of events that led directly to the war. Eleazar and the Zealots then controlled the Temple's inner court for virtually the whole of the war, sometimes by themselves, sometimes in concert with other revolutionary factions, prominently the group led by John of Gishala. Association with this Eleazar would tend to draw the family of Honi b. John near to the center of revolutionary events. It might suggest that they were priestly. It would further imply that they did not flee as refugees. Rather, along with numerous other insurgents, they chose to continue the war in the Judaean Desert. The caves of Murabbaʿat would accordingly take on a new aspect. But is the Eleazar of 4Q348 the same man as the factional leader?

Both Eleazar and Simon are exceedingly common names, a fact strongly warning against facile identification. On the other hand, adding to the name the evident revolutionary character of the dating formula would seem to improve the chances markedly. If this is not the Zealot Eleazar b. Simon, then this is a man of comparable radical views. Certainty is impossible absent further information, but we may cautiously begin to contemplate the Murabbaʿat First Temple documents in a different light. Attention then turns to the fourth and final significant figure in this frustratingly fragmentary source.

That figure is Bar Honi, mentioned last in the asyndetic listing of vendors or, at any rate, actors in line 15. The presence of this name would explain why this text is in the reconstructed archive—4Q348 would be Bar Honi's record of the transaction. This man was then arguably one of Honi b. John's four sons, as proposed from the other texts in his reconstructed archive: Absalom, Simon, John, or Hanina. The appellation Bar Honi was a kind of social convention. A study of the names "son of X" among the ancient Jews, conducted by Joseph Naveh, showed that a man of any social level might at different times be referenced by his formal name, his "handle" (usually connected to origin, occupation, characteristics, nature, or physical defect), or the expression "son of X." "People spent most of their lives," Naveh observed, "in informal and familiar surroundings, such as military units, working groups, or among friends, where there was a tendency to abbreviate and to drop one of the elements of the 'X son of Y' formula."[83] Thus Bar Honi was evidently a familiar, a friend to Eleazar b. Simon and others listed in the contract. This inference makes it yet more reasonable to suggest that he would have shared the revolutionary ideology they had agreed to declare by using the high-priestly dating.

In sum, the proposal is to assign eight documents to a reconstructed First Revolt archive of Honi b. John and family: *Mur* 18, 19, 25, 27, 32, 33, and 38 and 4Q348. A much more tenuous possibility would add an additional two manuscripts to the archive. These two are not certainly related between themselves, so one might accept one and reject the other. They are *Mur* 20 and 4Q346. *Mur* 20, a marriage contract, we have encountered above, noting that its dating formula (שנת חדה ע[שרה, "year eleven") would best be taken as a regnal dating, and that further the two best possibilities for the ruler in question were Claudius and Nero. Thus the year of its inscription would become either 51 or 65. Yardeni allowed that a first-century dating was possible on the basis of the letterforms.[84]

We know from the study of other surviving marriage contracts of this general period (e.g., *Mur* 21; *P.Yadin* 10) that the grooms or their *hypographeis* normally signed the document in first position. Accordingly, the sole surviving signature of *Mur* 20, located in first position, is probably that of the groom: יהודה בר יהו[, "Judah b. YHW[." In turn, it seems probable that the השנם of line 2 is his grandfather. If one tentatively restored the damaged patronym of the signature as יהו[נתן, "John," then *Mur* 20 lines 1–2 might be read and restored as follows, and further, the text assigned to the archive of Honi b. John: [1]בשבעה לאדר שנת חדה עשׂ]רה לקלדוס קסר בהרדונא אמר יהודה בר יהונתן] [2]בר מנשה מן בני אלישיב, “On the seventh of Adar, year ele[ven of Claudius, Caesar, in Haradona, Judah b. John] b. Manaseh from Bene Eliashib [said to . . .].” This is a hypothetical, but it accounts for the few data we have and would explain the text’s presence among the archives. The proposed Judah b. John would then plausibly be the brother of Honi b. John. If the text were dated to the reign of Claudius, he would be seen as getting married (again?) at the age of thirty or forty. The name of Honi’s and Judah’s paternal grandfather, Manaseh, would likewise emerge. This name then potentially ties together with 4Q346.

As with 4Q348, 4Q346 is of dubious connection with the site of Qumran. Indeed, as noted in the previous chapter, scholars today question whether any documentary texts come from the caves near that site, whereby it becomes necessary to explain the true provenance of any that do not. One cannot absolutely rule out proximate origin in the Cave of Letters or another Naḥal Ḥever cave, but the suggestion faces a serious objection. According to paleographic analysis, the documentary materials in question date to the first century B.C.E. or first century C.E.[85] Yet textual scholars and archaeologists are in nearly unanimous agreement that the Naḥal Ḥever caves were not occupied during those years.[86]

Given that a good case can be made for the association of 4Q348 with Murabbaʿat and the First Revolt, we have warrant to sift the other documents in the group 4Q342–348, 4Q351–354, and 4Q356–361, looking for additional such connections. Composed in Hebrew, Aramaic, and Greek, the writs are preserved in so fragmentary a condition that they offer little with which to work. However, 4Q346 does provide a few clues for the historian. It is an Aramaic deed of sale that Yardeni dated to the late first century B.C.E.[87] A certain Simon is the vendor, a Manaseh the purchaser. Since it was written during the years when a genealogical reconstruction would place any Manaseh who was grandfather of a putative Judah b. John, one might tentatively consider placing this text in the Murabbaʿat archive of Honi b. John and family.

The third proposed archive may be denominated the Archive of the Family of Dositheos b. Eleazar. Three documents potentially belong here: *Mur* 21, 30, and 31. At the heart of this archive is *Mur* 30, for it is the most complete and most suggestive of personal relationships, and so of possible relationships among the texts. The papyrus is a *Doppelurkunde* recording the sale of a sizable field (four dunams, or about half a hectare) in the vicinity of Jerusalem, together with its crops and trees. The seller is the eponymous Dositheos. Composed in excellent "Mishnaic" Hebrew, the contract is evidently to be dated—if Eshel and Cotton are correct—to the late autumn of 69 C.E., only eight months before the fall of Jerusalem to Roman forces. The price of the field, 88 *zuz*, is consistent with prices known from other contracts and rabbinic literature. Despite the reign of terror that Josephus portrays as existing within the city at this late stage of the revolt, then, no deflation of property values is evident. This fact is surprising and may say something about the people involved and their confidence in the war's outcome.

Another actor in the document is the vendor's wife, Salome b. Honi, who stipulates to the sale and clears the property from any liens of her own. This was necessary, as the wife might otherwise retain rights by virtue of her dowry or *ketubbah*. Upon divorce, the husband owed his wife both the repayment of her dowry, which monies he typically used freely while married, and all support that he had promised her in the marriage contract. The wife was legally entitled to extract what was due from her husband's properties, including monies realized from the sale of land or houses alienated after the marriage terminated; hence the need for Salome's statement indemnifying the purchase.[88]

As noted earlier, Salome seems to have been the daughter of Honi b. John. If valid, this connection is important, because the intermarriage of archival families would require that the various First Revolt occupants of the Murabbaʿat caves did not simply end up there by chance, haphazardly, each group making its way as best it could amidst the slaughter and chaos of Jerusalem's fall, only to have everyone look up when the dust had settled to find themselves together. Rather, these families were related. They had laid careful plans, devising joint survival protocols. The caves were prepared ahead of time as a desert refuge—should such become necessary—and when the time came, the families retreated to Murabbaʿat.

More than the surmise of Salome's paternity potentially links the families of Dositheos and Honi. Recall that in *Mur* 18, Abraham b. Hanin—in the present reconstruction, one of Honi b. John's sons, and thus Salome's brother—is said to be residing in Kislon in 55 or 56 C.E. According to *Mur* 30, the same village may be connected to the family of Dositheos as well. An attractive reading and reconstruction of lines 10–11 would be: [10]דוסתס בר אלעזר [11]בר אלׄ[עזר(?) מן כ]סׄלון ישׄ[ב בירושלים, "Dositheos b. Eleazar

b. Ele[azar from Ki]slon, resid[ing in Jerusalem."[89] Thus Dositheos's home village is revealed as Kislon, although he was living in the Judaean capital at the time of *Mur* 30. If this reconstruction is correct, one may reasonably deduce that members of Abraham's family, including his sister Salome, came to know Dositheos and his family in Kislon ten or fifteen years before the inscription of *Mur* 30. This acquaintance led to intermarriage between the two families. In turn, that relationship took them all to Jerusalem some years later, where they found themselves when the First Revolt erupted.

Mur 21 is an extraordinarily interesting *ketubbah* or marriage contract recording the union of one Menahem b. [PN] with a bride whose name has only partially survived, as [PN] b. Lazar. Milik noted the scribal peculiarities and concluded on that basis that the text was one of the earliest among the Murabbaʿat finds:

> The scribe's ductus is very peculiar. One may note especially the curved, rounded shapes of letters such as aleph, beth, daleth, samekh, sometimes lamedh, mem, nun, resh, tav; the very neat distinction between beth and kaph; the characteristic forms of heh, mem, tav; the alternation between final and medial forms; the varying thickness of the letters. These are clues that might suggest a relatively early date for this document (before the First Revolt?), unless these are merely mannerisms of the scribe.[90]

Several additional aspects of the manuscript layout and language mark it as peculiar. The lines are uneven and the beginning points rather helter-skelter. The Aramaic is notable for its verbal and nominal gender neutralization, for the use of the Greek loan νόμος (נמסא) for "law" instead of the דין normal to *ketubbot,* and for the use of the informal *nota accusativi* ית instead of the direct-object marker ל usual in the diction of the Aramaic contracts of this period. One gains the impression that this document expresses a generally more informal and quotidian Aramaic than the genre ordinarily adopted. Taken as a whole, these indications point to a nonprofessional scribe, and indeed, the signatures appear to verify that the writer was none other than the bride's father, Lazar b. Joseph—who wrote with an unpracticed or level 2 hand.[91]

Lazar is a hypocoristic for Eleazar, the name shared by Dositheos's father and grandfather. If Lazar b. Joseph is indeed related to Dositheos, he obviously could not be his father, Eleazar b. Eleazar. The suggestion is therefore that he may have been his grandfather. The family had retained this old *ketubbah* for two generations beyond its inscription. If this posited connection is correct, then it probably means that *Mur* 21 is one of the two oldest manuscripts among the surviving materials from Murabbaʿat.[92] For if Dositheos and Salome b. Honi as man and wife were wealthy Jerusalem property holders in 69 C.E., then they were perhaps born between 30 and 40. Receding approximately twenty years for the time between generations would put the birth of Eleazar b. Eleazar and his sister, [PN] b. Lazar, at about 10 C.E. The birth of Lazar b. Joseph would then fall about 10 B.C.E. Allowing for the typical female age of fifteen at marriage would place the nuptials of [PN] b. Lazar and Menahem b. [PN] in approximately the year 25 C.E. Together with its amateur authorship, this extreme age and the rural setting for its composition might explain the odd scribal and legal characteristics of *Mur* 21. All of this is of course rough-and-ready calculation, but it helps to imagine the social context within which this remarkable document may have come into existence.

Inclusion in the Archive of the Family of Dositheos b. Eleazar of the third proposed document, *Mur* 31, depends on the correctness of the posited linkage between Dositheos and Lazar b. Joseph. Accordingly, this is a very tentative attribution. The document is a fragmentary *Doppelurkunde*, probably recording the sale of some land, as 37 *zuz* changed hands. Yardeni dates the handwriting to the first century C.E.[93] A damaged phrase reads either "daughter of Joseph" (ברת יוסף) or, possibly, "the house of Joseph" (בית יוסף). Potentially, this Joseph is Lazar's father, and his daughter, Lazar's sister. If so, this text might be the very oldest of all the Murabbaʿat manuscripts, originating around the beginning of the Common Era.[94]

Table 2.1 and Figures 2.1, 2.2, and 2.3 summarize and illustrate the foregoing discussion of the three possible family archives.[95] Undoubtedly, some of the suggested connections and attributions are mistaken. The fragmentary state of the evidence virtually guarantees that any effort at historical and prosopographic reconstruction will make wrong turns. Nevertheless, the exercise has shown that it is reasonable to consider that perhaps eighteen documents discovered at Murabbaʿat have survived from First Revolt Jerusalem. They plausibly represent the archives of three families of that place and time who retreated in 70 C.E. to the Judaean Desert, probably to continue the fight along with other *sicarii,* Zealots, and like-minded freedom fighters. The families, like their texts, were intertwined: Cleopas b. Eutrapelus signed as a witness for Simon b. Hananiah, so binding the archives of their respective families; the family of Honi b. John intermarried with that of Dositheos b. Eleazar. Family members from one group find apparent mention

Table 2.1. Possible First Revolt archives among the Murabba'at texts

Archive	Document	Type/ language	Family member	Absolute/ internal date (C.E.)	Palaeographer's date (C.E.)
Family of Eutrapelus	*Mur 22*	Deed of sale/Heb	—	10/69	69
	Mur 26	Deed of sale/Ar	Eutrapelus b. Eutrapelus	—	1st/early 2nd
	Mur 29	Deed of sale/Heb	Cleopas b. Eutrapelus	8/67	67
Family of Honi b. John	*Mur 18*	I.O.U./Ar	Absalom b. Hanin	55/56	55
	Mur 19	Divorce/Ar	Miriam b. John	10/71	72
	Mur 25	Deed of sale/Ar	Hanina [b. Hanina?]	68/69	Ca. 68
	Mur 27	Deed of sale/Ar	[Hanina?] b. Hanina	—	1st/early 2nd
	Mur 32	Deed of sale/Ar	John [b. Hanina]	—	66–73
	Mur 33	I.O.U./Ar	Simon b. Hanin	—	1st/early 2nd
	Mur 38	Fragment/Ar	Hananiah b.[; Honi [b.	—	1st/early 2nd
	4Q348	Fragment/Heb	b. Honi	61/62	1st
Family of Dositheos b. Eleazar	*Mur 21*	Marriage/Ar	Eleazar b. Joseph	—	1st
	Mur 30	Deed of sale/Heb	Dositheos b. Eleazar	10/69	69
	Mur 31	Deed of sale/Heb	[Daughter] of Joseph	—	1st
Unattributed	4Q346	Deed of sale/Ar	Manaseh	—	Late 1st B.C.E.
	Mur 20	Marriage/Ar	Judah b. Jo[nathan?] b. Manaseh	12/51	66 or 117
	Mur 23	Deed of sale/Ar	—	—	1st
	Mur 28	Deed of sale/Ar	Joseph b. Gabinius	—	66–73

Note: Heb indicates Hebrew; Ar, Aramaic.

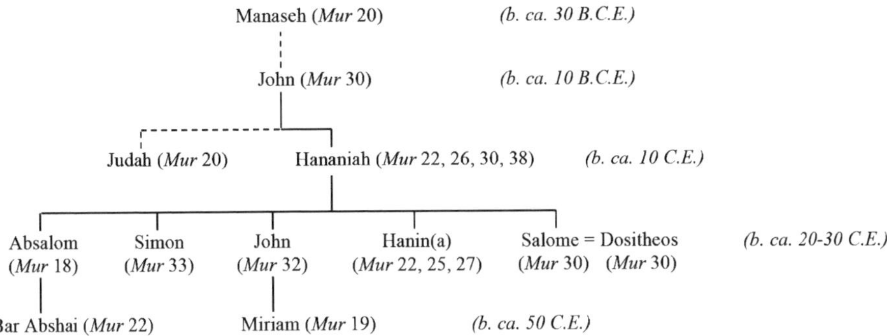

Figure 2.1. *The family of Honi (Hananiah) b. Jonathan.*

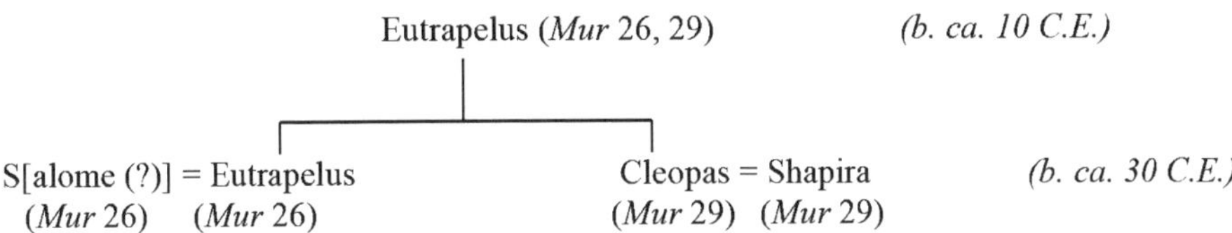

Figure 2.2. *The family of Eutrapelus.*

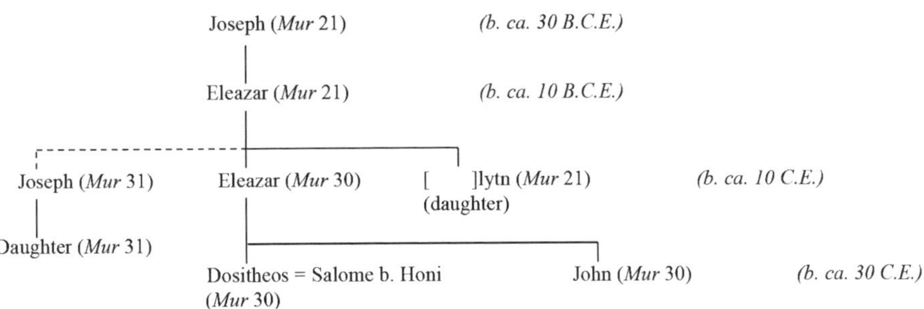

Figure 2.3. *The family of Dositheos b. Eleazar.*

in documents belonging to another group. The same scribal shop serviced all three families.[96] The picture that emerges differs notably from the reconstruction of Milik and de Vaux, who assigned only two or three manuscripts to a single putative First Revolt refugee family.

Instead, fully half of the personal documentary finds from Murabbaʿat arguably attach to one or another of the three families here identified. A fourth family archive, that of the Bene Galgula, certainly comes from the time of the Second Revolt and will be considered below. Yet these documentary archives were not the only late Second Temple materials unearthed in the Murabbaʿat caves. A fair number of literary works also came to light, composed in both Hebrew and Greek. The Greek writings are of particular interest, for analysis of these texts may contribute important facts about Greek language and literacy in antebellum Jerusalem—the home of Josephus.

Greek Literacy and Book Culture in First Revolt Jerusalem

When one considers the archives of the First Revolt that stem from Jerusalem, a striking anomaly begs for attention. Briefly remarked above, it deserves a bit of concentrated focus: *of all of the signatories of the Judaean Desert materials who signed or underwrote Semitic documents, only three ever signed in Greek* (Tables 1.2 and 1.3 in Chapter 1). Two of these were the brothers Eutrapelus: Eutrapelus *filius* and Cleopas. Not only did they sign in Greek, but with reasonably practiced hands, and so they were either clearly literary literates (Cleopas) or on the way to such (Eutrapelus).[97] Moreover, both were likely native to Jerusalem; Cleopas certainly was. He is designated in *Mur* 29 lines 10–11 as קלבוס בר אוטרפלוס מירשלים, "Cleopas b. Eutrapelus from Jerusalem." Personal provenance being a legal consideration in these ancient contracts, to say that someone was "from" a given place legally identified the person's place of origin. The intention was to distinguish that person from someone else who was merely "dwelling in" that locale.

Accordingly, Cleopas had been born in Jerusalem, so it was as a native of that city that he had attained literary literacy in Greek. Furthermore, judging from their behavior in a cultural situation that ordinarily called for Semitic signatures, both brothers were proud of their Hellenism. We have seen that Cleopas was also literate in Aramaic, but his Semitic signature was markedly less fluent, suggesting that his primary educational path had been the Greek *paideia*. These were Hellenists—yet at the same time, as demonstrated by their ultimate retreat to the desert to continue the war, men zealous for native Judaean traditions and polity. The two casts of mind were plainly compatible. The brothers Eutrapelus did not consider the Greek language "the tongue of the oppressor" but proudly proclaimed it their personal possession. Thus, within the corpus of this study, these men stand out as exceptional. So far as we have evidence, they represented a rare breed.

A second, conceptually related singularity is connected with the caves of Murabbaʿat. For here were found the only remnants of "pure" Greek literary culture unearthed in any of the Judaean Desert find-spots. That is to say, while a few literary materials clothed in Greek dress were discovered in Caves 4 and 7 near Qumran, none represented the Greco-Roman literary culture that flourished in contemporary Rome, Alexandria, and Oxyrhynchus.[98] Rather, these materials proved to be Jewish cultural artifacts, originally composed in Hebrew or Aramaic and merely translated into Greek: works such as 1 Enoch or the Books of Moses.[99] No literary works originally composed in Greek turned up at Masada, either;[100] nor was any discovered at Wadi Daliyeh, nor Naḥal Ḥever; nor at Jericho, Wadi Nar, Wadi Ghweir, Wadi Sdeir, Naḥal Ṣeʾelim, and Naḥal Mishmar. In this regard, Murabbaʿat was unique. Only here were found plays of the comedians, only here Greek historical or philosophical writings. Again, the heuristic question may serve, "Who took the texts to the caves?" The question is worth exploring in this regard, for in particular we want to know whether to attach this Greek literature to the First Revolt archives or to the Second.

The tentative thesis explored below is that the twin rarities are best regarded as a single phenomenon: Murabbaʿat's only known literary literates in Greek owned the only Greek literature to emerge from the Judaean Desert discoveries. Not only is this hypothesis reasonable prima facie, it is also consistent with all the textual facts in hand.

Benoit edited and published in *Les Grottes de Murabbaʿât* a total of thirteen Greek literary writings, all inscribed on papyrus, as was normal in the Mediterranean generally (*Mur* 108–112, 126–132, and 155). Most were exiguous, so fragmentary as to defy generic classification. All that could usually be said was that they were copied in literary hands and, so far as could be determined, laid out in the columnar format customary for Greek literature of the period.[101] A few were sufficiently preserved that a bit more analysis was possible. Benoit admired the hand of *Mur* 108 as "élégante, élancée, légèrement inclinée vers la gauche," suggesting that the work was perhaps "un texte philosophique."[102] (Benoit overlooked the work's meter; on the basis of its use of iambic trimeter, Jean Bingen subsequently identified it as a possible comedy.)[103] *Mur* 109, the recto of an opisthograph, Benoit thought might concern "un sujet d'ordre historique ou philosophique," resting this suggestion on the few legible vocables, παιδεία, μυθῶδες, and προγόν[οι?].[104] The verso contained another unidentifiable literary work, composed in a different, more cursive hand (*Mur* 110). On the basis of paleography, Benoit believed that all three of these copies quite likely derived from the years 50–100.[105] *Mur* 111, with only the single word καί extant among scattered letters, seemed likely to come from the same elegant and distinctive hand as *Mur* 109.[106] Accordingly, this work, too, might have been copied in the second half of the first century.

Subsequent paleographical analysis has fully affirmed Benoit's first-century dating of these four writings. In 1991, Edoardo Crisci published a thorough study of all the Greek writings discovered in Palestine and Mesopotamia and devoted several pages to these Murabbaʿat texts. Most notable in his discussion of *Mur* 108 was his comparison with a Greek fragment found at Masada: "Graphic analogies were also observed with the elegant writing of PMasada 741, whose terminus ante quem is the spring of 73 or 74 C.E."[107] Hannah Cotton and Joseph Geiger had published this work, better known as the Letter of Abaskantos to Judas, in the years since Benoit wrote, as a part of their treatment of the Greek and Latin materials of Masada.[108]

One of just two Greek papyri of any substance found in the ruins of Herod's desert redoubt, the letter concerns the sending of some lettuce requested by Judas—evidently resident at Masada—of his brother, Abaskantos, reasonably supposed by Cotton and Geiger to be living at En Gedi, the nearest source for such produce.[109] But Cotton and Geiger were unwilling to date the letter with any certainty to the Jewish habitation of Masada during the First Revolt. In their view, it may possibly have derived from that time but equally from any earlier point beginning with Herod's reign. Nothing in the paleography precluded a date considerably earlier than 74 C.E. Accordingly, given the notable similarity of the hands, one might be inclined to adjudge *Mur* 108 as likewise a product of the first century C.E. generally, and not necessarily just of that century's second half.

Crisci concurred with Benoit that *Mur* 109 and *Mur* 111 appeared to be products of the same scribe; he further concluded that a dating in the latter half of the first century or early second century was most likely.[110] For our purposes, however, something else that he said in discussing these two texts was even more interesting:

> Here, as in the writing of PMur. 108, the lower curves of epsilon and sigma are strongly oblique; epsilon in particular . . . has a characteristic shape, formed sometimes with the three strokes produced separately, at other times with the second and third fused into a single movement. The medial element is often ligatured with the following letter. Note also the form of alpha, with its eyelet sometimes extending beneath the base line of the writing. This feature is also

> present, as will be seen, in some of the Dura Europa texts. It finds its most exaggerated expression in certain Palestinian hands, and therefore—since it does not appear in the Egyptian papyri . . . *it may be understood as a peculiar feature of the Greek writing of that region, and in its most characteristic form, of Palestinian writing.*[111]

If the hypothesis we are exploring is correct, then, and these Greek writings are to be attached to First Revolt Jerusalem, it probably follows from Crisci's analysis that the texts were actually produced in that city as well. They were not imported; they were Palestinian copies. It was possible to obtain Greek literature in the Judaean capital in one way or another—whether by purchase, borrowing to copy, or another means—just as it was in Alexandria or Oxyrhynchus. Thus Josephus (to extrapolate one example) may reasonably be supposed to have obtained and read Thucydides while resident in Jerusalem and not merely later as, in Rome, he sat to compose his *Bellum judaicum* and contemplated the question of its proper model. Some measure of Greek literary culture evidently flourished in the very shadow of Herod's Temple.

Mur 112 is more difficult to date confidently by paleographic method than the texts discussed so far. Perhaps somewhat under the influence of de Vaux's dating theories, Benoit and Crisci focused on second-century *comparanda,* but each noted the existence of possible first-century analogs as well. The unidentified literary work, possibly concerning natural science or medicine, is inscribed on the verso of a scroll whose recto contains a legal process.[112] For the paleographers it was this legal process, *Mur* 113, that seemed to be the earlier writing, hence the more critical for dating.

The writ is too fragmentary to yield full analysis but involves two women with Jewish names, identified simply as Salome and Miriam, and a Roman veteran (ο]ὐετρανός) whose name is lost.[113] Benoit suggested that it might concern property boundaries and date from the first half of the second century C.E. Crisci considered its script "less typically Palestinian" than that of other Murabbaʿat papyri and suggested that it represented a typical bureaucratic majuscule of about the beginning of the second century, a characterization that would seem to leave open a somewhat earlier date if other evidence pushed in that direction.[114]

And two pieces of evidence appear to do so. First, the paleography of *Mur* 112, apparently the later text: important *comparanda* adduced by Benoit date well within the first century. If *Mur* 112 dates to the first century, then so must *Mur* 113. Particularly notable for Benoit because of close parallels was an otherwise unpublished papyrus from the second year of Domitian (82 C.E.), excerpted as an example in Schubart's standard work on Greek paleography.[115] Schubart himself remarked on this text: "It would be difficult to classify such a hand except for the date formula. Even an expert might be off by decades."[116] If this hand is difficult, even dangerous to date, then plainly its Judaean twin *Mur* 112 offers equal challenges—and prospects. *Mur* 112 might properly be dated several decades earlier than either Benoit or Crisci thought, and *Mur* 113 in train. We could well find ourselves in the mid-first century. Uncertainty is considerable. It would therefore be desirable, while not rejecting this evidence for first-century origins, to find some basis for dating other than the slippery science of paleography.

Perhaps such a method offers itself—and this, if acceptable, would be the second piece of evidence dating *Mur* 112 and 113 to the first century and therefore associating the opisthograph with First Revolt Jerusalem. This second dating approach relies upon a closer look at the legal writ, *Mur* 113.

It is a notable fact that many opisthographs known from Egypt exhibit the same pattern as that of *Mur* 112–113: a documentary text on the recto, a literary text on the verso. In fact, fully 17.9 percent of all the papyri discovered at Oxyrhynchus and published by 1989 manifest this pattern.[117] George Houston has commented, "Such recycling of documentary rolls is usually taken as a sign of an economy-minded collector, one who was trying to save money by having his copies made on secondhand rather than new papyrus."[118] Thus the owner of *Mur* 113 presumably presented the scribe this used piece of papyrus and asked to have the literary work inscribed on the back. What this fact means, of course, is that one may discover the name of the literary text's owner if it happens to be mentioned in the documentary text as extant—not, in theory, an unlikely possibility, since the names of principals frequently appeared more than once in documents they preserved. And how does one know which person of several who may appear was the owner of the papyrus? The trick is to connect a given person named in the document to one known from the archive that possibly included the text. Naturally, this step of the attribution process is precarious. Nonetheless, numerous successful examples of the approach dot the annals of Egyptian papyrology.[119]

The focus for *Mur* 113 becomes the woman Salome (שלום). Evidence suggests that this was the name of Eutrapelus b. Eutrapelus's wife. Unfortunately, the wife's name survives nowhere in her family's archive undamaged, but portions of it appear twice, and reasoned probability encourages a certain confidence that her name was, indeed, Salome. In *Mur* 26 line 18 the name appears most fully, written out as follows: ס[אנתת]ה (*three to four letters*) ברת (*three to four letters*)]ש, "*S*[. . . daughter of . . .]*s*, [his] wife."[120] The name appears again among the document's signatories on the verso.[121] Comparison with extant portions of the manuscript above and below the damaged name indicates that the letters lost from line 18 number ten or eleven. These letters will have spelled out the wife's personal name after the initial *sin/shin,* the term ברת, "daughter of," and her father's name except for its final letter. Excluding ברת, then, only seven or eight cursive Aramaic letters remain to fill out the names of both father and daughter. Accordingly, these must be reasonably short names. The ending of the patronym suggests that it was likely Greek, since Semitic names seldom end in *samekh,* whereas Semitic spellings of Greek names in the second declension, and sometimes the third, commonly do. But attempting to press beyond this inference regarding the father's name is pointless. The options are simply too numerous.

Not so for the daughter. The lacuna calls for a short name that was normally spelled with *shin* or, less likely since much less common, *sin* (or, just possibly, *samekh*—occasionally used elsewhere in place of *sin*). One must allow that the name could be Greek or Latin, expressed here in Aramaic guise. It seems reasonable to narrow the search to female names attested in Palestine between the time of Alexander the Great and the editing of the Mishnah, hence to utilize Ilan's *Lexicon* (*s.vv.*). What emerges is that six known names other than Salome are possible. When assessing probabilities, however, each of these others is subject to at least one potentially weighty objection.

Some are exceedingly rare. Here one would categorize the names Salina, Shilat, Storge, and Susanna. Salina is attested only once, in Greek lettering (Σαλίνα). Shilat (שילת) is likewise once attested. Storge, a Greek name, occurs once written out in Greek letters (Στοργή). Susanna (שושנה) occurs three times. Several of these rare names are also subject to a second objection, length. As configured in our scribe's hand, they would seem to be too long for this lacuna. If inserted, insufficient space would remain to complete the Greek patronym. These names would include Storge, if written as expected, סטרגה or סטורגה; Salina, סלינה; and Susanna. Here, too, one would likely categorize Shapira (שפירה), which occurs twelve times and would be an attractive alternative if not for its length. The third objection, that the name should be spelled with *samekh* in Semitic and therefore thus in *Mur* 26, also argues against two of the names already noted, Storge and Salina. It further applies to Sarah, which occurs eight times but, when written in Semitic letters, is always spelled with *samekh* (סרה) in our period. True, as noted, the homophonous *sin* could conceivably have been used to spell these names, and the first letter of the name as written in *Mur* 26 might be so construed. But this orthography is uncommon in late Second Temple Hebrew and Aramaic texts. The tendency is rather in the opposite direction, as with Sarah, rendered in the Bible שרה: words spelled in earlier times with *sin* were now regularly spelled with *samekh* instead.

These considerations conspire to push Salome to center stage. The name occurs fully sixty-three times, more than five times as frequently as its closest "rival" possibility, Shapira. Indeed, according to extant evidence Salome was second only to Miriam as the most common of all female names in Palestine during our period.[122] Since all of the other options are either very rare, too long, should be spelled with a *samekh,* or are open to more than one of these objections, Salome as the name of Eutrapelus's wife is clearly the option to be favored.

If the Salome of *Mur* 113 was Eutrapelus's wife, then possibly *Mur* 112 represented a literary work that her husband, or another literary literate in the family, desired to own. (As we have seen, Salome herself was illiterate, a *hypographeus* signing *Mur* 26 for her.) And if this connection is correct, it most plausibly follows that the other Greek literary works found at Murabbaʿat belong to the archive of the brothers Eutrapelus, too. But another possibility exists that must be considered before embracing this tentative conclusion. Among the Murabbaʿat papyri are two other women named Salome. Was either of them the woman referenced in *Mur* 113?

One of these women we have already encountered. She is Salome b. Honi, the wife of Dositheos b. Eleazar; they were two of the principals involved in the Hebrew contract *Mur* 30. Salome was illiterate. Dositheos signed the contract fluidly in Hebrew, with a level 3 signature. Thus, although his name is Greek, he clearly had pursued the kind of education that turned early to the Hebrew scriptures, such that he was now a literary literate, deeply conversant with the native Judaean literary tradition. One cannot eliminate the possibility that he may also have advanced so far in the Greek *paideia* that he could read Greek literature, in this case including *Mur* 112, but no positive evidence suggests this conclusion.

The second Salome was one of the Bene Galgula associated with the Second Revolt, to be discussed below. She and her brothers, Jesus and Jose, were the children of Yohanan Galgula. Jesus was commander under Simon b. Kosiba of a camp located at or near Herodium, and Jose also possessed a certain authority. The family evidently fled to the caves at Murabbaʿat as the revolt collapsed late in 135. This Salome's name appears in one or two documents belonging to the family's archive: *Mur* 115, a contract for remarriage composed in Greek, and possibly *Mur* 116, a second marriage contract written in that language. *Mur* 116 is very fragmentary and no signatures survive. *Mur* 115 retains three signatures on the verso in three different hands, each signing in Greek. Although damaged, the names can be read sufficiently to ascertain that none is that of Salome or her known brothers.[123] Consequently, we have no window into the question of whether or not this Salome or anyone in her family was a literary literate in Greek.

The study of ancient history necessarily involves more calculation and weighing of probabilities than one would wish. Evidence is typically scanty and must be treated like the proverbial stone squeezed for water. So it is with the question at hand. Eutrapelus's wife was likely, though not certainly, named Salome. Without question, literary literacy in Greek existed in her family. These are positive evidential factors. We know of no such literacy among the other depositors in these caves. Therefore, given the mere handful of people involved in the Murabbaʿat caches, it seems appropriate to suggest that *Mur* 112 and 113 belonged to the archive of the brothers Eutrapelus, rather than to another Salome or to another collection.

The remaining Greek literary papyri from Murabbaʿat are so fragmentary that brief consideration will suffice. Benoit characterized the hand of *Mur* 126 as "écriture littéraire soignée," with numerous first-century analogs from Oxyrhynchus, including *P.Oxy.* 1361, 1362, 1789, and 1806.[124] Crisci observed that the text was "penned in a round, vertical hand with a thick, uniform stroke, datable to the first or second centuries C.E."[125] *Mur* 127–129 all represented careful hands, all likewise being reminiscent of *Mur* 113 and so to be dated similarly to it. Comparing *Mur* 130–132 with that group, Benoit considered these latter "écritures bien différentes, mais toutes fort soignées."[126] Last, *Mur* 155 comprised thirty-six fragments sharing an identical exterior appearance and hand, hence was certainly a single manuscript; beyond a few isolated letters, however, no decipherment was possible. Although blank on the other side, the normal recto, the scribe had written it against the fibers on the verso. Benoit was uncertain that *Mur* 155 was a literary work at all; regarding hand and date, he noted simply, "L'écriture, aussi appliquée que malhabile, est d'un caractère neutre, difficile à dater."[127]

Paleographic dating is a messy and inexact business at times. Nevertheless, so far as that artful science is able to advise the historian in the matter at hand, the thirteen Greek literary texts from Murabbaʿat may all be regarded as at least possible—and a majority, as likely—first-century products. As we have seen, considerations of intrinsic probability also favor that dating. We evidently have to do with a small book collection, clearly dear to the hearts of its owners,[128] gathered in antebellum Jerusalem by Eutrapelus and perhaps other members of the family and eventually transported to the insurgents' common grave. That a Judaean Desert grotto would one day house and preserve their writings, destined to perish completely everywhere else, would scarcely have pleased the original Greek authors. Nor was this the end sought by the carrier readers, one presumes. But such are the ironies of history, as Herodotus observed: σκοπέειν δὲ χρὴ παντὸς χρήματος τὴν τελευτὴν κῇ ἀποβήσεται (One must look to the outcome of any situation: how did it turn out?).[129]

Recent years have seen intensified interest among scholars of ancient literacy in the question of book collections. They are frequently difficult to isolate and identify among the detritus of antiquity, but in a study published in 2009 George Houston proposed that collections could safely be discerned using either of two methods.[130] The first was to study ancient booklists.[131] These might be compiled for a variety of purposes, of course, but by applying certain criteria one may determine by process of elimination that the list in hand likely described an actual collection. For example, repetition of titles would rule out the notion that the list was a scholar's bibliography, a teacher's assignments, or a list of desiderata. These sorts of lists would have no reason to name a work more than once. Likewise, such lists would be unlikely to number opisthographs among their items. And any list devoted to the works of a particular author, but omitting titles that any scholar should have known, would be unlikely as an ancient bibliography.

Houston's second proposed method of isolating ancient collections was to identify concentrations of papyri found together in specific and identifiable archaeological sites. Such papyri would be found together because they were somehow discarded in antiquity as a unit.

Applying these methods, Houston identified eighteen ancient Greek book collections. On examining them he drew a number of interesting conclusions, although our concern at this juncture lies elsewhere. For in addition to Houston's inferences, close scrutiny of these collections draws out certain common characteristics that support the possibility that *Mur* 108–112, 126–132, and 155 (or some selection of those fragmentary papyri) constituted a personal library of Greek literature. First, it is clear that by modern standards ancient collections were frequently Lilliputian. Several of Houston's collections numbered fewer than ten items. Comparing also Anglo-Saxon booklists from English libraries, he observed, "Roman-era libraries varied in size along a wide range from just a few volumes to several thousands . . . collections of even a few dozen volumes might well be considered, and in fact were, impressive."[132] As a group of thirteen works, then, a putative Eutrapelus family library would be entirely respectable. Second, ancient collections were usually coherent, nucleating around the particular interests of their owners. Nevertheless, extrinsic, subliterary items such as grammatical works or commentaries were usual as well. The lamentable condition of the Murabbaʿat materials precludes much analysis along these lines, but the extant vocabulary of *Mur* 112 (e.g., πίνω, λιθάριον [drink, gemstone]) would countenance identification of its contents as comic or subliterary, perhaps magical or astrological.

Third, the Egyptian corpora often evidenced the same scribe preparing two, three, or even more of the books in a given collection.[133] That *Mur* 109 and *Mur* 111 were the work of the same person is therefore not merely reasonable, but—if they were indeed elements of a single collection—more or less a natural expectation. Fourth, within a number of the collections that Houston spotlighted, opisthographs comprised a notable percentage. This was in fact a kind of fault line in the evidence: some collections held many opisthographs, but most included none or almost none. It was not a matter of middle ground. Rather, certain owners gravitated to these cheaper scribal products, some of which may have been acquired as used books.[134] One of Houston's collections of this sort contained fifteen manuscripts, six of which were inscribed on the verso of documentary rolls (40 percent). Of forty-five books in a library of astronomical texts, eleven were opisthographs (24 percent); of 296 rolls in a third library, 51 were inscribed front and back (17 percent). Recalling that three of the thirteen works in the putative Eutrapelus collection were opisthographs (*Mur* 109, 110, and 112; at least 23 percent), the profile of the Murabbaʿat materials would seem to display several of the hallmarks of a particular kind of ancient personal library.

In all likelihood, it was only after Jerusalem fell in the late summer of 70 that Eutrapelus, his family, and most of the other freedom fighters evidenced by the texts retreated to their previously prepared hideaways, the caves of Murabbaʿat. Internally dated texts favor this conclusion. All three suggested families possessed texts executed in or near the year 69, and even late in that year: the family of Honi b. John, *Mur* 25 (between March 68 and March 69);

the family of Dositheos b. Eleazar, *Mur* 30 (ca. 3 October); and the family of Eutrapelus, *Mur* 22 (ca. 26 October).[135] The coin of Year Four unearthed by de Vaux and team also dates to that year and supports this *terminus post quem.* One cannot absolutely rule out a flight earlier in the year 70, but Titus and the Roman forces laid siege to Jerusalem at the Passover (late March) of that year and by May had ringed the city with a *circumvallum.* From that point very few people escaped. Moreover, as zealots both convinced and confident (else why still buy and sell land at normal prices?), it is questionable whether these families would have sought to flee before the destruction. After about a year in the caves, they were joined at Murabbaʿat by Miriam b. John, late in the fall of 71. Her writ of divorce while resident on Masada was dated around 13 October of that year (*Mur* 19), shortly after which she would have traveled the thirty kilometers north to resettle.

The chronology of the Roman pacification of the desert rebel groups following the fall of Jerusalem is imperfectly known. Rebels still held three major fortresses and formed other minor pockets of resistance in the wilderness. Nothing happened for about a year, while Sextus Vettulenus Cerealis, erstwhile commander of V Macedonia, acted as governor pro tempore and Vespasian pondered an official appointment. Late in 71, not long before Miriam's divorce, Sextus Lucilius Bassus arrived as the first of a series of praetorian legates. Within a few months, it is suggested, the experienced commander reduced Herodium. In the spring of 72 he turned his attention to Machaerus, where after an aborted siege the zealots surrendered on guarantee of safe conduct out. They promptly fled to the Forest of the Jordan to continue resistance. It was now the summer of 72. Before Bassus could follow up, he died, and a number of months passed before L. Flavius Silva could arrive to administer to Jewish hopes the coup de grâce.[136]

Thus we arrive at the spring of 73. It seems that the forces under Silva simply moved from north to south methodically eliminating each center of resistance, beginning with the zealots hiding in the Forest of the Jordan. The Romans had learned their lesson at Machaerus. Henceforth, no quarter would be given, but the Jews would be slaughtered to the last man, woman, and child. After enforcing this principle at the forest, Silva and his men arrived next at Qumran, where after a short, hopeless siege and, one supposes, satisfying slaughter, they burned the structures to the ground.[137] On the way to Masada they encountered the families at Murabbaʿat and other cave-dwelling insurgents. The three First Revolt families, and presumably others as well, had lived at the site and in nearby environs for about three years.[138] Entering the caves, the Romans killed any Jew they encountered. Mute testimony to their presence, it seems, is *Mur* 158, a fragmentary Latin document possibly dropped by one of the soldiers. Benoit dated the writing solidly within the first century C.E.[139] Poignant potential testimony of another sort is the child's sandal discovered by the modern archaeologists.

Arriving at the final and southernmost point of Judaean resistance, Masada, Silva and his soldiers set up camps surrounding the isolated peak and constructed a crude but effective *circumvallum.* The camps and the wall can still be seen. Scholars have often supposed that a protracted siege now began, but as John Roth has pointed out, its length, "was determined entirely by the time necessary to build the siege works required to overcome Masada's natural defenses."[140] Since the siege ramp the Romans constructed stood atop a natural shoulder adjoining the rock well up the cliff face, the amount of work necessary in order to approach the summit was greatly reduced. Moreover, the men of the Tenth Legion were experienced with siege ramp construction. Only a year earlier they had built one at Machaerus. On the basis of close analysis and numerous parallels, Roth estimated that the ramp may have been completed in as few as twenty-one days and the entire siege begun and ended in four to nine weeks. A siege begun in March would easily have been completed by Xanthicus 16 (ca. 16 April), the date that Josephus gives for the fall of Masada and the deaths of its nine-hundred-plus defenders.[141] The First Jewish Revolt had now been utterly extirpated. But the caves of Murabbaʿat would not be silenced. Sixty years later, Judaean voices would again echo from their depths.

Who Took the Texts to the Caves? Second Revolt Texts

"That the Roman world was once awash with documents is . . . clear, even if hardly any have survived. . . . Writing articulated the complex economic and administrative systems on which the empire, its cities, and their inhabitants depended. The Roman empire, and its societies, could not have functioned without it."[142] Greg Woolf's statements are as true of Judaea as of Egypt or of Rome itself, and if we seek to understand the Second Revolt materials from Murabbaʿat, they are of the essence. From the beginning Milik recognized such, albeit perhaps imprecisely.[143] Yet scholars have said little concerning the nature of these finds in the years since 1961, even though greater precision is wanted and, given the emerging understanding of the First Revolt discoveries, possible.[144] For our purposes, greater precision is essential, for these documents supply a great deal of information about Judaean language and literacy in the early second century C.E. To make optimal use of it, we must understand the data's historical setting as accurately as possible. A few background remarks may set the stage for that investigation.

As Judaea passed from governance by Herod and his son Archelaus to direct rule by Rome in one form or another (generally; variations involved Agrippa I and II), the administrative mechanisms remained essentially unchanged.[145] When, again, Judaea came to be held in the revolutionary grip of Simon b. Kosiba, the earlier structures were simply retained, although of course taxes and duties now made their way to the Jewish warlord as he picked the emperor's pocket.[146] During all of this time, and even earlier, Judaea was divided into administrative units that the sources call "toparchics" (e.g., 1 Macc 11:28). Two lists of those toparchies survive in literary sources, one in the *Bellum judaicum* of Josephus, another in the *Naturalis historia* of the elder Pliny.[147] They are largely identical, except that where Josephus lists eleven toparchies, Pliny enumerates just ten. Pliny omits Josephus's toparchies of Idumea and En Gedi, while including Jaffa (which Josephus saves for an appendix, as strictly speaking it was not in Judaea). The differences reflect chronology. Josephus wrote from his own antebellum experience of living in the land, whereas Pliny relied upon some sort of postbellum written source—a Roman *formula provinciae* or perhaps an officer's *commentarii.*[148] For our purposes, what is important is that both lists include Herodium.[149] For it was in Herodium that Jesus b. Galgula was appointed under Bar Kokhba as רוש המחניה (*Mur* 42 [*sic*]), "camp commander."[150] The combination of that appointment and that location explains much about the Second Revolt documents discovered at Murabbaʿat.

We know of Jesus b. Galgula from explicit mention in two additional Bar Kokhba letters as well, *Mur* 43–44, and perhaps from *Mur* 51, addressed to [PN b.] Galgula. We find apparent reference to a sister Salome in *Mur* 115, Σαλώμην Ἰωανου Γαλγούλα (Salome daughter of John Galgula, line 4).[151] Here she is contracting to remarry Eleazar b. Simon, from whom an unstated number of years earlier she had been divorced. Possibly *Mur* 116, another marriage contract involving a Salome and an Aurelius, also belonged to her, if—somewhat akin to Babatha's—one posits for her a very complicated romantic life.[152] A third member of the family, seemingly Jesus's brother, finds apparent mention in *Mur* 46: [1]מׄיונתׄן בן [מחנים] ליוסה [בן] גׄל[גולה] [2]שלום, "from John b. [Mahanaim] to Jose [b.] Gal[gula], greetings."[153] These, then, were the Bene Galgula: Jesus, Jose (short for Joseph), and Salome.

Their home village may have been Kephar-Barucha, some twenty kilometers southwest of Herodium, if the disputed reading that is part of the prescript in *Mur* 43 is rightly understood as a toponym: "From Simon b. Kosiba to Jesus b. Galgula, and to the men of Barucha [ולאנשי הברך], greetings."[154] The family seems to have been quite prosperous, for at her remarriage to Eleazar, Salome was able to command a dowry of fully 200 *zuz*. This was the stipulated rabbinic sum for a virgin, and double that usual for widows.[155] In any event, one would expect Bar Kokhba to have selected his commanders and administrators from the ruling class and thus to discover in Jesus b. Galgula and his family dressed-down Judaean analogs of a leading Roman family of Cicero's day, the sort of Romans who could boast consular and censorial ancestors and whose personal archives in the Republican period often housed as well the official records of the state.

For this is the thesis here propounded: *abstracting the materials that can be connected to the First Revolt archives, the attributable Murabba'at documentary finds represent what survives of the Archive of the Bene Galgula, which comprised their personal documents plus the state documents that Jesus had amassed in his role as chief administrator of the toparchy of Herodium in the period from the outbreak of the Second Revolt in 132 until early 135.* (Or, perhaps, some shorter portion of those years, ending in 135; we do not know when his appointment began.) The state documents constituted an official Second Revolt period archive of the toparchy of Herodium. Literary and documentary sources from the period of this study explicitly mention comparable archives or archival officials in other toparchic capitals, including Jerusalem, Jericho, and En Gedi.[156] One would certainly expect that an equivalent archive existed in Herodium as well. After all, Herodium was plainly a center of particular importance to the rebels, to judge from the unique character of the tunnels they dug deep into the mountain. Of all the hiding complexes known from the Second Revolt, only these tunnels allowed a person to walk upright. Large numbers of people were able to move around underground without being seen.[157] When the insurrection collapsed and the family fled to the desert, Jesus b. Galgula took all of these state materials with him in the expectation that he might someday need to give account of the various legal and political affairs to which they witnessed.[158]

Two sets of facts support this thesis. First, the scenario envisaged accords well with what is known of how officials in the Roman world often managed administrative archives. And second, the documents themselves evidence both *communal legal activity* and *administrative hierarchy*, as would be expected if the thesis were reasonably close to the historical reality.

"In any empire the size of the Roman, Chinese, or British, certain problems are common for the administration. Who is entitled to citizenship? Who pays the poll-tax? What is the annual revenue from a given area?"[159] The answers to these questions cannot be remotely approached for any area of the Roman Empire except Egypt, and even there only at certain times and places. Nevertheless, we do know something about administrative matters as they were handled in Rome itself; and the Egyptian system, while certainly not identical to those established in other provinces, did represent a considered Roman response to the common problems they faced everywhere, and so used judiciously—and without pressing details—it can serve as a very rough guide to what might be expected in Judaea.

In Egypt the Romans used a highly bureaucratic system substantially inherited from the Pharaohs, Persians, and Ptolemies but modified a bit for their own purposes.[160] A central administration with jurisdiction over all Egypt stood in Alexandria. Feeding that administration were two document streams, one whose fount was the Greek cities, the other flowing from the *Chora*. The latter was divided in descending order of hierarchy into nomes, toparchies, and villages, each replete with various titled officials. With Simon b. Kosiba poised at the apex, parallels in Second Revolt Judaea can be demonstrated only for the two or three lowest levels of this Egyptian pyramid. Limited as Judaea was to a mere eleven toparchies, the native unit of that name probably was the functional equivalent of the Egyptian nome. Accordingly, we can concentrate attention on the lower Egyptian courses, while nevertheless considering that the mechanism functioning during the Jewish Revolt was possibly more elaborate than our sources let us see.

In Egypt the village official or κωμογραμματεύς served for one year and was generally a resident of the village. (Recall that Petaus son of Petaus, the illiterate scribe whom we met in Chapter 1, was one such officeholder.) It seems that in some cases this office was a liturgy, in others, salaried and paid by the villagers. Copies or originals of many of the papers this official generated would make their way up the ladder to the τοπογραμματεύς (toparchic scribe). From there, documents often passed still further upward to the nome capitals and their archives, which contained official papers and correspondence, tax rolls, land registers, and census lists. Between 64 and 67, the Romans established a second type of archive, the Βιβλιοθήκη ἐγκτήσεων, to process and store separately records of land and slaves.

Many villages and every toparchy in Roman Egypt housed a combination notarial office and archival repository, termed by the sources γραφεῖον.

Here, under the supervision of an official who ran the office for a commission, hired scribes produced documents in both Demotic and Greek. They prepared tax records, petitions, reports, and the like for clients who visited the office. Each person involved in such transactions received a copy, while the originals were kept and eventually pasted into long papyrus rolls. Several additional written instruments layered the comprehensive records yet more thickly; all were dutifully reproduced and sent up to the next level. There as well stood a symmetrical system, where summary records were made based on the incoming documents; for land records, scribes copied out διαστρώματα, *Übersichtsblätter.* Odd as it may seem in the face of such meticulous record production, however, no well-organized filing system existed to store older records and facilitate reference to them. Materials were simply bunched together in wall slots or thrust into jars. Some of the frail papyri would disintegrate over time from the excessive heat in the depositories; others, more frequently consulted, lost their beginnings or suffered analogous wear damage. After several years had passed, the recovery of any particular item sought among this confused and crumbling menagerie was to a considerable degree a matter of luck.

At the lower levels only some γραφεῖα existed as dedicated architectural structures. Not uncommonly, the home of the presiding official served in that capacity as long as he held office. When he left, the records he had accumulated often left with him, the new official starting from scratch. Consequently, to find records of older transactions in an Egyptian village, one frequently had to know who had served during the given years and seek out their homes or those of their heirs. For such customs in Egypt we may take the example of Kronion, son of Apion, and his partner Eutuchas, who ran a village record office at Tetubnis from circa 43 to 52 C.E. As senior partner, Kronion kept the financial records of the office at his house, which also apparently served as the γραφεῖον. The office employed a variety of scribes, including night clerks and specialists who could compose in Demotic. Since records of Kronion's father's service as a notary were also found among Kronion's archive, he had evidently inherited the role. Obviously, neither set of records was ever passed on to successors.

Thus the archives of Egyptian officials would often embrace office records as well as personal documents. To take a second example: when discovered, the archives of a certain Aurelius Isodorus comprised his family's personal papers (documents he accumulated as a landholder and tenant) together with the public records of ten liturgical offices he held over the years 289–319.[161]

One Apollonius, a tax official responsible for the nome of Apollonopolis Heptakomia at the time of the Jewish rebellion of 117 C.E. and into the early reign of Hadrian, furnishes a third example. After seven years, he retired to his property in Hermopolis and took his official papers with him. His family archive was discovered commingled with these records of routine business, census reports, and court documents. The total was almost 150 papyri.[162]

The dynamics of officials and archives were not dissimilar in Republican Rome: "Although the Tabularium . . . showed a tendency to absorb records of various administrative origins, the idea of concentrating in one place the archives of different creators was alien to ancient and medieval times."[163] And while it is true that *leges* and *senatus consulta* found formal deposition in the *aerarium,* that small, boxy temple employed only a handful of clerks and served the documentary needs of few Romans. Rather, recordkeeping proceeded in accordance with the essential principles governing many other transactions of power conducted in Republican Rome. Its center was the great families. Each household included a separate room dedicated to this purpose, the *tablinum.* When public affairs necessitated consultation, arrangements were made with the requisite family, whose records (e.g., magistrates' day-books, *commentarii*) never left the family's custody. Indeed, as Phyllis Culham has noted, "the old senatorial families could expect their need for information to be met by archival resources in their own households and in those of their friends; they did not need an institution that might well work against their interests." Even with the coming of the empire, this familial system continued for some time. Matters that absolutely required to be made public were posted, and people consulted such postings as a matter of course. And, naturally, the family archives were by modern standards poorly organized and difficult to use.[164]

Given what we know of the ways of the Roman world, then, an official such as Jesus b. Galgula likely would have held the archive of Herodium in his own quarters. One would expect these archival holdings to be relatively substantial and to include both public and private, family materials. The public materials would be recognizable by their communal character, so distinct from that of private documents. One would also expect the administrative archive to manifest such fitful logic and elliptic organization as one actually perceives among the Second Revolt Murabbaʿat materials, even if—as is surely not the case—it were still possible to analyze all that once existed. But if the scenario suggested above were true, one would further expect at least some evidence of hierarchy among the public records. We do find precisely that.

Mur 94 is a bookkeeping summary in Greek of accounts, evidently taxes. It lists men, women, and slaves, the names followed by ciphers that specify taxes due in kind. As Baillet noted in his commentary on the text, such a summary would be composed utilizing subordinate records and accounts such as *Mur* 91. The latter Greek text records accounts of grain and lentils, listing names and amounts, and is crudely written. *Mur* 94, in contrast, possesses "écriture d'un style aisé et élégant."[165] Thus this summary appears to be the product of a more skilled scribe, employed presumably at the capital, Herodium, where he drew together reports such as *Mur* 91, sent in from one village or another within the toparchy.

Similarly composed in a beautiful hand, but in Hebrew, is the διάστρωμα, *Mur* 24.[166] Dated ca. 20 January 134, surviving portions of this summary record eleven lease contracts executed in Herodium by one Hillel b. Garis, possibly all on the same day. The leases are for plots of land of various sizes located in ʿIr Nahash, perhaps a latifundium, as observed earlier, and situated more than thirty kilometers due west of Herodium. Annual payment in kind by each sharecropper was to take place at Herodium. Each individual leaseholder would have been issued a personal copy of the relevant contract, of course, and Hillel for his part would have held separate copies of all eleven contracts. Herodium's status as capital presumably accounts both for the execution of the contracts so far distant from the lands being leased and for the superordinate character of the record prepared for archival storage there.

Given all the facts—Jesus b. Galgula as the camp commander at Herodium; that village's status as the longstanding capital of a toparchy; retention of earlier political organization during the Second Revolt; the presence of personal texts such as Salome's marriage contract(s); the many first-order public documents preserved amidst fewer but manifest second-order texts (*Mur* 24, 42, 94); and the potential explanatory clarity afforded the phenomena of the caches by analogy with administrative practices elsewhere in the Roman world—the most reasonable understanding of the whole would seem to be that proposed. These materials comprised the personal archive of the Bene Galgula, borne to the caves of Murabbaʿat for safekeeping together with the administrative archive of Herodium.

It remains to define briefly the contents of the combined holdings of Jesus and his family. The administrative archive is clearly broader than the preponderant Greek materials and seems to have been trilingual—not surprising, perhaps, given the historical circumstances and on the analogy of the bilingual Egyptian administrative materials. But before going further, the necessarily provisional character of this overview must be frankly stated. Many of the documents are fragmentary in the extreme. Precise genre assignments are often difficult; for the Greek texts, the process is often a surmise based upon the type of script. Still, general contours useful as guides to the present study emerge, and some of the documents shed special light on issues of Judaean language and literacy.

Although the discoveries at Murabbaʿat included a significant number of Aramaic compositions in addition to the First Revolt contracts, only three were sufficiently preserved to be recognizable as public documents, *Mur* 8–10.[167] All are accounts; the latter two evidently involve taxes. *Mur* 8 is different and especially notable in that it may furnish a rare glimpse into the literacy of the Judaean subelite.

Inscribed on a piece of fine leather by five different individuals, *Mur* 8 is most likely a receipt for about a month's supply of individual and troop rations, received at Herodium by at least seven guerrilla commanders (two men signed for two or more others).[168] A relative of this genre of military receipt is well known from Masada.[169] Certainty eludes, but reason suggests that such leaders would only occasionally be drawn from the village elite, instead normally emerging from the ranks as engagement with Rome manifested their martial qualities and tactical capacities. The document is full of errors and evidence of its ad hoc character: amounts to be issued are recalculated on the spot. Several of the signatories misspell their names and otherwise struggle to put matters in writing. That they responded to the requirement to sign for the grain with the choice of Aramaic is therefore the more telling. The text reads as follows:[170]

1. לבני̊ פסן סערין ס 20 ס 19 ק 3
2. ישוע <בר> אחי ס 40
3. טרפטח ס 16 ק1/2 א1
4. ישוע בר חרקק ג3 כה
5. יצוק בר מ{מ}נוח ובזוז ב̊ר̊[

[1]For the sons of PSN, barley: 20 *seah* 19 *seah* 3 *kab*. [2]Jesus <b.> Ahi 40 *seah*. [3]"Lentil(?)" 16 *seah* 1/2 *kab* א1 (*kab*). [4]Jesus b. Harqaq ג3 (*seah*) ה(5) *kor*. [5]Yasoq b. Manoah and Bazoz b.[. . .[171]

Two or more sons of PSN (an unknown PN) first signed for twenty *seah* of barley, a substantial amount given that one *seah* equated to something between 8.56 and 13.0 liters.[172] These men therefore requisitioned between 170 and 260 liters of barley—enough for a great deal of bread![173] Immediately, however, they reduced the amount they needed to nineteen *seah* and three *kab,* that is, 19.5 *seah,* but without erasing or otherwise disowning the higher number. Jesus b. Ahi misspelled his name, forgetting to write בר, "son of"; likewise, "Lentil" mangled his handle rather badly, if Yardeni is correct in suggesting that this is the intended word.[174] Instead of טרפטה, he should have produced טלופה or טלפה.[175] Presumably, the nickname referred to a birthmark or other physical characteristic reminiscent of the legume. Not the birth name he had once learned to write, however poorly, this moniker had never been practiced in "school." He did the best he could but clearly had a hazy understanding of the conventional relationships between Aramaic orthography and the phonemes of the language. (The interchange of the liquids *lamedh* and *resh* is a well-attested phenomenon of the Aramaic colloquial.)[176] Then either Yasoq b. Manoah or Bazoz b. [PN] (whichever signed for both) mistakenly repeated the first *mem* of Yasoq's patronym.

In addition to the problem with his name, Lentil originally signed for sixteen *seah* and one-half *kab* of barley, then increased it slightly to one *kab,* which number he inscribed twice, once with the requisite cipher and once with the letter *aleph.* Yet despite this evident concern for precision, he neglected to erase the earlier amount. Jesus b. Harqaq signed for three *seah,* it seems, although he failed to inscribe the abbreviation for that measure. He did write the number itself two different ways, however, both as a cipher and with the correct letter of the alphabet. Dispensing next with ciphers altogether, he used only the letter *heh* to record the number of *kor.*

These acts of signing, recalculating, and rewriting fairly transport the reader of *Mur* 8 into the living moment. To the traditional rabbinic portrait of a population learning to read scripture on its fathers' laps, however, this living moment offers no life. Beyond their numerous errors of commission and omission, the commanders' letterforms bespeak hands seldom put to pen. The sons of PSN, Jesus b. Harqaq, and the writer of line 5 all wrote at level 2, and so, while able (if that is not too generous a term, given their spelling struggles) to write their names, they would have fared better against Roman troops than against any text longer than a sentence or two. Defeat in the second instance was certain. The holy books of Israel lay far beyond their reading capacities, even if they could speak a vernacular dialect of Hebrew, a possibility their Aramaic signatures do not directly address. As for Jesus b. Ahi and Lentil, they were comrades not only in arms, but in capacity: both were βραδέως γράφοντες. All in all, the impression given by *Mur* 8 of the Judaean subelite is that among villagers, easy signature literacy would be a noteworthy accomplishment. Granted, this glimpse of a very small selection of that population amounts to little more than a sort of anecdote; even so, gather a series of anecdotes, and a narrative begins to emerge. We shall possibly gather another shortly.

As noted, Greek predominates in the administrative archive. *Mur* 89–107 are all accounts composed in Greek on leather employing documentary hands. Use of treated skin for documents differs from the norm in Egypt, of course, with its papyrus industry; it seems that in Judaea the difference in cost was not marked, and the choice hinged on availability or aesthetic factors.[177] Indeed, Judaeans utilized wood as well, as did others in the Mediterranean basin outside of Egypt (famously the Roman soldiers at Vindolanda), and even the occasional ostracon. *Mur* 89 is an account of payments, perhaps a tax record, roughly alphabetized; the surviving portions attach to iota. The same elegant scribe appears to have composed *Mur* 90, a record of payments *in natura.* Baillet cautiously suggested that *Mur* 98 and *Mur* 100, also accounts but extremely fragmentary, may have been additional products of the selfsame scribe.[178] If so, then this clerk was likely resident at Herodium.

Also evidently belonging to the administrative archive are *Mur* 92–93, *Mur* 96–97, and *Mur* 99, 101, and 102. All are public accounts of various sorts. Similarly, *Mur* 118–121 are fragmentary Greek accounts, inscribed on papyrus rather than skin. *Mur* 95 is a list of names, a public genre otherwise absent from the Greek materials but present among the Semitic administrative materials. Beyond these is another group of Greek texts inscribed on papyrus, so damaged that they cannot safely be characterized. One suspects that they, too, belonged to the administrative archive, as all are, as Baillet noted, "fragments avec écriture cursive" (*Mur* 133–154).[179] If so, more than forty Greek administrative documents survive.

Why were so many of the administrative materials produced by a revolutionary and nationalist government composed in Greek? The answer seems clear enough: Simon b. Kosiba had retained the mechanisms Rome had put in place over the previous century and more. The language of formal administration in the Roman East was Greek. Accordingly, Judaean scribes had long been trained to produce documents in the requisite language and genres, and they simply continued to operate during the revolt according to their training. By reason of this shared Roman standard, too, the genre characteristics of the texts produced in Judaea are in all essentials similar to those we know from Roman Egypt—in all essentials, but not in all details.

For in small ways interesting to the subject of this study, the Jewish origins of the documents come out of hiding.

Mur 97, for example, is an account of cereal payments *in natura,* possibly a record of sharecropping. Baillet described the hand as markedly poor,[180] and the Greek as poorer still. At one point the scribe lists the singular κάβον, that is, the measure *kab,* but in "agreement" with the number sixteen. This is manifestly an example of Semitic interference, since this agreement, so jarring in Greek, is correct in both Hebrew and Aramaic. A second listing juxtaposes the form σατά, *seah,* with the number one. Of course, the singular of this word in Greek is σάτον.[181] Baillet concluded of the scribe, "sans doute pense-t-il moins au pluriel de σάτον qu'à une transcription littérale de l'araméen סָאתָא = σατά et non σάτα" (doubtless he had in mind less the plural of [Greek] *saton* than a literal transcription of Aramaic *sata* [Greek accentuation changes accordingly]).[182] His inference seems broadly correct and clarifies that the linguistic interference for this scribe involved Aramaic, not Hebrew.[183] *Mur* 97 reveals something of the acceptable standard of Greek among the Judaean scribes in small villages. Clearly, the standard was not always very high. Presumably, this was a reflex of supply. Further, given the scribe's evident lack of skill, one is likely to have here a person who wrote Greek more closely approximating his speech than texts usually capture, simply because he knew no better. And so, albeit tenuous, we snatch a glimpse at the knowledge of Greek in a Judaean village.

We also see that ordinary village scribes trained for administrative positions did not always—perhaps, did not often—proceed very far with the Greek *paideia.* This observation is important mostly because it alerts us to the likelihood that as an index of literary literacy the handwriting of scribes may be misleading. A professional educational track was probably in place at times separate from the education in literary literacy that Cribiore's work documented. By means of apprenticeship the ancient Bartleby might acquire a practiced hand simply by dint of dull, methodical reproduction of the limited variety of genres required by customers, himself neither needing nor gaining anything beyond a rudimentary command of literary Greek, and without having copied the substantial quantity of literature that would be required to produce a layperson with an equally skilled hand. Doubtless something similar might also be said of scribes possessed of fluid Hebrew signatures.

Similarly offering a glimpse into actual language usage in Judaean villages is the Greek form φαλωνεί that occurs in both *Mur* 92 (line 3, Ἰούδας φαλωνεί) and *Mur* 94 (*bis,* lines 8–9, Σίμων φαλωνεί, Σαοῦλος φαλωνεί). In each case Greek would normally have used δεῖνα, "a certain one," and this is the meaning in these documents: a certain Judah, a certain Simon, a certain Saul. That is to say, these people were unknown or only partially identified to the scribe, so that their patronyms or equivalent identifiers could not be set down. The Greek form actually used is probably a Hebrew loan: the term פלוני occurs five times in biblical texts and is very frequent in rabbinic Hebrew.[184] If the term is indeed Hebrew, then the fact that these scribes, unable to retrieve δεῖνα, first fell back on Hebrew presumably indicates something about their personal speech habits. And this is so particularly in view of *P.Yadin* 28–30, Greek petitions prepared for Babatha in Mahoza—quite possibly, as it seems, by a Jewish scribe. These copies use δεῖνα a total of ten times.[185] On the other hand, φαλωνεί never occurs in the Babatha Archive. Thus one can evidence neither that φαλωνεί was a widespread replacement term among Jews nor that δεῖνα was unknown to writers of Greek in areas of Jewish habitation.

But does φαλωνεί certainly reflect Hebrew? An argument could be attempted that Aramaic underlies this Greek rendering. For one thing, Aramaic knows the cognate פְּלָנִי as far back as Official Aramaic.[186] It then continues in use for centuries, being attested in Syriac, Mandaic, Jewish Palestinian Aramaic, and Jewish Babylonian Aramaic.[187] The *omega* in φαλωνεί might arguably be seen as a reflex of /a:/, which in the Jacobite dialect of Syriac, for example, was pronounced as a mid-back vowel. Some evidence suggests that this shift was known in Palestine as well. Indeed, a supporter of this graphic possibility might cite the reading of Ἐλεαζώρ in *Mur* 94 itself.

Thus, an Aramaic origin for φαλωνεί is not impossible. All the same, it is neither probable nor the better interpretation of the evidence before us. For while the word פְּלָנִי almost certainly was an element in the lexicon of most Judaeans in this period, the suggestion that someone spelling it *ad aurem* would render it as φαλωνεί is not persuasive. The further suggestion that two different scribes would do so independently seems extremely improbable. For the orthography of Hebrew names in the Greek Murabbaʿat materials shows that the /a:/ was virtually never, if ever, represented with *omega,* but rather always with *alpha.* The form Ἐλεαζώρ that might seem to put the lie to this statement is probably not the correct reading, as Baillet acknowledged. Rather, the word in *Mur* 94 is better read as the hypocoristic Ἐλεάζ.[188]

Accordingly, the use of φαλωνεί in these manuscripts probably testifies both to the living use of Hebrew among Judaean village scribes and to a dynamic bilingual process by which these Greek documents came to exist. As each person stepped forward to pay the tax, his or her name was inscribed, and as was usual among ancient scribes, everything written was simultaneously vocalized aloud.[189] What seems to be indicated here is that although the scribe wrote the name in Greek, he vocalized it in Hebrew. So for *Mur* 92, for example, the scribe said יהודה פלוני, but wrote Ἰούδας φαλωνεί.

Seemingly in the same vein, the scribe of *Mur* 94 wrote of another person in line 15,]ωφηρα. Baillet restored the word as Σ]ωφηρά and analyzed it as "appellatif tiré de l'hébreu סוֹפֵר 'scribe' avec final א de l'état emphatique araméen" (a designation taken from Hebrew *sopher*, "scribe," with the final aleph of the Aramaic emphatic state [which makes nouns definite]).[190] This analysis would either have the writer mixing morphologies (very rare in situations of linguistic contact) or require the understanding that "scribe" had become for the Judaeans a mere title. No longer recognized as Hebrew, it was now felt to be Aramaic *status absolutus* and accordingly needed that language's postpositive article in order to become definite (the required grammatical *status* when apposed to a proper name as in lists). Neither option is attractive. Instead, one should consider restoring ἀσ]ωφήρα, analyzing as purely Hebrew, הסופֵרה, "the scribe" (f.). The nonreduction of *sere* (/e:/) would be expected if nominal accent in the writer's Hebrew vernacular were regularly penultimate—a possibility supported by considerable evidence.[191] And female scribes, while relatively uncommon in the Roman period, are attested elsewhere.[192] The presence of Ἰώσηπος ασωφηρ in *Mur* 103 line 1 then constitutes a parallel example of a person listed as a scribe, and simultaneously perhaps a fourth instance of a Judaean clerk writing Greek but vocalizing Hebrew: יוסף הסופר.

This last phrase turns our attention very naturally to the Hebrew documents in the Herodium archive, beginning with the letters. As Chapter 4 will treat the entire Bar Kokhba correspondence in some detail, we need mention here only a few points briefly. The Murabbaʿat deposits include at least seven such letters. Notably, unlike the Bar Kokhba missives found at Naḥal Ḥever—which also used Aramaic and Greek—the Murabbaʿat authors wrote only in Hebrew. All attempted bookhands; two were so successful as to be calligraphic. At least three of the letters were addressed to Jesus b. Galgula (*Mur* 42–44). Another, *Mur* 46, had as recipient his brother Jose. Otherwise, the names of the addressees are lost to damage, but the letters' presence in the archive speaks for itself and strongly urges that one or both of the brothers were intended for each of *Mur* 45, 47, and 48. In addition, Milik characterized the very fragmentary *Mur* 49–52 as possible letters, and nothing argues against that assessment except their miserable state of preservation. All are in Hebrew, all but one in chancellery hands, and one, *Mur* 51, may preserve the short form of one of the brothers' names in an address formula: לגלגלה, "to Galgula." Furthermore, Yardeni's correction of Milik's misreading and mistaken reconstruction of *Mur* 61 raises the possibility that it, too, was a Bar Kokhba letter.[193] If so, then the archive from Herodium would have contained as many as a dozen letters of official correspondence in Hebrew.

Also composed in Hebrew is the superordinate summary document, referenced previously several times, *Mur* 24. Comparatively well preserved, it invites scrutiny for what it may reveal concerning literacy. As noted, this document tabulates a series of subleases by Hillel b. Garis of plots in ʿIr Nahash, located in the region known as Har Ha-Melekh. Virtually all of this fertile region had earlier been imperial property but was now, evidently, fallen to Simon b. Kosiba as his personal possession.[194] Accordingly, the land was not sold but merely leased, rendering the lessees some sort of tenant. But which kind, precisely?[195] On this question closely parallel documents from contemporary Egypt may prove very helpful. Understood in the way these documents encourage, *Mur* 24 constitutes a second "anecdote" regarding the literacy of the Judaean subelite. Moreover, we may have in *Mur* 24 the largely unrecognized epigraphic presence of an early rabbi famous in rabbinic literature.

Consider the following extract from the text, the record of the sublease that comprises column E, with a few damaged words restored on the basis of verbatim parallels in the other columns:[196]

> [On the twentieth of] Shevat, year [tw]o of the redemption of [I]srael by Simon b. K[osib]a, Prince of Israel, in the army camp resident at Herodium: Judah b. Baba said to Hillel b. Garis, "I have of my own free will this day [le]ased (חכרתי) from you the parcel which was mine by my (former) lease in ʿIr Nahash, which you (now) hold on lease from Simon the Prince of Israel. I have leased this parcel from you (for a period) beginning this day and concluding with the end of the eve of the sabbatical year, five full years, five (full) years by [re]ckoning (שני מכסה[?]).[197] I [will] measure out [this] rent for you in [He]rodium [on the roof of the treasury year by year], wheat [pure and unadulterated], thr[ee *kor]s* and a *letek*. . . . The lease is hereby incumbent [up]on me [as stipulated above . . ." *(signatures followed).*

This text is transparently a Judaean counterpart to subcontracts of the following type from Roman Egypt, this one composed on 10 October 120, just a few years preceding (*P.Ryl.* 168):

> Petechon son of Hareos to Hermias son of Sabourion, greeting. I hereby have leased from you for only the current 5th year of Hadrian Caesar our lord, for the sowing of vegetable seed, three arouras from the imperial estate land that you hold on lease in the former allotment of Apollonios son of Agathinos, at a rent of three artabas by the oil makers' measure for each aroura that appears on the survey-map of the estate inspector, viz. the parcel that was cultivated in the past 4th year of Hadrian our lord by Phinion son of Tothes. I will measure out the rent in the month Epeiph, and when you carry away your half from the threshing floor it shall be new, pure, unadulterated, sifted and measured by the seven-*metra* artaba measure of Athena that is used by the estate. You remain responsible for the rental payable to the estate. [Date.] I, Dioskoros son of Didymos have written for him, who is illiterate.[198]

Milik believed that *Mur* 24 was a record of subleases contracted by b. Garis in Eleutheropolis, where he was "sans doute administrateur [*parnas*] du village."[199] By Milik's lights, then, *Mur* 24 was a record of a lease made by a government agent of land that he administered for Simon b. Kosiba. That sort of leasing method existed in Egypt, too, in dealing with imperial holdings. Designated officials in the nome capitals and villages would lease the lands in the name of the emperor. The lessees were known as "public farmers" and would ordinarily farm the lands themselves, although subleases in such cases were not unknown.[200]

Yet, despite the initial attractions of this thesis, Milik seems to have been wrong. *Mur* 24 was no government lease. For one thing, no warrant exists for Milik's confident assertion that Hillel b. Garis was a *parnas* or administrator serving under Bar Kokhba. Since Milik wrote, two texts explicitly attesting *parnasim* leasing the rebel chief's lands have come to light, and they differed from *Mur* 24 in their formulation. The texts are *P.Yadin* 42 and *P.Yadin* 44. In each case, the text explicitly declared the lessor a *parnas*.[201] *Mur* 24 made no such statement about Hillel at any point. In a precisely worded legal text this was a meaningful silence.

A second obstacle to Milik's view joins this first: *P.Ryl.* 168 was not a government lease. Its manifest parallels with *Mur* 24 urge that the latter was likewise no government lease but rather a Judaean analog to whatever sort of document *P.Ryl.* 168 itself was. In the case of the Egyptian text, we have the great advantage of knowing the details of the social context. By extrapolating to Judaea, we arrive at an understanding that seems to fill in the holes of Milik's explanation.

Stewards of the extensive imperial estates in Egypt sometimes preferred to use there the system for administering such lands that prevailed in North Africa.[202] In this system (to which *P.Ryl.* 168 witnesses), the estates were first leased out as expansive tracts of land to a small number of wealthy entrepreneurs. The imperial steward—and hence the emperor—sometimes got rental monies and taxes up front on the principal *bis dat qui cito dat* and were spared further immediate concerns. In turn, the middlemen would subdivide and sublease their lands, realizing in the end a considerable profit. Accordingly, lessees such as Petechon son of Hareos were well down the food chain, typically subsistence farmers who would farm the plots themselves.

It appears that *Mur* 24 tabulated the same sort of arrangement. A wealthy entrepreneur, Hillel b. Garis, subleased to at least eleven tenant farmers portions of a large tract of prime land in Har Ha-Melekh that he had himself leased from Simon b. Kosiba some time earlier. Duly tabulated, a record of the agreements was deposited in the appropriate government archive, in this case at Herodium, and so came eventually to be among the papers of Jesus b. Galgula. The small size of the portions subleased supports this interpretation, at the same time arguing against the idea that the lots in question would be further subdivided. In all likelihood, we meet here Judaean peasants, ordinary folk acquiring land from a former imperial latifundium to farm and so support their families.

The size of the plots is calculable if one accepts a reasonable hypothesis offered by Applebaum: the quantities of grain paid as annual rent in *Mur* 24 are equivalent to the amounts of seed-corn sown in each plot.[203] On the basis of a Talmudic source, we know the approximate values of the Judaean seeding measurements to which the *Mur* 24 numbers correspond if Applebaum is correct.[204] Plugging in those values, the plot of *Mur* 24 B works out in modern terms to 8 hectares; that of 24 D, to 11.4 hectares; and that of 24 E, our Judah b. Baba's land, to 6.6 hectares. Respectively, these lands would approximate to 16.5, 23.6, and 13.6 acres.[205] In the light of what we know about ancient crop yields and the sizes of farms needed to support single families in Roman Palestine, this acreage equates with smallholds. Depending upon which scholarly estimate one adopts, a family of six to nine people would need between three and seven hectares for subsistence.[206] Thus Eleazar the Shilonite of *Mur* 24 B, [PN] b. John of

24 D, and Judah b. Baba were evidently leasing the amount of land their families would need to farm just to survive.

If, as it seems, *Mur* 24 does show us Judaean peasants, so far as the text is preserved, it shows them to be illiterate. Unfortunately, only three of the columns are sufficiently extant that the final lines, where the signatures occurred, can be read or reconstructed. In each case (*Mur* 24 B, C, and D) the lessee needed to employ a *hypographeus.* The extreme regularity of the separate contracts' structures throughout the document, wherein only a few slight deviations distinguish otherwise identical wording as one moves from one to the next, gives impetus to the notion that this regularity carried over to the signatures: probably most of the other lessees were likewise unable to sign. Obviously, one cannot exclude the possibility that one or more of the signatories of the damaged columns did sign for themselves, but if so, it appears that such would have been the exception, not the rule. The loss of the lines that would have resolved this issue is therefore especially regrettable (though merely another of the many demonstrations within the present corpus of "Murphy's law of manuscript research": just when the most critical reading or ancient statement is at hand, the manuscript breaks off). Had column E come down to us intact, we might have known whether it was possible in ancient Judaea to be a rabbi and yet not read. In theory, why not? This was, after all, a world in which scribes were sometimes illiterate, γραμματεῖς, ἀγράμματοι.

That Judah b. Baba may have been such a rabbi, learned while unlettered, is not, however unlikely, impossible. That this principal of *Mur* 24 E was at least a rabbi, and a man known to us from rabbinic literature, is a markedly safer bet. Norman Golb has cautiously suggested the connection in correcting earlier scholarship's reading of the name as Judah b. Rabba. That was Milik's original reading in the only place in column E where the name can be read, line 4: [י]ה̊ו̊דה̇ ב̊ן̊ ר̇ב̇א.[207] Milik's numerous sigla signaled his doubts about the reading, an uncertainty that did not plague Yardeni. She offered the unencumbered [י]הודה בן רבא.[208] Nonetheless, fewer sigla cannot mandate fewer doubts. The primary problem is the patronym. Golb wrote of its initial consonant: "It may be observed under magnification that the ink has chipped away from the papyrus at the position of a bottom horizontal stroke . . . [yet] the edges of ink are discernible at that position. The enlargement makes clear that the first consonant of the cluster is not R (*resh*) but rather B (*beth*)."[209]

Golb's revision seems right: the name is [י]הודה בן בבא. Whether the proposed connection with the Tannaitic master was also right is, as always, a matter of probabilistic calculation. One point in its favor is the notable rarity of the father's name. In Second Temple sources it occurs just three times: a Baba known from Josephus, a Baba b. Baba (evidently his son) named in rabbinic literature, and a Baba mentioned in *P.Hever* 64.[210] Additional points in favor of Golb's hypothesis are that Judah b. Baba the Tannaitic master is known to have lived in the third generation of the Tannaim, circa 120–140 C.E., and that he was associated with Yabneh or Jamnia, in the general region of Har Ha-Melekh: the very time and place of the figure in *Mur* 24. As Golb observed, ʿIr Nahash was only about thirty-five kilometers distant from Yabneh. Since it was the most fertile region of Har Ha-Melekh, "it is not at all unlikely that at least some members of the Academy of Yabneh had agricultural holdings in the general vicinity of that place."[211] A number of Rabbi Judah b. Baba's decisions imply expert agricultural knowledge, still another factor to consider.[212]

Whether the two b. Baba's were one and the same we shall never know for certain. Golb's suggestion is nevertheless a useful reminder that, however rarely, on occasion a person does appear in epigraphic materials who is known also from surviving literary sources. If the lessee of *Mur* 24 was indeed the rabbi, we know the unfortunate sequel to his appearance in this Hebrew archival document. He died a martyr in the aftermath of the heralded but only temporary "redemption of Israel by Simon b. Kosiba, Prince of Israel."[213]

In addition to the letters and *Mur* 24, a half dozen other fragmentary documents seem to represent Hebrew components of the Bene Galgula archive. Some may be archival copies belonging originally to the administrative archive of Herodium; others, personal contracts that belonged to the family. In most cases one cannot be sure which is which. *Mur* 41 was certainly administrative, as it comprises a list of names.[214] It was composed in a mixture of cursive and bookhand letterforms, with the latter greatly predominant. *Mur* 7 was a Hebrew personal contract composed in a calligraphic bookhand; likewise, *Mur* 36, *Mur* 37, and *Mur* 174. *Mur* 39 and 40 preserve only two signatures each, and they are the same two signatures, those of the witnesses Simon b. Menahem and Dositheos b. Jacob. Presumably, these documents were two related contracts, somewhat akin to *P.Yadin* 44–46; as in that situation, so here, some of the witnesses were involved more than once. Simon signed in Aramaic, Dositheos in Hebrew. Given the extreme rarity of signatories affixing their John Hancocks to Aramaic contracts in Hebrew (only 2.4 percent did so; see Table 1.2), probably *Mur* 39–40 were composed in Hebrew—thus Dositheos's conforming signature. Simon simply didn't know the language and so signed in Aramaic, a common phenomenon in the present corpus. *Mur* 50 and *Mur* 58 are extremely fragmentary, but both definitely in Hebrew and both running against the grain in that they present cursive hands. For it is a striking fact that virtually all of the Second Revolt Hebrew materials from Murabbaʿat exemplify bookhands. In contrast, the Aramaic documents never do, nor the Hebrew from the First Revolt. These distinctions must be meaningful in some way and will receive further attention in Chapter 4. (Possibly, *Mur* 50 and 58 are First Revolt documents.)

In all, then, the administrative archive of Herodium contained twenty-two identifiable Hebrew documents, although as many as seven might instead have belonged to the private archive of the Bene Galgula. In addition, as we have seen, the public materials included at least three Aramaic documents (and doubtless others too fragmentary to identify any longer), together with some forty-five Greek manuscripts. To this considerable administrative archive, comprising seventy documents, one may add three Greek texts that belonged either to the family's private archive or to that of one or more other families who fled to the caves with them. *Mur* 114 is an acknowledgment of debt that Baillet believed was left behind by Roman troops during a brief stay in the caves. On the basis of the consular names, it seemed to date to 171 C.E.[215] Cotton and Werner Eck have since argued convincingly that it ought instead to be dated to the late 120s and so associated with the Second Revolt.[216] *Mur* 115 is Salome's contract of remarriage, and *Mur* 116 is another, much more fragmentary marriage contract, whether hers or that of another Salome.

Taken as a whole, in terms of both its contents and the proposed historical understanding—a military commander preserving the documents produced during his period of service, together with his private archive—the situation of Jesus b. Galgula finds a remarkable and thereby instructive parallel in the Abinnaeus Archive. Abinnaeus was a career military officer of the fourth century C.E. whose last assignment was as prefect of the cavalry and garrison commander at Dionysias in the Fayyum, in Lower Egypt.[217] His archive as recovered contained eighty-two documents, although it was once somewhat larger, substantial damage having afflicted certain pieces such that they could not be analyzed.[218] Among the surviving documents were letters from superiors, equals, and inferiors (cf. inter alia *Mur* 43, 46, and 42, respectively); personal contracts (doubtless present, though now hard to distinguish within the Murabbaʿat materials); and documents pertaining to the female members of the family (cf. inter alia *Mur* 115). As with b. Galgula, Abinnaeus in his military role was called upon to resolve local civilian disputes. Timothy Teeter has written:

> These two roles—both as commander of a garrison with de facto if not de jure responsibilities for the enforcement of order not only in respect to military, but also to purely civilian matters, and thereby as patron . . . help explain both the nature of his archive and the reason for its survival. The letters, petitions, contracts, etc., the mixture of public and private documents—a distinction which may not even have occurred to Abinnaeus—do not merely indicate these roles; their very maintenance as an archive, even after [his] retirement, was a function of those roles. His archival responsibilities extended beyond his mere tenure in office as it would for any Roman official and patron.[219]

And as it would, one might add, for many non-Romans—even a Judaean—in a Romanized Mediterranean world.

The only remaining possible components of the Archive of the Bene Galgula are the Hebrew literary texts, about which, unfortunately, little can be said with any degree of confidence. Seven literary texts are involved, including a phylactery (*Mur* 4) and a mezuzah (*Mur* 5), and none can be dated except by paleographic analysis. Milik assigned *Mur* 1, possibly a complete Torah scroll, to the beginning of the second century C.E.; likewise, the scroll of the twelve Minor Prophets, *Mur* 88. He offered no very definite suggestion for the phylactery or mezuzah; the other three texts, *Mur* 2 (Deuteronomy), *Mur* 3 (Isaiah), and the nonscriptural *Mur* 6, Milik dated to Herodian or even Hasmonean times, suggesting that they might have been taken to the caves by the First Revolt refugees.[220]

When Milik wrote, the numerous literary works from Qumran Cave 11, discovered only in 1956, had yet to be digested. Many of these manuscripts exemplify relatively late hands, from the period of 50 C.E. or even later, and from them we have come to know the later hands much better than in Milik's time.[221] All of the Cave 11 hands certainly antedate the destruction of Jerusalem in 70, but several nevertheless greatly resemble the hands of Milik's "second-century" Murabbaʿat texts. Consequently, one cannot rule out the possibility that the Torah scroll and the Minor Prophets scroll were actually among the archives of First Revolt families. Conversely, *pace* Milik, one cannot necessarily associate the earlier manuscripts with the earlier revolt. They might easily have been held in one or more collections for more than a century and taken to the caves by the Bene Galgula or others who went there with them. In Roman times book collections often survived intact for two or even three centuries, being passed down within a family or sold off to some outside collector.[222] Their histories could be circuitous, or as Martial would say, *habent sua fata libelli* (book scrolls have their own peculiar fates).

These considerations mean that paleography offers no real help in trying to decide who took these literary texts to the caves. Any of them could belong to either revolutionary era.

Nevertheless, if a certain amount of speculation be admitted, a suggestion or two may merit consideration. It is attractive to associate *Mur* 1 and *Mur* 88 with the Bene Galgula for one particular reason: they may be synagogue copies, especially *Mur* 1. A complete copy of the Torah such as it seems to be would be highly unwieldy for actual use by an individual, as it would be almost forty-six meters long when unrolled and devilishly heavy. Yet for communal use such a monster would be divinely symbolic, and with several men helping to handle it, markedly less unwieldy. The Herodium excavations uncovered a synagogue on the site that had been built by the revolutionaries who held the fortress during the First Revolt.[223] Both the fortress and the synagogue were evidently put to use again during the Bar Kokhba conflict and thus were functioning under Jesus b. Galgula as camp commander there. Such a synagogue would necessarily require scriptural texts. Putting two and two together, therefore, one might connect *Mur* 1 with that synagogue. When it became necessary to abandon the fortress, Jesus and the Jewish resistors would never have countenanced leaving a Torah scroll behind for the Romans to desecrate per their standard operating procedure. They would have taken the scroll along to their place of hiding. So too, perhaps, *Mur* 88—although, if this much smaller scroll were associated with the synagogue, it was apparently rescued by someone other than the camp commander and taken then to Murabbaʿat Cave 5.

Who among the First Revolt families might have possessed Hebrew books? We have noted earlier that several members of the family of Honi b. John were, so far as we have evidence, either illiterate altogether or literate only at a low functional level. None was a literary literate. The family of Eutrapelus did include literary literates, but so far as we know they possessed that level of literacy in no language but Greek. Cleopas's Aramaic signature, it will be recalled, was only at level 2. Accordingly, if any of the Hebrew books discovered at Murabbaʿat are to be associated with a known First Revolt family, it would seem that the family of Dositheos b. Eleazar emerges by process of elimination. But we might have arrived at the same destination by a more positive path of reasoning: Dositheos both possessed a fluid hand and knew Hebrew, to judge from *Mur* 30 and his signature there in the holy tongue. He was just the literary literate we need. Of course, given the many uncertainties involved with all of the foregoing analysis of the Murabbaʿat materials, this attribution warrants no great confidence. We may reasonably assume the presence of people invisible to us in the surviving evidence.

Putting these speculations aside, then, we may note that four distinct archives arguably emerge from the Murabbaʿat caches. All belonged to upper-class Judaeans. As extant, these four archives included altogether seven Hebrew literary works (at most, for these writings may well have belonged to people otherwise unevidenced). If one considers that the (as many as) thirteen Greek books may have completed one of these archives, then one is left with seven Hebrew works divided by three families. On average, then, on this very rough-and-ready calculation, the Murabbaʿat evidence suggests that an elite Judaean family might own a book or two. But the concept of "average" is probably inappropriate here. More likely, most families owned no books at all, whereas those who did read owned a median of three or four books.

Table 2.2 summarizes the foregoing analysis of the Murabbaʿat texts. The suggested division of the manuscripts between the two revolts is much more balanced than what de Vaux and his co-authors proposed in 1961. A significant number of manuscripts can reasonably be connected to Jerusalem in the years leading up to, and during, the First Revolt. A historical and logical coherence now characterizes the Second Revolt materials as well. These results have emerged simply by applying a two-pronged analytical instrument: first, the search for archives—which the history of this period and the evidence of other Judaean Desert discoveries argue should be in evidence; and second, attempting to answer a question: "Who took the texts to the caves?" The answers to this question have issued from the texts themselves—again, only to be expected if the question were a proper one. Doubtless this analysis has unknowingly embraced certain errors of fact and judgment. Still, allowing for the necessary give and take, the broader conclusions seem solid enough. The historical distinctions now possible promise to guide and add resonance to the statistical analysis of Chapter 5.

For now, the Eleusinian road leads on to Jericho.

Jericho: History of the Discoveries

The chance discovery in a cavern near Jericho of a complete wooden comb, a type typical of the Bar Kokhba period, led in 1986 to a two-day

Table 2.2. Murabba'at texts sorted by revolt

	First Revolt		Second Revolt			Indeterminate	
	Private documentary	Literary	Administrative/private documentary		Private documentary	Documentary	Literary
	Mur 18 Ar	*Mur* 108–13 Grk	*Mur* 8 Ar	*Mur* 7 Heb	*Mur* 114 Grk	*Mur* 160 Lat	*Mur* 1 Heb
	Mur 19 Ar	*Mur* 126–32 Grk	*Mur* 9 Ar	*Mur* 36 Heb	*Mur* 115 Grk	*Mur* 161 Lat	*Mur* 2 Heb
	Mur 20 Ar	*Mur* 155 Grk	*Mur* 10 Ar	*Mur* 37 Heb	*Mur* 116 Grk	*Mur* 162 Lat	*Mur* 3 Heb
	Mur 21 Ar	—	*Mur* 24 Heb	*Mur* 39 Heb	—	*Mur* 163 Lat	*Mur* 4 Heb
	Mur 22 Heb	—	*Mur* 41 Heb	*Mur* 40 Heb	—	—	*Mur* 5 Heb
	Mur 23 Ar	—	*Mur* 42 Heb	(?) *Mur* 50 Heb	—	—	*Mur* 6 Heb
	Mur 25 Ar	—	*Mur* 43 Heb	(?) *Mur* 58 Heb	—	—	*Mur* 88 Heb
	Mur 26 Ar	—	*Mur* 44 Heb	*Mur* 174 Heb	—	—	—
	Mur 27 Ar	—	*Mur* 45 Heb	—	—	—	—
	Mur 28 Ar	—	*Mur* 46 Heb	—	—	—	—
	Mur 29 Heb	—	*Mur* 47 Heb	—	—	—	—
	Mur 30 Heb	—	*Mur* 48 Heb	—	—	—	—
	Mur 31 Heb	—	*Mur* 49 Heb	—	—	—	—
	Mur 32 Ar	—	*Mur* 50 Heb	—	—	—	—
	Mur 33 Ar	—	*Mur* 51 Heb	—	—	—	—
	Mur 38 Ar	—	*Mur* 52 Heb	—	—	—	—
	Mur 158 Lat	—	*Mur* 61 Heb	—	—	—	—
	Mur 159 Lat	—	*Mur* 89–107 Grk	—	—	—	—
	4Q348 Heb	—	*Mur* 118–121 Grk	—	—	—	—
	(?) 4Q346 Ar	—	*Mur* 133–154 Grk	—	—	—	—
Total by type	20 texts	14 (?) texts	62 texts	8 texts	3 texts	4 texts	7 texts
Total by war	34 texts		73 texts			11 texts	

Note: Ar indicates Aramaic; Grk, Greek; Heb, Hebrew; and Lat, Latin.

excavation of the interior. Directed by Hanan Eshel, the excavation of Abi'or Cave, as it is known today, unearthed remains dating from three distinct periods: the Chalcolithic era, the fourth century B.C.E., and the first and early second centuries C.E. In 1993, as a part of the large-scale "Operation Scroll," Eshel and Boaz Zissu were asked to conduct another season of excavations at the site and along its cave-pocked ridge, Ketef Jericho. Additional finds emerged. In particular, a second important hollow, the Cave of the Sandal, proved to contain Bar Kokhba–period materials, including the skeletons of two couples—perhaps three—and several children. The two excavations thus proved that here, too, as in so many other regions of the Judaean wilderness, people had fled to the caves at the end of the Second Jewish Revolt seeking safety. Unfortunately, here they did not find it.

Glass vessels, nails, textiles, a needle, rope, and decayed portions of several types of leather sandals yielded themselves to the archaeologists. Gold rings, a golden earring, and a silver cosmetics spoon suggested that at least some of the refugees were elite. Notable were floral remains whose examination by Mordechai Kislev revealed that the rebels who fled to Ketef Jericho did so with inadequate supplies of food. This lack forced them to collect the wild fruits that ripen in the local wadis only in the months of September and October. Unlike some of the other refuge caves of the Bar Kokhba period, therefore, these caves were neither prepared beforehand nor supplied for long-term habitation. It seems that the rebels fled hurriedly in the autumn of 135 C.E., were discovered within a relatively short time, and were dispatched where they hid by Roman forces.

Of greatest interest for the present study are the documentary finds that emerged from Abi'or Cave and the area beneath its entrance, sifted to good effect. The 1986 excavation retrieved portions of six documents, and the 1993 excavation added to that number very considerably, though mostly only tiny fragments of texts. The total number of documents exceeded seventy. Included were two Aramaic writings of the late fourth century B.C.E. and Greek, Hebrew, and Aramaic products of the first and early second centuries of the Common Era.

Documentary Finds

Shortly after the discoveries were made, two preliminary studies alerted the scholarly world to several of the most important textual finds at Ketef Jericho.[224] A few years later, in 2000, the *editiones principes* of all of the texts appeared as a section of volume 38 in the series *Discoveries in the Judaean Desert.*[225] The most notable of the documents included *P.Jericho* 1, a well-preserved list of loans from the end of the fourth century B.C.E., important for helping to fill a gap in the understanding of the development of the Aramaic scripts; and *P.Jericho* 16, a Greek papyrus mentioning Hadrian and dated ca. 1 May 128 C.E.[226] *P.Jericho* 7 and *P.Jericho* 9 both seem to date to the reign of Domitian. The lower text of *P.Jericho* 7, an Aramaic *Doppelurkunde* recording the sale of a date crop, reads בעשרין וחמשה לטבת [שנ]ת תלת דמטס ק[סר, "On the twenty-fifth of Tevet, [ye]ar three of Domit(ian)us Cae[sar."[227] Thus this writ was inscribed in 84 C.E. Dating within a few years of it is *P.Jericho* 9, if Yardeni's very difficult reading of a portion of line 11 in the lower text can be sustained. With some reservations, she suggested דמטׄיׄנׄוׄסׄ קׄסׄרׄ (Domitian Caesar).[228]

These last three texts thus help to establish the chronological parameters of the Roman-period documents. Judging on the basis of paleography and the few explicit dates still extant, virtually all of the Roman-period texts seem to date to the years between the Jewish revolts, embracing the last third of the first century and the first third of the second. If this conclusion is valid, then the language usage in the Jericho documents makes an important contribution to the questions of this study. For here to be found are at least four—and perhaps significantly more than four—Hebrew documents. This is noteworthy inasmuch as these years were a time when, according to scholarly consensus, the Jews were drafting no legal documents in that language.

The exact number of Hebrew writings is problematic because the single designation *P.Jericho* 15 embraces more than thirty exceedingly fragmentary Semitic manuscripts, most without a single legible word. We know only that they are inscribed in cursive varieties of the Jewish script. It stands to reason that at least some were composed in Hebrew. In any event, as noted, *P.Jericho* 9 was a *Doppelurkunde* composed in Hebrew during the reign of Domitian. Add to that *P.Jericho* 11, very fragmentary, but either a deed or a letter written in the holy tongue; *P.Jericho* 14, unclassified but possibly a letter in the same language (שלחתי כסף, "I have sent money," can be read in fragment b, line 2); and *P.Jericho* 8/10. The intriguing final document Yardeni presented as two texts, each with its own number. Her discussion, however, drew attention to the identical hands—proving their origin with the same scribe—and offered the attractive hypothesis that *P.Jericho* 8, an Aramaic outer text belonging once to a double deed, and *P.Jericho* 10, a Hebrew inner, stemmed from the same document.[229] As no material joins were possible, she drew no definite conclusion. Neither shall we, but in either case we are left with four certain

Hebrew documents, and the reasonable prospect of others, all originating between the years 70 and 130 C.E.

In his popular work *Bar-Kokhba,* Yigael Yadin suggested that the use of Hebrew in documents written during the Second Revolt reflected a "change made by a special decree of Bar-Kokhba who wanted to restore Hebrew as the official language of the state."[230] As Cotton has noted, "an official act seems to have been necessary, given the overwhelming evidence for the currency of Aramaic in legal documents before this period."[231] These comments were based on the evidence then known and reflect what has become the consensus. Yet the Hebrew materials from Ketef Jericho give pause and seem to require a more nuanced understanding of language usage. It is important to remember that surviving pieces of evidence are partial, localized in their origins, and often attach to thin slices of time. *The use of Hebrew to compose documents might well have varied according to time and place.* In the region near Jericho, it appears that Hebrew and Aramaic were both used for contracts, letters, and the like—as far as we can tell, in roughly equal proportion. For the number of Jericho manuscripts definitely composed in Aramaic, six, is essentially the same as that for Hebrew.[232] Moreover, we have reason to think that the people of Jericho used Hebrew for documentary purposes over a long span of time, at least a century. That is to say, its use was evidently no response to the revolts against Rome, no reflection of concomitant high nationalist feeling. Indeed, not only was Hebrew used between the revolts, it was used well before the first uprising. The evidence for this fact is Khirbet Qumran ostracon 1 (KHQ1).

Discovered by James Strange in the winter of 1996 as he conducted soundings on the marl terrace south of the settlement at Qumran (a two-hour walk from Jericho), this damaged ostracon is apparently a deed of conveyance. The entire left side of the document is missing, and a number of problematic readings have made the text a focus of some controversy.[233] Nevertheless, a substantial amount of the wording is extant, and all scholars agree that the ostracon was inscribed in Hebrew in the second year of a missing era. A certain Honi b. PN conveys a list of items to an Eleazar b. PN. Precisely when this took place is unknown: the official editors defined the script as "Late Herodian" (i.e., 30–68 C.E.), whereas the leading authority on cursive Jewish scripts, Yardeni, characterized it as "an early Herodian semi-cursive written by an unskilled scribe."[234] Thus Yardeni's dating required a late-first-century B.C.E. or early-first-century C.E. time of origin. For our purposes precise dating, while desirable, is really not necessary. On either view, this ostracon likely antedates the First Revolt by decades. Clearly legible letterforms in the ostracon's second line spell out the place of origin: בירחו, "in Jericho." None dispute this reading.

Accordingly, well before the First Revolt, Hebrew was a language used in Jericho and its environs to inscribe documents of various sorts.[235] Alerted by this fact, we may reasonably suppose that other towns and villages in Judaea, places for which we have no comparable evidence, may well likewise have used Hebrew for legal texts interchangeably with Aramaic, despite the undoubted fact that Aramaic was the language in which the core legal traditions originally developed and were often passed on. At Beth ʿAmar, for example, we have recently discovered that Hebrew could be used for several consecutive lines within an Aramaic document. So it is possible that in this hamlet, too, a broader tradition of using Hebrew for legal purposes obtained in Roman times.

As stated, the total number of documents cached in Abi'or Cave in or about the year 135 amounts to approximately seventy, twenty-one in Greek being added to the forty or fifty Semitic texts. These seem to comprise individual, not administrative archives, so far as their lamentable state of preservation supports any judgment on the matter. Because the surviving portions are so broken, it is impossible to ascertain prosopographic connections between documents such as appear to exist at Murabbaʿat. Also, we find no clearly public documents—although, as noted earlier, mention is made of an archive in Jericho that held copies of private documents. A number of the Semitic compositions display previously unexampled letterforms. A distinct school of scribes apparently functioned in Jericho, following its own traditions.[236] One may observe a similar situation at Mahoza, as we shall see. Different regions, then, presumably would have trained students to write their names and all else that they learned to copy at school somewhat differently. Jericho accordingly warns of drawing conclusions about Judaean language and literacy that are too broad or insufficiently nuanced. One must allow for a substantial local factor.

Before leaving Jericho, one missing component of the caches requires notice: no literary texts emerged from any of the caves at Ketef Jericho. This is in marked contrast with the other Bar Kokhba sites of the Judaean Desert, all of which evidenced some literary material. The absence of books may, of course, be nothing but a kind of accident, an aspect of the *fata libelli* that Martial remarked. Discoveries may remain to be made; or perhaps these particular refugees just owned no books; or maybe those they did own failed to survive even in the piecemeal fashion of the documentary manuscripts. But another consideration may be relevant. The archaeologists remarked that the caves they explored evidenced severely disturbed, often inverted stratigraphy.[237] Because they were more accessible than most of the other Bar Kokhba refuge caves, these were frequently used and reused during the centuries spanning antiquity to the present. Subsequent temporary inhabitants, or ancient explorers of the Ketef Jericho caverns, may have removed literary texts as being valuable. In fact, we know of two specific occasions when hidden books were found near Jericho.

The first occurred in the early years of the third century C.E., and thus, if the books were a Bar Kokhba–period deposit, about a century after they were cached. We find the notice in the *Historia ecclesiastica* of Eusebius, who references the man's own writings and tells of Origen utilizing a Greek manuscript of the Psalms that was "found in a jar [πίθος] at Jericho" during the reign of Antoninus the son of Severus. Working in Caesarea on the coast of Palestine, Origen adopted this version of the biblical book as one of the final three of seven parallel columns comprising his *Hexapla* for the Psalter.[238] We cannot necessarily conclude, of course, that this manuscript was discovered in a cave, but that is possible, especially when one recalls that numerous of the Dead Sea Scrolls were sequestered in the so-called scroll jars, a type of pottery evidenced also in the Jericho region. In the case of the second ancient discovery of hidden books near Jericho, however, the connection to a cave is explicit.

About the year 800, Timotheus I, patriarch of Seleucia, composed in elegant Syriac a letter to his friend Sergius, metropolitan of Elam, in which he described the discovery, now some ten years old:

> For we have learned from certain Jewish men, reliable as recent catechumens to Christianity, that ten years ago books were found in the vicinity of Jericho in a cave, within a kind of house. They say that a dog belonging to an Arab who was hunting entered a cave [*neq'a*] following some animal, and did not come back out. Thus his master entered behind him and found a small dwelling [*baytuna*] in the interior of the cave, and great numbers of books therein. Thereupon he entered Jerusalem and made this fact known to the Jews, a throng of whom consequently went out and discovered books of the Old Testament and, in addition to them, other Hebrew books as well.[239]

After detailing some of the biblical perplexities that he hoped the books might help resolve, Timotheus went on to say, "That Hebrew fellow then told me, 'We found more than two hundred psalms of David among those books.'" So, this discovery evidently included apocryphal psalms of the sort known from the Qumran caves, a genre whose existing specimens give no suggestion of sectarian origins.

Whether either discovery of literature ought to be connected to Ketef Jericho is naturally very uncertain. But it does seem likely that the second set of books, in particular—which from the description apparently involved a refuge cave of the sort associated with Bar Kokhba materials—originally would have been associated with documents that were simply of no interest to the Jews who found the books. People who fled to the caves of Judaea in times of emergency took what they could carry—books, yes, as precious and valuable; but documents, too, as in some ways even more precious. Any family that fled with books and set up living quarters in a cave also would have taken contracts, receipts, and similar stuff of everyday life, if they had any. Perhaps the books once described should be paired with the documents now unearthed.

Or perhaps—to pose a fifth possible explanation for the absence of literary materials at Ketef Jericho—any books cached in the caves in antiquity were pilfered by bedouin in recent times. They, after all, had an impressive track record in the matter of manuscript discovery, easily outdistancing their scholarly competitors. Moreover, as we have seen, they chose not to provide, or perhaps no longer remembered, an accurate provenance for everything they discovered and sold to Western scholars. It is therefore just possible that we have in our possession a book or two from Ketef Jericho and just do not know it. During those years the discoveries were coming thick and fast, and mix-ups might easily have occurred in what one imagines as—at best—an ad hoc tribal filing system.

In February 1952, short months after Joseph Saad's adventures uncovering their trail to Murabbaʿat (ironically, in fact, while de Vaux, Harding, and team were actually excavating that site), the Taʿamireh bedouin discovered Qumran Cave 2. It was just a few meters south of the original cave. The archaeologists hurried north to rescue any remaining scraps from that cave. Later that summer the tribesmen were the first to Qumran Cave 4, mother lode of the Dead Sea Scrolls, which alone yielded some forty thousand manuscript fragments, eventually comprising more than 550 separate writings. And they plundered the cave right under the noses of de Vaux and fellow archaeologists while they labored a mere fifty meters away, excavating Khirbet Qumran. When the archaeologists looked up and realized what was happening, rushing then to halt the depredations and attempt some sort of scientific excavation of Cave 4, the bedouin simply went away and found Qumran Cave 6. As the breathless, frustrated, and increasingly frazzled scholars arrived tardily in their wake at that site, the bedouin slipped south again to initiate yet another replay of the now standard scenario.

Arriving at the region near En Gedi, roughly thirty-two kilometers south of Cave 6, they began to trace the bed of a seasonal river known as the Wadi Habra (Arabic) or Naḥal Ḥever (Hebrew). With uncanny skill and white-knuckle daring they succeeded in identifying several more manuscript-bearing caves in the cliffs rising more than six hundred meters above the wadi on either side. These materials are, if anything, even more important to the issues of the present study than the finds at Murabbaʿat. They and related discoveries along the wadis near En Gedi are the final stop in our metaphorical journey. To them we now turn.

3 En Gedi, Mahoza, and Kephar-Baru

Naḥal Ḥever and Environs: History of the Discoveries

For cliffs as high and as steep as those of Naḥal Ḥever and several of the parallel wadis north and south, the Taʿamireh bedouin had to prosecute their search using methods different from those employed at Murabbaʿat or in exploring the caves near Qumran. A small man or young boy skilled in rock-climbing would descend the vertical face from the top of the cliff with one end of a rope ladder clamped in his teeth, feeling blindly for hand- and footholds as he went. Of course, the least slip meant certain death, because potential ancient refuge caves were typically to be found about one hundred meters down from the cliff top, and six or seven hundred meters up from the wadi bed below. Locating a promising cave, the climber would anchor the ladder at its entry, allowing larger fellow tribesmen to clamber down the several hundred meters of swaying rope to aid in the investigation. By this death-defying method the tribe explored dozens of caves in 1951 and 1952, striking pay dirt more than once. Whether in the process they suffered casualties is unknown. In late July of 1952 the bedouin were once more shopping new wares to de Vaux, Milik, and their colleagues at the École Biblique et Archéologique Française de Jérusalem and ultimately to Harding and the Jordanian government. The wares they were shopping this time, however, were a bit of a problem. They had been discovered in Israeli territory, not Jordanian.

The response to this revelation was a Jordanian purchase nonetheless, followed by a covering tale equal parts truth and falsehood—clouded statements vague in their import but precise in their wording, care being taken to say nothing false in scientific publications, nothing true in personal discussion, except to the trusted few. Eventually, the disinformation spurred further exploration and greater discovery, with no little irony thrown in for good measure.

The ends of the present study require as accurate an apprehension as possible of the historical contexts surrounding the contracts and letters so as to frame the people being studied. Once again, we want to know who took the texts to the caves. Accordingly, we need to know *which texts came from which caves.* Earlier obfuscations cannot be tolerated if they can be penetrated. And indeed, close analysis and comparison of the statements the scholars in the know made in the early 1950s, laid alongside what can now be known from subsequent discoveries and the published texts themselves, permits substantial lifting of the veil they apparently attempted to throw over the facts. Notwithstanding, the following analysis is not a morality play. What the scholars did was questionable ethically, but not everyone will judge that, on balance, they acted wrongly. For by their actions these people obtained precious evidence that might otherwise have been lost to historical understanding.

The July materials that the bedouin took to the École Biblique included a dated Aramaic papyrus, a Greek document inscribed on skin, and fragments of a scroll of Genesis. Taken as it were "on consignment," the materials were duly photographed by Najib Anton Albina, scion of an old Latin family in east Jerusalem, who was the official photographer for virtually all of the Judaean Desert texts acquired by Jordan. As usual, he entered them in his photographer's notebook, recording the exact date ("7/25/52") and labeling them "Sedeir manuscripts."[1] That is, he understood them to derive from Wadi Sdeir, then partially in Jordanian territory, known in Hebrew as Naḥal David. Presumably, he got this information from the scholars who had questioned the bedouin. It appears today that this was an accurate attribution. All subsequent acquisitions from the recent bedouin finds would receive something else.

On 5 August the bedouin returned for payment and turned over additional texts that had been agreed upon. Among other things, this lot included Nabataean papyri. The authorities acquired two additional lots in that month of August, on the twenty-second and twenty-third.[2] These groups were sizeable. Among them were substantial fragments of a Greek translation of the Minor Prophets, later termed "a missing link" in the history of the Old Greek Bible. His log shows that Albina designated the first fragments of these new manuscripts that he photographed as "Seyyal manuscripts." This entry occurred on 1 September. The same label was then applied to each of eight subsequent entries involving the new caches as they came to be photographed, a process that took some time because the fragments had to be sorted and analyzed first. Thus the major part of the photography occurred in July 1956. By then, the existence of the new finds was widely known, for the scholars had announced them and even published preliminary editions of select portions.

"Seyyal" was Albina's spelling for the normalized English Wadi Seiyal, known in Hebrew as Naḥal Ṣe'elim. Between 1948 and 1967 it lay entirely within Israeli territory, and the bedouin had in fact searched this locale (or shortly would). The label created a safe fiction. The same label was attached to the photographic plates themselves. It was apparently agreed to say that the find-spot for the new Bar Kokhba–period materials was the Wadi Seiyal, although the scholars who knew the truth were careful never to put that claim in writing.[3]

What was the point of the fictitious label? For the bedouin, it allowed the profitable search of Judaean Desert caves to continue unimpeded, since according to Jordanian law it was not illegal for them to plunder antiquities in Israel. To search in Jordanian territory was, however, quite another matter. It was important that this latter possibility not be raised, so as to avoid persistent questioning by authorities outside the small group in the know. For the scholars, the fictitious label served to keep the actual location a secret known only to them. After all, since the find-spot lay in Israeli territory, they had no hope of conducting scientific excavations there. This way, they evidently calculated, any future bedouin discoveries would come to them, not to the Israelis, nor to anyone else. And that was exactly how it went.[4]

The month following the acquisitions, de Vaux composed a description of the new finds, part of a larger article on the continuing excavations at the site of Khirbet Qumran. He described the provenance as follows: "Another important lot has come from several caves that seem to be close to one another in a region that has not been certainly identified."[5] Significantly, he mentioned several caves and specified that they were apparently located very near one another. He then went on to say:

> Biblical texts in Hebrew are less numerous; they attach to Genesis, the Psalms and Numbers, and here as well is a complete phylactery. The newest discovery in the biblical domain is a Greek version of the Minor Prophets, concerning which P. Barthélemy gives a preliminary report in this same fascicle of the *Revue*. A Hebrew letter is addressed to Simon ben Kosiba, the leader of the

> revolt, Bar Kokhba. Two contracts in Aramaic are dated in the "3rd year of Israel's liberation in the name of Simon ben Kosiba." Two Greek documents supply dates in the Era of Provincia Arabia and two Aramaic documents follow the same chronology. Most surprising has been to find in this lot a series of Nabataean papyri, some rather lengthy, and furnishing more continuous text in that language than had been supplied by all the [Nabataean] inscriptions. But their cursive writing will require a considerable effort to decipher.[6]

De Vaux's description referenced the article by Dominique Barthélemy in that same issue of the *Revue Biblique.* Barthélemy was a Septuagint specialist attached to the École Biblique whom de Vaux and the Jordanian authorities had tapped to publish the *Greek Minor Prophets Scroll.* His twofold description of the find-spot for his text is worth comparing with de Vaux's statement. The first portion of the description appeared in the body of the article; the second, in an elaborating footnote:

> But during the second half of August 1952 the tireless Taʿamireh bedouin discovered within a new cave important fragments of a leather scroll that was deposited there during the Bar Kokhba Revolt.
>
> This [dating] is shown with sufficient certainty by the script of small fragments of Hebraized Aramaic papyri discovered in the same cave, as well as the coins and dated documents found in two other caves very nearby.[7]

Both scholars, then, stated that the new discoveries had originated in more than one cave. Barthélemy specified the number as three. The point is noteworthy since later scholarly descriptions became much less specific. Both men further indicated their understanding that the caves in question were near one another. Most important, the additional details added by the two scholars clearly evidenced that each knew that the true find-spot lay elsewhere than the Wadi Seiyal.

In de Vaux's case, the giveaway was the mention of a Genesis scroll. In retrospect, we know that no copy of Genesis can be meant other than the scroll Albina had photographed in July and labeled as coming from Wadi Sdeir. No great powers of deduction are required, as among the new discoveries this was the only copy of Genesis. Today, this scroll is published and designated Sdeir 1.[8]

Similarly, Barthélemy averred that explicitly dated material had come, not from the cave where the Minor Prophets scroll was discovered, but rather from two other nearby caves. The propinquity of these two other caves was of the essence to establish the historical significance of the prophets scroll.

For if the scroll were later than other known recensions of the Old Greek, those of Aquila, Theodotion, and Symmachus, then its importance would diminish considerably. Attachment to the first century C.E. or earlier was critical. Since only a general dating could emerge from the paleographic analysis of the few small Hebrew and Aramaic fragments found, as he said, in the same cave as the scroll, Barthélemy needed to reference the other caves so as to adduce, if possible, their geographic cohesion to his cave. By this means he could argue the connection of the deposits to one another and from the dated materials found in the other two derive a rather precise *terminus post quem non* for his own cave's holdings.

Barthélemy's allusion to "dated documents found in two other caves" must in part hearken back to the materials from the Wadi Sdeir, whence what we today label Sdeir 2. This is a dated Aramaic contract of the third year of Simon b. Kosiba and the only dated text in the Sdeir materials.[9] Accordingly, both scholars referred to the Sdeir finds precisely and truthfully, but obliquely, in terms deliberately obscure to their contemporaries. Their descriptions become clear only in retrospect. From the beginning the true find-spot for most of the new materials was believed to be in the Wadi Sdeir and two caves proximate to Sdeir, in "caves that seem to be close to one another," "caves very nearby."

Words may be elastic, but they can scarcely stretch to classify caves in the Wadi Seiyal as "close" to caverns in the Wadi Sdeir. Traveling south from Sdeir to Seiyal, following ancient roads along the coast of the Dead Sea, then turning westward into the wadi, measures more than twenty kilometers (cf. Figure 1.1). Caves in eastern portions of the Naḥal Ḥever, on the other hand, would accurately be described as neighboring those in the Wadi Sdeir. They stand about eight kilometers distant by the same method of reckoning. As we shall see, Naḥal Ḥever was in fact the place where the bedouin found most of the new texts.

Presumably, they had made this fact known, for the scholars took care with every new find to interrogate the bedouin concerning provenance. The tribesmen were seldom immediately forthcoming, of course, hoping for further finds and further sales; but eventually, they—or their middleman for most of the transactions, Khalil Iskander Shahin (better known as "Kando")—would reveal the truth, so far as they remembered it. Specifically queried on the point, John Strugnell (who arrived to help with the work at the museum in 1953) stated in February of 2000 that "the bedouin were questioned very thoroughly regarding the origin of the texts."[10] Elsewhere he wrote: "We were very careful not to confuse material identified to us as coming from different sites in the Judaean Desert. From the time of the arrival of the fragments in the museum we kept the various groups separate, never working on them in the same room . . . the ascriptions of fragments to caves should be treated as very reliable."[11] The scholars were confident that they knew from the bedouin the origins of the materials they worked on. We have seen that this confidence was sometimes misplaced, but such situations were the exception, not the rule.

About a year after the lots described were purchased, the bedouin arrived with yet additional materials. This was July 1953. Barthélemy wrote that these "additional fragments were purchased to complete the lot" ("autres fragments sont venus compléter ce lot") that had come, along with the Minor Prophets scroll, from a cave located south of those of Wadi Murabbaʿat.[12] This description of provenance indicated that no new find-spot was involved but was otherwise conspicuously less detailed than that of his first publication. Similarly, the Aramaist Jean Starcky, in publishing a preliminary study of a Nabataean document among the original items purchased, spoke of a group of texts "concerning which one lacks . . . the necessary precise details" ("sur lequel on manque . . . des précisions nécessaires").[13] In a series of publications Milik wrote variously of manuscripts whose provenance was uncertain ("dont le lieu de provenance exact n'est pas certain," "dont l'emplacement n'est pas jusqu'ici repéré avec certitude," "trouvé en 1952 en un lieu mal déterminé du Désert de Juda").[14] None of the scholars mentioned the Wadi Seiyal, the rather precise find-spot that their own official Jordanian records were listing. Only in 1987, when the origins in caves of the Naḥal Ḥever had become known and the true attribution was no longer at stake, did any of the scholars in the know use the term "Seiyal" in a publication. This was Strugnell, apparently intent on laying blame for that misleading attribution exclusively at the feet of the bedouin: "[The 'Seiyal' collection] was acquired in 1952–4 by the Rockefeller (or, as it was then called, Palestine) Archaeological Museum, from clandestine excavators who had shown little respect for political frontiers. They told us that the provenance of these documents was 'the Wadi Seiyal' and the collection was named accordingly."[15]

By 1953 the "clandestine excavators" in the Naḥal Ḥever had attracted the attention of others besides the scholars in Jordanian east Jerusalem. An amateur Israeli archaeologist investigating some caves near En Gedi, Uri Shoshani, heard that the bedouin were excavating caves in Naḥal Ḥever. He informed Yohanan Aharoni, then inspector of the Israeli Department of Antiquities, who organized and conducted a survey of the area from 25 November to 16 December 1953. Aharoni discovered two Roman siege camps overlooking caves on the eastern end of the wadi, a fact suggesting the importance of those anciently taking refuge within. Thus prompted, he explored one of the caves, a large cavern on the northern bank that later came to be known as the Cave of Letters. This exploration proved very discouraging, making evident as it did the thoroughness of the bedouin searches, which seemed to guarantee that nothing more remained to be found. Additional investigation appeared pointless, so the expedition returned to Jerusalem.

But Aharoni continued to ponder what he had seen. About eighteen months later, during the week of 2–9 May 1955, he returned to Naḥal Ḥever, this time to investigate the cave on the southern bank that lay opposite the Cave of Letters, beneath the second siege camp. This cave was extraordinarily difficult of access, and so, Aharoni reasoned, quite likely still pristine, undisturbed by the bedouin. Entering the cave after enormous exertions, Aharoni and his companions were struck a double blow. The first: underfoot before them lay strewn dozens of skeletons of men, women, and children, leading the archaeologists to dub this grotto the Cave of Horrors. These people had seemingly died of starvation or thirst under an intent Roman watch centuries ago. The second blow was more prosaic: the bedouin had already been here—indeed, even here, in this virtually inaccessible place. Despairing Israeli archaeologists accordingly forswore further exploration of the Judaean Desert caves, and apart from minor activity around En Gedi in 1956, nothing happened for nearly five years.[16]

The spur to new action was borne by the winds of rumor. Toward the end of 1959 a visiting American scholar, fresh from a visit in east Jerusalem with the scholars at the Palestine Archaeological Museum, crossed the border and entered west Jerusalem bearing news for Aharoni. The documents from an "unknown source" offered by the bedouin to Jordanian authorities had come, he revealed, from Wadi Seiyal (Naḥal Ṣe'elim). This southern locale lay well outside the earlier surveys that had focused on the northern part of the Judaean Desert of Israel. Aharoni immediately organized an expedition to the wadi, from 25 January to 2 February 1960, but found little of interest, locating only one small cave that the bedouin had failed to notice. Clearly a more extensive search would be needed.[17]

At this point Aharoni's nemesis, Yigael Yadin, entered the picture. The two men were bitter archaeological rivals, a rivalry rooted in events of a few years earlier when Aharoni had chafed under Yadin's leadership in excavations at Hazor. Since that time Aharoni had made the archaeology of the Judaean Desert his bailiwick, whereas Yadin had worked elsewhere. All concerned now recognized that a more extensive expedition to the desert was essential if the bedouin were to be forestalled from pillaging all of the region's remaining treasures. Nevertheless, Aharoni was not looking for Yadin's help. Nor was Yadin necessarily trying to insert himself. But earlier high positions in both the army and politics provided him casual access to powerful connections unmatched by Aharoni or any other Israeli academic. Yadin happened to mention to Prime Minister David Ben-Gurion that Aharoni had found little and that the bedouin incursions were becoming increasingly problematic. Ben-Gurion responded by ordering his chief of staff, Chaim Laskov, to intensify border patrols so as to keep the tribesmen out. But Laskov had a more elegant solution in mind. He went to Yadin, under whom he had once served, and made his proposal: Why not assemble a team of leading archaeologists and mount an all-out, large-scale expedition to explore all of the relevant wadis at one time? With the full logistical support of the army, which he now offered, it should be possible to search every cave in the area systematically.

Yadin liked the idea but was cautious of seeming to tread on Aharoni's toes. He therefore sent Laskov to the president of the Hebrew University, Benjamin Mazar, and to Joseph Aviram, secretary of the Israel Exploration Society. Enthusiastic in their support of the idea, these two men then formed the proposed team with Aharoni at its head. Under Aharoni would be Nahman Avigad, Pesach Bar-Adon, and . . . Yigael Yadin. Aharoni grudgingly let himself be persuaded to accept Yadin, but as he formulated plans to explore the ravines, he also carefully considered how to make certain that his rival would not overshadow him this time.

Under the joint auspices of the Hebrew University, the Department of Antiquities, and the Israel Exploration Society, the expedition was planned as a four-pronged affair. Each leader would direct an independent group working in a defined area, and each would have sole scholarly control over whatever he and his group found. Yadin suggested otherwise, that all the wadis be considered as a single huge expedition and that any publications be joint, but Aharoni angrily refused. Given first choice of where his group would work, Aharoni—convinced of excellent prospects by the disinformation that this was where the Jordanian texts originated—chose the northern bank of Naḥal Ṣe'elim. Avigad selected the southern bank of that same wadi. Bar-Adon picked next and chose Naḥal Mishmar and Naḥal Asael, two small, closely contiguous ravines. Aharoni thus left Yadin with what seemed by far the least attractive prospect—Naḥal Ḥever, which had already been closely investigated by Aharoni himself and found, so it seemed, picked bare. The irony that Aharoni had maneuvered Yadin's assignment to this true origin of most of the recent bedouin finds would shortly emerge, as would the fact that the tribesmen had unwittingly left the greatest discoveries untouched.

Because the army was needed elsewhere shortly, the expedition could last no longer than two weeks, but the army helped to extend archaeological work time by preparing beforehand the campsites where each group would bivouac. On 23 March 1960 the searching and digging commenced.

Avigad's Expedition A quickly determined that the southern bank of Naḥal Ṣe'elim had housed no refugees from the time of Bar Kokhba. Thereupon they uprooted and moved north to Naḥal David (Wadi Sdeir). Given time constraints, they could do no more than examine cursorily one cave on the western end of the valley, denominated the Cave of the Pool because of the plastered water tank anciently prepared at its entrance. (Recall the similar installation at Murabbaʿat.) Just inside the entrance near the pool an iron arrowhead was discovered protruding from the ceiling, dramatic evidence of a missile launched from outside at occupants of the cave. The Roman design of this weapon together with accumulated sherds of pottery demonstrated the cave's use during the time of the Second Revolt, presumably by notables from nearby En Gedi. But Avigad and his team found no texts.

Bar-Adon and his Expedition C examined dozens of caves, finally locating one on the southern bank of Naḥal Mishmar that had both been inhabited during the Second Revolt and escaped bedouin ravages. This was the Scouts' Cave, accessible only by ropes descending fifty meters from the cliff top. Along with pottery typical of the period, the cave contained fragments of glass vessels, remnants of a wooden box, pieces of an ancient leather jacket, delicate woven fabrics tinctured in blue and red, and portions of worn sandals once belonging to children and adults. A Greek papyrus—of high quality but badly creased, elegantly indited on both sides by a skilled scribe, apparently a record of grains dispersed—was also discovered.[18] The team further unearthed a fragment of a Hebrew or Aramaic document inscribed in semicursive lettering, though no complete word survived.

Together with his Expedition B, Aharoni identified four caves on the north bank of Naḥal Ṣe'elim that had been inhabited during the Bar Kokhba era. One of them, the Cave of the Skulls, had been thoroughly dug by the tribesmen. Gathered together within this cave were found seven skulls, disarticulated skeletons piled high alongside. Coins from the early third century C.E. suggested the time of this bizarre secondary burial. Closely searched as it was, the possibility that the Taʿamireh made some discoveries here cannot be excluded. Nevertheless, the pattern of these caves did not fit the descriptions de Vaux and Barthélemy had furnished, for the bedouin had bypassed two of Aharoni's four caves. Thus by no reckoning can these be the three caves of which they spoke.

These caverns supplied notable materials. The Cave of the Arrow concealed in one corner an arsenal of cane arrows. Cave 34, the Cave of the Scrolls, rewarded Aharoni with a fragmentary phylactery, portions of an Aramaic deed inscribed on papyrus, several Greek papyri, and a scrap of a leather scroll of Numbers.[19] Thus Aharoni was by no means denied his share of interesting discoveries, although none would suggest that they won him true glory. Together they cast a modest candle's glow at the entrance to dark corridors of the past. It was Yadin's discoveries that were to hurl fulgent beams far down those same corridors, Yadin who would claim the garland—in typical fashion, on a night that many present considered the greatest occasion of his illustrious career.

Shortly after Yadin's Expedition D arrived at Naḥal Ḥever it became clear that no new caves held any promise. With a certain air of resignation, therefore, Yadin put his crew to work in the Cave of Letters that Aharoni had explored just a few years earlier. This truly was an impressive cavern, extending back about forty-six meters into the earth, possessed of two entrances separated by a thick rock column and divided into three "halls" by narrow tunnels strewn with boulders fallen from the ceiling. On the second day a gruesome find served notice that careful exploration might yet yield significant rewards. In a small niche offshoot of Hall C a volunteer, Pinhas Prutzky, came upon a grouping of skulls placed in baskets. On the opposite end of the niche, gathered in other baskets, the jawbones and skeletons to which the skulls presumably belonged were piled together and wrapped in cloth embracing the baskets. Yadin believed that these were the remains of Bar Kokhba's warriors and their families, gathered and interred in this strange manner after the war by relatives. The similarity to Aharoni's dated find farther south, however, suggests that the bones may have received this treatment a century later at the hands of temporary occupants.

Rugs and textiles associated with the bones were among the earliest known of the Roman period. Among the textiles were tunics in relatively good condition, displaying bands (*clavi*) of varying widths that may have served, as with Roman tunics, to advertise the social rank of the ancient people they adorned. A child's linen shirt was found sufficiently intact that portions of the cloth tied off to create pockets still held herbs, spices, and seeds. The Talmud refers to such ties (קשרים); they often served young children as prophylactics and curatives.[20]

The chance discovery of a Bar Kokhba coin on the ridge outside the cave entrance led to a much more significant find that exemplified the matchless resources Yadin was able to bring to bear through his special connections. The commanding officer of the Israeli Southern Command and Yadin's longtime friend, Avraham Yoffe, visiting Yadin shortly after the coin was unearthed, suggested that the army supply the team with a military mine detector to ferret out buried coins and other metal objects. Within a day or two the mine detector arrived by helicopter and was in action, operated by two experienced technicians, and just hours later a persistent, continuous humming signaled the presence of subterranean metal. Excited but disciplined excavation shortly located a large basket secured by a palm-frond rope. Untied, the basket yielded nineteen carefully packed bronze objects: three incense shovels, various libation vessels, several bowls, keys, and, perhaps most significant, a *patera* 22.6 centimeters in diameter. At the center of this *patera* a medallion, encircled by a beaded pattern, displayed a familiar scene taken from Greek mythology: Thetis riding on a centaur, taking weapons to Achilles. Subsequent research showed that most of the objects probably derived from Capua, exact parallels being known from Pompeii and Herculaneum. Yadin believed that the revolutionaries had seized these cultic objects from a Roman unit or temple in the vicinity, but this is only one possibility. They may instead reasonably be associated with the hopes of a rebuilt Jerusalem Temple, where they were intended for use. Indeed, they may actually have served in the Second Temple, surviving the First Revolt destruction.[21] But more important than resolving this issue, for the present study at least, was Yadin's plausible deduction from the discovery: "It became clear that all these objects were deliberately packed and hidden underground. This indicated that the inhabitants of the cave at one time contemplated escape, and must have hidden their treasures in preparation for it. As we know now, their chance never came."[22] The fact of this deliberate hiding can help to unravel connections existing among the people who fled to the Cave of Letters with the objects, as we shall see. It also explains why the bedouin failed to find so much of what was in the cave.

On 3 April the great find of the first year's expeditions occurred. At the farthest remove of the cavern, the rear of Hall C, wedged tightly into a crevice between the wall of the cave and a large boulder, a goatskin bag came to light. Held loosely within it were a variety of cosmetic objects, jewelry fashioned from semiprecious stones such as carnelian and sardonyx, skeins of wool, a baby's tunic, a bronze mirror protected by a wooden case shaped like a table-tennis racket—and fifteen letters inscribed on papyrus and wood. Written in Aramaic, Hebrew, and Greek, the letters were carefully folded and secured with strings to form a bulging rectangular bundle. Yadin handled them as little as possible, gingerly lowering them into a small cardboard box. Two days later, he was in Jerusalem, seeking the assistance of James Biberkraut to open them without further damage.

Biberkraut was a preservation expert who had assisted Eliezer Sukenik, Yadin's father, in unrolling the brittle leather of the first Dead Sea Scrolls in the late 1940s. He had also worked with Yadin himself to open the badly decomposed *Genesis Apocryphon* in 1955. Now he and the archaeologist worked feverishly to separate and unfold the letters so that Yadin could decipher them at least preliminarily. Yadin's plan was to unveil the writers and contents of the missives, kept secret from everyone involved with the Judaean Desert expeditions (including the other leaders), at an evening of lectures scheduled for May at the residence of President Yitzhak Ben-Zvi.

When the evening came, a gathering of members of the Knesset, high-ranking military figures, scholars, and celebrities listened intently as each of the expedition leaders described the results of the 1960 season of excavations. Yadin, the most charismatic of the men and easily the most riveting speaker, was intentionally scheduled to speak last. His entertaining rendition of the numerous spectacular discoveries at Naḥal Ḥever was rendered mere prologue by final comments and accompanying slides. Projecting an image of the first epistle he had deciphered, Yadin read in a loud, clear voice the opening line (containing the phrase) שמעון בר כוסבה הנסי על ישראל: "Simon b. Kosiba, the 'president' [*nasi*] of Israel."[23] He then turned to Ben-Zvi and addressed him with dramatic tones, "Your Excellency, I am honored to be able to tell you that we have discovered fifteen dispatches written or dictated by the *last* president of Israel eighteen hundred years ago."[24] The audience, at first stunned, presently erupted in clamor and astonished applause. Sitting quietly were the other leaders, caught completely unawares. Aharoni's private thoughts can only be imagined.

Some of those present viewed Yadin's presentation as grandstanding, and of course they were right. But the next day Kol Israel broadcast news of the remarkable finds, and the newspapers headlined the letters and their discoverer. As Silberman has written, "It was as if a Swiss scholar had suddenly located the private papers of William Tell, or as if a British archaeologist had stumbled upon Robin Hood's personal correspondence."[25] The disinformation regarding Wadi Seiyal now had propelled Israel to discovery greatly overshadowing the Jordanian holdings, notable though they were; had allowed Yadin to triumph over his archaeological adversary; and had guaranteed a second season of Israeli excavations in the Judaean Desert.

For that season the same leaders headed a similar, four-pronged attack, although a great deal more preparation went into the logistics because of the first season's successes. Avigad and Expedition A returned to the Cave of the Pool and Naḥal David just above En Gedi. Under Aharoni the members of Expedition B were set to investigate the Cave of Horrors and the Roman siege camp above it. The Scouts' Cave in Naḥal Mishmar was the object of Bar-Adon's attentions as he led Expedition C. Yadin returned to the Cave of Letters, convinced that among the boulders, lying in their present positions since antiquity, additional hiding places might still be uncovered.

By means of new numismatic finds, Avigad's team was able to date the Roman-period occupation of the Cave of the Pool unequivocally to the time of Bar Kokhba. They deduced that an elite family from En Gedi had prepared the cave well in advance by constructing the efficient rainwater reservoir that gave the cave its name and by hauling into the cave huge *pithoi* to store food. The considerable remains suggested that the family lived in the cave for an extended period, but the absence of household articles and valuable objects seemed to mean that the fugitives survived the war and the Roman mop-up and finally left with everything worth taking. Not all of the refuge caves had become tombs.

Bar-Adon and his team found a few more very fragmentary materials from the period of the Second Revolt in the Scouts' Cave,[26] but the real treasure unearthed was an amazing hoard of more than four hundred articles dating to the Chalcolithic Period, almost all metal, but a few carved from hippopotamus tusks. Some years later a Chalcolithic temple was excavated not far away, to which archaeologists today assign these items with confidence.

Aharoni's team dug the entire Cave of Horrors down to the bedrock. This method disclosed various things the bedouin had failed to discover. Household items such as baskets, ropes, spindle whorls, gaming pieces, combs, needles, and nails came to light. Several ostraca were found near graves that the bedouin had disturbed. One was inscribed in semicursive Hebrew, שאול בן שאול שלו[ם], "Saul b. Saul; peace!" Within a nearby, undisturbed grave excavators came upon a Hebrew prayer, apparently composed in a more vernacular register of the language, rather than imitating biblical models; its extremely fragmentary condition, however, precluded certainty on this point.[27] Not far away were found thirteen small fragments of a once handsome leather scroll, most inscribed with elegant Greek lettering. These proved to be portions of the Minor Prophets scroll that Barthélemy had partially published in 1953 and so established beyond question that one of the three caves described by the French scholar had been the Cave of Horrors.[28] As a cave in Wadi Sdeir was another, the identity of only the third cave remained a question mark.[29]

Yadin's new work in the Cave of Letters soon replaced that question mark with an exclamation point. Near the newly cleared eastern entrance some fragments of papyrus with traces of Nabataean script were brought to light. Yadin wrote of them:

> These fragments . . . are of great importance in decisively corroborating the conjecture that several of the documents now in Jordan—the origin of which, according to scholars there, is "unknown"—were in fact found in the Cave of Letters. . . . Also discovered in the recess, in addition to the fragments of Nabatean deeds, was a small piece of a scroll of the Book of Numbers. . . . We may assume—as in the case of the fragment of Psalms found in the first season—that larger pieces of this scroll are now in Jordan.[30]

In this statement Yadin's skepticism regarding the postured ignorance of de Vaux, Barthélemy, Milik, Starcky, and the others was palpable. And he was completely correct in his surmise: the portions of the Book of Numbers that de Vaux had described in his initial statement ten years earlier, as well as the Psalms scroll he had referenced, have subsequently been matched with the portions Yadin discovered.[31] The identity of the third cave was now known.

On the first day of the 1961 excavations Yadin and his team made yet another spectacular discovery, comparable to that of the letters in the first year. Hidden beneath sizeable slabs of stone deliberately placed to conceal them were a basket and several water-skins, one on top of the other. The basket, itself a marvel of skilled artisanry, contained a jewelry box, wooden dishes shaped by a lathe, an iron sickle, a pair of women's sandals, several keys, and three iron knives. The left sandal of the pair was deformed, indicating that the woman had walked with a pronounced limp. Under the basket the water-skins, all badly decomposed, had let their contents slip out a bit, including a sack fastened with a twisting rope. Inside was a leather case packed tightly with papyri: the thirty-five documents of the Babatha Archive. Clearly, the sandals were also hers. Babatha b. Simon had lived with a notable disability.

Still farther down in the deposit was a fine leather purse decorated on both sides with a rosette design. Badly torn, the purse had once contained the batch of documents now strewn along the sloping bottom of the crevice. Six in number, these materials comprised the archive of Eleazar b. Samuel, including *P.Yadin* 44, the elegant Hebrew contract belonging to him with which we began this book. Since the basket, water-skins, and purse were manifestly a single deposit, one may reasonably conclude that Babatha—already twice widowed before the Bar Kokhba war broke out—had now found in Eleazar a prospective third husband, with whom she fled to the cave. Something of their stories shall occupy us shortly.

The road to publication for the principal Naḥal Ḥever texts, both those taken to the Palestine Archaeological Museum by the bedouin and those discovered by Yadin and Expedition D, proved to be long and winding. Yadin for his part almost immediately conceived a plan of publishing his final report in three volumes consisting of the nontextual archaeological finds, the texts, and a volume of plates of the documents.[32] He worked hard to bring the plan to fruition and did manage to produce the first and third of these promised books.[33] But he was never to complete the final report on the texts themselves.

Yadin started well, beginning work on the Semitic texts immediately and bringing in H. J. Polotsky to edit the Greek. In addition to the 1961–1962 summary articles in *Israel Exploration Journal* and the final report on the finds, he soon issued a historical synthesis of what he was learning in the *Jaarbericht Ex oriente lux*;[34] and, of course, he published in 1971 his popular volume *Bar-Kokhba*, which was immediately seized upon even by scholars because of its color photographs of unpublished documents. This volume contained many of his maturing ideas about the texts and their meaning. Unfortunately, for Yadin well begun was only half done. In the years following the excavations at Naḥal Ḥever, three events conspired to impede the appearance of the final report's third volume.

First, he led the excavations at Masada that became an Israeli national project in 1963–1965 and then spent time studying the materials, writing preliminary excavation reports and editing a Hebrew copy of the Wisdom of Ben Sira found there.[35] Second, with the fall of east Jerusalem and other territory to the Israelis during the 1967 Six-Day War, Yadin managed to get his hands on the principal manuscript of the *Temple Scroll*. This well-preserved and longest of the Dead Sea Scrolls had been held for many years at his home in Bethlehem by the bedouin middleman, Kando. Aware of the scroll's existence because of preliminary negotiations for its acquisition some years earlier (which had cost him $10,000), Yadin sent soldiers to Kando's home and seized it.[36] He spent the next ten years editing the complex work for publication in Modern Hebrew and then oversaw the issuing of the English *editio maior* a few years later. Third and finally, after the Yom Kippur War, politics in Israel led Yadin to reenter the center ring, and he stayed until 1981. Upon stepping away from that circus, he promptly announced that publication of the Naḥal Ḥever texts would become his scholarly priority, and so it did—but only for a short time. On 28 June 1984, at the age of sixty-seven, a seemingly healthy Yadin suddenly collapsed and died. Left in limbo were a number of significant projects, and a period of reorganization by colleagues and benefactors intent on publishing his legacy followed. Even before Yadin's death, Polotsky had withdrawn from the project of publishing the Greek materials because of his own declining health.[37] Matters needed to be reconceived from the ground up.

The Greek documents of the Babatha Archive soon devolved upon Naphtali Lewis. Lewis worked so quickly by the glacial standards that had become the norm for publication of Judaean Desert materials that his completion within five years caught the executors somewhat by surprise. Rather than wait for the Semitic texts, it was decided to publish the Greek items as a separate volume. Thus Yadin's projected volume three split to become two volumes, Lewis's *The Documents from the Bar Kokhba Period in the Cave of Letters: Greek Papyri* appearing in 1989. Reviewers were lavish in their praise of the book, which was composed of twenty-seven of the Babatha papyri.[38]

The Hebrew, Aramaic, and Nabataean texts that Yadin had discovered and to a certain degree deciphered fell initially to Joseph Naveh, doyen of Israeli epigraphers, and Jonas Greenfield, a leading philologist. They soon associated Ada Yardeni, then a doctoral student under Naveh; he reduced his own role symmetrically as hers grew. When Greenfield died unexpectedly in 1995,[39] Baruch Levine agreed to help complete the editing process, and several other eminent specialists in the fields impinged upon by the documents also lent their expertise to the final product: Hannah Cotton, who edited two Greek letters found among the Bar Kokhba *epistulae;* Geoffrey Khan, an Arabist; and Lawrence Schiffman, a scholar of rabbinics. *The Documents from the Bar Kokhba Period in the Cave of Letters: Hebrew, Aramaic and*

Nabatean-Aramaic Papyri appeared in 2002, containing thirty documents. A melancholy irony attaches to the fact that it took the wilderness texts forty years to cross the Jordan to publication. Reviewers were mostly happy simply to have them at last, and the excellence of their handling by the team that produced the volume left little of substance to criticize. As Hillel Newman commented, "The 'mere' task of deciphering and transcribing the cursive scripts in these papyri is so daunting . . . that Ada Yardeni's artful presentation of the material is nothing short of astonishing."[40]

The Ḥever texts that the bedouin had taken to the Palestine Archaeological Museum similarly took many years to reach the public eye. After the initial announcements of their discovery, and a brief flurry of publications focused upon the several texts initially released, silence descended. Ten years later Barthélemy published the *Greek Minor Prophets Scroll* after a fashion in *Les devanciers d'Aquila.* This book contained a transcription of the manuscript but was no edition in the usual sense. That task Barthélemy never completed, in 1982 ceding the text along with his notes to Emanuel Tov, a respected specialist in the Septuagint. Tov then produced a masterful edition that appeared as a volume in the series *Discoveries in the Judaean Desert.*[41] The remaining Greek materials were assigned to the Strasbourg papyrologist J. Schwartz, who died some forty years later, apparently without having taken the first step toward their publication. Publication of the Semitic texts followed a similar course of events—or perhaps better, nonevents. Milik and Starcky had charge of them and published essentially nothing over the years before the responsibility was finally transferred to others.

On one occasion Milik did break the silence. The virtuoso of the Murabbaʿat materials reported in 1956 that work on the Ḥever fragments "n'est guère avancée."[42] That same report summarized for specialists the contents of his assignment, in the process evidencing the truth of his admission: he offered almost nothing that had not already been said by de Vaux in his initial announcement. Then Milik turned his scholarly energies back to Murabbaʿat and the Dead Sea Scrolls and seems never to have returned to the Ḥever texts so hesitantly begun. Starcky, too: after publishing the preliminary edition of the Nabataean text noted above, he never published the other Nabataean materials. Privileged in addition with editing sixty-seven manuscripts of the Dead Sea Scrolls, he held the lot for thirty-five years and died without publishing any of those, either. Before he saw "the chariot of Israel and its horsemen" in 1988, he arranged for a younger colleague at the École Biblique, Émile Puech, to assume his mantle. Unfortunately, sixty years after their discovery, the remaining Nabataean texts have yet to appear in an *editio princeps*.[43]

As Starcky's texts passed to Puech, so Milik's to Greenfield. At one point, then, Greenfield was editing the Naḥal Ḥever Semitic texts of both groups, Yadin's and Milik's. When Yardeni came on board to help with the former, she simultaneously assumed the lion's share of work with the latter. Greenfield's death left the bedouin texts entirely in her hands. Three years earlier, Schwartz's moribund Greek materials had been reassigned to Cotton, and now she and Yardeni teamed to produce the single volume that would contain all of the formerly Jordanian documentary texts.[44] Their joint work, *Aramaic, Hebrew and Greek Documentary Texts from Naḥal Ḥever and Other Sites,* appeared in 1997.[45] Sandwiched between the covers of this volume were treatments of some fifty Semitic and fourteen Greek documents.[46] The publication of both groups of Naḥal Ḥever documents was at last complete.[47]

We can now return to the question that especially structured this exposition of the history of scholarship: *Which texts came from which cave?* For Yadin's discoveries the question is, of course, beside the point; but what of the bedouin discoveries? The answer now evident is that almost all of what they found derived from the Cave of Letters—an answer latent from the very beginning, actually, in Barthélemy's original characterization of the situation. Recall what he said in discussing the Second Revolt dating of the *Greek Minor Prophets Scroll:* "But during the second half of August 1952 the tireless Taʿamireh bedouin discovered within a new cave important fragments of a leather scroll that was deposited there during the Bar Kokhba Revolt. . . . This [dating] is shown with sufficient certainty by the script of small fragments of Hebraized Aramaic papyri discovered in the same cave, as well as the coins and dated documents found in two other caves very nearby." This description was precisely composed. The Frenchman said here that three caves were involved; that the cave in which the Minor Prophets scroll was found (now known as the Cave of Horrors) contained only small, undated fragments of material in the Jewish script; and that internally dated documents and coins came from two other caves, which we know today were (1) a grotto in the Wadi Sdeir (now thought to be Avigad's Cave of the Pool),[48] and (2) the Cave of Letters. But recall that the materials believed to come from Wadi Sdeir were the only ones that received an accurate attribution. These amounted to two Greek texts, a copy of Genesis, and an Aramaic contract. By process of elimination, therefore, we can deduce that Barthélemy and, presumably, the other scholars at the Palestine Archaeological

Museum believed at the time that essentially everything else they reported derived from a cave known today as the Cave of Letters. And they believed this because the bedouin told them so.

It is possible, of course, that the matter is somewhat more complicated. The tribesmen may have told only some of the truth. A few of the materials may actually have come from another cave or caves. Indeed, today we know that three of the documents eventually labeled as "Wadi Seyyal" likely emerged from another cave on the west end of Naḥal Ḥever, the Cave of the Tetradrachm.[49] But these three texts probably came to the scholars a year or more after the central descriptive statements appeared (Strugnell wrote, it will be remembered, of a process of bedouin retrieval that continued until 1954) and so impugn neither Barthélemy's 1952 portrait of the facts nor its implications. *Almost everything the bedouin produced came from the Cave of Letters.*

A small, strange detail of the story surrounding these discoveries further directs thinking to this end. When Yadin died, his executors found among his papers several fragments of *P.Hever* 61 and the whole of *P.Hever* 62, two Greek papyri later published by Cotton in DJD 27. Yadin's fragments of *P.Hever* 61 formed joins with portions that had been among the Jordanian holdings. Also among Yadin's *Nachlaß* was *P.Hever* 8, an Aramaic contract composed in Kephar-Baru. A second Kephar-Baru document, known since Milik's first publication of it as the "Kefar Bebayu Conveyance" (he misread the name), was among the first of the materials the bedouin took to the Jordanians. It was therefore embraced by Barthélemy's characterization and must have come from the Cave of Letters. Also found in Yadin's effects was a photograph, though not the text itself, of *P.Hever* 49, a Hebrew I.O.U. that can be shown to derive from En Gedi (see below).

In other words, among Yadin's papers stood a group of documents entirely lacking explanatory paperwork, all of which connect to the Cave of Letters or nearby En Gedi. The Israeli scholar doubtless obtained them either directly or indirectly from the same bedouin who had earlier dealt with de Vaux and team. What seems most likely is that Yadin seized these portions when he confiscated the *Temple Scroll* from Kando in 1967. They were of special interest to him precisely because he recognized—indeed, perhaps knew positively from Kando or others—their connection to his own discoveries in the Cave of Letters.

If it is true, then, that essentially all of the bedouin materials derived from the Cave of Letters, then the holdings of that cave were truly remarkable: more remarkable, in fact, than those of any of the Qumran caves except for Cave 4. The whole would amount to some forty-two Greek documents, seventy-one Hebrew and Jewish Aramaic documents, twelve contracts composed in Nabataean, and six literary scrolls: 131 writings.[50] They have the potential to inform this study in a myriad of ways. But as always, we first need to know, if possible, whose they were.

Archives of the Cave of Letters

We know for a fact that the Cave of Letters contained three archives carried there and hidden by Judaean refugees, because each was found in situ and intact. These are the Babatha Archive, the Archive of Eleazar b. Samuel, and the Archive of John b. Ba'yah. From the loose bedouin findings Hannah Cotton has plausibly reconstructed a fourth archive, the Archive of Salome Komaise. But after all the documents belonging to these corpora are abstracted, a considerable number of papyri found in the cave remain, scattered and disconnected in modern understanding no less than once they were on Albina's glass plates. These materials can scarcely have been as disconnected in ancient reality as they seem on initial modern inspection. They must possess interconnections. They surely belonged to one or more additional archives, for nothing else explains their presence in the cave—assuming we have now established that they did, in fact, essentially all come from that one cave, so that they are rightly regarded as a kind of "closed system" that must explain itself. Having suffered bedouin depredations like the Archive of Salome Komaise, they similarly require modern analysis with a view to reconstitution. Because many texts are very fragmentary, only tentative results are possible, numerous scraps necessarily being left to one side as lacking the essential information. Nevertheless, the historical circumstances of their deposition argue that a search for interconnections among the documentary dramatis personae is warranted. Pursued accordingly, the process seems to offer some reward, for in addition to the four archives noted, at least two others apparently emerge: one that may be labeled the Archive of Eleazar b. Eleazar, and another that one might call the Archive of the Bene ("Sons of") Hananiah.

Thus the thesis here is that *it is possible to discern a total of six archives among the deposits in the Cave of Letters.* Each calls for some comment: in the case of the four previously known, brief, focused on certain new deductions; in the case of the two newly reconstructed, more expansive, focused on explanation and defense of the decisions involved.

Since Yadin's original discovery the Babatha Archive has borne this name, but it was never fully descriptive. For along with her own many documents, Babatha held three belonging to Shelamzion, the daughter of her erstwhile husband Judah b. Khthousion by his other wife, Miriam. These documents were *P.Yadin* 18, Shelamzion's *ketubbah* or marriage contract; *P.Yadin* 19, a deed of gift that Judah bestowed upon his daughter; and *P.Yadin* 20, a renunciation of claims against Shelamzion issued by other family members not long after Judah's death. In addition, *P.Yadin* 7 was a deed of gift originally belonging to Miriam b. Joseph, Babatha's mother. Thus the so-called Babatha Archive was more precisely a family archive.

This fact must be kept in mind as one considers *P.Yadin* 8, whose inclusion has puzzled scholars because the text contains mention neither of Babatha nor of other previously established members of her family. As Hillel Newman has written, "We are still at a loss to explain the connection . . . to Babatha, and the reason for the preservation of P. Yadin 8 among her personal papers remains a mystery."[51] The matter no longer seems very mysterious, however, in light of the role frequently played by Judaean women as family archivists and given the relationships between principals and signatories that were common in general and that will unfold in specific in the pages that follow.

P.Yadin 8 records the sale of a white donkey (חמר חור) and a female animal (נקבה, perhaps a she-ass) by one brother to another. Both men bear the patronym Simon. This name was, of course, Babatha's own father's as well. Considering the evident familial character of her archive—and, too, that of Salome Komaise's (half of whose documents, it will be recalled, belonged not to her, but to other family members)—it only makes sense to suggest that these men were Babatha's brothers. As we shall see, Babatha likely had at least five brothers, several of whom served as witnesses to her documents. One of the brothers named here, Joseph b. Simon, probably also signed as a *hypographeus* in *P.Hever* 64, a papyrus belonging to Salome Komaise's papers.[52] He was apparently Salome's mother's second husband. A presumed third brother, Eleazar b. Simon, signed *P.Yadin* 8 as a witness (line 11). Thus the issue of the document's inclusion in Babatha's materials may reasonably be laid to rest.[53] This was a contract that, for reasons unknown, she now held for one of the two principals (both of whom would presumably at one time have possessed a copy).

The Archive of Eleazar b. Samuel is well defined, comprising six contracts concerned with farming in En Gedi. What has not been observed previously, but is of great interest for our purposes, is the fact that a single scribal family produced all of these contracts. Yardeni established in the *editio princeps* that the three Hebrew documents (*P.Yadin* 44–46) were the work of Joseph b. Simon. We noted above that his brothers Masabala and Sippon and his son Judah were among those who signed the contracts as witnesses and *hypographeis.* But one can go further: Eleazar b. Samuel's three Aramaic contracts also originated in the sons of Simon scribal shop in En Gedi.

The scribe of *P.Yadin* 42, in which Eleazar leased certain extremely valuable date plantations for the royal sum of 650 denarii per year, was none other than Masabala, military commander of En Gedi under Simon b. Kosiba. Masabala also penned *P.Yadin* 43, a receipt for one of Eleazar's lease payments for the same property. These documents stem from the first year of the revolt. Then, two years later, Mattat b. Simon, another member of the scribal family (who had formerly lived in Mahoza and signed there documents belonging to Babatha), scribed the sale of a vegetable garden for Eleazar (*P.Yadin* 47b).

In different publications Yardeni walked all around the edges of these suggestions for Masabala's role and Mattat's relation to him. She identified Mattat as the scribe of *P.Yadin* 47b. She further observed that he produced *P.Hever* 7 and *P.Hever* 13 (neither belonging to Eleazar b. Samuel's archive). Her discussions of *P.Yadin* 42–43 noted that one scribe was responsible for both,[54] and she even adduced, when analyzing *P.Hever* 7, that Mattat's hand was similar to the scribe's of the two Yadin papyri, commenting, "It is possible that the similarity results from a common scribal school."[55] Moreover, Yardeni remarked that the hand of Masabala b. Simon, who witnessed *P.Hever* 13, was akin to that of its writer, Mattat.[56] In short, she came very close to making the connections here proposed: Mattat and Masabala wrote with similar hands because they were brothers, presumably trained in the scribal arts by the same man, their father. During the years of the revolt, both resided in En Gedi, working in the same shop there. During the attested years before the revolt certain members of the family lived in En Gedi, others in Mahoza; Mattat was among the latter.

Eleazar b. Samuel was one of the family's good customers after the war broke out and seems to have had a special relationship with Masabala in particular. For not only did Masabala produce two of Eleazar's contracts, but he also acted as his *hypographeus* for *P.Yadin* 44, as we saw in Chapter 1. That it was Masabala who composed *P.Yadin* 42–43 (and indeed, a third document, the Hebrew *P.Yadin* 49, which belonged to the Archive of the Bene Hananiah) becomes evident upon close examination of those documents alongside his three preserved signatures (Figures 3.1–3.5). In addition to the general resemblance of the hands that strikes the reader immediately, a number of specific points are diagnostic. Perhaps the most important is the recumbent *sin/shin,* a very peculiar form that also characterizes the hands of other members of the family, including Mattat and his sons. Notably similar from text to text are the curved-back *nun*s and the left-hooked final forms of that same letter; the forms of *'ayin* and final *aleph;* the *daleth*s with very distinct pseudo-*keraia;* the forms of *peh* and *peh finale;* the squared *kaphs;*

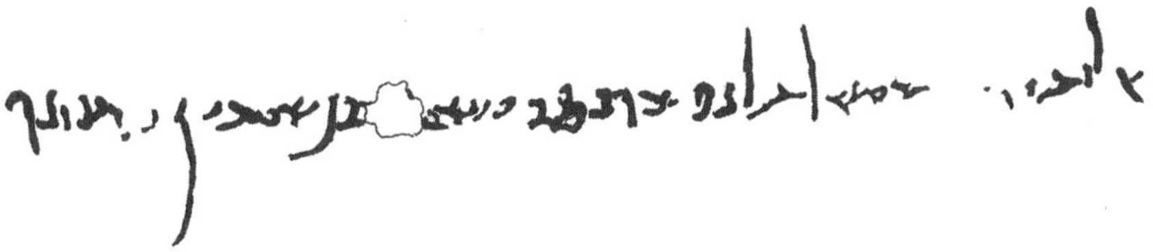

Figure 3.1. *Example of the hand of Masabala b. Simon,* P.Yadin *44:* אליעזר [בן] שמואל על נפשו כתב משבלה בן שמעון מרצונו.

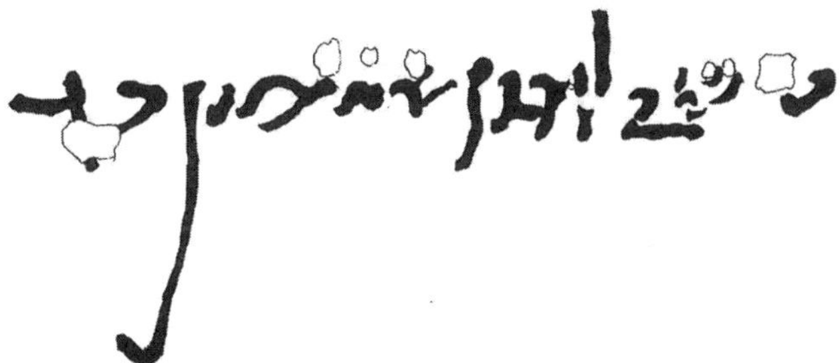

Figure 3.2. *Example of the hand of Masabala b. Simon,* P.Yadin *45:* משבלה בן שמעון עד.

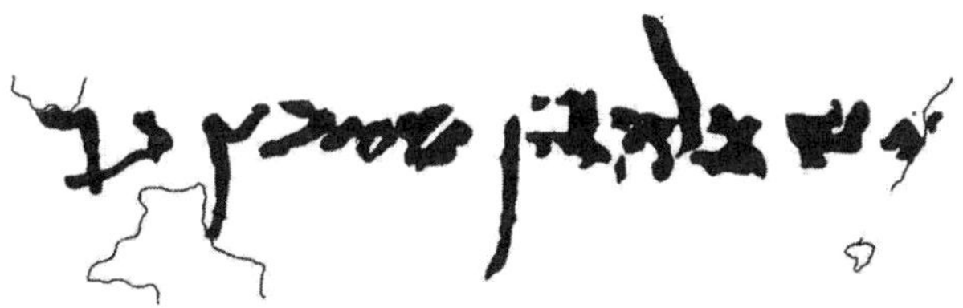

Figure 3.3. *Example of the hand of Masabala b. Simon,* P.Hever *13:* משבלה בן שמעון עד.

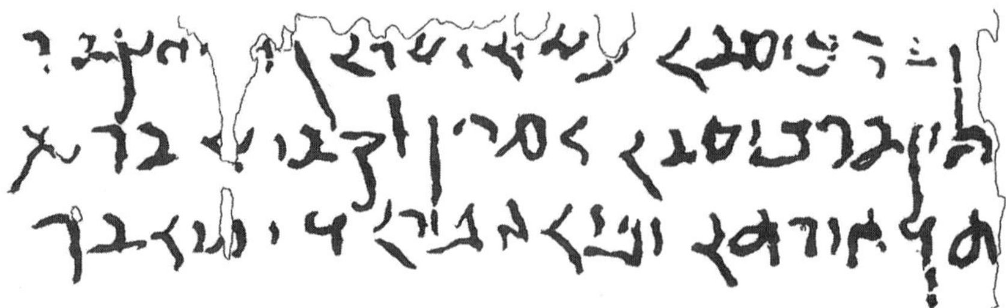

Figure 3.4. *Example of the hand of Masabala b. Simon,* P.Yadin *42 (selection, partial lines; Aramaic):*
[ו]ן בר כוסבא נשיא ישראל י[ה]וחנן בר
[ש]מעון בר כוסבא אמרין לקביש בר
]תך חורתא ופיא חפירא די הוא בר

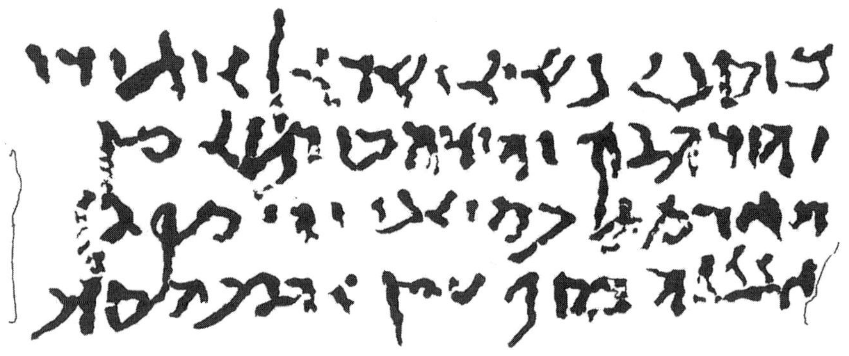

Figure 3.5. *Example of the hand of Masabala b. Simon,* P.Hever *49 (selection; Hebrew, on skin):*
כוסבא נשיא ישראל איתודי
יהודה בן יהודה סרטא מן
החרמת עמי אני יהוסף בן
חנניה כסף זוזין ארבעה סלע

and the somewhat jumbled appearance of the script. Masabala dashed these documents off quickly and carelessly. In the process he frequently manifested an idiosyncratic tendency to enlarge or extend letters at the end of a line (such as his signature) or at the end of units of meaning. One cannot miss the extremely long, curvilinear final *nun*s, for example, descending at times into the third line below.[57]

The Archive of John b. Ba'yah is strange in its contours. It consists of nothing but letters—fifteen in three languages: nine in Aramaic (*P.Yadin* 50, 53–58, 62–63), four in Hebrew (*P.Yadin* 49, 51, 60–61), and two in Greek (*P.Yadin* 52, 59). Considerable evidence indicates that John, like Masabala his co-commander and many of the other people known to us from these archives, was a person of means. Strangely missing, therefore, are the expected contracts and receipts for the purchase and sale of lands, crops, and the like. Further missing, as it seems, are the personal documents that the presumed women of his family would normally have carried, prominently their *ketubbot*. It is perhaps possible that such are actually present and simply not recognizable in the fragmentary portions from the cave that defy generic analysis. If so, however, since the letters were discovered undisturbed, this possibility would logically require two deposits by John and his family, only one of which the bedouin chanced upon. This seems an unlikely scenario. Other possibilities are that John had lost other documents in the chaos of the collapsing revolt, or that he carried other portions of his archive on his person during an attempt to break out of the cave after the Romans encamped above. Of course, John himself may never have been in the cave, and the documents likewise. Female members of the family are perhaps more likely final occupants and carriers. (Recall that his archive was found among a woman's effects in a goatskin bag.) The absence of expected documents is not limited to John's situation in any case. Materials are missing from Babatha's archive as well, and from Eleazar b. Samuel's (where are the lease receipts for the remaining monies due for Year One, and everything for Years Two and Three of the revolt?). In fact, as a matter of method we should avoid the assumption that all theoretically relevant documents for any particular point of inquiry have come to our hands. They may not merely have perished; they may—for reasons opaque at this remove—never even have existed.

The entrée for the reconstruction of an Archive of Eleazar b. Eleazar is the problem posed by *P.Yadin* 36, often known as *Papyrus Starcky*. Of the numerous bedouin-discovered Nabataean documents assigned to Jean Starcky in the 1950s, this was the sole text that the French Aramaist succeeded in bringing to print.[58] The question is, "To whom in the Cave of Letters did it belong?" The need to account for its presence in the cave, taken together with certain other evidences, leads logically to the present proposal.

In 2001 Ada Yardeni produced a fine new edition of *P.Yadin* 36 in which she joined several new fragments and offered improved readings and a clearer understanding of the legal situation described and implied by the text.[59] Her analysis of the latter was as follows. In 43 C.E. Nicarchus b. Neboma and his brother Buni, resident in Mahoza, having borrowed money from one Isimilik, owed him 400 *sela,* principal and interest. They had pledged as hypothec for the loan two stores and the cells within them (חנותא ותוניא די גוא מנהם), located in the agora, together with a palm grove (גנת תמריא) and its irrigation ditches. When they proved unable to repay the loan, Isimilik had a writ of seizure issued and took control of the property. By the time of *P.Yadin* 36, composed between 58 and 67, Nicarchus and Buni had died and Eleazar b. Nicarchus, heir to both men, had come to Isimilik to redeem the earlier writ and take the property back into the family fold. *P.Yadin* 36 is, then, the redemption of a writ of seizure. A *Doppelurkunde,* it once bore the signatures of at least five witnesses, but only one survives and is legible. That one signature, however, is possibly fortuitous, and critical to potential historical understanding. Written by an experienced hand in the Jewish semicursive of the time, it reads יהֹוסף בר יהודה כֹּ]תבה, "Joseph b. Judah hereby wi[tnesses]."[60]

Some seventy years later the palm grove redeemed by Eleazar b. Nicarchus apparently reappears as the γαννὰθ Νίκαρκος in *P.Yadin* 21 and *P.Yadin* 22, two Greek documents belonging to Babatha's archive.[61] (The grove is referenced by its Aramaic name, simply transliterated, so that Νίκαρκος does not decline.) Babatha has distrained the grove, formerly property of her deceased second husband, Judah b. Eleazar Khthousion, in lieu of dowry and debt monies that Judah's family owes her from his estate. The matter is under litigation reflected in these papyri. Yadin recognized the likely identity of the palm grove referenced in these three documents as early as 1962, opining, "In the course of time this garden [mentioned in Starcky's Nabataean text] came into the possession of Judah ben Elazar, Babata's second husband, and after his death, into that of Babata, in addition to other gardens."[62] G. W. Bowersock went a bit further in his 1991 review of Lewis's publication of the Greek portions of Babatha's materials: "A Jew by the name of Eleazar records a claim to property, and Eleazar's father bears the hellenic [*sic*] name of Nicarchus. These details for so small a place as Maoza and the likelihood that the text was abstracted from Babatha's cave make it certain that Nicarchus and his son Eleazar are related to Babatha's second husband. He was himself the son of an Eleazar."[63] Bowersock went beyond Yadin in drawing two inferences. First, he stipulated the manner by which the palm grove came to be a part of Babatha's husband's estate: he had inherited it. This was a reasonable inference, and likely to be right. But Bowersock's second inference was less felicitous. He seemed to imply with his wording that the Eleazar b.

Nicarchus of *P.Yadin* 36 should be identified with Judah b. Eleazar's father. This would mean, of course, that Judah's grandfather would be Nicarchus. Yet we know that Judah's grandfather was actually named Judah; evidently he had himself been named for this grandfather by the process of papponymy. The genealogy is explicit at *P.Yadin* 20:7–8, 27–28. Bowersock just overlooked this link, as it seems, if his words here are rightly understood.

Judah must have had a pair of Eleazars in the recent branches of his family tree, not just one. The first would be his father, Eleazar Khthousion b. Judah. The other would be the Eleazar b. Nicarchus of *P.Yadin* 36. Babatha's husband inherited the grove from his father, Eleazar Khthousion; but how had Khthousion himself obtained it? What was his relationship to Eleazar b. Nicarchus? Likely this man was his uncle, his father Judah's brother, and the man who had borne his own name in his father's generation (for in this culture names frequently recycled in families generation after generation).[64] As Eleazar b. Nicarchus had inherited from both a father and an uncle, so evidently his namesake, Eleazar Khthousion. The property listed in *P.Yadin* 36 passed to him from his agnate uncle. The proposed tie is drawn tighter by the lone surviving signature on *P.Yadin* 36, belonging as noted to Joseph b. Judah—none other, it seems, than another son of Khthousion's father: thus, the latter's brother, serving to witness a family transaction as is so common in these contracts. (For visual clarity on the proposed relationships, see Figure 3.6 below.)

These considerations both sharpen the focus and intensify the puzzle of the question we are pursuing regarding *P.Yadin* 36. To whom in the Cave of Letters did it belong? If the palm grove it mentions came ultimately to belong to Babatha, then was this Nabataean text part of her archive? Cotton and Yardeni originally thought so.[65] But the problem with this idea is obvious. Babatha's archive was found in situ, tied with twisted ropes. How could the bedouin have extracted a text from an ostensibly undisturbed archive; and even if that were possible, why would they want to do so, leaving the rest of the documents? Clearly, they did neither. For the connection to Babatha to be correct, a second deposit by Babatha would be necessary, one that the bedouin found. The suggestion is no more plausible in her case than was the similar notion with John b. Baʿyah above.

Yardeni evidently gave this problem more serious consideration in the four years intervening between her joint work with Cotton and her new edition of *P.Yadin* 36. She now offered a new analysis: "There is no information about the way in which the grove came into Yehuda's possession, but there is no reason to believe that *P.Yadin* 36 is part of the Babatha archive."[66] We cannot know how Babatha's husband obtained the grove, Yardeni now opined. In a note she then took issue with Bowersock's proposal that Judah inherited it from Eleazar b. Nicarchus. "[He] need not have inherited the palm grove; he could have bought it."[67] Perhaps; but her objection was really beside the point. For however Judah got the grove, either by inheritance or purchase, he evidently did get the grove. Therefore, why was *P.Yadin* 36 not a part of Babatha's archive—as, certainly, it was not? She had the property; why not the documentation?[68]

Here it is well to reintroduce a fact that has gotten lost in the scholarly discussion of this text. The property included more than a grove. It also included two stores. Hence a division of the property listed might well have occurred among the relevant heirs, in which Eleazar Khthousion distributed the grove to his son Judah, and *someone else received the stores.* That *P.Yadin* 36 was not part of Babatha's archive yet was found in the Cave of Letters reveals that another heir of Eleazar Khthousion (or at least someone holding that heir's papers) must have been in the cave. This person's archive included *P.Yadin* 36 because the possession of this document proved his or her ownership of the stores. In other words, the puzzle of *P.Yadin* 36 instigates a search for a missing relative of Judah b. Eleazar.[69] The contention here is that the missing person was named Eleazar b. Eleazar.[70] And he is not really missing at all. He has merely been overlooked.

We clearly encounter Eleazar b. Eleazar in *P.Yadin* 15, a deposition composed in Greek in which Babatha accuses the guardians of her orphan son, Jesus b. Jesus, of embezzling funds from the monies they controlled on his behalf. By this time (October 125 C.E.) Babatha had remarried, and her new husband, Judah b. Eleazar Khthousion, acted for the purposes of this document as her transactional guardian. Accordingly, when it came time for Babatha to subscribe the deposition, he could not also serve as her *hypographeus,* although he played this role for her in other documents. The man who did now sign was Eleazar b. Eleazar, and both his name and his role suggest a family connection. Toma b. Simon, likely Babatha's brother, and Jesus b. Jesus, a relative of hers by marriage (Figure 3.6), were among the witnesses, so family participation is otherwise evident. In subscribing the document, Eleazar wrote Greek, relatively uncommon in these documents, and did so with a practiced hand. He was apparently a literary literate in the language, therefore, although by literary standards his Greek was a bit subpar in its orthography and case usage. He penned: Ἐλεάζαρος Ἐλεαζάρου ἔγραψα ὑπὲρ αὐτῆς ἐρωτηθεὶς διὰ τὸ αὐτὴς[!] μὴ ἐδένα γράμματα (At her request, Eleazar the son of Eleazar wrote for her because she does not know letters).[71] Given his patronym and the prominence of the name Eleazar in the family genealogy as it can be reconstructed, this man was almost certainly the brother of Babatha's husband.

Confidence in this conclusion increases in light of *P.Yadin* 10, Babatha's *ketubbah* for her marriage with Judah b. Eleazar. Composed by the groom himself some time between about 123 and 125 (the date has not survived), this document shows that Babatha was wealthy indeed. Her dowry is four times the amount prescribed by the Mishnah as the norm for Judaean free women.[72] Signing the marriage contract is again Babatha's brother Toma b. Simon, along with a certain PN b. Yohanan, a third witness whose name is no longer legible, and, it seems, Eleazar b. Eleazar. As in *P.Yadin* 15, Eleazar acts as Babatha's *hypographeus,* and this in a document intrinsic to the intimacies of Jewish family life and therefore most likely to involve family members. The language of the contract is Aramaic, and Eleazar signs in the same tongue, once again with a practiced hand. He was evidently triliterate: Greek, Aramaic, and Hebrew. His signature is damaged, and Yardeni did not read the name in the *editio princeps,* but sufficient—and critical—letters survive, so as to give reasonable confidence in the reading: [22][בב]תא [ברת] שׁמ[עון] עׄל נפשׁהׄ [23][כת]בׄ אל[עזר] בׄרׄ אלעׄ [זר] ב[ ]ׄם מׄמׄרׄ[ה], "[Bab]atha [b.] Sim[on] hereby (witnesses) concerning herself; Ele[azar] b. Elea[zar wro]te . . . at her dictation."[73]

Thus, it is certain that an Eleazar b. Eleazar with connections to Babatha existed: probable brother and potential co-heir of Judah, likely brother-in-law of Babatha. Of course, his mere existence is not enough. We need to put him rather than some other relative in the Cave of Letters with Babatha, and to do that more is required than inference based on *P.Yadin* 36. We need documents that include his name or are otherwise plausibly connected to him personally. These documents should be sought among the loose materials unearthed by the bedouin, whence derived *P.Yadin* 36. For the hypothesis must be that the bedouin found and plundered an archive containing *P.Yadin* 36 and, potentially, other documents. The Archive of Eleazar b. Eleazar, if it existed, will need to be identified and reconstructed from the Ḥever papyri.

One may well begin with the Aramaic *P.Hever* 8a. This document was one of the initial batch of "Wadi Seiyal" materials, and Milik brought it to print in 1954. Subsequent scholarship has greatly improved his original readings and translation, culminating in Yardeni's treatment in DJD 27.[74] In this writ, dated to Year Three of the era of Simon b. Kosiba (i.e., 134–135), a certain Hadad b. Judah sells a house, but not the contiguous courtyard, to an Eleazar b. Eleazar. Given the undoubted association of this document with *P.Yadin* 36—both emerging from the same cave, peddled by the same bedouin traders, in the same early batch of materials in 1952—the identification of this Eleazar with the brother of Babatha's Judah seems highly likely. Strengthening this identification is the signature of one of the witnesses, presumably the vendor Hadad's brother. His name is Judah b. Judah. His presence here strengthens the proposed identification because his signature also appears on a document in Babatha's archive, *P.Yadin* 26, prepared four years earlier in Mahoza.[75] That the same witness would sign documents belonging both to Babatha and to the Eleazar b. Eleazar before us, in two different villages separated by a journey of a hundred kilometers, can hardly be coincidence. Given the role of family members in ancient contracts generally, one must strongly suspect that these three people were related.[76]

With *P.Hever* 8a ten years have passed since Babatha's marriage to Judah in Mahoza, and Eleazar no longer inhabits that town. He (and Judah b. Judah) now reside in Kephar-Baru in the Peraea (see Figure 1.1). Moreover, line 3 informs us that Eleazar is מן תמן, "from there": this town was his ἰδία, his legal place of origin. So we discover that he had always been an alien in Mahoza. Then, in line 2 the scribe annotates Eleazar as שטרא, "adjutant." This term may shed a good deal of light on the man, which in turn may help to assign to his archive additional documents found in the cave. Accordingly, the word requires some discussion.

The origins of שטר in both Jewish Aramaic and in Biblical Hebrew are disputed, some scholars arguing that the term was a borrowing from Akkadian, others that it was a Northwest Semitic cognate of the Mesopotamian word. Actually, the matter is complicated, evidence suggesting that according to which dialect of Northwest Semitic is in view, and depending on whether one focuses on nominal forms or on verbal, שטר may have been both a loanword and a cognate.[77] For our purposes we can note that the usage in our text appears to be verbal (*peal* participle, *status emphaticus* masculine singular); observe that, practically speaking, the verb is known only in Aramaic dialects that were in contact with Hebrew;[78] leave the etymological ins and outs to others; and focus on attested usage in Judaean texts.

In Biblical Hebrew only the participial form of שטר is attested, but it is common, used as a title. Officials so designated were associated with the management of local affairs by "the elders of the city" (e.g., Deut 16:18).

Conventionally translated "officers," שטרים were probably the actual executives of any given community. The method of communal organization described in the biblical texts carried over into the postexilic period and extended, probably, all the way into the Roman era.[79] In addition to other responsibilities, these "officers" had particular wartime functions. These functions, too, explicitly carried over into Hellenistic and Roman times. An example is 1 Macc 5:42: ὡς δὲ ἤγγισεν Ιουδας ἐπὶ τὸν χειμάρρουν τοῦ ὕδατος, ἔστησεν τοὺς γραμματεῖς τοῦ λαοῦ ἐπὶ τοῦ χειμάρρου καὶ ἐνετείλατο αὐτοῦς λέγων Μὴ ἀφῆτε πάντα ἄνθρωπον παρεμβαλεῖν, ἀλλὰ ἐρχέσθωσαν πάντες εἰς τὸν πόλεμον (And as Judah came to the stream of water, he stationed there certain officers of the army, commanding them, "Don't allow anyone to camp here; they must all come to the battle"). As Jonathan Goldstein has observed, the Greek γραμματεῖς τοῦ λαοῦ here probably translates an original Hebrew שטרי העם.[80] These officials stayed the faint-hearted from retreat before battle. The same portrayal appears in the *War Scroll* (1QM) 10:5–6: ו[ש]וטרינו ידברו לכול עתודי המלחמה נדיבי לב להחזיק בגבורת אל ולשיב ,כול מסי לבב, "And our [o]fficers shall speak to all those ready for battle, the willing-hearted, to the end that they hold fast to God's power, and to the end that the faint-hearted be stayed from flight." In his magisterial commentary on this idealized manual for eschatological holy war, Yadin surveyed the work's several other uses of שטר (which his translators rendered by the quaintly Victorian "provost") and compared them with the relevant passages in the Hebrew Bible. The Israeli archaeologist and general then concluded, "A review of the provosts' duties in the O.T. proves that they were equivalent to the adjutant general's branch and the adjutancy in today's armies, dealing with conscription problems, matters of law and order, transmission of orders, and supervising their execution."[81]

Given that as a verb שטר is virtually nonexistent in the Aramaic dialects apart from those in contact with Hebrew, the term may fairly be considered a lexical Hebraism in *P.Hever* 8a. In this connection one should add that the scribe of this text, John b. Eli, was also the scribe of *P.Hever* 8, composed in both Aramaic and Hebrew; so he knew the language of the term's origin.[82] As a Hebraism, שטרא presumably carried with it some measure of the military semantics its use in biblical and postbiblical Hebrew texts displays. In other words, Eleazar was an official of some sort in Kephar-Baru, and more narrowly, his responsibilities were at least partially military. At the time of the Second Revolt such can only mean that he had been placed in authority by Simon b. Kosiba. If so, Eleazar was an important man, a leader in the revolt, like Masabala b. Simon and John b. Ba῾yah in En Gedi and Jesus b. Galgula in Herodium. One might reasonably look, then, for his involvement in correspondence with Bar Kokhba in the manner of his co-commanders. As it happens, among the Ḥever papyri are found at least one, and possibly two letters.

P.Hever 30 is a badly effaced but essentially complete dispatch intended for Simon b. Kosiba, sent by an otherwise unknown Simon b. Mattaniah.[83] As the only surviving letter intended for, rather than coming from, the leader of the revolt, *P.Hever* 30 is naturally of great interest and will engage us at more length in Chapter 4. The Hebrew letter reports some bad news and suggests that the revolt was collapsing in the region whence it came. Among other things, Simon b. Mattaniah informs b. Kosiba that certain Gentiles who had previously been elsewhere—perhaps under another commander, now dead—have gathered or hidden in his vicinity (כנפו בי הגאים), some with him personally, others in a nearby town (בישוב).

On the verso of the letter an address tag survives, but barely, so effaced that it can be read only with considerable difficulty. The tag is composed of two names, that of the addressee (Simon b. Kosiba, written as לשעמון, "to Simon"), and that of an ostensible carrier. Yardeni noted, "With difficulty the first name may be read as אליעזר [Eliezer], rendering a different name than the sender."[84] She was sufficiently uncertain of this reading, however, that she printed only אל°°°°, and in fact one might also read אלעֿזֿרֿ, Eleazar. Fortunately, the distinction makes no difference: these were bi-forms of the same name, each demonstrably being used at different times for the selfsame individual.[85]

The connection of this letter to Eleazar b. Eleazar, if rightly inferred, argues that the letter was never delivered. For considering that *P.Hever* 30 somehow wound up in the Cave of Letters, the most natural interpretation of the facts would be that Eleazar was entrusted with delivering this letter to Simon b. Kosiba as an aspect of his military function in Kephar-Baru. Perhaps the revolt in the region of Kephar-Baru collapsed more rapidly, more completely than either Simon b. Mattaniah or Eleazar had expected, the hopelessness of the situation making itself fully apparent even as Eleazar was about to set out. Rather than deliver the missive, Eleazar elected to flee to the caves near En Gedi to try to save himself and his family. Equally possible is that word of Bar Kokhba's defeat at Betar reached Eleazar and precipitated the flight to the caves. In any event it seems clear that the letter was undelivered, for one would not expect a courier, as opposed to the sender, to retain a record-keeping copy. *P.Hever* 30 may with good reason be attached to Eleazar's archive.

Much more tentatively *P.Hever* 36 might be pondered as a possible second letter belonging to the archive.[86] In truth, it is uncertain whether this exceedingly fragmentary papyrus, comprising just the top margin, a single word on the first line (כוסבה, "Kosiba"), and a single letter on the second, is an epistle at all. The name Kosiba might equally derive from the date formula of a legal text. What can be offered more confidently is that the fragment derives from a Hebrew, not an Aramaic writing. No Aramaic legal writ in the materials of this study, whether from Murabbaʿat, En Gedi, Mahoza, or Kephar-Baru, was indited in a bookhand, whereas *P.Hever* 36 presents finely wrought, almost calligraphic lettering. During the period of the Second Revolt these sorts of hands are known only in Hebrew texts, though in both letters (e.g., *Mur* 46) and contracts (e.g., *P.Yadin* 44–46).[87] One can simply note the possibility that we have here a letter, adduce the derivative point that a Bar Kokhba letter would more likely attach to Eleazar than to any other figure whose name appears in the loose fragments of the Cave of Letters, and turn to another text in search of surer ground in defining Eleazar's possible archive.

With *P.Hever* 22 we find such ground, quite literally: this is a deed of sale involving land, and perhaps additional items on the property. The land was located in Kephar-Baru, for Judah b. Judah, the signatory to *P.Hever* 8a whom we discussed above, signed as a witness here as well. *P.Hever* 8a, it will be recalled, was explicitly contracted in Kephar-Baru. A second signatory to that contract, Simon b. Joseph, signs here, too. Moreover, a third witness, Yohanan b. Joseph, supplemented his signature with the phrase בכׄ[פר ברו, "in Ke[phar Baru." Careful study of the damaged papyrus shows that Eleazar b. Eleazar was the vendor in the transaction, selling to a Simon b. PN. This conclusion emerges by combination of two readings with a fact. The first reading is in line 7, אנהׄ אלע֯ז֯ר֯ לשמעון ("I, Eleazar, to Simon"). The second reading appears in the second signature on the verso of the contract, [אלעזר בר] אלע[זר על נפשה, "Eleazar b.] Elea[zar hereby (witnesses) concerning himself."[88] The fact: the first and second signatures on this type of *Doppelurkunde* were regularly those of the principals. The fact warrants combining the readings, the personal name of line 7 with the patronym of the principal. Fortifying the identification of this contract's Eleazar as our man is the surviving *lamedh* of אלע[זר here, the bookhand form of which is unusual in a semicursive script—unusual, yet identical with the form used by the Eleazar who signed Babatha's marriage contract (*P.Yadin* 10). Thus, a number of small details add up to a reasonable case for associating *P.Hever* 22 with the Archive of Eleazar b. Eleazar.

A sixth text possibly belonging to Eleazar's archive is *P.Hever nab* 2, the Nabataean contract that Yardeni published in a preliminary analysis, although it still awaits its *editio princeps* at the hands of Starcky's successor, Émile Puech.[89] In this deed of sale, dated by Yardeni to circa 100 C.E., a certain Salome sells property "by inheritor's right and by permission" to a Nabataean, Shaadilahi. Ill-defined, owing to the fragmentary state of the relevant lines of the papyrus, the property included wet and dry wood and ground along with sunny and shady areas. It may therefore have been located near the swamp mentioned in other texts from Mahoza. Salome did not sign for herself; she being illiterate, the scribe signed for her, in Nabataean Aramaic. Oddly and exceptionally, no patronym accompanies her personal name. Two other signatures are partially preserved, both the signatures of witnesses, both in the Jewish script. The first is composed of just a few legible letters. The second is the interesting one, more legible, though still uncertain in its reading. It is inscribed in a practiced hand, and one can tentatively make out אׄ[ל]עׄז[ר ב]רׄ יה[ו]דה כתבה, "Eleazar b. Judah hereby witnesses."[90] This might well be the signature of Eleazar Khthousion b. Judah, the father of Babatha's Judah. The text's dating to the turn of the century would fall within his presumed floruit, given that Babatha's archive shows his son's to have been a generation later, at about 120 C.E. Salome perhaps would have been a female member of Judah b. Eleazar's family, her very existence otherwise unsuspected.

P.Hever nab 2 would then align itself with *P.Yadin* 36, the other published Nabataean text from among the loose bedouin materials—signed, it will be recalled, by a Joseph b. Judah, best seen as Khthousion's brother. If correctly perceived, this alignment creates a strong presumption that all of the remaining unpublished Nabataean materials, *P.Hever nab* 3–6, likewise belong to this same grouping of materials: all within the Archive of Eleazar b. Eleazar.[91] Of course, bearing in mind that history and logic do not always get along very well, only the long-awaited full publication of the remaining papyri can confirm or confute this inference.

Possibly to be viewed as the final components of the Archive of Eleazar b. Eleazar are three documents that evidently did not belong to him personally. All three seem instead to find their nexus in one John b. Eli. The first we have already briefly encountered, *P.Hever* 8, a deed of sale composed in both Aramaic (the upper text) and Hebrew (the lower text).[92] John himself authored this document, just as he also composed *P.Hever* 8a, which belonged to Eleazar b. Eleazar. Thus John was a fellow resident of Kephar-Baru who knew Eleazar and wrote for him, as well as for himself. What requires explanation is the presence of John's own texts in the Cave of Letters.

Straightforwardly one could, of course, simply posit him as another one of the cave's residents in time of emergency. Perhaps as a friend of Eleazar he fled with him to the cave, carrying with him his own small archive that the bedouin found and rescued two millennia later. This possibility cannot be disproved. But a more elegant solution to the problem posed, because it both reduces the number of archives requiring reconstruction and also accords with the patterns for archiving them that we have seen were common in that culture, is to imagine that John had an unknown sister, PN b. Eli, who was married to Eleazar (so Figure 3.6). She would then be the archivist of the texts belonging to both men. As did Salome Komaise and Babatha, she would have held materials belonging both to her husband and to a brother. If this understanding is correct, then in addition to *P.Hever* 8, the daughter of Eli perhaps also carried *P.Hever* 10, a mutilated receipt belonging to a John, and *P.Hever* 26, a similarly fragmentary writ concerning barley, scribed by her brother John.[93]

In sum, the Archive of Eleazar b. Eleazar appears as a considerable and varied group of texts, possibly belonging to two men and held by a woman. The surviving evidence for its contours as laid out in the foregoing pages varies in its quality as in its quantity. Accordingly, the inclusion of some texts is more confident than that of others, just as some proposed connections are clearer than others. If nevertheless all of the suggested materials did belong to this collection, then Eleazar's archive assumes a profile similar to Babatha's in its richness: thirteen papyri, composed in three languages: Aramaic (*P.Hever* 8 [top], *P.Hever* 8a, *P.Hever* 10, *P.Hever* 22, and *P.Hever* 26), Nabataean (*P.Yadin* 36 and *P.Hever nab* 2–6), and Hebrew (*P.Hever* 8 [bottom], *P.Hever* 30, and *P.Hever* 36). Like Babatha's, this archive included writ from two villages distant from each other, texts likewise spanning multiple decades. The earliest component would be *P.Yadin* 36, dating to about 60; *P.Hever* 8, dating to the latter part of the third year of Simon b. Kosiba, so to 135, would be the latest. What is more, unlike Babatha's, the reconstituted Archive of Eleazar b. Eleazar would embrace Bar Kokhba correspondence alongside legal documents, in this distinctive resembling most the Archive of the Bene Galgula from Herodium.

Naturally, it is not essential to the basic thesis here proffered that all of these materials belonged to Eleazar's archive. All that need stand is the recognition that he or his archivist, holding some portion of the suggested papyri, was in the Cave of Letters with Babatha and twenty-odd other refugees. A great deal is explained if it does stand.

The fifth proposed archive of the Cave of Letters is that of the Bene Hananiah. It possesses an interest out of all proportion to its modest size. Although only two texts can be assigned to it with any degree of confidence, both are noteworthy, no less for general historical understanding than for the issues of this study. The clearest entrée to their consideration is actually through a third text that does not even belong to this archive, but to Babatha's; and it was not Babatha's own document, but rather belonged to Shelamzion, daughter of Babatha's second husband, Judah, and his other wife, Miriam b. Baʿyah of En Gedi.

On 5 April 128, in the village of Mahoza, the scribe Tehinah b. Simon composed Shelamzion's *ketubbah, P.Yadin* 18, writing it out in Greek. From a scribal standpoint this is one of the most complex and fascinating documents found in the Judaean caves, for nine separate individuals took part in various roles. The principals were Shelamzion's father, Judah, and the man to whom he had agreed to give her in marriage, the En Gedite Judah Cimber b. Hananiah b. Somala. Signing as witnesses were two other men bearing the patronym Hananiah, Simon and Joseph. They were almost certainly the groom's brothers. Both dwelled just this side of the divide separating literacy from illiteracy: βραδέως γράφοντες. Despite what might seem a dubious equipping for the task, one of these brothers, Joseph, served repeatedly in the Babatha Archive as a witness, laboriously scrawling the letters of his name on six separate occasions for her or her father. He also affixed his misspelled signature (יוהסף בר חנניה; it was nearly always thus) to one of the papyri in the Salome Komaise Archive, *P.Hever* 64. The earliest document on which Joseph b. Hananiah's name appears as witness is *P.Yadin* 6, which dates to 119. So by the time of Shelamzion's wedding, his family and Babatha's had known each other for at least a decade. Just shy of a decade hence, members of the two families would come together in a refuge cave. This contract helps explain why they would be together. They were, in fact, one family, intermarried.

If Joseph and Simon were challenged when it came to the art of the stylus, their brother the groom was not even in the contest. He could not write at all, although the fact has escaped scholarly notice. What happened when it came time for Judah Cimber to sign and subscribe the marriage contract is remarkably instructive for the interests of this study, and justifies a bit of a digression at this point.

At the bottom of the Greek contract both Judah Khthousion and Judah Cimber subscribed in Aramaic, verifying the contents of the Greek (more precisely, *establishing*—for the subscription actually effected the contract, as it stated the agreement of the principals). Beneath their subscriptions, the scribe signed, then the principals and the witnesses added their signatures. Just beneath Cimber's labored signature, יהודה קׄנׄבר כׄת[ב]יה,[94] a cryptic and badly damaged Greek phrase appears, inscribed in a hand different from that of the scribe. According to Lewis, it reads, . .[. . .] . . . τιτος χειρ——.[95] Annotating the reading, Lewis wrote, "The raised horizontal line appears to be a concluding flourish rather than a sign of abbreviation."[96] Cotton, however, offered a slightly different reading, . . . [. . .]τιτος χειρ——, and took the opposite view of the flourish: it was indeed a sign of abbreviation, concluding the Greek χειρ(οχρήστης).[97] She appears to be correct, for the letters preceding the flourish cannot be construed—she and Lewis agreed on this point—as μάρ(τυς). Lewis offered no suggestion for integrating this line of Greek into the list of signatures, and he left it untranslated.[98] This treatment is entirely understandable, for he had no reason to suspect that it was an abbreviation for χειροχρήστης: Cotton's article on the term in *P.Hever* 61, where it is written out in full, did not appear until six years later. In that article she demonstrated that the use in the Ḥever papyri is the earliest in surviving Greek, antedating by two centuries its next earliest documented occurrence, in the Neoplatonist philosopher Iamblichus (*VP* 161).[99] But like Lewis, Cotton made no suggestion for understanding what the Greek meant in context.

Yet the meaning is plain. What can be read besides the abbreviation is the remnant of a Greek patronym, the genitive of a third-declension name whose nominative ended in -τις, being formed from a stem terminating in the dental τ. An example of such a name for a Judaean would be Θάτις, known from Josephus and 1 Maccabees.[100] This person signed for Judah Cimber. Since the line occurs just beneath Cimber's name, he is the natural referent for the notation. Cimber could not sign, so a *hypographeus* signed for him. The phenomenon, as we have seen, was exceedingly common. Yet from this particular instance emerge several noteworthy points regarding language and literacy.

For one thing, it becomes clear that Cimber knew no Greek. He was not merely illiterate in the language; neither could he speak it. For if the point of the subscription were merely to affirm in writing that Cimber agreed with the foregoing contents of the contract, that could have been done in Greek, the language that the *hypographeus* wrote easily and flowingly. Instead, he produced a version of Cimber's agreement in a twisted and tortured version of the Jewish semicursive. Fluid when writing Greek, in attempting Aramaic the *hypographeus* was transformed into a βραδέως γράφων. The imperative motivating his hackneyed production can only be that he conceived his role as representing Cimber's own *speech,* as opposed to his mere assent. And he could not represent Cimber's speech writing Greek.

If this understanding is correct, then it would seem to follow that for these ancients the subscription encoded, more or less literally, legal "verbal assent." Accordingly, writers were constrained to inscribe a person's words in something approaching a spoken register, echoing the very words used. Unlike legal diction in general, therefore, the subscriptions potentially present us with fairly straightforward evidence of spoken language (potentially: the matter is complicated by the likelihood that people were often expressing verbally the gist of legal formulae as prompted by the scribe). This inference will come around for inspection again in Chapter 4, when we consider distinctions of dialect in the languages that the Judaeans of this period spoke and wrote.

Another thing: the phenomenon here before us, a Jewish scribe writing Greek easily while being nearly illiterate in Semitic, demonstrates that Judaean scribes were not necessarily trained in Aramaic before tackling Greek. Prima facie this might have been a reasonable suspicion, but here is hard evidence. We have pointed in Chapter 2 to other evidence tending in that same direction, and we also noted there that the inference might well apply to people other than scribes: indeed, to anyone deciding on education for literacy. One need only recall the Jerusalemites Cleopas and Eutrapelus, the sons of Eutrapelus. What begins to emerge, it seems, is a culture of "alternative literacies." People possessing sufficient funds and leisure to invest in an education would choose either Greek or Semitic, but not often both. This choice, so far as we can tell at this point, was based at least as much on pragmatic considerations as on ideology. We shall explore this issue, too, more fully below.

Returning for the present to the case of Judah Cimber, a bit more needs to be said. For here we have a son of an extremely wealthy Judaean family—Shelamzion presents him with a dowry 20 percent larger than Babatha's had been—who was illiterate in every language. Moreover, judging by their hands, his brothers Joseph and Simon, though they could sign their names, were no more capable than Cimber when it came to dealing with a scroll of the Jewish scriptures. This is a fact of more than merely "religious" import (to make for a moment a purely modern distinction). It would also seem significant for Judaean politics that men of this ilk—the leaders of village society by virtue of birth or money—could not deal firsthand with the foundational texts of the Jewish polity.[101] Potent in some ways, they were dependent in others, things that weighed heavily in the life of Roman Judaea. And we shall see that the Bene Hananiah were not isolated members of the upper class in these regards. What is more, Cimber was not simply illiterate, incapable of writing or reading Greek. Neither could he (nor his brothers?) speak the language of the overlords, with whom, as a member of the elite, he would have had at least occasional, potentially significant, dealings. We must then begin to wonder how the leaders of village life viewed the acquisition of Greek.

If on the one hand Cimber could not speak Greek, on the other he likely could speak a vernacular dialect of Hebrew. The foundation for this statement is *P.Hever* 49, the first of two extant papyri that belonged, so it seems, to the Bene Hananiah family archive that was taken to the Cave of Letters.[102] This is a promissory note composed in Hebrew on a scrap of poor-quality skin, rather than the usual papyrus. Here, Cimber's brother Joseph borrows a single tetradrachm (!) from a soldier and temporary resident, Judah b. Judah. Judah and his own brother, Jesus (who signs as witness), have come down to En Gedi early in the revolt (133 C.E.) for reasons unstated. Their origin is a place called Ha-Horemet (החרמת, vocalization uncertain), perhaps to be identified with modern Khirbet El-Makhrum, five kilometers northeast of Herodium (see Figure 1.1).[103] Scholars have not known that this document derived from En Gedi, for in exceptional fashion, it lacks the locale clause.[104] As argued above, however, the scribe of *P.Hever* 49 was Masabala b. Simon, who resided in En Gedi. Moreover, the final signatory can now be read as Judah b. Joseph, Masabala's nephew, an En Gedite and trained scribe who also signed *P.Yadin* 44 and *P.Yadin* 45.[105] His three signatures are identical, and as always, Judah here signed in Hebrew with a beautiful bookhand.

With his usual chicken-scratch handwriting Joseph b. Hananiah likewise signed the I.O.U. in Hebrew. That he signed it in the language of the contract indicates that he knew the language, something we could not have deduced from any of his signatures earlier in Mahoza, which were always in Aramaic. Moreover, because he signed as a βραδέως γράφων, it can hardly be the case that by his signature Joseph asserted knowledge of the holy tongue acquired by years of study. Rather, the signature probably means that he could speak a vernacular dialect, something like the Hebrew in which Masabala drafted the note. If Joseph could, his brothers Cimber and Simon likely could as well. In Roman Judaea, evidence is mounting to suggest, Hebrew was for many a home language (on which much more below).

For the present study one final aspect of *P.Hever* 49 comes to the fore. In lines 10–11, Joseph promises to repay the loan made in En Gedi "from my house and my other property" (והתשלם [מן] ביתי ומן נכסי). The statement evidences that Joseph owned property in that village, which was probably, as it was for Cimber, his place of birth. He must also have owned property to which he expected to return in Mahoza, since that was his home for many years. His brother Cimber is explicitly said in *P.Yadin* 18 to own property in both locales.[106] Judah b. Eleazar Khthousion, Babatha's second husband, likewise owned property in both places. Eleazar b. Eleazar, his brother, held contracts on property in both Mahoza and Kephar-Baru. We shall see that other members of the Judaean Desert village elite followed the same pattern of landholding in two or more villages. Not only does this fact demonstrate the extreme wealth of these leading families of the Bar Kokhba Revolt, it has other possible social implications as well. For example, Judah b. Khthousion had two wives, one in each village where he enjoyed holdings. Did others similarly practice polygamy, with families in each place where they spent time?

The second document here proposed as constitutive of the Bene Hananiah Archive is *P.Hever* 13. The scribe of this Aramaic writing is Mattat b. Simon, whom we encountered above. One of the two witnesses is Masabala b. Simon, presumably Mattat's brother, as noted. The commander's presence signals that the writ derives from En Gedi, which would in any case be likely, given that Mattat earlier scribed a document for Eleazar b. Samuel there (*P.Yadin* 47b). Produced on 20 Sivan of Year Three, *P.Hever* 13 dates some two years later than *P.Hever* 49 and—depending on whether the years of the war were calculated beginning from the first month, from the war's outbreak, or from the seventh month—is possibly the latest dated Bar Kokhba document to survive. The principals are one Shelamzion b. Joseph and Eleazar b. Hananiah, arguably Cimber's and Joseph's brother, the man who would have held this writ, and the presumed reason for its presence in the Hananiah family archive. Just what the document is, however, has been a matter of controversy.

The first reference to its existence appeared in Milik's 1956 survey of the contents of the "Wadi Seiyal" materials: "In another papyrus document a woman, Shelamzion berat Joseph, requests a divorce from her husband,

Eleazar bar Honi (or Honiah). The key clause is: 'That you should be notified concerning the act of divorce and repudiation on her part.'"[107] Thus Milik believed *P.Hever* 13 to be a divorce document, or גט. The conventional understanding has been, however, that Jewish women in antiquity could not divorce their husbands. Only men could issue letters of divorce. This understanding is based on numerous passages in rabbinic literature. In part impelled by such considerations, Jonas Greenfield, while preparing to publish this text along with the other Naḥal Ḥever papyri that had fallen to him, argued in several lectures in the early 1990s that *P.Hever* 13 was not a גט, but rather a שובר, or receipt, issued by Shelamzion on receiving the גט.[108] Greenfield and fellow-laborer Yardeni published a preliminary study of the text making this argument;[109] when Greenfield died, Yardeni then represented this position in her *editio princeps* in DJD 27.[110]

To be sure, more than just the weight of later Jewish legal understanding prompted Greenfield and Yardeni to recast Milik's view of *P.Hever* 13. The puzzling orthography of several critical words in the document arguably fortified their approach, suggesting to them that the scribe switched from person to person while composing a document ultimately at some variance from the standards expected in a writ of divorce. Thus, lines 3–5 say, "I, Shelamzion b. Joseph Qabshan of En Gedi, have no claims upon you, Eleazar b. Hananiah." Here, Mattat represented Shelamzion speaking in the first person. But he immediately juxtaposed in line 6a, די הוית בעלה מן קדמת דנן. The form בעלה seemed to Greenfield and Yardeni best understood as the noun בעל with a third-person feminine singular suffix, that is, "her husband" (*ba'alah*), yielding the phrase, "who were formerly her husband." Thus Mattat had switched and now spoke descriptively of Shelamzion in the third person while addressing himself to Hananiah. He then continued the second-person mode in lines 6b–7 but shifted addressees, directing to Shelamzion: ד[י] הוא לך מנה גט שבקין ותרכין, which the two Israeli scholars understood as "inasmuch as you have received from him a document of divorce and expulsion." Crucial to their interpretation was the form מנה—evidently the preposition מן with a third-person masculine singular suffix, "from him" (*minneh*). This understanding entailed that the document that Mattat was producing could not itself be the גט, since he here referenced Shelamzion's receiving such in the past. Hence Greenfield and Yardeni reasoned that *P.Hever* 13 must be some sort of writ describing and relating to a divorce decree. Rabbinic literature spoke of such documents on a few occasions, denominating them as "receipts," or שוברים. Conceived as documenting the payoff of the dowry, these writs were technically receipts for the woman's *ketubbah*. This was what Shelamzion was giving to Hananiah, not a divorce decree. She was affirming payment of her dowry.

With additional arguments and evidences largely drawn from rabbinic literature, Greenfield and Yardeni's reasoning seemed to make some sense of an admittedly knotty text. Nevertheless, Mattat's switch from first to third to second person—and back again to first person (line 8)—was unparalleled and struck some as a forced and unlikely construal.[111] It was also unclear why such a receipt was really necessary. Seemingly, all Judaean custom required in the present circumstance was that one cross out the *ketubbah*'s wording, so signaling the marriage document as invalid and annulling the concomitant dowry debt. A marriage contract of this sort defaced by diagonal lines (χιασμοί) is in fact preserved among the Judaean Desert finds (*P.Hever* 69, from Aristoboulias).[112]

Despite these objections, however, none of the critics could explain the apparent third-person forms written with *heh,* בעלה and מנה. Greenfield and Yardeni could claim that much, however precarious their resulting tightrope walk of a solution might seem. An uneasy standoff with the critics ensued. Was *P.Hever* 13 correctly understood or not?

If by "correctly understood" one means "as Greenfield and Yardeni argued," then the answer would seem to be no. A more elegant, possible linguistic explanation for the strange forms that gave rise to their interpretive configuration emerges from a peculiarity within *P.Yadin* 19, Judah Khthousion's postnuptial deed of gift to Shelamzion. Written in Greek by a Mahozan scribe whose command of that language was "notable for its erratic orthography, indiscriminate vowels . . . and insouciant case endings,"[113] the document contained some especially odd forms to which Lewis called attention in his commentary: "ὑπερῴαις, θυρίαις and πανταίοις present the following problem of interpretation. The reading of the diphthong αι is certain in all three instances, where the correct spelling requires οι. Are we to attribute this eccentric spelling entirely to the caprice or semi-literacy of the scribe, or do we glimpse here in his phonetic orthography a local peculiarity of pronunciation in which the sounds of αι /e/ and οι /i/ tended to be assimilated?"[114] Thus Lewis was essentially suggesting a tendency for /e/ = /i/ (at this date in the history of the Koine, more strictly speaking, /ɛ:/ = /œ:/),[115] either of which could be expressed by the grapheme αι in the scribe's *ad aurem* expression. One cannot help noticing that the phonological equation that Lewis posited for his Greek scribe would, if roughly operative in

Mattat's Aramaic in *P.Hever* 13, dissolve the dissonance created by that text's problematic orthography. That is to say, if Mattat pronounced Aramaic with a similar "local peculiarity of pronunciation," in which /e:/ (monophthong and monophthongized)[116] and /i:/ had in certain environments fallen together, and wrote intermittently with a phonetic orthography analogous to that of the scribe of *P.Yadin* 19, then *P.Hever* 13 could be read straightforwardly as a גט. Several considerations support this suggestion.

First, like the scribe of *P.Yadin* 19, Mattat was from Mahoza. So he and the scribe of this text would likely have pronounced Aramaic and Greek similarly to each other, including any local peculiarities. Second, the scribe was himself a "son of Simon" (his damaged signature cannot be read with confidence, Lewis rendering it .[.]. .ας Σίμω[ν]ος). As both were scribes and both were sons of Simon in the same small village, he was possibly Mattat's brother. It is perhaps not impossible—though the exiguous surviving traces give the notion very little encouragement—that he was actually Mattat himself (i.e., reading/restoring Μ[α]θίας). And third, the scribe's Greek was shaky, whereby his native tongue, likely Aramaic, would tend to interfere with it more frequently. In the case of *P.Yadin* 19, the scribe usually succeeded in producing the expected historical spellings, but on the three occasions that Lewis noted, his actual pronunciation induced him to write the aberrant forms. And that actual pronunciation, it is here proposed, derived from his native speech as substrate interference.

Applying the suggested phonological equations to the problematic forms of *P.Hever* 13 results in the following: עינגדה (written, line 5) = עינגדי (pronounced), בעלה (line 6) = בעלי, and מנה (line 7) = מני. This understanding decisively changes the meaning of the phrases in which בעלה and מנה appear. They now become more or less typical for a writ of divorce. One now has for line 6 די הוית בעלה (=בעלי) מן קדמת דנן, "who were formerly my husband." Line 6b–7 becomes ד[נה] הוא לך מנה (= מני) גט שבקין ותרכין, "This is a document of divorce and expulsion for you from me."[117] On this construction of the writ's language, *P.Hever* 13 would show that women in the Judaism of this period could indeed divorce their husbands, just as Ilan, on other grounds, has argued that it does.[118] If so, we have before us a strong disjunction from rabbinic law. We are again reminded of the treacherous difficulties involved with applying rabbinic literature to the texts and cultural history of Roman Judaea. Sometimes we can do it straightforwardly. Other times we cannot do it at all. Often we are somewhere in between—somewhere, but where? As we walk this path, we do well to remember that sand and quicksand look alike.[119]

The two documents proposed as the remnants of the Archive of the Bene Hananiah are thus of extraordinary interest both historically and linguistically. Note that *P.Hever* 13 and *P.Hever* 49 were both products of that same scribal shop, belonging to Masabala, Mattat, and their relatives, that had produced all of the surviving materials of the Archive of Eleazar b. Samuel. Accordingly, of the six archives that seem to be distinguishable among the findings from the Cave of Letters, two were entirely the products of the same family of scribes. These men evidently serviced a noteworthy segment of En Gedi's village elites. Included among those elites was the family of Salome Komaise, the central figure of the final archive from the cave, to which we now briefly turn.

Cotton reconstructed the Archive of Salome Komaise as consisting of seven documents. Of these, only three actually belonged to Salome herself: *P.Hever* 12 is an Aramaic receipt for the value of some dates, addressed to Salome by her brother and a business partner (חבר). It dates to the year 131 and is set in the town of Mahoza, where all but one of her archive's documents have their setting. *P.Hever* 64 is a Greek deed of gift in which Salome's mother, Salome Grapte, makes over to her daughter her own remaining property in Mahoza. *P.Hever* 65 is then Salome's *ketubbah* for her marriage to her second husband (at least, the second we know), Jesus b. Menahem, native of a village in the Peraea, near Livias. This document is also in Greek.

When Salome entered the cave near En Gedi in the fall of 135, she was carrying, in addition to the above, two papyri once belonging to her first husband, Shamoa b. Simon. (He appears to have been Babatha's brother and thus Salome's own cousin. We shall consider the reasons for believing in these relations shortly.) The documents were *P.Hever* 60, a rent receipt composed in Greek, and *P.Hever* 62, Shamoa's declaration of land for the census of 127 held by the governor of Arabia, Titus Aninius Sextius Florentinus. This, too, was a Greek document. In addition, Salome bore to the cave the Greek *P.Hever* 61, another land declaration of that same census belonging to a dead brother, and *P.Hever* 63, belonging to her mother. This last was Salome's renunciation of certain Mahozan properties in favor of her mother. Such was the extent of the Salome Komaise papers as reconstructed by Cotton.

Probably an eighth document ought to be added to this collection, *P.Hever* 7. This is an Aramaic contract for the sale of a house, courtyard, and appurtenances; the vendor is one Hazak b. Mattat, apparently the son of the scribe: once again, Mattat b. Simon.[120] The purchaser is Eleazar b. Levi. Levi, of course, was the name of Salome Komaise's father. Given the find-spot in the same cave with Salome's materials, Eleazar as her brother seems a logical inference. Salome was, after all, evidently archiving a veritable potpourri of family documents. It is therefore somewhat puzzling that neither Yardeni, in her edition of the text, nor Cotton, in her discussion of Salome's archive, even suggested the possibility of the proposed connection.[121] Perhaps the several uncertainties in the text motivated this restraint.

We do not know for certain where the text was composed, as the left half of the document, in which any toponyms would have appeared, has been sliced away by a knife, possibly in antiquity, more likely in modern times. All that can be read is the reference to Eleazar as dwelling in "the village of [. . ."—presumably, the place where the property was located and the contract agreed upon. We know, however, the date of this writ, Iyyar of Year Three, which equates to 134–135, and we know from the dating of *P.Hever* 13 that Mattat the scribe was living in En Gedi in that year. We should probably reconstruct the lacuna accordingly, אלעזר בר לוי . . . דיתב בכפר [עין גדי, "Eleazar b. Levi . . . who is living in the village of [En Gedi."[122] The likelihood that the text was produced in En Gedi then reinforces the suggestion that it be associated with Salome Komaise, since we know that with the outbreak of the revolt, she, and probably her mother, had gone to that village. Now it appears that a brother also repatriated, and purchased property there. Note that Mattat b. Simon the scribe had either done the same or else owned property in En Gedi already in the antebellum years. We learn from *P.Hever* 7 that as of 134–135 he had distributed some property to his heirs.

These, then, are the six archives recovered or reconstituted from the Cave of Letters. The ubiquitous Mattat appears in four of them: he signed *P.Yadin* 26 as a witness (Babatha Archive) and composed *P.Hever* 47b (Archive of Eleazar b. Samuel), *P.Hever* 13 (Archive of the Bene Hananiah), and *P.Hever* 7 (Archive of Salome Komaise). He also seems to be the scribe of *P.Hever* 14, a thumbnail-sized scrap of which survives.[123] Table 3.1 summarizes the contents of the two newly proposed archives, those of Eleazar b. Eleazar and the Bene Hananiah.

With at least a provisional understanding of these archives in place, we are at last in a position to explore in a bit more detail something of what can be known about the lives of the principals and witnesses who appear in the documents discovered in the Cave of Letters. We are dealing for the most part with a group of intermarried extended families—very rich and, evidently, powerful members of the village elites. As we shall see, among them were distinguished priests. These were the dramatis personae of a tragic tableau. These were the leaders of the Bar Kokhba Revolt.

Table 3.1. Newly reconstructed archives from the Cave of Letters

Archive	Document	Type/language	Family member	Date (C.E.)
Eleazar b. Eleazar	*P. Yad.* 36	Writ of redemption/ Nab	Eleazar b. Nicarchus	ca. 60
	P.Hev. nab 2	Deed of sale/Nab	Eleazar b. Khthousion	ca. 100
	P.Hev. nab 3	Unpublished/Nab	Unknown	Unknown
	P.Hev. nab 4	Unpublished/Nab	Unknown	Unknown
	P.Hev. nab 5	Unpublished/Nab	Unknown	Unknown
	P.Hev. nab 6	Unpublished/Nab	Unknown	Unknown
	P.Hev. 8	Deed of sale/Ar and Heb	John b. Eli	135
	P.Hev. 8a	Deed of sale/Ar	Eleazar b. Eleazar	134 or 135
	P.Hev. 10	Receipt/Ar	John b. Eli	ca. 120–135
	P.Hev. 22	Deposit/Ar	Eleazar b. Eleazar	132–135
	P.Hev. 26	Deposit (?)/Ar	John b. Eli	ca. 120–135
	P.Hev. 30	Letter/Heb	Eleazar b. Eleazar	135
	P.Hev. 36	Letter (?)/Heb	Eleazar b. Eleazar	132–135
Bene Hananiah	*P.Hev.* 13	Writ of divorce/Ar	Eleazar b. Hananiah	134–135
	P.Hev. 49	I.O.U./Heb	Joseph b. Hananiah	135

Note: Nab indicates Nabataean; Ar, Aramaic; and Heb, Hebrew.

People of the Cave of Letters

Most of the people mentioned in the materials that have survived from the Cave of Letters were born and lived out their lives in three villages that gazed upon the Dead Sea from three points of the compass: from the west, En Gedi; from the east, Kephar-Baru; and from the south, Mahoza (unless it was on the east; see below). By the end of the revolt, many of these people had been funneled into En Gedi, and one suspects that it was here that their ancestors had settled originally.

We are fortunate that En Gedi has been excavated and the results published.[124] The excavations revealed an oasis village extending over some forty dunams (almost four hectares), three or four times the normal expanse for a Judaean village at this time. Moreover, En Gedi was very densely settled, with houses closely compacted, often adjoining one another and sharing walls as a mechanism for ameliorating the murderous heat of summer months. On the basis of the size and density of the site, the excavators estimated that at its height, slightly after our period, the village housed about one thousand people—some two hundred families.[125] These people survived in part by harvesting the lumps of asphalt that regularly floated up from the floor of the Dead Sea and burst through the surface like a breaching whale. Indeed, such lumps could approach the size of a mature Beluga,[126] and the villagers would sally forth in small vessels, surrounding it in a scene reminiscent of whalers swarming over a carcass, securing and hauling it ashore to render it and sell the bitumen as caulk and sealant.

But at the focal point of the local economy were unique products shared only with Jericho and a very select few other places in the region of the Dead Sea: Judaean balsam, high-quality dates, and their derivatives. These derivatives were luxury goods for the most part, including aromatics, perfumes, sweets, and special alcoholic drinks, though use also included application to religious rites and medicines. The villagers were experts steeped in arcane agricultural know-how, and their ability to cultivate a variety of succulent dates has scarcely been equaled in modern times, let alone improved upon. According to the elder Pliny, when laid end-to-end, four of the premier "Nicholas" dates could stretch to a length of half a meter.[127] En Gedi was thus an export economy specializing in luxury goods. Many of these goods went to nearby Jerusalem while it still stood. Others went out of the country. Gaza was a convenient port, only two or three days distant, and is recorded as shipping balsam as early as the third century B.C.E. Flowing into the village were significant quantities of foodstuffs for a population that the local arable land could not fully support. The excavations unearthed many coins, showing that in contrast to most rural economic systems in Judaean antiquity, that of En Gedi was monetized. The En Gedi of Masabala, Judah b. Eleazar Khthousion, and their contemporaries was an exceptionally large, exceptionally rich village.

Among the discoveries at En Gedi was an Aramaic inscription set into the mosaic floor of a Byzantine-period synagogue. It included mention of a "secret of the village":

מן דגלי רזה דקרתה לעממיה דין דעינוה משוטטן בכל ארעה וחמי
סתירתה הוא יתן אפוה בגברה ההו ובזרעיה ויעקור יתיה מן תחות
שומיה

> Whoever reveals the secret of the village to the Gentiles—He whose eyes move to and fro upon the whole earth and see the hidden things shall set his face against that man and his descendants and uproot them from beneath heaven.[128]

The nature of this secret has been much discussed, but the most convincing interpretation sees it as related to the two central crops of the village economy:

> It could have included cultivation and irrigation regimes, planting and replanting methods, and the acquisition of propagation materials of especially useful cultivars. The secret(s) probably also included harvest and post-harvest technologies such as commercial product extraction; handling and packaging; utilization of the by-products; the grading and commercialization of the end products. The entire integrated system of agro-technical know-how probably included numerous secrets, many of which can no longer be imagined, as the balsam shrub is no longer cultivated. It is possible that the exact definition of the secret was purposefully worded vaguely and was meant to include future secrets, as the mosaic was made to last a long time, and indeed did.[129]

As En Gedi's peculiar agricultural situation was of long-standing and in no way limited to the Byzantine period, one must assume that the secret or secrets, if correctly interpreted, were of equal long-standing. They would always have needed to be protected if the villagers were to preserve their way of life. Hence En Gedi would have employed little if any slave labor, as slaves would lack incentive to keep the secrets. Inhabitants of the village in Babatha's time would have been free and for the most part also would have led lives tied to the economic system here described. They owned or leased the land on which these crops were cultivated and the factories and shops in which they were processed, just as their contracts and letters often either imply or explicitly describe.

The wealth of En Gedi was especially evident to the excavators from the high-quality construction of the houses. Most were of the type known as "courtyard houses." Hirschfeld has written of such structures, "In view of the investment required in planning and in the construction dimensions, this house-type seems to have been used exclusively by wealthy families."[130] Some of the En Gedi residences possessed mosaic floors, a find rare in Judaean village contexts. Most of the houses were single-story structures, but a few were discovered that rose two stories.

The most impressive of these two-story structures the excavators dubbed the Halfi House. Six rooms surrounded its spacious courtyard, at one end of which a masonry staircase ascended to a second story, where stood two additional rooms. Larger rooms below were floored with white mosaic, which was watertight and so could be flooded in the summer to create a kind of ancient air conditioning. At one end of the courtyard stood a plastered installation that the excavators believed functioned to extract balsam drops and to mix that essence with other oils as a part of the long process of manufacture. This house must have belonged to one of the wealthiest families in the village. In this connection it is notable that the En Gedi home that Judah b. Eleazar Khthousion gifted to his daughter Shelamzion was likewise a two-story courtyard structure (*P.Yadin* 19:14). They, too, must have been among the wealthiest property owners in the town. According to the same papyrus, their home was located directly across Aristion's Lane from a synagogue.[131] Such proximity has generally been highly prestigious in Jewish communities.

As for Mahoza, we know from the Babatha and Salome Komaise archives that the village was similar in its structures to En Gedi, at least partially composed of courtyard houses, some of which were two stories. Indeed, Salome Komaise had such a mansion deeded over to her by her mother.[132] Mahoza possessed palm groves and other plantations, including—most likely—balsam, along with a swamp, elaborate irrigation installations, a river, and various named plots.[133] Yet the precise location of Mahoza is still uncertain. The documents indicate that it was within reasonable proximity of Zoar, because that city was the capital village to whose territory Mahoza was assigned. Scholars have suggested competing options for the ancient settlement's placement.

The first option would locate Mahoza in the Ghor al-Safi, south of the Dead Sea and near Wadi al-Hasa. This is an oasis not unlike En Gedi in its natural endowments and would lend itself to the same sorts of agriculture practiced in the Judaean village. Advocates of this view propose that the village, or at least its plantings, ran more or less right up against the seashore, for two date groves in Mahoza bore the name Algifyamma (written as Ἀλγιφιαμμά, i.e., Aramaic על גיף ימא, "on the seashore").[134]

The second option on the table was proposed by Ernst Axel Knauf. He argued that the location in the Ghor al-Safi was unlikely because surveys in the region had discovered no substantial settlements for the period in question. His suggestion was to see Mahoza as located much farther north, on the Lisan that juts into the Dead Sea from the east: "Given its road connections (the shore of the Dead Sea was completely impassable until very recently between the Lisan and Kallirhoe/ez-Zarah), Mahoza would still have fallen into the District of Zoar, and it would not have been too difficult to travel from Mahoza to [Rabbat-Moab] on other affairs."[135] Knauf's view has been seconded by Konstantinos Politis, who places Mahoza at the ruins of Haditha. Immediately adjacent is an ancient cemetery, with burials of the same type found in the much larger Khirbet Qazone cemetery five kilometers to the southwest. Khirbet Qazone dates to the first to third centuries C.E.[136]

The third village associated with the prosopography of the Cave of Letters documents, Kephar-Baru, will henceforth acquire a higher profile in the historiography of the period if the proposals of the present study persuade. Previously, just two documents were generally connected to the site.[137] Now it will be as many as seven (see Table 3.1). Most scholars associate the site with the damaged Βα]αρου of the Madeba Map,[138] depicted as some four kilometers inland to the northeast of the hot baths of Callirrhoe. Josephus described the village, which he called Baaras, in a passage connected to Herod the Great's travel to Callirrhoe in desperate search for relief from his final illness:

> There is a place called Baaras, which produces a root bearing the same name. Flame-coloured and towards evening emitting a brilliant light, it eludes the grasp of persons who approach with the intention of plucking it, as it shrinks up and can only be made to stand still by pouring upon it certain secretions of the human body. Yet even then to touch it is fatal, unless one succeeds in carrying off the root itself, suspended from the hand. . . . In this same region flow hot springs, in taste widely differing from each other, some being bitter, while others have no lack of sweetness. . . . Hard by may be seen a cave, of no great depth and screened by a projecting rock, above which protrude, as it were, two breasts, a little distance apart, one yielding extremely cold water, and the other extremely hot.[139]

The name Baru evidently derives from the Semitic בער, which can mean "to burn" and is a transparent reference to the hot springs. (The spellings of the name without the medial *'ayin* in *P.Hever* 8 and 8a pose no problem for the identification, since the phoneme had fallen out of Judaean speech in most of the region, and graphic representation would thus easily be omitted by the nonprofessional scribe of these documents, John b. Eli.)[140] Josephus's description fits the hot springs of Hammamat Ma'in, which emerge into the narrow, fissured Wadi Zarqa Ma'in. Above the hot springs sit the remains of an ancient village known today as Manyat Umm Hasan. This was probably Kephar-Baru; it has yet to be excavated, and so little can be said of life there. Some five kilometers to the southeast stood the fortress of Machaerus, evidently destroyed by the Romans at the end of the First Revolt and so not inhabited by the rebels under Bar Kokhba. Eusebius seems to have known Kephar-Baru in his day and described it as a very large village.[141] Here,

Eleazar b. Eleazar and others of our cast of characters played out their roles during the Second Revolt.

This triad of Dead Sea villages—En Gedi, Mahoza, and Kephar-Baru—was home to four major family groupings appearing in the materials of the present study. Representatives of two of these families wound up in the Cave of Letters: the family of Judah b. Eleazar Khthousion, into which Babatha married, and Babatha's birth family, which included Salome Komaise and her mother, Salome Grapte. A third major grouping was the family of Eleazar b. Hita, signatory to *P.Yadin* 44, it will be recalled, and at one time a third military commander of En Gedi. At a later juncture he got into trouble with Simon b. Kosiba, and surviving letters suggest that Hita was eventually arrested and led to the leader of the revolt in chains. We have no evidence for deciding what became of him or his family when the revolt finally collapsed. The fourth family is that of Masabala: the sons of Simon, a priestly scribal clan. Scholars have said nothing concerning the possibility that members of this clan made their way to one of the Judaean caves, but, as we shall consider shortly, clues to its fate have survived, and they are connected with a particular cave.

Additional families occur, of course; the Judaeans who prepared the thirty-five known refuge caves as hiding places of last resort all likely constituted extended family units.[142] Yet these four are the most prominent in the extant documents. These are the families whose prosopography will factor most into the statistics and analysis of Chapter 5 and into the final conclusions. Brief attention to their stories is therefore both appropriate and necessary in order to form as precise an idea as possible of just whose language and literacy we are examining.

The families of Babatha and that of her second husband, Judah b. Eleazar Khthousion, have their nexus, obviously, in herself (Figures 3.6 and 3.7). But Babatha was a relative newcomer to the family scenes. By the time that she and Judah wed, his family had been on the scene in Mahoza for perhaps a century. The ancestral figure was one Neboma, known from *P.Yadin* 36. His name is recorded among Nabataeans and also at Palmyra but is unknown for Judaean men. It seems likely, therefore, that he was not Jewish, but probably Nabataean. Of his two sons, Nicarchus bore a Greek name unattested among Judaean Jews, and Buni is a short form of Benaiah, or possibly of Benjamin, both well-known, indeed biblical male names.[143] Accordingly, it appears that Neboma had married a Jewess. If so, the story of Babatha and her families begins with an ironic twist: an Arab marrying a Jew. Thereafter, all the

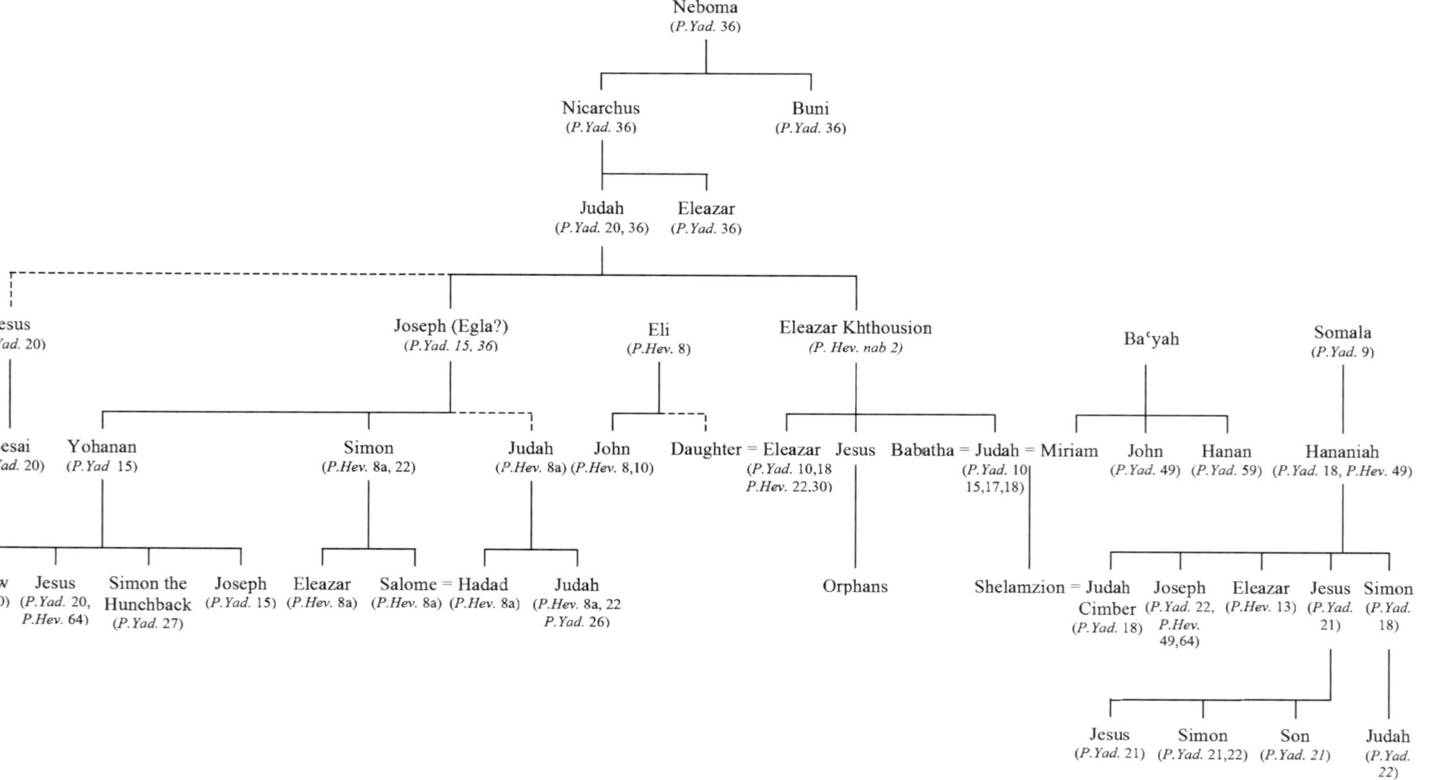

Figure 3.6. *Babatha and the family of Eleazar Khthousion.*

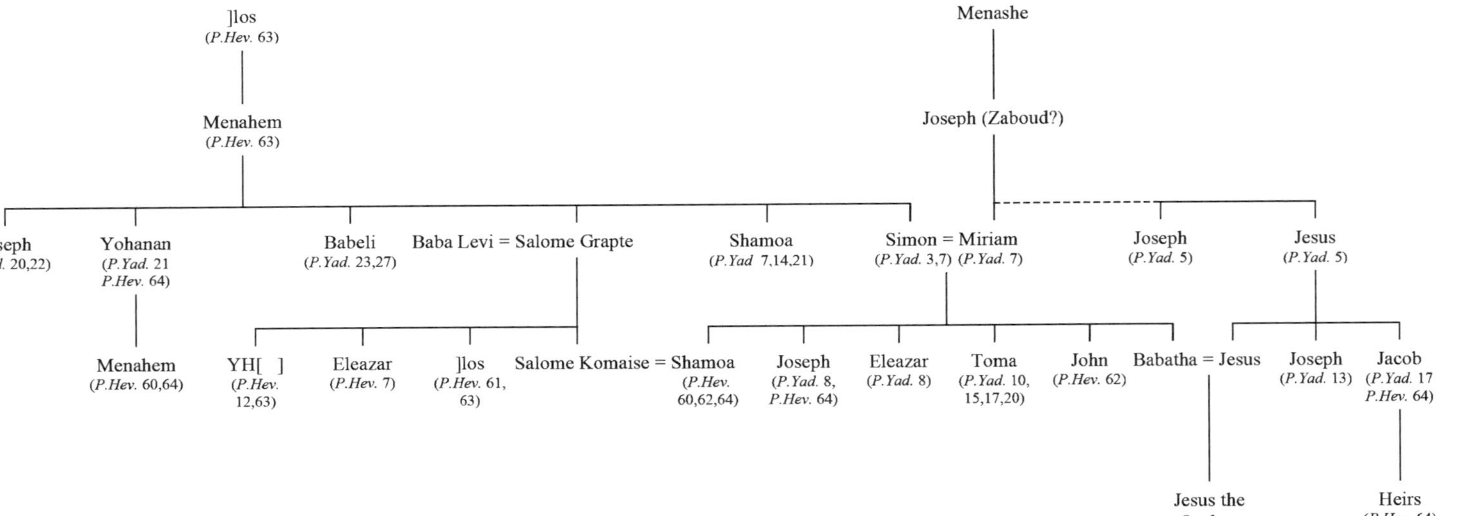

Figure 3.7. *The family of Babatha and Salome Komaise: a possible reconstruction.*

family names known to us are Jewish, but we are alerted to the possibility that some of the apparent Nabataean names in our materials may conceal people of mixed marriages. We are also alerted to the significant degree to which at least some Judaeans had integrated with those on the other side of an invisible border, a border whose political reality we cannot doubt but whose cultural reality was evidently more attenuated.

We have no way of knowing whether Neboma's Judaean wife represented the first wave of Judaean immigrants to the realm of the Nabataeans. But she is unlikely to have been the only one of her people residing at this time in Mahoza, and so the natural question becomes, "Why now?" Before attempting a tentative reply, one should perhaps emphasize that it *was* evidently now (unless earlier)—not decades later, in connection with the destruction of En Gedi during the First Revolt—that Jews came to live on the southern shores of the Dead Sea.[144] It was now, in the first decades of the first century C.E., that the family of Judah b. Eleazar Khthousion first put down roots in the kingdom of the Nabatu. These years coincide with the establishment at En Boqeq of an unguent factory under what Andrea Berlin has suggested were the auspices of the Nabataean royal family.[145] Judging from the archaeological evidence of concern for matters of ritual purity, that establishment included Jews, who presumably came to make a profitable living, bringing with them their knowledge of the secrets for balsam commercialization. It may be that at the same time, others from En Gedi settled in Mahoza with similar encouragement from the Nabataean elite, for mutual profit in the cultivation of balsam and dates. The documents from the Cave of Letters tell us, after all, that the king of the Nabatu owned gardens to grow these crops on what one can only imagine, given royal prerogatives, must have been prime real estate—as it happens, right next to gardens owned by our Judaean families.

In the generation after Nicarchus and Buni, the brothers Judah and Eleazar come into view, and from then on the family of Judah Khthousion was split between Mahoza, En Gedi, and, in the next generation, Kephar-Baru.[146] Judah and his descendants through Joseph Egla are attested in Mahoza, involved with Babatha in various ways, including acting as the guardian of her orphan son, Jesus. Eleazar b. Eleazar, as we have seen, resided at different times in Mahoza and Kephar-Baru, and an entire wing of the family can be reconstructed as living alongside him in the Peraean village. Judah b.(?) Joseph Egla was the father of that Judah b. Judah who signed several of Eleazar's documents. A brother of the former, Simon, settled in Kephar-Baru and signed Eleazar's documents, too. Judah b. Judah had a brother, Hadad, who evidently married Simon's daughter and thus his own cousin, Salome b. Simon. Marrying one's cousin was a frequent endogamous mechanism among the Judaeans of this period, albeit controversial in some circles, and was intended to keep property within the family. Babatha's first marriage to Jesus b. Jesus was likely of the same type, as was the marriage of Salome Komaise to her first husband, Shamoa.[147]

If one asks when Judah Khthousion's family first settled in Kephar-Baru, surviving evidence suggests that the answer is with his father, Eleazar Khthousion. The reason to believe so is the fact noted above, that Eleazar b. Eleazar claimed Kephar-Baru as his ἰδία. So he was born in that village. Yet we know from the documents that his father owned properties in both En Gedi and Mahoza. Assuming, as seems reasonable, that the elder Eleazar also owned property in the village where this son of his was born, it emerges that he was invested in three different locations, each several days' travel distant from the others. We begin to get some sense of what must have been a very considerable fortune and, too, a hint of what may have been rather interesting living arrangements. He evidently had families in more than one location. Did he then have more than one wife?

Babatha entered the family of the elder Eleazar through her marriage to his son Judah in about 125 C.E. The exact date of their union is unknown. Her *ketubbah* survived among her papers (*P.Yadin* 10) inscribed in Aramaic by this new husband, but the date is lost. She had previously been married to Jesus b. Jesus for about four years, terminating with his death in 124. As noted, by that marriage Babatha had a son, Jesus, who was likely little more than four years old upon her second marriage. If Yadin was correct that Babatha's was one of the eight female skeletons found in the Cave of Letters, all of whom were between the ages of fifteen and thirty, then she was probably born about 105 and married Jesus at about the usual age for women, fifteen. Supportive of this inference for her approximate birth date is the fact that in the land declaration of 127, *P.Hever* 62, her brother Shamoa b. Simon declared his age to be thirty. He would then have been about eight years her senior.

Much of what we know about Babatha's life derives from the records of a drawn-out dispute concerning the maintenance of her orphaned son. This maintenance was by means of monies generated by substantial property that would devolve to Jesus upon the age of majority, for the interim being managed by court-appointed guardians. At one point in the course of these disputes Babatha offered to mortgage some of her own property as hypothec against the orphan's money, which she wished to manage herself so as to provide for her son more richly. We learn thereby that she had considerable property in her own name. Additional evidence of her wealth comes from her property declaration of 127 (*P.Yadin* 16), which reveals that she held four palm groves in Mahoza whose existence we would not otherwise have suspected,[148] and from the litigation that followed the death of Judah b. Khthousion, when she distrained and held still other groves that had been his as payment for her dowry and a loan of 300 denarii she had made to Judah. In addition, she owned at least one (courtyard?) house in Mahoza (recall that three keys were found in her deposit in the cave), and as argued above, we cannot safely assume that her surviving papers alert us to all she may have possessed. We know from his land declaration that her brother Shamoa held in partnership with another brother, John b. Simon, as many as eleven pieces of land in Mahoza, and since the document is damaged, he may well have declared more. Further, it is evident that only landownership was being declared, so exempting factories, homes, donkeys (*P.Yadin* 8), and many other similar things that would have been needed and so must be factored into any reckoning. Moreover, Babatha's papers evidence three other brothers who lived in Mahoza—Joseph, Eleazar, and Toma—each of whom we may reasonably suspect owned substantial property.[149] From the surviving written materials it thus emerges directly and by implication that the family was prodigiously wealthy, and the archaeological discoveries associated with the archive supply a limited but complementary view of the same.

The large number and high quality of the clothes and housewares the archaeologists discovered in the Cave of Letters speak clearly to the wealth of Babatha and her extended families. But perhaps most emblematic of the fact was a set of three glass platters found hidden in a tiny horizontal crevice. Yadin described their opening and subsequent study:

> When we took out the plates we could scarcely believe our eyes. The glass was as translucent as if it had just been manufactured. . . . It is common to see ancient glass with patina created by dust and humidity throughout the ages; in fact, we like ancient glass for that very reason. But here in the cave, because of the absolute lack of humidity, no patina formed and the glass was preserved exactly as it was two thousand years ago . . . the large bowl was of particular beauty. It was manufactured by moulding, grinding and cutting. The circular facets contained within two thin lines, both on the centre of the underside and around the rim, all are *intaglio.* The edge has what is called a cut "bead and bar" pattern. Overall rotary polishing

> is evident. . . . Although glassware of similar technique from the Roman Empire is known, no complete specimen of that type has yet been found anywhere within its vast area.[150]

Here at the vanishing point of the Roman world was found one of the finest pieces of ancient glassware ever discovered, exceptional for its clarity and line. The value of the piece in its day must have been considerable, not merely because of that exceptional quality, but also because the bowl had been imported a great distance from an unknown workshop located more centrally to imperial culture. We might rather have expected one of the great families of Jerusalem to own such glassware—but of course, Jerusalem was lost to the Jews. Perhaps in Babatha we see the sort who had populated the city's upper strata when the Temple still stood, supporting a lavish life in the cultural capital by means of lands and factories in rustic villages.

Apart from the matter of her orphan son, a second arena of dispute in Babatha's life emerges from her archive. This involved Judah's other wife, with whom Babatha went to law after his death to decide issues of property he had held. Which wife was to get it? For our purposes the details are not as interesting as the fact of the question. Scholarship has been divided since the publication of the Greek portions of Babatha's archive over the social context of the dispute: was Judah a bigamist, whereby Babatha and Miriam b. Baʿyah of En Gedi were simultaneously his wives, or had he married Babatha only after divorcing Miriam? In the latter case it would be surprising that Miriam would be claiming his property upon Judah's death, presumably five years after her marriage to him had ended. Ordinarily, her dowry would by this time have long since been settled. But one can imagine circumstances in which wrangles with the family might have dragged on, just as in fact happened with Babatha.

The scholarly argument has really come to rest on just how applicable one thinks later rabbinic law ought to be in framing the issues. Ranon Katzoff argued against Naphtali Lewis's original assertion that Judah had two wives simultaneously[151] largely on the methodological axiom that the rabbinic texts portray a kind of "normative Judaism," which here rules to the contrary: "The mass of Jewish literature presents a picture of monogamous marriage."[152] Thus the issue of Judah's potential bigamy has been connected with larger methodological disputes roiling the study of ancient Judaism. But it need not be so. Lewis's argument was strictly philological and entirely convincing, and never received a direct response from Katzoff. Lewis pointed out that both women use an unambiguous Greek clause in characterizing Judah: "μου καὶ σου ἀνδρὸς ἀπογενομένου" (your husband and mine having perished). Both call Judah their husband: "the simple, unforced sense of [the clause] is that both women were wives (now widows) of the deceased, not one a wife and the other a divorcee."[153] Babatha was a second wife. Judah had two wives, one in En Gedi and another in Mahoza, and presumably split his time between them. This situation, it would seem, was at least partly a reflex of the economic circumstance that Judah was invested in two villages and needed to spend significant spans of time in each. Thus Babatha's question brings us to one of our own, adumbrated earlier: Why assume that Judah's situation was particularly unusual in either respect, property or wives? In fact, we know that it was not unusual respecting property.

We have seen that Judah Cimber of the Bene Hananiah, in-laws to Babatha, certainly owned property in both En Gedi and Mahoza. Probably Joseph b. Hananiah did as well. Babatha's Judah explicitly did, of course, and his brother Eleazar in Mahoza and Kephar-Baru. Their father Eleazar Khthousion may have been a property owner in all three villages in which his later family is attested; he certainly possessed valuable real estate in both En Gedi and Mahoza. Masabala and Mattat, brothers and sons of Simon, lived much of their lives in separate villages, with additional brothers attested in both En Gedi and Mahoza. We cannot be certain how this scenario began, but given the emerging pattern, it makes sense to suggest that their father may have owned property and had families in both villages. We have some reason to believe that Masabala and Mattat each spent time in the other's main location (indeed, it may be that these only *seem* to be their main locations), themselves becoming split property holders in the process. We observed earlier that Mattat owned a house and land in En Gedi, which by 134 or 135 were listed under the names of his heirs.[154] Living for years in Mahoza as he did, he must have possessed a home there as well, if not gardens or plots. In turn, Masabala, though residing in En Gedi, used the term ופיא (perhaps *wafiya*), "complete," when inscribing the Aramaic *P.Yadin* 42. The editors persuasively suggest that the word be seen as an Arabism from the root *w-p-y*, cognate with Hebrew יפה.[155] Masabala may have picked this term up while spending time in Mahoza, where the Nabataeans spoke both an Aramaic dialect and a form of Arabic and demonstrably peppered their Aramaic liberally with Arabisms.[156] Turning to Salome Komaise's family, we know that Jesus b. Menahem, her second husband, was a wealthy landholder from a town near Livias who also either already owned or expected to acquire property in Mahoza.[157] And her father, Baba Levi, evidently owned property not only in Mahoza, but also—to judge from *P.Hever* 7—in Bene Yirashel. The text describes Salome's brother, Eleazar b. Levi, as a wine seller (השפי) born in that otherwise unknown village.[158] As with Eleazar Khthousion, so too with Baba Levi: having a son born in a given village probably implies a period of residence in that locality and so for wealthy people also a home and, reasonably, lands, factories, or both.

Thus Judah's pattern of property ownership was more paradigmatic than peculiar. Our texts show many of the men of his class living in different villages at different times, evidently owning property simultaneously in more than one place, presumably moving back and forth to oversee their investments. *P.Yadin* 6, a Nabataean text, may illustrate their way of life.[159] In this agreement inscribed in the year 119 or 120, a certain Yohana b. Meshullam (like Judah, a resident alien born in En Gedi) agrees to work the lands that Judah held in Galgala, a subdivision of Mahoza. The text describes Yohana as providing his own seed, tilling the ground, and caring for the crops. Payment was to be in kind. He was thus an אריס, a tenant farmer. Judah's role is reminiscent of the Gospel parable of the rich absentee landlord who sends servants to collect his portion of the crops and faces a rebellion from wicked tenants (Matt 21:31–41).

If, then, Judah's ownership of property in different places was indeed a factor in his bigamy, we should consider whether his bigamy was perhaps equally paradigmatic as his property ownership. Was this simply the way of Judaean life in the region of the Dead Sea?

The documents suggest that Salome Komaise was one of four children born to Salome Grapte, all of them possibly of her union with Baba Levi (for his genealogy, see Figure 3.8). But one of the Komaise brothers may have been the fruit of an earlier marriage of Salome Grapte. His damaged name appears in *P.Hever* 12, a receipt for a tax on dates composed in 131 C.E. According to that text, Salome's receipt was issued by "your brother יח°° בר תשה and

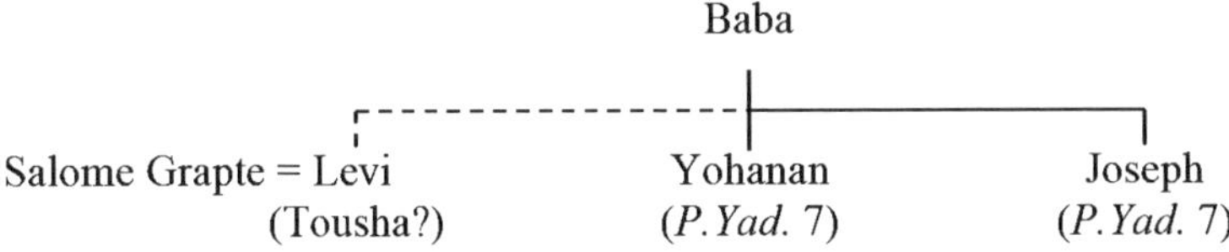

Figure 3.8. *The family of Levi b. Baba.*

my partner Simon" (lines 2–3).[160] The first element of her brother's name is damaged, and the vocalization of the patronymic element is unknown but *may* have been Tousha, a caconymous nickname evidently meaning "wimp" or "weakling."[161] This Tousha was likely Baba Levi himself—but if not, then it appears that Salome possessed a half-brother from her mother's putative first marriage. In that case, Salome Grapte would have had three husbands according to our texts: Tousha, Baba Levi, and finally Joseph b. Simon. More likely, though, there were only two. Picturing Salome and the Wimp together as a couple creates a vivid if incongruous image, as her name may mean "the Looker."[162]

When Salome Komaise came of age to marry, a union with a certain Shamoa b. Simon was arranged. Simon was Babatha's father's name, of course, but in itself that suggests nothing in particular, since the name was so common for Judaean men. But Shamoa is another matter. According to Ilan's *Lexicon,* the name was rare in the five hundred years covered, attaching to only four individuals besides our man here.[163] One of those four was Shamoa b. Menahem, almost certainly Babatha's agnate uncle, since he signed three of her documents and bore the same patronym as her father. The likelihood is therefore that "Shamoa" was for Babatha's clan a family name, and concomitantly that Salome Komaise was matched with her cousin, one of Babatha's five known brothers.

Of Shamoa's several appearances in our documents, one occurs in a pair of texts, *P.Yadin* 21–22, that record the same transaction from the perspectives of buyer and seller, respectively. These papyri clearly illustrate the intertwining of family and daily life that must have been the norm for both Salome Komaise and Babatha during their years in Mahoza and so invite a moment's attention. The occasion was Babatha's sale on 11 September 130 of the produce of the aforementioned three orchards that she had seized from Judah's estate when he died. Purchasing the dates was one Simon b. Jesus b. Hananiah, almost certainly the nephew of Cimber and Joseph and Eleazar, the Bene Hananiah so frequently intersecting Babatha's and her family's lives. What is especially interesting is that all but one of the eleven people who are involved with this sale in one way or another arguably belong either to the immediate family of Babatha or to that of Simon b. Jesus. Babatha is the seller; Simon b. Jesus b. Hananiah is the buyer; Shamoa b. Menahem, Babatha's agnate uncle and the brother of Salome Grapte, is the guarantor of the sale (her family is looking out for her in her widowhood); Jesus b. Jesus, Simon's brother, signs as one witness; PN b. Jesus, another brother, takes the same role; Yohanan b. Menahem, another agnate uncle of Babatha's, witnesses; our familiar friend Joseph b. Hananiah affixes once again his customary, gallinaceous John Hancock; one Joseph b. Menahem, presumably yet a third agnate uncle of Babatha's, signs as a witness; and finally, Judah b. Simon, the buyer's cousin, witnesses *P. Yadin* 22.

What is further interesting for our purposes is the range of literacy within the same families that these signatures attest. Babatha cannot sign, of course, and one Yohana b. Makhuta subscribes for her in fluid Nabataean script. Despite his name, he may have been a Jew—as a product of intermarriage à la the sons of Neboma, Nicarchus, and Buni—and even a relative of Babatha's. Otherwise, the Aramaic signatures of the men in both families toggle between levels 1 and 3, a fact that will require concentrated attention later. And finally, the only person certainly a member of neither family, the scribe Germanus b. Judah, proudly self-styled as a *libellius* (λιβλάριος), composed the two texts in a Greek notable mostly for its Aramaisms and false syllabification.

The latest document among Salome Komaise's archive is the Greek *ketubbah* attesting her marriage to Jesus b. Menahem in early August of 131, *P.Hever* 65. At this point her first husband Shamoa had been in the grave for nearly four years, and Salome may have been cohabiting for some time with Jesus in an ἄγραφος γάμος (marriage without a written contract).[164] Almost exactly a year later, Germanus b. Judah penned the latest document in Babatha's archive, *P. Yadin* 27. During that same summer of 132, scholars believe, the Second Revolt erupted in Judaea, and the conflict probably spread quickly to areas of the Nabataean realm.[165] The Judaeans living there evidently became personae non gratae, and if the actions of Gentiles during the First Revolt are any indication, they may even have come under attack from neighbors who saw this as an opportunity to seize Jewish property. In any event, our texts document the repatriation of Babatha, Salome, and every other Judaean whom we can follow. Our attention likewise moves from Mahoza to Judaea, and to some estimate of our two remaining prominent families. They are most apparent to us, at any rate, in En Gedi.

The family of Eleazar b. Eleazar b. Hita (Figure 3.9) we know principally through this same man, although other members of his family are evidently on view in documents involving him. Hita was Eleazar b. Samuel's partner, it will be recalled, in the repartitioning and subleasing of En Gedi lands documented by the Hebrew contracts *P.Yadin* 44–46. In the last of this series the partners lease to a certain Jesus b. Simon two sites known as "The Sullam"

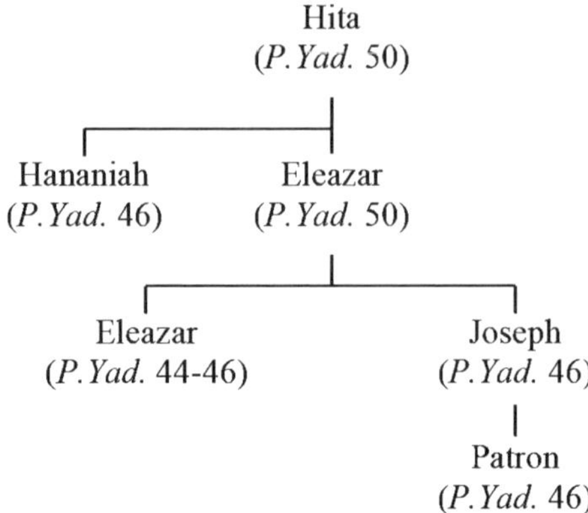

Figure 3.9. *The family of Eleazar b. Hita.*

and "The Bor" (i.e., "the ladder" and "the pit"), which had formerly been held by another member of the Hita family, Hananiah b. Hita. Included in the lease were date palms of the first quality (דקל טוב), other trees, and cropland. The witnesses to the contract include a PN b. Simon, presumably the brother of the lessee, Jesus, and two other men who were probably Hita's relatives: Joseph b. Eleazar, likely his brother, and Patron b. Joseph, that man's son and thus Hita's nephew. Both Joseph and Eleazar were more facile with the calamus than was Hita, the archetypal slow writer. They wrote at level 2. Thus none of the members of the Hita family for whom conclusions are possible was a literary literate, which is notable given that Eleazar b. Eleazar b. Hita was eminent in En Gedi, and extremely rich.

On the basis of one of the Bar Kokhba letters, *P.Yadin* 56, it seems that Eleazar was at one time a third military commander of the village under Bar Kokhba. Written by one of Simon's lieutenants, the letter is addressed ליהונתן בר בעין ולמסבלה ובר חיטה אחי שלם, "to John b. Baʿyah and Masabala and Bar Hita, my brothers: Greetings." The letter tells the men to pack up unnamed goods and some salt for transport by mule and to bring along with those things unspecified young men and a certain Theodosius b. Theodorus. Given the short form of the name here, some uncertainty attaches to the issue of just which member of the Hita family is in view: is this Eleazar b. Eleazar, or rather the father? The editors understood the man to be the former (although without explaining why),[166] and this seems the more likely option considering the reconstructed genealogy of the family and the age ranges that it would imply for Eleazar and his father.[167] If rightly understood, the signatures to *P.Yadin* 46 indicate that Eleazar b. Eleazar had a brother whose son was old enough to exercise legal functions. He was thus an adult. This understanding entails that, were he still living, the elder Eleazar would be in his late sixties at the least. This is not an age at which one would expect an ancient to assume military command in guerrilla-style warfare.

Sometime later and for reasons unknown, Eleazar ran afoul of Simon b. Kosiba. The letter *P.Yadin* 50, dispatched by Simon's lieutenant Simon b. Judah to John and Masabala, orders them to deliver "Eleazar b. Hita" to Bar Kokhba immediately.[168] They are to take care during the arrest that no harm befall Eleazar's "produce" (עמליה) or his date fruits, and—most especially—that no one goes near the balsam garden (לטמה, i.e., *ladanum*—a Latin loan) that Eleazar leases from the state. He is thus the only En Gedite whose name we know who is explicitly said to cultivate opobalsam, literally worth its weight in gold, as opposed to choice dates. Further, if any man in En Gedi sides with Eleazar and offers resistance to the letter's commands, John and Masabala are ordered to bind him, too, and send him to Bar Kokhba for punishment. The implications of this letter for the state of the revolt are grim indeed: military leaders are now defecting or insubordinate, and the possibility exists that soldiers in Simon's own army may take up arms in defense of Eleazar.

We do not know the sequel. The fact that none of the remaining thirteen letters sent to En Gedi names Eleazar as a co-commander, however, argues two things. First, the reference here in *P.Yadin* 50 is likely to Eleazar the son, not his father, since we have no reason to believe that actions involving the father would have meant the son's dismissal from command—and yet he is named in no further letters. Thus he was, in fact, removed—being punished, it would follow, for his own sins, not those of his father. And second, we should probably infer that all of the other letters to En Gedi were later, not earlier, than *P.Yadin* 50 and 56. We should have expected all three commanders to be referenced if any letters preceded our pair. Since as a partner in the subleasing described in *P.Yadin* 44–46 Eleazar was evidently in good standing when they were composed in approximately October/November of 134, it appears that for much of its last year the revolt was in extremis. This chronological inference will be of some value to us in our considerations in Chapter 4.

Masabala b. Simon and his family are particularly well attested in the materials that have descended to us (Figure 3.10). Masabala himself is

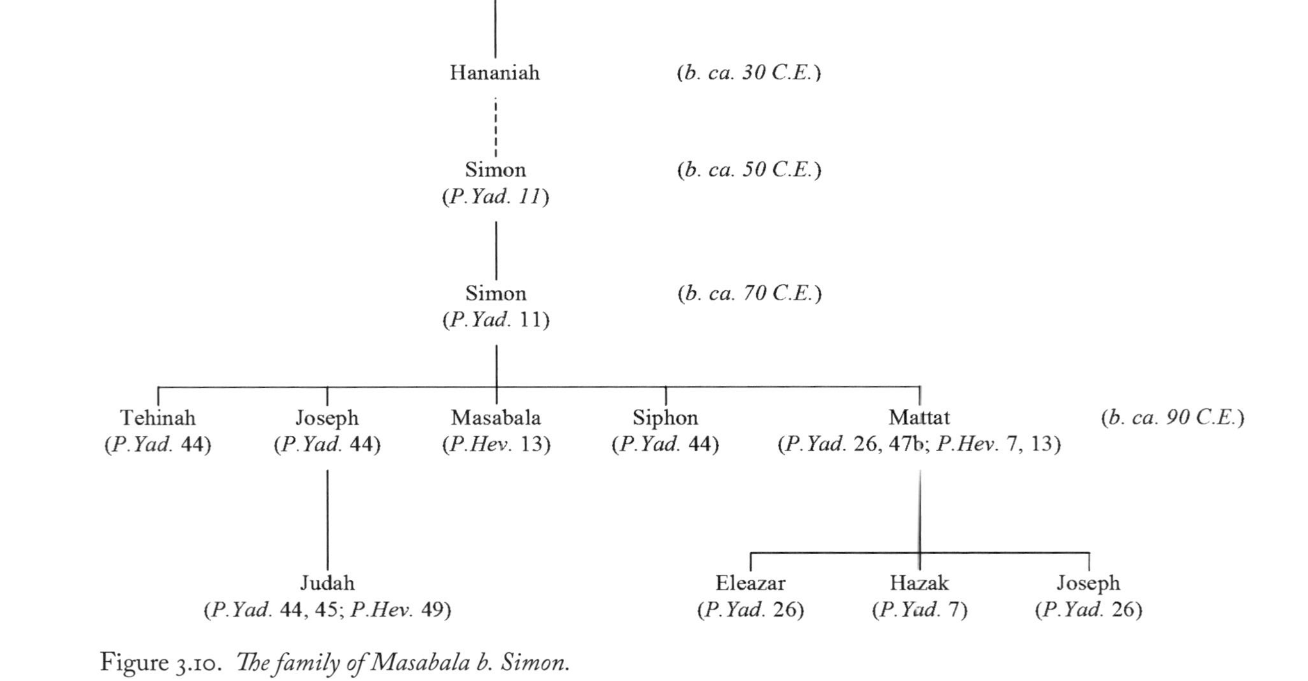

Figure 3.10. *The family of Masabala b. Simon.*

addressed in eight of the Bar Kokhba letters and is the subject of another, in addition to his scribal role already noted, so that he appears in one way or another in no fewer than fifteen documents.[169] In terms of surviving evidence, a probability exists that the patriarch of the family was another Masabala, probably born about the turn of the Common Era. He is the only other Judaean bearing that striking name in Ilan's extensive corpus.[170] Josephus referred to him at *B.J.* 5.532: "After these men a certain priest, Hananiah the son of Masabala, a man of the ruling class, and Aristeus the scribe of the Sanhedrin were executed, and along with them fifteen of the leading men from among the ordinary citizens."[171] Thus in 70 C.E. the revolutionary war leader Simon b. Giora executed Hananiah b. Masabala as part of a purge of elite opposition in the city. This man was one of the hereditary class of priests and was moreover of the highest station in society. Josephus called him ἐπίσημος, "eminent; of the ruling class," the very word-group he used elsewhere of his own family, which by his account was related to the Hasmoneans.[172] His usage would make Masabala b. Simon and the other sons of Simon members of that same elite priestly class to which Josephus himself belonged: the Judaean ruling class.[173] The notion that Simon b. Kosiba might have chosen as his own immediate subordinates men of this class is hardly surprising. Moreover, scholars have often noted the prominence evidently assumed by priests in the Second Revolt.[174]

That Masabala and his brothers should have been both priests and scribes was not unusual. Significant overlap existed between the two categories, even at the highest levels of Judaean society.[175] Our priestly scribes undoubtedly owned lands and gardens in En Gedi and Mahoza and, just possibly, an import-export business connected to trade on the Dead Sea. The Aramaic root סבל that underlies Masabala's handle-become-name was used in Judaean Aramaic for "porter" and occurs in Mas556, a letter sent circa 70 C.E. to Masada discussing supplies. Several of the Bar Kokhba letters also require Masabala and his co-commander(s) to supply the army. In any event, one presumes that the family's wealth was not amassed primarily by working as scribes; that trade was merely one of a number of irons in the family's fire. It is just that from our perspective this trade is very much to the fore, inasmuch as it resulted in the sons of Simon appearing in more than twenty separate documents—in many of them, several times—and in every one of the six surviving archives that may arguably be attached to the Cave of Letters. At most, as we shall see, only a few odd Semitic letters (γράμματα) have survived of the family's own archive or archives. Yet, Babatha aside, we nevertheless know its members better than we know anyone else within the Bar Kokhba materials.

The calligraphic handwriting that Joseph b. Simon used to compose *P.Yadin* 44–46, and that his brother Siphon and son Judah essentially duplicated in affixing their signatures to those documents, plainly shows that the family was used to producing book scrolls. Some of these scrolls may have been deluxe editions and so comparatively lucrative as items for a local, or perhaps regional, book culture. Even ordinary books were valuable, too expensive for many people, and so might provide a decent income provided one could obtain sufficient customers. Finding prospective buyers was doubtless easier in a wealthy village such as En Gedi. The sons of Simon also produced documents, as we have seen, and must have served many of the families of En Gedi and Mahoza in frequent transactions that required paperwork. If we want to imagine how their scribal shop in En Gedi may have functioned, we can perhaps begin with William Johnson's reconstruction of a typical situation in Roman Egypt:

> The financial feasibility of a "book trade" in fact makes much more sense if we try to re-imagine a *librarius* not as a "bookseller" but as a scribe or scribal shop that performs multiple functions: copying books to order from the (few) master copies maintained in stock; copying books to order from a master copy derived from a public library; selling used books, including those from auction; perhaps rarely (given the capital risks) making multiple copies in advance for books thought to have ready customers. This scenario is consistent with what we know of ancient artisan classes generally, and what we know of the modern scribal trade still surviving in, for instance, Arabic countries.[176]

We know nothing of public libraries in Roman Judaea,[177] and we have to factor in the production of documents alongside literary endeavor, but with those adjustments Johnson's picture may serve, as long as we are willing to be content with what is possible, a blurred rather than sharply etched image of ancient reality. We do know that people of the social class of our four families owned some books since literary works were found among their belongings in the Judaean refuge caves.

At the end, as the Second Revolt collapsed, at least two of these families fled to the caves in the nearby cliffs. Surviving members of the extended families of Babatha and Salome Komaise prepared the Cave of Letters as a refuge. They made their way to it sometime in the fall of 135, presumably (but not certainly) after the disaster of Bethar. As for the family of Eleazar

b. Hita, nothing is known. We have no evidence of them in any of the caves beyond their presence in the archives of others. But what of the family of Masabala, Joseph and their scribal brothers? A heretofore-unrecognized clue may offer a dark and deeply sad suggestion of their fates.

Aharoni's Cave of Horrors was one of the two or three most inaccessible of the refuge caves. The mouth of the cave lies some seventy-six meters beneath the lip of the plateau above. A drop of more than three hundred meters separates the entrance from the floor of the wadi below. The escarpment here is essentially vertical. No path down ever existed. Aharoni and his fellow excavators reached the cave via rope ladders eighty to one hundred meters long. Similarly, the ancient men, women, and children whose skeletal remains greeted the archaeologists upon their entry must have used ropes to drop supplies and lower themselves and their families. Ropes were found within the cave, in some cases still attached to the handles of broken pots.

We have already discussed the cave, and there is no reason to repeat what has been said. But one portion of Aharoni's report of Expedition B's findings calls for a closer examination. He wrote of certain graves found at the rear of the cave, some of them still pristine. These graves held the remains of people who died earlier than the majority of the inhabitants, whose skeletons were some distance away, strewn throughout the fore-portions of the grotto. Those in the rear had been laid to rest by family members, their presence demonstrating an appreciable period of cave habitation, long enough that weaker or older members of the group died before the final death watch instituted by the Roman forces camped directly above. Of these few people Aharoni wrote:

> Close by the graves, and apparently connected with them, we unearthed several ostraca. This material had been so severely damaged by the bedouin that, from the fragments recovered, we were able to reconstruct only one more or less complete inscription [here Aharoni described the writing noted earlier: Saul b. Saul; peace!]. . . . A second ostracon found in this part of the cave is also inscribed with the name of a person, though the letters are difficult to decipher and the reading therefore uncertain.[178]

Aharoni offered a conjecture or two concerning the reading but cautiously refrained from any certain suggestion. Only decades later was it possible to read this second ostracon with any degree of certitude. The scholar who succeeded in this decipherment was, unsurprisingly, Ada Yardeni.

In her *Textbook* published in 2000, Yardeni included a drawing, transcription, and translation of the ostracon that Aharoni had struggled to read.[179] Her drawing captured the flowing, semicursive script produced by a practiced, likely scribal hand: יהוסף בר שמעון, "Joseph b. Simon." Since the *Textbook* was intended as a paleographic analysis only, Yardeni offered no comment on the possible historical significance of this name in its archaeological setting. In 2004 Klaus Beyer published the second volume of *Die aramäischen Texte vom Toten Meer,* in which he included the ostracon, fully accepting Yardeni's reading but likewise offering no comment on what it might mean.[180] Otherwise, Yardeni's decipherment has gone unremarked, perhaps because it has not been placed within the context of the Naḥal Ḥever materials as a whole. No certainty can be possible, of course, but the question that leaps to mind is reasonable: Can this be the Joseph b. Simon who wrote *P.Yadin* 44–46?

In favor of the possibility is the self-evident importance of whomever was entombed in the Cave of Horrors. The Romans did not routinely station troops above the wadis to ensure the deaths of refugees in the caves. In fact, if the archaeology speaks truth, many such people escaped the caves alive. It therefore seems plain that the Romans believed they knew who was in the Cave of Horrors and the Cave of Letters, presumably because their identities and whereabouts had been betrayed by other Judaeans, perhaps under torture. The camps argue by their presence that the Romans wished to make examples of the leaders of the Second Revolt and had sought them with an animus. We know that John b. Baʿyah, one of the two military commanders of En Gedi, was in the Cave of Letters—or at least, his letters and some family members were. Perched like a nest of vultures right above was one Roman camp. A second camp was perched across the gulch above the Cave of Horrors. A certain symmetry attends the suggestion that within the second cave were known to be hidden the second military commander and his family. That would mean Masabala b. Simon, Joseph b. Simon, and other surviving sons of Simon and their extended families (evidently including one Saul b. Saul).

In any event, the inhabitants of the Cave of Horrors included members of the En Gedi elite, for it was only the elite who could afford to outfit the refuge caves, their wealth being attested by the archaeological finds. And the cave hid a family or related families rather than miscellaneous refugees, for the reasons argued earlier. And these people included one or more scribes, to judge from the fluency of the hand that inscribed the ostracon. And some of its inhabitants possessed the patronym "Simon." One of them was named

Joseph; likely, it was a member of his family who lovingly labeled the grave that held his body. And so his family was perhaps scribal.

The links in this chain of evidence and reasoning are by no means all equally solid, nor do all of them lead inevitably to the next. Still, we may have discovered the answer to the question of what happened to Masabala and his relatives. If so, we may also have discovered an answer to one of the guiding questions of this study: whose texts were they? In this case, the text is the Minor Prophets scroll inscribed in Greek, easily the most significant writing to emerge from the Cave of Horrors. The owner may well have been one of the sons of Simon—an elite priest, that is, and a rock-ribbed supporter of the revolt, a man trained to read and interpret the Hebrew scriptures: a nationalist intellectual. That such a man might expostulate from the Greek is of great interest and offers potential insight into language and literacy that will require further discussion later.

Any of Masabala's family who survived to flee, found in the Cave of Horrors not the life they pursued, but the death that pursued them. At least twenty-one people died there, ten adults (including at least three women) and eleven children.[181] Concerning those deaths Aharoni was circumspect, noting only that the absence of any signs of injury to the bodies showed that the Romans did not take the cave by force of arms, a conclusion that the inaccessibility of the cave would otherwise compel. Obviously, they did not surrender. Precisely how, then, did the inhabitants of the Cave of Horrors die—and for that matter, of the Cave of Letters?

Though we shall never know for certain, the answer to the question may be important for our estimate of these people. Several clues are suggestive. It should be borne in mind as we consider these possibilities that the common notion—that they despairingly gave themselves over to death by thirst or starvation—has always been as uncertain as any other answer.

Aharoni wrote in his report that the besieged inhabitants, realizing that the size of their cave precluded hiding their possessions from the victorious Romans, decided on a particular course of action:

> [They] evidently decided to make a great bonfire in the centre of the cave and destroy all their belongings in it—apart from the Greek scroll of the Twelve Minor Prophets which, together perhaps with some important documents, was buried between the rocks of the end chamber [where the burials were]. . . . Most of the utensils were found broken into pieces in the debris from the great fire . . . how intense the heat of this blaze was, can be seen from the warped glass bowl.[182]

One does not like to imagine how human beings would fare in proximity to glass-warping heat, not to mention the siphoning effect a large fire would have on the cave's oxygen, or the problem of smoke inhalation. The significance of the destructive fire may have been greater than Aharoni allowed: more than a guarantee that the Romans would never plunder their belongings, but rather a final act of defiance, a fiery prelude—or perhaps for all but one, postlude—to death by their own hands. The brilliance of the flames would easily have been visible to the Roman forces above and on the other side of Naḥal Ḥever. The meaning would have been clear, the thought processes perspicuous. Surrender being out of the question, all that remained was self-destruction, or a slow, agonizing death by thirst, all the while watching one's loved ones suffer hopelessly.

Aharoni's description was possibly intended to remind us of the words of Josephus's description of the final moments of the defenders of Masada, a description given in the form of Ben Jair's speech. According to the Jewish historian, this commander exhorted his comrades to take their own lives rather than submit to the brutality awaiting them and their loved ones the next morning at Roman hands: "But first, let us destroy both our possessions and the fortress in a fire, for the Romans will be grieved, I well know, neither laying hold of our persons, nor gaining the profit."[183] Josephus also portrays Jewish self-destruction in the face of what seemed even worse at Jotapata (*B.J.* 3.355–87), at Gamla (*B.J.* 4.78–81), and at the fall of Jerusalem (*B.J.* 6.280). His narratives have in recent years become greatly controversial; did these things really happen? To engage that controversy here is as pointless as to insist on the interpretation given above of the events at the Cave of Horrors. Nevertheless, one cannot doubt that a perfervid rebel such as Masabala would resonate with the words Josephus placed in Ben Jair's mouth.

On the opposite side of the wadi, the greater accessibility of the Cave of Letters may have dictated a different final scene to the tragedy. This cave could be reached by foot via an extremely narrow and dangerous descent. Yadin proposed, it will be recalled, that the inhabitants hid their documents and other valuables in preparing to flee. If one ponders the situation from the perspective of the rebels, it seems likely that he was right. For once the Romans established themselves above, an attempted breakout was the sole alternative to death by deprivation or self-destruction. Any attempt to flee, it would have been plain, was almost certain to fail—but only almost. The other options were certain death. The archaeological finds in the cave, including the surprisingly high proportion of female skeletons to male (eight to three), comports with the idea that some men did attempt to escape, probably at night. The footing would have been even more perilous in the dark, but they might have gained the element of surprise.

They would have exited the cave with their weapons, hoping to reach the escarpment above before the Romans discovered them and picked them off the cliff face with their archers. We shall never know whether the final revolutionaries failed to reach the top, or did succeed, only to perish there in hand-to-hand combat. Either way, their desperately hopeful families were evidently forced to turn back to await death in the cave. It would not have long delayed.

Did something like these scenarios actually happen? We can do no more than weigh the relatively meager evidence, calculate probabilities, imagine, and restrain imagination. But one verity is that nearly two millennia later, Yigael Yadin and his team of archaeologists succeeded in finding what Babatha and her families had hidden, what the bedouin had overlooked: the letters that were to give the cave its modern name. The Cave of Letters yielded these missives as the great treasure of the 1960 excavations. The fifteen letters from Naḥal Ḥever joined a dozen or so from Murabbaʿat. Yadin completed his excavations the following year. What remains two generations later, arguably, is full excavation of the letters themselves. Just as with the bedouin, so the first scholars on the analytic scene, for all that they did discover, may have left some of the greatest treasures behind. Beneath untested boulders, betwixt unexplored crevices lie data critical for the study of Judaean language and literacy. We turn to the task of excavation.

4 Epistolary Culture in Roman Judaea

The Bar Kokhba Letters in the Greco-Roman World

Fifty years have passed since the most recent discovery of dispatches included today among the Bar Kokhba letters, which together number as many as twenty-nine.[1] *Sixty* years have passed since the bedouin spirited the initial missives out of the caves of Murabbaʿat. Still, these documents have yet to receive thorough examination against the backdrop of their times, as products of the Greco-Roman world.

This statement intends no criticism. It is just a matter of fact. More than half a century on, these artifacts demand full analysis for what they are: letters of the Roman Mediterranean. The oddity owes to various factors. Dennis Pardee and his co-authors gave expression to one while introducing their 1982 study that embraced eight of the Hebrew missives: "The study of Hebrew letters as letters is in its infancy. Indeed, the same is true of letters in all the ancient Semitic languages. As a general statement, it may be said that ancient Semitic letters have been studied primarily from a philological or historical perspective, but not from a specifically epistolographic one."[2] Although important progress has been made since those words were set down, the study of Hebrew and Aramaic epistolography, if no longer in its infancy, has yet to outgrow its youth.[3] Work remains to be done on many fronts.

The ever-increasing specialization that characterizes modern academia has been a second factor inhibiting analysis of the Bar Kokhba letters as Greco-Roman artifacts. Cursory perusal of the bibliography on the letters will quickly bring to the fore that the vast majority of those writing on them have been Semitists and scholars of the Hebrew Bible. Since all but two of the Bar Kokhba letters are composed in Semitic languages, this scholarly self-selection is entirely understandable. For the most part, serious study of the letters demands exactly the sort of linguistic training that the majority of those writing on them have in fact got. But most scholars of the Hebrew Bible live at some remove from Greco-Roman times. They inhabit a mental world several centuries to the left on the timeline from the historical setting of these letters. Accordingly, they have tended to view the materials much more as Semitic letters than as products of the empire, as in continuity with ancient Near Eastern missives more than as cousins to the epistolary papyri from Roman Egypt or the letters of Cicero. Their situation has been one that all scholars share, of course: any given training conditions a person to ask certain kinds of questions, see certain phenomena, and not others. Only a tiny percentage of those applying themselves to the letters have been drawn from the realm of classics—itself a field in which, laid against its history of two millennia and more, the study of the formal features of Greek and Latin letters is of comparatively recent vintage.[4] Moreover, within classics the study of epistolography has become a specialization, further reducing the pool of potential comparatists.

A third factor of no small importance involves the publication history of these texts and an unfortunate loss of momentum. Three of the most complete of the Bar Kokhba letters from Murabbaʿat were published shortly after discovery, appearing in preliminary editions in 1953.[5] These texts drew comment from many of the world's leading Hebraists and biblical scholars, igniting a brush fire of discussion and back-and-forth. *Mur* 43, for example, featured in sixty-three treatments of one sort or another in the years before 1977; forty-seven of these dated to the 1950s.[6] The fire abated a bit, only to spring to new life with Yadin's discoveries and preliminary publications of the materials from the Cave of Letters. But his treatment of the letters in his articles and in *Bar-Kokhba* was more tease than substance. Of the fifteen letters belonging to the Archive of John b. Baʿyah, Yadin offered a peek at six, completely revealing just four.[7] Scholars were naturally reticent to attempt broad analytic conclusions on the basis of such partial data, most of which they could not check for themselves. As the 1970s came to a close, interest in the letters choked and died. The necessary oxygen—information—was simply not to be had. The words of Fergus Millar in 1993 were representative: "Three decades after the initial discovery the majority [of Yadin's texts] have remained unpublished. . . . Further comment on this extremely discreditable record would be superfluous."[8]

At the time Millar wrote, such feelings were widespread. People of necessity turned their attention elsewhere. Perhaps then it is unsurprising that little discernible new interest in the Bar Kokhba letters was stirred by Yardeni's *Textbook*, even though it was essentially a full publication, including hand-drawings, transcription, and translation. Nor did the appearance two years later (2002) of the *editio princeps* of Yadin's materials suffice to rekindle the flame.[9] The embers had grown cold. The momentum of the exciting early years had been forfeit.

These considerations may help to explain why comparison of the Bar Kokhba letters with the formal features of Greek and Latin letters such as the "frame" (*praescriptio* and farewell), subscriptions, folding, and addressing has been minimal—substantially nonexistent before Dirk Schwiderski's treatment of some of these things in 2000.[10] Comparison of the various processes involved in composing and delivering the letters has yet to occur. All of these elements hold potential for improved historical understanding of Simon b. Kosiba's administration and the course of the Second Revolt. More particular to this study, their analysis promises deeper penetration into questions of Judaean language and literacy. This promise motivates the following preliminary discussion.

The Letters as Greco-Roman Artifacts: First Steps

Serious study of Northwest Semitic epistolography took its start with the publication by Joseph Fitzmyer of "Some Notes on Aramaic Epistolography" in 1974.[11] This treatment became the conscious inspiration of articles in the next few years by Pardee on Hebrew letters and by his collaborator Paul Dion on comparative epistolography;[12] from their consultations with David Whitehead then sprang the joint *Handbook* of 1982. Fitzmyer was able to include in his analysis at least some information on eight of the Aramaic letters from the Cave of Letters, but the evidence dictated that he focus most of his attention on letters composed more than half a millennium earlier, the great majority of them found in Egypt: notably, the Elephantine Papyri, the Hermopolis Letters, and the Arsames Correspondence.

Fitzmyer separated the *praescriptio* (which meant for him expression of sender and recipient) from the initial greeting, which he reserved for separate treatment. Regarding the former, Fitzmyer found that the expression usual to the Bar Kokhba letters, "From X to Y," was one of five variations used by his corpus. This usage was shared, he thought, with the majority of the

Arsames letters and with two missives imbedded in the biblical text (Ezra 7:12 and Dan 3:31 are the relevant verses). In fact, however, Fitzmyer's grouping of all these texts as a single category was problematic in that, while the Arsames Correspondence used an expression *equivalent* to that of the Bar Kokhba letters, it was not verbally identical;[13] and the biblical portions as we have them are controversial of date and origin.[14] Thus within Fitzmyer's corpus, the *praescriptio* of the Bar Kokhba letters was effectively sui generis.

Similarly standing alone was the form of the initial greeting used by the writers of the Second Revolt correspondence.[15] The Aramaic Bar Kokhba letters say simply שלם, "Greetings" (literally, "peace"). Significantly more elaborate formulae characterized Fitzmyer's corpus elsewhere. Typical would be that of *BMAP* 13, שלם מראי אלהיא כלא [ישאלו] שגיא בכל עדן, "May all the gods earnestly [seek] my lord's welfare at all times," or that usual to the Arsames Correspondence, שלם ושררת שגיא הושרת לך, "I send you peace and much prosperity." Again unique within Fitzmyer's corpus, and in his judgment "hard . . . to explain," was the concluding salutation of the Bar Kokhba letters, either הוו שלם or הוא שלם, "Be well!"[16] Most other Aramaic letters lacked a final salutation altogether. A few private, as opposed to official letters, witnessed לשלמכי שלחת ספרא זנה, "I have sent this letter seeking your welfare" (frequent in the Hermopolis Letters). Thus the Bar Kokhba letters stood apart from earlier Aramaic epistolography in every feature of the frame.

On the Hebrew side of things, Pardee and his co-authors analyzed seven Bar Kokhba letters from Murabbaʿat together with the only Hebrew letter from the Cave of Letters then fully published with a photograph, *P.Yadin* 49. The great bulk of the letters to which they compared these Second Revolt writings originated in the last days of the Judaean monarchy, just before the kingdom fell to Nebuchadnezzar and the forces of Babylon. The Arad Letters date mostly to around 597 B.C.E. The Lachish Letters attach to 589 B.C.E. or so, when invasion was imminent. Both groups of earlier letters were written in ink on ostraca. Thus they were both much earlier and inscribed on a medium different from that of the Bar Kokhba missives. Because space on this medium was considerably more restricted than that available on papyrus, the writers of these letters tended to use shorter versions of the framing formulae than they might otherwise have chosen. For these reasons one might expect notable differences to emerge in comparison. But the earlier letters shared with the Second Revolt materials their basic character: all three groupings were military administrative documents. This fact gave special point to the comparison.

The scholars found that the Bar Kokhba letters identified both sender and recipient fully, whereas the earlier Hebrew missives rarely identified the sender at all and often relied on epithets rather than names to specify the addressee. Greeting formulae differed from group to group: Arad was unlike Lachish, and both were unlike the Bar Kokhba texts. Transitioning from the *praescriptio* to the body of the letter, the earlier materials regularly used ועת(ה), "and now," whereas the Bar Kokhba letters used ש, perhaps best understood as a particle of recitation and so left untranslated. The ostraca from Arad and Lachish contained no salutation formula. In contrast, the Second Revolt Hebrew documents mirrored their Aramaic counterparts in closing with variations on הוה שלום, "Be well!" Pardee and his co-authors concluded, "The chronological separation of the letters from ca. 600 B.C. and those from ca. A.D. 132–35 is, as one would expect, decisive: the two groups have entirely different formulae."[17] Whence the new conventions of the Bar Kokhba texts? Here the scholars refrained from any definite suggestion. "Much more data is needed for the transitions within both Hebrew and Aramaic epistolary traditions," they explained, "before we can come to a conclusion on the chronological factor in the changes (i.e., the epistolary formulation used in the Bar Kokhba period may have been operative for several hundred years for all we know)."[18] Here and there they did make brief allusion to the possibility of Greek influence but then pursued the matter no further.[19]

So matters stood when Schwiderski came on the scene some twenty years hence.[20] He began his discussion of the letters in the context of Hellenistic-Roman times with a reasonable a priori: "The Bar-Kosiba texts show that correspondence at the time of the Second Jewish Revolt did not remain fixed on a single language even within a particular group, but that Hebrew, Aramaic and Greek were used side by side. This synchronous use leads one to expect numerous formal similarities [among the letters]."[21] He proceeded to work his way systematically through the elements of the frame. In great detail he illustrated how the usage of the Second Revolt texts differed from earlier Northwest Semitic practice. Schwiderski showed that the typical opening form of the Aramaic Bar Kokhba letters,[22] פלני לאלמני שלם, "X [bids? sc. אמר] peace to Y," was extremely similar to the standard formula known from Greek letters beginning in the third century B.C.E., ὁ δεῖνα τῷ δεῖνι χαίρειν (sc. λέγει) ("so and so greets so and so").[23] He also assembled all the formulae used in the Bar Kokhba letters for the final salutation and set them against the Greek. The simplest versions were Hebrew הוה שלום /Aramaic הוא שלם,

"Be well!," precisely replicating Greek ἔρρωσο.[24] What Schwiderski said was not entirely new, of course. What was new was the thoroughness with which he said it. Earlier scholarship had suggested possibilities; Schwiderski offered demonstration. He concluded, "From the start one must expect substantial influence upon the Hebrew and Aramaic epistolary formulae coming from the Greek."[25]

Schwiderski then turned his attention to the "chronological factor in the changes" that Pardee, Dion, and Whitehead had recognized. How long had the epistolary formulae found in the Bar Kokhba letters been operative? Were they forms that had emerged only under the circumstances of the Second Revolt, as Alexander had tentatively suggested? In the years since those scholars had written, the materials from Masada and the Qumran caves had at last appeared in print, and these offered some new data on the issue that Schwiderski turned to good use. He found in the fragmentary Aramaic letter from Masada, Mas556, the one-word initial greeting formula שלם.[26] Since the letter could not reasonably postdate the destruction of the fortress at the end of the First Revolt, and since it was unlikely that this usage appeared here for the first time in Judaean history, Schwiderski concluded that he had evidence of Greek influence by the first century C.E.[27]

This was as far as he could go with epigraphic testimony, but letters imbedded within the literary texts from Qumran offered a chance to push the quest for the evidence of Greek influence farther back. Schwiderski found his most compelling argument on this score in 4Q550, sometimes known as *Proto-Esther*[a] (though more recently by the name *Jews at the Persian Court*). Imbedded in this writing was a putative letter from Darius I that bore a filing description derived from the first line of the interior text: פׄתׄגׄ[ם דר]יוש מלכא לעבדי שלטנא די כׄוׄלׄ [א]רעא שלם, "The lett[er of Da]rius the king to the ministers of the Empire in all the earth: Greetings!"[28] Here in this Aramaic text was the simple but telltale epistolary formula "X to Y," along with the familiar one-word greeting formula שלם that derived from Greek χαίρειν. Schwiderski, following Klaus Beyer, argued that this copy of *Jews at the Persian Court* could be dated on the basis of paleographic analysis to circa 50 B.C.E. and that the original composition was probably produced in the eastern Diaspora some 150 years before this copy's production.[29] Some scholars have suggested earlier dates for the original composition, but without considering Schwiderski's comparative method.[30] The Greek connection most reasonably supports a date for the work no earlier than the latter part of the third century, since one must allow a decent passage of time between the onset of rule by the Hellenes in the East and the appearance of Greek epistolary formulae in fictional Aramaic letters. Change of Semitic traditions would not likely have been immediate for documentary letters, after all, and these certainly would have preceded their literary cousins. Schwiderski's chronological conclusions were therefore convincing: "The exact time of origin of the *shalem* formula must remain open. Regarding its use for initial greeting as well as for farewell formulas, the origin may be placed somewhere between the end of the fourth century B.C.E. and the first century B.C.E. on the basis of the epigraphic sources. The literary text before us allows us to fix the time more precisely: somewhere within the third century B.C.E."[31] Schwiderski further argued that the use of Greek epistolary frames logically must have begun in Judaea with letters written in Greek. Here, he offered no specifics, but one need merely contemplate the fact that from the tail end of the fourth century B.C.E. until the mid-second century B.C.E., the region was directly ruled first by the Ptolemies, then by the Seleucids: empires that governed in Greek. Certain letters issued by those rulers still survive.[32] From Greek, Schwiderski opined, the formulae migrated in appropriate new dress to Aramaic epistolography. He ventured no suggestion as to dates, but it would be reasonable to consider for this practice a time no later than the years of Hasmonean hegemony, when, to take just one example, Alexander Jannaeus issued coins inscribed in both Greek and Aramaic. From Aramaic the usage passed into Hebrew, Schwiderski further argued, likely only at the time of the Second Revolt, when Hebrew again began to be used for letters, as an expression of nationalism.[33]

On the whole, Schwiderski's suggested chronology and direction of development are convincing. That Greek epistolary structures were birthed in Judaea by Greek letters is almost self-evident. That Aramaic practice was the source of Hebrew is also evident and emerges not merely on general considerations as he proposed, but from attention to specifics: the Hebrew letters not infrequently continue to use Aramaic words and phrases for the frames. This practice betrays the direction of influence. But on the question of when Hebrew letter writing may have begun, the German scholar's conclusions are less felicitous. As seen earlier, letters written in Hebrew possibly occur among the materials from Ketef Jericho (recall the very fragmentary *P.Jericho* 14, שלחתי כסף, "I have sent money"). Granted, the Jericho materials are too fragmentary to bear much weight; but the so-called Halakhic Letter (4QMMT), surviving in six copies among the Dead Sea Scrolls, robustly testifies to the epistolary use of Hebrew in the early first century B.C.E.[34] It seems that correspondence in Hebrew took place alongside that in

Aramaic, at least in certain times and places, and within particular—probably priestly—circles. In general, though, Schwiderski established what he set out to show. Aramaic and Hebrew frame formulae derived from Greek usage and were in place well before the dawn of the Common Era.

Writing the Bar Kokhba Letters

Yet the frames are a small part of a much bigger picture. The Bar Kokhba correspondence displays many equally fundamental points of contact with Greco-Roman epistolary conventions. These other connections have gone unremarked by scholars, but taken cumulatively they demonstrate two matters of conspicuous importance for the issues of our study. First, even among a people as singular as the Judaeans, a well-attested Mediterranean koine governing fundamental practices of letter writing had taken root. And second—a related, but nonetheless a distinct matter—*Roman Judaea was an epistolary culture,* conceivably no less so than was the Roman Egypt much better known to us through the papyri.[35]

One of these additional points of contact involves the inscription of the final salutation. Since many letters were produced by scribes,[36] even among the elites, it was customary for the person sending the letter to write out ἔρρωσο or the equivalent in his or her own hand—provided, of course, that the author was literate. This practice is commonly seen already in the royal correspondence of the Hellenistic period. After the king's chancery had prepared a preliminary draft of a given letter and then the letter itself, the king customarily added ἔρρωσθε with his own hand, and perhaps a bit more.[37] One reason this practice arose was to authenticate the letter, since the great bulk of it would be in a hand different from the author's. Seeing the author's handwriting would certify to the recipient that the missive was indeed the author's. With official letters the issue of genuineness could be acute, particularly in a time of crisis, but even with private correspondence fraud was not unknown. Much could hinge on proof of genuineness. The importance of this reassurance is particularly evident from statements in the letters of the apostle Paul.[38] And Apuleius—to take another example—accused of using magic to win a widow for his bride, counteraccused his opponent Aemilianus of authoring a letter that influenced her to marry: it was the letter, not magic—provided the letter were genuine. Thus he confronted Aemilianus: *Estne haec tua epistola? . . . estne tua ista subscribtio* [*sic*]? (Is this letter yours? . . . Is this subscription yours?).[39] Subscription was authorship.

Another purpose of personal subscriptions was to extend to a correspondent the author's care and esteem—as it were, to perfume the letter. Writing at least some words in one's own hand, if not the entire letter, was frequently perceived as a significant gesture of friendship. Cicero's correspondence explicitly testifies to the weight that might be given to this personal touch.[40] Among the Latin letters from Vindolanda are numerous instances where the authors added the closing greetings in their own hands, a fact evident from the different handwriting. The most famous example from the British site is perhaps one Claudia Severa's three lines elegantly subscribed to a birthday invitation, a manifest gesture of affection.[41]

The great majority of those Bar Kokhba letters sufficiently preserved to judge contain some form of personal subscription, usually in a hand differing from the body of the letter (Table 4.1).[42] One of these subscriptions holds particular interest. *Mur* 43 is a letter addressed from Simon b. Kosiba to Jesus b. Galgula and concerns the treatment of certain Galileans. When he published the *editio princeps* Milik suggested that these Galileans, mistreated by the Judaean locals—perhaps concerning supplies of foodstuffs—had gone to complain to b. Kosiba: "He took the matter to heart: a letter by his own hand, a solemn oath formula, a threat of shackles, [menacing] analogy to the case of a certain Ben Aphlul."[43] Milik said nothing about the hand of the subscription, which appears different from that of the body so far as its damaged condition permits a conclusion, but reconstructed the subscription in accordance with his proposal: [ש]מ̊וען ב[ן כוסבה] ע̊ל [נפשה], "Simon so[n of Kosiba], on [his own behalf]."[44]

Yadin subsequently discovered among the missives from the Cave of Letters the document now known as *P.Yadin* 50. This letter was subscribed by a man named Simon b. Judah in a hand differing from that of the body. On the basis of this discovery, the Israeli scholar questioned Milik's identification of the author of *Mur* 43:

> This signature [in *P.Yadin* 50], of [one of] Bar Kokhba's aides, is of great value; for had the letters been partially obliterated, leaving only the words, "Shim'on Bar . . ." there is no doubt that it would have been assumed immediately that this was the signature of Shim'on Bar Kosiba himself. But in view of the clearly legible "Shim'on Bar Yehuda," some doubt is cast on Milik's restoration of the signature of the letter found in Wadi Murabba'at. . . . None of the letters in our possession is signed by Bar Kosiba himself . . . it may be assumed that the person who signed the Murabba'at letter was another Shim'on.[45]

Table 4.1. Language and script in the Bar Kokhba letters

Designation	Sender(s)	Addressee(s)	Subscriber/ language of subscription	Language	Script	Level of hand
Mur 42	Jesus b. Eleazar, Eleazar b. Joseph	Jesus b. Galgula, "all Israel"	Jacob b. Joseph (?)/Hebrew	Hebrew	Bookhand	4
Mur 43	Simon b. Kosiba	Jesus b. Galgula, men of Kephar-Barucha	Simon b. Kosiba/ indeterminate	Hebrew	Bookhand	4
Mur 44	Simon	Jesus	None	Hebrew	Bookhand	4
Mur 45	—	—	—	Hebrew	Bookhand	4
Mur 46	John b. Mahanaim	Jose b. Galgula	John b. Mahanaim/ Aramaic	Hebrew	Bookhand	4
Mur 47	—	—	—	Hebrew	Bookhand	4
Mur 48	b. Galgula (?)	John b. Mahanaim	b. Galgula (?)/ Aramaic	Hebrew	Cursive	4
Mur 49	—	—	—	Hebrew	Bookhand	4
Mur 51	—	b. Galgula	—	Hebrew	Bookhand	4
Mur 52	—	b. Galgula	—	Hebrew	Bookhand	4
Mur 61 (?)	Simon b. Kosiba	—	—	Hebrew (?)	Bookhand	4
P.Hev. 30	Simon b. Mataniah	Simon b. Kosiba	Simon b. Mataniah/ Hebrew	Hebrew	Bookhand	4
P.Yad. 49	Simon b. Kosiba	Masabala, John b. Ba'yah, men of En Gedi	Anonymous writer Indeterminate	Hebrew	Cursive	3
P.Yad. 51	Simon b. Kosiba	Masabala, John b. Ba'yah, men of En Gedi	—	Hebrew	Cursive	3
P.Yad. 60	Simon b. Kosiba	John	—	Hebrew	Cursive	3
P.Yad. 61	Simon b. Kosiba	Men of Tekoa	—	Hebrew	Cursive	3

continued

Table 4.1. *Continued*

Designation	Sender(s)	Addressee(s)	Subscriber/ language of subscription	Language	Script	Level of hand
P.Yad. 50	Simon b. Kosiba	John b. Ba'yah, Masabala b. Simon	Simon b. Judah/Aramaic	Aramaic	Cursive	3
P.Yad. 53	Simon b. Kosiba	John b. Ba'yah	Anonymous writer/Aramaic	Aramaic	Cursive	3
P.Yad. 54	Simon b. Kosiba	John, Masabala	Samuel b. Ammi/Aramaic	Aramaic	Cursive	3
P.Yad. 55	Simon b. Kosiba	John, Masabala	None	Aramaic	Cursive	3
P.Yad. 56	Simon b. Kosiba	John b. Ba'yah, Masabala, b. Hita	Anonymous writer/Aramaic	Aramaic	Cursive	3
P.Yad. 57	Simon	Judah b. Manaseh	Anonymous writer/Aramaic	Aramaic	Cursive	2/3
P.Yad. 58	Simon	John, Masabala men of Kiryat-'Arbayya	Anonymous writer/Aramaic	Aramaic	Cursive	3
P.Yad. 62	—	—	—	Aramaic	Cursive	3
P.Yad. 63	Simon	—	None	Aramaic	Cursive	3
P.Yad. 52	Soumaios	John son of Beianos, Masabala	Soumaios/ Greek	Greek	Cursive	4
P.Yad. 59	Annanos	John	Annanos/ Greek	Greek	Cursive	4

The fact that Yadin published no photograph of his text made it impossible for scholarship to resolve the issue, but the matter was by no means as clear-cut as Yadin portrayed it, as Pardee and his co-authors saw: "If the signatures of *papMur* 43 and [*P.Yadin* 50] are not the same, this would perhaps indicate that Milik was correct in restoring *bn kwsbh* and that *sm'wn bn/br k(w)sbh* and *sm'wn br yhwdh* are two different persons, for it would be asking too much of coincidence to have three persons named Shimon writing letters from Bar Kokhba's camp."[46] Only with the 2002 publication of the *editio princeps* of *P.Yadin* 50, which included photographs, did it become possible to revisit the question. Perhaps because study of the Bar Kokhba letters had by then lost much of its early vitality, however, no one seems to have done so. A few minutes suffice to check the plate of *P.Yadin* 50, place it alongside that of *Mur* 43, and see that the signatures in question are not identical.[47] Even though the writing of the subscription in *Mur* 43 is damaged, the two hands are so distinctly dissimilar that this judgment seems certain. Different Simons autographed the two letters.

Accordingly, if one agrees with Pardee, Dion, and Whitehead that multiplying "writing Simons" in Bar Kokhba's camp is an implausible exercise, it becomes likely that the subscription to *Mur* 43 really did come from the leader's own hand. Milik's reconstruction of the subscription was wrong, we know today; in legal texts, the phrase על נפשה applies only to principals. Much to be preferred would be either [ש]מ̊וען ב[ר כוסבה כתבה] (Aramaic) or [ש]מ̊וען ב[ן כוסבה כתבו] (Hebrew), "Simon b. Kosiba commissioned it." The language of the subscription must remain uncertain given the damage, and inasmuch as people did not necessarily subscribe letters in the same language as the body (see Table 4.1). These sorts of formulae were often scrawled almost on autopilot, and since the default for Semitic letters was generally Aramaic, the odds perhaps favor that choice.

More interesting than the language is the measure of the script's fluency, now that we can reasonably suppose that in *Mur* 43 we do have Simon b. Kosiba's personal hand to evaluate. The letters turn out to be labored products: *mem* disproportionate, outsized compared with the others; final *nun* short and squat, notably inelegant. This is not the signature of a man at ease with a calamus. But neither was he a βραδέως γράφων. The leader of the Second Jewish Revolt possessed a level 2 handwriting. He had advanced sufficiently in his education to gain some exposure to the copying of literary works, but not far enough to write or read easily. That Simon b. Kosiba could have handled a text of the Jewish scriptures with aplomb is highly doubtful. He was not literate in the sense we usually mean today, that is, able to pick up a text and read with relative ease and substantial understanding. In short, Bar Kokhba was no literary literate. It seems a "messiah" did not have to be.

Folding and addressing letters was another aspect of epistolary production wherein Judaeans had departed from earlier techniques and now embraced the Mediterranean koine. Earlier Semitic procedure had been particular and elaborate:

> When the letter was completed, it would be turned recto-up and folded upward toward the top in a series of horizontal bands, so that the blank space left at the bottom of the verso could be flapped over and exposed. The address would be written on this space. The letter, now folded into one long narrow strip, would then be folded laterally into quarters or halves (in a few cases, thirds), bound with a string, and sealed with a lump of wet clay impressed with the seal of the writer. It was now ready for dispatch.[48]

Greco-Roman methods were notably different. Greek letters would similarly be folded accordion style, but most often vertically, not horizontally. The letters would typically have four to seven folds. Where it is still possible to discern, given their sometimes fragmentary preservation, the majority of the Bar Kokhba papyrus letters used this Greek method. Thus, *Mur* 43 has six vertical folds; *Mur* 46, six; *Mur* 47, three visible, some having been lost; *Mur* 48, two vertical folds remain, some lost; *P.Yadin* 49, six or seven vertical folds; *P.Yadin* 50, four vertical folds; *P.Yadin* 53, six vertical folds; *P.Yadin* 55, four vertical folds; *P.Yadin* 56, three vertical folds; and *P.Yadin* 63, five vertical folds. In contrast to the Greek East, Romans seem regularly to have rolled papyrus letters into a scroll shape rather than folding them,[49] and one Bar Kokhba letter, *Mur* 42, was discovered by the archaeologists treated that way: "rolled rather tightly from the bottom up, with the beginning of the text on the inside."[50] A few of the Bar Kokhba letters display horizontal folds, usually because they were inscribed on long narrow strips rather than more standard pieces of papyrus.[51]

Unlike the earlier Semitic letters, whose address was inscribed on the last strip of the verso after it was folded down—the address thus paralleling the body of the letter—Greek letters were turned over and rotated ninety degrees. The scribe would then address the letter on the verso, at right angles to the body of the letter.[52] This last is precisely the method of *P.Hever* 30, and evidently of *P.Yadin* 52.[53] The other Bar Kokhba letters lack addresses altogether, a common phenomenon as well with Greek and Latin letters. Often, the person delivering the letter knew the addressee and his or her whereabouts, and so no address was necessary.

In the matter of folding, *P.Yadin* 54 presents a special case because it was inscribed on wood. Yadin described this letter and how it was inscribed and folded in his preliminary report on the 1960 excavations in the Cave of Letters: "It is inscribed with two columns, written from right to left. An incision had been made down the back, so that the wood could be folded, and it thus formed a kind of pinax. There are nine lines of writing in the right-hand column, and eight in the left, written in well preserved ink except for a few places where the characters have become blurred, or where the ink was absorbed into the knots of the original wood."[54]

When they published the first batch of tablets from the site of Vindolanda in 1983, the editors, Alan Bowman and J. David Thomas, were aware of the Judaean tablet and Yadin's description. They wrote: "The Vindolanda letter format is identical. The leaf [their term for the thin slat of wood] is used with the broad dimension as the width, the grain running horizontally. It is written in two columns (from left to right, of course), of which the left-hand column tends to be broader than the right. The leaf is then scored down the centre and folded with the letter on the inner faces."[55] The virtual identity of technique here in letters originating from opposite ends of the Roman Empire is remarkable. Even the Vindolandan norm of beginning with a comparatively wide column, followed by a narrower second column, is replicated by the Judaean exemplar. *P.Yadin* 54 averages 26.4 letters and spaces in the first column, 22.4 in the second. Such congruence of detail strongly suggests that, had evidence from many intermediate points survived, the same patterns would have been replicated.[56] A standard Mediterranean technique existed and, mutatis mutandis, Judaea participated. One standardized aspect of these leaves was the two-column format, a format virtually unique to the medium, only very rarely seen in letters on papyrus.[57] Since it is presented in two columns, therefore, it appears that in addition to *P.Yadin* 54, *P.Yadin* 49—although inscribed on papyrus—replicates a draft originally set down on a wooden leaf. Bar Kokhba's writer used the leaf for the draft and then, presumably after authorial review and with requisite changes incorporated, produced the fair copy on papyrus.

Doubtless, use of these leaves was common, both in wooded imperial localities where papyrus was not readily available and elsewhere as a cheaper alternative to the Egyptian export.[58] Probably the latter factor was more important in Judaea.[59] The leaves, or "ink tablets," to introduce another term suggested by Bowman and Thomas, were cut from the sapwood of young trees using a very sharp knife possessing a long blade. According to the authors, when first cut the tablets were extremely supple and so could be scored and folded across the grain without breaking (whereas folding with the grain, modern experiment shows, causes tears). After treating the surface with beeswax to prevent the ink from spreading or leeching, the tablets were ready for inscription with a reed or metal pen.[60] Simon b. Kosiba's writers must have used similar techniques in preparing *P.Yadin* 49, *P.Yadin* 54, and possibly drafts of other letters.

More should be said about the matter of rough drafts, but this is best done under the broader rubrics of how Greco-Roman letters were *composed* and *delivered.* As noted, writing a letter would frequently involve more than the stated author. Use of scribes was routine. For private correspondence they were easy to find in the markets and at the town gates. Official correspondence, such as are most of the Bar Kokhba missives, normally relied on chanceries and offices of the *ab epistulis.* Since writers other than the author regularly had some role, and because questions of Judaean literacy are implicated, it is important for us to distinguish the possible levels of involvement by others. E. Randolph Richards made this aspect of epistolary preparation a subject of two books, the first and more technical of which has become a standard work.[61] He preferred to use the term "secretary" for writers other than the author, and this term is useful for us as well because it leaves open the theoretical possibility that some of Bar Kokhba's writers came from the ranks not of scribes, but of soldiers. Indeed, we shall propose that a fair number of his secretaries were writers of convenience who happened to be on hand when Simon needed to send a letter.

Richards described the role of any given ancient secretary as falling at one of several points along a spectrum: "At one extreme the secretary was a *transcriber* who had no input in the letter, taking strict dictation from the author. At the other extreme the secretary *composed* the letter for the author. Most letters fell somewhere in between [making the secretary a *contributor*]."[62] If the secretary were merely to transcribe, he either had to take dictation very slowly, essentially syllable by syllable, or—to move at a speed approximating normal speech—use shorthand. By the time of the Bar Kokhba letters, shorthand techniques existed for both Greek and Latin. Cicero evidently employed—indeed, may have invented—the so-called Tironian Notes,[63] and Seneca spoke of a system firmly in place for Latin by the first century C.E.: *Quid verborum notas quibus quamvis citata excipitur oratio et celeritatem linguae manus sequitur?* (What about the notes for words by which means speech, no matter how rapid, may be captured, and the hand can follow the rapidity of the tongue?).[64] Scholars who have treated the history of shorthand have argued about which was first, Greek shorthand or Latin.[65] For us, the point is moot in both senses of that word. We cannot doubt that Greek shorthand existed by the time of the Second Revolt, or that Judaeans were using it, because among the texts of the Wadi Murabbaʿat is one that employed it. This text is *Mur* 164.[66]

Discovered in two pieces that seem to have detached, *Mur* 164 had evidently been retrieved in antiquity from a pile of scraps to fashion a kind of pouch. Such were common in antiquity for conveying parcels of mail. An almost identical leather bag bore the Arsames Correspondence.[67] Presumably, *Mur* 164 once contained all or a portion of one of the archives taken to Murabbaʿat by the freedom fighters withdrawing there during the Jewish revolts. It is attractive to imagine that the substantial archive belonging to Jesus b. Galgula and family may have rested in its stomach, or perhaps the contracts and Greek books owned by the sons of Eutrapelus. In any event, inscribed on the scraps-turned-purse were two columns of writing totaling forty-seven lines, the letters distorted, often profoundly, by the leather's crumbled-torn-shrunken condition. The writing was manifestly tachygraphic nevertheless, Benoit observed, and very probably Greek, although decipherment lay outside his expertise: "Not only does one discern within it Greek letters such as delta, theta or phi . . . but one also recognizes various strokes that are similar to the known system of Greek tachygraphy. . . . A comparison shows many analogies of forms, along with some differences. It could be that we have here a somewhat personal variety."[68]

In theory, then, it is possible that when composing the surviving Greek letters Simon b. Kosiba or his lieutenants dictated viva voce to a secretary writing shorthand. One can find no evidence of the possibility within the texts, however, nor should we expect any if the secretary was competent. That is not the real point. What interests for our purposes is the antecedent fact: tachygraphy was at home in Judaea. The very survival of *Mur* 164 may imply appreciable dictation in day-to-day life. Here was a consequent striving for ways to make it easier, which in turn entails substantial letter writing in Greek. The actual physical remains have, of course, long since almost entirely turned to dust, blown hither and yon. Like Shelley's monument of Ozymandias, virtually nothing remains but the swirls. Virtually nothing—but not, nothing. In addition to *P.Yadin* 52 and 59, the two epistles belonging to John's Cave of Letters archive, fragments of as many as eight additional documentary Greek letters survive. These are Mas741, the Letter of Abaskantos to Judas that we encountered earlier; Mas745–746, representing two or three additional Greek letters; *P.Hever* 67, a letter mentioning timber; *P.Har Yishai* 2; *P.8Hever* 4; and *P.Jericho* 19.[69] All but the last probably derive from En Gedi. In addition to these ten are roughly twenty-five letters referenced and to some extent quoted by Josephus in *Antiquities* books 12–14.[70] Scanty as these surviving portions are—perhaps thirty-five letters, an almost incalculably small percentage, doubtless, of what once circulated—they nevertheless bear tangible witness. Judaeans wrote to other Judaeans in Greek. In that process, tachygraphy played a role. And so with *Mur* 164 we recover yet another piece of the puzzle: in these regards, Judaea was integral with the larger Mediterranean world. Its people used the forms and technologies of Greco-Roman epistolary culture.

To write in either Semitic language, however, use of shorthand was no option. No such system existed for Hebrew or Aramaic in antiquity, as far as we know. Accordingly, Bar Kokhba and the other writers were left with two possibilities, only one of which was easy. Human nature being what it is, the easier was logically the more likely choice, and the texts we have support the logic.

The difficult option necessitated for both author and secretary a return to their schooldays. After first acquiring the capacity to write the alphabet, they had as children proceeded to write syllables, sometimes by copying, and sometimes at their teacher's dictation. Thereby they had grown accustomed to think about both spoken and written language as fundamentally composed of syllables. If the secretary did not know shorthand, or sometimes for reasons of special care or necessity, the author would dictate and the secretary would transcribe syllable by syllable. Cicero once took the effort to write an especially important missive to M. Terentius Varro in this manner. As often, he shared his letter with Atticus, and then sought his literary friend's opinion: "But I ask you, did my letter to Varro please you more than a little? God forbid that I suffer through something like that again! For I didn't dictate to Tiro, who is accustomed to follow entire periods, but to Spintharus, one syllable at a time."[71] Tiro was able to follow entire periods and transcribe them at the speed of ordinary speech. On this occasion, Cicero had instead chosen to employ a different secretary, Spintharus, perhaps because he possessed an especially beautiful hand and Cicero wanted this letter to impress Varro on all levels. But the effort of syllable-by-syllable work had been so arduous that here with mock seriousness he vowed never to do it again. Not only was it time-consuming to dictate in this manner, it badly hampered fluid thought. Shorthand aside, however, if the secretary were in the role of transcriber, it was *syllabatim* or nothing.[72]

But the secretary might instead serve as a contributor, assisting the letter's composition in a wide variety of ways. Having the secretary so operate was far the easier choice for Hebrew and Aramaic, a choice that the surviving letters sometimes prove Simon b. Kosiba and his commanders made. One clue that a secretary was helping to compose is evidence of a rough draft.[73] Numerous exempla of draft epistles survive in both Greek and Latin.[74] The author would charge his secretary to produce a preliminary version from a more or less detailed set of instructions or notes. The draft complete, the author would check it, note needed changes, and order a fair copy produced and sent. In the Greco-Roman world, drafts would typically use cheaper materials than would the final version: an ostracon, for example, or a wooden tablet or leaf, to be superseded for the final version by papyrus.

We have already observed that *P.Yadin* 49 seems to signal by its bicolumnar format transfer from a rough draft on wood to the papyrus we have, simply because epistles on papyrus almost never used two or more columns, while those on leaves regularly did. A second indicator that this Hebrew letter began life on wood involves a strange detail of the columnar arrangement. Eight complete lines in the first or right-hand column precede six damaged lines, none complete, in the left. By their very essence, of course, columns are separated from one another by a break. What is peculiar to *P.Yadin* 49 is that the lines in the first column immediately begin to elongate so as to stretch across, erasing the break, precisely at the point where the lines in the second column cease to descend. Plainly, the secretary knew when setting down the first column that it was permissible to steal space to the left beginning with his seventh line—and he knew this because his rough draft, laid out in columns identical to the planned fair copy, modeled that possibility.

Another evidence of drafts can be a letter's structure. At times, the notes given the secretary are still detectible in the finished product. With the letter only modestly fleshed out, the ribs, as it were, show through clearly. Here again, the Bar Kokhba letters conform to their world. The Aramaic *P.Yadin* 50 ordering Hita's arrest exemplifies the point. The author, Simon b. Judah, wrote in the name of Bar Kokhba (a phenomenon we shall shortly discuss) and instructed his secretary to draft a letter dealing with three specific points. The ribs of these points poke through in the form of the repeated Aramaic particle די, and in the second and third instances, through fronting of the topic noun (*casus pendens*) immediately previous to the particle. Consider:

> Simon b. Kosiba to John b. Ba'yah and Masabala b. Simon: (I order) that [די] you send Eleazar b. Hita forthwith, prior to the Sabbath. Take care with his produce and what remains of his harvest. Anyone who offers resistance concerning this order, send to me, and I will punish him. As for his cattle, (I order) that [די] they are not to damage the date palms. If anyone offers

> resistance (to this order), I will punish you severely. As for his balsam plantings, (I order) that [די] no one go near them.
>
> (Second hand) Simon b. Judah commissioned it.

The structure is clearer in the Aramaic than decent English permits, simply די, ובערה די, and ולטמה די. The secretary evidently departed from Bar Judah with a three-point list of topics and went away to produce, presumably on an ostracon or reclaimed scrap of papyrus, some version of what we see here. Having checked that draft, Bar Judah made any changes he saw fit and authorized preparation and sending of the fair copy. His signature verified for John and Masabala in En Gedi that he stood behind the orders as originating with Simon b. Kosiba.

An epistolary twin to the rough draft is the file copy, that is, a second copy of a dispatched letter that an author would retain for recordkeeping. The "twins" were so close genetically that the rough draft might serve as the file copy. If the two were not one and the same, then—as with twins—telling them apart may be difficult for modern scholars and any others outside the original family circumstances. File copies can nevertheless often be distinguished. As known from archaeological discovery, they tend to be more complete versions of the final letter than is the draft, including more (or even all) of the frame matter that drafts normally exclude.[75] Moving from the documentary to the literary, the parade example of presumed file copies might be what we know as the letters of Cicero. We cannot be certain that file copies kept by Cicero, Tiro, or both lie at the heart of his *Epistulae ad Atticum*, *Epistulae ad familiares*, and *Epistulae ad Quintum fratrem*. The question has been one of long-standing controversy. Still, direct reference to a large archive of Cicero's letters to Atticus has come down to us in Cornelius Nepos's biography of the latter. Nepos indicates that he has seen the collection personally.[76] And Cicero sometimes refers in his correspondence to letters written by himself or others that he has archived and retrieved. These literary references to file copies are of some value to the argument. But the main reason to believe that such materials furnished much of Cicero's correspondence as it has come down to us is pragmatic. It is simply difficult for many scholars to imagine the considerable project of editing and publishing his letters succeeding otherwise. That originals were retrieved from each of more than one hundred different correspondents strains credulity; and if that were possible, and large numbers of people did keep letters they received for years afterward, then the very thoroughness of that putative recordkeeping itself encourages the collateral notion that the Roman elite would record letters they sent no less.[77]

Regardless of the decision one reaches regarding Cicero's published collections, none dispute that he did sometimes file copies of letters dispatched. Among the Bar Kokhba correspondence one similarly finds evidence that file copies were kept, if not always, at least sometimes. *Mur* 48 is probably an example. Poorly understood in the past because of its fragmentary condition and Milik's unintentionally misleading readings and restorations, with Yardeni's new edition its true nature came potentially into view.[78] In keeping with her purposes, however, the Israeli scholar offered no remark on the point—in fact, she left it untranslated into Modern Hebrew, presumably because of its fragmentary condition. It is indeed very fragmentary, but in a peculiar way, as Pardee and co-authors observed: "The letter is almost complete in outline but too fragmentary in detail to be further interpreted."[79] Outline, however, is all we need if our goal is merely to recognize what we are seeing, and with Yardeni's work the outline is sharp-edged.

Portions of seven lines remain on two fragments that once occupied the upper left hand corner of the Hebrew missive. The top and left margins are visible. The fragments do not join, but are separated by a break of only a letter or two, and align horizontally such that the lines can be read as continuous. The most critical of Yardeni's improvements over Milik's readings was her replacement of יוחני in line 1 with מחנים, so metamorphosing the contextually inexplicable name Yohane (a form of Joanna?) into the explicable, even expected Mahanaim.[80] This man was doubtless John b. Mahanaim, the En Gedi official known from *Mur* 46 and *P.Yadin* 44. Since his name stands at the end of line 1, and considering the formulaic character of the *praescriptio* that would precede it, two possibilities exist for reconstruction: (1) this is a letter *from* John to a superior, presumably Simon b. Kosiba. By both Greco-Roman convention and Judaean (*P.Hever* 30), letters from inferior to superior began by naming the recipient first, the reverse of letters between equals, or from superior to inferior. John's name would accordingly be in second position. Or (2) this is a letter *to* John from one of the Bene Galgula. He is accordingly named here later in the line, as the margin nears.

The second option is manifestly preferable. After all, the letter was found in the Archive of the Bene Galgula, not that of John b. Mahanaim. It should therefore relate to them and their affairs as authorities at Herodium, not to him and his at En Gedi. Nor have we any reason to think that a letter addressed to Simon b. Kosiba, and involving neither brother, would come to rest in their archive. History is unpredictable, of course, and we can be certain of nothing. But we lack warrant for believing that the brothers (or anyone else) ever received Simon b. Kosiba's correspondence as proxies. As usual, we deal in probabilities. Hence the first two lines should be read/restored something as follows:

[1][מיוסה בן גלגולה ליונתן בן] מחנים [בע]ין [2][גדי ca. 20]°י
שלום שמל̊[ח?]

> [From Jose b. Galgula to John b.] Mahanaim in E[n Gedi . . .] Greetings! (I ask that) sal[t (?) . . ."[81]

This letter may reflect a correspondence between Jose b. Galgula and John that we seem to see in *Mur* 46. In that letter the direction of movement was the reverse of this one, from John to Jose, and it seems that the letter before us was possibly either the letter that elicited *Mur* 46 or the reply to that letter. The first thing that John b. Mahanaim says in the other letter is, "I do not need your load of grain [עמרך]." Implied by that statement is an antecedent offer to supply it—likely extended in an earlier letter, perhaps the fair copy of our letter, *Mur* 48. If so, we have preserved in the Archive of the Bene Galgula vestiges of a correspondence moving between officials at two centers of the revolt, En Gedi and Herodium. Unsurprisingly, a principal topic they discussed was military supplies. The proposed restoration of "salt" (מלח) in line 2 of *Mur* 48 derives from the traces and the apparent occurrence of that word in line 4.[82] The forces at Herodium would need salt, of course, and En Gedi, as Simon b. Kosiba's port on the Salt Sea, was the principal supplier. Numerous other letters in the Bar Kokhba materials concern supplies for his forces, and salt is explicitly a topic of both *P. Yadin* 56 and *P.Yadin* 58, received at En Gedi by John b. Baʿyah and Masabala.

Mur 48 is then most likely a letter from Herodium and one of its commanders to John b. Mahanaim at En Gedi. But how do we know that it is a file copy, rather than the fair copy of a letter that was never sent? The short answer is, we do not know, not for certain. Still, several considerations suggest that *Mur* 48 is a file copy. For one, as noted, file copies were a regular feature of Greco-Roman correspondence. Prima facie we might expect to find some evidence of the practice in the Bar Kokhba letters. And it seems we do; arguably, the script of *Mur* 48 is precisely that.

Among the correspondence found at Murabbaʿat this letter alone is in a cursive hand. All others were set down in bookhands. The pattern of formal script at Murabbaʿat contrasts sharply with the situation of the letters Yadin found in the Cave of Letters. All fifteen of those letters were instead composed using semicursive letterforms (see Table 4.1). The difference between the sites is stark and unexpected, and it requires explanation.

We shall shortly consider the matter in detail, but to understand *Mur* 48 we must anticipate that discussion a bit and foreshadow a conclusion for which considerable evidence is offered below: the formally established protocols for letters between Simon b. Kosiba and his lieutenants and officials, and for correspondence among those underlings, were to use the Hebrew language and to compose in bookhand. These were ideals, not always possible to achieve in the day-to-day circumstances in which a need to communicate would generate a letter. In part, these protocols were an expression of the nationalism that fueled the revolt.[83] To write Hebrew in a literary script was deliberately to recall the appearance of the holy books and so was intended, as it seems, to express, arouse, and sustain nationalist sentiment. Not every Judaean letter writer was capable of conforming to the protocols, but in the case of the Herodium materials they were always met—except for *Mur* 48. Why was it different?

Several explanations for such variation in script are possible, of course, some entirely benign. The likely explanation here, however, in light of the totality of the Murabbaʿat letters, is that this was a file copy: never intended to circulate, so not calling for a bookhand, therefore efficiently and rapidly produced. If Jose or Jesus had wanted to send a fair copy, he would have employed a scribe to produce it according to the protocols, if possible. And at Herodium it generally was possible. We saw in Chapter 2 that skilled scribes were on hand at that topographic capital, composing Hebrew legal documents. *Mur* 24 was written there, as it states explicitly, and in a gorgeous calligraphic bookhand. Likewise, *Mur* 7 and *Mur* 174 probably derive from that site, both produced by the same scribe, who possessed a fine if not first-rate bookhand. Moreover, the writer of *Mur* 48 was a scribe who produced, in Milik's words, a "belle écriture cursive sans ligatures," a calligraphic cursive akin to the hand of *Mur* 26.[84] A scribe this skilled could presumably have managed some sort of bookhand if it were wanted.

So *Mur* 48 is probably not a fair copy never sent. Neither is it best seen as a rough draft. The letter includes the subscription and the frames, both typically excluded from drafts. The subscription is in a second hand, presumably the author's. Thus all the essential formal elements of a fair copy are here, as one would expect for a file copy. Milik characterized the two hands: "Le texte dénote la main d'un scribe professionnel, à opposer au *ductus* hésitant de la signature de l'envoyeur" (The text [itself] displays the hand of a professional scribe, as opposed to the hesitant ductus of the sender's signature).[85] This second, amateur hand may be that of Jose b. Galgula. Less likely, it is that of his brother Jesus. In line with the more probable option, a proposed reading/restoration is [יוסה בן גלגולה] כֹתבה, "[Jose b. Galgula] commissioned it."

Rough drafts and file copies may thus be clear evidence of secretarial contribution. What of the secretary as composer, Richard's third point on the spectrum of involvement? These were instances where the author tasked his helper to compose the letter, offering little or no help with the content other than to provide addressee and topic. At one point in his life, while in exile in 58 B.C.E., Cicero engaged his friend Atticus to carry on correspondence in his name for him. His profound depression at being away from Rome had sapped him of the intellectual and emotional energy necessary to engage in the intricate dance that epistolary interaction with the elite often represented. Thus he wrote to Atticus, "If there are people to whom you think letters ought to be sent in my name, I would wish you to do so and to take the necessary care" (*si qui erunt quibus putes opus esse meo nomine litteras dari, velim conscribes curesque dandas*).[86] In this instance Atticus was not really a secretary, of course—more like a lieutenant, and so a reasonably precise parallel, perhaps, to Simon b. Kosiba's officers. They too, we shall see, wrote in the name of another, either taking pen in hand or employing a secretary.

Another example of secretarial composition that we know from Cicero's correspondence involved his brother Quintus. It was Quintus's regular practice, apparently, to employ a bevy of secretaries to create his correspondence, and then to have his most trusted helper, Statius, check the letters for problems of various sorts. Before Statius had come to him, however, Quintus had no one in the role of quality control. In both cases Quintus was sending out missives upon which his own eyes had never rested: "Statius has informed me that letters used to be brought to you fully drafted, and that he would read them and inform you if they were problematic; but that before he came to you, letters went out indiscriminately. Accordingly, collections of selected letters exist and are subjected to criticism."[87]

P.Yadin 54 seems to reflect a situation not unlike that of Quintus. This was the letter on wood. It was written and subscribed by the same man, Samuel b. Ammi, about whom we know nothing more. We must assume that he was a lieutenant of Simon b. Kosiba's who was delegated to write and send a letter to En Gedi and its commanders. Whether Simon himself ever saw the letter we have no way of knowing, but he did not subscribe it. The *praescriptio* nevertheless says, "Simon b. Kosiba the prince over Israel, to John and to Masabala: Greetings!" John and Masabala were to receive the commands transmitted here as those of the prince himself, although Simon neither wrote nor dictated the missive. His lieutenant Samuel acted as secretary and composed *P.Yadin* 54 on a wooden leaf, probably first preparing a draft on another leaf or an ostracon that clarified the spacing for him. Thus he knew that the last line in each column of the fair copy would be blank and so made certain to center one word or phrase in each. In this way he guaranteed that no one could modify the letter without detection, adding words before it was received. This is not the only hint in the Bar Kokhba correspondence that security was a concern. Interception of couriers, spies, substitution of false letters for true, perfidious commands inscribed between the lines of actual: all were problems for wartime correspondence in the Greco-Roman world. Cassius, for example, wrote to Cicero from Syria in 43 B.C.E., "if my letters were not delivered, I have no doubt that Dolabella . . . seized my carriers and intercepted the letters" (*quod si litterae perlatae non sunt, non dubito quin Dolabella . . . tabellarios meos deprehenderit litterasque interceperit*); and some years earlier, in May of 49 B.C.E., Cicero had written to Atticus, "therefore after this I won't write to you about what I'm going to do, only about what I've done; for everybody seems to be a Corcyrean [spy], trying to overhear what I say" (*itaque posthac non scribam ad te quid facturus sim sed quid fecerim; omnes enim* Κωρυκαῖοι *videntur subauscultare quae loquor*).[88]

We have seen that *P.Yadin* 50, the letter ordering Hita's arrest, was composed by one hand and subscribed by another, that belonging to Simon b. Judah, again otherwise unknown. He, too, must have been a lieutenant of the prince, told to prepare and send the letter. An anonymous secretary actually inscribed the letter; Bar Judah composed it; but Simon b. Kosiba was, by ancient canons, the author. Accordingly, it declares, "Simon b. Kosiba to John b. Ba'yah and Masabala b. Simon." We have no warrant for assuming that the leader of the revolt reviewed the letter any more than Quintus did his. Review and correction would routinely have fallen to Bar Judah, the subscriber. This letter had in effect two secretaries.

Another variation on the motif of secretary as composer appears in *P.Yadin* 63, a badly damaged Aramaic epistle on papyrus. Self-described as a letter from Kosiba, lines 4–6 are salient here: כתבת לכון ושלחת לכון ית אגרתה ב[י]ד שמעון בר ישמעאל, "I am both writing and sending the letter to you through Simon b. Ishmael." The naming of the letter carrier is notable as another commonality with practice in the Greco-Roman world.[89] *P.Yadin* 63 bore no subscription, and needed none. Bar Ishmael would deliver the letter himself. He could carry greetings from the leader orally.

Taken with the explicit statement of the letter's method, the absence of authorial subscription in *P.Yadin* 63 is suggestive, spotlighting a feature of nearly a third of the letters in the Bar Kokhba correspondence. They either lack a subscription altogether, or while having one, have it only in the secretary's hand. No author subscribed them, most especially not Simon b. Kosiba. Accordingly, these letters supply us no direct indication of how he was involved. More importantly, they supplied none to the original recipients. Recall the problems of wartime security. Given the sorts of issues Cicero's letters make explicit, how could those recipients have known that an unsubscribed letter was genuine?

To some extent this problem may only be apparent, a mirage arising because we strain squinting to the distant historical horizon. These letters are problematic to us. They need not have been to them. Consider: at least some of the letters lacking authorial subscriptions likely were composed and delivered by the same person, by secretary-carriers functioning as did Simon b. Ishmael. The combination of roles in a single individual is well attested in the Greco-Roman world.[90] The notion explains much and would have obvious advantages. Oral information from a secretarial carrier known to the recipients could accomplish even more than subscriptions written in what appeared a familiar hand. Handwriting, after all, could be forged. Forged letters were a problem during times of conflict in the ancient Mediterranean.[91] We will return to the possibility of secretary-carriers when we consider the various aspects of letter delivery more fully below. For now our attention must turn to the clues that the lack of subscriptions furnish regarding the method by which Simon b. Kosiba produced these letters.

In this connection we should keep in mind that the phrase "Bar Kokhba letters" has always been something of a misnomer. Ostensibly, it speaks of letters that the leader of the Second Revolt either fully composed personally or was supposed to receive. In fact, however, we can confidently assert such direct involvement in just two instances we have so far discussed. One letter, *Mur* 43, he likely composed and subscribed, as noted. This and *P.Hever* 30, addressed to him, are the only certain "Bar Kokhba letters" in the primary sense that the expression would most naturally connote. Many of the others may be something else (see Table 4.1).

Eight are too fragmentary to label. We can say nothing about the prince's involvement. Three more were either probably or certainly epistles dispatched by one underling to another (*Mur* 42, 46, and 48). Simon b. Kosiba had no involvement with these letters. Add to them the three additional letters of the foregoing discussion that the leader merely commissioned, *P.Yadin* 50, 54, and 63. For at least the first two of these, the prince contributed little beyond address and general topic. That leaves eight letters into which Simon *might* have had direct input, perhaps dictating or giving detailed instructions.

The degree of involvement Simon b. Kosiba had in these remaining letters is actually somewhat opaque. Apart from two, *Mur* 44 and 45, all definitely had different writers, suggesting scattered origins or unstable circumstances. *P.Yadin* 49 seems to have been subscribed (damage is very considerable), but by the secretary.[92] Similarly, *P.Yadin* 53 bears a subscription in the same hand as the body, as do *P.Yadin* 56, 57, and 58. *P.Yadin* 55 has no subscription at all. Of these last six, then, different secretaries subscribed five, and one was sent without final greeting or authorizing comment. So far as the outward evidence indicates, Simon b. Kosiba need have involved himself personally no more with these letters than with *P.Yadin* 50, 54, and 63. On the other hand, we must allow for possible oral complements to the letters supplied by their carriers. Albeit invisible to us, a ghostly Kosiba could have been directly involved in any or all of them.

Mur 44 and 45 are of a different character than the six mystery letters just noted, even though the first lacks a subscription, the second the relevant lines. As witnessed by their bookhands, they are not merely secretarial, but scribal. Furthermore, the same scribe probably wrote them both, the only case in the entire correspondence of a repeat scribe.[93] The likelihood of their common scribal origin, their probable common addressee—Jesus b. Galgula, in the first instance certain—and their adherence to the Hebrew protocols together suggest these letters be joined with *Mur* 43. They are correspondence directly involving Kosiba himself. If so, he probably had a scribe accompanying him at the times these two letters were sent. Among other things, both missives evidently command Jesus b. Galgula to distribute grain from the national granary (אוצר) at Herodium, presumably to soldiers (cf. *Mur* 8 in Chapter 2). *Mur* 24 testifies that the granary contained stores amassed at least in part through taxation in kind of leaseholders. Bar Kosiba refers to the storehouse in both letters as "my house" (ביתי), a shortened form of the common expression (well known from biblical usage) בית אוצר.[94]

In sum, for a significant proportion of the Bar Kokhba correspondence, the data regarding precise compositional method allow more than one possible interpretation. Simon may have been directly involved, dictating or closely overseeing as many as ten of the letters—or as few as four. If the latter or something close to it, the Jewish warlord becomes another Quintus, spouting brief commands, sporting a bevy of secretaries. They take dictation, true, but mostly they contribute or even compose letters that are as much or more of them as of him. Reading such letters we are at some remove from the man himself. He may actually be nowhere in sight. If but four letters capture the man's own words, then "the Bar Kokhba letters" deserve that description only marginally more than "the Samuel b. Ammi correspondence." But it would not be surprising if so few letters directly attach to the prince. That reality would be at home in the patterns of Greco-Roman correspondence—so pervasive was the activity of the secretary.

Delivering the Bar Kokhba Letters

"It is common knowledge," wrote Eldon Jay Epp: "Letters in late antiquity were carried by family members, friends, acquaintances, employees, slaves, and soldiers; by businessmen or passing travelers headed for places of the letters' destinations; by soldiers given a letter-carrying commission; and by government postal services. Sometimes, too, letters were sent to an intermediary place or person, whence they would be forwarded to the addressee."[95] This clear and succinct statement of the postal options would, one imagines, substantially comprehend the possibilities in Roman Judaea no less than for the Egyptian late antiquity Epp was specifically describing. It certainly accords with what we know of delivery methods in the Greco-Roman period generally. If, as proposed here, Judaea between Pompey and Hadrian was a lively epistolary culture, in that regard homogeneous with the greater Mediterranean *oikoumene,* then it would doubtless be profitable to consider how each particular of Epp's description might play out. But such cannot be our purpose here. Because Epp's list was applicable more to times of peace than of conflict, only two of his methods call for discussion if we want to understand the delivery of the Bar Kokhba letters. Still, we should bear in mind that Judaea was not always at war. The full roster of options on offer was probably found there during the years 63 B.C.E. to 136 C.E.

We might first ask whether Simon b. Kosiba was able to take over an existing government postal system when the revolt broke out in 132. In the

East such systems had existed since the time of the Assyrian Empire.[96] The Persians inherited a structure of well-maintained roads, wayside stops at regular intervals to exchange chariots, and relays of riders reminiscent of the American Pony Express. Herodotus was famously impressed.[97] From the Persians the basic methods passed to Alexander and then, among others, the Ptolemies, and finally to the Romans in imperial times. Portions of a register from one of the Ptolemaic way stations survive. With familiar Egyptian bureaucratic thoroughness it catalogs postal items according to day and hour of arrival, names of the carriers to and from the station, and the parties corresponding.[98] The Roman *cursus publicus,* with its characteristic night quarters (*mansiones*) and staging posts (*mutationes*), was strictly for use by imperial authorities to convey official mail and authorized people. Most of what we know about it derives from literary descriptions, as archaeological evidence is sparse.[99] Its maintenance was an essential function of provincial government, and some measure of the system existed in Syria-Palestine by the time of Hadrian. We know, for example, that frequent letters passed between Bostra in Arabia and Karanis in Egypt, necessitating the use of a postal system in Judaea.[100] It may be that the revolutionaries under Simon were able to seize and utilize the Roman infrastructure for a season. By the time of the surviving correspondence, however—which seems in every case to date no earlier than the final eighteen months of the war—the revolt had so turned that sign of such a success is nowhere evident.

Thus we must explore the second of Epp's postal mechanisms that suggests itself as likely: the use of soldiers given a commission as postmen, or simply chosen for the task ad hoc as the need arose. In fact this method would also mirror Roman practice. Generals and governors typically dispatched their letters locally and to Rome via military personnel (especially *lictores* and *statores*). The Bar Kokhba correspondence offers a good deal of evidence regarding the people who carried the missives, and in general they, too, were soldiers, sometimes of high rank.

Mur 42 was probably borne by a certain Jacob b. Joseph, who may have been the scribe as well as the carrier. Sent by both *parnasim* of Beth-Mashiko to Jesus b. Galgula, military commander at Herodium, it was nevertheless composed as representing the voice of just one person, probably the first *parnas*/subscriber, Jesus b. Eleazar. This man notes that he would have delivered the letter himself except for the fact that "the Gentiles are near." He obviously means the Roman forces. The danger was considerable, and so the presumption would be that a citizen soldier, and quite possibly a younger man, received the commission to brave that danger, avoid the Romans, and deliver the letter. He evidently succeeded. That the man's name was Jacob b. Joseph depends on the following reasoning.

Mur 42, it will be recalled, was not just any letter; it was an epistolary affidavit addressing the contested issue of whether a particular cow had been rustled. This cow and its current holder, Joseph b. Ariston, were now resident in the military camp at Herodium. Jacob b. Judah, the previous owner living at Beth-Mashiko, affirmed that he did sell the cow to Joseph. It was not stolen. The two *parnasim* subscribed as commissioners of the letter, Jacob as principal (על נפשה) and two other men as witnesses using the usual Hebrew term for their role, עד. The final signatory was Jacob b. Joseph, the putative carrier. He wrote his name with a fluid scribal hand, a fact supporting Milik's original suggestion that he was the scribe. The letter is certainly a scribal product, following the protocols suggested above, written in Hebrew bookhand.

But Milik also based his suggestion on the word that followed Jacob's name, מעיד, which the Polish scholar rendered "greffier."[101] Pardee and co-authors demurred. Milik's term was imprecise. They noted the unparalleled use of מעיד by a signatory to a letter (or, one might add, legal document; still unique today, after full publication), which would not naturally describe a generic "clerk." The biblical usage, they observed, would suggest something like "one who causes to witness." Accordingly, they proposed the translation "notary," imagining that after another person scribed the document, this Jacob verified the signatures.[102]

Pardee and co-authors did not explain, however, just how they visualized the mechanics of the situation. Did Jacob b. Joseph notarize the letter before someone else carried and delivered it? If so, it is unclear how his testimony would make the letter any more credible in its affirmations than would the witnesses' signatures by themselves. In the many other contemporary legal materials, the signatures of witnesses always suffice. Notaries never sign as such, by whatever term described. Nothing in the legal situation here appears different on principle. Accordingly, something other than notarization is probably going on.

What makes most sense of מעיד is to suppose that Jacob was the scribe, that he also carried the letter, and that when he arrived in Herodium and presented the document, he either added his signature on the spot or offered testimony to support his earlier signature, testifying thereby to both the content and the genuineness of *Mur* 42. In other words, the term implies that he was questioned (or at least subject to being questioned) about matters not set down in writing and that he presented an affidavit on such matters. The word מעיד is unique because among surviving documents the situation in which it appears is unique: *Mur* 42 is the only epistolary affidavit, the only combination letter–legal document. The term reflects the corollary combination, oral-written, frequent to letters. The legal precision of its use should be respected in translation: מעיד might possibly be translated simply as "hereby witnesses,"[103] but to keep the legal distinctions clear in English as they are in Hebrew, and to reflect the presumed questioning, a better rendering for *Mur* 42 might be "affiant."

To have the scribe and militiaman Jacob carry the letter would serve the situation well in other regards also. It was common for a carrier, whoever he might be, to read the letter aloud to the recipients after arrival. A carrier-reader would naturally need to be literate, and, as is emerging, most Judaeans were not. Having the scribe deliver the letter was therefore a percentage play. It guaranteed a proper reading out, aided accurate interpretation through follow-up questions, and spared the necessity of finding someone else able to read and guide interpretation after delivery. A scribe who could avoid the Romans was plainly no wizened, gnarled old man. In the crisis of the revolt, anyone who was not those things was ipso facto a soldier. Thus the reasoning: Jacob b. Joseph, soldier and scribe, took the missive to Jesus b. Galgula at Herodium.

Yet the complexities *Mur* 42 presents regarding letter delivery are not so quickly disposed. There is the matter of the recipients. These are more numerous, more general, than first appears. Jesus alone is addressed in the *praescriptio,* but the farewell reads, "Be well—and all Israel!" (line 7). In the addition of the latter phrase this missive testifies to more than legal facts. It also evidences an important phenomenon in the Bar Kokhba correspondence, one that yet again situates that correspondence squarely within typical Greco-Roman practices. Plainly, *Mur* 42 was expected to be read aloud, and not just to Jesus and a few companion officers, but to "Israel," an assembly of soldiers in the camp. Presumably, citizen soldiers from Beth-Mashiko serving at Herodium under Jesus b. Galgula were among the intended. One or more of them had likely raised the whole issue of the cow's legal ownership in the first place. These men needed to be apprised of the matter's resolution.

The plurality of addressees directs attention to a tricky problem regarding the correspondence as a whole. As a glance at Table 4.1 will show, including *Mur* 42, six of the letters implicitly stipulate to a public reading, the presumptive audience usually being addressed separately from the immediate recipients: *Mur* 43 (men of Kephar-Barucha), *P.Yadin* 49 (men of En Gedi), *P.Yadin* 51 (men of En Gedi), *P.Yadin* 58 (men of Kiryat-ʿArbayya), and *P.Yadin* 61 (men of Tekoa). Likely a public reading is often intended even when no groups are specified, given the apposition in *P.Yadin* 49 lines 1–2: "From Simon b. Kosiba to the men of En Gedi, to Masabala and John b. Baʿyah," (משמעון בר כוסבא לאנשי עינגדי [*sic*] למשבלא וליהונתן בר בעין). One might infer from this apposition that other letters, explicitly addressed only to Masabala and John, implicitly intend the "men of En Gedi" as well, whatever be the phrase's precise referent: town council, war council, or other body of residents. The tricky issue raised by such plural addresses is this: were the postmen of the Bar Kokhba letters always conceived as mere *carriers,* or did they sometimes—perhaps even often—enjoy a much more exalted status, as *envoys*? The historical concomitants are especially significant in the latter case. Can one tell the difference from the letters themselves?

The answer to this last is arguably yes, often. Several factors help to distinguish the two categories of postmen in the Greco-Roman world.[104] One such factor is the character of the letter being delivered, private or official. Private letters ordinarily moved between individuals, not groups, and between people of the same or similar social status. Official letters, often public, naturally had a broader group of recipients and frequently involved differences of status. So if we have a letter in which authorities address groups, as in our six situations, that situation alone defines the bearer as more likely an envoy. A second factor, no less important, is the person of the sender. Simply knowing the social standing of the dispatcher may identify envoys. Kings and governors sent envoys, themselves distinguished; peasants, carriers, not. The recipient's status is equally determinative. Private letters required no lofty or well-regarded bearer. They just needed to arrive. A slave dedicated to the task (*tabellarius*) would do nicely, or a merchant traveling in the right direction. But official letters involved honor and prestige. They normally called for an envoy.

By these criteria the bearers of the letters invoking Simon b. Kosiba were in most cases envoys: the leader of the revolt, or those he commissioned, addressed locally prestigious officials, and on numerous occasions groups. The social corollary follows that the envoys would typically be distinguished Judaeans as well. In the context of the war, such status would attach to the village elites, men such as Eleazar b. Eleazar, the envoy named by the address in *P.Hever* 30 (assuming that our understanding of the letter's inscription is correct).

The bedrock principle regarding envoys in Greco-Roman society was that one held the envoy as if he (or, much more rarely, she) were the dispatching authority come in person. This meant that the envoy was received as having the sender's status, not his own. The *Didache* expressed the concept in Christian terms: πᾶς δὲ ἀπόστολος ἐρχόμενος πρὸς ὑμᾶς δεχθήτω ὡς κύριος (let every apostle who comes to you be received as the Lord) (2:4). The correspondence of Pliny the Younger and Trajan illustrates the same principle from secular writings. Shortly after his arrival in Bithynia, Pliny wrote to the emperor: *Quinto decimo kal. Octob., domine, provinciam intravi, quam in eo obsequio, in ea erga te fide, quam de genere humano mereris, inveni* (I entered the province, Lord, on the fifteenth day of October, the calends. There I found the respect and obedience directed toward you that you merit from humanity). Trajan's reply underscored the essence of the convention: *Nam et tu dabis operam, ut manifestum sit illis electum te esse, qui ad eosdem mei loco mittereris* (And you, too, take care that it be plain to them that I have chosen you, that I have sent you to them in my stead).[105] Similarly, when in 193 B.C.E. the praetor M. Valerius Messala wrote to the city of Teos of their envoy's arrival at Rome, assuring them ἡμεῖς δὲ τόν τε ἄνδρα ἀπεδεξάμεθα φιλοφρόνως (we have received your man in friendly fashion), all concerned understood that it was effectively the city leaders themselves who had been well received.[106] This basic principle, envoy equals sender, explains much about the authority borne by the Bar Kokhba letters. Even though their composition may often have represented minimal personal involvement by Kosiba, they were his. When read, it was Simon b. Kosiba's presence that was invoked. His was the voice heard.

A second fundamental principle regarding envoys was that they possessed great power to speak for those who sent them.[107] They had received instructions beyond the letter's contents. In Greek missives a common expression regarding this practice was τὰ δὲ λοιπὰ πυνθάνου τοῦ φέροντός σοι τὰ γράμματα (as for the rest, learn about it from the one who has brought you the letter), sometimes supplemented with a further explanation of the intimate relationship between envoy and sender, οὐ γὰρ ἀλλότριος ἡμῖν ἔστιν (for he is no stranger to us).[108] The Bar Kokhba letters contain equivalent expressions. For example, the final line of *P.Yadin* 63 (line 8) contains the damaged phrase די אמ[ר לכו]ן̊, "that he will sa[y to yo]u," doubtless the remains of an Aramaic analog to the τὰ δὲ λοιπὰ formula.[109] *P.Yadin* 53 is even clearer, in that virtually all it says is, "Everything that Elisha says to you, do for him, and exert yourself mightily with him in his ev[ery] undertaking" (דכל דאלישע אמר לך עבד לה והתשדר [*sic*] עמה [בכ]ל עבידה). Almost certainly, Elisha himself was the envoy who bore this letter from Simon b. Kosiba to John b. Baʿyah in En Gedi.

Envoys came, then, as bearers of messages, written and oral; as trusted agents of the authorities behind them; and—no minor point—as observers. For not only did they come from an authority, they returned. And when they got back, they reported. How had the letter been received? How had the envoy, and so the authority behind him, been treated? The potential dynamics were manifold. To recipients, envoys were far more formidable than couriers. They were to be respected; to be feared; to be manipulated; sometimes, to be bribed, or otherwise made to discover a new loyalty. Moreover, the line between envoy and spy was potentially a thin one, hence the ancient dictum, ὁ ἄγγελος καὶ κατάσκοπος καὶ κῆρυξ τῶν θεῶν (a messenger is at once both spy and herald from the gods).

M. Luther Stirewalt has shown that a particular protocol existed in the Greco-Roman world governing the procedures to be followed when envoys bearing official letters arrived.[110] An official presentation would lead to a public reading followed by oral reports. An example appears in Thucydides' description of the failed Sicilian expedition. At one point the general Nicias sent an official letter by chosen messengers to report to the Athenians what had happened: "The following winter the people sent by Nicias arrived at Athens. They shared the verbal messages with which they had been entrusted, and if anyone had a question, they answered it. They also delivered the letter. The city scribe came forward and read the letter to the Athenians, and it was as follows."[111] Nearly five hundred years later the Book of Acts describes essentially the same protocol as four envoys, Judas, Silas, Paul, and Barnabas, return to Antioch from a council at Jerusalem. They bear an official letter and are prepared to elaborate on what has happened in Judaea: "These men were sent out and arrived at Antioch. Gathering the congregation, they delivered the letter to them, and when they had read it, they rejoiced at its encouragement. Judas and Silas, also being prophets themselves, encouraged the brothers and sisters at length and fortified them."[112] Stirewalt summarized:

> Through the centuries, then, in different communities and settings, the official, administrative letter was treated consistently. It was prepared by competent, authorized persons and was carried by envoys who delivered it with ceremony appropriate to the particular assignment. It was addressed and delivered to a constituted body and read before that assembly or its representatives. Carriers

also delivered oral messages and answered inquiries related to the letter's content.[113]

Regarding the question of whether Kosiba possessed Stirewalt's "competent, authorized persons," that is, a chancery that prepared some of his letters, we shall say more shortly. For now, the matters of assembly and reading in Second Revolt Judaea beg brief comment, if only to illustrate the potential gains to historical understanding that a thorough consideration, not possible here, might offer.

Consider the case of *P.Yadin* 50, which we examined earlier for other reasons:

> Simon b. Kosiba to John b. Ba'yah and Masabala b. Simon: (I order) that you send Eleazar b. Hita forthwith, prior to the Sabbath. Take care with his produce and what remains of his harvest. Anyone who offers resistance concerning this order, send to me, and I will punish him. As for his cattle, (I order) that they are not to damage the date palms. If anyone offers resistance (to this order), I will punish you severely. As for his balsam plantings, (I order) that no one go near them.
>
> (Second hand) Simon b. Judah commissioned it.

If Stirewalt is correct in his synthesis of the protocols involved with Greco-Roman envoys, we must imagine that one or more high-status men arrived at En Gedi bearing this letter. It seems likely that troops accompanied. These men would escort Eleazar b. Hita back to Simon b. Kosiba after his arrest. John and Masabala would have assembled the "men of En Gedi" to receive the envoy with proper formality. In all likelihood people had an idea of why the envoys had come. Bar Hita and (as the letter delicately implies) certain followers had been insubordinate toward Kosiba, so compelling the dispatch of this embassy.

Perhaps the envoy(s) read the Aramaic letter aloud, though equally the En Gedites may have supplied the reader. Simon b. Judah's signature, no doubt recognizable to some among the assembled, assured the letter's genuineness—obviously critical and otherwise liable to challenge in a matter this delicate. One of the richest and most prominent men in the town, one of En Gedi's three military leaders, was being arrested and taken back to face justice, and if found guilty, likely execution at the hands of the prince.

As the letter was being read, the envoys must have watched the men of the town closely. How would they respond to its harsh demands? Would they make a move to resist? Just how far had En Gedi fallen from its erstwhile attachment to Kosiba? The troops may have stood with weapons drawn, prepared to arrest on the spot anyone manifesting disobedience. Doubtless, eyes fastened on Hita's group in particular. Albeit as a kind of miniature, the tense scene pictured by the letter recalls Cicero's attack on Cataline in the senate. The envoys possibly would have offered further threats, likely answered verbal challenges. Letter finished, Hita arrested, the "men of En Gedi" disbanded, the envoys presumably stayed long enough to ensure necessary measures regarding cattle, date palms, and balsam. In essence, the state was now confiscating Hita's properties, though that characterization is a bit imprecise, since it was only by lease from Simon that he held some of them.

Given that—as argued in Chapter 3—this letter was likely one of the earliest in the series of surviving missives held in John's archive, arriving after November 134, we may assume that a grudging compliance followed the letter and that the envoy reported it as such. For were such not the sequel, new commanders would presumably have been appointed, and additional letters on the matter might be expected. As it is, subsequent letters to En Gedi are full of threats for potential disobedience, perhaps in part reflecting the envoy's equivocal report on his return. Indeed, the notion that this letter and almost all the others that John or his wife took to the cave precede by mere months—and for the latest in the series, mere weeks—the collapse of the revolt fits well their content. Consider: to judge from its mention of Hita's produce and fresh harvest, this letter arrived in the late spring or early summer of 135. The revolt collapsed in the fall. Unless we are to suppose that we possess only the latest dispatches skimmed from a larger cache of letters received (which seems very unlikely), we should probably conclude that John b. Baʿyah and Masabala were commanders in En Gedi for little more than a year. Concomitantly, it seems that other, unknown commanders preceded them at En Gedi during the first years of the revolt.

Taking the letters as a whole, En Gedi plainly teetered on the brink of a break from the prince. Not far away, as we learn from the missives, Tekoa more than teetered. Refusing to fight, its men fled to take refuge in En Gedi. And find refuge they did. The En Gedites took them in and shared their homes, which Simon may have viewed as nothing but an act of incipient rebellion. Perhaps En Gedi was restrained from full-scale desertion only by the hopeless realization that no alternative to Simon and continued fighting remained. The time for possible rapprochement with Rome had long since passed. Unless stopped elsewhere, Roman forces would one day arrive at the

Salt Sea. Even so, the letters seem to show that it was progressively more and more difficult for Kosiba to keep En Gedi with him.

Letter Writing and Judaean Education for Literacy

It may be seen, then, that the Bar Kokhba letters are of a piece with Greco-Roman epistolography generally. The Judaean missives comport with those of the broader Mediterranean with regard to formal features: *praescriptio,* farewell, subscriptions, folding, and addressing. The processes of their production and delivery likewise comport. The letters evidence the various roles of the secretary possible in the contemporary world, whether as transcriber, contributor, or composer. They show signs of note taking, of rough draft production, of dictation, and of file copies. Even regarding the implied presentation of the letters by envoys, the Bar Kokhba letters fit the Greco-Roman world. One might explore several of these matters more fully, and note additional features such as the use of shorthand, but enough has been said in this preliminary discussion to establish the critical equation. The Judaeans between Pompey and Hadrian belonged to a Mediterranean koine of epistolary culture. Giving it their own stamp, shaping it to their own unique expression, it seems they used its methods as fully as did any other member.

And why should this equation matter to us? Because beyond its usefulness for exploring political and military realities such as how Simon b. Kosiba operated as prince, the equation sheds reflected light on questions of Judaean language and literacy. Where gaps exist in our understanding of the Judaean situation, we gain from the equation a certain warrant to approximate with fill-ins from elsewhere in the *oikoumene.* One such gap involves the specifics of educational content and method.

A commonplace in the study of Greco-Roman letters states that the methods used were geographically widespread and fundamentally static for hundreds of years, the centuries spanning the Diadochoi to Muhammad. The inference to be drawn from this extraordinary continuity is that people must have been educated in letter-writing techniques all along for it to be so. Education for literacy routinely included instruction in drafting letters. Thus John White has observed, "The number of epistolary conventions in papyrus letters, which retain their formulaic identity over several centuries, is sufficient evidence of a rudimentary instruction in letter writing."[114] Abraham Malherbe has concurred: "That the basic characteristics of the private letter are so faithfully preserved from the fifth century B.C. can only be explained as partly due to school instruction and the guides to letter writing."[115]

If letter writing was not just a scribal activity in the Greco-Roman world generally, then the equation would argue that it was not in Judaea, either. There, too, ordinary people were presumably educated for letter writing. As elsewhere, one would suppose, many at the higher levels, and sometimes those at the lower, acquired a basic ability to compose and read a formulaic letter. The equation suggests that if this was true in Egypt and Britain, likely it was equally true in the realm of Herod and the Roman procurators, the land of the First Jewish Revolt and the Second. *For detailed identity of method implies substantial identity of training to acquire that method.*

In the ancient world, literacy was a variety of technology, just as is computer literacy in ours. The principle governing technology in our world was more or less equally applicable in the ancient: in general, people master only as much of a technology as is of practical use. The equation urges that for at least the upper classes of Judaea, learning to write letters was a useful thing. It was something they needed to know—hence, we come round again to the basic point: *they lived in an epistolary culture.*

To be sure that we are on a firm footing, however, it would be highly desirable to undergird these broad cultural inferences with specific data derived from textual analysis. This is arguably possible through a closer look at certain of the Bar Kokhba letters. More: we can perhaps not only demonstrate that letter writing was taught, but also discover at what stage in the process of education that happened. The data emerge against the backdrop of a phenomenon already remarked. In contradistinction to those from Murabbaʿat, composed in bookhands, the Naḥal Ḥever letters were written entirely in cursive hands. Unlike the first group, the latter collection was also largely composed in Aramaic or Greek, not Hebrew. The only reasonable interpretation of these sharp differences is that the circumstances of Kosiba's letter production had changed. The ultimate reasons for the change we can deduce only with great uncertainty at best, but the proximate reason becomes plain under review. Whereas the Murabbaʿat letters were uniformly scribal products, most (perhaps all) of those from Naḥal Ḥever were not. Instead, they were the work of literate citizen soldiers, ordinary men trained to write letters as a part of their youthful educations. In order to see how this claim may be justified, it is necessary first to consider what was expected of Bar Kokhba–period letter writers—what we have labeled above, the protocols. Then we must take a closer look at what we actually get.

We noted in Chapter 2 that many scholars have regarded the use of Hebrew in the Bar Kokhba letters and other documents from that time as evidence that Simon b. Kosiba "restored" the language to official use as an act of nationalism.[116] We also saw that the materials from Jericho in particular would question a characterization using the term "restore," but with proper adjustment this view of the matter makes sense. After all, Hebrew was repeatedly pushed forward at critical junctures in the history of Judaea as a kind of call to the colors. The phenomenon is most on view in the written evidence best able to survive the climate, coins. We find the emerging Hasmonean state turning to Hebrew for most of its numismatic inscriptions. The script adopted was no form of the Jewish script used for routine, day-to-day writing, but rather paleo-Hebrew. It resembled the alphabet of First Temple times. This choice makes explicit the nationalistic thinking behind the coins, since that script alone was "purely" Hebraic, in contrast to the quotidian letterforms derived from Aramaic. During the First Revolt the rebels minting coins in Jerusalem and in hotbeds of resistance such as Gamla made the same choices of language and script. Those choices emerge yet again with the Bar Kokhba coins. The Hebrew language and a version of its most ancient script thus served repeatedly for numismatic propaganda, supporting claims to Jewish independence.[117]

So the first of the suggested epistolary protocols: a mandated preference for Hebrew—not merely signaled by the Bar Kokhba letters (Table 4.1), but advertised by the coins of the day. The Second Revolt language mandate was consistent with earlier political patterns. Yet it would have been futile to insist correspondents trod the path of the *numismata* a further step in pursuit of the paleo-Hebrew script, since virtually no one mastered it but specialized scribes (and the occasional mint master on a learning curve). What substituted was another nationalistic choice, the bookhand—even to illiterate Judaeans, familiar from the holy books. Use of this script was another protocol established under Simon's rule, a fact discovered at the nexus of three lines of evidence.

The first of these converging lines is the profile of actual usage: a significant majority of Hebrew letters from the time of the Second Revolt use the bookhand (eleven of sixteen, 69 percent).[118] One might be inclined to put little stock in this small sample, whatever the percentages. The apparent pattern might be just that—apparent, reflecting no actual ancient reality, a result of asymmetric preservation and discovery. After all, we know from the vastly larger sample of surviving Egyptian papyri that bookhands rather than documentary hands were sometimes used for both letters and contracts, usually for no discernible reason. Why should we think this Judaean situation any different?

Again, it is the profile of actual usage that presses the point. *Not a single one of the Aramaic letters, contracts, and other documents discovered in the Judaean Desert uses the bookhand.* In every case their scribes indited them with a cursive or extremely cursive script. Here we have as evidence not just sixteen, but in the neighborhood of two hundred texts. Of particular relevance among these are nine Aramaic Bar Kokhba letters, none in bookhand.[119] Nor do the Hebrew documents from First Revolt Jerusalem ever use a bookhand—always, a cursive variety (*Mur* 22, 29, 30, 31, 4Q348). Nor the Hebrew documents from first-century Jericho—cursive, always (KHQ1; *P.Jericho* 9, 10, 11, 14, and [whichever fragments may be Hebrew] 15). In fact, apart from the Bar Kokhba letters, Hebrew written with literary hands appears in just two categories of Judaean Desert material: literature, and—a most telling fact—*Second Revolt contracts: Mur* 7, 24, 36, 37, 39, 40, 41, 52, 174, and *P.Yadin* 44–46. The percentage of Second Revolt contracts written in Hebrew bookhands is even higher than that for the letters (twelve of thirteen, 92 percent). These considerations strongly support the proposed conclusion. Simon b. Kosiba mandated the bookhand for Hebrew documents.[120]

A second line of evidence derives from the personal practice of Simon b. Kosiba himself. It stands to reason that what the leader did as he acted officially might mirror his expectations of others. This is especially so because he did the same thing more than once. It carries weight that Hebrew bookhand appears in all three of the letters for which a really solid case can be made for immediate origin with Simon. The letters are *Mur* 43–45.

The first of these, it will be recalled, Simon signed. It is unique in this regard and so, of all the Bar Kokhba letters, the one most certain to come from him personally. *Mur* 44–45 were composed by the same scribe in a chancery hand. One letter from a scribe is a matter of opportunity; two, a matter of practice. Two letters from the same scribe probably means that Simon had the man with him in his troop. As the prince moved about, he needed to communicate with units in his guerrilla army, clumped as they were in scattered villages and hideaways. Archaeologists have unearthed rock-hewn hiding complexes in more than 125 Judaean settlements. Here the units of citizen soldiers gathered before and after launching strikes at Rome.[121] Simon must often have moved among these settlements to encourage the forces, to lead sorties, and to plot strategy, and while doing so he clearly maintained contact with other places by means of letter and envoy. We have epistolary evidence only for the last year of the conflict, but some sort of mobile chancery was presumably his regular practice from the outset. Hellenistic monarchs, governors, mayors, and at the top of the pyramid a bit later, Roman emperors all employed chanceries and *ab epistulis*.[122] It seems that we see Simon's chancery disintegrate before our eyes as we turn our gaze from the Murabbaʿat missives to those from Naḥal Ḥever. Amateurs now replace the royal scribes. To associate this disintegration with disintegration of the revolt itself is reasonable if speculative (more below). Returning to the main point: the letters most safely considered the prince's own follow, indeed, apparently exemplify the proposed protocols. Were it not for the first line of evidence, we might be inclined to dismiss the matter of a measly three letters. But given the patterns of usage generally, these missives from Murabbaʿat were best recognized for their special witness.

The third path of evidence and reasoning in support of the suggestion that protocols existed is, depending on how it is understood, potentially the most explicit. It calls to the bar the Greek letter to John and Masabala, *P.Yadin* 52. Hannah Cotton edited this letter in excellent fashion for the *editio princeps*, in the process solving several paleographic and linguistic cruxes that had bedeviled understanding since its initial publication by Lifshitz. Nevertheless, the global interpretation she offered raises a number of difficulties. The proposal here is that once those problems are resolved, the letter straightforwardly and explicitly alludes to at least the first of our protocols, and perhaps the second as well.[123] Cotton's translation is as follows, with the critical portion left untranslated for now (and all but the first name rendered according to the conventions of the present study):

> (First hand) Soumaios to John son of Baʿyah and to Masabala greetings. Since I have sent you Agrippa, hurry to send me wands and citrons, as much as you will be able to, for the camp of the Jews, and do not do otherwise. ἐγράφη δ[ὲ] Ἑληνεστὶ διὰ τ[ὸ] [ἡ]μᾶς μὴ εὑρηκ[έ]ναι Ἑβραεστὶ ἐ[γγρ]άψασθαι. Release him (Agrippa) more quickly on account of the festival, and do not do otherwise.
>
> (Second hand) Soumaios, Farewell.[124]

Cotton argued that *P.Yadin* 52 was a communiqué sent by a Nabataean.[125] She reasoned that it was necessary to explain why Greek was chosen for this letter rather than Semitic, and that this choice was explicable if made by a Nabataean, since, she said, the Judaean Desert discoveries show that Nabataeans wrote in Greek when not using Nabataean. Also, the name Soumaios was Nabataean, Cotton maintained, offering several clear examples of Nabataeans bearing that name. And third, marshaling perhaps her strongest argument, Cotton pointed out that the phrase "camp of the Jews" ([π]αρεμβολὴν Ἰουδ[αί]ων) would not have been an expression a Jew would have used; hence, the letter came from a Gentile.[126] Her last two points were not new in scholarship on the text, but her first argument was original, and the conclusion to which the constellation of points led her was noteworthy. Cotton proposed to understand the critical clause as, "It (the letter) was written in Greek because of our inability (to write?) in Hebrew letters." The Nabataean author could have written in a form of Aramaic linguistically intelligible to Judaeans, she urged, but only using the Nabataean script, which no ordinary Judaean could read. In turn, the Nabataean was ignorant of the script used for Hebrew and Jewish Aramaic.

The question mark Cotton attached to "write" expressed scholarly caution concerning the reading/restoration of ἐ[γγρ]άψασθαι. Cotton felt that neither the *alpha* nor the *psi* were entirely happy readings. Nevertheless, she cited Hayim Lapin with approval: "The sense requires a verb meaning 'writing' (or related action), and the traces at the end of the word are consistent with the middle aorist infinitive of γράφω," of which ἐγγράφω is a synonym.[127] "Furthermore," she noted, "the middle voice ἐ[γγρ]άψασθαι is very appropriate in such a context."[128] These linguistic judgments seem sound. Cotton's arguments for Nabataean authorship were a bit shakier.

The way that Cotton phrased her assertion that Nabataeans wrote in Greek was strictly accurate but precarious in what it suggested: "Nabataeans in the archives from the Roman province of Arabia, unless they sign their names in the Nabataean cursive script, do so in Greek letters."[129] Most readers would take her statement to imply that as a general populace Nabataeans made appreciable use of Greek, as otherwise her words have small point. But if one takes as evidence the Judaean Desert finds, as Cotton did, this natural inference proves mistaken. To begin with her writer: one assumes that the commander of a military troop would only occasionally be a scribe. So it is meaningful that laypeople as writers are virtually invisible in the Nabataean-related texts Cotton referenced. Almost all of the Nabataean writers in our texts are arguably scribes, mostly signing with level 4 hands, although occasionally a level 3 hand occurs (which may, of course, still be a scribal hand). In only two instances do we encounter laypeople writing in that tongue.[130] Thus, we have no real evidence regarding lay abilities among the Nabatu, although ancient analogies require that most tribespeople would have been much less adept as writers than were their scribes. And Nabataean scribes, while often possessed of beautiful hands in their own script, generally could not produce Greek. When they witnessed Greek contracts, they almost never signed in that language, instead inscribing Nabataean (which argues, according to one thesis of this study, that these signatories generally did not know Greek).

Take the example of *P.Yadin* 12, an extract from the official minutes of the Petra town council. The minutes were almost certainly written in Latin originally,[131] but this portion was excerpted and translated into Greek so that Babatha might depart with a copy that someone back home in Mahoza could read. Five Nabataean scribes present in Petra signed the extract, but only one in Greek. Similarly, *P.Yadin* 16, Babatha's land registration of 127, composed in good Greek by a (Nabataean?) scribe in Rabbat Moab, received signatures from five other Nabataean scribes—all, however, in Nabataean. In the same vein, Shamoa b. Simon's registration of that same year, *P.Hever* 62, likewise composed in Greek at Rabbat Moab, was signed by four Nabataeans. Just one was able to do it in the language of the document. Shifting the geographic scene, the Greek-writing scribes we know from Mahoza were not Nabataean, but Judaean, if names are any indication: Theenas son of Simon, Germanus son of Judah, and Thaddeus son of Thaddeus. The Nabataeans who produced contracts in Mahoza, Huwaru b. Awatu, Azur b. Awatu, and Yohana b. Makhuta, did so only in Semitic (cf. *P.Yadin* 1, 2, 3, 4, 5, 9).[132]

In sum, Nabataeans who signed Greek contracts overwhelmingly signed in Nabataean (twenty of twenty-three, 87 percent).[133] Those who signed Nabataean contracts signed in Nabataean or else could not sign at all (eighteen of eighteen, 100 percent: two illiterates, sixteen scribes).[134] Thus Cotton's implied point, that Nabataeans would routinely fall back on Greek when not writing Nabataean, is nearly without example even for scribes. Nabataeans precluded for some reason from use of their own language would routinely have nothing to fall back on. Indeed, the materials of the present study suggest that Judaeans would be significantly more likely to know Greek as a second or third language than would Nabataeans (see further Chapter 5).

Cotton spooled a thread of earlier scholarship in taking the name Soumaios as Nabataean. No doubt attaches to the possibility. The Abdharet b. Soumaios of *P.Yadin* 12 that she cited, for example, was undoubtedly Nabataean. But Soumaios appears to be a hypocoristic of the name Samuel. Such was Ilan's analysis, and she listed nearly a dozen forms in support of it, spelled variously Σαμαῖος, Σαμαίας, Σουμαῖος, Σειμαῖου, שאמי, שמי, and שאמי.[135] Samuel was not an uncommon Jewish name in Roman Judaea, according to that same onomastic expert. Twenty-six attested individuals bore the name in the centuries under review.[136] Thus, the hypocoristic Soumaios, while certainly compatible with the Nabataean hypothesis, is equally compatible with the notion of a Jewish writer of *P.Yadin* 52. The second possibility would seem far the more likely prima facie, given the demographics (it was, after all, a *Jewish* revolt) and the nationalist character of the conflict. Foreign commanders of Jewish troops? The idea that a perfervid rebel such as Masabala b. Simon would submit to military orders from a Nabataean—regarding a Jewish festival, moreover, hardly an ideologically neutral topic—seems incongruous. As time went on, he barely took orders from Simon b. Kosiba. Yet, however reasonable these objections as probabilistic arguments, the expression "camp of the Jews" has for numerous scholars, as for Cotton, clinched the matter. Jews would never originate such a way of describing Simon b. Kosiba and his soldiers.

Or would they? As it happens, a very natural possible explanation for the expression lies close to hand, in the Bar Kokhba letters themselves. When Agrippa arrived at En Gedi with the letter we know as *P.Yadin* 52 (and he probably was the carrier, as Cotton noted), he came with at least one companion, a pair of donkeys, and a second letter. This second letter, *P.Yadin* 57, has often been compared with our Greek missive, as the topics overlap. Both concern aspects of preparation for the Festival of Booths, celebrated in late September or early October. Read together, held together: both letters eventually found their way to the Cave of Letters as holdings of John b. Baʿyah's archive. What scholars have overlooked is that Soumaios, writer of *P.Yadin* 52, knew when he composed his brief that its recipients would be reading both missives. How might that fact affect his choice of words? Further, they have not considered what the arrival of the two letters as a package means for Soumaios's own location as he wrote. Before proceeding further, a translation of the Aramaic *P.Yadin* 57:

> Simon to Judah b. Manaseh at Kiryat-ʿArbayya: I am hereby sending to you two donkeys. You are to send two men with them to John b. Baʿyah and Masabala, so that they may load (the donkeys) with palm branches [ללבין] and citrons [אתרגין] and dispatch them to the camp, that is, to you. As for you, send some of your men to bring you myrtle branches and willows. Prepare the whole and send them to the camp, because the crowd is large. Be well![137]

When this letter was inscribed, it seems to say, Simon b. Kosiba was located in one "camp," Judah b. Manaseh in another, and yet a third was in view. Probably every significant concentration of Judaean soldiers during the Second Revolt was considered a "camp" (Hebrew, מחנה). The term was ideological and carried overtones of holy warfare, for which reason, one supposes, the Aramaic Bar Kokhba letters always use this Hebrew lexeme rather than one of the standard Aramaic equivalents.[138] Recall that Jesus b. Galgula is titled by *Mur* 42 as רוש המחניה, "camp commander," and that *Mur* 24 speaks repeatedly of "the camp resident at Herodium" (המחנה שיושב בהרודיס), of which we have argued Jesus was the commander. It may be that Kosiba was now at Herodium, as often suggested, since it was Judaean headquarters and near Jerusalem, the traditional center of pilgrimage for the festival. Yet we cannot be certain of the current military situation. He might equally well have been heading toward the festival and so writing from any one of the 125 other sites archaeology has identified as Second Revolt hiding places for soldiers. Each was a potential "camp," and the prince's leadership was of necessity peripatetic. Moreover, Herodium may not have been the designated site for the celebration. We do not know for a fact where that was. Herodium may even have fallen already (see below).

Agrippa took *P.Yadin* 57 with him when Judah b. Manaseh sent him to En Gedi. The purpose was to certify that the commands in *P.Yadin* 52, although issued with no mention of the prince, originated with Simon b. Kosiba. The official of that second dispatch, Soumaios, doubtless wrote at Judah's delegation, acting as a composing secretary and subscribing the letter (the actual scribe goes unnamed). Therefore, the camp from which Soumaios wrote was logically the one where Judah was in command: Kiryat-ʿArbayya. It was to this camp that b. Baʿyah and Masabala of En Gedi were ordered to send the palm branches (θύρσους/ללבין)[139] and citrons (κίτρια/אתרגין) mentioned in both letters, as Soumaios specifies: *to me* (μοι). There at Kiryat-ʿArbayya, in accordance with *P.Yadin* 57, Judah, Soumaios, Agrippa, and unnamed others would prepare the En Gedi elements along with the companion pair of local origin, the myrtle branches and willows. These together made up the "four kinds" typifying the Festival of Booths. From Kiryat-ʿArbayya they would send them on by donkey caravan to their final destination, "the camp" as designated by the prince (*P.Yadin* 57:4): a location either known to all or specified by Agrippa in oral supplement to the two letters.

The question for Soumaios as he directed the scribe of *P.Yadin* 52 was how to reference that final destination. For the week of the festival, the normally scattered and concealed guerrilla units would come together openly at that place, visible, vulnerable, a sealed tortoise daring to stretch forth its head. Obedience to their traditions required risking a type of attack that was the Romans' incomparable strength: set battle formation. Given the situation, Soumaios had to avoid the agreed location's familiar name, whatever that was. Interception of the letter was always a possibility. A natural alternative was to designate this unusual gathering of Judaean soldiers—and possibly of their wives and children, as would be normal during peacetime—according to what it was, the main camp, since everyone would be there (*P.Yadin* 57 describes the large group, אכלסה סגי, borrowing ὄχλος from Greek). That was just what he did, adopting παρεμβολὴν Ἰουδαίων, meaning *the* "Camp of the Jews" par excellence.[140] The fuller expression he chose, ἰς (i.e., εἰς) παρεμβολὴν Ἰουδαίων, was in keeping with a frequent use of the Greek preposition, as indicating ultimate purpose or destination.[141] Thus the letter was carefully worded, precise in distinguishing from one another the two camps, first Kiryat-ʿArbayya (μοι) and then the ultimate destination (εἰς).

If this way of understanding the two letters as a package is correct, then nothing any longer deters from what was always, from a cultural perspective, the most natural reconstruction of events. Simon b. Kosiba here ordered Jews to take steps for the coming Jewish Festival of Booths, probably in the autumn of the year 135. No Nabataean leadership was required. In the process, a Jew whose name was Samuel, known for familiar purposes as Shummai[142] (a variant of Shammai) or, as Greek would express it, Soumaios, had a scribe who happened to be available write a letter. One may imagine that his pool of potential writers was not large, given that most of the soldiers in any camp would have been illiterate at that level of function, and most "camps" were small because their village locations were small. The circumstances of the moment may well have been further restrictive of choices. A substantial portion of the soldiers had perhaps already departed Kiryat-ʿArbayya for the festival.

As a matter of the percentages, the cultural situation Soumaios faced was scarcely remarkable. Greek was a language in which many Judaean scribes were for pragmatic purposes competent. Over the preceding century and a half, the Roman administration had raised up many village scribes equipped for its needs. They were not always symmetrically trained in the Jewish script, as we have seen, and of those who were, only a certain, yet-smaller total percentage would have known Hebrew and been able to write letters in it. So Soumaios found himself with a scribe who knew Greek. He used the option he had. *P.Yadin* 52 went forth as a Greek epistle. Soumaios himself could sign in the language. Of the named recipients, Masabala, leader of an eminent priestly clan that evidently treasured a Minor Prophets scroll in Greek, likely would have read it without difficulty. *P.Yadin* 59, the other Greek letter among the Bar Kokhba correspondence, names John b. Ba'yah alone as recipient. The evident expectation was that he, too, could handle the language of Javan.

The end of the matter, then, is that Cotton's translation of the critical clause in *P.Yadin* 52 goes awry; ἐγράφη δ[ὲ] Ἑλῃνεστὶ διὰ τ[ὸ] [ἡ]μᾶς μὴ εὑρηκ[έ]ναι Ἑβραεστὶ ἐ[γγρ]άψασθαι was far more likely intended to communicate, "The letter was written in Greek because we were unable to write it in Hebrew." This was, of course, a kind of apology. The question is, concerning what, precisely: *for* writing in Greek, or for *not* writing in Hebrew?[143]

An apology for writing in Greek would probably imply a generalized, therefore ideological resistance to its use. No such ideology has become evident elsewhere in our texts. On the contrary, recalling the brothers Eutrapelus in Chapter 2, for example, we saw men who chose to keep fighting Rome after the destruction of Jerusalem in 70 C.E., zealous freedom fighters clearly, who yet manifested pride in their Hellenism. We have also seen that Jews of these years might choose to produce their marriage contracts in Greek (*Mur* 115–116, *P.Yadin* 18, and *P.Hever* 64 and 69). And the phenomenon of Jews writing Jews in Greek in *P.Yadin* 59 (revolutionary leaders) and elsewhere similarly argues that no nationalist animus was aimed at Greek. Such does not mean to say that no one at all regarded Greek as the language of the oppressor. But the evidence fails to support the idea of generalized resistance. Greek had a long history in Palestine before the coming of the Romans. No necessary connection existed between the two.

Accordingly, the better interpretation of the apology is that Soumaios apologized to John b. Ba'yah and Masabala for *not* writing in Hebrew. If so, then an expectation that he would seek to do so probably existed; ergo, we have essentially explicit the first of our protocols. Simon b. Kosiba mandated the use of Hebrew during the Second Revolt. Possibly implied as well is the second protocol—use of the bookhand. We may easily understand that the telegraphic expression natural to epistolary language would intend by Ἑβραεστὶ not only the language, but also its presentation. One cannot insist on that inference, but in light of the whole of the evidence, it would make good sense. Actual practice in general, and that of Simon b. Kosiba in specific, are unequivocal in supporting the existence of both protocols.

If the foregoing combination of data and analysis has brought us at least to the neighborhood, if not to the exact address where dwell the actual facts, then the letters from Naḥal Ḥever plainly demand some explanation. As tabulated in Table 4.1, not one of them follows both protocols, and 73 percent (eleven of fifteen) follow neither. We have already briefly touched upon a possible explanation. In contrast to the correspondence produced by scribes and preserved at Murabbaʿat, the materials from the Cave of Letters were mostly, or even entirely, amateur productions. Ordinary soldiers raised in an epistolary culture wrote them in different places at the behest of the peripatetic Kosiba, or at that of certain underlings to him. The reason this catch-as-catch-can practice became necessary late in the war apparently was that the commander's circumstances had deteriorated. Very tentative thoughts: Herodium may have fallen.[144] With it were lost the office and scribes of the chancery. Or, another signal defeat had been inflicted, perhaps that memorialized by the Hadrianic Arch at Tell Shalem.[145] Simon, in the meltdown of the rebellion and so likely more on the move now than ever, lacked both motive and means to attend to such minor details as the protocols.

Be these things as they may, the absence of the protocols from the Naḥal Ḥever correspondence is not the only reason to suspect their lay origins. The letters manifest numerous other phenomena difficult to square with professional production. Problematic or "substandard" elements occur in many of these dispatches, including aspects of planning/presentation, letterform, and language. The following is a very concise presentation of the most salient of these issues:

P.Yadin 49. Yardeni has observed that this letter was composed by a notably idiosyncratic hand, quite possibly using a block of wood.[146] The letters vary considerably in size, not normally the case in scribal hands of this period.

P.Yadin 50. The letters of this hand lean oddly forward; a *resh* sometimes looks like a *nun*, and *peh* is extraordinary as a closed loop. Nonstandard orthography includes שבה for שבתא, a backformation with "slippage" of *status,* since the context demands the meaning "the Sabbath." Similarly, one finds פרענת for expected פרענתא or פרענו. This is either a defectively spelled Hebraism (i.e., פרענות) or an "erroneous" Aramaic form (again, an issue of *status*).

P.Yadin 53. This letter is indited on the verso, letters perpendicular to the direction of the fibers: not an expected move by a scribe handed a perfectly good piece of papyrus. Further, the elements of the *praescriptio* are disordered, suggesting a writer trained at some point in composing letters, but who has seldom actually done it, and so forgotten certain basics.

P.Yadin 54. Written carelessly, this letter displays a large variety of letter-forms, and in varying sizes. These characteristics suggest a practiced but nonprofessional writer. Nonstandard spellings are numerous, including סלם for שלם (!), virtually inconceivable for a trained scribe, not unlike a modern writer misspelling "cat." The word התשכו for אשתחכו lacks standard metathesis, uses a *heh* for expected *aleph,* and leaves out the *heth.* The word תחדון renders תאחדון, and תיעבדון, תעבדון (*ad aurem*).

P.Yadin 55. Yardeni labeled this "a very peculiar . . . cursive handwriting."[147] The letters all lean forward and vary in the degree to which they do so. Size varies greatly. The writer failed to reckon space properly, such that letters in several lines lapse beneath their line at the left margin. An odd final *nun* in פרען‎תא (line 8) was caught on proof and corrected to פרענתא.

P.Yadin 56. This letter displays a very idiosyncratic hand, writing an extreme cursive. The writer rotated his *shins* ninety degrees to the right and produced a most peculiar *heh.*

P.Yadin 57. Yardeni commented on this letter, "slowly written with a practiced hand."[148] In fact, however, the level is at the margin of practiced, best judged a level 2/3. (Slow writing is normally diagnostic of nonprofessionals, of course, but this writer may have been aged, ill, or suffering a disability.) The large spacing between letters and words is further suggestive of a nonprofessional, as is the omission of the standard "Greetings!" (שלם) in the *praescriptio.*

P.Yadin 58. Yardeni argued that this letter was "written by an unprofessional . . . with a flat calamus held almost parallel to the line."[149] She also commented on the large spacing between the letters and the lines.

P.Yadin 60. The writer of this missive left large spaces between the letters, with considerable variation of size and form. He further miscalculated the length of three lines, being forced to finish them above or below the line at the left edge. Lines are also notably uneven.

P.Yadin 61. As with *P.Yadin* 58, this writer held the calamus flat and virtually parallel to the line,[150] a sure sign of a nonprofessional. Further diagnostic are the large spaces between the letters and the lines.

P.Yadin 62. This letter is extremely fragmentary, so no conclusions can be at all secure, but the large letter spaces evident would commonly apply to nonprofessional writing.

P.Yadin 63. Carelessly written, but by a practiced hand, this dispatch mixes cursive letterforms with formal. Large spaces stand between letters, words, and lines: all familiar characteristics of amateur writers.

Thus for at least twelve of the fifteen Cave of Letters epistles, we have good reason to suspect amateur authorship. This is so quite apart from the matter of the protocols. Factoring those in, the possibility grows appreciably. As amateurs, these writers did not know the bookhand, even when they could produce Hebrew. In these twelve amateur letters, we have exhibits A through L affirming Judaea as an epistolary culture. Their witness corroborates the numerous systemic indicators discussed earlier, namely, the detailed conformity of the Bar Kokhba letters to Greco-Roman epistolary practices. As the Mediterranean world was an epistolary culture generally, so, too, Judaea specifically.

A salient further point in this connection is that, apart from *P.Yadin* 57, all the postulated amateur dispatches were the products of level 3 hands (Table 4.1). Even the exception noted is just a half step, as it were, from the critical threshold of competence: level 3, equating to literary literacy. In point of fact, this level as a common feature among amateur letters is unsurprising. For in the Greco-Roman world, the curriculum seems often to have included instruction in letter writing within the second phase of schooling. This phase, recall, was the point where the student passed from the realm of the elementary teacher, or γραμματαδιδάσκαλος, to instruction by a γραμματικός. It was during these years of secondary education that the ancients acquired what we today consider normal reading ability. Because of the method by which reading and writing were taught, visible proof of this acquisition would regularly be a level 3 hand. In other words, the apparent fact that amateur Judaeans who wrote letters nearly all possessed level 3 hands is precisely what we might have predicted if Judaean pedagogy indeed mirrored Mediterranean techniques. In their world people who had acquired that level of literacy typically had some training in how to write letters.

Evidence that ancient secondary education included epistolary elements is largely indirect. The third level of training, that with a rhetor, required basic knowledge of letter writing as a prerequisite to certain exercises in *prosopoeia.* Advanced students wrote letters to help develop their abilities of literary character portrayal: "The purpose of the exercise was apparently to encourage flexibility and sophistication in style or mood, not in the technique of letter writing itself. Even though it was essentially rhetorical in intent, *prosopoeia* is probably the primary source of the so-called 'forged' letters ascribed to famous ancient people."[151]

Thus the exercises of the third level of instruction point backward to what must needs have been taught earlier, often at the second level, but sometimes even the first: basic letter-writing technique.[152] This prerequisite gave the student the capacity to appropriate the rhetor's instruction. Evidently, then, students generally learned to write letters no later than during study under the γραμματικός, or during an equivalent training within the family. Model letters used for, or resulting from, such instruction survive among the Egyptian papyri.[153] The Bologna Papyrus, dating to perhaps the third or fourth century C.E., presents eleven examples of different types of letters in both Greek and Latin and seems to have some connection to epistolary handbooks.[154] Two such handbooks have come down to us from the Greco-Roman world. The older of these, known as pseudo-Demetrius, is today frequently dated to the pre-Christian era and may go back as far as 200 B.C.E.[155] The primary goal of such handbooks was practical instruction in letter writing for advanced students—those in chancery and business schools. Elementary training must have preceded. We have no evidence for handbooks or advanced letter-writing instruction in Judaea, but elementary instruction is obvious in the regular formulae of the Bar Kokhba corpus. As a percentage of the population, the number of Judaeans able to write letters would have been roughly the same as those possessing level 3 hands.

Language and Letters: Hebrew

Among the Greeks and the Romans a range of opinions existed as to the proper linguistic register for letters. Since a letter was frequently conceived as a stand-in for a meeting with a friend,[156] it was commonly held that the language even of literary letters ought to be simple, mirroring the everyday speech natural to such encounters. Thus Cicero wrote to Papirius Paetus: *quid tibi ego videor in epistulis? Nonne plebeio sermone agere tecum? . . . epistulas vero cotidianis verbis texere solemus* (How do I present myself to you in letters? Don't I correspond in ordinary speech? . . . We really are accustomed to compose in everyday language).[157] Seneca shared this view: *Qualis sermo meus esset, si una sederemus aut ambularemus, inlaboratus et facilis, tales esse epistulas meas volo, quae nihil habent accersitum nec fictum* (I would have my language be such as we would use sitting or walking together, unadorned and simple. I want my letters to be the sort that have nothing far-fetched or contrived).[158] The younger Pliny also favored unadorned composition: *et pressus sermo purusque ex epistulis petitur* (In letters we seek plain, concise language).[159] Others preferred a register elevated somewhat above the vernacular, while yet avoiding literary niceties such as periods.[160] Of course, these opinions were not dicta. They represented the customs of epistolary culture. Everyone realized that matters such as the identity of the recipient and one's relationship to that person might well affect decisions of language. Cicero himself, for example, famously composed in a register much closer to the literary when he wrote to Caesar than he thought appropriate when writing to Paetus.[161] But in point of fact, most letters were rather ordinary products, what pseudo-Demetrius characterized as γραφομένων ὡς ἔτυχεν, "haphazardly written." Ordinary they were, as ordinary as a conversation.

Cicero's typical epistolary language may serve as one example of convention. Termed *sermo cottidianus* after his own appellation, this register reflected something of the speech of the Roman elites of the day. It was by no means street Latin, despite Cicero's casual characterization of it above as *sermo plebeius.* According to L. R. Palmer's analysis, the most pronounced characteristics of this educated but speechlike style were ellipse and rapidity. Also notable were much parataxis and parenthesis, the use of adjectives for adverbs, picturesque—even overblown—vocabulary, frequentive verb forms, and slang. These same things might be found in vulgar Latin speech.[162] That, of course, was precisely the idea.

What, then, of Judaea? With so many epistolary isobars connecting the practices there to those of the greater Greco-Roman world, was the tendency to compose letters in registers allied to speech yet another? The importance of the question is clear. For if it is answered in the affirmative, we gain an analytical entry point, enabling us to compare (something like) the registers people might use for day-to-day life with those needed for literary literacy. How wide was the gap between the Hebrew dialects spoken in Judaea and the literary forms of the scriptures? Similarly, how broad was the chasm between literary forms of Aramaic and village patois? If the linguistic distance was significant, as in coeval Egypt, then that would have obvious ramifications for literacy and its acquisition. The difficulty of acquiring it would certainly be a determining factor in how many people did in fact learn to read and write, and how well. It would also affect aspects of literate behavior involving illiterates, such as group reading. So: in general, was the Hebrew of the Bar Kokhba letters something like that of ordinary speech?

A significant proportion of the scholars most qualified to judge have from the very beginning answered this question, "Yes." Consider the words of J. T. Milik, for example, or those of Eduard Kutscher, *magistrorum magister* of mid-twentieth-century Hebrew and Aramaic philology. Milik thought that the letters proved a form of Mishnaic Hebrew (MH) to have been widely spoken in Roman Judaea:

> The thesis of scholars such as Segal, Ben Yehuda, and Klausner that Hebrew was a language spoken by the population of Judaea in Persian and Greco-Roman times is no longer mere hypothesis: it is an established fact. . . . One has the impression that Ben Kosiba sought to impose the dialect he and his fighters spoke as the only means of official and literary expression. Judah the Prince and his successors will do no more in their time than make the first attempt at raising Mishnaic to the rank of religious and legal language.[163]

Similarly, Kutscher:

> חשיבות גדולה עוד יותר מאשר לאיגרות הארמיות נודעת לאיגרות העבריות אשר כפי שתלמדנו חצצה חטופה כתובות של לשון חז"ל.
>
> Importance even greater than that of the Aramaic letters attaches to the Hebrew letters, which, as even a cursory glance informs us, were written in the language of the rabbinic sages.[164]

In Kutscher's 1961 study of the letters (still the only broad linguistic analysis, and so even today the standard), he reiterated several times his conviction that this Hebrew was for the letter writers a spoken tongue, "still a living language."[165] As known from the rabbinic materials, MH (and here, more specifically, the earlier period of the language, Tannaitic Hebrew) displays striking differences from the grammar of Biblical Hebrew (BH) in its Masoretic form. The verbal system is recast, with complete disappearance of the *vav*-consecutive narrative structures, along with loss of the infinitive absolute and basic volitive forms. Final *mem* has merged with final *nun*, such that masculine plurals now typically end with ין-, not ים-. The relative particle is ש, not אשר. The genitive particle של replaces the construct chain usual in the scriptural books. The word היה ("to be") now combines frequently with participles to create a durative meaning.[166] Yet this MH has come down to us first through scribal mechanisms and then, eventually, by means of printed books. In the earlier process, scribes often "improved" the manuscripts, replacing actual MH forms with more prestigious biblical equivalents. Similarly, printed versions of the Mishnah and other Tannaitic materials opted for "purer" forms of the Hebrew texts known to the publishers. Thus one cannot judge MH truly from printed editions, nor are these the ideal *comparanda* for the Bar Kokhba letters. Where possible, early, "unchanged" (i.e., less changed) manuscripts and fragments such as Codex Kaufmann and the Parma codices need to be consulted. Kutscher and his students, notably Moshe Bar-Asher, pioneered and developed this approach to the problems of MH. It was these purer Tannaitic materials that Kutscher specially sought out for his analysis of the Bar Kokhba letters. But even they displayed a form of the language at some variance from that of the Second Revolt missives, both grammatically and lexically. Accordingly, the letters do not differ from the rabbinic texts redacted between 200 and 250 C.E. because of scribal melioration tout à fait. Kutscher's conclusion was that the letters also hint at one or more dialects of Hebrew spoken in Judaea, different from the earliest MH attested in rabbinic sources—while, of course, nevertheless belonging to that language in essentials.

Accordingly, we should speak of proto-MH dialects in both the Hebrew letters and Hebrew legal writ surviving from the caves. The latter were composed in proto-MH because, in contrast with Aramaic, no special, more archaic legal dialect existed for Hebrew. Focusing on the letters, then, but with input from the legal materials, the following is a short sketch of salient aspects of the language most reasonably considered akin to the Hebrew vernacular.

First, a word on orthography: the letters display no standardization. Each man did what was right in his own eyes; no scribal king existed in Israel in those days. This is precisely what might be expected if a vernacular now had to be put to pen. Some writers did one thing, others another (in contrast to the somewhat more standardized Aramaic letters). We shall consider one or two details on this point a bit further on.

Tables 4.2–4.4 may assist consideration of certain features of the phonology. As Table 4.2 indicates, BH as transmitted by the Masoretes possessed twenty-three consonantal phonemes,[167] represented by twenty-two graphemes (ש represented both /ś/ and /š/, differentiated by the early medieval Masoretes using supraliner dots).[168] The vernacular dialects of Judaean Hebrew (Table 4.4) retained as few as seventeen consonantal phonemes, while preserving all of the classical graphemes—some of which many writers used incorrectly in historical terms, because the phonemes they had once represented no longer existed in the speech of the letter writers. The incorrect usage is, of course, our royal road to understanding things as they were.

Table 4.2. Consonantal phonemes of Masoretic Biblical Hebrew

		Bilabial	Dental/ alveolar	Palato-alveolar	Palatal	Velar	Pharyngeal	Glottal
Stops	Voiceless	p (פ)	t (ת)	—	—	k (כ)	—	ʾ (א)
	Voiced	b (ב)	d (ד)	—	—	g (ג)	—	—
	Emphatic	—	ṭ (ט)	—	—	q (ק)	—	—
Fricatives	Voiceless	—	s (ס)	š (שׁ)	—	—	ḥ (ח)	h (ה)
	Voiced	—	z (ז)	—	—	—	ʿ (ע)	—
	Emphatic	—	ṣ (צ)	—	—	—	—	—
	Lateral	—	ś (שׂ)	—	—	—	—	—
Nasals	—	m (מ)	n (נ)	—	—	—	—	—
Liquids	Lateral	—	l (ל)	—	—	—	—	—
	Nonlateral	—	r (ר)	—	—	—	—	—
Glides	—	w (ו)	—	—	y (י)	—	—	—

Table 4.3. Consonantal phonemes of Classical Attic Greek

		Bilabial	Dental	Velar	Glottal
Stops	Voiceless	p (π)	t (τ)	k (κ)	—
	Voiced	b (β)	d (δ)	g (γ)	—
	Aspirate	p^h (φ)	t^h (θ)	k^h (χ)	—
Fricatives	Voiceless	—	s (σ)	—	*h (ʿ)
Nasals	—	m (μ)	n (ν)	—	—
Liquids	Lateral	—	l (λ)	—	—
	Nonlateral	—	r (ρ)	—	—

(Essentially the same phoneme/grapheme situation also obtained in the Aramaic seen in the letters, and so in discussing the tables we will occasionally use Aramaic examples.) The characters א, ה, ח, and ע were now for many nothing but graphemes, serving as *Vokalträger* for an ancient writing system that did not generally represent vowels. The voiceless and lateral sibilants had merged, leaving only the voiceless dental/alveolar /s/, represented at times indifferently by the graphemes that earlier served for three phonemes (ס, ש). Lost or greatly attenuated were all of the pharyngeal and glottal consonants (known in traditional Semitic philology as "gutturals"). The fricatives had thus been enormously simplified.

Table 4.4. Consonantal phonemes of Judaean Semitic vernaculars (first to early second centuries C.E.)

		Bilabial	Dental/ alveolar	Palatal	Velar
	Voiceless	p (פ)	t (ת)	—	k (כ)
Stops	Voiced	b (ב)	d (ד)	—	g (ג)
	Emphatic	—	ṭ (ט)	—	q (ק)
	Voiceless	—	s (ס, שׂ, שׁ)	—	—
Fricatives	Voiced	—	z (ז)	—	—
	Emphatic	—	ṣ (צ)	—	—
Nasals	—	m (מ)	n (נ)	—	—
Liquids	Lateral	—	l (ל)	—	—
	Nonlateral	—	r (ר)	—	—
Glides	—	w (ו)	—	y (י)	—

Arguably, all of this change was in the direction of Greek and under its influence. It occurred in a trilingual environment in which Greek was a prestige language. Table 4.3 represents Classical Greek of a formal register as it existed in the Athens of Socrates.[169] As shown, it comprised fifteen consonantal phonemes, although in Koine as spoken in most of the East during our period the voiceless glottal fricative /h/ (the "rough breathing" of standard grammars) did not exist.[170] The Greek of Palestine was for most speakers psilotic. Hence the consonantal phonology of vernacular Judaean dialects, whether Hebrew or Aramaic, now came quite close to mirroring that of Koine Greek. Attic and Koine had never possessed much of an inventory of fricatives or glottals, nor any pharyngeals. Now the two major Semitic languages of Judaea had converged to present similar profiles.

Not all of these changes were everywhere found, differing somewhat regionally, but they all obtained at one place or another when Bar Kokhba arose to lead Judaea in revolt. In some villages all the changes were on display. Many of them we know to have been widespread. For others the evidence is less full, the situation correspondingly less well understood.[171] Examples and a bit of discussion will clarify.

In his article "On Formal and Informal Spelling of Unpronounced Gutturals," the Israeli epigrapher Joseph Naveh collected considerable evidence regarding the pharyngeal and glottal consonants in the Hebrew and Aramaic of our period.[172] He observed: "The 'spelling errors' of the unprofessional writers, and especially of those who wrote in vulgar cursive, provide abundant evidence on the language of the people who wrote these texts. . . . There is evidence that not only *alef*, but also *'ayin, ḥet* and *he* were not pronounced."[173] He cited the example of *P.Hever* 49, wherein one reads שאפרך בכל זמן שת[ומ]ר לי, "that I shall repay it to you at any time you [te]ll me." The writer, Masabala b. Simon, failed to inscribe the *'ayin;* one should have שאפרעך. Certainly as a priest and scribe Masabala knew the proper spelling. He was not one of Naveh's "unprofessional writers." Writing formally in a literary work, he would presumably have produced שאפרעך. But when writing vernacular Hebrew he was less bound by traditions of historical spelling and wrote at times *ad aurem,* just as Shakespeare did, for example, when signing his own will "Shakspear" in another situation of a vernacular lacking a standard orthography. The omission of *'ayin* is frequent in this period, as in the writing of Simon as שמון, סמון, סימו *et similia,* not שמעון.[174]

One of the signatories to *P.Hever* 49 was Joseph b. Hananiah. He regularly signed his name יוהסף rather than the "correct" יהוסף, because the *heh* was only a historical spelling and he was unable to locate its proper position by ear.[175] Jar inscriptions at Masada witness the same metathesis.[176] Naveh further showed that one gets *heh* serving as a *Vokalträger* (*mater lectionis*) in initial (הלעזר for אלעזר, Eleazar), medial (שהצלכם, "who are with you," *Mur* 43), and frequently, final positions (e.g., marking the Aramaic *status emphaticus,* אגרתה, "the letter," *P.Yadin* 63). This often happened where on historical grounds an *aleph* would be expected. The alternation between *aleph* and *heh* has sometimes led scholars to suggest that Aramaic *Aphels* appear in the Hebrew texts of this period. For example, in *P.Yadin* 45–46 both *"Aphel"* and the expected *Hiphil* forms of the verb חכר, "lease," appear (45:7, שהחכרתי; 45:14, אחכרתי; 46:8, אחכרתום). But the Aramaic forms are, of course, not really such: they are examples of nonstandard spelling, reflecting the loss of the relevant phonemes. The forms in *P.Yadin* 45 would be homonymous, being heard approximately as [akarti]. *"Hiphils," "Haphels,"* and *"Aphels"* are often no longer distinguishable if all one has to guide is the preformative.

Heh and *ḥeth* also interchanged in the writing of vernacular Hebrew (and Aramaic), although modern scholarly editions of the texts often disguise the fact. The scribe of *Mur* 44–45, for example, wrote without distinguishing between the letters graphically, as was common in this period. This lack of graphic distinction presents a real dilemma for modern editors, for the phenomenon is not merely a matter of graphemes. It often reflects the pronunciation, or rather, lack of it. In such situations, modern editions have generally represented *heh* or *ḥeth* according to the historical grammar. In fact, however, the scribe of *Mur* 44–45 heard no difference between these consonants and so did not distinguish them graphically. Naveh transliterated *Mur* 44 as written, without a single *ḥeth,* whereas Yardeni's edition, for example, assumed on historical grounds that the letter occurred eight times and transliterated accordingly.[177] For this scribe, however, and many other writers as well, hers was a distinction without a difference. "Correct" use of the graphemes was nothing but historical spelling.

Aleph had quiesced in many environments already within the biblical period, and so its frequent omission or representation by *heh* in the Bar Kokhba letters and contracts is completely unsurprising and requires little discussion. One example can perhaps suffice, the frequent spelling of מאמרה, "from his verbal statement," as ממרה (e.g., *P.Yadin* 44).

So much for the pharyngeal and glottal consonants; the loss of these phonemes is widely evidenced and so was apparently widespread. The situation with the sibilants is less clear-cut. That there were mergers involving them in various vernaculars of the broader region is undoubted. Phoenician, for example, still spoken in villages to the northwest, retained only a single sibilant (/s/) of a five-phoneme inventory formerly identical to that of BH.[178] Samaritan Hebrew had merged /ś/ and /š/ as /š/.[179] Indeed, variations in the realization of the sibilants had existed in the region since biblical times, as seen in the famous Shibboleth/Sibboleth alternation at the core of the story in Judges 12. The Bar Kokhba period evidence suggests that in at least some parts of Judaea, earlier voiceless and lateral fricatives had merged, leaving only /s/. This is probably the best explanation of the greeting in *P.Yadin* 54, סלם. We do not know the provenance of the letter, only that it was sent to En Gedi on the peripatetic Simon b. Kosiba's orders. Kutscher originally suggested that the surprising form was due to Greek influence; Healey has more recently opined that it is an Arabism.[180] Kutscher's explanation is the more elegant, since it is not just ad hoc: as seen, decisive Greek influence seems apparent in other aspects of the phonology. This understanding also applies to two forms that appear in the Beth ʿAmar text, סעלב and ארישתובול. The first word is the toponym familiar from other sources as Shaʿalabbim (see Figure 1.1). The second is the Greek personal name Ἀριστόβουλος, which by normal canons of orthography comes into Hebrew and Aramaic spelled with a *samekh,* אריסתובול.[181] The orthography for both forms here indicates /š/

> /s/. Greek influence has been suggested.[182] Regarding *sin* and *samekh,* their merger was well under way earlier and is fully complete in the letters and contracts. As evidence, one need go no further than the first lines of many of the letters and their rendering of Kosiba: כוסבה (*Mur* 43), כוסבא (*P.Yadin* 49), כשבה (*P.Yadin* 50), כ[ו]שבה (*P.Yadin* 55), and כוסבא (*P.Hever* 30).

Another feature of vernacular phonology that the Bar Kokhba letters and contracts reveal is neutralization of nasals in final position. The effect of this change was to make the decision whether to spell forms in Hebrew texts with *mem,* or rather with *nun,* largely a matter of the writer's whim or, perhaps, ideology. Thus *Mur* 22 twice presents אחרים, "others," and once אחרין; *P.Yadin* 44–46 evidence זוזין ("*zuz*"), דינרין ("dinars"), and ארבעין ("forty") alongside סלעים ("*selas*") and קשרים ("ties"). Examples of apparent randomness could easily be multiplied. But some writers made a decision to be consistent and used only one option exclusively. The scribe of the Hebrew *Mur* 44 always mimated his plural suffixes (שהצלכם ["who are with you"], ברגלכם ["on your feet"]) and always spelled the masculine dual/plural morpheme ים- (שמים ["heaven"], הגללאים ["the Galileans"], כבלים ["fetters"]). The lay writer of Hebrew *P.Yadin* 49 took the opposite tack, always nunating with the plural suffixes (לאחיכן ["for your brothers"], עליכן ["to you"], דברכן ["your matter"], etc.) and always spelling the masculine plural in "Aramaic" fashion, ין- (יושבין ["dwelling"], אכלין ["eating"], שתין ["drinking"], etc.).[183] These orthographic phenomena illustrate more than the proposed neutralization. They also underline the lack of a standard orthography for the vernacular Hebrew dialects. Plainly in these regards individuals spelled as the spirit moved them.

The same does not hold true for the Aramaic materials. Even though the neutralization of final nasals seems to have affected both languages equally, one almost never finds mimation in final syllables in the Aramaic texts.[184] For Aramaic, then, a more standardized orthography patently existed and was known to our writers, whether scribe or lay. Here is a strong indication that Judaean education for correspondence ordinarily trained people to write in Aramaic, not Hebrew. Therefore, called upon to substitute vernacular Hebrew when Simon b. Kosiba instituted his protocols, Hebrew speakers—used to writing only Aramaic—may often have found the new requirements too taxing to obey. For hyperliterate moderns, the required transfer of formulae and technique might seem straightforward, provided a person is fluent in both tongues. But most ancient literary literates were not comfortable with writing to the degree modern Westerners are. To compose under the stress of recent or foreseeable combat, on the spot, at the commander's orders, and in a way one had never been trained—these things asked much of the lay writer in particular. Thus the ratio of Hebrew letters among John b. Baʿyah's archive (four of fifteen, 26.7 percent) cannot be pressed as a straightforward measure of what percentage of the population knew vernacular Hebrew.

A feature affecting both Semitic languages was the weakening of the liquids. One may infer this attenuation by their assimilation or loss. For example, Jesus b. Simon, a principal to *P.Yadin* 46, signed to acknowledge his contractual obligations as follows: ישוע [בר] שמעון ענפשה. The form ענפשה (for על נפשה) illustrates the assimilation of the final *lamedh* of על to the initial *nun* of the following word, and Jesus wrote them as one term. The assimilation of word-final *lamedh* in Aramaic is well attested for centuries before our period.[185] Now it affected Hebrew as well. Similarly testifying to its weak pronunciation, writers omitted *resh* more often than any letter besides the "gutturals" in texts of all sorts during these years.[186] Such a weakening could result in a succession of two vowels, which the Bar Kokhba texts evidence might elicit a glide. This is probably the explanation for the spelling of the second element in the name of Kephar-Baru in *P.Hever* 8a. The writer, John b. Eli, spelled the name בריו, inserting the *yodh* as a glide.[187] No glide appears in the name as written in *P.Hever* 8 (ברו)—even though John authored both texts—but the actual pronunciation was presumably no different in the two cases. A similar process involving *lamedh* explains the strange form of the En Gedite deictic pronoun הלוו ("these") that Joseph b. Simon twice put to paper in *P.Yadin* 44 (lines 17–18).[188] The word is otherwise spelled הללו. Related to the weak pronunciation of *lamedh* and *resh* was their occasional confusion in spelling, whereby the form התשדר appears for התשדל (*P.Yadin* 53:3), and the imperial title ἀυτοκράτωρ was realized in *P.Yadin* 8:1 as אוטקלטור.

Another phonological phenomenon pervasive in the Bar Kokhba letters and other documents, and common to both languages, involves certain consonant clusters that occur in the Hebrew *Hitpael* and in the Aramaic *Hitpeel* and *Hitpaal* (and *Itpeel/Itpaal*) conjugations. In Masoretic BH, and generally in early literary Aramaic, the *tav* of the preformative that characterizes these conjugations is subject to metathesis before a sibilant. Thus, for example, התשמר* becomes השתמר, "be careful." This process applies to *samekh, sin,* and *shin.* Slightly different processes, involving metathesis and assimilation of voicing or emphasis, regulate the voiced *zayin* and the emphatic *tsade,* respectively.[189] These processes avoid disallowed consonant clusters and thus serve euphony. But our documents evidence virtually none of them.

Instead, verb forms creating these consonant clusters are consistently spelled without metathesis. Examples are *Mur* 49:3 ומתשדר, *P.Yadin* 7:16 אתזבן, *P.Yadin* 10:14 מתזנבן, *P.Yadin* 53:3 התשדר, and *P.Yadin* 54:6 התשכו [*sic*]. This difference from the literary norms entails that the problem of the stop/sibilant consonant clusters was solved in some other way, but scholars, while noting the odd orthography, have attempted no comprehensive explanation. The suggestion here is that the spelling disguises a full assimilation, in which the stop assimilated to the sibilant. The Aramaic *Hitpaal* masculine singular imperative התשדר in *P.Yadin* 53:3, for example ("exert yourself mightily"), might be heard approximately as [issadda] (incorporating as well the other phonological changes discussed above). Such total assimilation characterized Samaritan Hebrew, whose traditional pronunciation for the reading of the Torah probably goes back to Second Temple times, as well as later forms of Aramaic known from Palestine, namely, Jewish Palestinian Aramaic and Samaritan Aramaic.[190] In these Hebrew and Aramaic traditions, the assimilated stop, always written in the Bar Kokhba examples, is sporadically written but much more often suppressed. The relevance of the later Aramaic dialects to the argument here is that they seem to reflect earlier vernaculars, in accordance with a linguistic commonplace characterized by the eminent Aramaist Stephen Kaufman: "Literary language almost always reflects the colloquial speech of an earlier period."[191]

The famous problem of the meaning and form of ἐφφαθά in the New Testament (Mark 7:34) *may* also have its solution in the recognition of a similar, but even broader, assimilation of the stop of the preformative (i.e., the Greek perhaps represents what might be written in the Aramaic of the time as אתפתחה, feminine plural imperative, "Be opened!").[192] This broader assimilation likely continues the trajectory of the process proposed here. If so, then it offers another contemporary witness to the vernaculars of Roman Judaea. Total assimilation as an alternative to metathesis seems to be at least two centuries older than our texts, if scribal slips in the literary record are a fair indication,[193] and broader than Judaea, being attested as well in Nabataean Aramaic.[194]

A striking form that appears in the Bar Kokhba letters and contracts is אש in contexts where one would expect יש, the existential particle "there exists" (also used to express possession). For example, note *Mur* 44:2–3, שתשלח תבי חמשת כורין ח[טי]ן [ש]אש לביתי אצלך, "You are to send me—have brought—five *kors* of wheat held in my storehouse there with you," and *P.Yadin* 49:7–8, ושתעמרו במהרא משפינא שאש אצלכן, "and that you should pack up quickly from the ship that is at your location."[195] Masabala used the word in the Hebrew I.O.U. that he composed at En Gedi, *P.Hever* 49: כול שאש על השטר הזא, "everything that is in this writ" (line 12). Elisha Qimron has suggested that the form represents a phonological process, whereby initial [ye] > [e].[196] It may be that the spelling of the Aramaic existential particle, אית, also influenced the orthography.

A final feature of the phonology of these texts is the nasalization of final open syllables (at least in certain cases). The name "Judah," for example, not infrequently gets spelled "Judan" by nonprofessional writers.[197] For our purposes the best representation of this tendency, clearly a feature of living speech, may be the name John b. Baʿyah. The patronym is sometimes spelled בעיה (*P.Yadin* 53:2), but often the nasalization that speakers heard is present in the writing: Βειανοῦ (*P.Yadin* 26:3 and 52:2) and בעין (*P.Yadin* 49:2, 50:2, 51:2, and 56:1). This nasalization also explains, by the way, the English name Siloam, as in the Siloam Tunnel. The Hebrew of the toponym in the MT of Isa 8:6 is שִׁלֹחַ. The nasalized form familiar to us derives from the LXX transliteration of the name as Σιλωαμ. The translation of the Book of Isaiah from Hebrew into Greek is commonly placed in the first half of the second century B.C.E. If this dating is correct, then the nasalization of (at least certain) final open syllables antedates the Hebrew of our texts by nearly three hundred years. Jerome did not know the phenomenon, however, evidently not encountering it in the language of his Jewish informants in the fourth century C.E. He represented Siloam as *Siloa* (Vulgate). This nasalization is also absent, of course, from the languages of the Masoretes.

Turning to issues of morphology and morphosyntax, the Hebrew of the Bar Kokhba letters is, as noted, plainly part and parcel of Tannaitic Hebrew. Commonalities with the language of the Tannaim include use of the apocopated form of the imperfect of היה (יהו for יהיו); -מי ש, not -זה ש;[198] use of the participle for the future; אבית for בבית; אָמור *et similia* as active forms of the participle; אלו for BH אלה, "these"; and use of the proleptic suffix, for example, פרנסו של שמעון, "the *parnas* of Simon" (*P.Yadin* 44:6–7).

But this Hebrew is also unique, standing apart from Tannaitic in other aspects of morphology and morphosyntax, such as: the phrasal adverb לכול דבר used with לא to mean "not . . . at all" (e.g., *P.Yadin* 49:4); -בשל ש for "because" (*Mur* 46:7);[199] כל המה, "anything" (Aramaic מנדעם); -ש with the participle, for example, שיושב, "who dwells" (*Mur* 42:4), rare in Tannaitic texts;[200] and use of forms such as המך, "from you," where Palestinian Tannaitic texts use the equivalent, ממך.[201]

P.Yadin 51, for all that it is poorly preserved, nevertheless retains—among the few words that can be deciphered—a striking construct phrase. The beginning reads, "[From S[imo]n to [J]ohn in En <Gedi>, and *the rest of the En Gedites* (ושאר הענגדין): [Greetings!]" (lines 1–2).[202] The striking aspect of the italicized phrase is the placement of the definite article before the *nomen regens,* in contrast to Hebrew as generally known, which places the article in such phrases before the *nomen rectum.* Compound toponyms used to form gentilics, such as we have here, always follow this general rule, too. Thus, for example, in Masoretic BH "the Bethelite," a gentilic adjective derived from the name of the town Bethel (ביתאל), is expressed בית האלי (1 Kgs 16:34). The same process governs MH as known. So one would have expected here עין הגדין. But the formation we actually get does find more or less contemporary parallels. Several funerary inscriptions from Jerusalem, likely antedating the First Revolt, also attest it. One reads of Ammia the Beth Sheanite (הבשנית), Hanin the Beth Sheanite (הבשני), and Papias the Beth Sheanite (הבשני)—all formed "incorrectly."[203] Almost certainly this development occurred within colloquial Hebrew. It was no literary phenomenon. In fact, within colloquial Israeli Hebrew this ancient new formation has risen again. In the years since the nation's founding in 1948, the treatment of construct phrases as compounds has reappeared, although never taught in schools—resurrected, it seems, no less than the language itself.[204]

Another feature of the morphosyntax of the letters has likewise reappeared in Israeli Hebrew as spoken in the streets and on the playground. And again, the origin is not with the pen, but with the tongue. The feature is the replacement of literary Hebrew's את by -ת. In Masoretic BH the particle is very complex as regards both its morphology and its syntax, but in the most general way את is associated with accusative function.[205] Most often, it marks the definite direct object of a transitive verb and thus is followed by the definite article, -הַ, yielding the sequence [ʾet ha-]. In Israeli speech, this can become [ta-], an aphetic bound morpheme attached to the noun object. Seemingly, this same phonological and morphological process is seen in the letters and contracts from Bar Kokhba's time.[206] Thus, Simon b. Kosiba writes in *Mur* 43:3, "I call the heavens [i.e., God] as my witness" (מעיד אני עלי תשמים), where תשמים = את השמים. The deictic aspect of the particle shows itself in *Mur* 44:5–6, יהו בו אצלך תשבת הזו, "They will be in it with you there this Sabbath." Examples could easily be multiplied, as the form is very frequent. Indeed, according to Yardeni's indices, in the Bar Kokhba letters and other documents, -ת outnumbers את forty-three to five.[207] Usually, -ת

was what writers heard people say, and so in rendering vernacular Hebrew on papyrus or leather, -ת was what they wrote. Among these writers, the scribes, at any rate, well knew that this was not a BH form. In their minds they distinguished the language they were writing from the language of the scriptures. Interestingly, as with important features of the vernacular consonantal phonology, the development of -ת was shared with Punic and Neo-Punic.[208]

A syntagm of great interest appears in *P.Hever* 30, a letter that has not been well understood, but on which further progress seems to be possible. The commissioning official, Simon b. Mattaniah, captain of a troop under Simon b. Kosiba—quite possibly in the region of Kephar-Baru[209]—writes to the prince of certain events that have befallen revolutionary soldiers or "brothers." It is bad news. But the good news, Simon writes, is that "we were not among them" (לא היינו מִן בין להם).[210] The syntagm of interest is מִן בֵּין לְ, to mean "among." It is unique to the language of these letters. The closest biblical parallel is Ezek 10:2, 6 (*bis*) and 7, מִבֵּינוֹת לְ. In the standard editions of the Mishnah, the combination of מן and בין never occurs; but in Codex Kaufmann one finds some ten instances, though never precisely the expression used by Simon b. Mattaniah.[211]

We conclude this sketch of the Hebrew of the letters and related documents with a few comments on the lexicon. A full study of this aspect of the Bar Kokhba materials remains a *desiderandum*, but Nebe made a helpful start with his examination of the vocabulary of *P.Yadin* 44–46.[212] He found that of sixty-four nouns, forty-one are also BH, while twenty-three are not; of twenty-six verbs, twenty-one are also BH, five are not. About a dozen of the BH words now had new meanings—often, it seemed, under Aramaic influence. He documented as well much overlap with MH vocabulary. Isolated points made by Kutscher add to this picture, mainly in drawing distinctions between the language of the letters and that of the early rabbis. Thus, Kutscher noted the use of אזי for "then" rather than אז. The former is unknown in MH and is extremely rare in Masoretic BH (three occurrences): probably, he suggested, it occurs at all only because of textual contamination by scribes who spoke the vernacular we are describing. He noted also חפץ (=BH) for MH רצה, "want, will, be pleased"; ככה, "thus," rare in MH, common in BH; and מחוז for "port," rather than BH נמל or MH לימן (borrowed from Greek λιμήν).

The lexical connections with BH are open to more than one interpretation.[213] It may be that they represent dialect continuity with BH as it was spoken in former centuries, a continuity that existed in certain dialects of proto-MH but not in MH itself as that evolved. Or, they may instead represent intentional echoes of the biblical language, added to the letters by their authors as cultural insignia, much the way Cicero would sometimes vary the registers of his letters through lexical and grammatical choices he made.[214] Likely, both phenomena are alternately present. At our remove, we probably cannot hope to distinguish which is which.

Aramaic influence on the lexicon is very considerable. We noted in the first chapter that Segal had rather understated this influence, perhaps in unconscious overreaction to nineteenth-century claims that MH was an artificial language, more or less equal parts BH and Aramaic. Menahem Moreshet subsequently documented that 210 Tannaitic verbs "derived from" Aramaic.[215] Despite the methodological issues that cloud his sort of analysis, one cannot doubt the effect of contact with Aramaic as it emerges in the letters. Often, it is a matter of lexical extension, whereby Hebrew words, while retaining their old meanings, have added new ones from the sister language. Such extension is a common effect of bilingualism and multilingualism.[216] Examples from the Bar Kokhba materials include the following. In *P.Yadin* 49:3–4, the writer accuses the men of En Gedi of neglecting the war effort: לא דאגין לאחיכן לכול דבר, "you are not concerned for your brothers at all." This use of דאג is new, Kutscher observed; in BH the word means "to fear." However, דאג is often translated in Aramaic (e.g., Targum Onkelos) by יצף, which means both "fear" and "be concerned for." By extension, the Hebrew word also now meant both.

Two other interesting examples of lexical extension through Aramaic influence may occur in the understudied *P.Hever* 30. Simon b. Mattanah tells the prince about some (Nabataean?) allies, ידוע יהיה לך שׁכׄנפׄו בׄי הגאים שהיו [מ]ן °[ ], "Let it be known to you that the Gentiles who were [wi]th [. . .] have gathered with me" (lines 4–5).[217] The verb כנף (*si vera lectio*) is a hapax legomenon of uncertain etymology in BH; it appears in the *Niphal* in Isa 30:20, where it is usually translated "hide oneself."[218] In Aramaic, on the other hand, the root is relatively common and means "to gather, be assembled" in both Syriac and Jewish Babylonian Aramaic. This meaning yields a very plausible understanding for the Hebrew of *P.Hever* 30.

The second suggested example of lexical extension from the same communiqué appears in lines 6–7, where Simon informs the prince, [ואף] שנטרפו אחם מׄן כׄ[אן], "[And also] that brothers from h[ere] have been struck."[219] The word טרף in Hebrew means "tear," mostly of meat or animals being torn or devoured by wild beasts.[220] That meaning clearly is inappropriate in the present context. But several Aramaic dialects use the root to mean "strike"; in particular, Christian Palestinian Aramaic and Syriac. It seems, then, that proto-MH used the root similarly, a usage arising from bilinguals extending certain of the Aramaic semantics to the cognate root of their other language.

Lexical contact phenomena were not limited to Hebrew-Aramaic interplay, however. Less frequently, but nevertheless significantly, lexical extension could involve vernacular Hebrew and Greek. A good example is another phrase that has puzzled scholars, *Mur* 44:2–4: שתשלח תבי חמשת כורין ח[טי]ן [ש]אש לביתי אצלך בדעת, "You are to send me *bᵉda'at*—have brought—five *kors* of wheat held in my storehouse there with you." The meaning of the italicized syntagm, בדעת, is the crux. Normally, understood in terms of its constituents, it might mean something like "in knowledge," but that makes no sense here. Kutscher noted the opacity of the usage and criticized Milik's translation, while refraining from offering one of his own.[221] Yardeni was hesitant, translating it as "in/by consent(?)."[222]

A crucial clue to the writer's intention with the syntagm בדעת emerges by comparing it with parallel expressions in the Aramaic Bar Kokhba letters. The brief inscribed on wood, *P.Yadin* 54, is especially helpful. Observe that in both *Mur* 44 and *P.Yadin* 54 the prince is ordering the recipients to send something, and to do it in a certain manner. Concerning Hanin b. Ishmael, *P.Yadin* 54:8–9 tells John b. Ba'yah and Masabala to "send the man to me securely," that is, under guard: וית גברה תשלחון לי באספליא . A few lines later they are ordered to arrest Jesus the son of the Palmyrene and "send him to me securely," once again, under guard: ותשגרון לי באספליה (lines 14–15).[223] The Aramaic expression for "securely" (באספליה) is a calque/loan translation of a common Greek expression, ἐν ἀσφαλείᾳ.[224] The proposal here is that the Hebrew scribe of *Mur* 44 meant to say the same thing, only he did it not by loan translation, but by lexical extension.

The semantics of Greek ἀσφάλεια cluster around the concepts of security and safety. When an idea is held in this way, it may be described as a matter of *assurance* or *certainty,* as in Thuc. 2.11.3, οὔκουν χρή . . . καὶ ἀσφάλεια πολλὴ εἶναι μὴ ἂν ἐλθεῖν τοὺς ἐναντίους ἡμῖν διὰ μάχης (Therefore, certain as it may be that the enemy will not meet us in the field of battle . . .). Indeed, if a person holds an idea with assurance, then for that person the idea is generally the *truth.* The proem of Luke-Acts uses ἀσφάλεια in this sense: ἔδοξε κἀμοὶ . . . σοι γράψαι . . . ἵνα ἐπιγνῷς περι ὧν κατηχήθης λόγων τὴν ἀσφάλειαν (It seemed good to me also . . . to write to you . . . that you may know the truth about the things you have learned; Luke 1:3–4).[225] These nuances of the word overlap with the semantics of Hebrew דעת, which cluster around the concepts of knowing and understanding. That which is considered known is, of course, held by its possessor as a kind of truth. And what is known is, to varying degrees, certain. For a bilingual Judaean speaker of Greek and Hebrew, then, ἀσφάλεια and דעת could come to be equated in certain senses. It would be easy for that equation to expand; extension is nothing more than such expansion. The scribe of *Mur* 44 meant when he wrote for Simon, "You are to send me *b*ᵉ*da'at*—have brought—five *kors* of wheat held in my storehouse there with you," that the recipient, Jesus b. Galgula, should have the wheat transported "securely." Supplies were precious, and the enemy could not be permitted to interdict their transfer. He should transport it under guard. (In fact, the letter indicates that the prince supplied those men himself. One of them delivered the letter.) By extension, דעת had acquired a new meaning, increasing its semantic overlap with Greek ἀσφάλεια.

If the proposed analysis is right, then we seem to glimpse a highly functional Greek bilingualism, at least among elements of Judaean society—for absent such, this kind of usage would fail to communicate. Presumably, the writer expected that Jesus b. Galgula would understand the extension involved, so this was no Hebrew purist's way of avoiding the Greek loanword אספליה. Rather, the extension must already have existed among Judaeans generally. Considerable use of spoken Greek is thereby implied. Widely spoken Greek is also entailed by the convergence of phonology discussed above, if that analysis is correct—but we get ahead of ourselves. This is a topic for the next chapter.

We may now summarize what this rapid sketch of the letters and companion texts may tell us about the Hebrew they contain. Was that Hebrew close to the vernacular, as leading scholars such as Kutscher and Milik have held? It certainly possessed a substantially different verbal system vis-à-vis BH. Speaking merely of what can best be known about the phonology, that involving the consonants, a great deal had changed here, too. And, often because of contact with Aramaic and Greek, but also arising from internal dynamics, the lexicon was notably different from BH, though with much overlap. One might phrase the initial question another way. *If this was not a vernacular, then what was it?* When Simon b. Kosiba mandated the protocols argued for above, and writers responded with the Hebrew letters we possess, they manifestly proceeded rather differently than did medieval Jews, for instance, when they sought to create their own Hebrew correspondence. Seeking to cobble together a viable mechanism, these later writers drew a verb from the Torah here, a rare noun from Job there, mixing and matching as needed. The Roman Judaeans responded with something quite different. Where did their epistolary language come from, if it was not the spoken dialects that provided the resources? The language cannot reasonably be explained as a compounding of BH and the Aramaic of the time, since it contains numerous elements unknown from either, elements best explained as of colloquial origin. Scholars dubious of a living Hebrew in our period have yet to come to terms with this epistolary language.

We may also now roughly assess the distance between proto-MH and the language of the scriptures that stood at the center of Judaean education. Given the differences sketched above, that distance must have been daunting to young students. It appears comparable to the gulf separating Egyptian Koine from Homeric Greek, or today's regional dialects of the Middle East from classical Arabic. The differences are sufficiently profound that one has to wonder whether ordinary peasants, as uneducated speakers of vernacular Hebrew, could grasp much at all of the Torah they heard read aloud in the synagogue. The parallel situation with Arabic can be tested empirically. We know that, unless they receive a good education, speakers of modern Arabic dialects comprehend the reading of the Qur'an but little.[226] We shall need to speak further concerning this issue in Chapter 5.

Language and Letters: Aramaic

An even briefer linguistic sketch will need to suffice for the Aramaic of the letters, but since the issues involved here are less central to this study, perhaps that will be good enough. The dialect is sometimes termed "Judaean Aramaic," as noted earlier; as with any suggested label, this one raises issues of precision.[227] Scholars generally agree that the Aramaic of the letters is distinct from that of Judaean literary Aramaic on the one hand and Judaean legal language on the other.[228] They further tend to agree with Kutscher's point that "by its very nature, the language of [Aramaic] letters is closer to the spoken language than to the language of literature and legal texts."[229] The letters may thus fruitfully be combined with the Aramaic subscriptions to obtain the clearest view we are likely to get of the Aramaic vernacular during our period, though we are still, of course, some distance away.[230] As with the Hebrew letters, one can then compare the language to literary forms, gauge linguistic distance, and thereby estimate the steepness of a Judaean student's climb to Aramaic literacy.

As a general statement regarding the character of this Aramaic, one might note at the outset the prominence of late antique literary Aramaic in solving the problems the materials raise. In editing the subscriptions, for example, Greenfield and Yardeni repeatedly cited Sokoloff's *Dictionary of Palestinian Aramaic*—a masterwork dedicated to later (Byzantine period) texts—and Christian Palestinian Aramaic lexical forms.[231] So we are forcefully reminded of Kaufman's point quoted above: later literary language often points backward to earlier spoken forms.

In the area of consonantal phonology, the previous discussion of Hebrew applies here, too. In general, repeating ourselves would be unprofitable. But on one detail a bit of repetition for the sake of emphasis may perhaps be excused, given the centrality that distinctions between *Aphel*s and *Haphel*s and related forms commonly assume in Aramaic dialect classification. Comments such as the following, a part of the generally valuable "Grammar" portion introducing Yadin's Cave of Letters discoveries, are routinely found in studies involving our period: "The prefixed *aleph* marking the Aramaic causative stem (Aphel) replaced the *heh* of the Haphel characteristic of earlier phases of Aramaic. In the Aramaic reflected in the Naḥal Ḥever papyri, this process was virtually complete. Note, however, the prefixed *heh* in the unusual forms התשדר (53:3) and התשכו (54:6), as well as the difficult form היתי/ החת/הגס (54:3). Cf. also in an Aramaic subscription the form: הקחת (18:68; and see the NOTES *ad loc* in Yadin and Greenfield 1989:142)."[232]

One cannot make the foregoing distinction for our texts. No morphological process is to be seen here, however meaningful alternation of *Haphel* and *Aphel* may be in the Aramaic of other times and places. Here, it was a matter of phonology, and the graphic representations were "arbitrary." Either *aleph* or *heh* might have been chosen in each case where a decision was made, except that writers were to a greater or lesser degree influenced by their youthful training, adult habits, and perhaps additional factors to choose one or the other. As argued above, the phonemes these graphemes had once represented were now lost. Technically, therefore, speakers heard neither *Haphel*s nor *Aphel*s, but rather words that began with vowels, not consonants (even though the classic grammars assure beginners that Semitic words cannot begin with vowels!).

Outside consonantal phonology, numerous phenomena may be noted, naturally, where Hebrew and Aramaic are not the same. For such, the most illuminating counterpoint for our texts is the Aramaic of the Qumran writings (henceforth QA).[233] One notable distinction between the letters and literary texts is that our texts do not substitute nasalization for gemination, as the literary texts normally do. Thus one gets תתנון (*P.Yadin* 54:5), "you will give," not תנתנון as in QA and Masoretic Biblical Aramaic (BA); and the second-person masculine singular pronoun "you" is את (*P.Yadin* 57:3), not אנת(ה). A second noteworthy phenomenon is the tendency of at least some writers to insert a glide in certain environments before final open syllables in /a/. Thus for בבתה (Babatha), Babeli b. Menahem wrote בבתיה, and for גביחה, "the hunchback," גביחיה.[234]

Regarding morphosyntax and morphology, one notes the breakdown in the *status* distinctions still maintained by literary Aramaic. Thus the *status emphaticus* no longer reliably distinguishes definite nominal forms from indefinite (strictly, *status absolutus*). For example, *P.Yadin* 55:2 uses the form אגרתה to mean "a letter," just as Syriac might.[235] The subscription to *P.Yadin* 27 uses the month names in either *status,* evidently interchangeably (אלולא/תמוז, 27:11–12). Lay writers of legal texts often slip on this point too, indicating that the colloquial probably used the two *status* interchangeably in many situations.[236] Mirroring proto-MH, the jussive has been lost, no longer appearing in commands, whether negative or positive (e.g., *P.Yadin* 63:6, לא תעבד[ון] ל[ה], "you shall not do to him" [תעבדון for תעבדו]; *P.Yadin* 54:12, יקדון, "let [the houses] be burned," יקדון [for יקדו]).[237]

These texts use the particle ית (accusative function) in a way that Kutscher remarked as peculiar.[238] The particle is rare in Eastern Aramaic but rather common in Western Aramaic, so one might expect to see it in the letters. It is indeed common (twenty-five occurrences). Yet its syntax here does not accord with that of other Western representatives, seeming rather to be influenced, Kutscher observed, by the syntax of the Hebrew particle את. One even gets יתהון rather than the expected אנון ("them") as object of a verb (*P.Yadin* 54:5, 55:5, 55:6, 57:4 *bis*). We shall consider the issue of contact phenomena a bit more fully below.

Unique to these letters (although it also occurs in the Hebrew missives, apparently further evidence of education to write *Aramaic* letters) is the verbal form appearing in the salutation הוה שלם, "Be well!" For Aramaic generally, one would expect the *Peal* masculine singular imperative of a third-*heh* verb such as this to terminate in *yodh,* yielding (in Masoretic BA terms) הֱוִי (*hᵉwî,* in our period perhaps [ewi]). The orthography we actually get seems to imply הֱוֵה (*hᵉwê*). A termination in an /e/ is not entirely unknown in roughly contemporary literary Aramaic; the verb נשא ("lift, take up") in BA forms its masculine singular imperative as שֵׂא ([se]). But no other verb follows this pattern, and of course נשא is not a third-*heh* verb. Kutscher noted that, of all the comparable dialects, only Christian Palestinian Aramaic forms its *Peal* imperative in /e/, spelling it, however, with an *aleph* (e.g., רְמֵא, "throw!").[239] One might be inclined to see Hebrew influence in הוה שלם, since the spelling with *heh* is the norm for third-*heh* masculine singular imperatives in the sister language. Kutscher suggested the possibility. Yet the verb הוה is an Aramaic verb; and while it is not utterly unknown in Hebrew (it occurs four or five times in the fourteen hundred to sixteen hundred pages of printed Hebrew Bibles),[240] the normal verb for "be, become," היה, is the most common verb existing in that corpus. Further problematic, the roughly coeval Mishnah tractate *Avot,* an MH text, uses the Aramaic verb frequently, but "rightly" vocalized Aramaic-style, so far as spelling indicates (הוי). The best evidence for vernacular Hebrew of the time, then, does not support the notion of Hebrew influence on the Aramaic form. So it would seem most reasonable to turn back to the Christian Palestinian Aramaic parallel—except that there, precisely and uniquely for this verb הוה, the masculine singular imperative is always הֱוִי! Our form is unique, and almost certainly colloquial.

As noted, the lexicon of the letters and subscriptions is notable for its connections with later literary Aramaic. One finds, for example, the adverbial באפ[רי]ע, "immediately" (*P.Yadin* 55:5), known once from *Reichsaramäisch* but occurring half a dozen times in Jewish Palestinian Aramaic (spelled always בפריע).[241] An approximate synonym, שוה (*P.Yadin* 50:5), was known previously from Christian Palestinian Aramaic and Samaritan Aramaic. In the subscription to the Greek *P.Yadin* 15, Judah b. Eleazar Khthousion wrote, "In my presence [בקמי] Babatha affirmed all of the foregoing." The indicated syntagm appears elsewhere only in Christian Palestinian Aramaic and Samaritan Aramaic.

Loans from Greek are significant, given the modest bulk of material surviving in the letters and subscriptions. They include אספליא, as discussed earlier; אכלס, "army" or "crowd" (*P.Yadin* 57:5, ὄχλος); פרן, "dowry" (*P.Yadin* 18:71, φερνή); נמוס/נמוס, "law" or "custom" (*P.Yadin* 56:9 and 17:42, respectively, νόμος); אפטרפא, "guardian" (*P.Yadin* 27:12, ἐπίτροπος); and the legal calque לחשבן פקדון, "on account of deposit" (*P.Yadin* 17:41, calqued on εἰς λόγον παραθήκης, which occurs in the Greek of the text at 17:6 and 17:25). As these examples illustrate, the Greek vocabulary largely derives from the military and legal realms.[242] Borrowings from other languages include לטם (*P.Yadin*

50:12, *ladanum*) and דינר (*P.Yadin* 43:5, 47b:8, *denarius*) from Latin, and the verbs צחב, "object" (*P.Yadin* 50:8, 11, *ṣaḫiba*) and צפא, "clear (claims)" (*P.Yadin* 20:42, *ṣafā*) from Nabataean Arabic.

Hebrew contact phenomena are not limited to the lexicon but embrace morphology and syntax as well, demonstrating a profound interaction between the two Semitic tongues. Lexical Hebraisms would include חשבן, "account," at *P.Yadin* 17:41; עֵין, "weighed precisely," at *P.Yadin* 54:4; and הנסי, "the prince," as Simon b. Kosiba's title in the first line of the same letter. Similar is הבבלי, "the Babylonian"—a handle become a name—as Bar Menahem's self-identification in *P.Yadin* 27:13. Morphosyntactic Hebraisms include תדברו, "you shall lead," at *P.Yadin* 56:9; the expected Aramaic form תדברון occurs earlier in the letter, at line 3. Another is פרענת, "punishment" (*P.Yadin* 50:11), Hebrew for what should in Aramaic be either פרענותא or פרענו. A third example is the use of לא אנש to mean "no one," as regularly with Hebrew לא איש (*P.Yadin* 50:13). The Aramaic ואם לא (later אלא), "but if not," appears at *P. Yadin* 54:6 instead of the expected והן לא; אם is a Hebrew conditional particle.[243] In lines 2–3 of the same letter, the imperfect די תבחנון ותחדון is used as an imperatival ("you are to examine and seize")—regular usage in MH, but not in Aramaic. This use of the imperfect is common in the letters.

The penetration of Hebrew beyond the Aramaic lexicon and into the language's morphology and syntax is balanced by equal and greater penetration in the reverse direction. The Hebrew of the Bar Kokhba materials is notably more "Aramaized" than is "standard" MH as we know it through scribal transmission. Aspects of the lexical influence have engaged us above. Aramaic influence on the morphology would include the difficult כליהון/עליהון of *P.Yadin* 51:3. Although the correct reading of the noun or particle is debatable, the suffixed הון-, "their," is legible and appears in place of the expected Hebrew הם-. Similarly, one reads in *P.Hever* 30:5–6, [מן] קצתהון בישוב, "[some] of them are in the village."[244] Hebrew morphology would "normally" be מקצתם, with assimilation of the *nun* of מן and a mimating plural suffix. Indeed, the form קצת is itself a borrowing from Aramaic, though known already in BH.[245] Linguists consider this sort of borrowing—of inflectional morphology—to be rare.[246]

Scholars of our texts have sometimes seized upon the Aramaic influence on the Hebrew of the letters and other Bar Kokhba documents as evidence that many Judaeans no longer knew "real Hebrew." For example, speaking of the affidavit letter *Mur* 42, Eshel wrote: "An interesting feature of this document is that the *parnasim* attempted to write in Hebrew, but they incorporated Aramaic words and Aramaic syntax into the text. This document shows how hard it was for some people to express themselves in Hebrew."[247] This is a possible interpretation of the evidence, but it takes no account of the reverse phenomena—Hebrew affecting Aramaic—nor of other factors as well. A better interpretation would be that we have in the letters a reflection of the sort of Hebrew that people actually spoke in Judaean towns and villages. It was indeed an "Aramaized" Hebrew. But we also see a register akin to spoken Aramaic in the letters, and it is a "Hebraized" Aramaic. The whole must be weighed, not just the Hebrew. For we find Aramaisms in Hebrew, Hebraisms in Aramaic, code-switching, and many other phenomena familiar from situations of bilingualism, multilingualism, and language contact. Further, for Judaea one must factor Greek into the equation. We shall shortly consider the significant Semitisms in the Greek. And, as argued above, it seems that the consonantal phonology of the Semitic tongues had in Judaea converged notably on that of contemporary eastern Greek.

We shall discuss all these matters more fully in the final chapter. Here, however, we must return to the Aramaic as briefly sketched and suggest an answer to the question with which we began. Was colloquial Aramaic, so far as the letters and subscriptions reflect it, substantially different from the Aramaic of literature and legal writing? We can have no certainty concerning the answer, given our small linguistic sample, but the answer seems to be that the differences of register or dialect were not nearly so great as for Hebrew. Literary Hebrew would be unintelligible to a typical peasant. Literary Aramaic would usually not be, although it might be puzzling at times. Legal Aramaic would occupy a medial position. More needs to be said, but it is better said in a broader context, in which we bring together at last all that we have considered.

As we turn to that discussion, what reward, if any, has this preliminary excavation of the Bar Kokhba letters brought forth? The reader must judge the worth, but the following are the proposals of this study. Judaea was an epistolary culture, in that regard integrated within the greater epistolary culture that was the Roman Mediterranean in these years. The writing of letters was a regular part of education for literacy, but not usually in the first years. Only later, in the course of reaching the level of expertise we have called literary literacy, would one typically acquire the capacity to draft a simple letter. In Judaea, people usually wrote letters in a register akin to ordinary conversation. Usually they wrote in Aramaic. That was what they were trained to do. Scribes frequently wrote for them, however, and in those situations they might produce a Greek missive. A living Hebrew stood at the ready, and was occasionally called upon, but the typical layperson would not always feel comfortable turning that language to the written task.

But what were the odds that the typical layperson would even know the living version of the holy tongue? How did language and literacy really "work" in the multilingual Judaea of Herod, John the Baptist, Jesus, Josephus, and Simon b. Kosiba? We are at last ready to attempt an answer.

5 Language and Literacy in Roman Judaea

As the Curtain Rose: The Time of Pompey (63 B.C.E.)

We have worked in the preceding chapters to discover the people behind the names in our texts, investigating at some length a necessarily central question: Who took the documents to the caves? Arguably, we have arrived at some possible answers, and with them a sense of the social context for our materials. A brief review here of select historical processes and events that occurred before the curtain rose on our period—a glance at the mise-en-scène of the years before Pompey—may assist with that other dimension of context, chronology. Combining historical with social context, we can hope to have positioned a proper matrix within which to understand the data on which this chapter focuses.

None dispute that the Judaeans of the preexilic period were largely speakers of Hebrew. How did it happen, then, that by Roman times Aramaic was so pervasive in this region that, according to many scholars, it had become the language most people ordinarily spoke? To answer this question, two somewhat distinct models have been proposed: what one might call the "lingua franca model," and its competitor, the "languages-in-contact model."[1]

Perhaps the most prominent exponent of the lingua franca model has been Joseph Fitzmyer, but the view is widely held. In this scenario, Aramaic became the common language of Palestine largely as a reflex of political realities. Aramaic was used as the language of political administration in the Near East for centuries before the Judaean exile, beginning with the Neo-Assyrian Empire; the Neo-Babylonians and the Persians continued to use it as the lingua franca.[2] The Persian Empire stretched from Asia Minor to the region of the Indus. Throughout this territory, as diverse modern discoveries have shown, a fairly standardized form of Aramaic (*Reichsaramäisch,* or Official Aramaic) served for official communications and legal and economic documents.[3] At the center of this geographic region sat Judaea. Descendants of the Babylonian exiles had repatriated beginning in the 530s B.C.E., bringing with them from Babylon a spoken form of this standard language. By the end of the fifth century, Jewish mercenaries settled in Elephantine (at the first cataract of the Nile) were addressing letters to the Jerusalem leadership in Official Aramaic (CAP 30–32). Further testimony to its use by Judaeans in the years of Persian hegemony include the Moṣa stamp impressions, the Samaria Papyri from the Wadi Daliyeh, *P.Jericho* 1, and the Khirbet el-Qom documents.[4] Frank Polak has therefore argued:

> The social and cultural consequences of this situation can hardly be overestimated. Because of administrative and social exigencies, the entire Judaean community was affected by Aramaic. Real estate contracts, for instance, would be written in Aramaic, as they were in Elephantine and Samaria. Any complaint and judgment would have to be argued before the royal judges. Hence, Aramaic would be the preferred language of all persons doing business with the government, that is to say, probably the entire property-owning and professional part of the population, including even craftsmen. Thus Aramaic developed into the main language in administrative, legal and commercial contexts.[5]

In this fashion Aramaic became a prestige language. Polak went on to argue that producing documents in Aramaic would have been the main focus of scribal education in Persian-controlled regions, and so also at the provincial chancery in Jerusalem. Judaean scribes would no longer have learned the standard language of their bureaucracy in earlier times, a form of Hebrew—at least, not during the years of official training most scribes received. Only the most learned of the scribes would have advanced to the now arcane arts of formulating documents and producing literature in the ancestral tongue. The Aramaic lingua franca took root among the elite and spread thence to the lower classes as they sought to emulate the elites and accommodate themselves to the new linguistic realities. Following the breakup of the Persian Empire, this lingua franca changed and developed in a variety of directions, as is natural for spoken languages. So a number of local Aramaic dialects emerged among the Judaeans. According to Fitzmyer and his fellow travelers, representatives of these dialects are found in the Aramaic literary texts discovered near Qumran, in works such as the *Genesis Apocryphon* and the *Targum of Job* from Cave 11.[6]

Now certainly this approach has a ring of truth. But in portraying Aramaic influence on the Judaeans as coming almost entirely through a single channel—elite behaviors involving a superdialect—it overlooks broader historical and social realities. A more natural explanation, one that absorbs much of the lingua franca model but expands its too-narrow framework, is the languages-in-contact model.

Through various avenues Judaeans had been in contact with Aramaic speakers for centuries before the advent of Persian rule. The Israelite kingdom to the north was contiguous with Aramaic-speaking kingdoms from the beginning of the first millennium, presumably mediating some measure of Aramaic influence to the sister tribes in the south. At times, Aramaeans ruled both Israel and Judah; for example, Hazael, king of Damascus, is reported to have dominated both kingdoms in the late ninth century B.C.E.[7] As time went on, speakers of various Aramaic dialects settled in Transjordan as far south as Ramoth-Gilead.[8] Then in the eighth and seventh centuries B.C.E., forcible deportations by the Assyrians resettled Aramaic speakers from Mesopotamia in that region, in the area of Samaria, and along the coast, essentially surrounding the Hebrew-speaking Judaeans.[9] The results of language contact are sometimes evident. The Balaam text from Deir Alla in the Jordan Valley, for example—which perhaps dates to the early seventh century—displays a "mixed" form of Canaanite and Aramaic that has defied scholarly efforts at precise categorization.[10] As a means of guaranteeing that the routes stayed open, the Assyrians also stationed Aramaic speakers along the major trade routes passing into and out of Judaea. Judaean intermarriage with the peoples with whom they were in contact along all these borders and trade routes may be assumed; the practice is specifically condemned in biblical texts describing the period of repatriation under the Persians.[11] To all of these mechanisms of contact with Aramaic, the situation with the lingua franca can be added as yet another.

In the early centuries of its advance into Judaea, then, Aramaic entered by various avenues: by direct rule; through intermarriage, trade, and contact along the borders on three sides—and through the lingua franca. Doubtless various dialects of Aramaic were involved, such that the ultimate derivation of all Roman-period forms of Judaean Aramaic from the Persian lingua franca seems dubious on its face. The literary Aramaic used during the years between Pompey and Hadrian did, however, ultimately derive from Official

Aramaic: Jonas Greenfield argued for its classification as "Standard Literary Aramaic" (SLA), and his is a widely accepted counterpoint to Fitzmyer's approach.[12] SLA differed to varying degrees, but often markedly, from the spoken Aramaic Judaeans used.[13]

Thus, in the languages-in-contact model, Judaean literary Aramaic was not, as in the lingua franca model, essentially the spoken dialects dressed up in formal attire. Rather, SLA was a new Semitic koine that replaced earlier Official Aramaic.[14] As such, its use extended well beyond Judaea. Its impact can be seen in Syria, for example, as it affected the Old Syriac Gospels and early Syriac inscriptions,[15] and as it found expression in the most famous Palmyrene inscription, the bilingual Greek-Palmyrene taxation tariff of 137 C.E.[16] SLA books produced in Judaea may then arguably be taken as evidence for Wasserstein's pre-Hellenic "supra-national civilisation" continuing to express itself in "local aramaicised cultures" during the Roman period (more on this point later).[17]

The question of the character of Judaean Hebrew in the years leading up to Pompey is today more complicated than it used to be thought. Until about twenty years ago, something like the following stood as the consensus. The various forms of ancient Hebrew known to us could essentially be arranged along a time line. Earliest was Archaic Biblical Hebrew (ABH), mostly known indirectly through linguistic triangulation and onomastic analysis. Then came Standard Biblical Hebrew (SBH), sometimes called Early Biblical Hebrew (EBH). This was the language of the First Temple or preexilic scriptural writings. After the exile and return, a new form of Hebrew emerged, known as Late Biblical Hebrew (LBH). This was the Hebrew of Ezra, Nehemiah, Chronicles, and other postexilic scriptures. A developed form of LBH was to be found in the Hebrew materials discovered near Qumran. The Qumran Hebrew (QH) was a purely literary dialect, while vernacular Hebrew (to the degree that such existed, a contentious issue, as we have seen) was an early version or versions of MH.[18] Naturally, scholars argued for numerous variations on this somewhat simplified schema, but broadly conceived, this was the thinking.

Today, this edifice is under assault, much of the attackers' weaponry having been forged on the anvils of sociolinguists. The chronological conception retains many able defenders, willing to cede some territory to the attackers but well supplied and determined to weather the siege with citadel intact. It is not clear, however, to what degree they will succeed. The fiercest contests focus on two points of attack, with a third, more minor skirmish off to one side a bit. The relation of SBH and LBH is one of the major contests. A strong argument is being advanced that these ought not be seen as earlier and later forms of Hebrew, but rather as two synchronic styles. The second major contest is the relation of LBH to QH. Here, if not elsewhere, the assault seems likely to breach the walls: QH has been demonstrated statistically to attach to SBH, not LBH. The skirmish concerns whether or not QH represents a spoken dialect, and if so, its relation to proto-MH. A few details will aid consideration.[19]

Ian Young, Robert Rezetko, and Martin Ehrensvärd have spearheaded the charge regarding the relation of SBH and LBH. Their tactic has been the following. Relying upon literary analysis developed over the past century and more, they separated out certain scriptural books as "core EBH" and "core LBH." Analyzing both categories, they then arrived at statistical profiles of the grammatical features most characteristic of each. A crucial concept has been "accumulation": what is important is not the occasional appearance of a given grammatical feature, but rather its accumulation in one of the two categories. This method seemed to show that the presumed categories of SBH/EBH and LBH are not tight. They leak: some books generally considered "early" present profiles of features not greatly different from those considered "late." Other books are indeed distinct, appearing "early" or "late" as usually thought. The conclusion for which the authors then argued was that these data delineate stylistic, not chronological, distinctions. The two styles of writing Hebrew, each attested in both the preexilic and postexilic periods, were simply that: styles, both used in both periods. Issues of chronology must then be pursued using methods other than linguistic.[20]

This argument has raised important questions, but not without exposing its own Achilles heel: textual transmission. A fundamental difficulty for the entire enterprise is the need to take aim at distant, obliquely moving targets. The texts being analyzed were never static, once-for-all creations. We do not have *the* text, for example, of Exodus, but rather several forms of it (MT, LXX, Samaritan Pentateuch, 4QPaleo-Exodus^{m}). The shape of many scriptural books was in flux for hundreds of years; consequently, a series of intertwining literary editions is frequently in evidence, even though all that now survive are relatively late—and certainly fortuitous—textual exempla.[21] Doubtless additional literary editions ghost-trail back over the historical horizon. Moreover, *portions* of books underwent editing at different times by different hands. These books are not linguistic monoliths. Nothing precludes the possibility that reworking of an original SBH product, for instance, might leave it appearing much nearer to an LBH product. And, in a sense, it actually would be such.

For these reasons, counting accumulations of grammatical features book-by-book *in this corpus* may be flawed as a theoretical concept. It is too blunt a tool to use against the bewildering complexity of interlaced texts, copied and revised, revised and copied untold times, for centuries. We have a butter knife when we need a scalpel. How sharper tools might be possible, given present textual witnesses, remains unclear.[22] In any case, nothing in the data these authors have surfaced is truly incompatible with the notion that, to varying degrees, scribal author-copyists actively reworked earlier texts as they passed them down. Yet with that, we arrive at a form of the consensus.

And there are phenomena that the synchronic model explains less well than a version of the consensus can. Linguistic processes that appear reasonably transparent on the chronological approach cloud to opacity when considered matters of mere style. Scholars have proffered examples both lexical and syntactic. Verbal functions appear to fall away, balanced by the compensating rise of a new system to carry that semantic load.[23] It is much easier to believe that the falling and rising are real—matters of language change—than to see them as vagaries of style. The same applies to hyperarchaisms: misanalyses of what seem, on the chronological model, to be earlier sources, copied but then wrongly employed by what seem to be later ones.[24] How to account for that sort of thing as mere matters of style? On the issue of SBH and LBH, the citadel of the consensus begins to look secure.

One cannot say the same of the conflict at the second front. Here, Young, Rezetko, and Ehrensvärd made what was probably the strongest contribution of their study. Taking five-hundred-word samples of scriptural books alongside several of the principal Qumran writings, they showed that the latter were much more like EBH in their profiles than LBH.[25] The core LBH texts such as Ezra and Daniel exhibited twenty-two to twenty-five LBH features, whereas the core EBH Genesis and Exodus numbered just one to four. *Pesher Habakkuk* was nearly the same as the EBH book on which it commented: it displayed six LBH features, Habakkuk itself, five. The *War Scroll* sample had nine LBH features; the *Community Rule,* nine; and the *Damascus Document,* twelve—all similar to EBH books. The authors understood clearly what probably explains this common profile for the Dead Sea Scroll literature:

> How did late authors like Ben Sira or the authors of the Qumran documents write in a late form of EBH? . . . It is widely acknowledged that well before the end of the Second Temple period, the Jewish educational curriculum was based on biblical texts, and that the core texts were EBH texts such as the Pentateuch, Isaiah, the Twelve Prophets, and Psalms, with the Wisdom books of Job and Proverbs. Education thus involved mastery and memorization of core EBH books, with a corresponding mastery of their language.[26]

On the question of the continuity or discontinuity of LBH, then, the consensus seems to have been wrong. The language of Hebrew literature on the eve of Pompey's arrival was not a direct development from LBH. Rather, it was akin to Atticism, a *Kunstprosa* that could be acquired (usually imperfectly) only by substantial education—education of a sort available to the cultural elite, but not to the masses.

This resolution of the second conflict leads directly on to the related skirmish, focused on whether QH was a spoken dialect. The consensus has held that it was not, but rather a more or less artificial literary tongue; and Young, Rezetko, and Ehrensvärd's work has arrived, as described, at an intersection with this view. This convergence of conclusions reached by different paths is impressive—indeed, in the present state of the question, compelling. The arguments raised by such scholars as Elisha Qimron, favoring a spoken origin for QH, have shown nothing more definite than the presence of various unprovenanced archaisms and formerly unknown innovations in the Dead Sea corpus.[27] These are noteworthy phenomena, but in itself their presence is not decisive. More than one explanation of them is possible, including appeal to language change and development within literary (as opposed to vernacular) languages. One thinks of *Homerische Wörter*. The best explanatory synthesis of all the linguistic facts known at present may be that of Joshua Blau:

> In our view one has to take into consideration, when analyzing the Hebrew of the Dead Sea Scrolls, its very complex history, exhibiting various traditions, genres, fashions, scribal schools, and personal inclinations. Therefore, even conspicuous differences in orthography and morphology cannot automatically be ascribed to changes in the spoken language. One must not forget that *even dead languages, only used in literature, change*. . . . It seems expedient to analyze Qumran Hebrew in the light of the language of various mediaeval Middle Arabic texts. . . . The Neo-Arabic elements attested in the Middle Arabic texts reflect, to be sure, a living language, yet many deviations from classical Arabic proper exhibit changes that affected a language no longer

> spoken, yet still used as a literary device, and depend on various traditions, genres, fashions, scribal schools, and personal inclinations. . . . Rather than to invent a non-existent dialect, it is much simpler and much more convincing to attribute most of the linguistic features absent from biblical Hebrew occurring in Qumran Hebrew to changes that arose in the literary language of the Dead Sea Scrolls owing to scribal schools [and the other things listed], just as it happened in the Middle Arabic texts.[28]

The situation with Judaean Hebrew at the time of Pompey's irruption was thus notably similar to that of Aramaic. In both cases, literary dialects distinctly different from the vernacular dialects were in place. For Aramaic, SLA bestrode a presumed welter of spoken varieties of the tongue, probably differing more or less from village to village, although we may judge only via flash-quick glimpses of their variety in the letters, in the subscriptions, and through occasional scribal slips in legal and literary works. A somewhat different, more conservative dialect served for legal documents.

Writers working in Hebrew sought to produce literary texts in language that mimicked Moses and the Prophets. Steven Fassberg has made the attractive suggestion to call this form of Hebrew "Standard Literary Hebrew," thereby formalizing the parallel with the Aramaic situation.[29] In contrast, for day-to-day speech—to the extent that Hebrew was used for such (just how much will become clearer below)—Judaeans generally used one or more varieties of proto-MH.[30] Apart from very ill-attested minority tongues that may have been used by an occasional Judaean, such as Latin or an early form of Arabic, that leaves Greek.

The coming of Greek to Palestine is an oft-told tale requiring no detailed rehearsal here. Hengel amassed and analyzed much of the relevant data in *Judaism and Hellenism* (1974), as had Tcherikover earlier and in great detail in *Hellenistic Civilization and the Jews* (1959).[31] Hengel opined, "The final establishment and dissemination of the *koine* was probably the most valuable and the most permanent fruit of Alexander's expedition."[32] Perhaps so; in Alexander's wake, and further through the division and rule of his conquests by the Diadochoi, Greek came to dominate public and economic life in the East, as evidenced most thoroughly in Ptolemaic Egypt. Between roughly 300 and 200 B.C.E. the Ptolemies also ruled Judaea, with a bureaucracy perhaps less all encompassing than Egypt's, but no less Hellenophone. They were followed in the next century by the equally philhellene Seleucids. From the period of the Ptolemies, the Tobias materials within the Zeno papyri may be taken as emblematic of the situation within circles of the Jerusalem aristocracy, with whom Tobias and his family had long intermarried.[33] The history of the Tobiads in subsequent generations, passed down by Josephus, illustrates at various points the growing presence of Hellenism and Greek within the Jerusalem upper classes.[34] The *Letter of Aristeas,* though dating from a later period, portrays (and evidently expects readers to find believable) a situation in which Jewish master scribes, sent to Egypt in the mid-third century, possessed a thorough mastery of Greek language and literature.

Palestinian sources are unfortunately very sparse for the third century, but as Hengel noted, "From the moment when the sources for Palestine Judaism become fuller, with the books of the Maccabees, we come across an abundance of Greek names."[35] Significant figures bearing Greek names and ascribed to this period also appear in rabbinic literature, most notably Antigonus of Socho (*m. Avot* 1:3). Antigonus was no Jerusalemite but hailed from a tiny village some twenty-four kilometers southwest of that city. The penetration of the Greek onomasticon to such a depth of Judaean society by the early second century B.C.E. is impressive.

From this point on, the spread of Greek names is well documented. At the social pinnacle, all of the later Hasmoneans bore Hellenic names alongside their Hebrew ones.[36] This phenomenon of double naming seems to have become common, particularly in the upper classes. Since Hengel wrote, Ilan's *Lexicon* has laid bare eye-opening onomastic facts: in the period covered by her analysis, 27.3 percent of attested male names were Greek. For women, the number was much higher, fully 43.6 percent. Comfortably settled amidst the favorite male names were two Greek options, Alexander and Dositheus. The top ten Judaean female names likewise possessed a notable Greek flavor, with Berenice in seventh position. As a percentage of the total population, 14.5 percent of Judaeans possessed Greek names.[37] It is hard to imagine such ubiquity of Greek names correlating in no significant way with deeper and deeper social penetration of the language that supplied them.

By the time that Pompey arrived at the walls of Jerusalem in 63 B.C.E., then, Greek had been established for some two centuries, and as far as our evidence indicates, it advanced from strength to strength during the ensuing decades up to the Second Revolt. Unlike Aramaic and Hebrew, though, here we need not particularly concern ourselves with issues of dialect and superdialect. Judaean Greek was, as Naphtali Lewis observed, "in its essence the postclassical Greek *koine* familiar from other sources in the eastern Mediterranean."[38] Such is not to say, as Lewis further observed, that it lacked certain idiosyncratic features; but these are best taken up in more detail below. We turn, then, to the data of our study, embedded as they were in a matrix of considerable linguistic complexity—and therefore, as we shall see, of a commensurate complexity of literate habits.

Hebrew Language and Literacy

We took a brief look at Table 1.3 in Chapter 1, but it now invites closer scrutiny, both to ask further questions of the data and to analyze in greater depth those questions asked earlier. In no small part, this greater nuance rests upon the foregoing prosopographic analysis. Note that the table documents events, not individuals. It tabulates what happened on numerous occasions in ancient Judaea when individuals had an opportunity to sign their names to legal writs composed in Hebrew. Each time an individual was presented with such an opportunity, it was at least theoretically possible that he or she might sign differently from the last time. We cannot assume that a given person who had signed in Hebrew once, for example, would always produce the same result on another occasion, even though signing in the language of the writ (if possible) was customary. Accordingly, what must be counted are occasions, not people. In point of fact, eighteen principals were involved on nineteen occasions recorded in the table: Eleazar b. Eleazar b. Hita signed both *P.Yadin* 44 and *P.Yadin* 45. Thirty-six separate individuals were involved in forty-two instances as witnesses, *hypographeis,* and officials. (For a detailed conspectus of all of this study's data on language and literacy, tabulated by documents and by names of individuals, see Appendices A and B.)

One should also be aware that the percentages in Table 1.3 are calculated only after discounting the several instances of "other" that are recorded. "Other" in this table—and in Table 1.2—generally indicates one of two things: either that a person is known to have been a party to a contract, but with no vestige of the signature surviving; or, that although fragments of words are discernible, the language of the signature remains stubbornly indeterminate. For example, Hillel b. Garis was a principal to *Mur* 24, subleasing to at least eleven other individuals. Some of their signatures do survive; on the extant portions of the contract, however, his does not. Again, Simon b. PN signed *Mur* 37, but whether in Hebrew or Aramaic is impossible to say because the distinguishing word for "son" is lost.

In one unique instance an individual is known to have been a fluent writer but nevertheless chose to have a *hypographeus* sign for him. This was

Tehinah b. Simon of *P.Yadin* 44, about whom we shall have more to say presently. He also counts in Table 1.3 as "other." We can of course have no unqualified assurance that our data disguise no additional instances of this phenomenon. We must bear in mind that human behavior is seldom mechanical and so—regardless of strength of custom—never fully predictable. Our numbers are therefore not absolute, but rather are indicators of how Judaean society functioned.

On 25 percent of the occasions represented, principals signed in Hebrew—a respectable number, certainly, given the widespread scholarly contention that among the Judaeans of our period Hebrew had died out. Principals, after all, are more random as samples of the populace than are witnesses, the latter chosen for their ability to write (and, conceivably, for their linguistic ability). This percentage is respectable—but if one considers two additional factors, the number for principals may rise considerably. First, we should ask what percentage of the *literate* people signed in Hebrew, since it is obvious that we learn nothing concerning the language abilities of the illiterates by their failure to sign. For all we can determine, all eight of them may have known Hebrew. A fairer gauge of Hebrew knowledge among the principals is to consider only the literates as our pool. Of eight such, then, four instances of signing in Hebrew yield a number of 50 percent, twice the initial indication. At this point the second additional factor enters the picture: the mixed Aramaic/Hebrew signatures. Two of the eight literate principals signed in this fashion. Jacob b. Judah signed *Mur* 42, יעקוב בן יהודה על נפשה, "Jacob b. Judah hereby (witnesses) concerning himself." Similarly, Jesus b. Simon signed *P.Yadin* 46, ישוע̊ [ב]ן̊ שמעון ענפשה.[39] If it could be established that even such partial use of Hebrew signaled that a person knew the language, then six of eight signatures would so qualify, fully 75 percent. Is this a proper understanding of the phenomenon of language mixture?

Several factors suggest so. We must consider the formulaic character of these signatures to contracts, especially for frequent signers (both men wrote at level 3 and so probably did sign their names relatively frequently). Formulae are by their very nature routine. Routine often elicits a more or less automatic response. Thus, if it were normal for these men to sign in Aramaic, but they found themselves on these occasions involved instead with Hebrew writ, they might well act out of habit and sign a part of their attestations in the normal fashion. When we glance ahead a bit and consider the witnesses and *hypographeis* to Hebrew legal documents, what we find seems to support this view of things.

Five of those men signed in mixed Aramaic/Hebrew, in every case with the Aramaic element first. That is, each inscribed his name using the Aramaic word for "son" but then arguably focused a bit and, recalling the situation and its cultural expectations, followed with the Hebrew term for "witnesses." For example, Simon b. Joseph witnessed *P.Yadin* 44, שמעון בר יהוסף עד. If these people routinely used Aramaic in legal situations, self-reference by the Aramaic form of their names would be natural, all the more so if this were their quotidian manner of reference to themselves in general—if, that is, they most often spoke Aramaic and so were usually addressed by this form of their names. Moreover, by itself, use of the Hebrew term עד would presumably suffice to signal knowledge of Hebrew and thereby communicate the critical legal fact: the witness's ability to comprehend the contract when read out, and so in signing to affirm the written transaction as corresponding to the oral exchange that preceded it.

We saw in Chapter 1 excellent reason to believe that Aramaic was indeed the ordinary language, if not of speech, then at least of legal matters. Recall that an overwhelming percentage, virtually 100 percent of signers, produced Aramaic when failing to sign in the language of a Hebrew, Greek, or Nabataean contract (see further the tables for Greek and Nabataean below). Also, scribal slips further confirm that people were habituated to writing legal texts—and so, *ex hypothesi,* signing them—in Aramaic. For instance, composing *P.Hever* 49 in Hebrew, Masabala b. Simon first wrote Judah b. Judah's name as יהודה בר יהודה (49:4) but then overwrote the *resh* with a final *nun* to render the name as Hebrew, יהודה בן יהודה.[40] This was an emblematic mistake and correction. One finds no slips of the opposite sort, substituting or correcting from Hebrew to Aramaic in an Aramaic contract.

Perhaps in the same vein, but more likely as a matter of custom, extant contracts show that First Revolt Jerusalem scribes *always* set down proper names in Aramaic, even when producing Hebrew writ. In *Mur* 22 every proper name appearing in full—Ishmael b. PN, Hanin b. Honi, Joseph b. Adi, Bar Abshai, Hanin b. Hanina, Halifa b. PN—is written with בר. In *Mur* 30, the witnesses are first cataloged in Aramaic—Jonathan b. Joseph, Simon b. Simi, Jonathan b. Eleazar, and Jonathan b. Hananiah. There follow the vender, Dositheus b. Eleazar; a neighbor, Hanin b. Jonathan; and the vender's father-in-law, Honi b. Jonathan (the same man as the neighbor, doubtless, but with alternate appellative). In each case, the word for "son" is Aramaic.[41] Again, all surviving proper names in the Hebrew 4Q348, composed in Jerusalem, appear as Aramaic: Matthew b. Simon, Eleazar b. Simon, and Bar Honi.[42]

Presumably, the custom *was* the custom because in Jerusalem, Aramaic was the customary language of law. Yet the signatories in the city often signed Hebrew contracts in the holy tongue.

Accordingly, we are probably right to conclude that those in our data pool who witnessed Hebrew contracts, or signed them as principals but did so mixing Aramaic with their Hebrew, simply slipped. They might have signed in pure Hebrew. With what they did produce, they were claiming to know the language of the contract. This claim was likely to be true, because the family members and neighbors who were partners in the process would recognize a false claim. If this is valid reasoning, then, on 75 percent of the occasions in evidence, literate principals to extant Hebrew contracts claimed to know that language. Of course, we have just eight random instances. Does the evidence regarding the significantly more numerous witnesses comport with such a high percentage?

In a word, yes. At this juncture of the discussion it makes sense to shift our terms and begin talking of individuals as well as occasions. As noted, on 75 percent of the opportunities presented, literate Judaean principals signed Hebrew documents in Hebrew. These eight occasions involved five individuals, since one man signed twice. Hence, we know that five of seven Judaean principals who were signature literate claimed to know Hebrew. This amounts to 71.4 percent. When we turn to the witnesses, *hypographeis,* and officials, similar profiles of occasions and individuals emerge. If we start with occasions, then—as Table 1.3 documents—we can say that in twenty-four of thirty-nine instances these people signed Hebrew texts in Hebrew.[43] Adding in the five cases of mixed languages gives us twenty-nine of thirty-nine occasions, 74.4 percent.

These thirty-nine instances represent the actions of thirty-three separate individuals. Of these, twenty-seven evidently knew Hebrew. For twenty-four of them, this conclusion is straightforward, because they signed in that language. Three other men present more complicated facts. All three hail from First Revolt Jerusalem and, as it seems, a single scribal shop, since two of them appear in documents together, and the third man is apparently brother to one of the other two. Thus all three are scribes. The first person, Simon b. Shabi, both wrote the Hebrew *Mur* 22 and signed it as a *hypographeus.* In the latter case, however, he signed in Aramaic. He did essentially the same things in *Mur* 29, composing it in Hebrew but witnessing on his own behalf and signing as *hypographeus* for a principal in Aramaic. Similarly, John b. Joseph scribed the Hebrew *Mur* 30 and witnessed it on his own behalf in Hebrew. But he signed for a principal to that document in Aramaic.

Since the statements of the principals were constitutive of the contract, whereby their words were of the very essence, one might suggest that these Aramaic signatures as *hypographeis* intended to record the *ipsissima verba* of non-Hebrew speakers. If so, this would accord with what we have seen elsewhere: recall *P.Yadin* 18, wherein an unnamed *hypographeus* fluent when writing Greek signed instead in a clumsy Aramaic, evidently to capture the actual words of the groom, Judah Cimber; and the Beth ʿAmar text, whose scribe wrote the document in Aramaic, except for the acknowledgment of the widow from Shaʿalabbim, whose words he set down in Hebrew.[44] Of course, this suggestion would not account for Simon b. Shabi's signing as a witness in Aramaic. His behavior was perhaps the exception that proves the rule: when analyzing human behaviors, we cannot expect a lock-step march to the rhythms of custom. But it is worth noting that the essential legal facts were in evidence regardless: Simon's knowledge of Hebrew, and so of the writ's precise stipulations, were scarcely in doubt—he had authored the text!

The third man proposed as arguably knowing Hebrew, but with complicating factors, is Eleazar b. Shabi, the only surviving signatory to 4Q348. We suggested in Chapter 2 that given the extreme rarity of his patronym, he was likely the brother of Simon b. Shabi. As the brother of a scribe who demonstrably knew Hebrew, and moreover as a scribe himself, we may reasonably assume that Eleazar also knew Hebrew. This is no certainty. The men might have had different mothers, thus different home languages. But it seems highly probable. If so, his signing 4Q348 in Aramaic becomes another of the rare examples of nonconformity to the statistically demonstrable custom: signing in the language of the writ, if possible. The *relative* frequency of such deviation in the materials from Jerusalem is important to acknowledge. It may suggest a lesser degree of attachment in that city to custom strictly observed elsewhere. In any event, the data show that inhabitants of Jerusalem usually followed the principle so evident in Judaea as a whole. The deviation is merely relative.

For two of the three Jerusalem scribes, then, we can definitely affirm that, despite their occasional inconsistency in signing, they knew Hebrew of the sort we find in the documents. Eleazar b. Shabi is a likely third example of the same. If so, then we can say that fully twenty-seven of thirty-three witnesses, *hypographeis,* and officials knew the Hebrew language. This would amount to 81.8 percent of the pool. Adding to them the literate principals, five of seven of whom claimed this linguistic knowledge, would yield thirty-two of forty, or 80.0 percent. Further, the two types of signatories—principals, a more or less random group, though from a certain level of society; and witnesses, chosen because they could sign—display similar profiles. That similarity serves to reassure that the numbers may reasonably be thought to portray broader Judaean realities.

In comparison to most scholarly depictions, the numbers are surprisingly high. They would lend credence to the argument that knowledge of vernacular forms of Hebrew was essentially at a steady state—the language still being spoken in Roman Judaea about as widely as it had been in the core region of biblical Judah: that is, excluding the Mediterranean coast, in the areas south of Samaria and north of Idumea. The 20 percent of the population ignorant of the language could represent Jewish immigrants from regions that did not speak Hebrew, prominently Galilee and the Babylonian Diaspora, and an influx during our years of Gentile inhabitants, most of whom would speak Aramaic dialects or Greek.

Before that assessment seems warranted, however, we must deal with important complicating issues. For one, how "random" is our pool of witnesses? We have established that family members and friends would be heavily involved in creating legal writ. These would generally be laypeople, and so study of their behavior gives us a picture in miniature of the broader society, itself overwhelmingly lay.[45] But was there a relatively higher degree of scribal participation for the Hebrew documents? If so, the foregoing numbers could well be skewed somewhat. Yet the skewing is not a given. As a group, higher proportions of Judaean scribes than of the general population would presumably know Hebrew—*unless,* of course, nearly everyone could speak the language. This last is an important caveat. On the basis of our data alone, distinguishing which situation was the reality may be very difficult. After all, it was inevitable that, compared with the percentage of the population they represented, scribes would be disproportionately involved in contracts. That issue leads on to the second matter. Are we really dealing with claims to *speak* Hebrew, that is, to know *vernacular* Hebrew? Judaean education in these years focused on the scriptural books, composed in literary Hebrew. A number of our signatories may have known no vernacular Hebrew but may have studied enough of this literary heritage to produce at least short passages in that form of Hebrew. In view of the act's legal meaning, might such people sign contracts in Hebrew? If so, might they form an appreciable element in our pool?

Consideration of either congeries of questions requires a tabulation of writing levels—illustrating once again, incidentally, the inseparable connection between language and literacy when investigating either aspect of ancient Judaea. How can we tell whether or not people were signing in Hebrew as a consequence of their literary training? One approach is to draw together signatories among the witnesses who signed in Hebrew, but at levels lower than level 3, the level of literary literacy. Those signing at levels 1 and 2 would not have learned sufficient literary Hebrew to stake a claim at knowing the holy tongue *on that basis.* They could not have inculcated enough of the scriptural variety so as to be able to comprehend a markedly variant form of Hebrew, that of the contracts—a fortiori, when hearing it read out at normal speeds. To do that would require a true mastery of the written version, paired with rare quick-mindedness. It follows that signing in Hebrew would mean for signatories at levels 1 and 2 knowledge of a colloquial version, akin to the contract itself (in all cases, then, proto-MH).

Conversely, signatories who signed *in Aramaic* at level 3 or higher would be people who may actually have read, copied, and memorized enough literary Hebrew to stake the aforementioned claim—but nevertheless, refused to do so. And this refusal would occur in atmospheres of heightened nationalist sentiment, since the Hebrew corpus mostly consists of materials produced during two wars with Rome. As elaborated in the previous chapter, among Judaeans emotions of this sort regularly called forth greater public use of the ancestral language. Accordingly, one assumes that level 3 signatories would often feel some pressure to use Hebrew. Discovery of Aramaic signers in that group would reinforce the inference that people signed in Hebrew only if they comprehended the contract as read. It would underscore the fact that signatures bore legal weight. Legal proprieties were taken sufficiently seriously as to override nationalism. And since comprehending oral proto-MH would differ from reading and comprehending SBH, the existence of Aramaic signatories at level 3 or higher would further validate the argument that signing in Hebrew equated with a spoken knowledge, not merely the ability to read. So what do we find? Table 5.1 tabulates the relevant data.

This table records individuals, not occasions. As shown, eight of twenty-four, or 33.3 percent of the signatories who chose to sign in Hebrew, signed at levels 1 or 2. This amounts to at least 75 percent of the total number of signatories at those levels who signed in any language (which tends to the notion that finding Hebrew signatories was not appreciably harder than finding signatories at all). Then, note that six witnesses signed at level 3 in Aramaic, which likewise amounts to 75 percent of the total signatories in that language. The high percentage suggests that the phenomenon was not

Table 5.1. Signatories to Hebrew documents: witnesses, *hypographeis*, and subscribers

Level	Sign in Hebrew (%)	Sign in Aramaic (%)	Sign (language indeterminate)	Totals per level (%)
1	2 (8.3)	1 (12.5)	0	3 (8.3)
2	6 (25.0)	1 (12.5)	2	9 (25.0)
3	4 (16.7)	6 (75.0)	2	12 (33.3)
4	12 (50.0)	0	0	12 (33.3)
Total	24	8	4	—

rare. Significant numbers of literate people chose not to sign in Hebrew, even though they could read it. All in all, given the limitations inherent to our corpus, it seems fair to conclude that *signing in Hebrew meant that one spoke proto-MH.*

Were scribes more involved in witnessing Hebrew documents than they were for Aramaic? If so, must we revise downward the estimate that roughly 80 percent of Judaeans spoke a colloquial form of Hebrew? An initial reconnoiter indicates that the answer to the first question is, "Yes." Scribal witnesses comprise 33.3 percent of the total witnesses to Hebrew contracts, compared with 11.8 percent for Aramaic writ (see Table 5.4). One way to address this issue is to isolate witnesses who signed Hebrew documents at level 3 or below: how many of them signed in Hebrew? The answer is twelve, among a total of twenty signatories signing in any language at or below level 3. Adding to that total the principals who signed in Hebrew (five of seven) yields seventeen of twenty-seven knowing Hebrew (63.0 percent). It thus appears that disproportionate scribal participation in Hebrew document production may have skewed our earlier estimate upward some 15–20 percent. A safer figure for Judaeans speaking a vernacular would seem to be 60–65 percent.

Yet two further considerations may act as counterweights to hoist that revised estimate back up somewhat. First, our sample includes the unique set of Hebrew contracts produced at En Gedi by Masabala b. Simon and his family, *P.Yadin* 44–46. Almost all of the other documents in our corpus were "singletons"; the statistical punch of such a set of three related texts, involving many of the same people, will obviously tend to be stronger than that of any three unrelated texts. *P.Yadin* 44–46 were the products of a scribal family working on behalf of a family member, Tehinah b. Simon of Mahoza. As a percentage, therefore, scribal involvement in these documents was extremely high and conspicuously affected the total picture. If one removes these documents and all of those participating—scribes or not, Hebrew signatories or not—the remaining data profile for Hebrew writ comes much more nearly to resemble that of Aramaic contracts. We end up with 17.4 percent scribal involvement for Hebrew, over against 11.8 percent for Aramaic. The skewing effect may be markedly smaller than first appears.

Add to that consideration the fact that the stated figure for Aramaic is (in a certain way of thinking) artificially low. Fewer scribes participated in producing Aramaic materials because a significant number of laypeople sidestepped the professionals to produce their own documents in that language, as we shall show when we take up the issue specifically. In contrast, few people felt comfortable doing the same in Hebrew because, aside from certain localities such as Jericho, it was not customary to put the vernacular to pen. Nonprofessional writers educated to level 3 learned to compose documents such as letters and (probably) simple contracts in Aramaic, but not in proto-MH. We considered this phenomenon when we examined the Bar Kokhba letters. Arguably, then, producing Hebrew contracts required more scribal involvement than the proportion of those knowing the language would properly suggest.

Assessing the potential effect of these counterweights on our figures is difficult. To attempt definitively to do so seems unwise. Better simply to suggest that our data show that 65–80 percent of Judaeans spoke a form of Hebrew. Hebrew vernaculars were plainly still alive and well in the years between Pompey and Hadrian, and it would be possible to mount an argument that the language was essentially as widely used among Judaeans as it had ever been. We shall not attempt that argument here, however. Suffice it to say that among a populace of about one million, somewhere *between 650,000 and 800,000 people spoke proto-MH.* The materials of this study evidence vernacular Hebrew in use across all sectors of Judaean society: cities (Jerusalem, Jericho), large villages (En Gedi, Kephar-Baru), and small villages (Tekoa, Beth ʿAmar, Beth-Mashiko). Even in the time of Bar Kokhba, the ancestral tongue was widely known indeed, and in two strikingly different varieties: proto-MH and literary Hebrew.

Linguistic analogy would suggest that Hebrew as spoken would probably differ somewhat from place to place within Judaea. Given the fortuitous character of the discoveries in the Judaean Desert, however, dialectal characteristics are hard to distinguish with any confidence. It does not help that we are ignorant of the ancient provenance of most of the Bar Kokhba letters, our best evidence for the vernacular. We cannot say to what degree they illustrate a single grammar, or more than one. We do not know whether the new expressions any given letter uses were in widespread use or peculiar to a particular village. But we can say that the strong differences between SBH and proto-MH would often render the former unintelligible to the uneducated peasant who spoke a dialect of the latter. Thus Judaea was virtually a textbook case of classic diglossia.

Charles Ferguson popularized the term *diglossia* in a seminal article published in 1959.[46] There he defined this sociolinguistic phenomenon as follows:

> Diglossia is a relatively stable language situation in which, in addition to the primary dialects of the language (which may include a standard or regional standards), there is a very divergent, highly codified (often grammatically more complex) superposed variety, the vehicle of a large and respected body of literature, either of an earlier period or in another speech community, which is learned largely by formal education and is used for most written and formal spoken purposes but is not used by any sector of the community for ordinary conversation.[47]

Ferguson studied four proposed examples of diglossia, in which a high (H) language or dialect coexisted with a low (L) variety: classical and vernacular Arabic, as in most Arab countries; French and Creole, in Haiti; standard and Swiss German, in Switzerland; and *Katharevousa* and *Dhimotiki* in Greece. In each instance, a large body of literature existed in H, while L often did not even have a written form (or if it did, it was not standardized). Children learned L from their mother's knee, H at school. In Ferguson's definition of diglossia, the H variety was not used by any sector of the community for ordinary conversation but was the vehicle of most kinds of writing.

In the decades subsequent to Ferguson's article, hundreds of additional studies on diglossia have appeared. In 1967, Joshua Fishman proposed an expanded definition wherein two or more languages or language varieties existed in functional distribution within a speech community.[48] Thus, as often used today, the term diglossia embraces the coexistence of all forms of speech in a community, whether of different languages, dialects, or social varieties. Indeed, the different expansions of meaning given diglossia by various scholars have sadly drained the term of much of its usefulness.[49] Further, with the increased emphasis among linguists on the concept of register, some have held that an analysis in terms of speech continuum is a better way to explain Ferguson's speech behavior and language choices.[50]

Nevertheless, if—while fully acknowledging the issues raised by scholars—we hold firmly to Ferguson's original, narrow definition (known today as "classic diglossia"), the application to ancient Judaea is readily apparent. Most of what Ferguson delineated concerning his four speech communities describes equally well what we find in Roman Judaea. Two strongly divergent varieties of Hebrew stood in complementary distribution: proto-MH for speech (L), and SBH for (much) writing (H). Presumably, the vernaculars were learned in the home. Only the educated elites would be at home with H. Peasants would come in contact with it when they heard the scriptures read in the local synagogue and so over the course of many years acquire a measure of understanding, much as Arab peasants do today with the classical Arabic of the Qur'an. But on many occasions they would need considerable explanation of what they heard.

Judaean society presents intricacies of a sort that Ferguson did not discuss with his examples, given the presence beyond Hebrew of different forms of Aramaic, and of Greek. But sticking for the moment to the situation with Hebrew, Ferguson's analysis is helpful. This was a situation of classic diglossia.

How, then, did Judaeans use the H form of Hebrew, precisely? In other words, how did Hebrew literacy work, and what were its functions in their culture? The answer begins to come clear if we consider the book scrolls found along with the documentary writings of the Bar Kokhba deposits. We discussed in Chapter 2 the small library of (as many as) thirteen Greek book rolls that may have been associated with the brothers Eutrapelus. These materials deserve further consideration in order to appreciate how unusual they were, and we shall give them such attention shortly. Putting them aside for the present, however, Table 5.2 tabulates all of the other literary texts discovered in the Bar Kokhba caves.

As the table illustrates, the Eutrapelus library aside, a total of nineteen literary works emerged from the caves associated with the Second Revolt. The *Greek Minor Prophets Scroll* from the Cave of Horrors, *8Hev* 1 XIIgr, is the solitary text not composed in literary Hebrew. The Murabbaʿat finds consisted of five book scrolls properly so-called and two "talismanic" literary miniatures, the sort typically encased and displayed by pious Jews of the period, whether their owners could read them or not: a mezuzah and a phylactery. These writings may have shared Jerusalem as their provenance, if they date to the First Revolt. But since one cannot distinguish with any

Table 5.2. Book scrolls in the Bar Kokhba caves

Number	Murabba'at	Wadi Sdeir	Naḥal Arugot	Naḥal Ḥever	Naḥal Ṣe'elim
1	*Mur* 1 Gen–Num (Deut?)	*Sdeir* 1 Gen	*Arug* 1 ArugLev	*P.Hev* 1a Num[a]	*34Se1* Phylactery
2	*Mur* 2 Deut	—	—	*P.Hev* 1b Ps	*34Se1* Num
3	*Mur* 3 Isa	—	—	*P.Hev* 2 Num[b]	—
4	*Mur* 4 Phylactery	—	—	*P.Hev* 3 Deut	—
5	*Mur* 5 Mezuzah	—	—	*P.Hev* 5 Phylactery	—
6	*Mur* 6 Unidentified Literary Text	—	—	*P.Hev* 6 Eschatological Hymn	—
7	*Mur* 88 XII	—	—	*8Hev* 1 XIIgr	—
8	—	—	—	*8Hev* 2 Prayer	—

confidence whether they were deposits of the First Revolt, the Second, or a mixture of both, their origins remain a mystery that almost begs speculation. If conveyed to the caves by Jesus b. Galgula and his family, for example, then these book rolls might represent products of the small village of Kephar-Barucha. That would be an interesting fact in itself, with obvious implications for the debated question of how numerous books were in Roman Judaea. For if even tiny villages might house a variety of books, then we might incline to think that the nation as a whole swarmed with them. But we cannot say whence the books, nor therefore can we approximate how many archival owners to associate with them.

All of the other cave deposits are almost certainly to be associated with elite refugees fleeing En Gedi to the numerous caves that puncture the escarpments northwest and southwest of the village. Apart from two phylacteries, ten book scrolls were discovered. Those from the Wadi Sdeir (Naḥal David) and Naḥal Arugot represent one archive each. The finds from Cave 34 in the Naḥal Ṣe'elim likely also derive from one individual's belongings, although it is plainly possible that two residents each owned one book. Thus we have three or four archives. To these we must add the findings from the Cave of Horrors and the Cave of Letters in Naḥal Ḥever.

Little survived the fiery destruction that the inhabitants of the Cave of Horrors inflicted on their possessions. The writings that did escape can be attributed to no particular individual, although possible association with the family of Masabala b. Simon is attractive. Again, with two texts, we have at most two archives, making a total of four to six book owners to this point. All are anonymous. The literature from the Cave of Letters, however, may arguably attach to someone we can name.

Yadin's team discovered pieces of the Psalms scroll and one copy of Numbers lying loose on the floor of the cave, evidently torn from their rolls as the bedouin spirited them out.[51] This fact supports three possible scenarios. Either the scrolls from which these fragments originated constituted a special deposit, concealed at some remove from the other archives in the Cave of Letters; or the scrolls were integral to one (or perhaps more) of the archives the bedouin removed; or some combination of these two options obtained. No particular warrant favors the first option nor, by parity of reasoning, the third. On the contrary, many ancient personal archives contained both documentary and literary items. Economy of explanation suggests the second scenario, although we cannot simply dismiss the others. Their existence necessarily casts additional doubt upon any tentative conclusion we may reach in pursuing the connection to a known archive.

As argued in Chapter 3, one may recognize three defensible archives among the loose materials from the Cave of Letters that the bedouin supplied the scholars in the early 1950s. And we must confine ourselves to the loose materials, since the bedouin obviously *discovered* the archive(s) that contained the books, just as they did those from which the loose materials derived. Undisturbed archives such as Babatha's or John b. Baʿyah's cannot have been the origin of the book scrolls. One reconstituted archive is that of Salome Komaise, reconstructed by Hannah Cotton (and, possibly, augmented in our own discussion). This archive, it will be recalled, was actually a family archive and contained writ belonging to Salome, to her mother Salome Grapte, and to two Komaise brothers. We lack evidence concerning the brothers' literate habits; both women, however, we know to have been illiterate. Accordingly, we can be quite confident that neither Salome Komaise nor her mother owned any books, and while we cannot say the same regarding her brothers, neither have we any positive reason to believe they did.

A second reconstituted archive, we suggested above, may be connected to the Bene Hananiah—that of Joseph who signed so many of Babatha's documents, and his family. This archive comprised just two documents, important though they are, *P.Hever* 13 and *P.Hever* 49 (Table 3.1). Both concern affairs in En Gedi, after the family members had repatriated. It seems that documents they presumably possessed regarding properties in Mahoza had been lost, or were no longer of use, perhaps owing to events involved with the revolt. This was apparently a truncated archive, which reduces the chances that it included books. But none of the Bene Hananiah whom we have reason to place in the cave was a known literary literate anyway. Judah Cimber was illiterate, Joseph b. Hananiah a βραδέως γράφων. Eleazar b. Hananiah signed nothing we have and so cannot be analyzed. Withal, family ownership of book scrolls is dubious, their removal to the cave more so.

Regarding the third reconstructed archive, on the other hand, we have excellent reason to believe the central figure (or his survivors) might have carried books to the cave. This was Eleazar b. Eleazar, Babatha's brother-in-law by her marriage to her second husband, Judah b. Eleazar Khthousion. His archive contained as many as thirteen documents, composed in Nabataean, Aramaic, and—significantly—Hebrew (Table 3.1). Further, Judah was a literary literate, evidenced by level 3 signatures in both Aramaic and Greek. He could read books. If he was indeed the envoy assigned to carry *P.Hever* 30 to Simon b. Kosiba, then we gain more reason to see him as both a reader and a speaker of Hebrew. That letter was written in proto-MH, and by the norms of the time its carrier might expect to be called upon to read and elaborate the message it contained. Thus, given our known possibilities, the books found in the Cave of Letters most likely belonged to Eleazar b. Eleazar and his family.

On that assumption, Table 5.2 tabulates the literary portions of five to seven archives from En Gedi, plus one or more archives from Murabbaʿat. The inference that follows from the ratio of books to archives is that it was not uncommon for elite families to own books. For we must consider that some of the evidence is missing. Only some of the families' possessions (including other books) made it to the caves, and only some of what did, survived to be discovered. The prosopography of the known inhabitants of these caves perhaps authorizes greater precision: among the elite, most nuclear families probably did not own any books, but most extended families did. Those Judaeans who did own books, we can further infer, ordinarily owned Hebrew books, and they usually owned fewer than five of them. A small minority (the sons of Eutrapelus and, possibly, Masabala and his family) could boast of Greek literary productions. Notably and perhaps surprisingly absent is anything composed in literary Aramaic. We will need to explore the possible meaning of this absence more fully below.

Table 5.2 also indicates that the Judaean elite most often chose to possess the books of Moses, the Torah. Of the fifteen book scrolls proper discovered in the Bar Kokhba caves, eight of them belonged to this division of the Jewish scriptures (53.3 percent).[52] The Psalter is also represented (one copy), as are the Prophets (three). Three "extrabiblical" books are found as well, but other than Psalms, no copies representing the so-called Writings (כתובים), the third division of the Masoretic Hebrew Bible. These data are consistent with what archaeologists discovered at Masada, where fifteen book scrolls survived the centuries to be recovered during the 1963–1965 excavations.[53] One scroll was an opisthograph, so the compositions totaled sixteen. Seven writings belonged to the categories of Torah, Psalms, and Prophets, the Torah again predominating and totaling 25 percent of the discoveries. Eight or nine Masada writings would today be categorized as "extrabiblical," though the ancient readers may well have held a different view on the matter.[54] Like the Bar Kokhba materials, the Masada book scrolls were Hebrew compositions. Not one is Greek, and the single outlier—denominated by the editors as an "unclassified (Aramaic?) fragment"—is actually a Hebrew text.[55]

Accordingly, taking Masada together with what was found in our caves, we have thirty-one book scrolls. All but one were written in Hebrew. Of the thirty Hebrew compositions, all but one were written in the H variety, Fassberg's Standard Literary Hebrew. Only *8Hev* 2 Prayer was composed in the L, proto-MH.[56] If these data are to be trusted, *Hebrew was plainly the usual language of literature in multilingual Roman Judaea.* The Dead Sea Scrolls, which we will discuss more fully when we take up Aramaic language and literacy, further support this inference. More than 80 percent of them are in the holy tongue.

Because Hebrew was the usual language of Judaean literature, it served as the primary vehicle for expressing a great deal of the society's self-understanding. By the time of Bar Kokhba, elements of that literary expression, unique in the Roman world for its impact, were more than a thousand years old. Augustan writers such as Virgil and Livy had lately begun to fashion in Latin something of a Roman equivalent to this story, but the mythic power of the Hebraic expression, as history has judged, was without peer. Fergus Millar has distilled the essential point well:

> In the second and third centuries two legions were stationed in the province now known as Syria Palestina, which we call more naturally Judaea. The steady concentration of force there—a few auxiliary cohorts in the early first century; one legion after the great Jewish revolt of A.D. 66–74; two legions in the 120s—was not accidental. It was a direct response to something which in this case is beyond all question. That is, a national religion and tradition,

> a national identity and capacity for independent state-formation. It is worth stressing how exceptional all this is: one of the most successful achievements of Greco-Roman civilization was the removal of the memories and identities of the people it absorbed. *Alone of all the peoples under Roman rule, the Jews not only had a long recorded history but kept it, re-interpreted it and acted on it.* That is what gives the *Antiquities* of Josephus, beginning at the Creation and following Jewish history continuously to the outbreak of the revolt in 66, a claim to be regarded as the most significant single work written in the Roman Empire.[57]

If Greek was the language in which Josephus told their story to the Romans, Hebrew was the language in which the Judaeans told it to themselves. Hebrew literature was the great medium by which they "kept it, re-interpreted it" and urged themselves to "act on it." Without Hebrew literature, the Son of the Star, Simon b. Kosiba—to take but one example—would have been inconceivable. The man, his revolt, and its aims were inseparable from the larger story of the "chosen people" and their understandings of what the God of Israel intended for them. When we ask ourselves how Hebrew literacy functioned in the culture, this must be our primary answer. It was the language of the story. But that is not, of course, the only answer to the question.

Hebrew literacy also served to fashion and sustain elites, as literacy did elsewhere in the Greco-Roman world. William Johnson has recently shown how owning and reading Latin and Greek books helped create an elite in Rome, and important aspects of his discussion carry over to Judaea and Hebrew books by analogy.[58] Greco-Roman book rolls were, in his words, "designed for clarity and for beauty, but not for ease of use, much less for mass readership."[59] Neither functionality nor thrift was a driving force in book preparation. Rather, typical scrolls from Egypt used just 40–70 percent of the writing surface that might have carried text.[60] Aesthetic display and even conspicuous consumption were evidently often important. Annette Steudel's 1991 reconstruction of the Psalms scroll found in the Cave of Letters may serve to illustrate the impressive character of numerous ancient Judaean books.[61] Her analysis indicated that the surviving fragments derive from columns 3–16 of a much larger original that stretched to seventy-five or eighty columns, measuring seven meters end to end. Inscribed in an exquisite bookhand, the scroll provided generous margins above and below each column, equally generous spaces standing between the columns. Emanuel Tov has shown that no fewer than thirty of the Dead Sea Scrolls were such deluxe editions. More particularly, of the scriptural book scrolls from the Bar Kokhba caves sufficiently well preserved to analyze, *every one* was such a manuscript.[62]

One purpose of such luxurious books, Johnson persuasively argued, was to establish social distance between their owners and the everyman all around them. Owning books of this stamp was akin to driving a high-end Mercedes-Benz today. It announced who one was and lodged a public claim to elevated status. As to social context, Johnson commented, "The bookroll was often used in a display setting."[63] In Rome, this could mean a reading performed by a lector at a dinner party, friends and associates gathered to admire and appreciate the occasion and its sponsor. In Judaea, the display setting could be the weekly reading in the local synagogue, where illiterate peasants might admire a man like Eleazar b. Eleazar, his beautiful scroll unrolling to his right as he proclaimed the sacred text in rumbling stentorian tones.[64]

What mattered most for elite formation was not mere ownership, of course, but the combination of owning, reading, and being able to discuss books. Learning to read a Greek or Roman book was arduous, in part because the text was presented as a "river of letters": in *scriptio continua,* with individual words frequently spilling over from one line to the next. Commas, underlining, italics, headers, indents, distinctions between capital and small letters—all were absent, as were many other aids readers take for granted today. And Roman elites learned to read aloud using a "special speech," what Quintilian called *orthoepeia,* a kind of "muffled song." Even history, Quintilian considered *carmen solutum*—poetry freed from the constraints of poetic meter.[65] Thus the witticism attributed to Caesar, spoken to someone offstage: *si cantas, male cantas; si legis, cantas* (If you're singing, you're singing badly; but if you're reading, you're good).[66] As Rex Winsbury has argued, this special speech was frequently denominated by the verb *cantare* and so distinguished from what the plebs spoke, denominated by *dictare:* "The average Roman would probably know a toff as soon as he opened his mouth—nothing, historically, very unusual about that."[67] In a world still overwhelmingly oral in its orientation, the reader was to bring the text to life, rouse it from supine hibernation, and release it animate once more. The letters were dead. Only the sounds lived. Reading books was therefore a kind of performance, even in private. The ultimate goal that Roman education for literacy pursued was not, as for us, reading swiftly and silently. It was reading well aloud. Winsbury further observed: "Roman books were not, in themselves, necessarily the final objective of the exercise, as they would be if they were modern books that formed part of a corpus of 'literature.' They were, as their most important function, a stage between two sets of oral activity—the original oral presentation of the 'work' and some future (if, at any given moment, not yet fixed) oral recreation of it."[68] In important ways, therefore, ancient books were more akin to a modern musical score than to a modern book. They served as an *aide mémoire,* a useful memorandum—to be consulted as needed, content already very familiar.

Johnson has analyzed Quintilian closely on these matters and demonstrated the latter's understanding that the reader's role was a difficult one, requiring many years of literary education just to acquire basic competence. The literature studied in the process was itself often difficult and demanded considerable advanced training, for the reader-in-the-making would be asked not merely to sound the words properly, but to explain the fine points of the content—for, in Quintilian's view, the former was impossible without the latter. Thus, as Johnson summarized, "the need for thorough reading, the need for rereading, the requirement of worthwhile reading, the need to understand in meticulous detail before internalizing what is read."[69] That final stage, to internalize, is of course Carr's "writing on the tablet of the heart." Much else here may also apply to Judaea.

As with Romans on the path to literary literacy, so, too, Judaean elites would need to master a difficult body of literature presented in a challenging format and learn to reanimate it with a pronunciation markedly different from that of ordinary speech. The Judaean correspondent to the Greco-Roman river of letters, *scriptio continua,* was a Hebrew text embodying the canons of an archaic grammar and using a great many obscure and forgotten words. In scribal writing as many as half a dozen of the twenty-two Semitic letterforms might be ambiguous. Orthography could be spare as well, creating still greater ambiguity. Intrinsic linguistic difficulties were daunting enough, but like Greco-Roman learners, Judaeans had first to clear the hurdle of the way the language was presented.[70]

One especially prominent linguistic issue for prospective readers was that—as discussed in the previous chapter—vernacular Hebrew dialects in our period had lost as many as one-third of the consonantal phonemes found in SBH. Whereas the literary language used twenty-three to twenty-five consonantal phonemes, day-to-day forms of Hebrew made do with about seventeen.[71] Recall that the Bar Kokhba letters and other materials indicate that in many locales during these years א, ה, ח, and ע > ∅. In fact, our earlier discussion purposely simplified matters, in that we postponed discussing the original polyphony of ח and ע. Substantial evidence indicates that the grapheme ח represented not only a voiceless pharyngeal fricative (/ḥ/), but also a voiceless uvular fricative (/ḫ/). Similarly, the grapheme ע represented not only a voiced pharyngeal fricative (/ʿ/), but also a voiced uvular fricative (/ġ/).[72] The phonemes represented by the two graphemes merged at different points in Hellenistic and Roman times, but ח, in particular, apparently retained two literary realizations into the second century C.E.[73] Josephus, for example, seems to have known both.[74] All of these "extra" phonemes are known to us because they survived in one or more reading traditions that we can examine.[75] The simple fact of this survival entails two corollaries: first, that Judaean reading traditions in our period were much more conservative than ordinary speech. And second, that these conservative Hebrew reading traditions were studied and preserved, taught and passed down within certain circles, presumably elites having in many cases priestly and Temple connections. For only elites would have sufficient wealth, ergo leisure, to devote themselves to such studies. Formal public reading would have used these standards, probably with some variation geographically and socially. So Judaeans learning to read would have had to master as many as eight consonants extinct in their vernaculars, and in the case of three polyvalent graphemes (ח, ע, and ש) would have had to learn by brute memorization *verse-by-verse* which consonantal pronunciation to supply where. This aspect alone would have been enormously arduous and time consuming.

Probably some students would also have been confronted with a reading tradition that syllabified Hebrew very differently from the form they spoke. A similar situation exists today in Israel's Samaritan community.[76] Many members speak Israeli Hebrew (as well as a Samaritan dialect), but they must learn to read the Torah using a quite different system of consonants, vowels, and syllables. Indeed, a reading of the Torah according to the Samaritan system is utterly unintelligible to non-Samaritan native speakers of Israeli Hebrew. Something of a window into the situation that may have existed for ancient Judaean readers is perhaps afforded by a close analogy, comparing the Tiberian Masoretic vocalization of Gen 11:6a with that of the Samaritan tradition.[77] The portion comes from the story of the Tower of Babel, and means, "And Yahweh said, 'Behold, they are one people, and they all have one language.'"

ויאמר יהוה הן עם אחד ושפה אחת לכלם

Tiberian rendering: wayyōmer ʾĂDŌNAY hēn ʿam ʿeḥaḏ wəśāpā ʾaḥaṯ ləḵullām
Samaritan rendering: wyåumer ŠEMÅ an ʿam ʿâd wašfa ʿat ălkallimmă

Essential elements of both of these systems certainly existed already in Roman Judaea, though the fullest evidence for the traditions is later.

Study of the Old Greek transliterations of proper names demonstrates the existence of yet a third system of syllabification in use during the third and second centuries B.C.E., and quite possibly spanning our period. Three random examples, set alongside simplified transliterations of the equivalent Tiberian Masoretic vocalization for comparison, are Ρεβεκκα for Rebecca (רִבְקָה/Rivkah), Χαλαννι for Calneh (כַּלְנֶה/Kalneh), and Ιοθορ for Jethro (יִתְרוֹ/Yitro). Not only are the vowels supplied different in the two traditions being compared, but the number of syllables often varies as well. Jerome's renderings show still additional systematically variant forms, as do those of Origen's *Hexapla*.[78] Although we frequently do not know all that we might wish of the relevant chronology and geography of use for these various reading traditions, likely some readers in Roman Judaea would have had to cope with the sort of syllabification issue that modern Samaritans face. If so, this would have constituted another significant impediment to performing the scriptures aloud in acceptable fashion.

Then there was the problem of knowing what archaic Hebrew words meant.[79] Just as with modern translators, ancient oral readers could not evade the issue of an opaque text. Both needs offer something. The Hebrew reader had to resolve two related, but not exactly identical problems: how to vocalize and so pronounce an unknown word, and what it meant. As far as we know, they possessed neither dictionaries nor word lists, and so other sorts of resources had to be brought to bear. Often, the ancient readers would solve the linguistic riddles they found in the scriptural writings by drawing upon vernacular Hebrew and Aramaic. For example, Edward Cook has observed that the LXX of Isa 53:10 translates a rare Hebrew word for "bruise" as though it were a homonymous Aramaic term, "purify."[80] Similarly, Jan Joosten has compared the Old Greek translation with the contextual use of difficult scriptural words within the Dead Sea Scrolls and spotlighted in the two corpora numerous identical lexical solutions for rare terms.[81] These were solved on the basis of proto-MH. Perhaps the problem solvers arrived at identical solutions simply because they relied upon identical resources to discover them ad hoc. But one suspects that at least sometimes the answers presented were the same because they were prepackaged elements of reading traditions that were widespread, known to various groups.

For the years between Pompey and Hadrian, the only surviving description of the process by which Judaeans learned to read the Torah and other scriptures occurs in one of the sectarian writings discovered near Qumran, *Rule of the Congregation* (1QSa), lines 6–8. Most specialists believe that the description adheres closely to antecedent patterns of priestly education. Since priestly education was, as Carr has shown, precisely the well from which all education in Judaea had begun in Maccabean times to draw, this description is probably more applicable to the whole of Judaea than its sectarian origins would initially suggest. Incorporating the reconstructions proposed by Lawrence Schiffman, the text reads as follows:

ומן נע[וריו ילמ]דהו בספר ההגי וכפי יומיו ישכילוהו בחוק[י]
הברית ו[לפי שכלו יי]סרו במשפטיהמה

> And from ear[liest childhood] they are to ins[truct] him in the Torah; according to age, they are to enlighten him in the commandment[s] of the covenant; and [according to his capacity, they] are to teach (him) their legal understandings.[82]

Training for Hebrew literary literacy is described as beginning with the Torah and in earliest childhood (נעורים; cf. Job 31:18)—presumably as early as five. Note that the Judaean author was no more interested in describing the actual initial stages of training for literacy—copying the alphabet, syllables, and sentences; writing one's name—than were the Greco-Roman writers who described education, Libanius, Quintilian, and Plutarch. The text begins with what interested the author, reading the Torah. It does not specify the timing of the stage beyond initiation into the book of Moses but simply indicates that as the child got older, education progressed to the "commandments of the covenant." Schiffman suggested that this phrase meant the practical application of the numerous commandments of the Torah.[83] Given what we are able to infer about educational processes on other grounds, including both comparative evidences and the archaeological findings, one would think that such "application" might well embrace instruction in the Prophets. Undoubtedly, study of both the Torah and "the commandments" included learning more than how to vocalize and pronounce the words, and what difficult words meant, challenging though all that was.[84] At least elementary broader interpretive aspects of the text would also be in view, as these were inseparable from oral performance of the content, which often included discussion. Here began mastery of the Judaean equivalent of Quintilian's fine points of the text.

Apparently not everyone would receive further education beyond this second stage, but only those with sufficient capacity. Perhaps most lay education would cease at this divide. After the description above, the lines of 1QSb that follow proceed to describe mustering into the ranks of adult membership at age twenty. Subsequent stages of life follow in the text, each marked out by a person's age at entry. Thus the text tacitly indicates that the time from early childhood until adulthood—many years, fifteen or more—was given over to training for reading and interpreting. This is a priestly ideal, of course, and includes works beyond the scriptures. Learning to read the Torah and some of the Prophets would presumably take a shorter period of time. Still, the schema broadly accords with a Tannaitic parallel attributed to Judah b. Tema in the Mishnah: "Five years old, the scriptures; ten years old, the Mishnah; thirteen years old, the commandments; fifteen years old, further scriptural derivations [תלמוד]."[85]

Judaean readers of Hebrew confronted problems of format, language, and literature fully as formidable as those facing readers in Rome or Alexandria. In all three Mediterranean social settings, long years of training were required before a person might read publicly without blunder and the accompanying shame. Since in general only the wealthy could afford to own books and to provide their children the years of tutelage needed to read them, skilled readers came to form self-perpetuating elites. In Judaea in particular, two distinct types of elite seem to be connected to Hebrew literacy.

One type, the "scribes and Pharisees" of the Gospel narratives, was "professional." The scribes, often priests, had been on the scene since time immemorial; the Pharisees were relative newcomers. They had instigated in the second century B.C.E. a kind of coup against priestly scribal power. A number of factors were involved, of course, but in no small measure both groups were elite in our period by virtue of their control over religiously authoritative texts composed in a language now only dimly intelligible to many Jews. They possessed considerable political power that waxed and waned and assumed new forms over time. Other literate interpretive movements came and went as well, and likewise competed for power. After the fall of the Second Temple, the rabbinic movement was one such. This relation between literacy, power, and "professionals" was hardly unique to Judaea. Various other Greco-Roman societies also gave rise to scribal classes that were empowered by their virtual monopolies on interpretation of religious texts. Everywhere this sort of relation between power and literacy involved the intertwined phenomena of control over access to texts and control exercised through texts. The 1994 book *Literacy and Power in the Ancient World* contained several essays exploring these issues, including one by Martin

Goodman focused on Judaea.[86] His essay was a modest first step in dealing with these complex social realities.[87] They require further study, but this is not the place.

It is the second type of elite connected with Hebrew literacy that calls for more focused attention here, especially because it seems to have escaped earlier notice. This elite emerges from the data of our study and has, in fact, already occupied us at some length in previous chapters. It is the wealthy householders, the people called in the Gospels οἰκοδεσπόται and in rabbinic literature often denominated בעלי בית. Rich landowners, they are portrayed in the New Testament as possessing parcels of land worked by tenants and slaves and as hiring queued day laborers to work their vineyards.[88] Obviously, it is not the existence of this landowning elite that is newly delineated by our data. What is new is their specific connection to literary literacy.

In our study, these are people such as Eleazar b. Eleazar and his brother, Judah, and other men among the extended families of Babatha and Salome Komaise. These men and their peers are often found as the principals in the documents we have been sifting. They were the sorts of people who owned—and presumably read—at least some of the Hebrew books archaeologists discovered in the Bar Kokhba caves. If we want to isolate and analyze these householders in our data, we can do it most directly by drawing together the principals who signed in either Hebrew or Aramaic at level 3. In theory, of course, level 3 signatures may sometimes attach to scribes, but since we have come to know the family connections of the great majority of our signatories, we can be confident that this possibility constitutes at most a tiny portion of our sample. Table 5.3 includes the numerical information we need. After abstracting women and scribes (level 4) from the principals, it can be seen that of forty-six nonscribal male principals, twelve signed at level 3.[89] This amounts to 26.1 percent of a representative cross-section of property-holders. A second approach is also useful in establishing the size of this elite: consider the witnesses who signed in Hebrew and Aramaic at level 3. This information can be derived from Table 5.4. Here one finds that forty of eighty-one (49.4 percent) of the witnesses and *hypographeis* signed at level 3. These people were not random participants but were selected from literate members of society, most often other village property-holders. Thus we are looking at the same segment of society in both categories but must further sift the witness category in order to arrive at an estimate of what proportion of the property-holders they represent. Sifting is possible by turning to Table 5.3.

Table 5.3. Literacy levels by language: principals

Level	Hebrew	%	Aramaic	%	Greek	%	Nabataean	%	Total	%	% (Scribes abstracted)	% (Scribes and women abstracted)
Illiterate	8 (6 males, 2 females)	50.0	13 (8 males, 5 females)	31.0	7 (5 males, 2 females)	77.8	1 (female)	50.0	29	42.0	46.0	35.8
1	2	12.5	4	9.5	0	0.0	0	0.0	6	8.7	9.5	11.3
2	2	12.5	12	28.6	0	0.0	1	50.0	15	21.7	23.8	28.3
3	4	25.0	8	19.0	1	11.1	0	0.0	13	18.8	20.6	24.5
4	0	0.0	5	11.9	1	11.1	0	0.0	6	8.7	—	—
Total	16	100	42	100	9	100	2	100	69	99.9	99.9	99.9

Table 5.4. Literacy levels by language: witnesses, *hypographeis,* and subscribers

Level	Hebrew	%	Aramaic	%	Greek	%	Nabataean	%	Total	%	% (Scribes abstracted)
1	3	8.3	16	21.1	15	25.0	3	33.3	37	20.4	23.6
2	9	25.0	23	30.3	7	11.7	3	33.3	42	23.2	26.8
3	12	33.3	28	36.8	39	58.3	3	33.3	78	43.1	49.7
4	12	33.3	9	11.8	3	5.0	0	0.0	24	13.3	—
Total	36	99.9	76	100	60	100	9	99.9	181	100	100.1

On the basis of Table 5.3 and with women and scribes abstracted, it can be seen that approximately 65 percent of male principals were signature literate. This would have been the pool of householders who could potentially sign documents. It was from this 65 percent that the witnesses to our materials were drawn. It follows that the 49.4 percent of the witnesses and *hypographeis* tabulated in Table 5.4 as signing at level 3 represent a percentage of the 65 percent who could sign at all. Put another way, roughly half of the witnessing householders who were literate at all were, in fact, literary literates. We can set the figure of 32.1 percent (49.4 percent of 65 percent) alongside the 26.1 percent of principals who were literary literates. The two numbers are congruent; by combining them, we gain a perspective derived from 127 individuals, three times the number of principals alone.

It will be less burdensome now to speak in terms of round numbers. To this point, our data suggest that approximately a quarter to a third of οἰκοδεσπόται were able to read Hebrew books. But if we are to estimate the importance of this fact for understanding the social function of Hebrew literacy, we need if possible to discover what proportion of the total Judaean population these people might constitute. To do so, however, we are forced to step directly into the briar patch that overgrows the overlap of ancient demographics and economics. Among the prickliest of the problems is that a great deal of the economic behavior of the Roman world is poorly understood. This is nonetheless the broader framework within which the economics of our region is necessarily analyzed. The inevitable result is uncertainty and controversy on all of the basic issues. Accordingly, what is said here must be seen as very tentative, needing appropriate adjustment if and when understanding of the ancient economic facts improves.

The approach that has dominated analysis of ancient Judaean realities has been the "primitivist" model of Moses Finley,[90] which largely accords with the social scientific analysis of ancient societies by Gerhard Lenski.[91] The accord is perhaps not surprising, as both scholars applied Marxist theory. This approach would hold that Judaeans comprised a great mass of productive agricultural peasants supporting a tiny, mostly urban, nonproductive elite of government officials, military personnel, wealthy landowners, priests, Temple functionaries, and intellectuals. This ruling class comprised 1–2 percent, together with a "retainer" class (scribes and Pharisees, for example) that amounted to another 5 percent. Peasants thus composed about 90 percent of the populace. Their main aim in life was to achieve what Anthony Saldarini called "wantlessness."[92] They survived on the slimmest of margins, being relieved by the elite of virtually all the small surplus they did manage to produce. Included among the farmers who made up the vast majority of village residents were various skilled artisans, but their poverty and low social standing were comparable to those of the farmers. Thus Lenski, in particular, portrayed the urban elite as a parasitic class of oppressors who took but did not give.

Scholars of the Roman world have significantly criticized and modified this model as it has been applied elsewhere, but their criticisms have yet to be carried over fully to analysis of Judaea.[93] The primitivist model predicts grinding, systemic poverty, but this picture does not seem to jibe very well with the totality of what we know about Judaea. In Herod's period, for example, the economy appears notably richer than simple grain production by peasants would foster. The precise level of wealth remains elusive, but Herod's building projects created jobs for workers in the quarries, masons, transportation workers, plasterers, carpenters, and many other artisans and laborers. His sons after him instituted and continued various projects, principally the Temple, where construction work went on for some eighty years. The Temple was at the hub of considerable economic activity, including livestock farming to supply its sacrifices.[94] Large sums from diasporate Jewry wended their way to the Temple in the form of the annual Temple tax and votive offerings. Much of this money then flowed out into the Judaean economy via wages to the thousands of Temple workers and purchases by Temple officials. Pilgrims traveling to the Temple further boosted its economic effect by spending in Jerusalem and nearby regions for transportation, food, lodging, and other personal needs. The wealth and fame of Jerusalem were proverbial in the Roman world.[95] The primitivist model also neglects to consider trade and manufacture, when we know that a merchant class (however small) did exist. Caesarea Maritima, after all, was the largest and most sophisticated port in the Levant. The model further makes certain assumptions about the structure of land tenure, holding that large estates were the dominant mode of agricultural settlement. For the years between Pompey and Hadrian, however, archaeology does not support this assumption. Our own study, just to take one example, portrays wealthy landowners with numerous smaller holdings scattered among several villages.

It seems, therefore, that Judaea does not fully fit the model, and its application requires what Fabian Udoh has called "trimming the foot to fit the shoe."[96] More recent studies of the broader Roman world have proposed (for at least certain places) a third population group, situated between Lenski's tiny elite and the peasant masses, a group of as much as 20 percent of the population, somewhat akin to a modern middle class.[97] In this newer, more nuanced model, the elite of 3–5 percent would still control most of the economic assets, but many people would live well above subsistence. Such people might have been able to afford the education necessary to become literary literates. Whether this is the view that will ultimately best explain the Judaean economy remains to be seen, but it would account for the wealth that seems to emerge in studies on the ground, wealth discordant with Lenski's approach. Some degree of wealth, as we have seen, was typically a prerequisite in the Greco-Roman world for acquiring the capacity to read books.

Thus we have two models for understanding the economics of Judaea in our period. The primitivist model of Finley and Lenski would locate our οἰκοδεσπόται within the oppressor elite, an elite comprising as a whole about 8 percent of the total population. The contending model would locate them within the upper quadrant of the population. We cannot really estimate what proportion of the 8 percent or 25 percent would be made up of wealthy householders, who would in any case overlap to some extent with the scribal class (recall Masabala b. Simon and family). For our purposes, such precision does not really matter. A useful thought experiment is possible without that precision. We want a reasonable estimate of how many people might have read Hebrew books; potentially a respectable, though indeterminate proportion of those people would have been our householders. We can work with the numbers of 8 percent and 25 percent and reason from there.

Let us assume that the estimate of the total population as one million is roughly accurate (see Chapter 1, note 157). We cannot be sure that it is, of course; we are admittedly still in the briar patch. But this is only a thought experiment, and so we can cautiously proceed. Of that one million, about one in five would be adult males, using the calculus common for ancient demographic estimates (for every man, one woman and three children). That would mean two hundred thousand men in ancient Judaea, sixteen thousand constituting the ruling elite and their retainers on the primitivist model. In the competing view, the number would be fifty thousand. These would be the people most likely to have sufficient education as to read books, although our data suggest that only about 30 percent of the householders among them would actually have acquired that skill.

What would such numbers mean on a village level—at En Gedi, for instance? En Gedi was a very large village, recall—some three to four times the ordinary size (forty dunams). And it was very rich. Because of these aberrations from the norm, it is not an ideal site for our experiment; but its matchless advantage is that we know things about this village and its inhabitants that we cannot proceed without. The excavators estimated the population of En Gedi at its height, somewhat later than our period, at about one thousand. The round number is convenient—a bit too high, but we are speaking in approximations anyway. Of one thousand people, approximately two hundred would have been men who might be householders. In the primitivist model, about sixteen En Gedi men would be predicted to be members of the elite; in the competing version, about fifty. Dividing these numbers by the 30 percent of householders whom our data suggest were literary literates, we get about five such men predicted for En Gedi by the primitivist model and about fifteen by the more recent economic model. Now, how do these numbers square with our data and the archaeological findings?

In the primitivist approach, five men and their families would be the candidates for escape to the caves carrying their books. What we actually find, referencing Table 5.2, is five to seven En Gedi archives with books. Thus, if the primitivist approach were roughly correct, we would incline to conclude that we had discovered the hideouts of virtually all the book-owning literary literates living in En Gedi when it fell. Prima facie, that seems very unlikely, given the chaos of war on the one end and the vagaries of survival and discovery on the other. Considering En Gedi's unusual wealth, we might double the number of literates—yet still, the archival ratio would seem improbable. Beyond that estimate of probability, positing a mere five literary literates for En Gedi ill accords with the evidence of Mahoza. Many of the Judaean inhabitants of that village had some demonstrable genealogical connection with En Gedi, so this second village is especially à propos in balancing our considerations. If we limit ourselves to the extended families of Babatha and Salome Komaise living in that village—a village presumably much smaller than En Gedi and with a majority of the inhabitants Nabataean—we find at least twelve fully literate Judaean expatriates inhabiting Mahoza during the years 120–130 C.E.: Joseph b. Menahem, Babeli b. Menahem, Shamoa b. Menahem, Simon b. Menahem, Toma b. Simon, Judah b. Eleazar Khthousion, Eleazar b. Eleazar, Judah b. Judah, Simon b. Joseph, Besa b. Jesus, Judah b. Simon, and Jesus b. Jesus.[98]

On the other hand, the more recent competing model would predict about fifteen literary literates for a typical village the size of En Gedi. If we double the number on account of that village's atypical wealth, the resulting thirty readers of Hebrew books begin to look more proportionate to the archives discovered and to the documented count at Mahoza. (Although even thirty may appear too few if we consider that the Mahozans in evidence represent just two extended families—or indeed, with their intermarriage, one.) On the basis of this thought experiment, we begin to appreciate how a scribal family such as the sons of Simon might have economic incentive to train as many of its members in the calligraphic bookhand as it did. Hebrew books, while often valuable, elite-adorning luxury products, may have been common enough sights even in obscure (and presumably small) villages such as Beth-Mashiko. Even there, Jacob b. Joseph produced a tolerable bookhand in writing *Mur* 42. One would assume he possessed that hand because, although dwelling in a village of three hundred or fewer, he nonetheless had occasion to use it.

More to the point of the question being pursued, this thought experiment encourages the idea that the second elite connected to Hebrew literacy—relatively wealthy householders—was of appreciable size. Much is very approximate and uncertain. Still, if it is plausible to think that expansive, rich villages such as En Gedi could boast dozens of these people, it is just as plausible to suppose that ordinary, small villages would be home to a few. These householders probably owned the books used in the village synagogue. They likely read them with their extended families, and perhaps neighbors, on days other than the Sabbath. They unrolled them to teach their sons (and very rarely, daughters) to read. It stands to reason that these οἰκοδεσπόται would represent a formidable social counterweight to the scribal class in the interpretation of the holy books. They, too, could animate the books in the telling of the story. Village scribes and priests would not be the only people empowered by their ability to mediate the words of the God of Israel. And the sons and daughters of these householders would absorb the Mosaic and prophetic narratives as they listened to their fathers, uncles, and brothers read and discourse. They need not be literate themselves to drink it all in, to remember and meditate, to ponder ספר ההגי "indoors and out of doors, in their lying down and their rising up" (Deut 6:7). Illiterates no less than literates might write on the tablets of their hearts.

One thinks of Naphtali Lewis's withering assessment of Babatha as he wrote, "However we estimate Babatha's social position because of her wealth, by no stretch of the imagination can this rustic, *illiterate* woman be classed among persons in high places."[99] Perhaps; but Babatha's illiteracy would not dictate that she lack culture. Literary literates surrounded her at home: her father, brothers, cousins, and eventually her husbands. As a member of a family stamped as elite no less by its literacy in archaic Hebrew than by its wealth, no less by the possession of books than by that of Roman glassware, Babatha b. Simon, daughter of a Mahozan householder, may have been more of a match at law for the Herodian Julia Crispina than Lewis imagined.

Aramaic Language and Literacy

Many scholars of our period have argued for Aramaic being the most widespread language in daily use in Judaea, and Table 1.2 supports that view. It shows that when Judaeans were given an opportunity to sign texts composed in that language, they signed in Aramaic, if they could sign at all, with overwhelming frequency. Thus, of literate principals, twenty-nine of thirty (96.7 percent) signed in Aramaic, and a similar percentage of the witnesses did the same. These numbers are much higher than the corresponding numbers for Judaean signatories of Hebrew, Greek, and Nabataean contracts and in themselves argue for the dominance of Aramaic as the ordinary Judaean language of signature literacy. This conclusion is reinforced by a point noted at the outset of this study, but worth repeating: when Judaeans were unable to sign any non-Aramaic contract in its own language, overwhelmingly they signed in Aramaic (ninety-four of ninety-five, 98.9 percent).[100]

The lone principal recorded by Table 1.2 as signing an Aramaic contract in a language other than Aramaic was Eutrapelus b. Eutrapelus. He signed *Mur* 26 with a practiced hand in Greek, which may have been the only language in which he was literate. We have seen that he and his brother Cleopas (who could sign in both Greek and Aramaic) may reasonably be taken as highly Hellenized inhabitants of Jerusalem, who were perhaps proud of their Hellenism. The solitary person in the witness category who signed an Aramaic contract in Greek was one PN b. PN, signatory to *P.Yadin* 8 in Mahoza. We can say nothing more about his situation because damage to the signature makes him impossible to identify, but his rare action simply underscores the main point.

Three other witnesses signed Aramaic contracts in Hebrew or in a mixture of Hebrew and Aramaic. Two of these anomalies occurred in the same writ, *P.Hever* 13, the divorce document that Shelamzion b. Joseph handed Eleazar b. Hananiah in En Gedi in 134 or 135. Written by Mattat b. Simon, it was signed by Mattat's brother, Masabala, military commander of the site, and in the holy tongue. In point of fact, Masabala never signed any text in any language but Hebrew—likely an expression of his militant nationalism. Presumably, the commander's action influenced PN b. Simon likewise to sign in Hebrew. (This was not Masabala's brother, as he lacked the expected scribal hand.) The mixed signature belonged to one Simon b. Joseph, an inhabitant of Kephar-Baru who affixed his John Hancock to *P.Hever* 8a in Aramaic but then switched to Hebrew when inscribing the word for "(hereby) witnesses" (עד). We never encounter Simon again. His is the sort of inconsistent action we expect to come across occasionally in the study of any group, but still: Judaeans almost universally signed Aramaic contracts in Aramaic. They did so, arguably, not just because it was customary, but also because it was comfortable. Aramaic was the language in which they learned to sign their names at the earliest stage of training for literacy—at least, if they were pursuing the "Semitic curriculum," not the Greek. Indeed, the evidence of the present study strongly argues that for ordinary Judaeans, *Aramaic was the primary language of daily writing.* They signed their names in it, wrote their letters in it, and at times, as we shall see, even composed legal writ in it. True, under Roman aegis, a good deal of Judaea's legal work got done in Greek. So far as we have evidence, though, that option always required a scribe to do the writing. Ordinary people wrote in Aramaic. This fact begs the question: apart from signatures, was that difficult for them? How much education would be needed to apply Aramaic to writing tasks in whatever realms Judaeans did so?

As discussed in the previous chapter, to the extent that is possible at all, the Aramaic Bar Kokhba letters and legal subscriptions are probably our best sources for taking the measure of vernacular Aramaic. We saw that the linguistic distance between SLA and the language of the letters was appreciable but less jolting than that between SBH and proto-MH. Because our focus was on the letters, we did not consider the evidence of Aramaic legal writ for the question—nor is this the place for a full-blown analysis. Yet a few remarks seem in order, since the issue of whether Judaeans wrote Aramaic essentially as they spoke it continues to be a matter of scholarly controversy,[101] and since the answer is plainly important in deciding who could potentially write. And we do learn some significant details from the Aramaic legal texts that happen not to be in evidence in the other documents of our limited corpus. The evidence we get comes from scribal inadvertence, and—especially rich—from the labored efforts of lay writers who at times attempted to write in the legal language. They clearly struggled more with legal texts than with letters, and this was so, it seems, because letters much more nearly approximated their vernaculars.

One vernacular phenomenon that reveals itself sporadically in the Aramaic legal materials is gender neutralization. This is a common characteristic among the Semitic languages generally: epicene forms appear in certain grammatical categories of a spoken dialect, while in the related literary dialect the corresponding forms are distinguished for gender.[102] Ordinarily, masculine forms substitute for feminine. Neutralization of this sort in Semitic especially affects feminine plurals of the verbs and pronouns (the forms least frequently called for in routine discourse). In our materials, the gender neutralization has extended to the feminine singulars of those categories: masculine singular appears for feminine singular in the imperfect of verbs and with the possessive suffix.[103] Also evidently reflecting vernacular Aramaic usage in the contracts are the ubiquitous nonstandard forms of the derived stem infinitives. For example, SLA and the legal dialect used קטלה and אקטלה/הקטלה as the infinitives of the *Pael* and *Haphel/Aphel,* respectively. Commonly, the Western Aramaic *mem*-preformative equivalents מקטלה and מקטלה (with different vocalization) replace these standard dialect forms in the contracts; even "Syriac" options such as מקטלו are attested at Mahoza and En Gedi.[104] In the realm of syntax, *P.Yadin* 10 offers a glimpse of a writer's vernacular expression in parallel with the equivalent standard expression. At line 6, Judah b. Eleazar Khthousion mistakenly wrote מה אנון, "which are," for the legal dialect's normal די הימון, used correctly at line 18.[105] This was evidently a scribal error of the type known as an "error of mind." Here, synonymous expressions familiar to a copyist may through inadvertence be substituted for the wording of a text being copied as its words flow from eye to mind to pen (more on Judah as a copyist shortly).

Other dialect features alien to the standard legal diction crop up regularly in the Bar Kokhba materials. Presumably, these mostly represent irruptions of the vernacular. For example, in *Mur* 26 line 8 one finds אחה for standard אחוהי, "his brother," and in the next line עלה, "on it," for standard עלוהי. Perhaps these Jerusalem alternatives arose by metanalysis; they do not represent a single phonological development. In *P.Yadin* 10 we discover a metathesized form of the root חסן, "to possess (as property)," conjugated—note—as a nonstandard Western Aramaic derived stem infinitive, למס[ח]נה (line 7, probably *Aphel*).[106] This metathesis was previously familiar from Jewish Palestinian Aramaic and Samaritan Aramaic, and so our earlier refrain sounds anew: many of the Bar Kokhba dialect forms find explanation in later Aramaic literary dialects, which themselves crystallize earlier vernaculars. Unless it is simply a graphic error, the strange infinitival form לתהך that appears in *P.Yadin* 42 line 8 for the expected למהך, "to walk," is new. It forcibly reminds us of the probability that numerous Judaean vernacular lexical and grammatical forms would appear bizarre, if only we could get a look at them. But we seldom get a glimpse because the formal dialects excluded them. We see in a glass, darkly, and we know in part.

As with the letters, the legal texts contain many loanwords—not part of the older legal dialect. These words point to vernacular derivation. A fair percentage derive from Hebrew. Not a few terms come from Arabic, probably via intercourse with Nabataeans. From Hebrew one finds אם (*Mur* 20, and often); שפה for מרק, "clear (of claims)," *P.Hever* 9, a contract from Yakim; and פותח, "opens," *P.Yadin* 47. Four Hebrew loans occur in a single contract, *P.Yadin* 7, Babatha's father's gifting of property to her mother: the root נחל, "to inherit," unknown otherwise in Aramaic; שבועה, "sworn statement";[107] אנוש, "man" (although it does occur in Nabataean); and בַּגָּד, "clothier." This last example is particularly interesting, as the Hebrew term occurs in neither SBH nor MH. This was a word that lived, as it seems, only in one or another dialect of proto-MH. Particularly in light of the other loans, this fact suggests that Hebrew was spoken among Mahozan Judaeans—hardly surprising, but noteworthy. No one there ever wrote in it, not even his name (though we have seen that the village was home to at least a dozen Judaeans who could read the literary language).

P.Yadin 7 is further notable for its many Arabisms. The editors suggest fully sixteen different loans.[108] One Arabism that appears in several Bar Kokhba documents is especially interesting. This is yet another term for "clear (of claims)," צפא, used in *P.Yadin* 47 line 10, in an infinitival form (presumably *Pael*). The Arabic verb is *ṣafā*, "be pure." The word צפא occurs in two Nabataean contracts, *P.Yadin* 2 and 3, as well as in Besa b. Jesus's Aramaic subscription to the Greek *P.Yadin* 20. Two explanations for these facts seem possible. Either Judaeans and Nabataeans conversed in a mutually intelligible form of Aramaic in Mahoza, En Gedi, and other villages near the Dead Sea; or Judaeans in contact with Nabataeans were learning a form of Arabic that Nabataeans used. The first possibility seems more likely given the semantics of the loanwords. If so, then evidently a vernacular rather different from SLA and the legal dialect is in view.

We may attempt a cautious synthesis at this juncture, realizing that our limited corpus requires tentative and modest assertion. It can be hazardous to generalize when so much is unknown. Still, adding the features discussed above to those surveyed in Chapter 4, we seem further to affirm that striking contrasts existed between literary and legal Aramaic on the one hand (formal Judaean Aramaic) and the colloquial forms on the other (vernacular

Judaean Aramaic). Status distinctions were lost in the latter; Syriac morphosyntax can give us some notion of the possible mechanisms that might have been used in lieu of such. Though with significant overlap, the formal and informal lexica were distinct: many words we know well from Jewish and Christian Palestinian Aramaic and other written dialects were already in spoken use. Loans from Greek and Arabic characterized the vernaculars, whereas the formal Aramaic dialects, having taken form before quotidian contact with Greek in particular, excluded such terms. Hebraisms could be found in both vernacular and literary forms of Aramaic. Masculine grammatical forms had expelled less common feminine counterparts from the vernacular. Verbal forms unknown to the formal dialects were common in the colloquial. All in all, it seems likely that ordinary Aramaic-speaking peasants would often find formal Aramaic puzzling. They could not always navigate it with easy comprehension even when they were literary literates who could read Hebrew. This disconnect is evident from surviving efforts by laypeople to copy documents composed in the legal dialect.

That Judaeans did write and copy documents in Aramaic is worth repeated emphasis.[109] The materials of this study clearly show that the primary function of Judaean literacy in Aramaic was practical production of documents, beginning with signing one's name, which people learned to do in Aramaic, not Hebrew. For better-educated people, Aramaic literacy then extended to creating letters and legal writ. We saw in Chapter 4 reasons to believe that essentially all of the Aramaic Bar Kokhba letters were lay products. Among the Aramaic legal texts, at least *Mur* 8, *Mur* 19, *Mur* 21, *Mur* 27, *Mur* 34, *P.Hever* 8 and 8a, *P.Hever* 26, *P.Hever* 9, and *P.Yadin* 10 were likely the same.[110] Presumably, other texts in our corpus were also produced without scribes, but the fragmentary condition in which they survive precludes analysis to demonstrate the point.

P.Yadin 10 affords an excellent example of the difficulties that a literary literate might face in copying an Aramaic legal document. This was Babatha's *ketubbah* for her marriage to Judah b. Eleazar Khthousion, who scribed the writ. In theory, of course, he might have written it out from memory, but that would be a surprising feat for a man who was not a scribe, and in fact the pattern of errors in the document proves instead that he followed an exemplar as best he could. Whence the exemplar? Handbooks of notarial practice did exist in our period, and Judah may have obtained one for his purposes.[111] At least as likely, however, is that he simply copied another *ketubbah* from the family archives, making such changes as necessary. Almost from the outset it did not go well. In line 6 he wrote עלך when he meant לך (or, technically, לכי), evidently under the influence of עלי immediately following. His eye skipped. In the next line he wrongly inscribed the masculine singular imperfect תצבא for the feminine singular imperfect תצבין, "you may wish" (they would have sounded similar because of the nasalization of final open syllables discussed earlier). Judah was likely vocalizing audibly as he wrote, normal ancient practice—a practice that may explain some of his errors, such as the foregoing. When he came to the second word of line 9, Judah inserted an entire clause by mistake, a line and a half (מה . . . חורין), evidently because his eye traveled back to the equivalent in his *Vorlage* of the end of line 6, where the mistaken insertion properly stood. This was not his only instance of misplaced clauses. At the end of line 15, Judah wrote ומתזנן מן ביתי מן נכסי, "provided for from my house and possessions," his eye having skipped back to the equivalent of the end of line 10, where the phrase belonged. Then in lines 17–18 Judah transposed two clauses, the pledging clause and the exchange clause generic to proper *ketubbot*.

But clausal sequence was not the sum of Judah's problems. In lines 13–14 he had all sorts of orthographic and grammatical issues trying to inscribe the phrases regarding the rights of daughters born to the couple to Judah's support. Most of these errors may be connected to the phenomenon of nasalization mentioned above.[112] In place of the proper [בנ]ן נק[ב]ן [י]חוין יתבן ומתזנן מן נכסי, Judah wrote [בנ]ן נק[ב]ן [י]הוא יתבא ומתזנן מן ביתי מן נכסי, "female children will live and be provided for from my house, my possessions." As he would do in line 15, Judah telescoped מן ביתי מן נכסי; only the latter belonged. At the end of line 14, he set down ואם, "and if," but then mistakenly wrote it again as the first word of line 15—a clear case of parablepsis. Then at the end of line 16, Judah wrote ד[י ת]מר, "(at any time) that you say," using the masculine singular imperfect for Babatha instead of the feminine singular. We have no way of knowing which stood in the *Vorlage,* itself conceivably not a scribal product; but at some point in the chain of transmission, we should expect the text to have read ד[י ת]מרין. Here, vulgar usage intruded.

Even these examples do not exhaust the store of Judah's errors in *P.Yadin* 10; still others might be brought forward. But perhaps the horse is long since dead. In any case, it was not just Judah—other literary literates and near literary literates experienced similar difficulties in copying documents. John b. Eli, writer of *P.Hever* 8, *P.Hever* 8a, and *P.Hever* 26, struggled mightily at points, as studies of his documents have shown.[113] Jacob b. Simon b. Diqna, author of *P.Hever* 9, sometimes had trouble reading his *Vorlage* and so imported nonsense words into his contract.[114] And Lazar b. Joseph, who composed for his daughter the *ketubbah* that we know as *Mur* 21, also erred in copying.[115] Presumably, these examples suffice to prove the point: even literary literates found composition in proper legal Aramaic challenging. Partly this was a matter of practice. Partly the problem was linguistic. The exercise called for writing in a dialect they did not speak. Letters, as we have seen, were a different matter. Because epistolary language approximated to the vernacular, lay writers could carry them off more successfully.

Thus the practical functions of Aramaic literacy; but what of the artistic? Was Aramaic turned to literary use for ordinary Judaeans? Prima facie, the idea seems reasonable and attractive, given that virtually all Judaeans spoke a form of the language. Was Aramaic the vehicle of a vulgar literature that circulated in less exalted circles than those that read archaic Hebrew, so difficult to master? Even though the formal language often contrasted starkly with what we know of the vernaculars, the distance was not so great as that separating literary and colloquial Hebrew. Presumably, lesser efforts would need to be devoted to its mastery. People who could not afford the education needed to animate the Hebrew scriptures and related writings might have been able to summon the time and money necessary to achieve literary literacy in Aramaic. Historical literacy studies offer numerous parallels for such in bilingual and multilingual settings. One might think, for example, of the explosion of vernacular literature in Dante's Italy, when processes of *volgarizzamento* gave a population of city-state dwellers, illiterate in Latin, translations and new works in Italian.[116] In Ferguson's terms, these books were intended for those who lacked sufficient education to read the H language. Now they could read the L. Was an Aramaic literature in Judaea something of an equivalent? Scholars have proposed versions of this notion in the past. For instance, the authors/editors of the new Schürer suggested as much when they conceded that "it is beyond dispute that biblical Hebrew enjoyed a literary revival during the centuries in question," but described Aramaic as "the principal language, spoken and written, used by Palestinian Jews during the inter-Testamental age."[117] A closer look at the contextualized data of our study may be clarifying.

Perhaps the most helpful materials for contextualizing the Bar Kokhba cave deposits are another group of Roman-Judaean deposits, the Dead Sea Scrolls. Scholars have lately begun to realize that the physical phenomena connected with the scrolls almost certainly point to a number of individual deposits rather than a single panicked flight to the caves by scroll-salvaging Essenes, hiding books removed from a central library at the site of Qumran.

In 2007, Daniel Stökl Ben Ezra subjected the paleographic ages suggested by the various editors of the scrolls to statistical analysis. His conclusion: "The average age of the dated scrolls from Cave 4 and from Cave 1 differs to such an extent from that of the manuscripts of Caves 2, 3, 5, 6 and 11 that the possibility that they are all randomly chosen samples of the same 'population,' the same library, becomes improbable . . . it can be shown statistically to be highly unlikely that the manuscripts from Caves 1 and 4 are random samples coming from the same collection as those [in the other caves]."[118]

Ben Ezra's analysis assumed the truth of the long-held consensus that the Qumran manuscripts were taken from the site of Qumran and hidden during the First Revolt in order to save them from advancing Roman armies. This consensus would entail that the books from the site were held in common; thus, when dispersed, they should appear within the separate caves as more or less homogeneous deposits. On the contrary, Ben Ezra's analysis proved that the paleographic facts of the manuscripts render the consensus scenario extremely unlikely. The deposits were strongly heterogeneous; the scrolls in the "early" caves were judged by their editors to be much older than those in the "late" caves. Accordingly, Ben Ezra suggested two deposits at different times: an earlier one in Caves 1 and 4 and a later one in the other caves. But he may not have gone far enough. Apparently unaware of Ben Ezra's study, Stephen Pfann argued in the same year that, judging by their paleography, the materials from Caves 3 and 11 also stand apart from those of the other caves: "The scrolls from both caves 3Q and 11Q represent the remnants of relatively young libraries. The scrolls of these two caves are among the latest from Qumran; 83% of the 11Q scrolls and 100% of the 3Q scrolls date to the first century AD. In fact 65% of the approximately 50 combined manuscripts from caves 11Q and 3Q date from the last 25 years before the fall of Jerusalem. The first-century scripts of these scrolls also tend to be particularly elegant and stately."[119] Many of these books verged on luxury editions and thus were especially comparable to the Bar Kokhba deposits. Pfann went on to say: "It appears to be high time to abandon the monolithic approach to the caves that assumes a common owner or origin for all the caves. Rather, each cave must be assessed on its own merits."[120]

This suggestion distills common sense and is the best approach regardless of what view a particular scholar may hold on the nature of the Qumran site and the so-called Essene hypothesis. Today, the relation of the scrolls to the site is much disputed; therefore, the usefulness of the archaeology of the site for interpreting the scrolls is moot. But the applicability of the archaeology of the individual caves in which the scrolls were found is indisputable. This is not the place for a full discussion, but a quick survey of salient aspects of the cave deposits other than paleography is important in order to show that it is reasonable to view the Qumran materials as a *group of deposits,* not as one single deposit. (Whether or not the deposits are Essene is beside the point for our purposes.) These various deposits can then be profiled and the profiles compared with those of the Bar Kokhba caves. We want to assess the general character of the Qumran collections over against those of our study. In particular, our interest in the profiles lies in the presence or absence of literary texts in Aramaic, and what the results might mean for understanding literate behaviors in Roman Judaea.

The Qumran cave deposits differ notably among themselves in what they suggest about the processes behind the sequestration of the texts. In Cave 1, for example, ten "scroll jars" were discovered arrayed in orderly fashion lining one wall of the grotto. Seven well-preserved scrolls were found inside the jars (other caves contained similar jars—Cave 3 had forty—but none of those jars held any manuscripts; they were usually empty). The inference would be that the hiding of the texts in Cave 1 was a calm, well-considered process. In contrast, the hundreds of scrolls unearthed in Cave 4 were discovered strewn in disarray on the cave floor, worm-eaten, badly decomposed, and jarless. The manner of their hiding implies panicked stashing and flight. Similarly, Cave 3 was one whose ceiling, recent excavations have shown, collapsed many centuries before the scrolls were hidden there. What remained was an "open recess, exposed to daylight, not a deep and dark cave, suited for hiding precious writings. [Materials] were simply heaped behind the rocks. . . . This was not a good place to choose, if the idea was to find a hiding place for an active library." The impression one gains from this description by Joseph Patrich, the excavator, is of a temporary cache by people in a hurry to flee, who evidently intended to return fairly shortly for their valuables, but never did.[121]

Caves 7 through 10 contained food remains and oil lamps, indicating that these caves were each inhabited for a short time, presumably by refugees of the war. Most of the other caves were uninhabitable. Several were actually animal lairs. From the perspective of its contents, Cave 8 looked much like a Bar Kokhba cave: three scrolls (two scriptural), a phylactery, and a mezuzah. One might think that this was one man's or one family's collection of books. Cave 9 preserved a single unidentifiable scrap of inscribed papyrus, with no trace of any jars. Cave 10 contained nothing but an ostracon inked with ten mostly indecipherable Semitic letters. And Cave 7 was especially distinctive: nineteen manuscripts, *all* in Greek, *all* on papyrus. Put together, the other caves totaled only six additional Greek writings out of more than nine hundred books (all six from Cave 4, actually). Further, the vast majority of Dead Sea Scrolls were animal-skin products. Most of the cave deposits included no or almost no papyrus books. Cave 4, the mother lode of the discoveries, was exceptional in that it did count among its roughly 680 scrolls, 90 written on papyrus. But Cave 1 totaled just 2 of 80; Cave 2, none of 33; Cave 3, none of 15; Cave 5, none of 35; and Cave 11, 1 of 31. Cave 6 then struck a discordant note in alliance with Cave 7, 64.5 percent of its contents being papyrus books (20/31). These differences are striking.

Differences of script and format also distinguished cave from cave. Books composed using previously unknown cryptic scripts (Cryptic A, B, and C) turned up in two caves: Cave 4, with fifty-three such writings (almost 8 percent of its total holdings), and Cave 11, with one. None of the other caves held any cryptic writings at all. Caves 4 and 1 included among their holdings opisthographs (seventeen and one, respectively). (Recall that we saw in Chapter 2 that the patterns in this regard as known from Egyptian discoveries are that most collections include no such writings, whereas a few personal collections include a high percentage of these cheaper products.) None of the other caves held any.

The material culture associated with the various caves also differed notably. Two examples will have to suffice. First, the textiles yielded by three of the caves: in Cave 11, the textiles were bleached white and bore indigo stripes; those in Caves 1 and 4 were not bleached but were simply off-white cloth and did not have stripes.[122] The people involved seem not to have been a single group and may well have represented different social classes, if the stripes are taken into account. And second, there is the matter of the phylacteries. A fair number were found in the caves—at least thirty, deposited in Caves 1, 4, 5, 8, and perhaps elsewhere (several of uncertain provenance were obtained from the bedouin).[123] What is odd about the phylacteries is the seemingly capricious variation in their contents. Some contained the scriptural portions that later rabbinic Judaism would declare normative; others encased much longer passages of the Torah; still others excluded the portion otherwise universal—at the very heart of the content of such tefillin—the Shema. A full study of the materials by David Rothstein in 1992 concluded that the diversity of content and order of presentation were inconsistent with a theory that any one group had hidden the scrolls. He wrote, "It appears probable that the [authors and owners] . . . constituted a broad spectrum of Palestinian (and diaspora) Jewry."[124] Since it is virtually certain that the phylacteries belonged to individuals involved with the deposits, the differences in the phylacteries logically entail that the caves where many were found (Cave 1, eight phylacteries, and Cave 4, twenty-one) contain composite collections belonging to numerous people, people who evidently differed in their understandings of something as fundamental to Jewish life as these tefillin but were cooperating to save their lives and their precious books. If this reasoning is correct, then it is also no coincidence that the largest cave deposits were found in those caves housing the greatest number of phylacteries.

Table 5.5 summarizes much of the foregoing discussion.[125] Boldface print calls attention to some of the most notable anomalies. Although other explanations could conceivably be defended, it appears most reasonable to think that the Qumran deposits represent numerous individual collections.[126] Further reasonable is the idea that most or all of the caves housed books belonging to wealthy individuals and their families. That such people might own between five and thirty-five books is consistent with evidence for Hellenistic and Roman book collections generally, as we saw in Chapter 2. Caves 1 and 4, on the other hand, more likely contained the composite holdings of numerous and disparate families or individuals. If the phylacteries found in Cave 4 may be taken as indicating very roughly how many individuals sought to save their manuscripts by hiding them in this cave, then something like twenty-one libraries are represented by the roughly 680 texts: an average of 32 books apiece, consonant with the other cave holdings.

Table 5.5 shows that most of these collections included Aramaic literature, in contrast to the Bar Kokhba collections—which, recall, held none. (Recall that no Aramaic literary texts were found at Masada, either.) Except for Cave 8, the Qumran cave deposits were very large compared with the cave holdings near En Gedi and at Murabbaʿat. Also (and speaking loosely, in deference to the danger of anachronism), the table shows that almost all of the Qumran collections embraced a great deal of nonscriptural material, whether in Hebrew or in Aramaic—again, in stark contrast to what Table 5.2 illustrates for the Bar Kokhba deposits. The Bar Kokhba book owners read almost exclusively those writings that came later to constitute the Hebrew Bible. The Qumran owners also read much scripture, but most of them held a majority of books that have historically been regarded as "nonbiblical" (roughly 70–80 percent of each deposit). And the owners of most of the collections compared in Table 5.5 were more than merely literary literates. They were hyperliterates.

Table 5.5. Profiles of the Dead Sea Scroll deposits by cave

Cave	No. of mss.	Paleography (median age)	Greek mss. (no./%)	Papyrus mss. (no./%)	Paleo-Hebrew mss.	Opisthographs	Cryptic mss.	Scriptural mss. (no./%)	Aramaic mss. (no./%)
1	**80**	**34 B.C.E.**	0/0.0	2/2.5	1	1	0	16/20.0	11/13.8
2	33	19 C.E.	0/0.0	0/0.0	1	0	0	17/**51.5**	2/6.1
3	15	19 C.E.	0/0.0	0/0.0	0	0	0	3/20.0	2/13.3
4	**680**	**38 B.C.E.**	6/0.9	90/**13.2**	9	17	**53**	146/21.5	105/15.4
5	25	28 C.E.	0/0.0	0/0.0	0	0	0	7/28.0	2/8.0
6	31	**50 C.E.**	0/0.0	20/**64.5**	2	0	0	8/25.8	4/12.9
7	19	N/A	19/**100.0**	19/**100.0**	0	0	0	1/5.3	0/0.0
8	5	N/A	0/0.0	0/0.0	0	0	0	2/**40.0**	0/0.0
11	31	25 C.E.	0/0.0	1/3.2	2	0	1	9/29.0	3/9.7

Thus, excepting Cave 7, each collection included a majority of writings composed in SBH—the conquest of which would, for most people, present sufficient challenge that its accomplishment might signal a stop. Except for Caves 7 and 8, however, these owners also read SLA. Further, most evidently handled one or more of the following: Greek, paleo-Hebrew script, and cryptic scripts. Accordingly, in a world where only a minority of people could even sign their names, these book owners read two or three languages and were conversant with multiple scripts. On the basis of their profiles, the Dead Sea Scroll deposits look like the holdings of serious Judaean intellectuals. Most of these owners, it would seem, were scholars. Their collections look different from those of such householders as fled to Murabbaʿat and the other text-bearing refugee caves of the Second Revolt.

Nick Veldhuis has proposed the term "scholarly literacy" to describe a similar sort of phenomenon in Mesopotamia. Scholarly literates were virtually always scribes in those earlier cultures. They were interested in collecting and preserving rare words and recondite uses of individual cuneiform signs. They applied their knowledge of arcana to compose colophons, royal inscriptions, commentaries, and related texts that stood as a kind of "meta-literature" alongside the literary heritage of their time. Veldhuis observed, "By studying and employing earlier sign forms the scribes not only maintained the accessibility of ancient texts, in particular publicly accessible monumental texts, they added a layer of complexity to the writing system, which could be used to set a text apart from ordinary writing." Veldhuis's scholarly literacy stood over against what he called "functional literacy," which might be, and often was, acquired by nonscribal householders: archaeologists have uncovered numerous texts in private homes. Functional literacy, which used a relatively small number of cuneiform signs, sufficed for reading or writing letters and business documents in particular. These were the sorts of things ordinary people needed to do.[127]

It is attractive to think that Judaean culture in the years of our study also knew a scholarly literacy that stood over against the pragmatic literacy of ordinary, though reasonably prosperous householders. Ordinary literacy was challenging enough. One would progressively learn to write one's name in Aramaic; to comprehend, copy, and compose Aramaic documents such as *ketubbot* and letters; and, ultimately, to read a sacred literature composed in an archaic tongue. Scholarly literates would superpose upon such foundations knowledge of additional literatures and writing systems, thereby "adding a layer of complexity" to Judaean literary culture and (by use of arcane scripts) "setting a text apart from ordinary writing." They would also, of course, set themselves apart from ordinary writers and readers, which was likely no less important. Such people might intone imperiously from a book composed in Cryptic A, its alien letterforms impervious even to fluent literary literates who might look over their shoulders: numinous writing, exalting the reader, defying and humbling the listener. These processes and their masters are on display in the Qumran deposits. Also on display there—and, as far as our evidence allows us to say, only there—is a notable literature composed in SLA. In most of the caves this literature comprised, on average, 10 percent of the holdings.

The contextual evidence suggests, we may now see, that the readers of Aramaic literary works were seldom ordinary folk. Rather, they were scholars. Ordinary folk, if they read at all, read SBH (or, as we shall see, much less often Greek). In Judaea in the years between Pompey and Hadrian, *Aramaic literature was the preserve of an elite guild of scholars.*

It had not always been so. We have sketched something of the history above. In the later years of Persian dominion and in the days of Alexander and his successors, the situation was likely as Elias Bickerman portrayed it: "We may postulate that about 300 B.C.E. every Jew who could read was more or less proficient in [literary] Aramaic."[128] What happened to overthrow this norm was the challenge of advancing Greek civilization and, ultimately, the refusal of the Jews to assimilate fully to broader Greco-Roman culture. Instead, they rallied to their own pre-Hellenistic literature and adopted a countercultural design, telling their own story and substituting Hebrew writings for the Greek *paideia* that triumphed everywhere else in the East. SBH elbowed SLA to one side, and knowledge of the latter dialect became much less general. The option for Judaeans who sought an alternative to literary literacy in Hebrew came to be Greek, not Aramaic. Only scholars retained literary Aramaic, and the works that they composed in it reflected and nourished their own specialized "meta-literary" and technical interests, on the one hand, and on the other, their continued participation in the broader Aramaic culture arrayed to the north and east.

The Aramaic writings that survived among the Qumran deposits reveal this development. They tend to be of three sorts, although the categories overlap somewhat: first, pre-Maccabean works from a time when SLA was still dominant; second, technical writings on topics such as divination and magic; and third, a few specific genres for which Aramaic had established itself, rather as Greeks often used Ionic for scientific writings and Homeric for epic. All of these writings were the domain of specialized priests and elite scribes, not literate householders. In the first category, the Qumran caches included copies of Tobit, early "pseudo-Daniel" works (4Q242), and early Enochic literature such as the *Book of the Watchers*. In the second, one finds 4Q318, a brontologion; 4Q559, a chronograph; 4Q561, a physiognomic horoscope; and 4Q560, a remnant of a book of incantations to be used for exorcism. A good example of the third category is the testamentary genre, with its quasi-legal formulation harkening to the legal realm where Aramaic still held sway as the norm. Works of this sort attaching among others to Levi, Amram, and Qahat (heroes in particular, one imagines, to priestly and scribal sorts) survived in the caves of Qumran. A significant number of the Aramaic writings have connections of one kind or another to the broader Aramaic-writing culture of Syria to the north and Babylon to the east.

In a classic study Abraham Wasserstein drew attention to this broader Aramaic-speaking civilization and continued Judaean membership in it via the Aramaic language. He uncovered an interesting reflection of this reality:

> The large extent of the overlap of [Greek] loanwords in Jewish Aramaic and in Syriac is significant; no less significant is the fact that both of these Aramaic dialects also share the results of certain internal Aramaic developments in the case of these Greek loanwords. This suggests, not that the Rabbis had borrowed these words directly from Greek, but rather that they found them ready-made, readily available, in the Aramaic *koine*, which they shared with their non-Jewish ... non-Greek-speaking neighbours not only in Palestine but in the whole region both before and after the Christian period.[129]

Virtually all Judaeans spoke one dialect or another of Aramaic. Expressing a lively epistolary culture, they wrote letters in the tongue. On occasion, those sufficiently trained and economically motivated would copy or even compose Aramaic legal writ, doing the best they could to reproduce its older idiom. But ordinary householders did not read Aramaic literature any more than most modern Westerners read books such as *The Speed and Power of Ships*. Aramaic books were, it seems, left to the Judaean analog of nautical engineers.

Greek Language and Literacy

Table 1.4 shows the results of instances wherein Judaeans signed Greek legal texts. Thus, it considers instances, not individuals. Ideally, they would have signed in Greek, but principals were never able to do so—although the numbers here are so low as to mean essentially nothing. The two instances of principals signing were two different signatures by the same man, Babatha's husband, Judah b. Eleazar Khthousion (*P.Yadin* 17 and 18). As is evident, he was illiterate in Greek and so signed in Aramaic. (Eleazar b. Eleazar, his brother, was in fact able to sign in Greek, and did so at level 3, but not as a principal.)

The statistics regarding the literate behavior of the witnesses and *hypographeis* are more meaningful and more revealing. We see that literate Judaeans generally could not sign in Greek. Three times in four they would instead affix an Aramaic John Hancock to Greek writ. They were therefore notably less signature literate in Greek than in Aramaic or Hebrew. But 25 percent of the time Judaean witnesses *were* able to produce Greek, a number twice that of their Nabataean counterparts. Nabataeans nearly always signed in Nabataean. Hence we may reasonably consider, as argued in Chapter 4, that Judaeans were substantially more likely to have some Greek as a second or third language than were tribesmen of the Nabataean realm.

Can we say more? Perhaps; Table 5.6 leads our inquiry on. This table documents individuals, not instances. It shows that apart from principals, a total of sixty-nine different Judaeans witnessed or otherwise played a writing role in Greek contracts. Of these sixty-nine, we can judge the fluency level of sixty signatures, whether in Greek or Aramaic; the other nine are too damaged to assess. We further find that of these sixty-nine individuals, twenty-one (30.4 percent) were capable of producing a Greek signature. This datum allows us to make a very rough and tentative estimate concerning Greek in our population. Recalling that according to our data, as discussed above, some 65 percent of male Judaean householders were signature literate, we can estimate that about 19.8 percent of Judaean men of that class had learned enough Greek to sign in it (i.e., 30.4 percent of 65 percent). Now, this number is likely exaggerated. The stronger the desire to find signatories who could sign in the contractual language, the less random our sample may be.[130]

Table 5.6. Signatories to Greek documents: witnesses, *hypographeis,* and subscribers

Level	Sign in Greek	%*	Sign in Aramaic	%*
1	0	0.0	14	33.3
2	2	11.1	7	16.7
3	16	88.9	18	42.9
4	0	0.0	3	7.1
Indeterminate	3	—	6	—

*Percentages calculated with "indeterminate" abstracted.

But if even 10 percent of Judaean house-holding men had studied Greek in order to sign, this would be a notable fact—if it were a fact.

Table 5.6 makes the facticity dubious: people evidently *did not learn Greek merely to sign.* Note that nearly 90 percent of those who signed in Greek did so at level 3. This is a much higher percentage than those signing in Aramaic, as the table illustrates: only about 40 percent of Aramaic writers were that fluent. More than half of these witnesses who learned to write in Aramaic failed to carry their training to the level of literary literacy. They could participate in the literate culture to some degree, indeed, one presumes, generally to the degree their affairs required. But they could not read a book. In contrast, Judaeans who applied themselves to Greek had as their goal the ability to read it with some ease. This fact also entails that those studying Greek often studied it longer than those on the Semitic track pursued their educations. We seem to be looking at further evidence for the notion of "alternative literacies." In parallel with a Semitic track, which would eventually lead to the ability to read the scriptures in SBH, an alternative path evidently existed that trained people in Greek, all the way to literary literacy. And people who started down this path often—in our data, almost always—stayed on it all the way to true reading ability.

Table 5.6 also shows that of sixty-nine signatories, sixteen could sign at level 3 in Greek (23.2 percent). Subject to the same caveats as our numbers above, it follows that 15.1 percent of male Judaean householders could read literature composed in Greek. Halving the number to compensate for the likely bias in our sample still leaves us with a rough-and-ready estimate that 7–8 percent of the elite male population—much of it, per our data, in the countryside, not the big cities—could read the language of Plato. But did they read Plato himself?

The contextualized materials of this study would argue, "Very seldom." We have touched on many of the relevant facts in Chapter 2, but a quick review may be useful. In contrast to Greek documentary materials, which were common, very few Greek literary texts of any kind were numbered among the various discoveries in the Judaean Desert. No literary works originally composed in Greek turned up at Masada, nor were any discovered at Wadi Daliyeh, Naḥal Ḥever, Jericho, Wadi Nar, Wadi Gweir, Wadi Sdeir, Naḥal Ṣe'elim, or Naḥal Mishmar. In this regard, Murabbaʿat was unique. We have proposed that among the finds that may properly date to the First Revolt, one Murabbaʿat archive, that of the brothers Eutrapelus, held as many as a dozen Greek literary works. Though the bulk of these fragmentary writings have so far defied precise identification, several belonged to the classical genres that contemporary Alexandrians or inhabitants of Oxyrhynchus were reading. These books might have graced the shelves of contemporary Athenians. But no other Judaean archives or book deposits contained Greco-Roman literature of the sort that the refined sensibilities of a Cicero or a Plutarch might have found appealing. Greek writings were discovered, to be sure; but they were *Judaean works in Greek dress.*

Accordingly, the unique deposit of Qumran Cave 7, with its nineteen literary scrolls, included only copies of Exodus, the Letter of Jeremiah, and 1 Enoch, so far as plausible identifications can be made. Similarly with the small number of Greek materials among the deposits of Qumran Cave 4: 4Q119 is a manuscript of Leviticus, as is 4Q120. 4Q121 is a copy of Numbers; 4Q122, of Deuteronomy. 4Q126 is too fragmentary to be identified; 4Q127 is a parabiblical work related to Exodus. These rolls may have been the holdings of a single family, now commingled with numerous other collections stashed in that cave. We may reasonably suspect that both Qumran Cave 7 and the Greek materials of Qumran Cave 4 represent the books of Judaeans who read their scriptures in Greek—an alternative literacy.

In this connection it remains to consider *8Hev* 1 XIIgr, the *Greek Minor Prophets Scroll* from the Cave of Horrors. This luxurious book may have belonged to the priestly scribal family of Masabala b. Simon. (Recall: we have reason to believe that his family was in that cave; we also know that he received letters inscribed in Greek [*P.Yadin* 52]. Further, his putative father, Simon b. Simon, signed *P.Yadin* 11 in that language, and his brother, Tehinah b. Simon, composed Greek legal writ.) Tov's study of the Minor Prophets scroll clearly demonstrated that it was a Septuagintal form of the text, but was substantially revised in the direction of the emerging proto-MT.[131] In other words, it was a Hebrew text in Greek dress, the dress newly fitted as tightly as possible. The *Greek Minor Prophets Scroll* is another example of the apparent phenomenon of alternative literacy.

It seems, then, that a certain percentage of the Judaean population was ingesting its native traditions in the language of Javan. The signatories to our materials who signed at level 3 presumably aspired, not to read Greco-Roman works, but rather to animate their own literary heritage. The broader phenomenon underlying their education represented a significant response by Judaean society to the overwhelming attractions of Greek culture. Seen from one perspective, to be sure, to some degree Judaeans became Hellenized; seen from another, however, they Judaized Hellenism in equal measure. The later rabbis recognized this turnabout as fair play. They gave Greek translations their imprimatur as scripture, something they withheld from written Aramaic translations of holy writ.[132] The fifth-generation Tanna, R. Eleazar b. Eleazar ha-Qappar, validated current reality when he opined, "May the words of Shem be spoken in the language of Japheth in the tents of Shem" (יהיו דבריו של שם נאמרים בלשונו של יפת באהלי שם).[133] A very old view, at least as presented, appears in the tractate *Megillah* of the Mishnah. A leader during the First Revolt, Simon b. Gamaliel, is said to comment on a legal position that plainly must be at least as ancient as he: "No difference exists between (holy) books, *tefillin* and *mezuzot,* except that the books may be written in any language, whereas *tefillin* and *mezuzot* may be written only in Hebrew. Rabban Simon b. Gamaliel says, 'Also, the only other language in which the (holy) books are permitted to be written is Greek.'"[134]

Opposed to the anonymous legal tradition, the stricter opinion of the celebrated Pharisee held that scriptural books were properly composed, if not in Hebrew, only in Greek. These sorts of dicta were seldom prospective, seeking to forestall some anticipated legal infelicity. Rather, they were reactions to actual practices. The passage implies that by the mid-first century C.E., if not earlier, significant numbers of scriptural writings composed in Greek were circulating in Judaea. This fact can only mean that some people found it easier to comprehend Septuagintal Greek than SBH. The former was not far distant linguistically from the koine of the period, except for its frequent Semitisms—presumably no problem for the readers and listeners in question. In contrast, SBH was sufficiently remote from colloquial Hebrew that untutored Hebrew-Greek bilinguals might well have preferred to hear Moses speak "in the language of Japheth."

The famous Theodotus inscription strongly suggests that the associated synagogue in Jerusalem operated in Greek during the decades before the Temple's destruction.[135] The inscription speaks of activities that took place in the synagogue, including "reading of the Law and teaching of the commandments" (εἰς ἀνάγνωσιν νόμου καὶ εἰς διδαχὴν ἐντολῶν). Greek copies of the scriptures such as we have in the Minor Prophets scroll and 4Q119–122 would have been needed. (None of the aforementioned texts was copied much later than the beginning of the first century C.E., according to Peter Parsons.)[136] According to the Book of Acts, a Greek-speaking "Synagogue of the Freedmen" in the same city came early to include followers of the Way.[137] New Greek translations of the scriptures by Aquila and Symmachus, more closely adhering to the Hebrew text now preferred more than the Old

Greek, appeared in the course of the next century. They derived from rabbinic circles or closely allied groups.[138] By the third century C.E. and the editing of the Tosephta, we get explicit and approving testimony that synagogues in a variety of locales were conducting their services in Greek perforce: "A synagogue of Greek speakers—if they have someone who can read it, they are to begin (the reading of scripture) in Hebrew (and continue in Greek). (A second opinion): They begin and end in Hebrew (with Greek in the middle). If they have but one man who can read Hebrew, then only he reads."[139] Contextualized, our data suggest that the efflorescent use of Greek for the public reading of the holy books in the second and third centuries had its roots in the period between Pompey and Hadrian. Some of our householders pursued a Greek *paideia,* but not precisely that of Egypt and Rome. They focused on their own sacred and ancient traditions. Presumably, they read to their families and their communities just as did other scribes and householders who read the scriptures in SBH. Only, these men read in Greek. If this reasoning is correct, it entails that listeners could comprehend, and thus that significant amounts of Greek were spoken (on which more below).

Learning to read literary Greek texts in Judaea was no easier than learning to do so elsewhere. One still faced the familiar river-of-letters presentation and, doubtless, long hours spent learning to interpret.[140] The presentation style is noteworthy given that Judaeans wrote Hebrew and Aramaic literature with spaces between words. They did not transfer this convenience to Greek books they copied or wrote, instead mirroring the Roman reception, wherein the more ancient style of writing with separate words gave way to the Greek technique (even for Latin). Reading Greek literature in Judaea was thus no more a democratic process, open to all, than was reading in SBH, or reading Greek in other places. The activity was inherently and intentionally elitist.

Why would anyone want to make the enormous effort to learn to read the scriptures in Greek? No single answer may be expected for this question, but for some people, it would doubtless have been a matter of efficiencies. Greek was the language in which Rome administered the Judaean province. Before that, Herod had used the language for that purpose, and earlier the Seleucids and Ptolemies. Thus, for centuries local leaders who regularly interacted with the governing authorities had found some acquaintance with Greek not merely helpful but necessary. For certain city and village elites, acquiring knowledge of Greek was an element of training for their positions in life. Much could be accomplished with just a utilitarian oral command of the tongue. But a certain percentage of householders found it necessary to journey some distance down the road to Greek literary literacy in order to function politically and economically. They needed to sign tax documents, for example, and to read letters and other predictable and uncomplicated texts. To circle back after progressing nearly to the second stage of a Greek *paideia* in order to undertake a second track of education, thereby to read SBH, would have demanded resources of motivation, time, and effort that relatively few possessed. It was more efficient simply to keep going with Greek, provided that one had the fundamental desire to read the scriptures at all. Where it existed, this desire would have been the fruit of religious sentiments that pervaded the culture.

And, too, we must bear in mind the social prestige that the language of the Hellenes enjoyed everywhere in the Mediterranean basin. Acquiring not just a speaking knowledge, but an ability to read the language well publicly, mattered. This prestige factor is evident from the "display element" we observed in Chapter 1 when examining surviving Greek inscriptions from Jerusalem. The upper classes in particular sought to associate themselves with the dominant political and social powers. Much of the impetus to Greek, in other words, reprised the earlier impetus to Imperial Aramaic: to command the language of the "winners" was more and more both a practical necessity for many and a desirable affectation for others.

Summarizing his impression of the realities behind the Greek ossuary inscriptions included in his study, Rahmani suggested that Judaean knowledge of Greek "was probably limited to everyday speech and in general did not include a profound familiarity with the language, its grammar or its literature; this is similar to the level of Greek evidenced at Bet Shearim at a somewhat later period."[141] The materials of the present study substantially corroborate the essentials of this view, while illustrating that actual facility with Greek varied greatly. A fair number of Rahmani's short inscriptions displayed issues with orthography or morphology. But was the intermittent haziness concerning Greek morphology, and especially with proper use of the cases, simply a matter of incomplete mastery of the language? Or was it rather the case that a diglossia existed for Judaean Greek, with an L form characterized among other things by simplification of the cases, and an H form equating with the standard koine?

Both incomplete mastery and diglossia have been urged as explanations for the Greek of the Judaean scribes from Mahoza. (These approaches are not, of course, intrinsically incompatible, but no scholar has attempted an approach combining the two.) One might summarize Naphtali Lewis's assessment of certain scribes with a single word, insouciance. Germanus b. Judah, author of *P.Yadin* 20–27, possessed according to Lewis "a large, clear hand, but . . . only limited mastery of Greek morphology and accidence."[142] A second scribe, the PN b. Simon who wrote *P.Yadin* 19, Lewis characterized as having an "even, flowing hand notable for its erratic orthography, indiscriminate vowels . . . and insouciant case endings."[143] Thus, for Lewis the aberrant grammar of these scribes followed no discernible pattern. In contrast, Stanley Porter argued for a diglossic method to the grammatical madness, calling as his premier witness the scribe of *P.Hever* 64:

> The cases used reveal that the author consistently changes the dative case to the genitive or accusative, and the genitive to the accusative case. This is the general tendency of the Greek language with regard to cases, with the dative case being assimilated with the genitive, and then the genitive being assimilated with the accusative. Far from being unmindful of case endings and grammatical gender, the author is entirely consistent, both in terms of his own idiolect and in terms of the tendencies of Greek language development.[144]

Neither Lewis nor Porter provided many details. Consequently, in attempting to decide between their opposed positions, a few examples are in order. If we examine PN b. Simon and *P.Yadin* 19, the data seem to justify Lewis's label of "limited mastery." The writer uses the dative for the genitive, the accusative for the genitive, the genitive for the accusative, and at other times employs the cases, particularly the dative, correctly.[145] No evident pattern emerges. Similarly, Germanus b. Judah displays a potpourri of errors. In *P.Yadin* 20, he writes ὁμολογοῦμεν συνκεχωρηκέναι . . . καὶ τοὺς σὺν αὐτῆς οἰκίαι for the expected ὁμολογοῦμεν συνκεχωρηκέναι . . . καὶ τὰς σὺν αὐτῇ οἰκίας (lines 27–30). In the same writ he produces instances of the genitive for the accusative case (e.g., εἰς . . . νότου, lines 30–31) and has occasional trouble keeping track of antecedents, affecting number agreement (ἐκδικήσωμεν . . . ἀντιλέγων, lines 35–39). In general, Germanus is especially fond of the genitive case, using it at various times for the nominative (e.g., μηνῶν τελίων τρῖς instead of μῆνες τελείοι τρεῖς, *P.Yadin* 27:11), for the dative (e.g., ἐπὶ Ἀτερίῳ Νέπωτι πρεσβευτοῦ καὶ ἀντιστρατήγου rather than πρεσβευτῷ καὶ ἀντιστρατήγῳ, *P.Yadin* 23:14–15), and for the accusative (e.g., ἀπέσχον παρά σου . . . ἀργυρίου δηναρίων ἕξ for ἀργυρίου δηναρίους ἕξ, *P.Yadin* 27:8–9). Germanus makes errors that appear random—the products of insouciance or ignorance.

The case of *P.Hever* 64 is unique for the profundity and variety of scribal mistakes. The text's original editor, Hannah Cotton, remarked: "the Greek of No. 64 is singularly ungrammatical and non-idiomatic. The scribe pays no attention to case endings and gender. . . . At times, the Greek is so poor that the text can be understood only when translated back into Aramaic."[146] Her wording implied insouciance or ignorance, not a patterned idiolect such as Porter claimed to find. Close analysis seems to favor Cotton's perspective over his. True, as Porter noted, several instances of genitive for the dative case do occur.[147] But in another instance, the reverse is evident, the dative appearing for the genitive.[148] The accusative appears where one would expect now the nominative, now the genitive, now the dative: it is an all-purpose case.[149] Thus, Porter's broad claim that "the author is entirely consistent" is simply not in evidence. This lack of patterning means that the better explanation for the bad Greek is not diglossia, but imperfect mastery.

Yet these writers possessed reasonably fine hands: they wrote bad Greek with a flourish. Their knowledge of the lexicon, while imperfect,[150] exceeded their mastery of Greek morphology. Their native Semitic languages had not habituated them to the concept of case endings. Still, for all its imperfections, the Greek these scribes had acquired served the practical needs of their situation well enough. What was important was Greek, not perfect Greek.

Not that all the Greek was bad. Tehinah b. Simon, Masabala's brother there in Mahoza, wrote correct, idiomatic Greek, albeit with an outward appearance less pleasing than his grammatically challenged peers produced. He was the person responsible for *P.Yadin* 13–15 and 17–18. Lewis described his "grammatical *Koine* Greek interspersed with occasional locutions of non-Greek origin," represented via a hand "easily legible but rather coarse and graceless in appearance."[151] Tehinah knew Greek well, but even he wrote (and presumably spoke) a form of the language that reflected centuries of contact with Semitic.

The documents from Mahoza illustrate the startling rapidity with which Roman provincial government asserted its ways following annexation of the Nabataean kingdom in 106 C.E.[152] Immediately, Greek replaced Nabataean as the language of legal affairs (although interestingly, some Nabataean documents did continue to be produced for years).[153] In general, scribes who had previously worked in Nabataean, Judaean Aramaic, or both[154] now had an economic incentive to learn Greek, and the facts show that even in a backwater village such as Mahoza, it was possible to obtain instruction. The quality of that instruction may have been questionable, however, and it is evident that not all learned equally well. Perhaps the quality of instruction was not the only issue. Germanus, PN b. Simon, and the scribe of *P.Hever* 64 may have been grown men when the annexation occurred. They were, it seems likely, somewhat in the situation of old dogs needing to learn new tricks. The study by modern linguists of language acquisition suggests that attaining a true mastery of Greek after about the age of thirteen to fifteen would have been very difficult for these ancient scribes.

Proponents of the so-called Critical Period Hypothesis argue that the human brain is predisposed for language learning until approximately the onset of puberty. At that time, perhaps because of hormonal changes and their effects on the brain, people cease to learn language with the casual ease of young children. From this point on, they must depend on more general learning abilities to acquire a second or third tongue. A variety of studies have shown that older learners nearly always speak their new language with what native speakers regard as a "foreign accent." Mastery of syntax and morphology is also less complete for virtually all such people. Vocabulary is the least problematic element for older learners.[155] We cannot be sure, of course, that certain of our scribes were in the situation of old dogs, but the sorts of successes and failures they had with Greek would fit this explanation. Moreover, if they had begun their careers as scribes working with the Semitic languages, that training would have occupied a number of years, their earliest and most formative. With the coming of Rome, Germanus, PN b. Simon, and some of their *confrères* would have needed to double back and initiate a second *paideia.*

Since these men were scribes, and (except for Tehinah) not necessarily socially elite, neither of their curricula may have been as full as the acquisition of acceptable literary reading proficiency described earlier would require. Yet some of the Judaean elite undoubtedly found themselves needing to pursue "tandem literacies." The phrase would likely describe the learning history of Masabala b. Simon and his brothers, for example. As a group, they produced or received documents in Hebrew, Aramaic, and Greek and apparently owned literature in both Hebrew (*8Hev* 1 Prayer) and Greek (*8Hev* 2 XIIgr). Similarly, Eleazar b. Eleazar wrote both Aramaic and Greek at level 3 and was evidently capable as well of reading aloud and explaining proto-MH letters such as *P.Hever* 30. As argued above, he may well have owned Hebrew books, both scriptural and nonscriptural (*P.Hever* 6).[156] Masabala's co-commander at En Gedi, John b. Baʿyah, received letters composed in Hebrew, Aramaic, and Greek; presumably, these letters were read aloud by envoys or locals, and John understood them. Also addressed to John was the one semipersonal letter extant among the Bar Kokhba correspondence, *P.Yadin* 57, and *it was written in Greek.* Composed by one Hanan, the letter displays a fluent, scribal-level hand but was no secretarial product. Rather, Hanan took pen to papyrus himself, signing with a flourish, "Hanan. Be well, brother!"[157] If Hanan were John's biological sibling, as seems quite possible, then the significant degree of education in the Greek language that he plainly received suggests that John, too, had immersed himself in that *paideia.*

Accordingly, we either know for a fact or, as in John's case, can reasonably suspect that each of these men had gained both Semitic and Greek educations, pursued all the way to literary literacy. They would be able to exposit the archaic Hebrew scriptures and to handle Judaean literature couched in Greek, such as the Minor Prophets scroll. Masabala, John, and Eleazar were all village officials and may have been such even before the revolt. Simon b. Kosiba evidently took over much of the Roman administration of the province, after all; village leadership structures may simply have been another. If so, the education these men received may cautiously be generalized and considered fairly common for their ilk throughout Judaea.

As we have seen, the process of acquiring an ability to animate ancient literature in either Greek or Hebrew was very intense—for most people, in fact, more or less all-consuming for a significant stretch of one's youth. It was no mean feat to learn to read in either literary language, and only a relatively small number ever accomplished it. By what process are we to imagine, then, that the Masabalas and Eleazars ascended to socially rarified heights in *both* traditions? A gifted few, one supposes, might attempt Parnassus and Sinai simultaneously. But most elite youngsters who needed dual literacy probably pursued one track, and afterwards, in their early teens, took up the other. This Judaean practice we may call, for want of another expression, tandem literacies, and it brings us back to the Critical Period Hypothesis. For if it were the practice in Judaea for certain elites to pursue Semitic learning and then, only after acquiring literary literacy in Hebrew, to undertake a form of the Greek *paideia,* then frequently such learners would commence instruction in reading Greek after reaching puberty. Training in Moses and the Prophets would occupy them to that point. This scenario would mean that Judaean tandem-literates might often control Greek less well than, say, typical members of the contemporary Roman elite, who often began to learn Greek before they could read Latin.

A famous passage in the *Antiquities* of Josephus may be taken as supporting this hypothetical reconstruction of Judaean education for dual literacy:

> And now I take heart from the completion of my proposed work to assert that no one else, either Jew or gentile, would have been equal to the task, however willing to undertake it, of issuing so accurate a treatise as this for the Greek world. For my compatriots admit that in our Judaean learning I far excel them [κατὰ τὴν ἐπιχώριον καὶ παρ' ἡμῖν παιδείαν διαφέρειν]. After acquiring a knowledge of Greek grammar, I labored strenuously to command both Greek prose and poetry—yet my native habit of speech prevented me from pronouncing the language properly [τὴν δὲ περὶ τὴν προφορὰν ἀκρίβειαν πάτριος ἐκώλυσεν συνήθεια]. . . . Consequently, although many people have laboriously undertaken this training, at most two or three have succeeded to reap the harvest of their labors.[158]

Josephus adds this statement at the end of his extensive work, seemingly as an address to listeners rather than readers, since readers would not hear his oral expression. It therefore seems likely that the original setting was that of a *recitatio* in Rome about the year 95 C.E.[159] and that the Judaean expatriate felt compelled in that cultured context to apologize for his imperfect Greek, marred as it was by a "foreign accent." Plainly, he was reading the final portion of the *Antiquities* to his audience personally rather than employing a lector. Obvious to all, his pronunciation was an embarrassment and could not be ignored. This was the time of the early Second Sophistic, and language issues were enormously important to the cultured class at Rome, doubtless focusing Josephus yet more intensely on his perceived shortcomings. (He was not the only easterner to harbor such self-doubts and to comment about pronunciation difficulties; Lucian of Samosata was another Aramaic speaker who came to Greek after a native *paideia,* speaking with a worrisome accent.)[160]

Josephus's comments here reference a two-step process to his own education, an education that he boasts prepared him as few others to write a work like the *Antiquities.* He had achieved a mastery of Judaean learning, acquiring the ability to read and interpret the Hebrew scriptures at a high level of expertise. He had also progressed through the several stages of a Greek *paideia,* beginning with grammar and ending with a thorough study of Greco-Roman writings. He notes the rarity of his situation, seeming in particular to mean a Judaean knowing classical prose and poetic works. If this is his meaning, the contextualized data of this study would support his claims, as we have seen: very few Judaeans studied Greek works of the classical canons. Josephus was no less given to rodomontade than was Cicero, but for once his self-assessment may be taken as factual. Not many could do what he had done.

He does not clearly spell out the sequence involved in his advancement to dual literary literacy. Nevertheless, in light of the Critical Period Hypothesis his pronunciation issues strongly suggest that before puberty Josephus had insufficient exposure to Greek to achieve native or near-native speech patterns in that language. If this inference is correct, it would follow that the Judaean priest and erstwhile general began life with the Semitic curriculum and did not undertake Greek in any serious way before his early teens. Josephus thus affords a well-lit example of how tandem literacies might play out among the highest Judaean elites. Masabala and the sons of Simon apparently stem from the same hegemonic priestly sector of society as Josephus, and similarly evidence literary literacy in both traditions.

Of course, constraints of time, money, ability, and motivation dictated that most Judaean potential literary literates choose between the two linguistic paths. For them, the question would have been one of alternative literacies, not tandem literacies. And a notable percentage of the village property-owning class, as our data indicate, chose to learn to read Greek rather than Hebrew. The same data promise to give some indication of the degree to which Greek was spoken, as opposed to being a language of signatures or reading. Spoken Greek is obviously a separate issue.

Recall that according to Table 5.6, twenty-one of sixty-nine signatories to Greek writ were able to sign in Greek. Presumably, those signing in Greek understood the contract as it was read aloud to them. The remainder of the literates signed in Aramaic. Nearly a third of the male householders who composed the majority of the signatories were able to muster enough Greek to affix their names in the language of the contract (30.4 percent). Now, we do not know how much canvassing those responsible did in order to round up people who could sign in Greek. We must allow that some searching may have occurred, which means that we would need to discount the 30 percent somewhat. On the other hand, it seems equally probable that some portion of the Aramaic signatories comprehended the Greek contract when it was read out in that tongue but simply could not sign in it. We have no means of deciding whether these two factors cancel each other out, but we are probably on reasonably safe ground if we let the straightforward figure stand for a moment as an approximation.

A second issue arises from the nature of our data: the question of class and language usage. Given that the materials of this study derive very largely from the householder class of Judaea, we must consider that our 30 percent arguably able to comprehend spoken Greek—and thus, in most cases, to speak it with at least a modicum of facility—would possibly not hold true farther down the social ladder. And because women virtually never sign in any language, we cannot analyze whether they spoke Greek to the same degree the men in the property-owning class did.

Let us then, for the sake of argument, simply put everyone else aside except for propertied-class males. Adopting as more probable the "anti-primitivist" model for the Judaean economy discussed previously, we would locate these men as representative of the top quartile of the population socially and economically. Working with the earlier assumption of a population of one million, we would thus have 9,900 speakers of Greek (200,000 males × 25.0% × 19.8%). This figure is self-evidently not nearly the whole, for it assumes that no women, no children, and no people of any but the elite classes spoke Greek. If even half the men spoke some Greek with their families, we would have 24,750 speakers. And the presence of this many speakers at the apex of the social pyramid would over time have a substantial trickle-down effect, so that the number would not be static. If, say, the second quartile of the population spoke Greek half as much as the top quartile, the number would be 37,125. If the third quartile embraced half as many Greek speakers as the second, the number would be 43,313; of the fourth by the same reasoning, 46,407. On the basis of our data and even these minimalist numbers, we come away with the impression of a *considerable amount of Greek spoken in Roman Judaea.* No solid quantification is possible, but this impression is buttressed by other considerations touched on earlier.

A weighty consideration is the phonological convergence between Greek and Judaean Semitic argued above. This sort of general linguistic change, one attested widely and presumably affecting all social classes, would seem to be impossible in the absence of a substantial critical mass of Greek speakers extending over time. A second supporting consideration is the fact that Judaeans wrote both official and personal correspondence to each other in Greek. As discussed, this sort of communication is often closer to speech practices than are other forms of writing. The Judaean Desert discoveries include ten such letters, rescued from the oblivion that still holds countless others: *P.Yadin* 52 and 59, the two epistles belonging to John b. Baʿyah's Cave of Letters archive; Mas741, the Letter of Abaskantos to Judas, and Mas745–746, representing two or three additional Greek letters; *P.Hever* 67, the letter mentioning timber; *P.Har Yishai* 2; *P.8Hever* 4; and *P.Jericho* 19. The connection of these Greek letters to Judaean speech is fortified when we recall that the Letter of Abaskantos, likely written either at Masada or

En Gedi, contained the term μαρούλιον, not a literary word in our period but still used for "lettuce" in Modern Greek today. This is the impress of colloquial Greek in mid-first century Palestine.

In the years spanning Pompey and Hadrian, Greek was evidently spoken less in Judaea than were either Aramaic or Hebrew. But it was a significant presence nonetheless. Scholars have often posited that one would hear it in the large cities, and on our evidence this posit appears true. Even in the small villages, however, a "χαίρειν" would sound over the hubbub to merge with shouts of "שלום." Scholars have allowed for this reality far less often. Greek texts and writers in this study derive from Jerusalem and Jericho, large population centers, true. Yet they derive no less—in fact, much more—from Herodium, Beth-Bassi, Aristoboulias, En Gedi, Kephar-Baru, and Mahoza, mere villages all. About 30 percent of men at the helm of village life could speak at least some Greek, if our data are rightly interpreted. Between one-third and one-half of those people could read the language, many of them well enough to handle books. To paraphrase the nineteenth-century British witticism, Greek may not have been well liked, but it was liked. What had Athens to do with Jerusalem? Much, and in Judaea itself.

Literacy Rates

Introducing the weighty volume *Ancient Literacies* in 2009, William Johnson wrote as follows:

> The most widely referenced general book remains William Harris' *Ancient Literacy* (1989), a thoughtful, immensely learned, and important book, which, however, focuses narrowly on the question of what percentage of people in antiquity might have been able to read and write. The moment seems right, therefore, to try to formulate more interesting, productive ways of talking about the conception and construction of "literacies" in the ancient world—literacy not in the sense of whether 10 percent or 30 percent of people in the ancient world could read or write, but in the sense of text-oriented events embedded in particular sociocultural contexts.[161]

These words typified one of the genera of scholarly responses to Harris's book, documented in Chapter 1: a certain lifting of the nose, but usually not before dispatching in Harris's direction some perfumed praise. (The other broad response, recall, was to dispatch the praise without nasal involvement.) One can understand why many scholars might feel as Johnson did about Harris's approach and its "narrow" focus on concrete questions. Surely there are "more interesting, productive" inquiries. After all, why should it really matter to anyone whether 10 percent of first-century Cretans, say—or, rather, 20 percent—could read? Surely, any next question asked after discovering the correct number, whatever that number might be, would prove much more interesting than the number itself. (Still, one cannot help suspecting as well that if the number of ancient readers that Harris had discovered were higher, closer to reifying the halcyon, book-loving past that many classicists long inhabited in their imaginations, the matter would have proved a good deal less dull.) In any case—if this disdain for counting how many could actually read makes some sense for broad swathes of Greco-Roman antiquity, and for virtually every people under Roman aegis, there is one place for which it does not make sense: Judaea.

Judaea alone possessed, as Millar put matters, all of the following elements: "a national religion and tradition, a national identity and capacity for independent state-formation." As he went on to say, they "alone of all the peoples under Roman rule . . . not only had a long recorded history but kept it, re-interpreted it and acted on it."[162] At the center of Judaean identity, tradition, and rebellious pursuit of state formation was a book: essentially, their constructed history, constantly read and interpreted at every level of society. This book was integral to every significant social movement or political idea that arose in Judaea during the years from Pompey to Hadrian. Therefore, while it is as true for Judaea as anywhere else that many other interesting questions can and should be asked about the functions of different literacies, here as perhaps nowhere else Harris's focus—pursuing the actual number of readers—necessarily becomes a first principle, imposing itself on the historian, willing and interested or not.

The weight of the issue does not mean that it is a light matter to arrive at a number. We have already noted the theoretical thorn bushes of economic structure and demographic analysis that overgrow this path. We must do with rough-and-ready estimates, but at least we do have some quantifiable elements with which to work. So: how many Judaeans were literate, in the several senses of that concept addressed by our data? We look back at Tables 5.3 and 5.4 for answers.

Table 5.3 tabulates the writing capacities and levels of the principals to all the legal materials of this study, by language, for each of the four languages in which we have written materials involving Judaeans. Under the category "illiterate," the table further distinguishes gender—a factor that becomes irrelevant for other categories of writing ability, since no women fit into any of them. That is to say, 100 percent of the female principals of this study were unable to sign their names, and so naturally none fits into any higher category of literate behavior. Given that the population of our study was largely the property-owning class, and especially (but not only) its rural representatives, the table brings to the fore some additional points of interest.

Note that about half of all principals were entirely illiterate: twenty-nine of sixty-nine (twenty-nine of sixty-three discounting scribes). Nineteen men and ten women could not sign their names. The next level of writing ability, representing the βραδέως γράφοντες, embraced about 10 percent of our lay population (11.3 percent if we include only men and no scribes). The combination of these two categories yields the inference that for elite ancient Judaeans, illiteracy brought no social stigma. A good many of the upper quartile of the population fell into this category. If it had carried social opprobrium, one would not expect the number to be so high. Yet the fact that more than 10 percent nevertheless made the effort to learn to write their names, and so to participate in literate culture, albeit minimally, suggests that people often felt some satisfaction, perhaps even pride, at wielding the stylus.

A noteworthy percentage of the populace arrived at level 2 but did not advance to true ability to read. More than a quarter of the male principals fall in this category. If we count only literate males, the number is 44.1 percent (fifteen of thirty-four). The size of this group raises the question, "What advantage would a person gain by advancing beyond mere signature literacy, yet not all the way to literary literacy?" For a certain number, of course, the decision would have been a matter of economics. They simply got all the education their families could afford to give them, and this is where it halted. But one must suspect that the choice was frequently based on other considerations. A man who functioned at level 2 could not only sign his name, but also, with some effort, copy a legal document. Lazar b. Joseph, writer of *Mur* 21, exemplifies such a person. He copied out his daughter's *ketubbah* even though he possessed only limited graphic skill. People at this level might sometimes be able to compose letters. The secretary of *P.Yadin* 57 provides a possible example here. He wrote "slowly with a practiced hand," according to Yardeni's analysis.[163] Slow writers are, of course, generally unskilled; the lack of practice is why they write slowly. Since he was able to produce decent letterforms, this man may have been elderly, sick, or disabled. But it is also possible that the writer was simply an advanced level 2 hand, on the cusp of level 3. These examples illustrate that level 2 writers could take part in significant ways in the literate culture of Judaea, doing things that no level 1 writer could undertake. They might read short, predictable documents such as letters and certain legal writ. Their writing ability would save them the fees required to hire scribes to produce these and similar documents.

But it seems likely that advancing to level 2 was also desirable so that students might gain a deeper acquaintance with Moses and the Prophets. These were the literary texts that students began slowly to read, copy, and memorize once they acquired modest ability with the cursive script. Even though many stopped short of truly functional reading ability, whatever knowledge of archaic Hebrew they gained would stand them in good stead for the rest of their lives. Unlike the typical peasant, level 2 writers would probably have understood a good deal of the strange language of the scriptures when hearing them read, simply by virtue of the grammatical and lexical explanation that accompanied their moderate exposure to the texts. This would have been true especially for speakers of proto-MH. In proceeding from level 1 to level 2, the ability of future property-owning men to participate in the legal and religious lives of their communities was meaningfully enhanced. Yet, by ceasing short of level 3, these people saved the time, enormous labor, and top-heavy expense of the years of additional education they would need to read and expatiate to the standard.

Nevertheless, Table 5.3 shows that nearly one in four property-owning men *could* read and expatiate to the standard (thirteen of fifty-three, 24.5 percent). If this percentage were generalized throughout the Judaean communities, it would suggest that among the elite, most extended families included at least one fully literate male. This relative abundance of readers would serve both the families' interests, in representing their higher-level written affairs, and the communities', in providing public readers to lead worship and instruction. Families would doubtless gain additional social prestige by providing these leaders. That such considerations were important to Judaeans seems to emerge from the calculation that *nearly 40 percent of men who were literate at all were literary literates* (thirteen of thirty-four; that is, discounting illiterates as given in the table). Note as well that if the literate males from all three levels are taken together, the figure of approximately 65 percent emerges in answer to the question, "What percentage of householding men were in any way literate?" (This is the figure foreshadowed earlier in the chapter.)

All of these percentages concerning principals are within shouting distance of the *comparanda* for witnesses to the documents of this study, as Table 5.4 shows. The figures in this table are somewhat higher across the board than are their correspondents among the principals, but given our sample sizes, the differences are fairly modest. For example, 49.4 percent of the male householder witnesses who were literate at all were literary literates—comparable to the figure for principals. Similarly, 17.6 percent of literate male principals were βραδέως γράφοντες, whereas for witnesses the number was 23.7 percent. What these relatively narrow ranges seem to indicate is that the individuals tabulated by Tables 5.3 and 5.4 were indeed broadly representative of Judaean male householders in general. Accordingly, we may be more confident in the reliability of the data.

Buoyed by this confidence, we can combine certain of the data in the two tables to create a larger and more representative sample. For the witnesses, recall, were mostly chosen as meeting the dual criteria of ability to sign and membership in the family. In combining with them that portion of the principals who were literate, we are pooling more individuals from the same social group: nonscribal, literate males of the elite. This combination yields 190 individuals literate at one of the three levels.[164] We can then calculate that among literate male householders, fully 47.4 percent were literary literates (90/190); 30.0 percent signed at level 2 (57/190); and 22.6 percent were βραδέως γράφοντες (43/190). On the basis of these numbers, it becomes possible to generate an approximate reply to our initial question: how many Judaeans were literate, in the several senses of that concept?

Of course, only Judaean males will be in view—and then, only those belonging to the elite, of which wealthy householders were reasonably representative. We have briefly noted that very few women were literate by any definition; we will shortly consider the matter in more detail, but for now we exclude females. Further, the scant evidence that has emerged in this study concerning subelite literacy has indicated that they might sometimes be able to sign, even on occasion at level 2; but they were mostly illiterate.[165] We have no reason to think that they could read books. Thus, this estimate—once again, more of a thought experiment than a hard number, given all the poorly understood social and economic variables—can consider only elite Judaean men.

If we recall that roughly 65 percent of elite males were literate; and if we then calculate, per our combined data, that 47.4 percent of that subgroup were literary literates; and further estimate, following the anti-primitivist model, that the top quartile of the population belonged to the broad category of elite, we get a figure of 7.7 percent male literary literates in Roman Judaea. Accordingly, it seems a safe statement that *between 5 and 10 percent of Judaean men in the years dividing Pompey from Hadrian were able to read books.* The ability to read with some ease, as books demand, is one common definition of literacy. Of course, for the total population the number would become just a fraction of this percentage. The apparent fact that women were more or less universally illiterate instantly halves the percentage. And we have no means whereby to assess such missing categories as the slave population, about whose literate behavior the next fact we get will be the first.[166] Still, the data we have argue that a reasonably high percentage of the Judaean male elite could read a book: about 30 percent (47.4 percent of 65 percent). For the full adult population, the same data suggest, the figure was far, far lower—probably on the low side of the range between 2.5 and 5 percent. Since Western culture has often been broadly characterized as rooted in Periclean Athens and the Jerusalem of Hillel and Jesus, no small irony accompanies the notion that just one person in forty in either city ever cracked a book.

Yet the ability to read is only one possible definition of literacy. A second possible definition—one more fitting the way Greco-Roman civilization itself regarded the matter (recall Petaus son of Petaus)—is the ability to sign one's name. Here, the number would be that same 65 percent of the male elite, yielding a total of something like 32,500 men of the total population (65 percent of 25 percent of 200,000). Putting children aside, then, this number would entail that *about 16 percent of Judaean adults were signature literate.* A good many elite men would possess reading and writing skills ranging somewhere between the antipodes of signature literacy and true reading. Per the present study, this intermediate category would embrace perhaps 19.5 percent of elite males.

It is today a commonplace that the Greco-Roman world was a literate world populated by illiterates. Society functioned by means of multiplied documents that ordinary, unlettered people could neither initiate nor respond to by themselves. Judaea was plainly no exception to this standard reality. Even centuries later, in early modern England (to take just one example), the ancient commonplace still applied. The usefulness of this sort of parallel is in helping us to imagine what the subelite data absent from our study of Judaea might have shown us. Depositions taken in England between 1530 and 1730 required that deponents sign or mark the documents. The levels of illiteracy within different social groups are instructive. No clergy failed to sign; they were 100 percent signature literate. Gentry likewise could nearly always sign their names (98 percent). Slightly more than half of those involved in trade and crafts could affix a John Hancock (56 percent); but only 21 percent of farmers, 15 percent of laborers, and 11 percent of women could accomplish that task.[167] Thus, centuries after our period, Western subelites remained mostly illiterate even when judged by that least demanding of standards, signature literacy. William Harris was right to draw the parallels. We can scarcely imagine that Judaea, whose elites were notably less literate than early modern England's, exceeded that nation's percentages farther down the social scale. Illiteracy among its ordinary peasants was probably nearly universal. Materials harvested from more or less contemporary Egypt buttress this inference:

> More than nine-tenths of the contracts and subscriptions drawn up at the *grapheion* in the agricultural village of Tebtynis in the 30's and 40's A.D. mention that at least one party to the transaction was unable to write the acknowledgment and to pen a signature; over two-thirds of the cultivators of public lands at the village of Lagis were unable to sign a joint declaration that the lands for which they were responsible had not been inundated for cultivation in 164; two-thirds of the cavalrymen in the squadron Veterana Gallica in 179 did not know letters, when asked to write an acknowledgment for receipt of their yearly hay allowance; over two-thirds of the citizens who applied for distributions of grain in the district capital of Oxyrhynchos in the later 3rd c[entury] asked others to write their applications for them.[168]

A literate society filled with illiterates—especially women: that was Roman Judaea in a nutshell. The following women were involved as principals with the documents of this study: Salome b. Honi (*Mur* 30), Shapira b. Jesus (*Mur* 29), Babatha b. Simon (*P.Yadin* 10 and many others), Salome Komaise b. Levi (*P.Hever* 63), Salome Grapte b. Menahem (*P.Hever* 64), Miriam b. Jacob (Beth ʿAmar), Salome b. Simon (*P.Hever* 8a), and Salome (no additional identifier; *P.Hever nab* 2). Eight women, none signature literate: the pattern speaks for itself and is resoundingly echoed by the statistics for other roles. Of approximately 225 Judaeans who served as witnesses and *hypographeis* in these materials, just one was a woman, the aforementioned Julia Crispina, evidently a Herodian and so perched at the very apex of the social pyramid. Out of nearly ninety scribes and secretaries named or implicated in our study, only one was female—and that identification was uncertain (*Mur* 94:15, ἀσ]ωφήρα, perhaps Hebrew הסופֵרה).[169]

How did such female illiterates and the many male members of their unlettered cohort negotiate life in the document-driven Judaea of our period? Ann Hanson's characterization of the coeval Egyptian scene was equally descriptive of the region to its east: "Common interests bound families, friends and even peripheral associates together into alliances of self-interest and self-protection. This pattern of trust and reliance was operative throughout the ancient world at all social levels and in many different spheres of public and private activity."[170] To avoid fraud and deception by literates, illiterates turned to close relatives and family members, to friends and business associates, and as a last resort to professional scribes known to be trustworthy. In the foregoing pages we have seen all of these relationships in play, with the families and friends of illiterates involved in their documents and safeguarding their interests again and again. In fact, it has been these connections that have undergirded most of the prosopographical analyses proposed.

Thus for documents, the ephemera of daily life; but what of literature and books? Here, the boundaries between literacy and illiteracy in the Greco-Roman world were not nearly as clear-cut as they were for legal writ. This realization has grown steadily in the years since Harris wrote and was the animating force behind Johnson's comments above regarding "text-oriented events." Such events do not require that everyone involved be able to read a text; indeed, they do not necessarily require a physical text at all. As Mary Carruthers observed in her seminal work *The Book of Memory:* "A book is not necessarily the same thing as a text. 'Texts' are the material out of which human beings make 'literature.' For us, texts only come in books, and so the distinction between the two is blurred and even lost. But, in a memorial culture, a 'book' is only one way among several to remember a 'text,' to provision and cue one's memory with 'dicta et facta memorabilia.' . . . A book is itself a mnemonic."[171] People may easily learn by listening to literature, and, having learned, retain a literary work or some portion of it in memory. These people need not be able to read or write, but they are clearly participating in literary culture. Indeed, Carruthers made a trenchant point when she continued, "I think it is probably misleading to speak of literary culture as a version of 'literacy' at all. The reason is simply this—as a concept, literacy privileges a physical artifact, the writing-support, over the social and rhetorical process that a text both records and generates, namely, the composition by an author and its reception by an audience."[172] The ancient book was for many experienced readers a mere mnemonic, or, as suggested earlier, a sort of musical score, waiting to be reanimated. That animation would connect its author with a new audience and, in an ideal sense, reproduce the original occasion of the work's completion and performance. In Judaea this understanding was perhaps complicated by the fact that many of the books most widely read were believed to have God as their ultimate author. But Carruthers's point does not thereby lose all force. Judaea, like the Greco-Roman world generally and like medieval Europe, was a memorial culture.[173]

For the educated, the point of learning to read was to engrave on the tablet of one's heart those works that the culture had valorized. For one's entire life, reading remained *intensive,* not *extensive* as it is today.[174] An educated man would read and reread the same books again and again; normally, these books were those learned as a child and adolescent. For people such as Seneca, this was as it should be: *Distringit librorum multitudo . . . probatos itaque semper lege, et si quando ad alios deverti libuerit, ad priores redi* (Having many books is a distraction. . . . Rather, always read the tried and true ones, and if at some point you are tempted to turn aside to others, go back to the first group!).[175] Anyway, there simply were not that many different titles around.[176] The presence of about 360 different nonscriptural books among the Dead Sea Scrolls (mostly lacking sectarian elements) might suggest that no more than a thousand Semitic works circulated in the Judaea of our period. Josephus famously contrasted the parsimonious Judaean situation with the myriads of writings competing among the Greeks.[177] Since almost no inhabitants of this world possessed libraries in each of several villas as did Cicero, for many literary literates coming upon something new to read probably lay outside routine. A concerted effort was required to obtain new material.[178] In Judaea the books of scripture, particularly Moses and the Prophets, were the scrolls commonly encountered by villagers. Some could read them; everyone could hear them read; and anyone could remember what they said. Thus the distinction between orality and literacy begins to lose focus when we come to books. In this world orality and literacy met at literary performance, and afterward, bound by memory, walked together. Did anything of actual importance distinguish the "literate," who read aloud and then recited from memory a book or portion learned, from the "illiterate," who listened, learned, and then recited the same portion? Most of us would think not.

But here is a place where ancient Judaea stood apart from the rest of its world and so confounds modern intuitions. Ancient Judaeans specifically chose to "privilege the writing-support" over the social and rhetorical processes it involved. As far as many of them were concerned, the written text *was* distinct from that which the mind held, and it was paramount. The mindset that attached itself to inscribed text begins to make itself apparent already in later portions of the writings we call biblical. Phrases such as

ככתוב בספר תורת משה, "as it is written in the Book of the Law of Moses," and ככתוב בתורת יהוה, "as it is written in the Law of Yahweh," proliferate at the hands of postexilic writers and editors. In literature composed during the years of our study, expressions similar in their intent to focus on written text appear in the Dead Sea Scrolls and the New Testament. One gets כי כן כתוב, "for thus it is written"; כאשר כתוב, "as it is written"; and X אשר כתוב בספר, "that is written in book X," alongside καθὼς γέγραπται, καθὼς ἐστὶν γεγραμμένον, and ὡς γέγραπται.[179] Frequent in the slightly later Tannaitic materials are citation formulae such as תלמוד לומר, "scripture says." These and equivalent expressions were so frequent in the literature of Roman Judaea that counting them becomes pointless.

No clearer witness to this Judaean mindset focused on the *written text* survives than the story of Rabbi Meir preserved in the Tosephta. It was required of Jewish men to read the Scroll of Esther (or hear it read) at the time of the Festival of Purim. Rabbi Meir was a third-generation Tanna and so an approximate contemporary of Simon b. Kosiba: "It once happened that Rabbi Meir went to Asya to intercalate the year, and failed to find there a Scroll of Esther inscribed in Hebrew. So he wrote it out from memory and then read from the scroll."[180]

It mattered that the scriptural text be inscribed. Mere oral recitation would not suffice. The book had to be *read,* not merely said. Because the text as written was of the essence, so too was the ability to read it. Therefore, literacy as distinct from orality must matter to the historian, as it did to the ancient Judaeans. Who was literate and how many are questions that help map the fault lines of that society. Many illiterates could and did participate in literary culture in Judaea of those years. We have no reason to view skeptically Josephus's claims that most of the populace knew the Law of Moses. Many of them heard it read in the synagogue and elsewhere, perhaps in the homes of householders, all of their lives. Like a great many in the history of Western literacy, ancient Judaeans mostly absorbed books with their ears.[181] Only a small number could read them or explain what was written. These few became or maintained themselves as the people that a Caesar would have said mattered. Power, influence, and informal as well as formal leadership attached to the ability to read. It was the very scratches on the scroll that were the word of God—θεοῦ δόγματα, as Josephus put it.[182] By deciphering and declaiming those scratches, a canny reader might lay claim to a people's destiny, even their eternity, throughout history a plenipotent combination for ruling elites. Among a largely illiterate People of the Book, to read was to lead. Therefore, at least for Judaea, Harris's approach to literacy, "focus[ing] narrowly on the question of what percentage of people in antiquity might have been able to read and write," was exactly right as the first question. And yet, for Judaea he offered no answer. In the foregoing pages, we have attempted to make good that oversight as far as possible. The limitations of the evidence are, of course, severe; the complexity of the social and linguistic patterns, daunting.[183]

On that November day long ago in En Gedi, the nine men gathered could have had no notion that what they wrote would so long endure. Nor could they have known that what they wrote would finally come to matter less, perhaps, than how they wrote it. Masabala b. Simon, fluidly staking with his cursive hand an insistent claim to Hebrew as quotidian norm; Tehinah, his brother, withholding his idiomatic Greek γράμματα so often found elsewhere, in deference (so it seems) to similar wartime sentiments; Joseph, the calligraphic scribe, not long hence to lie dead in a cave, memorialized for the ages by an Aramaic inscription placed tenderly on his chest; Eleazar b. Hita, scrawling his chicken-scratches, inelegant as a child's but still inscribed in the same tongue that Moses had used. Not far away, somewhere in the village, perhaps Babatha b. Simon limped home to await the return of her new man, Eleazer b. Samuel, a party who wrote nothing at all that day. They wrote then, and we read now. Ordinary moments for them, surely, but fossilized by unendurable tragedy. Of such is history.

Appendix A

Significant Documents of the Bar Kokhba Discoveries: Signatories and Writers

Signatories and Writers

Abbreviations are as follow: p, principal; w, witness; h, *hypographeus;* s, scribe; sub, subscriber; frag., too fragmentary to judge. For languages, (A), Judaean Aramaic; (H), Hebrew; (N), Nabataean Aramaic; (G), Greek; (L), Latin; (I), illiterate. For writing levels, 1, alphabetic hand; 2, unpracticed hand; 3, practiced hand; 4, scribal hand.

Date, designation, locale, character	Document language	Writers or signatories—role, language used, writing level
Middle to late first century B.C.E., 4Q345, unknown, deed	Aramaic	Hosea b. [PN]—p (I) Ishmael b. Simon—h/s (A) 3
Late first century B.C.E., 4Q346, unknown, deed of sale	Aramaic	[PN b. PN]—s (A) 4
55/56 C.E., *Mur* 18, Tsuba, I.O.U.	Aramaic	Zachariah b. Yohanan—p (I) Joseph b. [PN]—h/s (A) 4 Joseph b. Yohanan—w (A) 2 Yohanan b. [S]imon—w (A) 2
55–70 C.E., *Mur* 33, Jerusalem(?), loan bill	Aramaic	Simon b. Hanin—p (I) Cleopas b. E[utrapelus]—w (A) 2 [PN] b. [PN]—s/h (A) 4
58 C.E., *Mur* 23, unknown, bill of sale	Aramaic	[PN] b. [PN]—p(?) (A) 2 PN b. PN—p(?) (frag.) Yohanan b. [PN]—w (A) 2 [PN] b. [PN]—w (A) 3 [PN b. PN]—s (A) 4
58–67 C.E., *P.Yadin* 36, Mahoza, redemption of writ of seizure	Nabataean	Joseph b. Judah—w (A) 3 [PN b. PN]—s (N) 4
61–62 C.E., 4Q348, Jerusalem, deed	Hebrew	Eleazar b. Shabi—w (A) 3

continued

Date, designation, locale, character	Document language	Writers or signatories—role, language used, writing level
66–70 C.E., *Mur* 26 + *P.Hever* 50, Jerusalem(?), deed of sale	Aramaic	Eutrapelus son of Eu[trapelus]—p (G) 2 Sh[elam(zion?)] b. [ ]us—p (I) [PN] b. Sim[o]n—h (A) 3 [PN] b. [PN]—w (A) 2 (signed in A, annotated in H) [Eleazar?] b. MSHH—s (A) 4 [PN] b. [PN]—w (A) 1
66–70 C.E., *Mur* 27, Jerusalem(?), sale of property	Aramaic	[Haninah(?)] b. Haninah—p (A) 3 [PN] b. [PN]—w (A) 3 [PN b. PN]—s (A) 4
67 C.E., *Mur* 29, Jerusalem, deed of sale	Hebrew	Cleopas son of Eutrapelos—p (G) 3 Shapira b. Jesus—p (I) Simon b. Shabi—h (A!) 4 Simon b. Shabi—s/w (H/A!) 4 Joseph b. SGYHN—w (A) 2 Simon b. Zekariah—w (H) 2
69 C.E., *Mur* 30, Jerusalem, sale of property	Hebrew	Dositheus b. Eleazar—p (H) 3 Salome b. Honi—p (I) [John b. Joseph]—h (A!) 4 John b. Joseph—s/w (H) 4 Saul b. Jo[seph(?)]—w (H) 4 Dionytas b. [PN]—w (frag.) 3
69 C.E., *Mur* 22, unknown, sale of property	Hebrew	Joseph b. Adi—p (I) Sim[on b. Shabi?]—s/h (H/A!) 4 Sim[on? b. [PN]]—w (frag.) 3 [PN] b. [PN]—w (H) 3 [PN] b. [PN]—w (H) 4
71 C.E., *Mur* 19, Masada, bill of divorce	Aramaic	Joseph b. Nicus—p (A) 2 Eleazar b. Malka—w (A) 2 Joseph b. Malka—w (A) 2 Eleazar b. Hananah—w (A) 2 [PN b. PN]—s (A) 3
74 C.E.(?), Beth 'Amar, acknowledgment of payment of debt	Aramaic/ Hebrew	Miriam b. Jacob—p (I) Joseph b. Simon—w (A) 3 Judah b. Zechariah—w (A) 3 Joseph b. Jacob—h/s (A; H/A) 4

Date, designation, locale, character	Document language	Writers or signatories—role, language used, writing level
72–127 C.E., 4Q344, unknown, acknowledgment of debt	Aramaic	Eleazar b. Joseph—p/s (A) 4 [PN] b. Joseph—w (A) (frag.)
81–96 C.E., *P.Jericho* 9, unknown, deed of sale	Hebrew	[PN] b. [PN]—w (H) 4 Yohanan b. [PN]—w (H) 4 [PN b. PN]—s (H) 4
84 C.E., *P.Jericho* 7, unknown, sale of date crop	Aramaic	Joseph b. Yohanan—p (A) 1 Yohanan b. Simon—w (A) 4 Joseph b. [PN]—w (A) 4 [PN b. PN]—s (A) 4
94 C.E., *P.Yadin* 1, Mahoza, debenture	Nabataean	Muqimu—p (N) 3 Abadamanu—p (N) 3 Zaidu b. Shahru—w (N) 3 Taimu b. Huwaru—w (N) 4 [PN b. PN]—w (N) 3 Wanah b. Halafilahi—w (N) 3 Huwaru b. Awatu—s (N) 4
99 C.E., *P.Yadin* 2, Mahoza, sale of property	Nabataean	Abiadan—p (I) [PN] b. Zaidu—p/h (N) 2 [PN b. P]N—w (N) (frag.) [PN b. PN]—w (N) 4 P[N b. PN]—w (N) 3 [PN b.]ilahi—w (N) 4 Azur b. Awatu—s (N) 4
99 C.E., *P.Yadin* 3, Mahoza, sale of property	Nabataean	Abiadan—p (I) [PN] b. LTH—h (N) 3 Archelaus b. [PN]—w (N) 3 Wahabilahi b. Mushalimu—w (N) 3 Wahabdushara b. Shulay—w (N) 3 Zabadbaal b. Zabadion—w (N) 3 Azur b. Awatu—s (N) 4
99 C.E., *P.Yadin* 4, Mahoza, guarantor's agreement(?)	Nabataean	[PN b. PN]—p (I) [PN b. PN]—h (A) (frag.) [PN b. PN]—w (A) 2 [PN b. PN]—w (A) (frag.) [PN b. PN]—w (A) (frag.) [PN b.] Joseph—w (A) 2 Azur b. Awatu—s (N) 4

continued

Date, designation, locale, character	Document language	Writers or signatories—role, language used, writing level
First century C.E., *Mur* 21, unknown, marriage contract	Aramaic	Menahem b. [Mattat(?)]—p (I) [Lazar] b. Joseph—p/h/s (A) 2 [P]N b. [Lazar]—p (I) [PN] b. [PN]—h (A) 4 [PN] b. [M]attat—w (A) 1 [PN] b. Yohanan—w (A) 1 [PN] b. [La]zar(?)—w (A) 2
First century C.E., *P.Jericho* 8, unknown, deed	Aramaic	[PN b. PN]—s (A) 4
First century C.E., *P.Jericho* 10, unknown, deed of sale(?)	Hebrew	[PN b. PN]—s (H) 4
First century C.E., *P.Jericho* 11, unknown, deed of sale	Hebrew	[PN b. PN]—s (H) 4
First century C.E., *P.Jericho* 12, unknown, deed	Aramaic	[PN b. PN]—s (A) 4
First century C.E., *P.Jericho* 14, unknown, deed(?)	Hebrew	[PN b. PN]—s (H) 4
First or early second century C.E., *Mur* 31, unknown, deed of sale(?)	Aramaic	Simon b. [PN]—p (A) 3 [PN b. PN]—s (A) 4
First or early second century C.E., *Mur* 34, unknown, deed of sale(?)	Aramaic	[PN b. PN]—p/s (A) 2
First or early second century C.E., 1Mish 3, Mahoza, deed(?)	Aramaic	[PN b. PN]—p (A) 2 [PN] b. Dorymenes—w (A) 3 [PN] b. [PN]—w (A) 2 [PN b. PN]—s (A) (frag.)
First or early second century C.E., *P.Hever nab* 2, Mahoza, deed of sale	Nabataean	Salome—p (I) PN. b. PN—h/s (N) 4 [PN] b. [PN]—w (A) 3 Eleazar b. Judah—w (A) 3
First or early second century C.E., *P.Hever* 9, Yaqim, deed of sale	Aramaic	Jacob b. Simon b. Diqnah—p/s (A) 3 [PN] b. [PN]—w (A) 1 [PN] b. [PN]—w (A?) 1 [PN] b. Joseph—w (A) 2 Simon b. [PN]—w (A) 1

Date, designation, locale, character	Document language	Writers or signatories—role, language used, writing level
First or early second century C.E., *P.Hever* 9a, Yaqim, deed(?)	Aramaic	[PN] b. [PN]—w (A) 1 Jacob b. Simon b. Diqnah—p/s (A) 3 (with several other hands)
First or early second century C.E., *P.Hever* 11, unknown, marriage contract(?)	Aramaic	[PN] b. [PN]—p (A?) (frag.) [PN b. PN]—s (A) 4
First or early second century C.E., *P.Hever* 21, unknown, deed of sale	Aramaic	[PN] b. [PN]—w (A) 3 [PN] b. Yohanan—w (A) 3 [PN b. PN]—s (A) 4
First or early second century C.E., *P.Hever* 22, Kephar-Baru, deed of sale	Aramaic	[Simon b. PN]—p (frag.) [Eleazar b.] Eleazar—p (A? frag.) 3 [PN] b. Eleazar—w (A) 1 Yohanan b. Joseph—w (A) 3 [Judah b.] Judah—w (A) 3 Sim[on] b. Joseph—w (A) 3 [PN b. PN]—s (A) 4
First or early second century C.E., *P.Hever* 23, unknown, deed of sale	Aramaic	[PN b. PN]—s (A) 4
First or early second century C.E., *P.Hever* 24, unknown, marriage contract(?)	Aramaic	Simon b. [PN]—w (A) 2 Joseph b. [PN]—w (A?) 1 [PN b. PN]—s (A) 4
First or early second century C.E., *P.Hever* 24a, unknown, deed of sale	Aramaic	[PN b. PN]—s (A) 4
First or early second century C.E., *P.Hever* 25, unknown, deed of sale	Aramaic	[PN] b. [PN]—w (A) 3 [PN] b. [PN]—w (A) 3 [PN] b. [PN]—w (A) 2 [PN b. PN]—s (A) 4
First or early second century C.E., *P.Hever* 32 + 4Q347, unknown, deed	Aramaic	[PN b. PN]—s (A) 4
First or early second century C.E., 34Se 3, unknown, deed	Aramaic	[PN b. PN]—s (A) 4
First or early second century C.E., *Mur* 25, unknown, deed of sale	Aramaic	[PN] b. Yohanan(?) —p (A) (frag.) [PN] b. [PN]—w (A) (frag.) [PN] b. [PN]—w (A) (frag.) [PN b. PN]—s (A) 4

continued

Date, designation, locale, character	Document language	Writers or signatories—role, language used, writing level
First or early second century C.E., *Mur* 37, unknown, deed of sale(?)	Hebrew	Sim[on b. PN]—p 2 (frag.) P[N b. PN]—p 2 (frag.) [PN b. PN]—s (H) 4
First or early second century C.E., *Mur* 38, unknown, deed of sale(?)	Aramaic(?)	[PN] b. Eleazar—p (A) 1 Matthew b. Rabbah—w (A) 1 Hananiah b. [PN]—w (A?) 1 Yohanan b. [PN]—w (A?) 1 Marion b [PN]—w (A?) 1 Jesus b. [PN]—w (A) 1
First or early second century C.E., *Mur* 36, unknown, deed of sale(?)	Hebrew	[PN] b. Jesus—p (A) 2 [PN] b. Jesus—p (A) 2 [Sa]ul b. [PN]—w (A) 3 [PN b. PN]—s (H) 4
First or early second century C.E., *Mur* 39, unknown, deed(?)	Hebrew(?)	Simon b. Menahem—w (A) 3 Dositheus b. Jacob—w (H) 2
First or early second century C.E., *Mur* 40, unknown, deed(?)	Hebrew(?)	Simon b. Menahem—w (A) 3 [Dositheus] b. Jacob—w (H) 2
First or early second century C.E., *Mur* 113, unknown, summons and reply(?)	Greek	[PN b. PN]—s (G) 4
First or early second century C.E., *Mur* 116, unknown, marriage contract	Greek	[PN b. PN]—s (G) 4
First or early second century C.E., *P.Jericho* 2, unknown, deed of sale	Aramaic	[PN b. PN]—w (A) 2 [PN b. PN]—w (A) 1 Mahanaim b. [PN]—w (A) 3 [PN b. PN]—w (A) 2 [PN b. PN]—s (A) 4
First or early second century C.E., *P.Jericho* 3, unknown, deed of sale	Aramaic	[PN] b. Shimon—p/w(?) (A) 4 [PN b. PN]—p/w(?) (A?) 4 [PN] b. Honiyah—p/w(?) (A) 4 [PN b. PN]—s (A) 4
First or early second century C.E., *P.Jericho* 4, unknown, deed of sale	Greek	[PN b. PN]—s (G) 4
First or early second century C.E., *P.Jericho* 19b, unknown, deed(?)	Greek	[PN] son of [PN]—w (G) (frag.) Judas son of [PN]—w (G) (frag.) [PN] son of [PN]—w (G) (frag.) [PN b. PN]—s (G) 4

Date, designation, locale, character	Document language	Writers or signatories—role, language used, writing level
First or early second century C.E., *Mur* 28, HRMNH, sale of property(?)	Aramaic	[Titus] b. [PN]—p (A) 4 [Sim]on b. Phineas—p (A) 2 [PN b. PN]—s (A) 4
110 C.E., *P.Yadin* 5, Mahoza, deposit	Greek (copy of an Aramaic original)	Language of individual signatories uncertain: some G, some A (no published photograph) Honi b. Simon—p Joseph b. Yohanan—w Eleazar b. Judah—w Simon b. Manun—w Simon b. [PN]—w Judah b. Corainnus—w Tehina b. Tamman—s (A)
110 C.E.(?) , *P.Yadin* 31, Mahoza, contract(?)	Greek	[PN] b. Simon—w (A) 2 [PN] b. [PN]—w (A) 3 [PN b. PN]—w (A) 1 [PN b. PN]—sub (A) 1 [PN b. PN]—s (G) 4
115 C.E., *Mur* 114, Jerusalem, loan on hypothec	Greek	[PN b. PN]—s (G) 4
116 C.E., *P.Jericho* 13, unknown, deed(?)	Aramaic	[PN b. PN]—s (A) 4
117 C.E.(?), *Mur* 20, Harodona, marriage contract	Aramaic	Judah b. P[N] b. Menaseh—p (A) 2 [PN b. PN]—s (A) 4
119 C.E., *P.Yadin* 6, Mahoza, tenancy agreement	Nabataean	Joseph b. Hananiah—w (A) 1 Eleazer b. Halatiah—w (A) 1 Yohana b. Makhuta—s (N) 4
120 C.E., *P.Yadin* 7, Mahoza, deed of gift	Aramaic	[Simon] b. Menahem—p (A) 3 [PN b. PN]—w (A) (frag.) [PN] b. Menahem—w (A) 3 [PN b. PN]—w (A) 2 [PN b. PN]—w (A) (frag.) [PN b. PN]—w (N) 4 [PN] b. Simon—s (A) 4
122 C.E., *P.Yadin* 8, Mahoza, purchase contract	Aramaic	Bar Simon—p (A) 2 John b. Ishmael—sub (A) 3 Eleazar b. Simon—w (A) 2 Eleazer b. Halatiah—w (A) 1 [PN] son of [PN]—w (G) 2 Yohanan b. Makhuta—s (A) 4

continued

Date, designation, locale, character	Document language	Writers or signatories—role, language used, writing level
122 C.E., *P.Yadin* 9, Mahoza, waiver(?)	Nabataean	Joseph b. [PN]—p (A) 2 [PN] b. [PN]—w (A) 2 Judah b. Simon—w (A) 1 [PN] b. [PN]—sub (N) 4 Yohana b. Makhuta—w/s (N) 4
122–125 C.E., *P.Yadin* 10, Mahoza, marriage contract	Aramaic	Judah b. Eleazar—p/s (A) 3 Babatha b. Simon—p (I) Eleazar b. Eleazar—h (A) 3 Toma b. Simon—w (A) 3 [PN] b. Yohanan—w (A) 2 [PN] b. [PN]—w (A) (frag.)
124 C.E., *P.Yadin* 11, En Gedi, loan on hypothec	Greek (copy of Greek original)	Gaius Julius Procles—p (G) 2 Kallaios son of John—w (G) 3 Onesimos son of Jannaeus—w (G) 3 John son of [PN]—w (G) 3 Joseph son of Saeas—w (G) 3 Simon son of Simon—w (G) 3 Theodorus son of Matthew—(G) 2 Judah b. Eleazar—sub (A) 3 Justinus—s (G) 4
124 C.E., *P.Yadin* 12, Petra, extract from council minutes	Greek (translated from Latin original)	Nubi b. Walat—w (N) 4 Walu b. [PN]—w (N) 4 Abdobdat b. Shuheiru—w (N) 4 [PN] b. Abdisay—w (N) 4 Abderetas son of Soumaios—w (G) 4 [PN b. PN]—s (G) 4
124 C.E., *P.Yadin* 13, Mahoza(?), petition to the governor	Greek (copy of Greek original)	[PN b. PN]—s (G) 4
124 C.E., *Mur* 115, Bethbassi of Herodium, remarriage contract	Greek	P[N] son of [PN]—w (G) 3 P[N] son of [PN]—w (G) 3 Amra[m] son of [PN]—w (G) 3 [PN b. PN]—s (G) 4
125 C.E., *P.Hever* 60, Mahoza, tax or rent receipt	Greek	Reisha—sub (A) 2 [PN b. PN]—s (G) 4

Date, designation, locale, character	Document language	Writers or signatories—role, language used, writing level
125 C.E., *P.Yadin* 14, Mahoza, summons	Greek	Yohana b. Makhuta—w (N) 4 Shamoa b. Menahem—w (A) 3 Thaddaius son of Thaddaius—w (G) 3 Joseph b. Hananiah—w (A) 1 Tehinah son of Simon—s (G) 4
125 C.E., *P.Yadin* 15, Mahoza, deposition	Greek	Babatha b. Simon—p (I) Eleazar the son of Eleazar—h (G) 3 Judah b. Eleazar—h/sub (A) 3 Yohana b. Makhuta—sub (N) 4 Bar Egla (Alex?)—sub (A) 1 Joseph b. Bar Egla—h/sub (A) 3 [PN b. PN]—w (A) 3 Thaddaius son of Thaddaius—w (G) 3 Joseph b. Hananiah—w (A) 1 Toma b. Simon—w (A) 3 Jesus b. Jesus—w (A) 1 Tehinah son of Simon—s (G) 4
125 C.E., *P.Yadin* 28–29, unknown, judiciary rule	Greek (translated from Latin)	[PN b. PN]—s (G) 4 (*P.Yadin* 28–30 = three copies of Latin *Vorlage*, copied by two scribes)
125 C.E., *P.Yadin* 30, unknown, judiciary rule	Greek (translated from Latin)	[PN b. PN]—s (G) 4
125 C.E., *P.Yadin* 33, unknown, petition	Greek (copy of Greek original)	[PN b. PN]—s (G) 4
125–128 C.E., *P.Yadin* 32, Mahoza, contract(?)	Greek	[Tehinah son of Simon]—s (G) 4
125–128 C.E., *P.Yadin* 32a, Mahoza, contract(?)	Greek	[PN b. PN]—s (G) 4
127 C.E., *P.Hever* 61, Rabbat-Moab, declaration of land	Greek (copy of Greek original)	[PN] son of Levi—p/sub (I) Hunainu son of Saadilahi—h (G) [PN b. PN]—s (G) 4

continued

Date, designation, locale, character	Document language	Writers or signatories—role, language used, writing level
127 C.E., *P.Hever* 62, Rabbat-Moab, declaration of land	Greek (copy of Greek original)	Wahabilahi b. Abdilahi—w (N) 4 [PN] b. Awatu—w (N) 4 Eutychus son of Abdobu—w (G) 3 [PN] b. [PN]—w (N) (frag.) [PN] b. [PN]—w (A) 2 [PN b. PN]—s (G) 4
127 C.E., *P.Hever* 63, Mahoza, renunciation of claims	Greek	[PN b. PN]—s (G) 4
127 C.E., *P.Yadin* 16, Rabbat-Moab, registration of land	Greek (copy of Greek original)	Babatha b. Simon—p/sub (I) Judah b. Eleazar—h/sub (A) 3 Priscus—sub (L) Abdu b. Muqimu—w (N) 4 Mantanta b. Amru—w (N) 4 Awdel b. [PN]—w (N) 4 Yohana b. Abdobdat Makhuta—w (N) 4 Shaharu b. Mugdayu—w (N) 4 [PN b. PN]—s (G) 4
128 C.E., *P.Yadin* 17, Mahoza, deposit	Greek	Judah [b. Eleazar]—p (A) 3 [Jacob] b. Jesus—w (A) (frag.) Eleazar b. Eleazar—w (A) 3 Toma b. Simon—w (A) 3 [PN] b. Judah—w (A) 2 Joseph b. Hananiah—w (A) 1 Eleazar b. [PN]—w (A) 1 Judah b. Eleazar—sub (A) 3 Tehinah son of Simon—s (G) 4
128 C.E., *P.Yadin* 18, Mahoza, marriage contract	Greek	Judah b. Eleazar—p (A) 3 Judah Cimber—p (I) [PN] son of [PN]—h (A) 1 sub (G) 3 Simon b. Hananiah(?)—w (A) 1 Eleazer b. Halatiah—w (A) 1 Joseph b. Hananiah—w (A) 1 Wanah b. Ishmael—w (N) 1 Judah b. Eleazar—sub (A) 3 Tehinah son of Simon—s (G) 4

Date, designation, locale, character	Document language	Writers or signatories—role, language used, writing level
128 C.E., *P.Yadin* 19, Mahoza, deed of gift	Greek	Eleazer b. Halatiah—w (A) 1 Corainnus b. Jesus—w (A) 1 Jesus b. John—w (A) 2 Soumaios son of PN—w (G) 3 [PN] b. [PN]—w (A) (frag.) Judah b. Judah—w (A) 3 Eleazar(?) b. Joseph—w (A) 2 Judah b. Eleazar—sub (A) 3 [PN b. PN]—s (G) 4
129 C.E., *P.Hever* 64, Mahoza, deed of gift	Greek	[Salome b. Menahem]—p (I) Joseph [b. Simon]—h (A) (frag.) Reisha b. Judah—w (A) 2 Malik b. [PN]—w (N) 4 Jesus b. Yohanan—w (A) 1 Timadushra b. Abdharetat—w (N) 4 Joseph b. Shulai—w (A) 3 Joseph b. Hananiah—w (A) 1 [PN b. PN]—s (G) 4
130 C.E., *P.Yadin* 20, Mahoza, concession of rights	Greek	Joseph b. Menahem—w (A) 3 Jesus b. Yohanan—w (A) 1 Mattiyah b. Yehohanan—w (A) 3 Thaddaius son of Thaddaius—w (G) 3 Shabi b. Taymilahi—w (N) 3 Yohana b. Makhuta—w (N) 4 Besai b. Jesus—sub (A) 3 Julia Crispina—sub (G) 3 Germanus son of Judah—s (G) 4
130 C.E., *P.Yadin* 21, Mahoza, purchase of a date crop	Greek	[One to three names missing] Jesus b. Jesus—w (A) 3 [PN] b. Jesus—w (A) 1 Joseph b. Hananiah—w (A) 1 Yohanan b. Menahem—w (A) 1 Simon b. Jesus—sub (A) 2 Shamoa b. Menahem—sub (A) 3 Germanus son of Judah—s (G) 4 Shamoa b. Menahem: filing note on verso (A) 3

continued

Date, designation, locale, character	Document language	Writers or signatories—role, language used, writing level
130 C.E., *P.Yadin* 22, Mahoza, sale of a date crop	Greek	Babatha b. Simon—p/sub (I) Yohana b. Makhuta—h/sub (N) 4 Joseph b. Menahem—w (A) 3 Judah b. Simon—w (A) 3 Jesus b. Jesus—w (A) 3 Joseph b. Hananiah—w (A) 1 Germanus son of Judah—s (G) 4
130 C.E., *P.Yadin* 23, Mahoza, summons	Greek	Eleazar b. Simon—w (A) 3 Joseph b. Mattat—w (A) 4 Eleazar b. Mattat—w (A) 4 Thaddaius son of Thaddaius—w (G) 3 Eleazar b. [PN]—w (A) 1 Germanus son of Judah—s (G) 4
130 C.E., *P.Yadin* 24, Mahoza, deposition	Greek	Germanus son of Judah—s (G) 4
130 C.E., *P.Hever* 69, Aristoboulias, marriage contract (canceled)	Greek	Joseph son of PN—w (G) 3 Soulaios son of Eleazar—w (G) 3 Maro—w (G) 3 [PN b. PN]—s (G) 4
131 C.E., *P.Yadin* 25, Mahoza, summons and countersummons	Greek	[PN] b. [PN]—w (A) (frag.) [PN] b. [PN]—w (A) (frag.) [PN] b. [PN]—w (A) (frag.) Germanus son of Judah—s (G) 4
131 C.E., *P.Yadin* 26, Mahoza, summons and reply	Greek	Eleazar b. Halatiah—w (A) 1 Mattat b. Simon—w (A) 4 Joseph b. Mattat—w (A) 4 Judah b. Judah—w (A) 3 Eleazar b. Mattat—w (A) 4 Germanus son of Judah—s (G) 4
131 C.E., *P.Yadin* 34, Mahoza, petition	Greek (copy of Greek original)	[PN] b. Taymilahi—w (N) 3 Germanus son of Judah—s (G) 4
131 C.E., *P.Hever* 65, Mahoza, marriage contract	Greek	[PN b. PN]—s (G) 4
131 C.E., *P.Hever* 12, Mahoza, receipt for dates	Aramaic	[PN b.] P[N]—s (A) 3

Date, designation, locale, character	Document language	Writers or signatories—role, language used, writing level
132 C.E., *P.Yadin* 27, Mahoza, receipt	Greek	Babatha b. Simon—p/sub (I) Babeli b. Menahem—h/sub (A) 3 Eli b. [PN]—w (A) 3 Germanus son of Judah—s (G) 4
132 C.E., *P.Yadin* 35, Mahoza, summons(?)	Greek	[PN] b. [PN]—w (A) (no published photograph)
132 C.E., *P.Yadin* 42, En Gedi, lease agreement	Aramaic	Yohanan b. Jesus Marion—sub (A) 2 Horon b. Ishmael—sub (A) 2 Masabala b. Simon—s (A) 4
132 C.E., *P.Yadin* 43, En Gedi, receipt	Aramaic	Horon b. Ishmael—sub (A) 2 Yohanan b. Jesus Marion—sub (A) (frag.) Masabala b. Simon—s (A) 4
132–135 C.E., *P.Hever* 10, unknown, receipt for payment of fine(?)	Aramaic	Bar Shulai—s/sub (A) 3
132–135 C.E., *Mur* 42, Beth-Mashiko, letter of affidavit	Hebrew	Jesus b. Eleazar—sub (A/H) 2 Eleazar b. Joseph—sub (A/H) 1 Jacob b. Judah—p (A/H) 3 Saul b. Eleazar—w (H) 2 Joseph b. Joseph—w (A/H) 1 Jacob b. Joseph—s/w (H) 4
132–135 C.E., *Mur* 43, unknown, letter	Hebrew	Simon b. Kosiba—sub (frag.) 2 [PN b. PN]—s (H) 4
132–135 C.E., *Mur* 44, unknown, letter	Hebrew	[PN b. PN]—s (H) 4
132–135 C.E., *Mur* 45, unknown, letter	Hebrew	[PN b. PN]—s (H) 4 (same scribe as *Mur* 44?)
132–135 C.E., *Mur* 46, En Gedi, letter	Hebrew	John b. Mahanaim—sub (A) 3 [PN b. PN]—s (H) 4
132–135 C.E., *Mur* 47, unknown, letter	Hebrew	[PN b. PN]—s (H) 4
132–135 C.E., *Mur* 48, Herodium, letter	Hebrew	Jose b. Galgula(?)—sub (A) 3 [PN b. PN]—s (H) 4
132–135 C.E., *Mur* 49, unknown, letter	Hebrew	[PN b. PN]—s (H) 4

continued

Date, designation, locale, character	Document language	Writers or signatories—role, language used, writing level
132–135 C.E., *Mur* 51, unknown, letter	Hebrew	[PN b. PN]—s (H) 4
132–135 C.E., *Mur* 52, unknown, letter	Hebrew	[PN b. PN]—s (H) 4
132–135 C.E., *Mur* 61, unknown, letter(?)	Hebrew	[PN b. PN]—s (H) 4
132–135 C.E., *Mur* 174, Herodium(?), I.O.U.	Hebrew	[PN b. PN]—s (H) 4
132–135 C.E., *Mur* 7, Herodium(?), contract	Hebrew	[PN b. PN]—s (H) 4 (same scribe as *Mur* 174)
132–135 C.E., *Mur* 8, unknown, account	Aramaic	Signatory for Bene PSN—p (A) 2 Signatory for Jesus—p (A?) 1 Lentil—p (A) 1 Jesus b. Harqaq—p (A) 2 Signatory for Yasuq b. Manoah and Bazuz b. [PN]—p (A) 2
132–135 C.E., *P.Hever* 30, Kephar-Baru(?), letter	Hebrew	Simon b. Mattaniah—sub (H) 3 [PN b. PN]—s (H) 4
132–135 C.E., *P.Yadin* 49, unknown, letter	Hebrew	[PN b. PN]—s (H) 3
132–135 C.E., *P.Yadin* 50, unknown, letter	Aramaic	Simon b. Judah—sub (A) 2 [PN b. PN]—s (A) 3
132–135 C.E., *P.Yadin* 51, unknown, letter	Hebrew	[PN b. PN]—s (H) 3
132–135 C.E., *P.Yadin* 52, unknown, letter	Greek	Soumaios—sub (G) 2 [PN b. PN]—s (G) 4
132–135 C.E., *P.Yadin* 53, unknown, letter	Aramaic	[PN b. PN]—s/sub (A) 3
132–135 C.E., *P.Yadin* 54, unknown, letter	Aramaic	Samuel b. Ammi—s/sub (A) 3
132–135 C.E., *P.Yadin* 55, unknown, letter	Aramaic	[PN b. PN]—s (A) 3
132–135 C.E., *P.Yadin* 56, unknown, letter	Aramaic	[PN b. PN]—s/sub (A) 3
132–135 C.E., *P.Yadin* 57, unknown, letter	Aramaic	[PN b. PN]—s/sub (A) 3

Date, designation, locale, character	Document language	Writers or signatories—role, language used, writing level
132–135 C.E., *P.Yadin* 58, unknown, letter	Aramaic	[PN b. PN]—s/sub (A) 3
132–135 C.E., *P.Yadin* 59, unknown, letter	Greek	Hanan [b. Bayah?]—s (G) 4
132–135 C.E., *P.Yadin* 60, unknown, letter	Hebrew	[PN b. PN]—s (H) 3
132–135 C.E., *P.Yadin* 61, unknown, letter	Hebrew	[PN b. PN]—s (H) 3
132–135 C.E., *P.Yadin* 62, unknown, letter	Aramaic	[PN b. PN]—s (A) 3
132–135 C.E., *P.Yadin* 63, unknown, letter	Aramaic	Simon b. Ishmael—s (A) 3
133 C.E., *P.Hever* 49, En Gedi, promissory note	Hebrew	Joseph b. Hananiah—p (H) 1 Menahem b. [PN]—w (H) 3 Jesus b. Judah—w (A) 3 Judah b. Joseph—w (H) 4 Masabala b. Simon—s (H) 4
134 C.E., *P.Yadin* 44, En Gedi, lease of land	Hebrew	Eleazar b. Eleazar—p (H) 1 Eleazar b. Samuel—p (I) Masabala b. Simon—h (H) 4 Tehinah b. Simon—p (does not sign) Sifon b. Simon—h (H) 4 Elem b. Judah—p (I) Joseph b. Simon—s/h (H) 4 Judah b. Joseph—w (H) 4 Eleazar b. Judah—w (A) 1 Simon b. Joseph—w (A/H) 4
134 C.E., *P.Yadin* 45, En Gedi, lease of land	Hebrew	Eleazar b. Eleazar—p (H) 1 Masabala b. Simon—w (H) 4 Judah b. Joseph—w (H) 4 Sifon b. Simon—w (H) 4 Joseph b. Simon—s (H) 4
134 C.E., *P.Yadin* 46, En Gedi, lease of land	Hebrew	Jesus b. Simon—p (H/A) 3 [PN] b. Simon—w (H) 3 Petrus b. Joseph—w (H) 2 Joseph b. Eleazar—w (A/H) 2 Joseph b. Simon—s (H) 4

continued

Date, designation, locale, character	Document language	Writers or signatories—role, language used, writing level
134 C.E., *P.Yadin* 47 and 47b, En Gedi, sale contract	Aramaic	Two scribes: PN b. PN—s (A; 47) 4 Mattat b. Simon—s (A; 47b) 4
134 C.E., *Mur* 24, Herodium, lease of land	Hebrew (register of original Aramaic [?] leases)	Hillel b. Garis—p (no signature extant) Eleazar the Shilonite—p (I) Halifa b. Joseph—p (I) [PN] b. John—p (I) (language of *hypographeis* unknown) [PN b. PN]—s (H) 4
134–135 C.E., *P.Hever* 7, En Gedi(?), deed of sale	Aramaic	Mattat b. Simon—s (A) 4
135 C.E., *P.Hever* 8, Kephar-Baru, deed of sale	Aramaic (Upper) and Hebrew (Lower)	John b. Eli—p/s (A/H) 3
134–135 C.E., *P.Hever* 8a, Kephar-Baru, deed of sale	Aramaic	Salome b. Simon—p (I) Eleazar b. Mattatah—h (A) 3 Hadad b. Judah—p (A) 3 Simon b. Joseph—w (A/H) 3 Eleazar b. Simon—w (A) 3 Judah b. Judah—w (A) 3 John b. Eli—s (A) 3
134–135 C.E., *P.Hever* 13, En Gedi, waiver of claims	Aramaic	Shelamzion b. Joseph—p (I) Mattat b. Simon—s/h (A) 4 [PN] b. Simon—w (H) 2 Masabala b. Simon—w (H) 4
134–135 C.E., *P.Hever* 14, En Gedi, deed(?)	Aramaic	[PN b. PN]—p (I) [PN b. Sim]on—h (A) 3 Mattat b. Simon—s 4
134–135 C.E., 4Q359, En Gedi(?), deed	Aramaic(?)	[PN b. PN]—s (frag.) 3
134–135 C.E., *P.Hever* 26, Kephar-Baru, deed of deposit	Aramaic	Je[su]s [b. PN]—p (I) [John b. Eli]—h/s (A) 3 [PN] b. [PN]—w (A) 3
135 C.E., Sdeir 2, unknown, promissory note	Aramaic	Saul b. Rabba—p (I) [PN] b. Hezekiah—h/s (A) 3 Judah b. Ishmael—w (A) 2 Joseph b. [PN]—w (A) 3

Appendix B
Signatories and Writers Listed by Name

Abbreviations are as follow: p, principal; w, witness; h, *hypographeus;* s, scribe; sub, subscriber; frag., too fragmentary to judge. For languages, (A), Judaean Aramaic; (H), Hebrew; (N), Nabataean Aramaic; (G), Greek; (L), Latin; (I), illiterate. For writing levels, 1, alphabetic hand; 2, unpracticed hand; 3, practiced hand; 4, scribal hand.

Number	Name	Role, language used, level	Language of text	Designation of text	Remarks
1	Abadamanu	p (N) 3	Nabataean	*P.Yadin* 1	
2	Abderetas son of Soumaios	w (G) 4	Greek	*P.Yadin* 12	
3	Abdobdat b. Shuheiru	w (N) 4	Greek	*P.Yadin* 12	
4	Abdu b. Muqimu	w (N) 4	Greek	*P.Yadin* 16	
5	Abiadan	p (I)	Nabataean	*P.Yadin* 2	
		p (I)	Nabataean	*P.Yadin* 3	
6	Amra[m] son of [PN]	w (G) 3	Greek	*Mur* 115	
7	Archelaus b. [PN]	w (N) 3	Nabataean	*P.Yadin* 3	
8	Awdel b. [PN]	w (N) 4	Greek	*P.Yadin* 16	
9	Azur b. Awatu	s (N) 4	Nabataean	*P.Yadin* 2	
		s (N) 4	Nabataean	*P.Yadin* 3	
		s (N) 4	Nabataean	*P.Yadin* 4	
10	Babatha b. Simon	p (I)	Aramaic	*P.Yadin* 10	
		p (I)	Greek	*P.Yadin* 15	
		p/sub (I)	Greek	*P.Yadin* 16	
		p/sub (I)	Greek	*P.Yadin* 22	
		p/sub (I)	Greek	*P.Yadin* 27	

continued

Number	Name	Role, language used, level	Language of text	Designation of text	Remarks
11	Babeli b. Menahem	h/sub (A) 3	Greek	*P.Yadin* 27	
12	Bar Egla (Alex?)	sub (A) 1	Greek	*P.Yadin* 15	
13	Bar Shulai	s/sub (A) 3	Aramaic	*P.Hever* 10	
14	Bar Simon	p (A) 2	Aramaic	*P.Yadin* 8	
15	Besai b. Jesus	sub (A) 3	Greek	*P.Yadin* 20	
16	Cleopas b. E[utrapelus]	w (A) 2	Aramaic	*Mur* 33	
	Cleopas son of Eutrapelus	p (G) 3	Hebrew	*Mur* 29	
17	Corainnus b. Jesus	w (A) 1	Greek	*P.Yadin* 19	
18	Dionytas b. [PN]	w (frag.) 3	Hebrew	*Mur* 30	
19	Dositheus b. Eleazar	p (H) 3	Hebrew	*Mur* 30	
20	Dositheus b. Jacob	w (H) 2	Hebrew(?)	*Mur* 39	
	[Dositheus] b. Jacob	w (H) 2	Hebrew(?)	*Mur* 40	
21	Eleazar b. Eleazar	h (A) 3	Aramaic	*P.Yadin* 10	
	[Eleazar b.] Eleazar	p (frag.) 3	Aramaic	*P.Hever* 22	
	Eleazar son of Eleazar	h (G) 3	Greek	*P.Yadin* 15	
22	Eleazar b. Eleazar	w (A) 3	Greek	*P.Yadin* 17	
23	Eleazar b. Eleazar	p (H) 1	Hebrew	*P.Yadin* 44	
		p (H) 1	Hebrew	*P.Yadin* 45	
24	Eleazar b. Halatiah	w (A) 1	Nabataean	*P.Yadin* 6	
		w (A) 1	Aramaic	*P.Yadin* 8	
		w (A) 1	Greek	*P.Yadin* 18	
		w (A) 1	Greek	*P.Yadin* 19	
		w (A) 1	Greek	*P.Yadin* 26	
25	Eleazar b. Hananah	w (A) 2	Aramaic	*Mur* 19	
26	Eleazar b. Joseph	p/s (A) 4	Aramaic	4Q344	

Number	Name	Role, language used, level	Language of text	Designation of text	Remarks
27	Eleazar(?) b. Joseph	w (A) 2	Greek	*P.Yadin* 19	
28	Eleazar b. Joseph	sub (A/H) 1	Hebrew	*Mur* 42	
29	Eleazar b. Judah	w (A) 3	Nabataean	*P.Hever nab* 2	
30	Eleazar b. Judah	w (A) 1	Hebrew	*P.Yadin* 44	
31	Eleazar b. Malka	w (A) 2	Aramaic	*Mur* 19	
32	Eleazar b. Mattat	w (A) 4	Greek	*P.Yadin* 23	
		w (A) 4	Greek	*P.Yadin* 26	
33	Eleazar b. Mattatah	h (A) 3	Aramaic	*P.Hever* 8a	
34	[Eleazar?] b. MSHH	s (A) 4	Aramaic	*Mur* 26 + *P.Hever* 50	
35	Eleazar b. [PN]	w (A) 1	Greek	*P.Yadin* 17	
36	Eleazar b. [PN]	w (A) 1	Greek	*P.Yadin* 23	
37	Eleazar b. Samuel	p (I)	Hebrew	*P.Yadin* 44	
38	Eleazar b. Shabi	w (A) 3	Hebrew	4Q348	
39	Eleazar b. Simon	w (A) 2	Aramaic	*P.Yadin* 8	
		w (A) 3	Aramaic	*P.Hever* 8a	
		w (A) 3	Greek	*P.Yadin* 23	
40	Eleazar the Shilonite	p (I)	Hebrew	*Mur* 24	
41	Elem b. Judah	p (I)	Hebrew	*P.Yadin* 44	
42	Eli b. [PN]	w (A) 3	Greek	*P.Yadin* 27	
43	Eutrapelus son of Eu[trapelus]	p (G) 2	Aramaic	*Mur* 26 + *P.Hever* 50	
44	Eutychus son of Abdobu	w (G) 3	Greek	*P.Hever* 62	
45	Gaius Julius Procles	p (G) 2	Greek	*P.Yadin* 11	Roman

continued

Number	Name	Role, language used, level	Language of text	Designation of text	Remarks
46	Germanus son of Judah	s (G) 4	Greek	*P.Yadin* 20	
		s (G) 4	Greek	*P.Yadin* 21	
		s (G) 4	Greek	*P.Yadin* 22	
		s (G) 4	Greek	*P.Yadin* 23	
		s (G) 4	Greek	*P.Yadin* 24	
		s (G) 4	Greek	*P.Yadin* 25	
		s (G) 4	Greek	*P.Yadin* 26	
		s (G) 4	Greek	*P.Yadin* 34	
		s (G) 4	Greek	*P.Yadin* 27	
47	Hadad b. Judah	p (A) 3	Aramaic	*P.Hever* 8a	
48	Halifa b. Joseph	p (I)	Hebrew	*Mur* 24	
49	Hanan b. Bayah	p/s (G) 4	Greek	*P.Yadin* 59	
50	Hananiah b. [PN]	w (A?) 1	Aramaic(?)	*Mur* 38	
51	[Haninah(?)] b. Haninah	p (A) 3	Aramaic	*Mur* 27	
52	Hillel b. Garis	p	Hebrew	*Mur* 24	No signature extant
53	Horon b. Ishmael	sub (A) 2	Aramaic	*P.Yadin* 42	
		sub (A) 2	Aramaic	*P.Yadin* 43	
54	Hosea b. [PN]	p (I)	Aramaic	4Q345	
55	Hunainu son of Saadilahi	h (G)	Greek	*P.Hever* 61	
56	Huwaru b. Awatu	s (N) 4	Nabataean	*P.Yadin* 1	
57	Ishmael b. Simon	h/s (A) 3	Aramaic	4Q345	
58	[Jacob] b. Jesus	w (A) (frag.)	Greek	*P.Yadin* 17	
59	Jacob b. Joseph	s/w (H) 4	Hebrew	*Mur* 42	
60	Jacob b. Judah	p (A/H) 3	Hebrew	*Mur* 42	
61	Jacob b. Simon b. Diqnah	p/s (A) 3	Aramaic	*P.Hever* 9	
		p/s (A) 3	Aramaic	*P.Hever* 9a	With several other hands

Number	Name	Role, language used, level	Language of text	Designation of text	Remarks
62	Jesus b. Eleazar	sub (A/H) 2	Hebrew	*Mur* 42	
63	Jesus b. Galgula(?)	sub (A) 3	Hebrew	*Mur* 48	
64	Jesus b. Harqaq	p (A) 2	Aramaic	*Mur* 8	
65	Jesus b. Jesus	w (A) 1	Greek	*P.Yadin* 15	
66	Jesus b. Jesus	w (A) 3	Greek	*P.Yadin* 21	
		w (A) 3	Greek	*P.Yadin* 22	
67	Jesus b. John	w (A) 2	Greek	*P.Yadin* 19	
68	Jesus b. Judah	w (A) 3	Hebrew	*P.Hever* 49	
69	Jesus b. [PN]	w (A) 1	Aramaic(?)	*Mur* 38	
70	Je[su]s [b. PN]	p (I)	Aramaic	*P.Hever* 26	
71	Jesus b. Simon	p (H/A) 3	Hebrew	*P.Yadin* 46	
72	Jesus b. Yohanan	w (A) 1	Greek	*P.Hever* 64	
		w (A) 1	Greek	*P.Yadin* 20	
73	John b. Eli	p/s (A/H) 3	Aramaic	*P.Hever* 8	Aramaic upper and Hebrew lower
		s (A) 3	Aramaic	*P.Hever* 8a	
	[John b. Eli]	h/s (A) 3	Aramaic	*P.Hever* 26	
74	John b. Ishmael	sub (A) 3	Aramaic	*P.Yadin* 8	
75	John b. Joseph	s/w (H) 4	Hebrew	*Mur* 30	
	[John b. Joseph]	h (A!) 4	Hebrew	*Mur* 30	
76	John b. Mahanaim	sub (A) 3	Hebrew	*Mur* 46	
77	John son of [PN]	w (G) 3	Greek	*P.Yadin* 11	
78	Joseph b. Adi	p (I)	Hebrew	*Mur* 22	
79	Joseph b. Bar Egla	h/sub (A) 3	Greek	*P.Yadin* 15	
80	Joseph b. Eleazar	w (A/H) 2	Hebrew	*P.Yadin* 46	

continued

Number	Name	Role, language used, level	Language of text	Designation of text	Remarks
81	Joseph b. Hananiah	w (A) 1	Nabataean	*P.Yadin* 6	
		w (A) 1	Greek	*P.Yadin* 14	
		w (A) 1	Greek	*P.Yadin* 15	
		w (A) 1	Greek	*P.Yadin* 17	
		w (A) 1	Greek	*P.Yadin* 18	
		w (A) 1	Greek	*P.Hever* 64	
		w (A) 1	Greek	*P.Yadin* 21	
		w (A) 1	Greek	*P.Yadin* 22	
		p (H) 1	Hebrew	*P.Hever* 49	
82	Joseph b. Jacob	h/s (A; H/A) 4	Aramaic/ Hebrew	Beth 'Amar	
83	Joseph b. Joseph	w (A/H) 1	Hebrew	*Mur* 42	
84	Joseph b. Judah	w (A) 3	Nabataean	*P.Yadin* 36	
85	Joseph b. Malka	w (A) 2	Aramaic	*Mur* 19	
86	Joseph b. Mattat	w (A) 4	Greek	*P.Yadin* 23	
		w (A) 4	Greek	*P.Yadin* 26	
87	Joseph b. Menahem	w (A) 3	Greek	*P.Yadin* 20	
		w (A) 3	Greek	*P.Yadin* 22	
88	Joseph b. Nicus	p (A) 2	Aramaic	*Mur* 19	
89	Joseph b. [PN]	h/s (A) 4	Aramaic	*Mur* 18	
90	Joseph b. [PN]	w (A) 4	Aramaic	*P.Jericho* 7	
91	Joseph b. [PN]	w (A?) 1	Aramaic	*P.Hever* 24	
92	Joseph b. [PN]	p (A) 2	Nabataean	*P.Yadin* 9	
93	Joseph b. [PN]	w (A) 3	Aramaic	Sdeir 2	
94	Joseph b. SGYHN	w (A) 2	Hebrew	*Mur* 29	
95	Joseph b. Shulai	w (A) 3	Greek	*P.Hever* 64	
96	Joseph b. Simon	w (A) 3	Aramaic/ Hebrew	Beth 'Amar	
97	Joseph [b. Simon]	h (A) (frag.)	Greek	*P.Hever* 64	
98	Joseph b. Simon	s/h (H) 4	Hebrew	*P.Yadin* 44	
		s (H) 4	Hebrew	*P.Yadin* 45	
		s (H) 4	Hebrew	*P.Yadin* 46	

Number	Name	Role, language used, level	Language of text	Designation of text	Remarks
99	Joseph b. Yohanan	p (A) 1	Aramaic	*P.Jericho* 7	
100	Joseph b. Yohanan	w (A) 2	Aramaic	*Mur* 18	
101	Joseph son of PN	w (G) 3	Greek	*P.Hever* 69	
102	Joseph son of Saeas	w (G) 3	Greek	*P.Yadin* 11	
103	Judah b. Eleazar	p/s (A) 3	Aramaic	*P.Yadin* 10	
		sub (A) 3	Greek	*P.Yadin* 11	
		h/sub (A) 3	Greek	*P.Yadin* 15	
		h/sub (A) 3	Greek	*P.Yadin* 16	
	Judah [b. Eleazar]	p/sub (A) 3	Greek	*P.Yadin* 17	
	Judah b. Eleazar	p/sub (A) 3	Greek	*P.Yadin* 18	
		sub (A) 3	Greek	*P.Yadin* 19	
104	Judah b. Ishmael	w (A) 2	Aramaic	Sdeir 2	
105	Judah b. Joseph	w (H) 4	Hebrew	*P.Hever* 49	
		w (H) 4	Hebrew	*P.Yadin* 44	
		w (H) 4	Hebrew	*P.Yadin* 45	
106	[Judah b.] Judah	w (A) 3	Aramaic	*P.Hever* 22	
	Judah b. Judah	w (A) 3	Greek	*P.Yadin* 26	
	Judah b. Judah	w (A) 3	Aramaic	*P.Hever* 8a	
107	Judah b. Judah	w (A) 3	Greek	*P.Yadin* 19	
108	Judah b. P[N] b. Menaseh	p (A) 2	Aramaic	*Mur* 20	
109	Judah b. Simon	w (A) 1	Nabataean	*P.Yadin* 9	
110	Judah b. Simon	w (A) 3	Greek	*P.Yadin* 22	
111	Judah b. Zechariah	w (A) 3	Aramaic/ Hebrew	Beth 'Amar	
112	Judah Cimber	p (I)	Greek	*P.Yadin* 18	
113	Judas son of [PN]	w (G) (frag.)	Greek	*P.Jericho* 19b	
114	Julia Crispina	sub (G) 3	Greek	*P.Yadin* 20	Herodian
115	Justinus	s (G) 4	Greek	*P.Yadin* 11	Roman
116	Kallaios son of John	w (G) 3	Greek	*P.Yadin* 11	

continued

Number	Name	Role, language used, level	Language of text	Designation of text	Remarks
117	[Lazar] b. Joseph	p/h/s (A) 2	Aramaic	*Mur* 21	
118	Lentil	p (A) 1	Aramaic	*Mur* 8	
119	Mahanaim b. [PN]	w (A) 3	Aramaic	*P.Jericho* 2	
120	Malik b. [PN]	w (N) 4	Greek	*P.Hever* 64	
121	Mantanta b. Amru	w (N) 4	Greek	*P.Yadin* 16	
122	Marion b. [PN]	w (A?) 1	Aramaic(?)	*Mur* 38	
123	Maro	w (G) 3	Greek	*P.Hever* 69	
124	Masabala b. Simon	s (A) 4	Aramaic	*P.Yadin* 42	
		s (A) 4	Aramaic	*P.Yadin* 43	
		s (H) 4	Hebrew	*P.Hever* 49	
		h (H) 4	Hebrew	*P.Yadin* 44	
		w (H) 4	Hebrew	*P.Yadin* 45	
		w (H) 4	Aramaic	*P.Hever* 13	
125	Mattat b. Simon	s (A) 4	Aramaic	*P.Hever* 7	
		s (A; 47b) 4	Aramaic	*P.Yadin* 47b	
		s (A) 4	Aramaic	*P.Hever* 14	
		s/h (A) 4	Aramaic	*P.Hever* 13	
		w (A) 4	Greek	*P.Yadin* 26	
126	Matthew b. Rabbah	w (A) 1	Aramaic(?)	*Mur* 38	
127	Mattiyah b. Yehohanan	w (A) 3	Greek	*P.Yadin* 20	
128	Menahem b. [Mattat(?)]	p (I)	Aramaic	*Mur* 21	
129	Menahem b. [PN]	w (H) 3	Hebrew	*P.Hever* 49	
130	Miriam b. Jacob	p (I)	Aramaic/ Hebrew	Beth ‘Amar	
131	Muqimu	p (N) 3	Nabataean	*P.Yadin* 1	
132	Nubi b. Walat	w (N) 4	Greek	*P.Yadin* 12	
133	Onesimos son of Jannaeus	w (G) 3	Greek	*P.Yadin* 11	
134	Petrus b. Joseph	w (H) 2	Hebrew	*P.Yadin* 46	

Number	Name	Role, language used, level	Language of text	Designation of text	Remarks
135	[PN b.]ilahi	w (N) 4	Nabataean	*P.Yadin* 2	
136	[PN] b. Abdisay	w (N) 4	Greek	*P.Yadin* 12	
137	[PN] b. Awatu	w (N) 4	Greek	*P.Hever* 62	
138	[PN] b. Dorymenes	w (A) 3	Aramaic	1Mish 3	
139	[PN] b. Eleazar	w (A) 1	Aramaic	*P.Hever* 22	
140	[PN] b. Eleazar	p (A) 1	Aramaic(?)	*Mur* 38	
141	[PN] b. Hezekiah	h/s (A) 3	Aramaic	Sdeir 2	
142	[PN] b. Honiyah	p/w(?) (A) 4	Aramaic	*P.Jericho* 3	
143	[PN] b. Jesus	p (A) 2	Hebrew	*Mur* 36	
144	[PN] b. Jesus	w (A) 1	Greek	*P.Yadin* 21	
145	[PN] b. John	p (I)	Hebrew	*Mur* 24	
146	[PN] b. Joseph	w (A) (frag.)	Aramaic	4Q344	
147	[PN b.] Joseph	w (A) 2	Nabataean	*P.Yadin* 4	
148	[PN] b. Joseph	w (A) 2	Aramaic	*P.Hever* 9	
149	[PN] b. Judah	w (A) 2	Greek	*P.Yadin* 17	
150	[P]N b. [Lazar]	p (I)	Aramaic	*Mur* 21	
151	[PN] b. [La]zar(?)	w (A) 2	Aramaic	*Mur* 21	
152	[PN] b. LTH	h (N) 3	Nabataean	*P.Yadin* 3	
153	[PN] b. [M]attat	w (A) 1	Aramaic	*Mur* 21	
154	[PN] b. Menahem	w (A) 3	Aramaic	*P.Yadin* 7	
155	[PN b. PN]	s (A) 4	Aramaic	4Q346	
156	[PN] b. [PN]	p(?) (A) 2	Aramaic	*Mur* 23	
157	PN b. PN	p(?) (frag.)	Aramaic	*Mur* 23	
158	[PN] b. [PN]	s/h (A) 4	Aramaic	*Mur* 33	
159	[PN] b. [PN]	w (A) 3	Aramaic	*Mur* 23	
160	[PN b. PN]	s (N) 4	Nabataean	*P.Yadin* 36	
161	[PN] b. [PN]	w (A) 1	Aramaic	*Mur* 26 + *P.Hever* 50	
162	[PN] b. [PN]	w (A) 2	Aramaic	*Mur* 26 + *P.Hever* 50	Annotated in H
163	[PN b. PN]	s (A) 4	Aramaic	*Mur* 27	

continued

Number	Name	Role, language used, level	Language of text	Designation of text	Remarks
164	[PN] b. [PN]	w (A) 3	Aramaic	*Mur* 27	
165	[PN] b. [PN]	w (H) 3	Hebrew	*Mur* 22	
166	[PN] b. [PN]	w (H) 4	Hebrew	*Mur* 22	
167	[PN b. PN]	s (A) 3	Aramaic	*Mur* 19	
168	[PN b. PN]	s (H) 4	Hebrew	*P.Jericho* 9	
169	[PN] b. [PN]	w (H) 4	Hebrew	*P.Jericho* 9	
170	[PN b. PN]	s (A) 4	Aramaic	*P.Jericho* 7	
171	[PN b. PN]	w (N) 3	Nabataean	*P.Yadin* 1	
172	P[N b. PN]	w (N) 3	Nabataean	*P.Yadin* 2	
173	[PN b. PN]	w (N) 4	Nabataean	*P.Yadin* 2	
174	[PN b. P]N	w (N) (frag.)	Nabataean	*P.Yadin* 2	
175	[PN b. PN]	h (A) (frag.)	Nabataean	*P.Yadin* 4	
176	[PN b. PN]	p (I)	Nabataean	*P.Yadin* 4	
177	[PN b. PN]	w (A) 2	Nabataean	*P.Yadin* 4	
178	[PN b. PN]	w (A) (frag.)	Nabataean	*P.Yadin* 4	
179	[PN b. PN]	w (A) (frag.)	Nabataean	*P.Yadin* 4	
180	[PN] b. [PN]	h (A) 4	Aramaic	*Mur* 21	
181	[PN b. PN]	s (A) 4	Aramaic	*P.Jericho* 8	
182	[PN b. PN]	s (H) 4	Hebrew	*P.Jericho* 10	
183	[PN b. PN]	s (H) 4	Hebrew	*P.Jericho* 11	
184	[PN b. PN]	s (A) 4	Aramaic	*P.Jericho* 12	
185	[PN b. PN]	s (H) 4	Hebrew	*P.Jericho* 14	
186	[PN b. PN]	s (A) 4	Aramaic	*Mur* 31	
187	[PN b. PN]	p/s (A) 2	Aramaic	*Mur* 34	
188	[PN b. PN]	p (A) 2	Aramaic	1Mish 3	
189	[PN b. PN]	s (A) (frag.)	Aramaic	1Mish 3	
190	[PN] b. [PN]	w (A) 2	Aramaic	1Mish 3	

Number	Name	Role, language used, level	Language of text	Designation of text	Remarks
191	PN b. PN	h/s (N) 4	Nabataean	*P.Hever nab* 2	
192	[PN] b. [PN]	w (A) 3	Nabataean	*P.Hever nab* 2	
193	[PN] b. [PN]	w (A?) 1	Aramaic	*P.Hever* 9	
194	[PN] b. [PN]	w (A) 1	Aramaic	*P.Hever* 9	
195	[PN] b. [PN]	w (A) 1	Aramaic	*P.Hever* 9a	
196	[PN] b. [PN]	p (A?) (frag.)	Aramaic	*P.Hever* 11	
197	[PN b. PN]	s (A) 4	Aramaic	*P.Hever* 11	
198	[PN b. PN]	s (A) 4	Aramaic	*P.Hever* 21	
199	[PN] b. [PN]	w (A) 3	Aramaic	*P.Hever* 21	
200	[PN b. PN]	s (A) 4	Aramaic	*P.Hever* 22	
201	[PN b. PN]	s (A) 4	Aramaic	*P.Hever* 23	
202	[PN b. PN]	s (A) 4	Aramaic	*P.Hever* 24	
203	[PN b. PN]	s (A) 4	Aramaic	*P.Hever* 24a	
204	[PN b. PN]	s (A) 4	Aramaic	*P.Hever* 25	
205	[PN] b. [PN]	w (A) 2	Aramaic	*P.Hever* 25	
206	[PN] b. [PN]	w (A) 3	Aramaic	*P.Hever* 25	
207	[PN] b. [PN]	w (A) 3	Aramaic	*P.Hever* 25	
208	[PN b. PN]	s (A) 4	Aramaic	*P.Hever* 32 + 4Q347	
209	[PN b. PN]	s (A) 4	Aramaic	34Se 3	
210	[PN b. PN]	s (A) 4	Aramaic	*Mur* 25	
211	[PN] b. [PN]	w (A) (frag.)	Aramaic	*Mur* 25	
212	[PN] b. [PN]	w (A) (frag.)	Aramaic	*Mur* 25	
213	[PN b. PN]	s (H) 4	Hebrew	*Mur* 37	
214	P[N b. PN]	w (frag.) 2	Hebrew	*Mur* 37	
215	[PN b. PN]	s (H) 4	Hebrew	*Mur* 36	
216	[PN b. PN]	s (G) 4	Greek	*Mur* 113	
217	[PN b. PN]	s (G) 4	Greek	*Mur* 116	

continued

Number	Name	Role, language used, level	Language of text	Designation of text	Remarks
218	[PN b. PN]	s (A) 4	Aramaic	*P.Jericho* 2	
219	[PN b. PN]	w (A) 1	Aramaic	*P.Jericho* 2	
220	[PN b. PN]	w (A) 2	Aramaic	*P.Jericho* 2	
221	[PN b. PN]	w (A) 2	Aramaic	*P.Jericho* 2	
222	[PN b. PN]	p/w(?) (A?) 4	Aramaic	*P.Jericho* 3	
223	[PN b. PN]	s (A) 4	Aramaic	*P.Jericho* 3	
224	[PN b. PN]	s (G) 4	Greek	*P.Jericho* 4	
225	[PN b. PN]	s (G) 4	Greek	*P.Jericho* 19b	
226	[PN b. PN]	s (A) 4	Aramaic	*Mur* 28	
227	[PN b. PN]	sub (A) 1	Greek	*P.Yadin* 31	
228	[PN] b. [PN]	w (A) 3	Greek	*P.Yadin* 31	
229	[PN b. PN]	w (A) 1	Greek	*P.Yadin* 31	
230	[PN b. PN]	s (G) 4	Greek	*Mur* 114	
231	[PN b. PN]	s (A) 4	Aramaic	*P.Jericho* 13	
232	[PN b. PN]	s (A) 4	Aramaic	*Mur* 20	
233	[PN b. PN]	w (A) 2	Aramaic	*P.Yadin* 7	
234	[PN b. PN]	w (N) 4	Aramaic	*P.Yadin* 7	
235	[PN b. PN]	w (A) (frag.)	Aramaic	*P.Yadin* 7	
236	[PN b. PN]	w (A) (frag.)	Aramaic	*P.Yadin* 7	
237	[PN] b. [PN]	sub (N) 4	Nabataean	*P.Yadin* 9	
238	[PN] b. [PN]	w (A) 2	Nabataean	*P.Yadin* 9	
239	[PN] b. [PN]	w (A) (frag.)	Aramaic	*P.Yadin* 10	
240	[PN b. PN]	s (G) 4	Greek	*P.Yadin* 12	
241	[PN b. PN]	s (G) 4	Greek	*P.Yadin* 13	
242	[PN b. PN]	s (G) 4	Greek	*Mur* 115	
243	[PN b. PN]	s (G) 4	Greek	*P.Hever* 60	
244	[PN b. PN]	w (A) 3	Greek	*P.Yadin* 15	
245	[PN b. PN]	s (G) 4	Greek	*P.Yadin* 28	
		s (G) 4	Greek	*P.Yadin* 29	

Number	Name	Role, language used, level	Language of text	Designation of text	Remarks
246	[PN b. PN]	s (G) 4	Greek	*P.Yadin* 30	
247	[PN b. PN]	s (G) 4	Greek	*P.Yadin* 33	
248	[PN b. PN]	s (G) 4	Greek	*P.Yadin* 32a	
249	[PN b. PN]	s (G) 4	Greek	*P.Hever* 61	
250	[PN b. PN]	s (G) 4	Greek	*P.Hever* 62	
251	[PN] b. [PN]	w (A) 2	Greek	*P.Hever* 62	
252	[PN] b. [PN]	w (N) (frag.)	Greek	*P.Hever* 62	
253	[PN b. PN]	s (G) 4	Greek	*P.Hever* 63	
254	[PN b. PN]	s (G) 4	Greek	*P.Yadin* 16	
255	[PN b. PN]	s (G) 4	Greek	*P.Yadin* 19	
256	[PN] b. [PN]	w (A) (frag.)	Greek	*P.Yadin* 19	
257	[PN b. PN]	s (G) 4	Greek	*P.Hever* 64	
258	[PN b. PN]	s (G) 4	Greek	*P.Hever* 69	
259	[PN] b. [PN]	w (A) (frag.)	Greek	*P.Yadin* 25	
260	[PN] b. [PN]	w (A) (frag.)	Greek	*P.Yadin* 25	
261	[PN] b. [PN]	w (A) (frag.)	Greek	*P.Yadin* 25	
262	[PN b. PN]	s (G) 4	Greek	*P.Hever* 65	
263	[PN b.] P[N]	s (A) 3	Aramaic	*P.Hever* 12	
264	[PN] b. [PN]	w (A)	Greek	*P.Yadin* 35	No published photograph
265	[PN b. PN]	s (H) 4	Hebrew	*Mur* 43	
266	[PN b. PN]	s (H) 4	Hebrew	*Mur* 44	
267	[PN b. PN]	s (H) 4	Hebrew	*Mur* 45	
268	[PN b. PN]	s (H) 4	Hebrew	*Mur* 46	
269	[PN b. PN]	s (H) 4	Hebrew	*Mur* 47	
270	[PN b. PN]	s (H) 4	Hebrew	*Mur* 48	
271	[PN b. PN]	s (H) 4	Hebrew	*Mur* 49	
272	[PN b. PN]	s (H) 4	Hebrew	*Mur* 51	

continued

Number	Name	Role, language used, level	Language of text	Designation of text	Remarks
273	[PN b. PN]	s (H) 4	Hebrew	*Mur* 52	
274	[PN b. PN]	s (H) 4	Hebrew	*Mur* 61	
275	[PN b. PN]	s (H) 4	Hebrew	*Mur* 174	
		s (H) 4	Hebrew	*Mur* 7	
276	[PN b. PN]	s (H) 4	Hebrew	*P.Hever* 30	
277	[PN b. PN]	s (H) 3	Hebrew	*P.Yadin* 49	
278	[PN b. PN]	s (A) 3	Aramaic	*P.Yadin* 50	
279	[PN b. PN]	s (H) 3	Hebrew	*P.Yadin* 51	
280	[PN b. PN]	s (G) 4	Greek	*P.Yadin* 52	
281	[PN b. PN]	s/sub (A) 3	Aramaic	*P.Yadin* 53	
282	[PN b. PN]	s (A) 3	Aramaic	*P.Yadin* 55	
283	[PN b. PN]	s/sub (A) 3	Aramaic	*P.Yadin* 56	
284	[PN b. PN]	s/sub (A) 3	Aramaic	*P.Yadin* 56	
285	[PN b. PN]	s/sub (A) 3	Aramaic	*P.Yadin* 57	
286	[PN b. PN]	s/sub (A) 3	Aramaic	*P.Yadin* 58	
287	[PN b. PN]	s (H) 3	Hebrew	*P.Yadin* 60	
288	[PN b. PN]	s (H) 3	Hebrew	*P.Yadin* 61	
289	[PN b. PN]	s (A) 3	Aramaic	*P.Yadin* 62	
290	PN b. PN	s (A; 47) 4	Aramaic	*P.Yadin* 47	
291	[PN b. PN]	s (H) 4	Hebrew	*Mur* 24	
292	[PN b. PN]	p (I)	Aramaic	*P.Hever* 14	
293	[PN b. PN]	s (frag.) 3	Aramaic(?)	4Q359	
294	[PN] b. [PN]	w (A) 3	Aramaic	*P.Hever* 26	
295	[PN] b. Shimon	p/w(?) (A) 4	Aramaic	*P.Jericho* 3	
296	[PN] b. Sim[o]n	h (A) 3	Aramaic	*Mur* 26 + *P.Hever*	
297	[PN] b. Simon	w (A) 2	Greek	*P.Yadin* 31	
298	[PN] b. Simon	s (A) 4	Aramaic	*P.Yadin* 7	
299	[PN] b. Simon	w (H) 3	Hebrew	*P.Yadin* 46	
300	[PN] b. Simon	w (H) 2	Aramaic	*P.Hever* 13	
301	[PN b. Sim]on	h (A) 3	Aramaic	*P.Hever* 14	
302	[PN] b. Taymilahi	w (N) 3	Greek	*P.Yadin* 34	

Number	Name	Role, language used, level	Language of text	Designation of text	Remarks
303	[PN] b. Yohanan	w (A) 1	Aramaic	*Mur* 21	
304	[PN] b. Yohanan	w (A) 3	Aramaic	*P.Hever* 21	
305	[PN] b. Yohanan(?)	p (A) (frag.)	Aramaic	*Mur* 25	
306	[PN] b. Yohanan	w (A) 2	Aramaic	*P.Yadin* 10	
307	[PN] b. Zaidu	p/h (N) 2	Nabataean	*P.Yadin* 2	
308	[PN] son of Levi	p/sub (I)	Greek	*P.Hever* 61	
309	[PN] son of [PN]	h/sub (A) 1; (G) 3	Greek	*P.Yadin* 18	
310	[PN] son of [PN]	w (G) (frag.)	Greek	*P.Jericho* 19b	
311	[PN] son of [PN]	w (G) (frag.)	Greek	*P.Jericho* 19b	
312	[PN] son of [PN]	w (G) 2	Aramaic	*P.Yadin* 8	
313	P[N] son of [PN]	w (G) 3	Greek	*Mur* 115	
314	P[N] son of [PN]	w (G) 3	Greek	*Mur* 115	
315	Priscus	sub (L)	Greek	*P.Yadin* 16	Roman
316	Reisha	sub (A) 2	Greek	*P.Hever* 60	
	Reisha b. Judah	w (A) 2	Greek	*P.Hever* 64	
317	Salome	p (I)	Nabataean	*P.Hever nab* 2	
318	Salome b. Honi	p (I)	Hebrew	*Mur* 30	
319	[Salome b. Menahem]	p (I)	Greek	*P.Hever* 64	
320	Salome b. Simon	p (I)	Aramaic	*P.Hever* 8a	
321	Samuel b. Ammi	s/sub (A) 3	Aramaic	*P.Yadin* 54	
322	Saul b. Eleazar	w (H) 2	Hebrew	*Mur* 42	
323	Saul b. Jo[seph(?)]	w (H) 4	Hebrew	*Mur* 30	
324	[Sa]ul b. [PN]	w (A) 3	Hebrew	*Mur* 36	
325	Saul b. Rabba	p (I)	Aramaic	Sdeir 2	
326	Shabi b. Taymilahi	w (N) 3	Greek	*P.Yadin* 20	
327	Shaharu b. Mugdayu	w (N) 4	Greek	*P.Yadin* 16	

continued

Number	Name	Role, language used, level	Language of text	Designation of text	Remarks
328	Shamoa b. Menahem	w (A) 3	Greek	*P.Yadin* 14	
		sub (A) 3	Greek	*P.Yadin* 21	Also added filing note on verso
329	Shapira b. Jesus	p (I)	Hebrew	*Mur* 29	
330	Sh[elam(zion?)] b. [ ]us	p (I)	Aramaic	*Mur* 26 + *P.Hever* 50	
331	Shelamzion b. Joseph	p (I)	Aramaic	*P.Hever* 13	
332	Sifon b. Simon	h (H) 4	Hebrew	*P.Yadin* 44	
		w (H) 4	Hebrew	*P.Yadin* 45	
333	Signatory for Bene PSN	p (A) 2	Aramaic	*Mur* 8	
334	Signatory for Jesus	p (A?) 1	Aramaic	*Mur* 8	
335	Signatory for Yasuq b. Manoah and Bazuz b. [PN]	p (A) 2	Aramaic	*Mur* 8	
336	Simon b. Hananiah(?)	w (A) 1	Greek	*P.Yadin* 18	
337	Simon b. Hanin	p (I)	Aramaic	*Mur* 33	
338	Simon b. Ishmael	s (A) 3	Aramaic	*P.Yadin* 63	
339	Simon b. Jesus	sub (A) 2	Greek	*P.Yadin* 21	
340	Sim[on] b. Joseph	w (A) 3	Aramaic	*P.Hever* 22	
	Simon b. Joseph	w (A/H) 3	Aramaic	*P.Hever* 8a	
341	Simon b. Joseph	w (A/H) 4	Hebrew	*P.Yadin* 44	
342	Simon b. Judah	sub (A) 2	Aramaic	*P.Yadin* 50	
343	Simon b. Kosiba	sub (frag.) 2	Hebrew	*Mur* 43	
344	Simon b. Mattaniah	sub (H) 3	Hebrew	*P.Hever* 30	
345	Simon b. Menahem	w (A) 3	Hebrew(?)	*Mur* 39	
		w (A) 3	Hebrew(?)	*Mur* 40	
346	[Simon] b. Menahem	p (A) 3	Aramaic	*P.Yadin* 7	

Number	Name	Role, language used, level	Language of text	Designation of text	Remarks
347	[Sim]on b. Phineas	p (A) 2	Aramaic	*Mur* 28	
348	Sim[on? b. PN]	w (frag.) 3	Hebrew	*Mur* 22	
349	Simon b. [PN]	p (A) 3	Aramaic	*Mur* 31	
350	Simon b. [PN]	w (A) 1	Aramaic	*P.Hever* 9	
351	[Simon b. PN]	p (frag.)	Aramaic	*P.Hever* 22	
352	Simon b. [PN]	w (A) 2	Aramaic	*P.Hever* 24	
353	Sim[on b. PN]	p (frag.) 2	Hebrew	*Mur* 37	
354	Simon b. Shabi	h (A!) 4	Hebrew	*Mur* 29	
		s/w (H/A!) 4	Hebrew	*Mur* 29	
	Sim[on b. Shabi?]	s/h (H/A!) 4	Hebrew	*Mur* 22	
355	Simon b. Zekariah	w (H) 2	Hebrew	*Mur* 29	
356	Simon son of Simon	w (G) 3	Greek	*P.Yadin* 11	
357	Soulaios son of Eleazar	w (G) 3	Greek	*P.Hever* 69	
358	Soumaios	sub (G) 2	Greek	*P.Yadin* 52	
359	Soumaios son of PN	w (G) 3	Greek	*P.Yadin* 19	
360	Taimu b. Huwaru	w (N) 4	Nabataean	*P.Yadin* 1	
361	Tehinah son of Simon	s (G) 4	Greek	*P.Yadin* 14	
		s (G) 4	Greek	*P.Yadin* 15	
		s (G) 4	Greek	*P.Yadin* 17	
		s (G) 4	Greek	*P.Yadin* 18	
	[Tehinah son of Simon]	s (G) 4	Greek	*P.Yadin* 32	
	Tehinah b. Simon	p	Hebrew	*P.Yadin* 44	Could have signed but did not

continued

Number	Name	Role, language used, level	Language of text	Designation of text	Remarks
362	Thaddaius son of Thaddaius	w (G) 3	Greek	*P.Yadin* 14	
		w (G) 3	Greek	*P.Yadin* 15	
		w (G) 3	Greek	*P.Yadin* 20	
		w (G) 3	Greek	*P.Yadin* 23	
363	Theodorus son of Matthew	w (G) 2	Greek	*P.Yadin* 11	
364	Timadushra b. Abdharetat	w (N) 4	Greek	*P.Hever* 64	
365	[Titus] b. [PN]	p (A) 4	Aramaic	*Mur* 28	
366	Toma b. Simon	w (A) 3	Aramaic	*P.Yadin* 10	
		w (A) 3	Greek	*P.Yadin* 15	
		w (A) 3	Greek	*P.Yadin* 17	
367	Wahabdushara b. Shulay	w (N) 3	Nabataean	*P.Yadin* 3	
368	Wahabilahi b. Abdilahi	w (N) 4	Greek	*P.Hever* 62	
369	Wahabilahi b. Mushalimu	w (N) 3	Nabataean	*P.Yadin* 3	
370	Walu b. [PN]	w (N) 4	Greek	*P.Yadin* 12	
371	Wanah b. Halafilahi	w (N) 3	Nabataean	*P.Yadin* 1	
372	Wanah b. Ishmael	w (N) 1	Greek	*P.Yadin* 18	
373	Yohana b. Abdobdat Makhuta	w (N) 4	Greek	*P.Yadin* 16	
		s (N) 4	Nabataean	*P.Yadin* 6	
		s (A) 4	Aramaic	*P.Yadin* 8	
		w/s (N) 4	Nabataean	*P.Yadin* 9	
		w (N) 4	Greek	*P.Yadin* 14	
		sub (N) 4	Greek	*P.Yadin* 15	
		w (N) 4	Greek	*P.Yadin* 20	
		h/sub (N) 4	Greek	*P.Yadin* 22	

Number	Name	Role, language used, level	Language of text	Designation of text	Remarks
374	Yohanan b. Jesus Marion	sub (A) (frag.)	Aramaic	*P.Yadin* 43	
		sub (A) 2	Aramaic	*P.Yadin* 42	
375	Yohanan b. Joseph	w (A) 3	Aramaic	*P.Hever* 22	
376	Yohanan b. Menahem	w (A) 1	Greek	*P.Yadin* 21	
377	Yohanan b. [PN]	w (A) 2	Aramaic	*Mur* 23	
378	Yohanan b. [PN]	w (H) 4	Hebrew	*P.Jericho* 9	
379	Yohanan b. [PN]	w (A?) 1	Aramaic(?)	*Mur* 38	
380	Yohanan b. [S]imon	w (A) 2	Aramaic	*Mur* 18	
381	Yohanan b. Simon	w (A) 4	Aramaic	*P.Jericho* 7	
382	Zabadbaal b. Zabadion	w (N) 3	Nabataean	*P.Yadin* 3	
383	Zachariah b. Yohanan	p (I)	Aramaic	*Mur* 18	
384	Zaidu b. Shahru	w (N) 3	Nabataean	*P.Yadin* 1	

Notes

Chapter 1. *Status Quaestionum* and the Present Study

1. See for the provinces H. Eshel, B. Zissu, and G. Barkay, "Sixteen Bar Kokhba Coins from Roman Sites in Europe," *Israel Numismatic Journal* 17 (2010): 91–97.
2. The literature on the Second Revolt (132–136 [?] C.E.) is extensive, and many aspects of the war, including its causes, precise dating, and extent, are the subjects of vigorous scholarly debate. The primary sources from the Roman side are Cass. Dio 69.12.1–2 and SHA *Hadr.* 14. Among the best studies representing the "maximalist" perspective on the war's scope and importance (essentially the view taken here) are those of Werner Eck, notably "The Bar-Kokhba Revolt: The Roman Point of View," *JRS* 89 (1999): 76–89, and "Hadrian, the Bar-Kokhba Revolt, and the Epigraphic Transmission," in *The Bar Kokhba War Reconsidered: New Perspectives on the Second Jewish Revolt Against Rome* (ed. P. Schäfer; Tübingen: Mohr Siebeck, 2003), 153–70. A good short summary of the issues with bibliographic guidance is Hanan Eshel, "The Bar Kochba Revolt, 132–135," *CHJ* 4 (2006): 105–127.
3. Euseb. *Chron.* 86.
4. Yigael Yadin et al., eds., *The Documents from the Bar Kokhba Period in the Cave of Letters: Hebrew, Aramaic and Nabatean-Aramaic Papyri* (JDS 3; Jerusalem: Israel Exploration Society, the Institute of Archaeology, Hebrew University, and the Shrine of the Book, Israel Museum, 2002), 42–54.
5. To avoid ponderous repetition of the phrases "son of" and "daughter of," while not prejudicing issues of language, this study shall use "b.," thus abbreviating variously Hebrew and Aramaic בן, בת, בר, and ברת. When either Greek or Latin is the language in question, "son of" and "daughter of" are used. For analysis and normalization of names (with a few exceptions for reasons of the argument) this study follows the magisterial work by Tal Ilan, *Lexicon of Jewish Names in Late Antiquity. Part I. Palestine 330 BCE–200 CE* (Tübingen: Mohr Siebeck, 2002).
6. Eglatain has sometimes been understood not as a determinant of Mahoza, i.e., as part of the village of Mahoza's name, but rather as the district to which Mahoza belonged; see e.g., G. W. Bowersock, "The Babatha Papyri, Masada, and Rome," *JRA* 4 (1991): 340–41. This understanding does not seem to be

correct; thus H. Cotton and J. C. Greenfield, "Babatha's *Patria:* Mahoza, Mahoz 'Eglatain and Zo'ar," *ZPE* 107 (1995): 126–34.

7. On the contract as constitutive of the agreement, see Lawrence Schiffman, "Witnesses and Signatures in the Hebrew and Aramaic Documents from the Bar Kokhba Caves," in *Semitic Papyrology in Context* (ed. L. Schiffman; Leiden: Brill, 2003), 178–79, and cf. Asher Gulak, *Das Urkundenwesen im Talmud im Lichte der Griechisch-Ägyptischen Papyri und des Griechischen und Römischen Rechts* (Jerusalem: Rubin Mass, 1935), 15–24. Witnesses were in a similarly constitutive role in the Egypt of this period; cf. M. Depauw, "Autograph Confirmation in Demotic Private Contracts," *ChrEg* 78 (2003): 66–111.

8. Eleazar here wrote his name followed by a phrase, על נפשו, which admits of more than one possible understanding. Several scholars have discussed it over the years, as forms of it (including Aramaic על נפשה) are known from other documents besides the Bar Kokhba corpus. The first systematic study was that of J. J. Rabinowitz, "A Legal Formula in Egyptian, Egyptian-Aramaic and Murabbaʿat Documents," *BASOR* 145 (1957): 33–34. He believed the expression would mean "for himself," i.e., that the person signed with his own hand. Yadin and the coeditors of *Hebrew, Aramaic and Nabatean-Aramaic Papyri* argued that it means "on his own behalf" and that the phrase would not necessarily imply the presence of the person at the signing (52–53). If this view was correct, it would also mean that the use of this phrase by a *hypographeus* would not necessarily indicate anything about the writing ability of the signatory, since he might write well but simply be unable to attend the signing of the writ. *But this view does not, in fact, seem to be correct.* The translation given above understands the phrase as elliptical. The suppressed verb is מעיד, "witnesses," and since the act of signing was a kind of speech-act vitalizing the contract as in force, "hereby witnesses" is an attempt to capture the meaning מעיד communicated. This understanding would certainly require that the signatory be present and entail that a signatory's use of a *hypographeus* would usually indicate an inability to sign with his own hand. The reason for seeing the Judaean phrase as elliptical is that the full form of the expression has surfaced elsewhere in several third-century Syriac contracts from the region of the middle Euphrates. These contracts share many elements with the protocols of our texts, as indeed do Greek legal texts known from Egypt of the time. It is evident that this entire region was heir to customary ways of law that found local expression while maintaining broad continuity with each other. For example, like our texts, these Syrian contracts frequently contain signatures in a language different from that of the contract itself. Of nineteen intelligible texts among the mostly Greek *Papyrus Euphrates* materials, ten display at least some involvement by Syriac writers. Two of the contracts are entirely in Syriac, as is *P.Dura* 28, discovered in the 1930s at Dura-Europus. The latter text evidences a *hypographeus* signing for a certain Marcia Aurelia Matarata b. Samnai, who was illiterate. He wrote for her *'al naphsha sahda,* "hereby witnesses concerning

herself," that is, concerning her role or actions as a principal, stated in the writ (*P.Dura* 28 verso line 1). The verbal form is a participle, appropriate for such a speech-act. In the same way, Baishu b. Taymu signed *P.Euphr.* 19 at lines 1 and 5 on the verso, *'al naphshe sahed,* "hereby witnesses concerning himself." The Syriac expressions suggest that *P.Yadin* 44 should be understood as suppressing an equivalent Hebrew participle, hence מעיד. Elsewhere among our texts the implicated Judaean Aramaic expression would be identical to this early Syriac, על נפשה שָׂהֵד. For the Syriac contracts, see C. Bradford Welles, Robert O. Fink, and J. Frank Gilliam, *The Excavations at Dura-Europus. Final Report V.I: The Parchment and Papyri* (New Haven, Conn.: Yale University Press, 1959), 142–49 and Plates XXIX, LXXI (*P.Dura* 28); J. Teixidor, "Deux documents syriaques du IIIe siècle J.-C., provenant du moyen Euphrate," *CRAIBL* 1990: 146–66 (*P.Euphr.* 19); Teixidor, "Un document syriaque de fermage de 242 après J.-C.," *Sem* 41–42 (1991): 195–208 (*P.Euphr.* 20); and for the mixed-language and Greek texts, *P.Euphr.* 1–18, see D. Feissel and J. Gascou, "Documents d'archives romains inédits du moyen Euphrate (IIIe s. après J.-C.)," *Journal des Savants* 1995: 65–119; D. Feissel, J. Gascou, and J. Teixidor, "Documents d'archives romains inédits du moyen Euphrate (IIIe s. après J.-C.)," *Journal des Savants* 1997: 3–57; and D. Feissel and J. Gascou, "Documents d'archives romains inédits du moyen Euphrate (IIIe s. après J.-C.)," *Journal des Savants* 2000: 157–208.

9. Plaut. *Pseud.* 29–30.
10. Herbert Youtie, "βραδέως γράφων: Between Literacy and Illiteracy," *GRBS* 12 (1971): 239–61 (repr., *Scriptunculae* [Amsterdam: Adolf M. Hakkert, 1973], 2: 629–51); R. Calderini, "Gli ἀγράμματοι nell'Egitto greco-romano," *Aeg* 30 (1950): 34–36.
11. The editors found this reference confusing, saying that it is "problematic, in the first instance, since the contract involves more than one person in each pair, and up to this point, formulation has been in the third person plural. Who, then, is the single speaker in the first person?" (Yadin et al., eds., *Hebrew, Aramaic and Nabatean-Aramaic Papyri,* 50). They tentatively proposed that the reference is to Eleazar b. Eleazar, but the mention seems clearly to reference Masabala as the issuing official.
12. Yigael Yadin, "Expedition D—The Cave of the Letters," *IEJ* 12 (1962): 227–57, and הממצאים מימי בר כוכבא במערת האיגרות (JDS 1; Jerusalem: Israel Exploration Society, 1963).
13. This expression is unique in the Judaean Desert texts and therefore of uncertain meaning. In accordance with biblical usage, it might be translated "by the command" or "pursuant to the will" (cf. Pss 40:9; 103:21; Ezra 10:11, etc.). The parallel expression found ubiquitously in this and other such contexts is מאמרו, lit., "at his word." In a legal text one would expect precise wording, so the two expressions are presumably not free variants. The suggestion here is that this is the one instance attested among these texts where a principal or witness was not

actually present. Thus this will have been the legal formula used by a *hypographeus* to express an absentee principal's acknowledgment of his obligations. If so, it would be the Judaean equivalent to the Syriac *men puqdana d-* that appears in *P.Euphr.* 6–7 lines 37–38, "Aurelius Lela b. Belsin hereby witnesses *at the request of* [*men puqdana d-*] Belsin the *oikonomos.*" The word *puqdana,* lit., "command," is a semantic parallel to Hebrew רצון.

14. Herbert Youtie, "ΥΠΟΓΡΑΦΕΥΣ: The Social Impact of Illiteracy in Graeco-Roman Egypt," *ZPE* 17 (1975): 201–21 (repr., *Scriptunculae Posteriores* [Bonn: Rudolf Habelt, 1981], 1: 179–99); T. J. Kraus, "(Il)literacy in Non-Literary Papyri from Graeco-Roman Egypt: Further Aspects of the Educational Ideal in Ancient Literary Sources and Modern Times," *Mnemos.* (Ser. 4) 53 (2000): 327–29.
15. Ada Yardeni noted that after Eleazar's signature, "the word עד ('witness') is followed by one or two letters, the meaning of which is obscure" (Yadin et al., eds., *Hebrew, Aramaic and Nabatean-Aramaic Papyri,* 42). Her transcription of the damaged word, "witness," however, actually recognized two possible readings (*Papyri,* 44), one in Hebrew (עד) and one in Aramaic (שהד). Close study of the word under substantial magnification clarifies the situation; the second reading is correct. Eleazar wrote with an irregularly formed *shin* (ש) and a final *dalet* (ד) that terminated with a considerable curvilinear downward flourish that impinged on the line below and there obscured another word, of which Yardeni wrote, "[it] has not been deciphered so far" (*Papyri,* 42). It is possible to read that word as עָלא, "he went up," with the somewhat irregular (but still quite common) use of *aleph* rather than *heh* as the final *mater lectionis.*
16. A very few scholars dissented from this view in the nineteenth and early twentieth centuries, including T. Nöldeke, *Die semitischen Sprachen* (2nd ed.; Leipzig: Halle, 1899), 25, and S. D. Luzzatto, "Über die Sprache der Mischnah," *Literatur-Blatt des Orients* 7 (1846): 829–32; 8 (1847): 1–5, 46–48, 55–57. See the discussion in Angel Sáenz-Badillos, *A History of the Hebrew Language* (trans. J. Ewolde; Cambridge: Cambridge University Press, 1993), 162–63.
17. Gustav Dalman, *The Words of Jesus* (trans. D. M. Kay; Edinburgh: T&T Clark, 1909), 6.
18. Ibid., 11.
19. Cited from the introduction to the *Lesebuch* by William Chomsky, "What Was the Jewish Vernacular During the Second Commonwealth?," *JQR* 42 (1951–1952): 194.
20. Theodor Zahn, *Introduction to the New Testament* (trans. M. W. Jacobus; 3 vols.; Edinburgh: T&T Clark, 1909), 1:7.
21. Wilhelm Gesenius, *Geschichte der hebräischen Sprache und Schrift* (Leipzig: F. C. W. Vogel, 1815), 44–47; "Die Herrschaft der Seleuciden und der neue Einfluß eines aramäischredenden Volkes scheint allmählich die letzten Spuren vertilgt zu haben" (44).

22. Emil Schürer, *A History of the Jewish People in the Time of Jesus Christ* (trans. J. MacPherson; 5 vols.; Edinburgh: T&T Clark, 1885), 2:8.
23. The evidence was scarcely on view, however, and because of publishing delays the scholars could not examine the entirety for themselves until many years later. The relevant volumes of the final report of the Masada excavations appeared in 1989. These are Y. Yadin and J. Naveh, *Masada I, The Yigael Yadin Excavations 1963–1965, Final Reports: The Aramaic and Hebrew Ostraca and Jar Inscriptions* (Jerusalem: Israel Exploration Society and the Hebrew University of Jerusalem, 1989); and H. Cotton and J. Geiger, *Masada II, The Yigael Yadin Excavations 1963–1965, Final Reports: The Latin and Greek Documents* (Jerusalem: Israel Exploration Society, 1989). Before that time scholars perforce relied primarily upon the preliminary report by Y. Yadin, "The Preliminary Report of the 1963/64 Season," *IEJ* 15 (1965): 1–120, and Yadin's book, popular though with many useful photographs, *Masada: Herod's Fortress and the Zealots' Last Stand* (London: Weidenfeld and Nicolson, 1966).
24. "Dass zu Beginn unserer Zeitrechnung die herrschende Sprache in Palästina das Aram[äisch], nicht etwa das Hebr[äisch], war, kann nach den heutigen Erkenntnissen über die Geschichte des Aram[äisch] keinem Zweifel unterliegen"; Franz Rosenthal, *Die Aramäistische Forschung* (Leiden: Brill, 1964), 106.
25. Thus, e.g., the incredulous statement of Matthew Black, *An Aramaic Approach to the Gospels and Acts* (3rd ed.; Oxford: Clarendon, 1967), 47: "It would seem from this description of Hebrew in the time of Christ as a 'free, living language' and a 'normal vehicle of expression' that Dr. Wilcox [referring to *The Semitisms of Acts* (Oxford: Oxford University Press, 1965), 14] intends us to understand that Hebrew was in fact a spoken Palestinian language in New Testament times, and not merely a medium of literary expression only or a learned language confined to rabbinical circles"; or Klaus Beyer, *Die aramäischen Texte vom Toten Meer* (2 vols.; Göttingen: Vandenhoeck & Ruprecht, 1984–2004), 1:55, 58: "Bedenkt man, daß in den größeren Städten auch das Griechische gebraucht wurde, so ist es schwierig, eine Gegend zu finden, wo zur Zeit Jesu noch Hebräische gesprochen worden sein könnte. . . . Gesprochen hat man das Hebräische in Palästina seit 400 v. Chr. nicht mehr." Note also H. Ott, "Um die Muttersprache Jesu Forschungen seit Gustaf Dalman," *NT* 9 (1967): 1–25.
26. James Barr, "Which Language Did Jesus Speak?—Some Remarks of a Semitist," *BJRL* 53 (1970/71): 13.
27. J. A. Emerton, "Did Jesus Speak Hebrew?," *JTS* 12 (1961): 190.
28. J. A. Emerton, "The Problem of Vernacular Hebrew in the First Century A.D. and the Language of Jesus," *JTS* 24 (1973): 16.
29. Harris Birkeland, *The Language of Jesus* (Oslo: Jacob Dybwad, 1954), 11 (emphasis his).
30. Ibid., 39.

31. Ibid., 12.
32. Barr, "Remarks," and Emerton, "Did Jesus Speak Hebrew?," were responses in whole or in part to Birkeland's study. Note also the reviews by A. S. Kapelrud, *NTT* 55 (1954): 251, and H. Ljungunann, *STK* 31 (1955): 122–23. The eminent Semitist J. Cantineau was persuaded by Birkeland and lauded his work in a separately titled review, "Quelle langue parlait le peuple en Palestine au premier siècle de notre ère?," *Sem* 5 (1955): 99–101.
33. Birkeland, *Language of Jesus,* 22.
34. Note the assessment of Segal's role by Eduard Y. Kutscher, "Mischnisches Hebräisch," *Rocznik Orientalistyczny* 28 (1964): 36: "A. Geiger, der Verfasser der ersten wissenschaftlichen Grammatik dieser Sprache, hat behauptet, sie sei nie eine gesprochene Sprache gewesen, und sei von den Rabbinern geschaffen worden. Die darauf folgende Polemik dauerte fast 70 Jahre, bis M. H. Segal dieses Problem endgültig in bejahendem Sinne löste."
35. As observed by Eduard Y. Kutscher, *A History of the Hebrew Language* (ed. R. Kutscher; Leiden: Brill/Jerusalem: Magnes, 1982), 118.
36. Segal's first exposition of the problem was "Mishnaic Hebrew and Its Relation to Biblical Hebrew and to Aramaic," *JQR* 20 (1908–1909): 647–737. This was followed by Segal, *A Grammar of Mishnaic Hebrew* (Oxford: Oxford University Press, 1927; 2nd corrected printing, 1957), 5–18, and finally, by דקדוק לשון המשנה (Tel Aviv: Devir, 1936), 4–17.
37. Segal, *Grammar,* 6–7.
38. Ibid., 8, 49–50. Modern scholarship considers the debt to Aramaic to be notably greater than Segal allowed, particularly in light of the research of Menahem Moreshet, לקסיקון הפועל שנתחדש בלשון התנאים (Ramat-Gan: Bar Ilan University Press, 1980). Moreshet did a much more thorough job of exploring the relationships between the Mishnaic Hebrew verb and various dialects of Aramaic. See the comments in Chapter 4 below.
39. This is not a question that Segal himself asked in so many words but is an attempt to capture his point with a hypothetical example.
40. Thus, e.g., Jehoshua M. Grintz, "Hebrew as the Spoken and Written Language in the Last Days of the Second Temple," *JBL* 79 (1960): 32–47, who argued on the basis of new analysis of the Gospel of Matthew and of Josephus's use of the terms γλῶττα Ἑβραίων and Ἑβραίων διάλεκτον.
41. The first was 4QMMT, published in 1994, almost forty years after its initial very partial description. See Elisha Qimron and John Strugnell, *Qumran Cave 4.V. Miqsat Ma'ase ha-Torah* (DJD 10; Oxford: Clarendon, 1994), esp. 65–108 for the language.
42. "La thèse de savants comme Segal, Ben Iehuda et Klausner, d'après lesquels l'hébreu mishnique a été une langue parlée par la population de la Judée aux époques perse et gréco-romaine, n'est plus une hypothèse, elle est un fait établi. Plusieurs actes de Murabba'ât sont rédigés en mishnique; ils sont cependant

moins nombreux que ceux en araméen. Mais le mishnique est la seule langue de correspondance"; J. T. Milik in P. Benoit, J. T. Milik, and R. de Vaux, eds., *Les grottes de Murabba'ât* (DJD 2; Oxford: Clarendon, 1961), 70. Cf. Milik's influential popular work, *Ten Years of Discovery in the Wilderness of Judaea* (London: SCM, 1959), 130. Since Milik wrote, some of the correspondence among the newer finds from this period is indeed in Aramaic, and even in Greek, but this fact scarcely affects Milik's essential point.

43. Chaim Rabin, "The Historical Background of Qumran Hebrew," *ScrHier* 4 (1958; repr., 1965): 144–61, esp. 145–48.

44. The literature is extensive and no effort is made here to be complete. In addition to some of the works cited above, representative studies would include Hans Rüger, "Zum Problem der Sprache Jesu," *ZNW* 59 (1968): 113–22; J. Fitzmyer, "The Languages of Palestine in the First Century A.D.," *CBQ* 32 (1970): 501–31 (repr., *A Wandering Aramean: Collected Aramaic Essays* [Missoula, Mont.: Scholars Press, 1979], 29–56); Emil Schürer, *The History of the Jewish People in the Age of Jesus Christ (175 B.C.–A.D. 135)* (ed. G. Vermes et al.; 3 vols.; Edinburgh: T&T Clark, 1973–87), 2:20–28; Philip Edgcumbe Hughes, "The Languages Spoken by Jesus," in *New Dimensions in New Testament Study* (ed. R. N. Longenecker and M. C. Tenney; Grand Rapids, Mich.: Zondervan, 1974), 127–43; P. Lapide, "Insights from Qumran into the Languages of Jesus," *RevQ* 8 (1975): 483–501; Ch. Rabin, "Hebrew and Aramaic in the First Century," CRINT 1.2:1007–39; G. Mussies, "Greek in Palestine and the Diaspora," CRINT 1.2:1040–64; G. H. R. Horsley, *New Documents Illustrating Early Christianity* (5 vols.; North Ryde: Ancient History Documentary Research Centre, Macquarie University, 1981–1989), 5:19–26; Bernard Spolsky and Robert L. Cooper, *The Languages of Jerusalem* (Oxford: Clarendon, 1991), 18–33. Further literature may be found in Nahum Waldman, *The Recent Study of Hebrew* (Cincinnati: Hebrew Union College Press, 1989), 91–98. For the role of Latin, not otherwise considered in this study since evidently very few Judaeans spoke it, see the contrasting studies by W. Eck, "The Presence, Role and Significance of Latin in the Epigraphy and Culture of the Roman Near East," in *From Hellenism to Islam* (ed. H. M. Cotton et al.; Cambridge: Cambridge University Press, 2009), 15–42, and B. Isaac, "Latin in Cities of the Roman Near East," in ibid., 43–72.

45. Seth Schwartz, "Language, Power and Identity in Ancient Palestine," *P&P* 148 (1995): 3, has spoken of the role of Hebrew as follows, "Hebrew, no longer commonly spoken, became a *commodity,* consciously manipulated by the leaders of the Jews to evoke the Jews' distinctness from their neighbors, and the leaders' own distinctness from their social inferiors" (emphasis his).

46. Robert Gundry, "The Language Milieu of First-Century Palestine," *JBL* 83 (1964): 405, emphasis his.

47. Lester Grabbe, *Judaism from Cyrus to Hadrian* (2 vols.; Minneapolis: Fortress, 1992), 1:158.

48. On Phoenicia, see John D. Grainger, *Hellenistic Phoenicia* (Oxford: Clarendon, 1991), 77–83, 108–110: "Greeks in Phoenicia remained Greek, and the local Phoenicians accommodated them by learning their language. But only in the cities: the countryside remained Phoenician, in language and in culture" (109); and cf. Fergus Millar, "The Problem of Hellenistic Syria," in *Hellenism in the East* (ed. A. Kuhrt and S. Sherwin-White; Berkeley/Los Angeles: University of California Press, 1987), 110–33. For Egypt, see Naphtali Lewis, *Greeks in Ptolemaic Egypt* (Oxford: Oxford University Press, 1986; repr., Oakville: American Society of Papyrologists, 2001), passim; Lewis, *Life in Egypt Under Roman Rule* (Oxford: Oxford University Press, 1986; repr., Oakville: American Society of Papyrologists, 1999), 18–83; and Roger S. Bagnall, *Egypt in Late Antiquity* (Princeton, N.J.: Princeton University Press, 1993), 230–60.
49. A. W. Argyle, "Greek Among the Jews of Palestine in New Testament Times," *NTS* 20 (1973–1974): 88. Argyle was particularly influenced by the evidence of S. Krauss's list of Greek loanwords in rabbinic literature, *Griechische und Lateinische Lehnwörter im Talmud Midrasch und Targum* (2 vols.; Berlin: S. Calvary, 1898–1899; repr., Hildesheim: Georg Olms, 1964). His trust may have been misplaced. Note the devastating review of Krauss's method in Haiim Rosen, "Palestinian KOINH in Rabbinic Illustration," *JSS* 8 (1963): 56–73, esp. 57.
50. E.g., Eric Meyers and James Strange, *Archaeology, the Rabbis and Early Christianity* (Nashville, Tenn.: Abingdon, 1981), 82, "The majority of Jewish families could read and write Greek and did so even for family business"; Stanley Porter, "Jesus and the Use of Greek in Galilee," in *Studying the Historical Jesus: Evaluations of the State of Current Research* (ed. B. Chilton and Craig A. Evans; Leiden: Brill, 1994), 123–54, esp. 142.
51. Mark Chancey, *Greco-Roman Culture and the Galilee of Jesus* (Cambridge: Cambridge University Press, 2005), 122–65; quotations on pp. 123 and 135, respectively.
52. For discussion and the texts, see Carl R. Holladay, *Fragments from Jewish Hellenistic Authors* (3 vols.; Atlanta: Scholars Press, 1983–1995).
53. Cf. Moses Hadas, *Hellenistic Culture: Fusion and Diffusion* (New York/London: Columbia University Press, 1959), 36, "The most forceful evidence that Greek had become the vernacular comes from epigraphy." Epigraphic finds are also the focus in the thorough (though now outdated) analysis by J. N. Sevenster, *Do You Know Greek? How Much Greek Could the First Jewish Christians Have Known?* (Leiden: Brill, 1968), esp. 96–175. An excellent recent overview of the Greek evidence is provided by Pieter W. van der Horst, "Greek in Jewish Palestine in Light of Jewish Epigraphy," in *Hellenism in the Land of Israel* (ed. J. J. Collins and G. Sterling; Notre Dame, Ind.: University of Notre Dame Press, 2001), 154–74.
54. Hannah M. Cotton et al., *Corpus Inscriptionum Iudaeae/Palaestinae: A Multilingual Corpus of the Inscriptions from Alexander to Muhammad. Volume I: Jerusalem. Part 1: 1–704* (Berlin/New York: De Gruyter, 2010) (henceforth *CIIP*).

55. Thus Gideon Foerster, "Ossilegium and Ossuaries: The Origins and Significance of a Jewish Burial Practice in the Last Decades of the 1st Century B.C. and the 1st Century A.D.," in *Abstracts of the XVth International Congress of Classical Archaeology* (Amsterdam: Allard Pierson Museum, 1998); Lee Levine, *Jerusalem: Portrait of the City in the Second Temple Period (538 B.C.E.–70 C.E.)* (Philadelphia: Jewish Publication Society, 2002), 264–65, and Jodi Magness, *Stone and Dung, Oil and Spit: Jewish Daily Life in the Time of Jesus* (Grand Rapids, Mich.: Eerdmans, 2011), 152–54.
56. Amos Kloner and Boaz Zissu, *The Necropolis of Jerusalem in the Second Temple Period* (Leuven: Peeters, 2007).
57. For Jericho, see R. Hachlili, "The Goliath Family in Jericho: Funerary Inscriptions from a First-Century A.D. Jewish Monumental Tomb," *BASOR* 235 (1979): 31–65, and L. Y. Rahmani, *A Catalogue of Jewish Ossuaries in the Collections of the State of Israel* (Jerusalem: Israel Antiquities Authority/Israel Academy of Sciences and Humanities, 1994). Rahmani's collection of nearly 900 ossuaries (227 with inscriptions, 89 of them Greek) substantially overlaps the materials in *CIIP* but unlike the latter includes evidence from areas other than Jerusalem.
58. The linguistic categories as given in the table differ slightly from the categorization offered in *CIIP*. For reasons that are unclear, sometimes the editors of this volume have presented Aramaic materials as "Hebrew"; at other times, the reverse has occurred. On occasion, judgments differ because of ambiguous readings or lexical understandings. The category "Indistinct Semitic" here describes inscriptions that could be either Hebrew or Aramaic; generally, these consist of nothing but proper names.
59. Thus the argument of, e.g., Lee Levine, *Judaism and Hellenism in Antiquity* (Seattle: University of Washington Press, 1998), 76, who for reasons unstated sees this sort of calculation as furnishing a minimum.
60. *CIIP*, 548.
61. The fact is even explicitly stated on rare occasions. For example, *CIIP* no. 471 reads, "Joseph b. Saul, 2 *revaim;* Simon, 4 *meot.*" A mason had recorded that two men, presumably the two whose bones were found within the ossuary, each paid for a portion of the cost.
62. E.g., *CIIP* nos. 125, 219, 266, 324, 325, 331, 339, 343, 353, 451, and 592.
63. E.g., *CIIP* nos. 175, 178, 232, 369, 383, and 516. In this last instance, the names on the lid and the box were juxtaposed not only to identify the deceased among the numerous clients for whom work was being done, but also to serve as mason's marks to align the lid properly.
64. E.g., *CIIP* nos. 74, 134, 189, 293, 317, 343, 499, and 504. A pellucid example of this phenomenon was published subsequent to this volume of *CIIP;* cf. Boaz Zissu and Yuval Goren, "The Ossuary of 'Miriam Daughter of Yeshua Son of Caiaphas, Priests [of] Ma'aziah from Beth 'Imri,'" *IEJ* 61 (2011): 74–95.
65. E.g., *CIIP* nos. 98, 487, 534, 551, and 581.

66. The titles were not infrequently in Hebrew, demonstrating the prestige accorded to the holy tongue. Note in addition to the examples cited above, e.g., *CIIP* nos. 70, 244, 534, and 565.
67. Tessa Rajak, *Josephus: The Historian and His Society* (London: Duckworth, 1983; repr., Philadelphia: Fortress, 1984), 57. Consider by analogy the situation of the Roman Jews: "At Rome, the Jewish community seems to have been truly diglossic in Greek and Latin during the period in which it was producing epitaphs [third and fourth centuries C.E.]. While the language of some epitaphs was no doubt dictated by the ease with which people spoke Latin or Greek, often the choice seems to have been rather different: A quasi-pagan Latin epitaph or a distinctively Jewish Greek one" (David Noy, "Writing in Tongues: The Use of Greek, Latin and Hebrew in Jewish Inscriptions from Roman Italy," *JJS* 48 [1997]: 311). The language of the epitaph was not reflexively a matter of one's home language. Incidentally, Noy showed that the epitaphic use of Hebrew or Aramaic by Roman Jews in these years was exiguous. Only 3 percent of the epitaphs use those tongues.
68. *CIIP* nos. 609–692, but not including the thirty-four inscribed stone weights, as the government issued them. These were therefore public inscriptions. It should be noted that with the weights abstracted the sample of *instrumenta domestica* from Jerusalem is not very large, totaling just thirty-nine inscriptions.
69. Most of the excavation reports and inscriptions can be found in Benjamin Mazar (Maisler), *Beth She'arim: Report on the Excavations During 1936–1940. Volume I: Catacombs 1–4* (New Brunswick: Rutgers University Press, 1957); Moshe Schwabe and Baruch Lifshitz, *Beth She'arim. Volume II: The Greek Inscriptions* (New Brunswick: Rutgers University Press, 1974); and Nahman Avigad, *Beth She'arim: Report on the Excavations During 1953–1958. Volume III: Catacombs 12–23* (New Brunswick: Rutgers University Press, 1971).
70. "Καί γ' ἐλθ[ὼν ε]ἰς Ἅδην Ἰοῦστο[ς . . . αὐτ]όθι κεῖμα[ι], / σὺν πόλλοισιν ἑοῖς, ἐπὶ ἤθελε Μοῖρα κραταιή. / Θάρσει, Ἰοῦστε, οὐδεὶς ἀθάνατος." These are the final three of seven lines. The inscription is no. 127 in Schwabe and Lifshitz, *Greek Inscriptions,* 97–107.
71. Avigad, *Beth She'arim,* 230.
72. *t. 'Abod. Zar.* 4:3.
73. Cf. the words of Robert Goldenberg, speaking specifically of the destruction of the Jerusalem Temple in 70 C.E.: "Indeed, many must have reacted to the catastrophe with despair and total abandonment of Judaism. Apostates from Judaism received little notice in antiquity from either Jewish or non-Jewish writers, but ambitious individuals are known to have turned pagan before the war, and it stands to reason that many more did so after its disastrous conclusion." Thus his "The Destruction of the Jerusalem Temple: Its Meaning and Consequences," in *CHJ* 4:198.
74. Dorothy J. Thompson, "Literacy and Power in Ptolemaic Egypt," in *Literacy and Power in the Ancient World* (ed. Alan K. Bowman and Greg Woolf; Cambridge: Cambridge University Press, 1994), 67–83.

75. The evidence for Jewish use of Greek discovered in rabbinic literature suffers from similar problems of dating. It is simply too late to apply it with any confidence to the late Second Temple period. For valuable discussion of that evidence, see the studies by the master Talmudist Saul Lieberman: *Greek in Jewish Palestine: Studies in the Life and Manners of Jewish Palestine in the II–IV Centuries C.E.* (New York: Jewish Theological Seminary of America, 1942); *Hellenism in Jewish Palestine* (New York: Jewish Theological Seminary of America, 1950); and "How Much Greek in Jewish Palestine?," in *Biblical and Other Studies* (ed. A. Altman; Cambridge, Mass.: Harvard University Press, 1963), 123–41; for methodological assessment, note James Barr, "Hebrew, Aramaic and Greek in the Hellenistic Age," in *CHJ* 2:110–11 and 111 n. 1.
76. Rachel Hachlili, *Ancient Jewish Art and Archaeology in the Land of Israel* (Leiden: Brill, 1988), 103.
77. Avigad, *Beth She'arim,* 231–32.
78. Ibid., 233–35.
79. Ramsay MacMullen, "The Epigraphic Habit in the Roman Empire," *AJP* 103 (1982): 233–46, and "Frequency of Inscriptions in Roman Lydia," *ZPE* 65 (1986): 237–38.
80. Fergus Millar, "Local Cultures in the Roman Empire: Libyan, Punic and Latin in Roman Africa," in his collected essays, *Government, Society, & Culture in the Roman Empire* (ed. Hannah Cotton and Guy Rogers; Chapel Hill: University of North Carolina Press, 2004), 249–64 (a slightly modified form of the essay of the same title originally was published in *JRS* 58 [1968]: 125–51); Ramsay MacMullen, "Provincial Languages in the Roman Empire," in MacMullen, *Changes in the Roman Empire: Essays in the Ordinary* (Princeton, N.J.: Princeton University Press, 1990), 32–40, and Maryline Parca, "Local Languages and Native Cultures," in *Epigraphic Evidence: Ancient History from Inscriptions* (ed. John Bodel; London/New York: Routledge, 2001), 57–72.
81. Martin Hengel, *Judaism and Hellenism* (2 vols.; Tübingen: J. C. B. Mohr, 1973; trans. John Bowden; Philadelphia: Fortress, 1974). Among the most significant reviews and responses (some to the earlier edition) were those of J. G. H. Lebram, *VT* 20 (1970): 503–24; A. Momigliano, *JTS* 21 (1970): 149–53; L. H. Feldman, *JBL* 96 (1973): 371–81; and F. Millar, *JJS* 29 (1978): 1–21.
82. The reader certainly gains the impression from the most recent assessment of the debate, *Hellenism in the Land of Israel* (above, note 53), that Hengel more and more carries the day. He himself wrote: "My thesis of Judaism and Hellenism can surely be supplemented, improved, and sometimes corrected. And I hope that this will happen by new evidence again and again, but it must not be revised" ("Judaism and Hellenism Revisited," in *Hellenism in the Land of Israel,* 29). A lengthy statement of the opposing position by L. H. Feldman, "Contacts Between Jews and Non-Jews in the Land of Israel," in Feldman, *Jew and Gentile in the Ancient World* (Princeton, N.J.: Princeton University Press, 1993), 3–44, concluded just as

unequivocally, "In day-to-day life in the Holy Land throughout the Hellenistic and Roman periods . . . relatively little Greek influence of importance impressed itself upon the Jews" (42).

83. Emerton, "Problem of Vernacular Hebrew," 17.
84. For orientation, see Harvey Graff, "Introduction," in *Literacy and Social Development in the West: A Reader* (ed. Harvey Graff; Cambridge: Cambridge University Press, 1981), 1–13; and Graff, "Introduction," in *Literacy and Historical Development* (ed. Harvey Graff; Carbondale: Southern Illinois University Press, 2007), 1–11. Pages 417–39 of the latter volume comprise a substantial bibliography concerning the study of historical literacy, focused on Western Europe and the United States.
85. Eric Havelock, *The Literate Revolution in Greece and Its Cultural Consequences* (Princeton, N.J.: Princeton University Press, 1982). Note also his *Preface to Plato* (Oxford: Oxford University Press, 1963) and *The Muse Learns to Write: Reflections on Orality and Literacy from Antiquity to the Present* (New Haven, Conn.: Yale University Press, 1986).
86. Reading can be scientifically shown to shape the human brain, an aspect of the brain's "plasticity." A fascinating exploration is Stanislas Dehaene, *Reading in the Brain: The Science and Evolution of a Human Invention* (New York: Viking, 2009).
87. The dual characterization presented here is especially indebted to Rosalind Thomas, *Literacy and Orality in Ancient Greece* (Cambridge: Cambridge University Press, 1992), 1–28. For an interesting and nuanced consideration of the "fundamentalist" view, sometimes known as "the literacy hypothesis," note David R. Olson, "Why Literacy Matters, Then and Now," in *Ancient Literacies: The Culture of Reading in Greece and Rome* (ed. W. A. Johnson and H. N. Parker; Oxford: Oxford University Press, 2009), 385–403.
88. William V. Harris, *Ancient Literacy* (Cambridge, Mass./London: Harvard University Press, 1989).
89. Ibid., 3. This was the principal definition adopted by UNESCO in 1977.
90. Ibid., 7–8.
91. Ibid., 11–12, emphasis his.
92. Ibid., x and 328, respectively.
93. The figures in this paragraph are found in ibid., 328–32.
94. E. G. Turner, *Greek Papyri: An Introduction* (Oxford: Oxford University Press, 1967; paperback with supplementary notes, 1980), 78.
95. J. David Thomas, review of W. V. Harris, *Ancient Literacy*, *EHR* 108 (1993): 429–30, quotation on p. 430.
96. Her review appeared in *JHS* 111 (1991): 240–1, quotations on p. 241.
97. Rosalind Thomas, review of W. V. Harris, *Ancient Literacy*, *JRS* 81 (1991): 182–83, quotations on p. 182.
98. E.g., Christopher Bruell, review of W. V. Harris, *Ancient Literacy*, in *Review of Politics* 52 (1990): 466–69.

99. One is reminded of the comments of the sociologist of religion Rodney Stark, who does a good deal of regression analysis and similar statistical study in his work. Writing in *Cities of God* (San Francisco: HarperSanFrancisco, 2006), he argued: "Many of the really significant historical questions *demand* quantitative answers. They do so because they involve statements of proportion: they turn on such words as *none, few, some, many, most, all,* along with *never, rarely, seldom, often, usually, always,* and so on" (209, italics his). In reaction to those who turn up their noses at numbers, he wrote, "When it comes to proportional statements, the opinions of those who wouldn't count, shouldn't count" (222).
100. E. J. Kenney, review of W. V. Harris, *Ancient Literacy, CR* 41 (1991): 168–69, quotations from both pages, respectively. Kenney is the author of "Books and Readers in the Roman World," in *CHCL* 2, 3–32.
101. J. H. Humphrey, ed., *Literacy in the Roman World* (Journal of Roman Archaeology Supplementary Series no. 3; Ann Arbor, Mich.: Journal of Roman Archaeology, 1991). In the absence of the usual introductory remarks, the review of the volume by John Bodel in *JRA* 83 (1993): 183–84 provides helpful synthesis. For trenchant comments concerning the Greek side of Harris, note Roger S. Bagnall, *Everyday Writing in the Greco-Roman East* (Berkeley: University of California Press, 2011), 2–3, and for more detail Lucio del Corso, "I documenti nella Grecia classica tra produzione e conservazione," *Quaderni di Storia* 56 (2002): 155–89; Harvey Yunis, ed., *Written Texts and the Rise of Literate Culture in Ancient Greece* (Cambridge: Cambridge University Press, 2003); del Corso, "Materiali per una protostoria del libro e delle pratiche di lettura nel mondo Greco," *Segno e testo* 1 (2003): 5–78; and Ana Missiou, *Literacy and Democracy in Fifth-Century Athens* (Cambridge: Cambridge University Press, 2011).
102. The words of Nicholas Horsfall are representative on this score, "The nature and density of the epigraphic material from a given site is determined not merely by its educational and economic level in antiquity but by the skill of the excavators, the competence of the editors, by the circumstances of destruction, where applicable, and by the benevolence of geology and climate towards the survival of the writing materials once in use." Thus his "Statistics or States of Mind?," in *Literacy in the Roman World,* 67. Similarly, Tim Cornell insisted: "The surviving epigraphic evidence is unrepresentative, biased and misleading. These limitations and distortions cannot be overlooked by the historian, who must engage in a constant struggle to break free of the tyranny of the evidence. . . . The great weakness of W. V. Harris' book, I fear, is that it does not attempt to go beyond the evidence" ("The Tyranny of the Evidence: A Discussion of the Possible Uses of Literacy in Etruria and Latium in the Archaic Age," in *Literacy in the Roman World,* 33). In the absence of further explanation Cornell's criticism in particular seems unfair, even irresponsible, though perhaps he only meant to be clever.
103. Horsfall, "Statistics or States of Mind?," in *Literacy in the Roman World,* 59.

104. Horsfall complained, "I suspect we might have learned a good deal from analysis site by site of our major collections of archives and papyri . . . it does soon become clear that, given Harris' general approach to the evidence, the discovery of such small, solid bodies of material, in however many provinces, is more or less irrelevant to him" (ibid., 60). Other critics of Harris's work weighed in from this same perspective, e.g., Leonard A. Curchin, "Literacy in the Roman Provinces: Qualitative and Quantitative Data from Central Spain," *AJP* 116 (1995): 461–76.
105. The quotations in this paragraph are from Horsfall, "Statistics or States of Mind?," 62, 63, 68, and 76. Noteworthy in terms of his criticisms is Horsfall's article on Petronius, "'The Uses of Literacy' and the *Cena Trimalchionis:* I & II," *GR* 36 (1989): 74–89, 194–209.
106. James Franklin, "Literacy and the Parietal Inscriptions of Pompeii," in *Literacy in the Roman World,* 77–98, quotations from pp. 81 (first two) and 97 (third). The application of graffiti to the issues of literacy is perhaps not as straightforward as Franklin believed. See the studies in J. A. Baird and Claire Taylor, eds., *Ancient Graffiti in Context* (London/New York: Routledge, 2011).
107. Mary Beard, "The Function of the Written Word in Roman Religion," in *Literacy in the Roman World,* 58.
108. Alan K. Bowman, "Literacy in the Roman Empire: Mass and Mode," in *Literacy in the Roman World,* 119.
109. Keith Hopkins, "Conquest by Book," in *Literacy in the Roman World,* 134.
110. Ibid., 134–35, emphasis his.
111. Harry Y. Gamble, *Books and Readers in the Early Church* (New Haven, Conn.: Yale University Press, 1995), 248 n. 10 (emphasis added). Note also Rosamond McKitterick, "Introduction," in *The Uses of Literacy in Early Medieval Europe* (ed. Rosamond McKitterick; Cambridge: Cambridge University Press, 1990), 1–10.
112. Catherine Hezser, *Jewish Literacy in Roman Palestine* (Tübingen: Mohr Siebeck, 2001). The much more general work by Alan Millard, *Reading and Writing in the Time of Jesus* (New York: New York University Press, 2000), should also be noted.
113. Hezser, *Jewish Literacy,* 36. On p. 35 and elsewhere she did, however, approvingly cite the study and conclusions of Meir Bar-Ilan, "Illiteracy in the Land of Israel in the First Centuries C.E.," in *Essays in the Social Scientific Study of Judaism and Jewish Society* (ed. S. Fishbane, S. Schoenfeld, and A. Goldschlaeger; Hoboken, N.Y.: Ktav, 1992), 2:46–61. His was a noteworthy study. Bar-Ilan proceeded on the axiom of an inverse relation between literacy and urbanism and attempted to arrive at estimates of the percentages of the Jewish population living as rural agriculturalists, inhabiting small towns, and dwelling in the "highly urban" centers such as Jerusalem. He argued that whereas one could not discover directly how many Jews could read, direct evidence

did exist for demographic patterns. Factoring in comparative literacy and demographic data largely taken from modern studies, Bar-Ilan estimated that virtually all rural people would have been illiterate; that the literacy rates in smaller towns such as Tiberias may have been 2–15 percent; and that highly urban areas would have seen steady rates of 10 percent. Since seven of every ten Jews lived in rural settings, he asserted, "it is no exaggeration to say that the total literacy rate in the Land of Israel at that time (of Jews only, of course), was probably less than 3%" (55).

114. Hezser, *Jewish Literacy,* 36.
115. Ibid., 43; note also 75, "Rabbinic literature is the major source of information on the contents and forms of ancient Jewish elementary education, but the evidence is scattered and scanty and may reflect rabbis' wishful thinking more than actual circumstances."
116. The points in this paragraph derive from ibid., 67, 72, 237, 287, 289, and 446–47.
117. Ibid., 39.
118. She came closest in comments in ibid., 231.
119. The quotations in this paragraph derive respectively from Rajak's review in *JJS* 56 (2005): 154; Snyder's in *JBL* 121 (2002): 562; and Bar-Ilan's review, n.p. [cited 4 April 2007]. Online: http://faculty.biu.ac.il/~testsm/hezser.html.
120. Fergus Millar, "Transformations of Judaism under Graeco-Roman Rule: Responses to Seth Schwartz's 'Imperialism and Jewish Society,'" *JJS* 57 (2006): 146.
121. Seth Schwartz, *Imperialism and Jewish Society, 200 B.C.E. to 640 C.E.* (Princeton, N.J.: Princeton University Press, 2001), and Nicole Belayche, *Iudaea-Palaestina: The Pagan Cults in Roman Palestine (Second to Fourth Century)* (Tübingen: Mohr Siebeck, 2001).
122. Schwartz, *Imperialism,* 129 (emphasis added). The heart of the argument in the two books is Schwartz, ibid., 129–61, and Belayche, *Iudaea-Palaestina,* 49–170.
123. Hezser, *Jewish Literacy,* 89. She makes similar statements on pp. 39, 79, 88, 450, 474, and 497.
124. For Egypt, see Raffaella Cribiore, *Writing, Teachers, and Students in Greco-Roman Egypt* (Atlanta: Scholars Press, 1996), esp. 3–33. For Palestine, see below.
125. On this point note the discussions in Teresa Morgan, *Literate Education in the Hellenistic and Roman Worlds* (Cambridge: Cambridge University Press, 1998), and Raffaella Cribiore, *Gymnastics of the Mind: Greek Education in Hellenistic and Roman Egypt* (Princeton, N.J./Oxford: Princeton University Press, 2001), passim. Expert reaction has found this view of the papyri versus literature persuasive in general: on Morgan, see, e.g., M. B. Trapp in *CR* 50 (2000): 219–20; Peter van Minnen in *Mnemosyne* 53 (2000): 620–25; and Robert Lamberton in *CJ* 95 (1999): 88–92; and on Cribiore, see Lamberton, *CJ* 100 (2004): 107–10; Mary Lefkowitz in *Education Next* 3, no. 2 (Spring, 2003): 89–90; and Teresa Morgan in *American Historical Review* 108 (2003): 233.

126. Hezser, *Jewish Literacy,* 500, 422, 425–26, 422, and 500, respectively.
127. E.g., note Nahman Avigad, *Hebrew Bullae from the Time of Jeremiah: Remnants of a Burnt Archive* (Jerusalem: Israel Exploration Society, 1986); Robert Deutsch, *Messages from the Past: Hebrew Bullae from the Time of Isaiah Through the Destruction of the First Temple* (Tel Aviv: Archaeological Center Publications, 1999); Robert Deutsch and André Lemaire, *Biblical Period Personal Seals in the Shlomo Moussaieff Collection* (Tel Aviv: Archaeological Center Publications, 2000); and Robert Deutsch, *Biblical Period Hebrew Bullae: The Josef Chaim Kaufman Collection* (Tel Aviv: Archaeological Center Publications, 2003).
128. These are separate literary works, not copies. Many nonsectarian writings do exist in multiple copies, including *Enoch* (twenty-four copies), *Aramaic Levi* (nine), *Instruction* (eight), *New Jerusalem* (seven), *Visions of Amram* (six), *Apocryphal Jeremiah* (six), *Proto-Esther* (six), *Pseudo-Ezekiel* (six), *Apocryphal Joshua* (five), *Apocryphal Moses* (five), and *Mysteries* (four).
129. These numbers are based upon the list of manuscripts in Emanuel Tov et al., *The Texts from the Judaean Desert: Indices and An Introduction to the Discoveries in the Judaean Desert Series* (DJD 39; Oxford: Clarendon, 2002), 27–114, and Tov, *Revised Lists of the Texts from the Judaean Desert* (Leiden: Brill, 2009). Given the fragmentary condition of many of the texts, the numbers are unavoidably somewhat uncertain, but the precise number is not the point here.
130. Bagnall has made a useful contribution to methodology here. "Arguments from silence, or relative silence," he has written, "have played an important role in modern discussions of subjects like literacy and archives. . . . It is, I think, possible to show that many, even most, of the gaps in the record can be explained archaeologically" (*Everyday Writing,* 28). He then proceeded with an example, demonstrating on pp. 28–53 that as a measure of what once existed, the surviving documentation of Hellenistic Egypt is utterly misleading.
131. Only one text has been identified from which another may have been copied, and that identification (4QDan[b] from 4QDan[a]) is extremely tentative. See E. Ulrich, *The Dead Sea Scrolls and the Origins of the Bible* (Grand Rapids, Mich.: Eerdmans, 1999), 148–62, and on the question of *Vorlagen* more generally see E. Tov, *Scribal Practices and Approaches Reflected in the Texts Found in the Judean Desert* (Leiden: Brill, 2004), 29–30.
132. Such features include use of cheap materials such as poor quality papyrus sheets or leather scraps, wax or wood tablets, or sherds, rather than expensive scrolls; rough handwriting and wide lines; failure to calculate space precisely, resulting in the need to write in the margins and on the reverse; and inept language, with much crossing out and reworking evident. In addition, considerable positive evidence exists to show that we are dealing with copies: Tov, *Scribal Practices,* 28–29. Nothing suggests that the production of literary autographs among Second Temple Jews differed much from the processes in contemporary Rome, about which a bit more is known. Three stages were usually involved: (1) The

production of a draft copy; (2) a stage of correction, criticism, and revision, during which it was common to solicit input from others; and (3) production of copies produced in polished fashion by scribes. For the Roman evidence, see M. McDonnell, "Writing, Copying and Autograph Manuscripts in Ancient Rome," *CQ* 46 (1996): 469–91, esp. 486. Only the third stage is evident among the Dead Sea Scrolls. Issues of circulation and the means of textual reproduction are important when one considers the problem of *autographa;* see the incisive discussion by R. J. Starr, "The Circulation of Literary Texts in the Roman World," *CQ* 37 (1987): 213–23.

133. On these points in general, see Tov, *Scribal Practices,* 57–124, 131–248.

134. For a good discussion and references, see ibid., 20–24. Most recently, Ada Yardeni has argued that some fifty manuscripts were copied by a single scribe whose work is found in several of the Qumran caves as well as at Masada; see "A Note on a Qumran Scribe," in *New Seals and Inscriptions, Hebrew, Idumean and Cuneiform* (ed. M. Lubetski; Sheffield: Sheffield University Press, 2007), 287–98.

135. For fuller discussion of the points in this paragraph, see Michael O. Wise, "Accidents and Accidence: A Scribal View of Linguistic Dating of the Aramaic Scrolls from Qumran," in *Thunder in Gemini* (Sheffield: JSOT Press, 1994), esp. 119–46, with literature cited. On deluxe editions in particular, see Tov, *Scribal Practices,* 125–29.

136. Plin. *Nat.* 5.73. On this theory, see immediately below.

137. For further analysis of the social, geographical, and chronological issues involving the scrolls, and for arguments defending the numbers and percentages cited in this paragraph, see Michael O. Wise, "Dating the Teacher of Righteousness and the *Floruit* of His Movement," *JBL* 122 (2003): 53–87.

138. One cannot assume sectarian origin for any work merely because it was found at Qumran. The words of Hartmut Stegeman in "Die Bedeutung der Qumranfunde für die Erforschung der Apokalyptik," in *Apocalypticism in the Mediterranean World and the Near East* (ed. D. Hellholm; Tübingen: Mohr-Siebeck, 1983), 511, are representative of current thinking in the field: "Als 'spezifische Qumrantexte' können zunächst nur solche Werke aus den Qumranfunden gelten, die der Gestalt des 'Lehrer der Gerechtigkeit' eine autoritative Funktion beimessen, die die spezifische Ordnung der Qumrangemeinde kennen, auf andere Weise der Sonderstellung in Rahmen des Judentums reflektieren oder wegen ihres formalen oder terminologischen Konnexes mit solchen Schriften diesen *notwendigerweise* zuzuordnen sind" (emphasis his). For similar approaches, see C. A. Newsom, "'Sectually Explicit' Literature from Qumran," in *The Hebrew Bible and Its Interpreters* (ed. W. H. Propp, B. Halpern, and D. N. Freedman; Winona Lake, Ind.: Eisenbrauns, 1990), 167–87; L. Schiffman, *Reclaiming the Dead Sea Scrolls* (Philadelphia/Jerusalem: Jewish Publication Society, 1994), 34; D. Dimant, "The Qumran Manuscripts: Contents and Significance," in *Time*

to Prepare the Way in the Wilderness: Papers on the Qumran Scrolls (ed. D. Dimant and L. Schiffman; Leiden: Brill, 1995), 23–58; and G. Boccaccini, *Beyond the Essene Hypothesis* (Grand Rapids, Mich.: Eerdmans, 1998), 59–67.

139. Hezser, *Jewish Literacy,* 426. See also p. 146, etc.
140. Many of those who once argued in their writings for the older paradigm now acknowledge the wider provenance of the caches. Note, e.g., Philip Davies: "The huge variety of scribal hands throws the theory of a small scribbling sect into some doubt. . . . We certainly do *not* know where these . . . manuscripts were written, only where they were found" (emphasis his). Thus his "Reflections on DJD XVIII," in *The Dead Sea Scrolls at Fifty: Proceedings of the 1997 Society of Biblical Literature Qumran Section Meetings* (ed. R. A. Kugler and E. M. Schuller; Atlanta: Scholars Press, 1999), 156. Note also the words of scrolls editor-in-chief Emanuel Tov, "Hebrew Biblical Manuscripts from the Judaean Desert: Their Contributions to Textual Criticism," *JJS* 39 (1988): 5, "It now seems likely that many, if not most, of the [scriptural] texts found in this region were copied in other parts of Palestine, so that most of them can be taken as Palestinian texts."
141. On this last, note the comment of Snyder in his *JBL* review, 561: "The N[ew] T[estament] literature might have been profitably consulted. Even if some of the writers are beginning to leave the Jewish ambit to varying degrees, their habits of textual usage must still reflect their Jewish background."
142. Hezser, *Jewish Literacy,* 240, 230.
143. 11Q10 and 4Q157 (Job) and 4Q156 (Leviticus). Milik said of the latter: "Il n'est pas sûr que les deux morceaux aient appartenu à un targum *sensu stricto:* version araméenne de tout un livre biblique. Ils pourraient provenir d'un ouvrage liturgique ou rituel où certaines parties seraient des traductions littérales de quelques sections du Pentateuque" (J. T. Milik, *Qumrân Grotte 4 II* [DJD 6; Oxford: Clarendon, 1977], 86).
144. On this legal legacy, see the comments of Douglas M. Gropp et al., *Wadi Daliyeh II: The Samaria Papyri from Wadi Daliyeh* (DJD 28; Oxford: Clarendon, 2001), 19–32, esp. 32, and the full study by Andrew D. Gross, *Continuity and Innovation in the Aramaic Legal Tradition* (Leiden: Brill, 2008), passim.
145. Abraham Wasserstein, "Non-Hellenized Jews in the Semi-Hellenized East," *Scripta Classica Israelica* 14 (1995): 111.
146. Hezser, *Jewish Literacy,* 230 n. 31.
147. In 2002 new documents came to light in the environs of En Gedi in a cave on the north side known as the Har Yishai Cave. These were two very poorly preserved Greek documents, whose precise character is difficult to determine with certainty, though their association with the Bar Kokhba revolt is clear from the archaeology of the cave. See R. Porat, H. Eshel, and A. Frumkin, "Finds from the Bar Kokhba Revolt from Two Caves at En Gedi," *PEQ* 139 (2007): 35–53, and for the texts N. Cohen, "New Greek Papyri from a Cave in the Vicinity of En Gedi," *Scripta Classica Israelica* 25 (2006): 87–95. Further, in

2004 bedouin found a fragment of Leviticus in a small cave in Nahal Arugot; see Hanan Eshel, Yosi Baruchi, and Roi Porat, "Fragments of a Leviticus Scroll (ArugLev) Found in the Judaean Desert in 2004," *DSD* 13 (2006): 55–60. In 2009, bedouin discovered an archive in a cave south of Hebron, of which one text, known as the Bet ʿAmar text, has been published. See E. Eshel, H. Eshel, and A. Yardeni, "שטר משנת ארבע לחורבן בית ישראל," *Cathedra* 132 (2009): 5–24.

148. N. Lewis, ed., *The Documents from the Bar Kokhba Period in the Cave of Letters: The Greek Papyri* (JDS 2; Jerusalem: Israel Exploration Society, the Hebrew University of Jerusalem, and the Shrine of the Book, 1989); Y. Yadin and J. C. Greenfield, eds., *The Documents from the Bar Kokhba Period in the Cave of Letters: Aramaic and Nabatean Signatures and Subscriptions* (JDS 2; Jerusalem: Israel Exploration Society, the Hebrew University of Jerusalem, and the Shrine of the Book, 1989); H. M. Cotton and A. Yardeni, eds., *Aramaic, Hebrew and Greek Documentary Texts from Nahal Hever and Other Sites, with an Appendix Containing Alleged Qumran Texts* (DJD 27; Oxford: Clarendon, 1997); J. Charlesworth et al., eds., *Miscellaneous Texts from the Judaean Desert* (DJD 38; Oxford: Clarendon, 2000); and Yadin et al., eds., *Hebrew, Aramaic and Nabatean-Aramaic Papyri.*

149. Thus, e.g., H. Eshel, M. Broshi, and T. A. J. Jull, "Four Murabbaʿat Papyri and the Alleged Capture of Jerusalem by Bar Kokhba," in *Law in the Documents of the Judaean Desert* (ed. R. Katzoff and D. Schaps; Leiden: Brill, 2005), 45–50, on *Mur* 22, 25, 29 and 30; see also Eshel's earlier consideration of the matter, "Documents of the First Jewish Revolt from the Judaean Desert," in *The First Jewish Revolt* (ed. A. Berlin and J. A. Overman; London/New York: Routledge, 2002), 157–63; and see further discussion in Chapter 2 below.

150. Ada Yardeni makes the case regarding 4Q347 and 4Q359 in DJD 27, 283–84. Further evidence for confusion among the lots purchased from the bedouin comes from her join of *P.Hever* 50 with *Mur* 26; see ibid., 123–29. On 4Q348, see H. Eshel, "4Q348, 4Q343 and 4Q345: Three Economic Documents from Qumran Cave 4?," *JJS* 52 (2001): 132–35, and Chapter 2 below. For the nomenclature *P.Hever,* as opposed to *XHev/Se,* see H. Cotton, "Documentary Texts from the Judaean Desert: A Matter of Nomenclature," *Scripta Classica Israelica* 20 (2001): 115–16. The use of *P.Hever* is not only less ponderous, but also accords with the usage of John F. Oates, Roger S. Bagnall, Sarah J. Clackson, Alexandra A. O'Brien, Joshua D. Sosin, Terry G. Wilfong, and Klaas A. Worp, *Checklist of Greek, Latin, Demotic and Coptic Papyri, Ostraca and Tablets,* http://scriptorium.lib.duke.edu/papyrus/texts/clist.html, June 2011.

151. A. J. T. Jull, D. J. Donahue, M. Broshi, and E. Tov, "Radiocarbon Dating of Scrolls and Linen Fragments from the Judean Desert," *ʿAtiqot* 28 (1996): 85–91.

152. Only 3Q15, the *Copper Scroll,* is a certain exception. "Rebukes Reported by the Overseer" (4Q477), while is may have its origins in a documentary situation, is presented as a literary text (literary format, bookhand). The extremely

fragmentary Aramaic (?) writing 6Q26, typically identified as an account or contract, is possibly a literary work that makes use of documentary conventions, as, e.g., the Aramaic 4Q245 does in analogous fashion. On the documentary aspects of the latter, see Michael O. Wise, "4Q245 (PsDan[c] Ar) and the High Priesthood of Judas Maccabaeus," *DSD* 12 (2005): 322–23, 348. Further noteworthy is the fact that no fragments of these documentary texts were discovered by R. de Vaux and the excavation team when, in the wake of the bedouin searches, they recovered more than seventy manuscripts from Cave 4; thus S. Pfann, "Reassessing the Judaean Desert Caves: Libraries, Archives, *Genizas* and Hiding Places," *Bulletin of the Anglo-Israel Archaeological Society* 25 (2007): 149.

153. The words of Naphtali Lewis are à propos, "In Greek documents of the Hellenistic and Roman periods an individual is normally identified by name, father's (and/or mother's) name and city or village of origin (ἰδία, Latin *origo*)." Thus his "In the World of P. Yadin: Where Did Judah's Wives Live?," *IEJ* 46 (1996): 257. Cf. also M. Rostovtzeff, *The Social and Economic History of the Roman Empire* (2nd ed.; Oxford: Clarendon, 1957), 518. The point is as true of the Semitic texts from Judaea.

154. ʿIr Nahash (עיר נחש) of *Mur* 24 seems to have been such a latifundium, though the identification as such has apparently not been made previously. The term עיר is sometimes used in the Mishnah (e.g., *m. ʿErub.* 5:6) to refer to either (1) nucleated villages attached to large estates or (2) farmsteads turned into an agglomeration of homes by the addition of settlers or other increase in population. See the discussion by S. Applebaum, "Economic Life in Palestine," in CRINT 1.2:643.

155. Schürer, *The History,* 2:192–94.

156. In no particular order, unidentified or imprecisely located toponyms include Sophphate[ ] (in the district of Livias), Beth ʿAsahu, Beth ʿ[ ] (apparently a subdivision of En Gedi), Beth-Mashiko (near Kephar-Barucha), Ha-[ ] (probably near Jerusalem), Kephar Signah (in southern Galilee; cf. Beyer, *Aramäischen Texte,* 1:306–7, and Joseph Naveh, על חרס וגומא [Jerusalem: Magnes, 1992], 84), Ha-Nablata (*si vera lectio*), Bene Eliashib, and Bene Yirashel. (The vocalization of several of the foregoing is uncertain.) Regarding the last name in the list, בני ירשאל (*P.Hever* 7), Ramon Katzoff has argued cogently for its preference over the reading adopted in the *editio princeps,* "Bene Yisrael" (בני ישראל), "children of Israel." Yardeni had noted the correct reading but adopted the second option on the assumption of metathesis. Katzoff pointed to Bene Berak for a parallel but did not advert to the penultimate toponym in our list, Bene Eliashib (found in *Mur* 20), also previously misunderstood. The accumulating evidence now favors its interpretation as a place-name as well. See Katzoff's review of Cotton and Yardeni, DJD 27, in *Scripta Classica Israelica* 19 (2000): 319.

157. Ancient demographic analysis is notoriously tricky. The best modern studies build on the foundation laid by Tertius Chandler, *Four Thousand Years of*

Urban Growth: An Historical Census (Lewiston, N.Y./Queenston: Edwin Mellen Press, 1987). Estimates for the population of Palestine during the period of this study have ranged as widely as the methods employed. For a review of these estimates, see the study by M. Broshi, whose own imminently sane approach proceeds from the grain-growing capacity of the various regions Jews inhabited. His suggested population of approximately one million is adopted here. See his "The Population of Western Palestine in the Roman-Byzantine Period," *BASOR* 236 (1979): 1–10; reprinted and updated in his *Bread, Wine, Walls and Scrolls* (Sheffield: Sheffield Academic Press, 2001), 93–109.

158. For the reasoning justifying the identification with the top quartile and the number 250,000, see the discussion of the ancient Judaean economy in Chapter 5.

159. On the ubiquity of the names mentioned in this paragraph, see Ilan, *Lexicon,* 56–57.

160. The extremely useful prosopography in Yadin et al., eds., *Hebrew, Aramaic and Nabatean-Aramaic Papyri,* 387–90, is notable for (and suffers from) such reticence. An early prosopographical study by David Goodblatt deserves honorable mention: "A Contribution to the Prosopography of the Second Revolt: Yehudah bar Menasheh," *JJS* 38 (1987): 38–55. Publication of many additional documents has since made most of his deductions obsolete, but his application of the method was salutary.

161. R. Taubenschlag, *The Law of Greco-Roman Egypt in the Light of the Papyri 322 B.C.–640 A.D.* (2nd ed.; Warsaw: Panstwowe Wydawnictwo Naukowe, 1955), 171 nn. 6–7; Youtie, "ΥΠΟΓΡΑΦΕΥΣ," 213.

162. Youtie, "ΥΠΟΓΡΑΦΕΥΣ," 213–14; cf. 207–9 (with nn. 20–21), 220; Youtie, "ΑΓΡΑΜΜΑΤΟΣ: An Aspect of Greek Society in Egypt," *CP* 75 (1971): 170, 173.

163. E.g., one of the subscribers to *P.Yadin* 15, Yohanan b. Egla, largely unable to sign, employed his son Joseph as *hypographeus:* יהוחנן בר אלכה ביד יהוסף ברה (Egla wrote only בר אלכה and misspelled his own name, metathesizing the *lamedh* and the voiced palatal *gimel,* then substituting the unvoiced palatal *kaph* for the latter). Babatha b. Simeon required a male relative or close friend to act as her κύριος (designated in Aramaic as אדון) on several occasions; note *P.Yadin* 15:24, 17:40, and 22:34. On all of these citations, see Yadin and Greenfield, *Documents: Signatures and Subscriptions,* 139–47.

164. The Tosephta is cited according to M. S. Zuckermandel, *Tosephta* (Jerusalem: Wahrmann Books, 1970).

165. For a full description of the process of production and related issues, see E. Koffmahn, *Die Doppelurkunden aus der Wüste Juda* (Leiden: Brill, 1968), 10–20.

166. The text of *t. Git.* 6:9 is disturbed in the manuscript tradition. For a reasoned discussion leading to the understanding adopted here, see S. Lieberman, תוספתה כפשוטה. סדר נשים (repr., New York/Jerusalem: Jewish Theological

Seminary of America, 1995), 8:899–900. Cf. *m. Git.* 8:10 and Schiffman, "Witnesses and Signatures," 183.

167. Many more details on the concord of names among participants to the documents may be gleaned in Appendix A.
168. Ann E. Killebrew, "Village and Countryside," in *The Oxford Handbook of Jewish Daily Life in Roman Palestine* (ed. C. Hezser; Oxford: Oxford University Press, 2010), 194–95.
169. It should also be noted that one is not always dependent on names alone to establish familial connections. Other facts that emerge concerning people within the contracts act as a check on identifications that might otherwise be suggested and so help one avoid mistaken conclusions. For example, family members will sometimes share idiosyncratic letterforms, evident from their signatures. Other diagnostic criteria will appear in the discussion in succeeding chapters.
170. For purposes of this analysis, mixed Hebrew/Aramaic signatures are counted as Hebrew. For a justification of this procedure, see Chapter 5 and the detailed discussion of the Hebrew data.
171. For the translation of עיברית as "Hebrew letters" or possibly as "Aramaic," see the discussion by M. Hengel, *Between Jesus and Paul: Studies in the Earliest History of Christianity* (Philadelphia: Fortress, 1983), 10 and notes. That the meaning is unlikely to be the obvious is evident in view of the overwhelming Jewish tradition, well attested by rabbinic literature, that legal documents were couched in Aramaic, not Hebrew.
172. The only exception to this rule in the known corpus is the Bet ʿAmar text, wherein the language changes from Aramaic to Hebrew, then back again. The Hebrew was evidently intended to capture the verbatim acknowledgment of the widow involved at that point. See further Chapter 5.
173. גט שכתבו עברית ועדיו יונית יונית ועדיו עברית . . . כשר.
174. Unfortunately, this line of approach cannot help with the problem of Judaean knowledge of Greek. A person able to speak Greek would not necessarily be able to write Greek, even if he or she could produce an Aramaic signature.
175. Emerton, "Problem of Vernacular Hebrew," 17.
176. David Vincent, *The Rise of Mass Literacy: Reading and Writing in Modern Europe* (Malden, Mass.: Polity, 2000), 1–26.
177. R. S. Schofield, "The Measurement of Literacy in Pre-Industrial England," in *Literacy in Traditional Societies* (ed. J. Goody; Cambridge: Cambridge University Press, 1968), 311–25. Schofield went on to pursue the method in a number of subsequent studies, themselves frequently cited, including "Dimensions of Illiteracy in England 1750–1850," in Graff, *Literacy and Social Development,* 201–13. Here he showed that the percentage of men unable to sign at marriage declined in the years 1850–1911 from more than 30 percent to 1 percent, and of women from more than 45 percent to 1 percent.

178. Schofield, "Measurement," 318–19.
179. David Cressy, *Literacy and the Social Order: Reading and Writing in Tudor and Stuart England* (Cambridge: Cambridge University Press, 1980).
180. Ibid., 53.
181. Ibid., 56.
182. Ibid., 53. In his study "Levels of Illiteracy in England, 1530–1730," *Historical Journal* 20 (1977): 2, Cressy further observed of signature literacy, "It is, of course, an unsatisfactory criterion, but as a measure that is 'universal, standard and direct' it provides a fruitful starting place."
183. Kenneth Lockridge, "Literacy in Early America 1650–1800," in Graff, *Literacy and Social Development,* 183–200; E. Jennifer Monaghan, *Learning to Read and Write in Colonial America* (Boston: University of Massachusetts Press, 2005), esp. 383–86; Roger Collins, "Literacy and the Laity in Early Medieval Spain," in *The Uses of Literacy in Early Medieval Europe* (ed. R. McKitterick; Cambridge: Cambridge University Press, 1990), 125; Margaret Mullet, "Writing in Early Mediaeval Byzantium," in McKitterick, *Uses of Literacy,* 162; Rab Houston, "The Literacy Myth? Illiteracy in Scotland, 1630–1760," *P&P* 96 (1982): 81–102; D. Vincent, *Literacy and Popular Culture: England 1750–1914* (Cambridge: Cambridge University Press, 1989), 52–54; and Anthony J. Barbieri-Low, "Craftsman's Literacy: Uses of Writing by Male and Female Artisans in Qin and Han China," in *Writing & Literacy in Early China* (ed. Li Feng and Prager Branner; Seattle/London: University of Washington Press, 2011), 370–99.
184. M. T. Clanchy, *From Memory to Written Record: England 1066–1307* (2nd ed.; Malden, Mass.: Blackwell, 1993), 51. In an adaptation taken from the first edition, Clanchy expressed his reasoning more clearly: "In medieval England possession of a seal bearing the owner's name comes closest to the modern criterion of making the ability to sign one's name the touchstone of literacy. Although the possessor of a seal might not be able to write, he or she was a person familiar with documents and entitled to participate in their use." Thus his "Literate and Illiterate; Hearing and Seeing: England 1066–1307," in Graff, *Literacy and Social Development,* 22.
185. The full study is H. Youtie, "Pétaus, fils de Pétaus, ou le scribe qui ne savait pas écrire," *ChrEg* 41 (1966): 127–43.
186. Youtie, "ΑΓΡΑΜΜΑΤΟΣ," 171.
187. *P.Petaus* 11.35–37: "μὴ εἶναι δὲ καὶ αγράμματον αὐτόν, ἀλλὰ ὑπογράφειν οἷς ἐπιδίδωσι στρα(τηγῷ) καὶ ἄλλοις βιβλίοις τῆς κωμογρα(μματείας)."
188. Youtie, "ΑΓΡΑΜΜΑΤΟΣ," 172.
189. Harris, *Ancient Literacy,* 278–79.
190. Cribiore, *Writing, Teachers, and Students,* 146.
191. Ibid., 98–99; cf. Kim Haines-Eitzen, *Guardians of Letters* (Oxford: Oxford University Press, 2000), 63: "It appears that schoolchildren, and scribes at the

earliest levels, were taught a multifunctional basic hand, very close to the hand we find in private letters. It is only with advanced training that those who were to become professional scribes would learn a cursive writing (that aided speed) and/or the careful strictly bilinear hand that book dealers might wish to exhibit in their commercial copies." For further remarks on the relationship between personal hands and both literary and documentary types, see Wilhelm Schubart, *Griechische Palaeographie* (1925; repr., Munich: C. H. Beck'sche Verlagsbuchhandlung, 1966), 146–55.

192. The literary sources support this progression (Quint. *Inst.* 1.1.27, 34–35; Sen. *Ep.* 94.51). Hermas, as portrayed in The Shepherd of Hermas, seems to be a person who could copy graphically but not always construe the words so as to read: ἔλαβον ἐγώ, καὶ εἴς τινα τόπον τοῦ ἀγροῦ ἀναχωρήσας μετεγραψάμην πάντα πρὸς γράμμα· οὐχ ηὕρισκον γὰρ τὰς συλλαβάς, *Vis.* 2.1.4.

193. These are the terms used in the literary sources. Cribiore, *Writing, Teachers, and Students,* 13–14, shows that somewhat different terminology is not uncommon in the papyri.

194. Cribiore, *Gymnastics,* 192–219. Morgan, *Literate Education,* 313, provides a handy list of the most common authors in school texts.

195. K. Vossing, "Staat und Schule in der Spätantike," *Ancient Society* 32 (2002): 249–50.

196. Such was especially the case if, as often, students learned to read a language or form of language that they did not speak: Roman schoolchildren, for example, acquiring literacy initially via Greek, or speakers of the koine learning Attic. "Written-oral diglossia continues to hamper student progress in reading in modern times and surely posed difficulties for ancient learners in a far more rigid educational milieu" (Cribiore, *Writing, Teachers, and Students,* 9); see also Morgan, *Literate Education,* 100–110, 165–67.

197. Dion. Hal. *Comp.* 25, trans. Usher, LCL.

198. Cribiore, *Writing, Teachers, and Students,* 152.

199. Ibid., 33, 111–12.

200. Quint., *Inst.* 1.1.21.

201. Cribiore, *Writing, Teachers, and Students,* 116–17. For qualifications as to how the term βραδέως γράφων should properly be used, see Ann Hanson, "Ancient Illiteracy," in *Literacy in the Roman World,* 170. For additional definitional considerations, perhaps somewhat idealistic, see Thomas J. Kraus, "'Slow Writers'—βραδέως γράφοντες: What, How Much, and How Did They Write?," *Eranos* 97 (1999): 86–97.

202. Another attractive term for this kind of literacy, relevant especially in the Jewish context, is "sacred-text literacy." It required specialized training beyond the linguistic. For discussion, see B. Spolsky, "Triglossia and Literacy in Jewish Palestine of the First Century," *International Journal of the Sociology of Languages* 42 (1983): 102–4.

203. N. Gonis, review of R. Cribiore, *Writing, Teachers, and Students in Graeco-Roman Egypt*, *JRS* 88 (1998): 187. Cf. Morgan, *Literate Education*, 66–67, "In the Roman west, in Latin or Latin and Greek speaking areas, literate education is recognizably the same as in Egypt at a similar date."
204. Karel van der Toorn, *Scribal Culture and the Making of the Hebrew Bible* (Cambridge, Mass.: Harvard University Press, 2007), 56, with literature cited. For more detail on Mesopotamian education, note Dominique Charpin, *Reading and Writing in Babylon* (trans. Jane Marie Todd; Cambridge, Mass.: Harvard University Press, 2010), 17–67.
205. Toorn, *Scribal Culture*, 68 and citations; David Carr, *Writing on the Tablet of the Heart* (Oxford: Oxford University Press, 2005), 65–77.
206. Carr, *Writing*, 47–60, 111–73; Toorn, *Scribal Culture*, 75–104.
207. Milik, DJD 2, 92.
208. Ibid., 178.
209. Carr, *Writing*, 242. For literature and a full discussion of all of the abecedaries and alphabetic name lists, but discounting the notion that any are school exercises, see Hezser, *Jewish Literacy*, 85–88.
210. Yadin and Naveh, *Masada I*, 44–45. The editors were puzzled that these labels are written in Nabataean letters. In the light of what we now know from the Babatha materials, wherein one observes several Jews trained to write in Nabataean fashion as they lived in Mahoza, it seems reasonable to suggest that these men were from that region or similar villages of mixed Jewish and Nabataean habitation. They had come to be among the fighters and refugees at Masada because they repatriated to join the First Revolt. A similar explanation probably lies behind the fragmentary Nabataean letter 4Q343.
211. Carr, *Writing*, 260–61. For a largely positive and instructive reaction to Carr's proposals, see Richard A. Horsley, *Scribes, Visionaries and the Politics of Second Temple Judea* (Louisville, Ky.: Westminster John Knox, 2007), esp. 71–129.
212. Carr, *Writing*, 271.
213. For a similar approach in a much different context, see Herbert Hunger, *Schreiben und Lesen in Byzanz. Die byzantinische Buchkultur* (Munich: Beck, 1989), 82–85, with plates. Hunger sought to infer education and class backgrounds on the basis of people's use of majuscule or minuscule Greek lettering and their skill in producing it.
214. For this term and its conception, see H. Gregory Snyder, *Teachers and Texts in the Ancient World: Philosophers, Jews and Christians* (London: Routledge, 2000), 11, 186–205 and 215.

Chapter 2. Jerusalem, Herodium, Jericho, and Environs

1. The story of the discoveries presented here is largely based upon de Vaux's account in DJD 2, 3–50, and John Allegro, *The Dead Sea Scrolls: A Reappraisal* (2nd ed.; Middlesex: Penguin, 1964), 37–41, 179–87. For the numismatic evidence of a

trove or troves said to come from the Wadi Murabba'at, see J. T. Milik and H. Seyrig, "Trésor monétaire de Murabba'ât," *Revue numismatique* 6 (1958): 11–26; for the results of the 1968 survey that located an additional Roman-period cave and a Roman road in the area, see Zvi Greenhut, ed., "P. Bar Adon Excavations in the Judaean Desert," *'Atiqot* 9 (1984): 50–82; for the graveyard discovered near the caves in 1993, see Hanan Eshel and Zvi Greenhut, "Hiam El-Sagha: A Cemetery of the Qumran Type, Judaean Desert," *RB* 100 (1993): 252–59. Convenient current appraisals of the Murabba'at materials can be found in Ephraim Stern, "Murabba'at, Wadi: Archaeology," *EDSS* 1:581–83, and Hanan Eshel, "Murabba'at, Wadi: Written Material," *EDSS* 1:583–86.

2. Thus Y. Yadin, *Bar-Kokhba: The Rediscovery of the Legendary Hero of the Second Jewish Revolt Against Rome* (New York: Random House, 1971), 28.
3. The preliminary report by Harding appeared within just a few months and gave an interesting initial impression of the archaeological finds, not in fact fundamentally modified before publication in the *editio princeps:* G. Lankester Harding, "Khirbet Qumran and Wady Murabaat: Fresh Light on the Dead Sea Scrolls and New Manuscript Discoveries in Jordan," *PEQ* 84 (1952): 104–9.
4. The archaeologists uncovered only *Mur* 1, 2, 4, 42, 72, 78, a portion of 115, and 164; all the rest came by purchase.
5. Turned to great comedic effect by Tony Harrison in his play "The Trackers of Oxyrhynchus."
6. Allegro, *Dead Sea Scrolls,* 182–83.
7. On the question of the signature, see Chapter 4.
8. In February of 1962, the director of the museum of the Studium Biblicum Franciscanum reported that the museum had purchased from bedouin several fragments of a papyrus contract said to come from Murabba'at. J. T. Milik was to publish the I.O.U. That article never appeared, however, and only in 2008 did the document see the light of day. The team of scholars who published it suggested that it be numbered in sequence with the known Murabba'at texts, hence *Mur* 174. This suggestion is followed here. See E. Eshel, H. Eshel, and G. Geiger, "Mur 174: A Hebrew I.O.U. Document from Wadi Murabba'at," *SBFLA* 58 (2008): 313–26.
9. The actual number of the discoveries was somewhat higher. Of the Arabic fragments, most measuring less than a centimeter across, only three of forty-eight were considered worthy of publication.
10. Substantive reviews were not numerous but include J. Bingen, *ChrEg* 36 (1961): 409–12; M. Delcor, *VT* 12 (1962): 219–23; G. R. Driver, *HibJ* 60 (1961–1962): 164–67; L. H. Feldman, *CW* 55 (1962): 172; S. H. Hooke, *JTS* n.s. 13 (1962): 126–28; and H. Michaud, *RevQ* 3 (1961–1962): 285–92.
11. For a bibliography of the preliminary studies, see Dennis Pardee et al., *Handbook of Ancient Hebrew Letters* (Chico, Calif.: Scholars Press, 1982), 122–39 for the Murabba'at Bar Kokhba letters, and Reuven Yaron, "The Murabba'at Documents," *JJS* 11 (1960): 157 n. 2 for the legal documents.

12. Ada Yardeni, *Textbook of Aramaic, Hebrew and Nabataean Documentary Texts from the Judaean Desert and Related Material* (2 vols.; Jerusalem: Ben-Zion Dinur Center for Research in Jewish History, 2000).
13. Milik, DJD 2, 67. Milik also allowed that *Mur* 32, a very fragmentary deed (of purchase?) or I.O.U. might date to the earlier revolt. The hand seemed early: "Écriture cursive peut-être plus ancienne que celle des documents de la Second Révolt et même que celle de 18 (55/56 ap. J.C.)" (DJD 2, 149); however, he also observed similarity with the hand of *Mur* 30, which he believed dated to 134. Accordingly, he refrained from definitively assigning *Mur* 32 to either period.
14. "Il est donc possible qu'à la fin de la Première Guerre Juive ou au lendemain de cette guerre les grottes aient été le refuge d'une famille juive fuyant les Romains ou de zélotes continuant la résistance"; de Vaux, DJD 2, 48.
15. Here, too, one might note the hoard that came to light outside the excavations, although it lacked any known connection to the manuscript-bearing caves. Purchased from the bedouin, the hoard included 119 Nabataean drachmas, 51 imperial dinars, and 33 tetradrachmas of Trajan. Milik and Seyrig remarked, "Ce trésor est apparu sur le marché de Jérusalem en 1952 . . . d'après des renseignements dignes de foi, le trésor a été découvert au wàdi Murabba῾ât. . . . Les monnaies décrites ne constituent qu'une partie du trésor. Les deniers, notamment, étaient beaucoup plus nombreux, et quelque deux cents d'entre eux, vus chez des antiquaires, n'ont pu être étudiés ("Trésor," 11).
16. "Le témoignage concordant des monnaies et des textes nous révèle la nature de cette occupation: pendant la Seconde Guerre Juive, Murabba῾at a été le repaire d'un groupe de révoltés en lutte contre les Romains. Certains des objets qu'ils y ont abandonnés, les petites sandales d'enfants, les fuseaux et les fusaïoles, les peignes montrent qu'ils s'y étaient réfugiés avec leurs familles"; de Vaux, DJD 2, 48.
17. "L'ère sous-entendue est évidemment celle de l'Éparchie (de la Province d'Arabie, de Bosra), qui commence le 22 mars 106"; Milik, DJD 2, 106.
18. "Kann sich nicht vorstellen, daß nach der Eroberung durch die Römer im Jahre 73 n. Chr. ein jüdische Schneidebrief dort ausgestellt worden ist"; Koffmahn, *Doppelurkunden*, 43.
19. "Dies kann nur die 'Ära der Freiheit' des Jüdischen Krieges gegen die Römer gewesen sein, insbesondere, da wir aus Fl. Josephus Bell. l.c. wissen, daß in Masada eine Gruppe unnachgiebiger Patrioten, die sogenannten Sikarier, sich noch drei Jahre lang nach dem Fall Jerusalems gehalten haben. Masada war die einzige Stadt, in der es ein "Jahres sechs" seit der Befreiung beziehungsweise Rückeroberung im Jahre 66 n. Chr. gegeben hat"; ibid., 44; cf. 148–55. Note also her earlier "Zur Datierung des aramäisch/hebräisch Vertragsurkunden von Muraba῾at," *WZKM* 59/60 (1963–1964): 127–32, esp. 128–31.
20. Yadin, "Preliminary Report," 119 n. 112.
21. Yadin, *Bar-Kokhba*, 188–89.

22. Reuben Yaron, "The Mesadah Bill of Divorce," in *Studi in onore di E. Volterra* (6 vols.; Milan: A. Giuffrè, 1971), 6:433–55; Beyer, *Aramäischen Texte,* 1:307; Yadin and Naveh, *Masada I,* 9–11; Cotton and Geiger, *Masada II,* 1–2, and Hannah Cotton, "The Languages of the Legal and Administrative Documents from the Judaean Desert," *ZPE* 125 (1999): 224 (this is evidently Cotton's final, considered view; in between the two publications noted, she had been swayed by P. Freeman, "The Era of the Province of Arabia: Problems and Solution?," in *Studies in the History of the Roman Province of Arabia: The Northern Sector* [ed. H. I. MacAdam; BAR International Series 295; Oxford: Clarendon, 1986], 38–46, to readopt Milik's dating; thus in H. M. Cotton, W. E. H. Cockle, and F. G. B. Millar, "The Papyrology of the Roman Near East: A Survey," *JRS* 85 [1995]: no. 288 and n. 15; cf. her joint work with Yardeni, DJD 27, 148 and nn. 81–82); David Goodblatt, "Dating Documents in *Provincia Iudaea:* A Note on *Papyri Murabba'at* 19 and 20," *IEJ* 49 (1999): 249–59; H. Eshel, "Documents of the First Jewish Revolt," 158–59; Eshel, "The Dates Used During the Bar Kokhba Revolt," in *Bar Kokhba War Reconsidered,* 94–95; and Eshel, Broshi, and Jull, "Four Murabba'at Papyri," 48–49.
23. Milik, DJD 2, 111.
24. Koffmahn, *Doppelurkunden,* 45–46.
25. Beyer, *Aramäischen Texte,* 1:309.
26. Goodblatt, "Dating Documents," 255.
27. Beyer, *Aramäischen Texte,* 1:312. In point of fact, portions of four surviving signatures can be read on the badly effaced verso of *Mur* 23. Of the three where one can determine the language used, all are apparently Aramaic. The signature to which Beyer referred should be read as]◦ יהוחנן בר̇ (line 3).
28. Ibid., 1:316.
29. Eshel, "Documents of the First Jewish Revolt," 157–63.
30. D. T. Ariel, "A Survey of the Coin Finds in Jerusalem (Until the End of the Byzantine Period)," *LASBF* 32 (1982): 273–326, esp. 293; and H. Gitler, "A Comparative Study of Numismatic Evidence from Excavations in Jerusalem," *LASBF* 46 (1996): 317–62, esp. 328. Archaeologist have unearthed more than fifteen thousand coins in Jerusalem, among which are numbered only three overstruck by the insurgents.
31. The story of this discovery is most easily followed up in H. Eshel, "Aelia Capitolina, Jerusalem No More," *BAR* 23.6 (1997): 46–48, 73.
32. Eshel, "Documents of the First Jewish Revolt," 158.
33. See also his other study published in the same year, "מספר הערות על כוהנים גדולים בסוף ימי הבית השני," *Zion* 64 (1999): 499–500. Eshel later had second thoughts about this suggestion and urged that 4Q348 be understood as a Qumran text; thus his "4Q348, 4Q343 and 4Q345," esp. 134. The connection to Murabba'at is nevertheless more likely (see below).
34. Cotton and Yardeni, DJD 27, 283.

35. Yardeni, ibid., 302.
36. Eshel, "Documents of the First Jewish Revolt," 160.
37. Emanuel Tov, "The Greek Biblical Texts from the Judaean Desert," in *The Bible as Book: The Transmission of the Greek Text* (ed. S. McKendrick and O. O'Sullivan; New Castle, Del.: Oak Knoll, 2008), 101, opined that texts from find-spots other than Qumran may have been sold as coming from that site in order to inflate their price.
38. Cotton, "Languages," 219–31.
39. Milik had originally read the formula as "Year One," i.e., 131 C.E., as he suggested, or (according to a different scheme for the years of the revolt, followed by Yardeni), 132. See DJD 2, 118 and note ad loc, 120.
40. The only exception would be the text now known as *P.Hever* 8a, which says simply, "20 Adar, Year Three of the freedom of Israel." Prepared by the same scribe who wrote *P.Hever* 8, where the date is explicit as "Year Three of the freedom of Israel in the days of Simon b. Kosiba," no doubt can attend its attribution to the Second Revolt.
41. Cotton, "Languages," 224. In fact Cotton was mistaken on this point, as the number five could equally well apply to regnal dating, either by a Roman emperor (e.g., Nero) or by a Jewish high priest, as in 4Q348. Of the second option Cotton had, of course, no reason to be aware.
42. Here the term "archive" is intended to designate documents (and sometimes literary texts) gathered as a group in antiquity. The term is sometimes used by papyrologists to describe texts gathered around an individual, institution, court case, etc. by modern scholars, but that is not the usage proposed here. For further consideration of definitional issues, note, e.g., A. Martin, "Archives privées et cachettes documentaires," in *Proceedings of the 20th International Congress of Papyrologists, Copenhagen, Denmark, 23–29 August, 1992* (Copenhagen: Museum Tusculanum Press, 1994), 569–77. Martin proposed using the term "dossier" for the modern groupings. See also O. Pedersén, *Archives and Libraries in the Ancient Near East* (Bethesda, Md.: CDL Press, 1998), 2–3 and 2 n. 2, for further literature.
43. Scholars may have prematurely given up on the attempt; cf. Yaron as early as 1971, "The Mesadah Bill of Divorce," 434: "The papyri from Wadi Murabba'at are unrelated to each other; no archive can be put together."
44. The reference to documents being "attached" (קשורין) to one another seems to mean physically bound to one another with glue or thread, as was the habit in the Greco-Roman world.
45. M. A. Friedman, "Contracts: Rabbinic Literature and Ancient Jewish Documents," in CRINT 2.3b, 423–60.
46. Such practices were common in contemporary Egypt, as evidenced by many personal archives discovered there. The Adler papyri, for example, comprise the archives of a mortician and embalmer, Petesis, preserved by several generations of his family; and the papers of a certain Peteharsemteus were kept successively

after his death by his eldest son, Totoes, and then by his oldest grandson. These same two men also held the documents of their brothers, sisters, and wives. For discussion and bibliography, see Ernst Posner, *Archives in the Ancient World* (Cambridge, Mass.: Harvard University Press, 1972), 157.

47. The editors of the archive do not connect the principals of this document to Babatha. For fuller discussion of the suggestion that these were her brothers, see Chapter 3.

48. Jonas Greenfield, "The Texts from Nahal Se'elim (Wadi Seiyal)," in *The Madrid Qumran Congress* (ed. J. Trebolle Barrera and L. Vegas Montaner; 2 vols.; Leiden: Brill, 1992), 2:661–65.

49. H. M. Cotton, "The Archive of Salome Komaise Daughter of Levi: Another Archive from the 'Cave of Letters,'" *ZPE* 105 (1995): 171–208; Cotton, DJD 27, esp. 158–237.

50. See the discussions by Tal Ilan, "Women's Archives in the Judaean Desert," in *The Dead Sea Scrolls Fifty Years After Their Discovery* (ed. L. H. Schiffman et al.; Jerusalem: Israel Exploration Society and the Shrine of the Book, 2000), 755–60; and Sigrid Peterson, "Caves, Documents, Women: Archives and Archivists," in ibid., 761–72.

51. In the *editio princeps* of *Mur* 29, Milik read Cleopas's signature as Κ[λέο]πος Εὐτραπέλ[ο]υ χειρὶ ἑαυτοῦ γ(έγραφα); DJD 2, 142. P. J. Sijpesteijn subsequently offered a slight correction, to read ἐ<μ>αυτοῦ γ(έγραφα) ("A Note on P. Murabbaʿat 29," *IEJ* 34 [1984]: 49–50). Cotton has read Eutrapelus's signature in *Mur* 26 as [13]Ευ[. . .]Ευ[[14]χει(ρὶ) ε.[. . .]. .[, DJD 27, 128, and 129, "Note on the Greek Signature." Close study of the photograph under magnification suggests, however, that Eutrapelus simply "lined out" his signature and that otherwise what he wrote may be read and restored as follows: Ευ——Ευ[——?] χει(ρὶ) ἐμ[αυτ]. .[. The Semitic spelling of his name without patronym appears in line 13 of the outer contract, אוטרפלס.

52. Ilan, *Lexicon,* 55 (total individuals) and 280 (Εὐτραπέλος). The other Εὐτραπέλος is a man whose name is inscribed on a Jerusalem ossuary published by Clermont-Gannau in 1883 and dated as "pre-70 C.E." See now *CIIP* no. 515, where the name is described as an "altogether uncommon Greek name." It was not only rare in Judaea; it was rare, period. Accordingly, it seems very possible that the ossuary belonged to the father of our Eutrapelus and Cleopas.

53. Simon also serves as *hypographeus* for the illiterate Shapira b. Jesus in *Mur* 29, then signs his own signature as a witness: שמעון בר שבי שׂה[ד] . Between the words שבי and שהד, Simon inserted what appears to be a large, stylized *samekh,* perhaps representing the word ס(פר), "scribe." In both cases the hand is recognizably that of the body of the contract. Regarding the suggestion that Simon was the scribe of *Mur* 22, note in addition to the surviving portion of that text's signature (where he again served as *hypographeus*) שמ[, that the letterforms of the outer text of this *Doppelurkunde* are strikingly similar to those of the signatures of Shapira and

Simon in *Mur* 29. Thus the proposal to read and restore his signature in *Mur* 22 as שמ]וען בר שבי[מ̇מרה or, less probably, שמ]וען כתב[מ̇מרה.

54. Cf. Applebaum, "Economic Life," 663: "A high proportion of city-dwellers cultivated holdings in the immediate vicinity of the town, and the urban upper class's economic basis was almost invariably landed property."
55. The matter hinges on the reconstruction of 4Q348 below. Also possible is that some members were born in Kefar Signa, others in Jerusalem, and others perhaps yet elsewhere. Miriam is associated with a toponym of uncertain reading in *Mur* 19.
56. The text may also be a deed of purchase, but those types of contract were usually, to judge from what survives, *Doppelurkunden. Mur* 32 has no signatures on the verso, unlike the double contracts, and so is more likely an I.O.U. in its ordinary "simple" format.
57. Yardeni, *Textbook,* 1:35, 2:24.
58. Neither Milik nor Yardeni remarked on the damaged letters apparently belonging to signatures beneath Hanina's in *Mur* 27. Beyer (*Aramäischen Texte,* 1:313) did discern some illegible letters and also proposed to read a name, ח̇נ̇ין. Under magnification of the digitized image, the preferable reading of the letters beneath [?חנינא] ב̇ר חנינה על נפשה is [PN בר PN] ש̇הד, "[PN b. PN] hereby witnesses," and beneath that [מן] ח̇ברן, "from Hebron," the provenance of the nameless witness. The argument placing *Mur* 26 in Jerusalem also involves new readings. According to line 6 of that document, in the lower text, one of the owners of property bordering the lot being sold was אלעזר בר מש̇חי. (Yardeni, *Textbook* 1:37, read only בר מ◦חי and did not make the proposed connection.) This neighbor appears to have been the scribe of the text, for it is possible to read line 29 as [אלעזר] בר מ̇שחה̇ כתב ספריא, "Eleazar b.] MSHH wrote the contracts." Since immediately below the scribe's name his provenance is explicit, "from Jerusalem" (מן ירושלם), it follows that the contiguous property he owned was also almost certainly in that city. Ergo, the contract was written there, too. The reason for the unusual specification of his native provenance may have been the fact of the many refugees who had swollen wartime Jerusalem. In that situation, confusion and uncertainty about people's normal residence could have prompted particular care; the other two witnesses also have specified provenance, the second witness being said to come "from the city" (מן הקרי̇[ה] or just מן הקרי̇), presumably Jerusalem.
59. Yardeni, *Textbook,* 1:29–30, 2:22 (*Mur* 25) and 1:31, 2:23 (*Mur* 27).
60. Although the scribe/*hypographeus* is anonymous by reason of damage to the document, the critical reading of a *kaph* ensures that Simon himself was not the scribe, which would otherwise be an obvious possibility. The reading: שמעון בר חנין על נפשא כ̇]תב PN בר PN ממרה[, "Simon b. Hanin hereby (witnesses) concerning himself; [PN b. PN] wro[te at his dictation]."
61. Neither Milik nor Yardeni read the entirety of the crucial lines relevant to the witness. Beyer, *Aramäischen Texte,* 1:317, made suggestions that are correct on

important points, but the reading proposed here is new. In particular, the one surviving letter of the patronym has not previously been deciphered. Cleopas's hand was idiosyncratic, his letterforms personal, so that the *aleph* is not a certain reading (and is marked accordingly). Also, the reading of קלובו proposed here may equally be קלופו; that possibility would not, of course, endanger the equation with Κλέοπος. Note that in *Mur* 29, Cleopas's name appears twice in the Hebrew text, spelled by the scribe as קלבוס (lines 1, 11): i.e., not the Semitic form, but rather a Semitic spelling of the Greek form. See Yardeni, *Textbook,* 1:48–50.

62. Ilan, *Lexicon,* 28.
63. On such pairs, with specific comments regarding the name Κλέοπος, see Richard Baukham, *Jude and the Relatives of Jesus in the Early Church* (Edinburgh: T&T Clark, 1990), 17.
64. Milik, DJD 2, 153: "L'attribution de fragments . . . ne repose que sur le critère matériel de la qualité du papyrus."
65. Milik's explanation for the spelling, offered on the basis of what was known at the time, seems far-fetched today: "Hypocoristique de Hanan ou de Hannun formé par addition de l'afformante hypocoristique grecque -ιν = -ιον," ibid. For further discussion of nasalization in such forms, see Chapter 4 below.
66. Yardeni, *Textbook,* 1:56, read this name as מ̇°°א. Close examination suggests that her proposed *mem* is really an ordinary three-stroke cursive *het,* with extraneous ink having leaked between the right and middle strokes owing to the writer's lack of facility with the technology of writing. Similarly, excessive ink has bled from the reed pen to the right of the *nun,* obscuring the letter's true identity.
67. Yardeni, DJD 27, 301, attempted no reading here.
68. The rabbis acknowledged that customary law differed from place to place and recognized the validity of different customs for legal documents. Cf. e.g., *m. Ketub.* 4:12, where the laws of the marriage contract (*ketubbah*) differ between Jerusalem and outlying Judah. Note also the beginning of tractate *Gittin* in the Mishnah for regional differences.
69. Readings follow Yardeni, *Textbook,* 1:51–55 and 1:46–47, respectively.
70. Yardeni, DJD 27, 300.
71. *Exempli gratia* only; the first year is equally possible.
72. Strangely, scholars have not previously attempted to read the names of the witnesses. The reading here then prompts the reconstruction of the name at the end of line 14.
73. Ilan, *Lexicon,* 213. A related "Nabataean" form, שביו, is also attested once, on a jar discovered at Masada. Note that the reading of the names on the ossuaries is somewhat uncertain; thus *CIIP* nos. 148–49.
74. On the manuscript tradition and possible Talmudic intersections, see conveniently Schürer, *The History,* 2:230–31 and nn. 11, 16.
75. On all of these options see Ilan, *Lexicon,* 425–26. Ilan here reads Eshel, "כוהנים גדולים," 499–500, as suggesting the equation with Commodus. In fact, however, he

nowhere does more than equate with Josephus's Καμυδός. He does not explain the name's derivation. Thus the Roman equation, implicitly acceptable to her, becomes Ilan's own. J. C. VanderKam, *From Joshua to Caiaphas: High Priests After the Exile* (Minneapolis: Fortress, 2004), 454–55, finds Eshel's suggestion attractive, while noting its uncertainty. He also remarks the possibility of reading the name as נ]דביוס, thus dating 4Q348 to the reign of Ananias b. Nedebaeus (48–59 C.E.). That possibility can fit equally well with the proposals below for the date of 4Q348, probably putting it in the late 50s.

76. Schürer, *The History,* 2:232 and n. 19.
77. See VanderKam, *From Joshua to Caiaphas,* 475–76, for a recent summary of the few facts known about the man.
78. *Life* 17, trans. Thackery, LCL.
79. Eshel, "4Q348, 4Q343 and 4Q345," 133.
80. 1 Macc 13:41–42.
81. For judicious discussion, see M. Goodman, *The Ruling Class of Judaea* (Cambridge: Cambridge University Press, 1987), esp. 137–51.
82. On Eleazar b. Simon and the Zealots, see John Price, *Jerusalem Under Siege* (Leiden: Brill, 1992), 17–19 and 102–74.
83. Joseph Naveh, "Nameless People," *IEJ* 40 (1990): 108–23, quotation from p. 117.
84. Yardeni, *Textbook,* 1:119–20, 2:54.
85. See the paleographic discussions attached to each text by their editor, Yardeni, in DJD 27, 285–317.
86. An exception is Richard Freund, *Secrets of the Cave of Letters* (New York: Humanity Books, 2004), passim. His arguments have yet fully to persuade any colleague who has responded in print. Eshel, "כוהנים גדולים," 500n. 22, allowed the possibility ("אי אפשר לפסול לחלוטין את האפשרות") that 4Q348 might derive from Naḥal Ḥever.
87. The text is published in DJD 27, 296–98.
88. This was the rule of אחריות נכסים; cf. *Ketub.* 10.6 and the remarks of Yaron, "Mesadah Bill of Divorce," 450–51.
89. Yardeni, *Textbook,* 1:28; 2:51, offered [10]דוסתס בר אלעזר [11]בר֯ א°[   ]°לון°°[. Cf. Cotton, "Languages," 224, where she suggested a connection between *Mur* 30 and Kislon but without proposing a reading.
90. "Le *ductus* du scribe est très particulier. On notera surtout les formes courbes et arrondies des lettres comme *aleph, bet, dalet, samek,* parfois *lamed, mem, nun, resh, taw;* la distinction très nette entre *bet* et *kaph;* les formes caractéristiques de *hé, mem, taw;* l'alternance des formes finales et médianes; le module varié des lettres: autant d'indices qui pourraient suggérer une date relativement haute pour ce document (avant la Première Révolte?) à moins que ce ne soit maniérisme de scribe"; DJD 2, 114.
91. That Lazar is the writer emerges from several other elements of the contract in addition to the signatures, which themselves may be fully reconstructed and understood only in light of these other elements. The reasoning may begin with

the fact, at first puzzling, that Lazar indicates in line 18 that he "confirms everything that is written above." Normally, this is the legal statement of a principal, who agrees to all that has been stipulated and says so, then signs. Thus Lazar is in some sense a principal, who, like the groom, stipulates to the contract's conditions. Then, a reading in line 2, not suggested by Yardeni, indicates the relationships—Lazar is the father of the bride: thus,]תון ברתֹ [ל]עֹ[זר. Taken with these clues, line 3 suggests that Lazar has given Menahem something, probably the money of the *mohar* or dowry (again, Yardeni has not offered a full reading):]י[הב לעזר לֹמנ[ח]םֹ כ[סף זוזין, "Lazar hereby [g]ives to Mena[he]m mo[ney, *zuzin* . . .]." Finally, one notes that the hand of the second signatory to the contract is that of the writer. In fact, this same person also signs for the first principal, doubtless the illiterate groom, Menahem. Another *hypographeus* then signs for the bride. The first witness bears a patronym that may be reconstructed, hypothetically, as Mattat ([PN בר מ]תת שׁהֹ[ד]). The spacing for the signature of the groom requires that he, too, bore a short patronym, further suggesting the possibility that this first witness was his brother and that the groom's short patronym was therefore also Mattat. The following readings/reconstructions for the first two lines of the signatures result: line 1, [מנחם בר מתת על] נפשה; line 2, [כתב לעזר בר י]הוסף ממֹרֹ[ה], "Menahem b. Mattat hereby (witnesses) concerning himself; Lazar b. Joseph wrote at his request." Lazar is then remarkably father of the bride, principal, scribe, and *hypographeus* all at once, a combination of roles without parallel in the materials of the Judaean Desert.

92. Excepting 4Q346, if it is from Murabba'at.
93. Yardeni, *Textbook,* 1:34; 2:23.
94. On the other hand, the sole surviving signature on the verso reads ש]מעון [בר PN]. It is the signature of a principal, since it appears in line 2 of the signatures. Possibly this could be the Simon b. Hanin of *Mur* 33, who, being illiterate as seen above, would have written here by the hand of a *hypographeus.* In that case, *Mur* 31 would belong to the Archive of the Family of Honi b. John. The fact that the document was written in Hebrew may also support this second option, since we have little evidence for the use of that tongue in legal texts written in times not arguably connected to the wars with Rome (but see below on Jericho). In the case of this second option, the text would probably fall to the 60s C.E.
95. The paleographer's dates in Table 2.1 derive from the discussions in Yardeni, *Textbook.* The "unattributed" texts either cannot be connected to a specific archive or are so tenuous that it did not seem appropriate to make a definite proposal in the table, even though possibilities are discussed above. The dotted lines in Figures 2.1 and 2.3 characterize the most tentative proposed genealogical connections.
96. As proposed above, Eleazar b. Shabi, a scribe involved with 4Q348 (a text attached to the Archive of the Family of Honi b. John), had a brother, Simon b. Shabi,

who was the scribe of *Mur* 22 and 29. The latter two texts belonged to the Archive of the Family of Eutrapelus. Also listed in the text as a witness intended to sign *Mur* 29, but not in the end a signatory, was John b. Joseph. He and Simon b. Shabi were thus potentially related in some way. In just what way becomes clear with *Mur* 30, of which John was the scribe, evident from the fact that the hand of the document is the same as that signing both for the illiterate principal, Salome b. Honi, and as the witness, "John b. Joseph." A second witness to *Mur* 30 signed his name in Hebrew in a fluent scribal hand and was likely John's brother: שאול בן יהו[סף עד] ("Saul b. Jo[seph(?) hereby witnesses]"). *Mur* 30 belonged to the Archive of the Family of Dositheos b. Eleazar. Seemingly, then, all four men worked in a single scribal shop in Jerusalem that served these families.

97. See Appendix B for details.

98. For a conspectus, see Tov, "Greek Biblical Texts," 98–99.

99. Thus 4Q119 is a manuscript of Leviticus, as is 4Q120. 4Q121 is a copy of Numbers, 4Q122 of Deuteronomy. 4Q126 is too fragmentary to be identified; 4Q127 is a parabiblical work related to Exodus. 7Q1 is a manuscript of Exodus, 7Q2 of the Letter of Jeremiah. The identifications of 7Q3–19 are disputed, with the best suggestions seeing the very fragmentary portions as the likely remains of Septuagintal manuscripts or else of Greek translations of 1 Enoch; see, e.g., C. H. Roberts, "On Some Presumed Papyrus Fragments of the NT from Qumran," *JTS* n.s. 23 (1972): 446, and E. Puech, "Sept fragments grecs de la Lettre d'Hénoch (I Hén 100, 103 et 105) dans la grotte 7 de Qumrân (= 7QHéngr)," *RevQ* 18 (1997): 313–23.

100. A possible exception is Mas739, extremely fragmentary, but apparently containing the word ὄμματα. Since this word is a poetic term, rare in prose, Cotton and Geiger suggest this may be the remains of a literary text. If so, it remains unidentified, but the word does appear in LXX Proverbs. See Cotton and Geiger, *Masada II,* 81–82.

101. Strictly speaking, Benoit allowed that *Mur* 126–32 might also be calligraphic notarial hands (DJD 2, 262). Not enough papyrus survived to determine whether the texts were columnar.

102. Quotations from DJD 2, 234.

103. Bingen, review of Benoit, Milik, and de Vaux, 410 (n. 10 above) wrote: "Le 108 . . . n'est pas un texte philosophique; il conserve à mon avis, les restes d'un genre littéraire un peu inattendu à Murabbaʿat, quelques lambeaux de trimètres iambiques que je ne puis identifier. . . . Le fragment (a) contient le premières syllabes plus ou moins mutilées de 23 vers." He went on to propose that lines 11–14 seemed to belong to a prologue. Withal, however, he concluded, "La métrique, autant qu'on puisse en juger, ne favorise pas l'attribution à une comédie sans l'écarter pour autant." Austin, *CGFP* 359–60, included *Mur* 108 but placed it in the category *dubita.*

104. DJD 2, 237.
105. "D'autre part, 108 et 158, peut-être aussi 109 et 110, dont l'écriture paraît suggérer plutôt la deuxième moitié du Ier siècle, pourraient bien se rattacher à une occupation lors de la Première Révolte, qui est attestée par ailleurs" (DJD 2, 209).
106. "L'écriture ressemble beaucoup à celle de 109, au point qu'on hésitâte à ne pas les identifier" (DJD 2, 237).
107. "Analogie grafiche si rilevano anche con l'elegante scritture di PMasada 741, il cui termine *ante quem* è la primavera del 73 o 74 d.c."; E. Crisci, "Scritture greche palestinesi e mesopotamiche (III secolo a.c.–III d.c.)," *Scrittura e Civiltà* 15 (1991): 139.
108. Cotton and Geiger, *Masada II,* 85–88.
109. The word used for "lettuce" is probably to be read as μαρπο[ύλι]α. The term is uncommon, as the editors observe, known to LSJ only from the *Geoponica* and the very late Alexander Trallianus. They deduce, "Its occurrence here seems to attest its existence in spoken language, and this is confirmed by its survival in Modern Greek" (88). Accordingly, a reasonable hypothesis taking account of all of the evidence would be that some Greek was spoken at En Gedi in the first century C.E.
110. Crisci, "Scritture greche," 141.
111. "Anche qui, come nella scrittura di PMur. 108, le curve inferiori di *epsilon* e *sigma* presentano un andamento fortemente obliquo; *epsilon* in particolare (soprattutto in PMur. 109) ha una forma caratteristica, realizzato ora coi tre tratti separati l'uno dall'altro, ora con il secondo e il terzo fusi in un movimento unico; l'elemento mediano, infine, è spesso in legamento con la lettera successiva. Va segnalata anche la forma di *alpha,* con l'occhiello talora sporgente al di sotto del rigo di base della scrittura . . . questa caratteristica—che è presente anche, come si vedrà, in alcune scritture di Dura Europos—raggiunge la massima esagerazione in alcune stilizzazioni grafiche palestinesi, e dunque, poiché non la si trova nei papiri d'Egitto . . . *essa si configura come un elemento proprio della scrittura greca di quest' area geografica, e, nella sua forma più esemplare, della scritture palestinesi*"; ibid., emphasis added.
112. The suggested possibilities are Benoit's. Legible are forms of πίνω, φλέγμα, and λιθάριον (*si vera lectio*).
113. DJD 2, 239. Cotton, "Languages," 229, likened *Mur* 113 to *P.Yadin* 26, while noting that the former is "very fragmentary and undated." Apparently she did not find the paleographic arguments convincing.
114. Crisci, "Scritture greche," 146.
115. Benoit, DJD 2, 238; Schubart, *Griechische Palaeographie,* 56–57, labeled as Abb. 31. Schubart notes that the work is designated as Berliner Pap. P. 11743 (57 n. 1).
116. "Es dürfte schwer sein, eine solche Hand genau einzureihen, und ohne die Jahreszahl könnte auch der Kenner sich um Jahrzehnte irren"; Schubart, *Griechische Palaeographie,* 56.

117. Julian Krüger, *Oxyrhynchos in der Kaiserzeit* (Frankfurt: Peter Lang, 1990), 161: "414 [Stücke] sind beidseitig beschrieben, also 31,7%. Von diesen enthalten 180 oder 13,8% literarische Texte auf der Vorder-und Rückseite, während bei 234 Papyri oder 17,9% die Texte auf Vorder-und Rückseite verschiedener Art sind (Urkunde/literarischer Text)." Cf. also M. Lama, "Aspetti di tecnica libraria ad Ossirinco: copie letterarie su rotoli documentari," *Aeg* 71 (1991): 55–120, esp. 93, and more generally M. Manfredi, "Opistografo," *Parola del Passato* 38 (1983): 44–54.

118. G. W. Houston, "Papyrological Evidence for Book Collections and Libraries in the Roman Empire," in *Ancient Literacies: The Culture of Reading in Greece and Rome* (ed. W. A. Johnson and H. N. Parker; Oxford: Oxford University Press, 2009), 257.

119. A very ancient example concerns the Chester Beatty papyri of Ramesside period Deir el-Medineh, which several generations of workers on the necropolis copied, collected, restored, used as writing materials, and sometimes cut up: P. W. Pestman, "Who Were the Owners, in the 'Community of Workmen,' of the Chester Beatty Papyri?," in *Gleanings from Deir el-Medina* (ed. R. J. Demaree and J. J. Janssen; Leiden: Nederlands Instituut voor het Nabije Oosten, 1982), 155–72. Willy Clarysse described several archives containing literary works that could be attached to individuals by the proposed process or analogs: one belonged to an Akousilaos, σιτολόγος δημόσιος of the village Lusimachis in the reign of Tiberius; another belonged to Laches, a prosperous second-century farmer in the vicinity of Tebtunis; and a third was owned in the mid-sixth century by one Dioskoros and his brothers in the village of Aphrodito, near Panopoites; thus "Literary Papyri in Documentary 'Archives,'" in *Egypt and the Hellenistic World: Proceedings of the International Colloquium, Leuven—24–26 May 1982* (ed. E. van 'T Dack, P. van Dessel, and W. van Gucht; Leuven: Orientaliste, 1983), 43–61. A particularly interesting example is that of Aurelia Ptolemais, a literate woman of the third century C.E. whose archive comprised, along with various documents, two portions of the *Iliad* and two recherché writings, the *Sikyonika* and Africanus's *Kestoi*. Roger Bagnall identified her as the owner of the literary works using the general approach noted in "An Owner of Literary Papyri," *CP* 87 (1992): 137–40. Other examples appear in F. Kenyon, "The Library of a Greek at Oxyrhynchus," *JEA* 8 (1922): 129–38; E. Turner, "Roman Oxyrhynchus," *JEA* 38 (1952): 78–93; and P. W. Pestman, "The Official Archive of the Village Scribes of Kerkeosiris: Notes on the So-Called Archive of Menches," in *Papyrus Erzherzog Rainer (P. Rainer Cent.): Festschrift zum 100-jährigen Bestehen der Papyrussammlung der Österreichischen Nationalbibliothek* (Vienna: Verlag Brüder, 1983), 127–34. For cautionary remarks concerning the approach, note Peter van Minnen, "Boorish or Bookish? Literature in Egyptian Villages in the Fayum in the Graeco-Roman Period," *JJP* 28 (1998): 106–7.

120. Yardeni, *Textbook,* 1:37–39.
121. [ ]ס על [נפ]שה כתב [27]◦◦[ ]◦[ ]ן ממרה,[26] "[Salome (?) daughter of . . .]*s* hereby witnesses concerning herself; [ ]*n* wrote at her dictation." Yardeni, *Textbook,* 1:40, did not read the *samekh* of the patronym, hence did not suggest the identification with the wife.
122. Ilan, *Lexicon,* 57.
123. What can be read are Ἀναν[, Δα[, and Ἀμρα[. Milik noted that many Jewish names may be associated with the remaining letters of the first two (e.g., Anani, Ananias, Daniel, David) and that the third may represent Amram (DJD 2, 254). The latter, though rare, is attested in the Jewish onomasticon of Second Temple times; see Ilan, *Lexicon,* 203. One should note that the first name, if read as Ananos, is a shortened form of Ananias (חנניה), not of Yohanan (so Ilan, *Lexicon,* 100). Thus this individual is not Salome's father.
124. DJD 2, 262–63.
125. "Vergato in una scrittura rotonda e verticale, dal tracciato spesso e uniforme, databile tra li I e il II secolo d.c."; Crisci, "Scritture greche," 142.
126. DJD 2, 263.
127. Ibid., 267.
128. Clarysse, "Literary Papyri," 60–61: "The survival of literary texts among the documents is not a matter of mere chance: the texts which survived in this way were not the most interesting ones from a literary point of view, but were often those the owners wanted to keep close to hand . . . texts to which they were personally committed." Cf. the remarks of D. Obbink, "Readers and Intellectuals," in *Oxyrhynchus: A City and Its Texts* (ed. A. K. Bowman et al.; London: Egypt Exploration Society, 2007), 282.
129. Hdt. 1.32.9.
130. Houston, "Papyrological Evidence," 233–67. Note also his "Grenfell, Hunt, Breccia, and the Book Collections of Oxyrhynchus," *GRBS* 47 (2007): 327–59.
131. Conveniently, Rosa Otranto has published nineteen such lists in *Antiche liste di libri su papiro* (Rome: Edizioni di storia e letteratura, 2000).
132. Houston, "Papyrological Evidence," 246 n. 40.
133. For a recent listing of Oxyrhynchus scribes with multiple surviving scrolls, see William A. Johnson, *Bookrolls and Scribes in Oxyrhynchus* (Toronto: University of Toronto Press, 2004), 16–32.
134. Raymond Starr, "The Used-Book Trade in the Roman World," *Phoenix* 44 (1990): 148–57, doubted that such really existed but offered no convincing alternative explanation for Horace, Epist. 1.20.13. Addressed to his book as though to a young slave, Horace's line reads *aut fugies Uticam aut vinctus mitteris Ilerdam,* which Ps.-Acron *ad* 1.20.9 understood to mean *fient ex te opisthographae epistolarum.*
135. The modern dates are not precise even though the manuscripts are dated precisely in ancient terms. The reason is that the Jews of this period did not use

precalculated intercalation of the luni-solar calendar. Rather, they depended on the sighting of the new moon and agricultural phenomena, e.g., the ripening of the barley, to trigger adjustments. Rabbinic discussions show that months and days were inserted at convenience until well into the second century C.E. See E. J. Bickerman, *Chronology of the Ancient World* (Ithaca, N.Y.: Cornell University Press, 1968), 26.

136. The chronology of events in this paragraph follows E. Mary Smallwood, *The Jews Under Roman Rule* (Leiden: Brill, 1981), 331–36.

137. The date of Qumran's destruction is as contested as most other aspects of study of the scrolls and the site. The conventional position set out in the 1950s and still held by many scholars has been that the site fell in 68 C.E., when Roman forces encamped at Jericho and, espying Qumran, marched out and destroyed it. For this view the coins have been the only real evidence. But Ya'akov Meshorer, dean of ancient Jewish numismatics, has recently reexamined all of the evidence from the coins found at the site and argued compellingly for a later date, 73 C.E. Speaking of several city coins and mintings by Vespasian struck in 73, he noted: "These finds should be compared with the finds from Masada, where the same coins were discovered in the destruction level of 73 C.E. I am under the impression that Qumran reached its end at the same time that Masada did. . . . All the coins found [at Qumran] are the typical types used by the local population until 73 C.E., similar to the finds at Masada." See his "Numismatics," *EDSS* 2:619–20 (quotation from p. 620).

138. It is attractive to attach *Mur* 122 to this period of cave dwelling, most probably to the Eutrapelus family. Portions of three legible lines survive on this papyrus, and it seems to be a school exercise. The reasons for this categorization, tentatively that of Baillet as well (DJD 2, 261), are repetition of the same formula twice in three lines; numerous erasures and erroneous spellings; and the hand, distinctly that of a learner. Crisci, "Scritture greche," 147, described the hand thus: "esemplificano un grado di abilità grafica molto elementare . . . caratterizzato da forme incerte e grossolane e *ductus* impacciato." The young student, as one imagines this person, was learning to write and read Greek in the normal manner but was still at a relatively early stage in the process. In line 1 he or she wrote ἡδόρακα when ἠγόρακα was doubtless intended and repeated the error again in line 2. Then the student had to erase and correct two letters in the two words of line 3. In that same line the word χειρός was misspelled as χιρός but not corrected. So many mistakes in such a short text (five blunders for eight legible words!) would be rare for any but a student (Cribiore, *Writing, Teachers, and Students,* 91–96). While it is possible that *Mur* 122 dates to the Second Revolt habitation, that seems to have been a much shorter, continuously terror-filled period during which normal modes of existence would be improbable. The Second Revolt refugees fled to the caves only in the last months of the war. For a considerable stretch of the three-year First Revolt habitation,

in contrast, the freedom fighters were neither harried nor hunted and would probably want their children's education to proceed, if for no other reason than to occupy them constructively. As the family of Eutrapelus included literary literates in Greek, to suppose that it was they who were educating their children to read the language seems a natural speculation.

139. DJD 2, 270. In point of fact, Baillet's remarks on the paleographic dating of the other Latin documents from Murabbaʿat, *Mur* 159–163, allow the possibility that all of these documents attach to the First Revolt period; so DJD 2, 272–74.

140. J. Roth, "The Length of the Siege of Masada," *Scripta Classica Israelica* 14 (1995): 87.

141. Considerable debate has attended the question of the date of Masada's fall. The traditional date has been 73 C.E., but in recent years a number of scholars have defended a date of 74. It seems that the question has been resolved by finds at the site itself in favor of the traditional date. For discussion, see Cotton and Geiger, *Masada II,* 21–23, "Excursus on the Date of the Fall of Masada."

142. Greg Woolf, "Literacy or Literacies in Rome?," in *Ancient Literacies,* 46.

143. DJD 2, 69; 123. On the latter page Milik wrote of *Mur* 24, "Le διάστρωμα de Mur 24 provient probablement des archives d'Éleuthéropolis . . . il fut ensuite emporté dans le grottes du Désert de Juda par les rebelles fuyant devant l'offensive romaine, ou plutôt après la guerre, par les légionnaires romains, en vue d'une réutilisation future."

144. But note Cotton, "The Roman Census in the Papyri from the Judaean Desert and the Egyptian κατ' οἰκίαν ἀπογραφή," in *Semitic Papyrology in Context,* 119: "The parchment fragments from Wadi Murabbaʿat (*Mur* 89–107) . . . on the most plausible interpretation are lists of taxes in money and kind received by the administration." This statement is true so far as it goes, but it leaves many other texts to be explained.

145. For discussion see, e.g., M. Stern, "The Province of Judaea," CRINT 1.1:340–46.

146. Scholars are in general agreement on the retention of structures. Cf. e.g., Cotton, "Ein Gedi Between the Two Revolts," *Scripta Classica Israelica* 20 (2001): 151: "The leases and subleases found among the documents from Wadi Murabbaʿat and Naḥal Ḥever (as well as implied in some of Bar Kokhba's letters to his men in Ein-Gedi) suggest that Bar Kokhba took over the imperial domain in the places recorded." She referred to *Mur* 24 and *P.Yadin* 43–46 as leases/subleases and to *Mur* 46 and *P.Yadin* 49, 50–51, 53–60 as letters.

147. *B.J.* 3.54–6, *Nat.* 5.14.70.

148. For discussion of the evidence as understood before the publication of the finds at Naḥal Ḥever, see M. Stern, *Greek and Latin Authors on Jews and Judaism* (2 vols.; Jerusalem: Israel Academy of Sciences and Humanities, 1976–1984), 1:475–81. Those discoveries have shed considerable new light on the situation and are the basis for the chronological division suggested above; see Benjamin Isaac, "The Babatha Archive: A Review Article," *IEJ* 42 (1992): 67–69.

149. That Herodium was still serving as the capital village of a toparchy in 124 C.E., on the eve of the revolt, is explicit in the writ of remarriage, *Mur* 115, contracted ἐν Βαιτοβαισσαιας . . . τοπαρχείας Ἡρωδείο[υ] (line 2).

150. *Mur* 24 speaks repeatedly of the "army camp resident at Herodium" (המחנה שיושב בהרודיס). This, it seems obvious, was the camp of which Jesus was the commander. *Mur* 42, sent to Jesus by two *parnasim* of a village subordinate to Herodium, Beth-Mashiko, establishes as well that Jesus was empowered over what might seem civil matters and that he outranked high civil administrators.

151. Possibly Salome was Jesus's niece, as Ilan concluded (*Lexicon,* 137). She understood the name Galgula as the grandfather's handle, retaining Yohanan as Salome's father. The grammar and usage for such nicknames allow either interpretation. If Ilan was correct, another otherwise unattested brother emerges for Jesus. It may be noted that Milik was aware of both possibilities and argued for the one preferred here; DJD 2, 252.

152. Benoit wrote of Aurelius, "on ne peut dire s'il est un Romain ou un Juif affranchi ou fils d'affranchi" (DJD 2, 254). Bingen (note 10 above) thought him simply a Jew with a Roman name: "je crois qu'il ne s'agit probablement ni d'un citoyen romain, ni d'un affranchi" (411).

153. This reconstruction seems not to have been suggested previously, but it arises almost of itself from the combination of that which can be read, the length of the lacunae, and the notion that Judaeans kept family archives. John b. Mahanaim is known from the Naḥal Ḥever papyri as a *parnas* of Simon b. Kosiba in En Gedi.

154. For discussion of the reading, see Pardee et al., *Handbook,* 130, with bibliography.

155. *Mur* 115 line 5 and *m. Ketub.* 5:1; cf. Mordechai A. Friedman, "Babatha's *Ketubba:* Some Preliminary Observations," *IEJ* 46 (1996): 58–60.

156. For Jerusalem, note Josephus, *B.J.* 2.427. For Jericho, note *P.Jericho* 16 line 18 and the phrase indicating archival copying, ἔσχον [τούτου τὸν ἴσον], together with the comments by editor H. Cotton, and *P.Jericho* 18 line 1,]◦ φύλαξ ἀνέλαβον ταύτης τῆς ταμικῆς τὸ ἀν[τί]γρ[αφο]ν, with Cotton's comments (DJD 38, 95, and 99, respectively). (For a somewhat different reading of *P.Jericho* 18, note Jean Gascou, "The Papyrology of the Near East," in *The Oxford Handbook of Papyrology* [ed. Roger S. Bagnall; Oxford: Oxford University Press, 2009], 489 n. 44). For En Gedi consider *P.Yadin* 19 line 26, τευχίζει αὐτὴν διὰ δημοσίων, in Lewis, *Documents: Greek Papyri,* 84 and n. ad loc. 87.

157. Amos Kloner and Boaz Zissu, "Hiding Complexes in Judaea: An Archaeological and Geographical Update on the Area of the Bar Kokhba Revolt," in Schäfer, ed., *Bar Kokhba War Reconsidered,* 186.

158. A similar historical situation seems to lie behind *P.Se'elim* 4 and 5. The first is a census list from Judaea or, less likely, Arabia; the second, an account of grains. Both are public documents in Greek. As with Galgula's public materials, these seem to be the remnants of an archive preserved by the responsible official as he

fled to the caves when the Second Revolt collapsed. For the texts, see Cotton, "Roman Census," 105–22, and her *editiones principes* in DJD 38, 217–28.

159. W. E. H. Cockle, "State Archives in Graeco-Roman Egypt from 30 BC to the Reign of Septimius Severus," *JEA* 70 (1984): 106.
160. The present description of the Roman Egyptian bureaucracy depends upon Posner, *Archives,* 136–59; Cockle, "State Archives," 106–22; and F. Burkhalter, "Archives locales et archives centrales en Egypte romaine," *Chiron* 20 (1990): 191–216. Burkhalter offered certain corrections to Cockle's treatment, but these details do not impinge on matters here.
161. Posner, *Archives,* 155.
162. C. H. Roberts, "The Greek Papyri," in *The Legacy of Egypt* (ed. J. R. Harris; 2nd ed.; Oxford: Clarendon, 1971), 383–89.
163. Posner, *Archives,* 4.
164. The content of this paragraph derives from Phyllis Culham, "Archives and Alternatives in Republican Rome," *CP* 84 (1989): 100–115 (quotation from p. 105); Claude Moatti, *Archives et partage de la terre dans le monde romain (IIe siècle avant–Ier siècle après J.C.)* (Rome: Palais Farnèse, 1993), 99–104; and Claude Nicolet, "À la recherche des archives oubliées: une contribution à l'histoire de la bureaucratie romaine," in *La mémoire perdue: à la recherche des archives oubliées, publiques et privées, de la Rome antique* (ed. S. Demougin; Paris: Sorbonne, 1994), v–xvi.
165. Baillet, DJD 2, 224.
166. Milik, DJD 2, 122–34; Yardeni, *Textbook,* 1:107–12, 2:50–51.
167. *Mur* 35, 62, and 65–67 are all Aramaic documents in cursive script, too fragmentary to characterize. In addition, another nine documents are so badly damaged that all one can say is that they are Semitic; distinction between Aramaic and Hebrew is no longer possible (*Mur* 55–57, 59, 60, 64, and 68–70).
168. The discussion here is of fragment 1. Fragment 2 is a single partial line consisting only of ciphers, but it does seem to indicate that other individuals besides those listed on fragment 1 drew rations. One of the Bar Kokhba letters, *Mur* 43, discusses grain being issued by Simon b. Kosiba and his agents; see Chapter 4.
169. Mas557–584. See Yadin and Naveh, *Masada I,* 52–57.
170. The suggested reading builds upon those of Milik, DJD 2, 87–89, and Yardeni, *Textbook,* 1:217; 2:77, between themselves substantially different, and offers numerous interpretations different yet again.
171. One *seah* = six *kab* = thirty *kor.*
172. Magen Broshi, "Agriculture and Economy in Roman Palestine: Seven Notes on Babatha's Archive," *IEJ* 42 (1992): 235 and nn. 30–31.
173. The Mishnah indicates that standard daily human consumption would be the bread made from one-half *kab* of wheat, or from a whole *kab* of barley, the inferior grain. Factoring in other foods for meals, weekly consumption per head

would be perhaps four *kab.* If so, then the sons of PSN sign for sufficient barley to feed five men for forty days, i.e., approximately 205 "days" worth of barley. Jesus b. Ahi drew enough to supply fourteen men for a month. Similarly, Lentil signs for an amount that would feed five men for nearly thirty-five days. Jesus b. Harqaq seems to have individual rations amounting to thirty days' worth. For the data, see *m. Pe'ah* 4:7, 8:5; *m. Ketub.* 5:8; *t. Pe'ah* 4:8; and the discussion in Ze'ev Safrai, *The Economy of Roman Palestine* (London/New York: Routledge, 1994), 105–7.

174. *Textbook* 1:217, translating as "עדשים (?)." It may be that she was thinking of the actual food. Whatever the intended term, the Aramaic written form here is unambiguously singular, not plural; surely no one would sign for a single lentil. The singular makes sense only if taken as a nickname, and the text's structure, composed as it is of proper names and ciphers, supports this inference as well. One of the participants in *P.Yadin* 7 bore a similar Aramaic nickname, שיפונא, derived from Greek σιφώνιον, a kind of oat (*P.Yadin* 7 verso line 77). Eleazar b. Eleazar b. Hita, whom we met in Chapter 1, had a grandfather whose handle, חיטא, meant "wheat." In an agricultural society such names must have been relatively common.

175. The former occurs in Jewish Palestinian Aramaic and Jewish Babylonian Aramaic, the latter in Jewish Babylonian Aramaic and Syriac; see Michael Sokoloff, *A Dictionary of Jewish Palestinian Aramaic* (Ramat-Gan: Bar Ilan University, 1990); Sokoloff, *A Dictionary of Jewish Babylonian Aramaic* (Ramat-Gan/Baltimore: Bar Ilan University/John Hopkins University Press, 2002); and C. Brockelmann, *Lexicon Syriacum* (Edinburgh: T&T Clark, 1895), s.v. In his dictionary of Judaean Aramaic, Sokoloff offers a different reading for the word in question, טרפסה, and glosses it, "a type of legume (etym. unkn.)"; *A Dictionary of Judean Aramaic* (Ramat-Gan: Bar Ilan University, 2003), s.v. The reading, however, is clearly טרפטה.

176. See Chapter 4 for additional examples and discussion.

177. For a consideration of relative costs, note M. Haran, "Book-Scrolls at the Beginning of the Second Temple Period: The Transition from Papyrus to Skins," *HUCA* 54 (1983): 111–22; for other considerations, note N. Lewis, *Papyrus in Classical Antiquity* (Oxford: Clarendon, 1974), 61.

178. DJD 2, 230–31.

179. Baillet used the phrase to characterize three groups of fragments, DJD 2, 263–66.

180. DJD 2, 229: "L'écriture est grossière, tracée d'une main malhabile et avec un calame épais."

181. LSJ list LXX Hag 2:17, Matt 13:33, and Josephus, *A.J.* 9.4.5 (= 9.85). BDAG add the Lukan parallel 13:21.

182. DJD 2, 230. Baillet's distinction of Greek accent here must be taken with a grain of salt. As James Moulton and Wilbert Howard noted long ago: "The current accentuation of Semitic words is . . . often governed by pure caprice. The only

intelligible principle would be to set the accent always on the tone-syllable of the original Semitic. Our difficulties in that case would arise only where words had been partially Hellenised" (*A Grammar of New Testament Greek Vol. II: Accidence and Word Formation* [Edinburgh: T&T Clark, 1920], 59). That "intelligible principle" would be fine if it only were, as Baillet seems to have assumed, intelligible. In fact, we do not know that the Masoretic principle of accent on the ultima of most nominal forms actually applied to the Aramaic speech of Bar Kokhba's time. Note Kutscher's comments regarding both Hebrew and Aramaic, intertwined in this period as they were, in *The Language and Linguistic Background of the Isaiah Scroll (I Q Isa*[a]*)* (Leiden: Brill, 1974), 40–41, 110, 196, and 333–39. See further Chapter 4.

183. For a similar situation of interference, here involving Demotic and Greek, cf. Willy Clarysse, "Egyptian Scribes Writing Greek," *ChrEg* 68 (1993): 186–201.
184. 1 Sam 21:3; 2 Kgs 6:8; Ruth 4:1; 1 Chr 11:27, 36. Questions have been raised about several of these readings and other possible occurrences of פלוני; cf. *HALOT* s.v.
185. *P.Yadin* 28:1, 2, 5, 9, 12; 29:1, 2, 4, 5, 8, 10, 11; 30:1, 2, 3, 4, 8, 14, 18, 19.
186. *DISO*[2] 1995, 916.
187. Sokoloff, *Jewish Palestinian Aramaic* and *Jewish Babylonian Aramaic,* s.v.
188. Baillet, DJD 2, 226–27.
189. For the oral component of ancient scribal work, cf. e.g. Bruce Metzger and Bart Ehrman, *The Text of the New Testament: Its Transmission, Corruption and Restoration* (4th ed.; New York: Oxford University Press, 2005), 26–27 for general discussion and 257–58 for "errors of the mind." For further discussion of the mental aspect that might lead to such linguistic "slips" as we may see here, note J. Andrieu, "Pour l'explication psychologique des fautes de copiste," *Rev. Ét. Lat.* 28 (1950): 279–92.
190. Baillet, DJD 2, 227.
191. See note 182 above.
192. For Palestine one thinks particularly of Origen and his "girls trained for beautiful writing" ("κόραις ἐπὶ τὸ καλλιγραφεῖν ἠσκημέναις," Euseb., *Hist. eccl.* 6.23), but there are numerous others. See Haines-Eitzen, *Guardians of Letters,* 41–52.
193. Milik had read *Mur* 61 line 2 as שמעה ברו]. Further, he had joined the four fragments of the papyrus such that he believed a line preceded this name, on which could perhaps be read או, "or" (DJD 2, 170, and Plate L). Yardeni, *Textbook* 1:59, questioned both the reading and the joins of the fragments. She presented the fragments as separated; evidently her personal examination found that the alignment of the fibers does not support Milik's joins. She offered no readings except for the name on fragment א, now read as שמעון]. However, her fragment ג can be read as כו]; thus one might propose a near join of the two fragments, yielding מן] שמעון [בן] כו[סבא, i.e., "from] Simon [b.] Ko[siba]," and thus the incipit of a letter sent by the guerrilla chief. Equally possible, of course, the

ostensible letter may have been sent *to* the rebel commander, and this was an archival copy.

194. The region was the very heart of the revolt. See Kloner and Zissu, "Hiding Complexes," 216.

195. Rabbinic literature knows several distinct types, though it appears that none may precisely conform to the modes of this somewhat earlier period. There were the אריס, who paid his rent as a fixed percentage of the harvest, generally a third or a half (e.g., *m. Pe'ah* 5:5); the סוכר and the חוכר, each of whom paid a fixed amount, the former in coin, the latter in kind (e.g., *m. B. Mesi'a* 9:2 and *t. Demai* 6:2, respectively); and the שתלא, first made explicit in the Babylonian Talmud (e.g., *B. Mesi'a* 109a–b), but perhaps implicit already in *t. B. Mesi'a* 9:17–18. See the discussion by Applebaum, "Economic Life," 659. The Judaean Desert texts use only the term חכר and use it more broadly than does rabbinic literature.

196. Readings follow Yardeni, *Textbook,* 1:107; cf. Milik, DJD 2, 131–32.

197. The meaning of this phrase is uncertain. Milik passed over it without annotation, translating it as "années fiscales" (DJD 2, 131); Yardeni, *Textbook,* 2:50, agreed but noted the uncertainty while translating, "years of tax (?)." Both scholars seemed to assume an essential equivalence of מכסה with מכס, "tax, toll," but that is a highly questionable equation. Both terms occur in Biblical Hebrew, and they are not equivalent there; in the biblical sources, מכס means "tax" (Num 31:28, 37, 38, 39, 40, 41), but מכסה means "reckoning, computation" (Exod 12:4, Lev 27:23)—so on both *HALOT* s.vv. Subsequently, early rabbinic literature uses מכס (pl. מכסאות) in the biblical sense (e.g., *Abot R. Nat.* ch. 28), while מכסה never occurs. Probably the biblical מכס is a loanword via Babylonian *miksu,* pl. *miksatu,* "share of yield, customs, dues." The term מכסה is then a secondary, inner-Hebrew development. On the issue of this loan, see Paul Mankowski, *Akkadian Loanwords in Biblical Hebrew* (Winona Lake, Ind.: Eisenbrauns, 2000), 93–94. If this reasoning is correct, then the term מכסה is likely being used here in its biblical sense, and the proposed translation reflects this conclusion. The point seems to be that the time to the lease's end is not actually five full years but closer to four and one-half. Nevertheless, the time will be reckoned as five years, and the rent will be commensurate. In fact, this was a fair contract. The operative time for the agricultural aspects is being reckoned by the agricultural calendar, which began the year in September, and not by the regnal calendar, which began the year in March and by which the contract is dated. Normally, wheat was sown in the early winter, in December, to take advantage of the rainy season. This contract is dated ca. 8 February. Strongly implied, therefore, is that the land has already been planted and that this lease is for land recently taken from the emperor, with whose agents Judah b. Baba had presumably signed an earlier, now voided, contract. Note that the contract may say as much, stipulating that this land was b. Baba's "by my (former) lease." (Unless, as often, the note of previous ownership was merely an identifier.)

198. Translation by Lewis, *Life in Egypt,* 75. For additional examples of such texts from Egypt, see conveniently Naphtali Lewis and Meyer Reinhold, *Roman Civilization: Selected Readings* (2 vols.; New York: Columbia University Press, 1955), 2:184–85.
199. DJD 2, 123.
200. Lewis, *Life in Egypt,* 74.
201. *P.Yadin* 42 line 2 and *P.Yadin* 44 line 6.
202. Lewis, *Life in Egypt,* 74–75.
203. Applebaum, "Economic Life," 659 n. 10.
204. According to *b. 'Erub.* 23b, a *bet seah* (the area sown by a *seah* of wheat seed) was fifty by fifty cubits. In modern metric terms, a *bet seah* would then work out to 625 square meters. A *bet kor* would be thirty times bigger, 18,750 square meters. Thus Broshi, "Agriculture and Economy," 234.
205. Recall that one hectare is equal to 10,000 square meters.
206. These representative estimates are those of William Arnal, *Jesus and the Village Scribes* (Minneapolis: Fortress, 2001), 107, and Arye Ben-David, *Talmudische Ökonomie: Die Wirtschaft des jüdischen Palästina zur Zeit der Mischna und des Talmud* (New York: Hildesheim, 1974–), 1:44–46, respectively. Given the relative paucity of ancient archaeological and textual evidence and the disagreements between different modern methods of calculation, one must allow a considerable margin of error, such that the numbers above probably represent single-family farms—especially if the second family were larger than nine.
207. DJD 2, 131.
208. Yardeni, *Textbook,* 1:107.
209. Norman Golb, "Is a Tannaitic Master Referred to by Name in the Simeon Ben Kosiba Papyri?," 2 (cited 10 January 2008). Online at Oriental Institute of the University of Chicago, "The Dead Sea Scrolls and Other Hebrew MSS Project," http://www-oi.uchicago.edu/OI/PROJ/SCR.
210. Ilan, *Lexicon,* 80.
211. Golb, "Tannaitic Master," 3.
212. For a conspectus of all of the traditions, see I. Konovitz, מערכות תנאים (3 vols.; Jerusalem: Mosad Ha-Rav Kok, 1967), 3:18–23, and note particularly G. A. Wewers, "Rabbi Jehuda-ben-Baba: Skizze zum Problem der Individualüberlieferung in der frühen rabbinischen Literatur," *Kairós* 19 (1977): 81–115.
213. *b. Sanh.* 14a.
214. As Milik noted, the same hand wrote out all the names, so this cannot be a group of signatures to a contract (DJD 2, 154). Milik did not know in which language *Mur* 41 was composed; Yardeni succeeded in reading בן in line 6 and so established the exiguous document's language (*Textbook,* 1:57).
215. DJD 2, 240–43.
216. H. M. Cotton and W. Eck, "*P. Murabba'at* 114 und die Anwesenheit Römischer Truppen in den Höhlen des Wadi Murabba'at nach dem Bar Kochba Aufstand,"

ZPE 138 (2002): 173–83; Cotton, "The Bar Kokhba Revolt and the Documents from the Judaean Desert: Nabataean Participation in the Revolt (*P.Yadin* 52)," in Schäfer, ed., *Bar Kokhba War Reconsidered*, 137–40.

217. T. D. Barnes, "The Career of Abinnaeus," *Phoenix* 39 (1985): 368–74.

218. Harold Idris Bell, *The Abinnaeus Archive: Papers of a Roman Officer in the Reign of Constantius II* (Oxford: Clarendon, 1962).

219. Timothy Teeter, "Papyri, Archives, and Patronage," *CB* 80 (2004): 31.

220. For Milik's dating of these works: *Mur* 1, DJD 2, 75; *Mur* 88, 183; *Mur* 2, 78; *Mur* 3, 79, and *Mur* 6, 86.

221. F. García Martínez, E. J. C. Tigchelaar, and A. S. van der Woude, *Manuscripts from Qumran Cave 11 (11Q2–18, 11Q20–30)* (DJD 23; Oxford: Clarendon, 1997).

222. Houston, "Papyrological Evidence," 259–61.

223. V. C. Corbo, *Herodion I: Gli Edifici della Reggia-Fortezza* (Jerusalem: Studium Biblicum Franciscanum, 1989). Corbo believed that revolutionaries transformed a great Herodian triclinium (hall 15) into the synagogue only during the Second Revolt. However, scholarship generally has seen the transformation as likely happening already during the First Revolt, when, to judge from the coins, rebel presence was notably stronger than it was in the Bar Kokhba era. See the comments of Joseph Patrich, "Corbo's Excavations at Herodium: A Review Article," *IEJ* 42 (1992): 243.

224. Hanan Eshel and Hagai Misgav, "A Fourth Century B.C.E. Document from Ketef Yeriho," *IEJ* 38 (1988): 158–76; Esther Eshel and Hanan Eshel, "קטעים משתי תעודות ארמיות למערת אביאור בתקופת מרד בר כוכבא," *EI* 23 (1992): 276–85.

225. DJD 38, 1–113. The editors were Hanan and Esther Eshel, Hagai Misgav, Nahum Cohen, Ada Yardeni, and Hannah Cotton. Reviews have been few and insubstantial, perhaps because of the extremely fragmentary state of the written evidence. As Sidnie White Crawford noted in *HS* 42 (2001): 367, "This is not a volume that stands on its own as a collection, but it is a necessary and important reference work for wider investigations."

226. Note the study by R. Haensch, "Zum Verständnis von P.Jericho 16 gr.," *Scripta Classica Israelica* 20 (2001): 155–67.

227. The reading follows Yardeni, DJD 38, 57.

228. Ibid., 69 ad loc. On the same page she noted of the two extant signatures on the verso, "Only *br*, 'son of' in lines 15 and 16 and the name Yohohanan in line 16 can be read." This was a rare blunder, for the patronyms are both clearly בן (that is, Hebrew and not Aramaic בר), as one might expect on a Hebrew contract such as this is. Both signatures are fluent, perhaps scribal.

229. Ibid., 63 and 71. Yardeni did not note the parallel, but if indeed this was a single document with an Aramaic outer text and a Hebrew inner text, then it mirrors *P.Hever* 8, also a bilingual *Doppelurkunde* but with languages the reverse of the Jericho text. The point will warrant further discussion below.

230. Yadin, *Bar-Kokhba,* 181.
231. Cotton, "Languages," 221.
232. Aramaic texts of the Roman period are *P.Jericho* 2, 3, 7, 8, 12, and 13.
233. The *editio princeps* was published by Frank Moore Cross and Esther Eshel in Stephen J. Pfann et al., *Qumran Cave 4.XXVI: Cryptic Texts and Miscellanea, Part 1* (DJD 36; Oxford: Clarendon, 2000), 497–507. Before this publication, however, a preliminary study by the two editors, "Ostraca from Khirbet Qumran," *IEJ* 47 (1997): 17–28, elicited a considerable scholarly response, both positive and negative. The foremost reply taking issue with the principal conclusions was that by Ada Yardeni in the next fascicle of the journal, "A Draft of a Deed on an Ostracon from Khirbet Qumran," *IEJ* 47 (1997): 233–37. For the normally reserved Israeli scholar, her objection to their analysis was sharply worded: "In my view, the editors' hand copy is based on a mistaken reading of the text and is, therefore, misleading, especially to those unfamiliar with the variety of letter forms, as well as the formulae, in the Hebrew and Aramaic deeds from the Judaean desert. Accordingly, their transcription and translation cannot be accepted" (236).
234. Cross and Eshel, DJD 36, 497; Yardeni, "Draft of a Deed," 233.
235. Many priests lived in Jericho in Second Temple times, and this fact may be connected with a greater use of Hebrew. On the priestly connection, see J. Schwartz, "On Priests and Jericho in the Second Temple Period," *JQR* 79 (1988): 23–48, esp. 26–27.
236. For discussion of some of these odd letterforms, see Yardeni, "הכתב בשני קטעי השטרות ממערת אביאור," *EI* 23 (1992): 327–30.
237. Eshel and Zissu, DJD 38, 5–6.
238. Euseb., *Hist. eccl.* 6.16., "ἔν γε μὴν τοῖς Ἑξαπλοῖς τῶν Ψαλμῶν μετὰ τὰς ἐπισήμους τέσσαρας ἐκδόσεις οὐ μόνον πέμπτην, ἀλλὰ καὶ ἕκτην καὶ ἑβδόμην παραθεὶς ἑρμηνείαν, ἐπὶ μιᾶς αὖθις σεσημείωται ὡς ἐν Ἱεριχοῖ εὑρημένης ἐν πίθῳ κατὰ τοὺς χρόνους Ἀντωνίνου τοῦ υἱοῦ Σευήρου." Note the discussion of G. Mercati, "D'alcuni frammenti esaplari sulla Va e Via edizione greca della Bibbia," *Studi e Testi* 5 (1901): 28–46.
239. The letter was edited for publication by Oskar Braun and appeared in *Oriens Christianus* 1 as "Ein Brief des Katholikos Timotheos I" (1901): 300–313. In the same fascicle of the journal Braun published a biographical and bibliographic essay on Timotheus, "Der Katholikos Timotheos I und seine Briefe," 138–52. The portions quoted are taken from the letter in Braun's edition, 304 lines 11–19 and 306 lines 15–16, respectively. Note that the manuscript is slightly corrupt at two points of the first quotation: "in a cave, within a kind of house" renders *btura bbayta had,* suggested for the manuscript's *btura bayta had;* "in addition to them, other Hebrew books as well" renders *wastar menhon sephre d'ebraye,* for the manuscript's *wastar mene besephra d'ebraye.*

Chapter 3. En Gedi, Mahoza, and Kephar-Baru

1. The notebook appears as Appendix 1 in *The Dead Sea Scrolls on Microfiche, Companion Volume* (ed. E. Tov; Leiden: Brill, 1993), 155–62. The entry in question appears on p. 157. Doubtless neither the Jordanian authorities nor the scholars ever imagined that this notebook would become available for general inspection.
2. The precise statements of chronology appear in Milik, *Ten Years,* 16.
3. "Those directly in charge of the documents at the time of their discovery never made this claim in print." Thus the suspicious tone of the discussion by Hannah Cotton and Ada Yardeni in the introduction to their joint work, DJD 27. The quotation appears on p. 1. These two scholars pressed the matter no further and never referenced the crucial portions of the initial statements noted below.
4. Hanan Eshel, "A Survey of the Refuge Caves and Their Legal Documents," in *Halakhah in Light of Epigraphy* (ed. A. I. Baumgarten et al.; Göttingen: Vandenhoeck & Ruprecht, 2011), 139, has recognized some of the issues but has not offered a convincing explanation for the facts of the deception. In particular, he did not consider the initial scholarly descriptions.
5. "Un autre lot important est sorti de plusieurs grottes qui paraissent voisiner dans une région qui n'a pas été sûrement identifiée"; R. de Vaux, "Fouille au Khirbet Qumran," *RB* 60 (1953): 85. The article was completed, according to the subscription, on 30 September 1952.
6. "Les textes bibliques en hébreu sont peu nombreux; ils appartiennent à la Genèse, aux Nombres et aux Psaumes et, ici encore, il y a un phylactère complet. Le plus nouveau, dans le domaine biblique, est la version grecque des Petits Prophètes sur laquelle le P. Barthélemy, dans ce même fascicule de la *Revue,* donne une première information. Une lettre en hébreu est adressée à Shimeʿon ben Kosebah, le chef de la Révolte, Bar Kokeba. Deux contrats en araméen sont dates de la '3e année de la libération d'Israël au nom de Shimeʿon ben Kosebah.' Deux documents grecs donnent l'ère de la Province d'Arabie et deux documents araméens suivent la même chronologie. Le plus étonnant a été de trouver dans ce lot une série de papyrus nabatéens, certains assez longs et fournissant plus de textes continus en cette langue que n'en avaient donné toutes les inscriptions. Mais leur écriture cursive demandera un gros effort de déchiffrement"; ibid., 85–86.
7. "Mais au cours de la seconde quinzaine d'août 1952, les infatigables bédouins Taʿamré ont découvert dans une nouvelle grotte du désert de Juda d'importants fragments d'un rouleau de parchemin qui y avait été déposé lors de la révolte de Ben Kosebah" and "C'est ce qu'indique de façon suffisamment certaine l'écriture des petits fragments de papyri hébréo-araméene trouvés dans la même grotte ainsi que les monnaies et documents datés trouvés en deux autres grottes toutes proches"; D. Barthélemy, "Redécouverte d'un chaînon manquant de l'histoire de la Septante," *RB* 60 (1953): 19, and n. 2, respectively. Barthélemy's subscription stated that this article was completed on 19 September 1952. Greenfield, "Texts

from Nahal Se'elim," 661–62, later claimed, "When Barthélemy first discussed the discovery of the Greek text . . . Wadi Seiyal was given as the place of discovery." This statement was mistaken; no such attribution appeared.

8. Published by Catherine Murphy in DJD 38, 117–24.
9. Edited by Ada Yardeni in DJD 38, 125–29.
10. The statement occurred in a personal letter to Emanuel Tov, reported in the latter's "Greek Biblical Texts," 120 n. 11.
11. John Strugnell, "On the History of the Photographing of the Discoveries in the Judean Desert for the International Group of Editors," in *Dead Sea Scrolls on Microfiche,* 124.
12. Barthélemy, *Le devanciers d'Aquila* (Leiden: Brill, 1963), 163.
13. J. Starcky, "Un contrat nabatéen sur papyrus," *RB* 61 (1954): 161.
14. J. T. Milik, respectively, "Le travail d'édition des manuscrits du Désert de Juda," in *Volume du Congrès, Strasbourg 1956* (VTSup 4; Leiden: Brill, 1956), 20; "Deux documents inédits du Désert de Juda," *Bib* 38 (1957): 245; DJD 2, 75.
15. John Strugnell, in the preface to E. Tov, *The Greek Minor Prophets Scroll from Naḥal* Ḥever *(8HevXIIgr)* (DJD 8; Oxford: Clarendon, 1990). Strugnell wrote as editor-in-chief of the project to publish the Judaean Desert materials of all sorts, subscribing the preface as written in June 1987.
16. This and the foregoing paragraph depend largely on Yadin, *Bar-Kokhba,* 30–31.
17. This paragraph and the following discussion of the Israeli expeditions of 1960 and 1961 derive from N. Avigad, "Expedition A," *IEJ* 11 (1961): 6–10; Y. Aharoni, "Expedition B," *IEJ* 11 (1961): 10–24; P. Bar-Adon, "Expedition C," *IEJ* 11 (1961): 24–35; Y. Yadin, "Expedition D," *IEJ* 11 (1961): 36–52; N. Avigad, "Expedition A—Nahal David," *IEJ* 12 (1962): 169–83; Y. Aharoni, "Expedition B—The Cave of Horror," *IEJ* 12 (1962): 186–99; P. Bar-Adon, "Expedition C—The Cave of the Treasure," *IEJ* 12 (1962): 215–26; Yadin, "Expedition D—The Cave of the Letters," 227–57; Yadin, *Bar-Kokhba,* passim; Yadin, ממצאים, passim; and Neil Silberman, *A Prophet from Amongst You: The Life of Yigael Yadin, Soldier, Scholar, and Mythmaker of Modern Israel* (Reading, Mass.: Addison-Wesley, 1993). The chapter "Cave of Letters" in the last mentioned (pp. 247–69) is invaluable for its interviews with various participants.
18. Published by B. Lifshitz, "The Greek Documents from Nahal Seelim and Nahal Mishmar," *IEJ* 11 (1961): 59–60; *editio princeps* by Cotton in DJD 38, 203–4. It is now designated 1Mish 2.
19. Apart from the phylactery, published by Aharoni in the initial report, all these texts were published decades later in DJD 38.
20. E.g., *b. Shabb.* 66b.
21. For the connection to the First Revolt, see Freund, *Secrets of the Cave of Letters,* 135–46.
22. Yadin, *Bar-Kokhba,* 110.
23. This was *P.Yadin* 54, the Aramaic letter engraved on wood. Spelling is as indicated.

24. Quotation from Silberman, *Prophet,* 261.
25. Ibid., 262.
26. These comprised 1Mish 1 and 1Mish 3 and a few inscribed but almost illegible ostraca. The first was a Hebrew document, perhaps a letter, of which only the semicursive word ניתנו, "they were given," remained. The second was a palimpsest contract of some kind, the underlying language being Greek, with portions of three signatures in Aramaic surviving. That of the first witness was [PN] b. Dorymenes (בר דרמנס, i.e., Δορυμένης). This name also appears in *P.Yadin* 7, where mention is several times made of "the heirs of Joseph b. Dorymenes" (lines 6, 37, 38). The latter text dates to 120 C.E. and was produced in Mahoza. As these are the only two occurrences of the name in Palestine in the years covered by Ilan's *Lexicon* (273), it appears likely that the man who witnessed 1Mish 3 was related to the heirs of *P.Yadin* 7 and himself came from Mahoza, probably via En Gedi. Thus we gain some notion whence the occupants of the Scouts' Cave. For 1Mish 1 and 1Mish 3, see Bar-Adon, מערת המטמון (Jerusalem: Bialik Institute and Israel Exploration Society, 1971), 227–30.
27. The principle remaining indicator of the language is the form מברכין. Plurals with final *nun* are not unknown in Biblical Hebrew, but they are much more common in Mishnaic Hebrew, particularly in participles. See the edition in DJD 38 by Michael Morgenstern, 167–69.
28. B. Lifshitz, "The Greek Documents from the Cave of Horror," *IEJ* 12 (1962): 201–7.
29. Recall that two caves in Wadi Sdeir (Naḥal David) have in very recent years yielded materials to excavators. Excavated in 2002, the Har Yishai Cave contained eleven Bar Kokhba coins, a dozen arrowheads, a number of arrow shafts, pottery, stone and glass vessels, and the remains of woven textiles; the prize from this cave were two fragmentary Greek papyri from the Second Revolt period, discovered buried along with eight of the coins in a leather purse. The nearby Sabar Cave was explored at the same time. It concealed a cloth pouch in which were deposited nine Second Revolt–period coins. Neither of these caves, however, is likely to be the one from which the bedouin recovered the materials brought to the Palestine Archaeological Museum, as neither manifests the evidences typical of clandestine digging. On the caves, see Porat, Eshel, and Frumkin, "Two Caves at En Gedi"; on the papyri, see Cohen, "New Greek Papyri" (chapter 1, note 137).
30. Yadin, "Cave of Letters," 228–29.
31. Peter Flint, DJD 38, 133–34.
32. Thus explained in his "Cave of Letters," 227 n. 1.
33. The first volume appeared more or less simultaneously in both Modern Hebrew (ממצאים) and English, *The Finds from the Bar-Kokhba Period in the Cave of the Letters* (Jerusalem: Israel Exploration Society, 1963). A portion of the third volume, *The Documents from the Bar-Kokhba Period in the Cave of Letters: Plates* (Jerusalem: Israel

Exploration Society/Institute for Archaeology, Hebrew University/Shrine of the Book, Israel Museum, 2002), Yadin had already prepared and printed in England in 1963, but it was only issued with the Semitic texts nearly forty years later.

34. "The Nabatean Kingdom, Provincia Arabia, Petra and En-Geddi in the Documents from Naḥal Ḥever," *JEOL* 17 (1964): 227–41.
35. *The Ben Sira Scroll from Masada* (Jerusalem: Israel Exploration Journal and the Shrine of the Book, 1965).
36. Yadin told the story of his fascinating, and sometimes even dangerous, decade-long pursuit of the scroll in *The Temple Scroll: The Hidden Law of the Dead Sea Sect* (London: Weidenfeld and Nicholson, 1985), 8–55. For additional details that Yadin could not reveal in his lifetime, see Hershel Shanks, "Intrigue and the Scroll: Behind the Scenes of Israel's Acquisition of the Temple Scroll," *BAR* 13 (1987): 23–27.
37. He did manage to publish two preliminary reports, "The Greek Papyri from the Cave of Letters," *IEJ* 12 (1962): 258–62, and "שלוש תעודות מארכיונה של בבתה בת שמעון," *EI* 8 (1967): 46–51. In addition, his transcriptions came to Lewis's hands.
38. Actually, twenty-eight Greek papyri appeared in the book, but one turned out to belong to the archive of Salome Komaise. Among the most important reviews were Bowersock, "Babatha Papyri," 336–44; M. Goodman, "Babatha's Story," *JRS* 81 (1991): 169–75; Isaac, "Babatha Archive," 61–75, to which Lewis replied in "The Babatha Archive: A Response," *IEJ* 44 (1994): 243–46; and A. Wasserstein, "Lewis, Yadin and Greenfield, Documents from the Cave of Letters," *JQR* 84 (1994): 373–77. Wasserstein had earlier reacted in particular to Lewis's treatment of *P.Yadin* 18 in "A Marriage Contract from the Province of Arabia Nova: Notes on Papyrus Yadin 18," *JQR* 80 (1989): 93–130, to which Lewis replied in "The World of P. Yadin," *BASP* 28 (1991): 35–41.
39. Greenfield published a number of important preliminary studies before he died. These included "לצורת המקור בשטרות הארמיים מואדי מורבעאת ומנחל חבר," in שי לחיים רבין, *Studies on Hebrew and Other Semitic Languages Presented to Professor Chaim Rabin on the Occasion of His Seventy-Fifth Birthday* (ed. M. Goshen-Gottstein, S. Morag, and S. Kogut; Jerusalem: Academon, 1990), 77–91; "The 'Defension Clause' in Some Documents from Nahal Hever and Nahal Se'elim," *RevQ* 15 (1992): 467–71; "'Because He/She Did Not Know Letters': Remarks on a First Millennium C.E. Legal Expression," *JANES* 22 (1993): 39–44; and, with Hannah Cotton, "Babatha's Property and the Law of Succession in the Babatha Archive," *ZPE* 104 (1994): 211–24, and "Babatha's *Patria*," 126–34.
40. Hillel Newman, "Old and New in the Documentary Papyri from the Bar Kokhba Period," *Studia Classica Israelica* 23 (2004): 239.
41. E. Tov, DJD 8.
42. Milik, "Le travail," 20.
43. Starcky's Nabataean text has now been joined with the fragments discovered during Yadin's excavations and is known as *P.Yadin* 36. Of the other Nabataean

texts brought by the tribesmen, *P.Hever nab.* 2–6, only the first has been published in a preliminary way. Yardeni included the work in her *Textbook* (1:290, 2:95).

44. Cotton published a series of preliminary publications dealing with many of the documents in the run-up to the *editiones principes,* and she was thereby able to profit from scholarly interaction that could be incorporated into the joint volume. Most notable among these preliminary studies might be the following: "Another Fragment of the Declaration of Landed Property from the Province of Arabia," *ZPE* 99 (1993): 115–21; "A Cancelled Marriage Contract from the Judaean Desert (XHev/Se Gr. 2)," *JRS* 84 (1994): 64–86; "Rent or Tax Receipt from Maoza," *ZPE* 100 (1994): 547–57; "Loan with Hypothec: Another Papyrus from the Cave of Letters?," *ZPE* 101 (1994): 53–60; and "Archive of Salome Komaise," 171–208.
45. Substantive reviews included R. Bagnall, *BASP* 36 (1999): 129–38; G. W. Bowersock, "More Hadrianic Documents from the Judaean Desert, and the Bar Kokhba Revolt," *JRA* 14 (2001): 656–60; J. J. Collins, *JR* 79 (1999): 169–70; R. P. Gordon, *JTS* 52 (2001): 204–5; and R. Katzoff, *Scripta Classica Israelica* 19 (2000): 316–27.
46. Not including the "Qumran" documentary texts that Yardeni also published here.
47. That of the literary texts found in the caves of that wadi was complete in 2000 with DJD 38, 137–66, 173–200.
48. Y. Baruchi and H. Eshel, "Another Fragment of Sdeir Genesis," *JJS* 57 (2006): 136–38; Eshel, Eshel, and Geiger, "Mur 174," 314; H. Eshel, *Ein Gedi* (Jerusalem: Carta, 2009), 88–89.
49. The three manuscripts are *P.Hever* 9, an Aramaic contract anciently originating in Yakim; *P.Hever* 9a, a fragmentary Aramaic document involving the same hand and so presumably also from Yakim; and *P.Hever* 69, a Greek work from Aristoboulias. Both ancient locations were near the Cave of the Tetradrachm, which was certainly used as a Bar Kokhba refuge cave and certainly dug by the bedouin. See D. Amit and H. Eshel, "A Tetradrachm of Bar Kokhba from a Cave in Naḥal Ḥever," *Israel Numismatic Journal* 11 (1990–1991): 33–35.
50. The number is necessarily somewhat imprecise because of the extremely fragmentary state in which some documents survived. Thus it is not always clear whether two fragments represent one, or perhaps two, manuscripts.
51. Hillel Newman, "P. Yadin 8: A Correction," *JJS* 57 (2006): 335. Cf. N. Lewis, "The Complete Babatha: More Questions than Answers," *Scripta Classica Israelica* 22 (2003): 191–92.
52. The matter is uncertain as the signature is badly damaged ([כתב] יׄהׄוׄס[ף בר שמעון] [ממרה]), but the man signing served as *hypographeus* for Salome Grapte, a typical role for a husband, and we know from the body of the text that her second husband bore the name Joseph b. Simon.
53. It is other aspects of the text that are more problematic. The main issue may be stated succinctly: as the editors conceived it, *P.Yadin* 8 is a purchase contract in which Joseph b. Simon buys the donkey. Yet, they understood lines 7–8 as a

defension clause in which Joseph is the subject. But why would his name appear here? Normally, it was vendors who needed to stipulate to this role, so as to indemnify the purchaser against putative counterclaims. The editors then restored a passive verb, "I, Joseph b. Simon, am cleared." Such a statement is without parallel in other known purchase contracts and is, as noted, exceedingly odd on the face of it: the vendor should be speaking here. Newman accordingly argued that Joseph must have been the vendor, not the purchaser, a notion hinging on the vocalization of the Aramaic זבן in line 3 (Newman, "Correction," 330–36). But his solution raised difficulties in other lines of the contract and so was far from perfect. The following considerations may help. First: Yardeni's reading of Joseph's signature is very difficult; she read יׄהׄ[וס]ףׄ בׄרׄ [שמעו]ןׄ, for which there is clearly insufficient space in line 10, and which concords poorly with the forms of the first two letters of the suggested Joseph's name. Better is בׄרׄ [ש]מׄעׄ[ו]ן. Joseph does not then sign the contract at all—reasonable for a buyer when, as here, the contract is being issued under the watchful eye of an official collecting taxes, John b. Ishmael; which means that Bar Simon must be understood as the vendor. Then, second: reading Bar Simon's signature as suggested could give in lines 3–4 [3]זבן יהוסׄף בר שׄמעון מׄן אחׄ[והי] [4]<אחוהי> ב[ר שמ]עון חמר חדה, "Joseph b. Simon bought from his bro[ther] <his brother> Ba[r Sim]on one donkey." That is, no further nomenclature is missing from line 3. Rather, the scribe inadvertently repeated a word, a common scribal error. This suggestion makes sense of what can be read and of the syntax (Newman's option would have required לאחוהי in line 4, a problem he does not address). Then, third: it would make sense to read and restore Bar Simon's name with an appropriate verb for "clear" in lines 6–7, e.g., [6][ואצפא] [7]אנׄהׄ בׄ[ר שמעו]ןׄ, "[And] I, Ba[r Simo]n, [will clear] (these purchases)," etc. His name fits the space here much better than the editors' suggested יׄ[הוסף בר שמעו]ןׄ in any case, and fits the letter traces just as well. This solution would have Joseph b. Simon (lines 5–6) and his brother Bar Simon (lines 6–8) each speaking in turn in the first person and would produce a defension clause normal in all respects. For the *editio princeps,* see Yadin et al., eds., *Hebrew, Aramaic and Nabatean-Aramaic Papyri,* 109–13. On defension clauses generally, see E. Y. Kutscher, "New Aramaic Texts," *JAOS* 74 (1954): 233–48, esp. 247–48; R. Yaron, "On Defension Clauses of Some Oriental Deeds of Sale and Lease, from Mesopotamia and Egypt," *BO* 15 (1958): 15–22, and, more narrowly focused on lexical aspects, Greenfield, "Defension Clause." Incidentally, because of its damaged condition, Bar Simon's signature cannot be matched with any of Babatha's brothers' surviving signatures. Thus his precise identity remains unclear.

54. Yadin et al., eds., *Hebrew, Aramaic and Nabatean-Aramaic Papyri,* 143, 151.
55. Yardeni, DJD 27, 20 n. 7. Here she misidentified the common scribe of *P.Yadin* 42–43, suggesting Horon b. Ishmael, one of two issuing officials for the documents. Five years later, she had changed her mind, labeling the scribe "unknown" (previous note).

56. Ibid., 70: "The handwriting of the second [witness] is somewhat similar to that of the scribe [Mattat b. Simon]."
57. To compare the scripts letter-by-letter one may usefully consult the charts for *P.Yadin* 42–43 and *P.Hever* 49 that Yardeni provides in her *Textbook* 1:18, 104, and 106, respectively.
58. Starcky, "Contrat nabatéen." Along with reproach for failing in his obligations to publish, Starcky deserves credit for deciphering the previously unknown cursive Nabataean letterforms.
59. A. Yardeni, "The Decipherment and Restoration of Legal Texts from the Judaean Desert: A Reexamination of *Papyrus Starcky* (*P.Yadin* 36)," *Scripta Classica Israelica* 20 (2001): 121–37.
60. Regarding the translation of the phrase, note that כתבה is often a functional equivalent to שהד in the Aramaic of the Judaean Desert materials, occurring in materials from Jericho and Masada in addition to Mahoza.
61. *P.Yadin* 21:10 and *P.Yadin* 22:11.
62. Yadin, "Cave of Letters," 242 n. 21.
63. Bowersock, "Babatha Papyri," 340.
64. The cultural expectation is imbedded in the story that the Gospel of Luke relates regarding the birth and, eight days later, the naming of John the Baptist: "They were going to name him Zechariah after his father, but his mother spoke up: 'No!' she said. 'He is to be called John.' 'But,' they said, 'there is nobody in your family who has that name'" (Luke 1:59–61, NEB).
65. DJD 27, 3.
66. Yardeni, "Decipherment and Restoration," 128.
67. Ibid., 128 n. 23.
68. In the context of the foregoing discussion, note the absence of a document that by rights should have been in Babatha's archive: a papyrus once belonging to Judah showing his right to the grove. *It becomes increasingly evident that some legal rights and obligations were established in writing, and others by oral agreement.* In this connection compare *P.Dura* 126 of the year 235 C.E. In this document recording the decision of a tribune about a property dispute between two brothers, it is specifically stated that the disputed division had taken place somewhat earlier "[according to the cus]tom of the village, orally" ([κατὰ τὴν συνή]θειαν τῆς κώμης ἀγράφως, lines 1–2). In a similar vein, *P.Dura* 32, a divorce document of 254, states in line 14 that a soldier, Julius Antiochus, will henceforth raise no claim against his former wife, Aurelia Amimma, regarding anything "written or unwritten" (περὶ ἐνγράπτου ἢ ἀγράπτου).
69. One other suggestion has appeared in the scholarship. Hanan Eshel argued in "Another Document from the Archive of Salome Komaise Daughter of Levi," *Scripta Classica Israelica* 21 (2002): 171, that *P.Yadin* 36 belonged to the archive of Salome. His view was adopted by Jacobine Oudshoorn, *The Relationship Between Roman and Local Law in the Babatha and Salome Komaise Archives* (Leiden: Brill,

2007), 14 n. 38, and Hannah Cotton, "Continuity of Nabataean Law in the Petra Papyri: A Methodological Exercise," in *From Hellenism to Islam,* 155–56. This suggestion cannot be correct, however, as no reconstruction of Salome's family tree yields a connection with Judah b. Eleazar's family. Instead of attaching to Babatha's husband, Salome's kinship to Babatha comes through Babatha's own birth family, as will be shown below.

70. This man should not be confused with Eleazar b. Eleazar b. Hita of *P.Yadin* 44 and other texts, for two reasons: (1) for this identification to be correct, Hita the grandfather would need to be identified with Judah b. Nicarchus, the father of Eleazar Khthousion, an equation unsupported by any surviving document; and (2) more importantly, the signatures of the Eleazar we are suggesting and the grandson of Hita are entirely different. The latter, it will be recalled, verged on illiteracy (level 1 signature); our man wrote fluently, as will emerge below. For implied support of the mistaken equation, cf. the prosopography in Yadin et al., eds., *Hebrew, Aramaic and Nabatean-Aramaic Papyri,* 387.
71. *P.Yadin* 15:34–35, Lewis's reading.
72. *m. Ketub.* 1:2, 4:7, and 5:1. For discussion, see Shmuel Safrai, "שתי הערות לכתובתה של בבתא," *Tarbiz* 65 (1996): 717–19.
73. In Yadin et al., eds., *Hebrew, Aramaic and Nabatean-Aramaic Papyri,* Yardeni read for line 23 [ ]° אל[ ] אׄלו/י בׄר [ ]ׄם מׄמׄרׄ[ה].
74. Yardeni, DJD 27, 34–37, Plate 3 and Figures 4–5.
75. Judah's hand is practiced and distinctive, with curvilinear letterforms and a left-leaning ductus. Yardeni in Lewis, *Documents: Greek Papyri,* 114, read only יהודה בר [ ], but close study of the accompanying Plate 35 clearly evidences יהודה בׄרׄ יׄהׄוׄדׄהׄ. Tal Ilan, "Witnesses in the Judaean Desert Documents: Prosopographical Observations," *Scripta Classica Israelica* 20 (2001): 175–76, noted the possible identity of the Judahs of *P.Hever* 8a and *P.Yadin* 26 but without suggesting a reading. She further argued that the Judah b. Judah who signed *P.Yadin* 19 was the same individual; in that case, however, while making due allowance for the fact that a given person's signature may differ considerably from one time to the next, the letterforms, their size and ductus are so unlike our Judah b. Judah's that we must be dealing with two different men.
76. Judah b. Judah may plausibly be related to Eleazar. He may be the grandson of the Joseph b. Judah who signed *P.Yadin* 36, above; if so, he would be Eleazar's second cousin. See Figure 3.6 and associated discussion.
77. For the evidence of attestation, see *DISO*^{2} (1995), 1123–24, where a bibliography on the paleographic issue of the reading in *P.Hever* 8a may also be found. For etymological discussion regarding both Hebrew and the Aramaic dialects, see Stephen Kaufman, *The Akkadian Influences on Aramaic* (Chicago: University of Chicago Press, 1974), s.v. and 101 n. 352, and Mankowski, *Akkadian Loanwords,* 142–44.
78. John Healey, *Aramaic Inscriptions and Documents of the Roman Period* (Oxford: Oxford University Press, 2009), 132, seems unaware of the rarity in an otherwise

helpful treatment of *P.Hever* 8a. Apart from dialects in contact with Hebrew, only Palmyrene evidences this root שטר as a verb (homonymous roots meaning "be stupid" and "smear, spread out" exist but require no discussion here). For the Palmyrene usage, see Delbert Hillers and Eleonora Cussini, *Palmyrene Aramaic Texts* (Baltimore: Johns Hopkins University Press, 1996), 414. The verb is twice attested but in both instances uncertain.

79. R. de Vaux, *Ancient Israel* (2 vols.; New York: McGraw-Hill, 1965), 1:155, 225, 251, 2:394; Schürer, *The History,* 2:184–85.
80. J. Goldstein, *I Maccabees* (Garden City, N.Y.: Doubleday, 1976), 303: "Our author probably used the word [שטר] found at Deut 20:5–9, Josh 1:10 and 3:2."
81. Y. Yadin, *The Scroll of the War of the Sons of Light Against the Sons of Darkness* (trans. Batya and Chaim Rabin; Oxford: Oxford University Press, 1962), 152.
82. John as the scribe of both these texts and of *P.Hever* 26 is Yardeni's conclusion, DJD 27, 26. John b. Eli was also quite possibly Eleazar's brother-in-law, for reasons we shall consider presently.
83. The *editio princeps* was Yardeni, DJD 27, 103–4, with Figure 18 and Plate 20. Oddly, the publication contained virtually no analysis of the philological issues raised. Despite the damage to many words, it seems that a good deal more can be got from the text than Yardeni sought to draw out. See the comments in Chapter 4.
84. Ibid., 103.
85. See Ilan's discussion of the name Eleazar in her *Lexicon,* 65–79, esp. 71 n. 8, where she documents the interchange of names with various people known by both. She does not observe that in *P.Yadin* 47a and 47b, our Eleazar b. Samuel is referenced by both forms: as Eliezer generally, but in 47b line 2 as Eleazar. The editors, who wrote lacking the great boon of Ilan's data, were puzzled by the fact ("we cannot identify this otherwise unmentioned Elazar" [Yadin et al., eds., *Hebrew, Aramaic and Nabatean-Aramaic Papyri,* 167]), but the matter now seems clear.
86. *Editio princeps* Yardeni, DJD 27, 112 and Plate 22.
87. On this point see discussions in Chapter 2 and Chapter 4.
88. All of the readings suggested in this paragraph are new; cf. Yardeni, DJD 27, 85.
89. Yardeni, *Textbook,* 1:290–91, 2:95.
90. Yardeni, ibid., 290, offered יה[ו]דה כתבה °°°[°°°]°.
91. Eshel, "Another Document," 171, recognized the likelihood that all of the unpublished Nabataean contracts and *P.Yadin* 36 belong to a single archive but supposed that the archive was that of Salome Komaise. We have argued above and will further argue below that this supposition is wrong because Salome Komaise was unrelated to Judah, Babatha's husband, and so would not have inherited through his line.
92. M. Broshi and E. Qimron, "A House Sale Deed from Kephar Baru from the Time of Bar Kokhba," *IEJ* 36 (1986): 201–14; Yardeni, DJD 27, 26–33 and Plate

2. Yardeni joined several new fragments to the text as published by Broshi and Qimron and offered various improved readings and reconstructions.

93. Both edited by Yardeni in DJD 27, respectively 54–56 and Plate 7, and 95–96 with Plate 17.
94. Thus Yardeni, *Textbook* 1:142; her reading in the earlier Lewis, *Documents: Greek Papyri,* 79, was different. The later reading appears correct.
95. Lewis, *Documents: Greek Papyri,* 79.
96. Ibid., 82.
97. Cotton, "Subscriptions and Signatures in the Papyri from the Judaean Desert: The ΧΕΙΡΟΧΡΗΣΤΗΣ," *JJP* 25 (1996): 40 n. 48. Cotton noted that she had seen a photograph of the portion in question. Unfortunately, it is absent both from Lewis's collection of plates and figures and from the slightly different assemblage of photographs of the Greek documents in Yadin's volume of plates.
98. Lewis, *Documents: Greek Papyri,* 81.
99. Cotton, "Subscriptions and Signatures."
100. Ilan, *Lexicon,* 434. The *chirocrista's* actual name, whatever it may have been, does not occur elsewhere in the Babatha Archive.
101. Note here Josephus, *A.J.* 20.264: "παρ' ἡμῖν . . . μόνοις δὲ σοφίαν μαρτυροῦσιν τοῖς τὰ νόμιμα σαφῶς ἐπισταμένοις καὶ τὴν τῶν ἱερῶν γραμμάτων δύναμιν ἑρμηνεῦσαι δυναμένοις." See Steve Mason's comments on πολιτεία in Mason, *Flavius Josephus: Translation and Commentary. Volume 9, Life of Josephus* (Leiden: Brill, 2001), XLVII–XLIX, and cf. Werner Jaeger, *Paideia: The Ideals of Greek Culture* (3 vols.; trans. G. Highet; Oxford: Oxford University Press, 1943), 2:320–47.
102. As noted above, only a photograph of this document, not the text itself, was found among Yadin's papers after his death. The original document is now located in the Hecht Museum in Haifa, according to Eshel, "Survey," 143. The first publication was M. Broshi and E. Qimron, "שטר חוב עברי מימי בר כוכבא," *EI* 20 (1989): 256–61. Treatments by P. Segal, "לפירוש שטר החוב העברי מימי בר כוכבא," *Tarbiz* 60 (1990): 113–18, and J. Naveh, על חרס וגומא, 86–89, followed by a substantially revised version of the original edition by the initial editors, "A Hebrew I.O.U. Note from the Second Year of the Bar Kokhba Revolt," *JJS* 45 (1994): 286–94, greatly improved understanding. Yardeni then published a version in DJD 27, 121–22 and Plate 27, and five years later offered a slightly different reading in Yardeni, *Textbook* 1:18–19, 2:19. Most recently Beyer, *Aramäischen Texte,* 2:258–59, made some interesting observations and also proposed a few alternative readings.
103. This identification was suggested by Eshel, Eshel, and Geiger, "Mur 174," 317. Cf. C. R. Conder and H. H. Kitchener, *The Survey of Western Palestine: Memoirs of the Topography, Orography, Hydrography, and Archaeology, Vol. III, Sheets XVII–XXVI, Judaea* (London, 1883; repr., Jerusalem: Kedem, 1970), 120. Another possible identification was made by Naveh: Ha-Horemet may have been the name of a temporary or movable military camp ("'החרמת' עשויה להיות שם של מחנה צבאי," חרס וגומא, 86 n. 12).

This suggestion is made more attractive by the association of the root חרם with the Hebrew Bible's holy war narratives.

104. The identification of its provenance casts doubt on the suggestion by Hanan Eshel, urged in several of his publications, that the latter stages of the Bar Kokhba Revolt saw a precipitous deflation of land values. For this text can now be seen to derive from an En Gedi that evidences, in documents composed later than itself, normal land prices (e.g., *P.Yadin* 44–46). See inter alia Eshel, "Dates," 103–4, and "Bar Kochba Revolt," *CHJ* 4:121.

105. Broshi and Qimron originally read this signature in line 17 as יׄהׄדוה בן יׄהׄוׄדׄ[ה] עׄלׄ [נפשה]. This is not the expected formula for a witness to contracts from Roman Judaea, but rather that of a principal. Their second edition offered instead, יׄהׄדוה בן יׄהׄוׄדׄ[ה] עׄ°]. For that edition Yardeni had provided the hand-drawing, offering reconstructions of damaged letters consistent with the editors' readings. But Yardeni offered יׄהודה בן יׄהׄו°[ ]עׄדׄ in DJD 27, and her new hand-drawing, modified from the original, proposed no reconstructions for the damaged letters of the patronym. She reprised this new reading and hand-drawing in her *Textbook*. Study under high magnification suggests that the signature be read as יׄהודה בן יׄהׄוׄסׄ[ף] עׄדׄ. Comparison with Judah b. Joseph's other signatures confirms the reading.

106. ὑπαρχόντων ὧν τε ἔχει ἐν τῇ αὐτῇ [πα]τρίδι αὐτοῦ καί ὧδε, lines 17–18 of the inner text; similarly, lines 52–54 of the outer text.

107. "Dans un autre document en papyrus, une femme, Salamsiyon berat Yehoseph, demande le divorce de son mari El'azar bar Honi (ou Honyah). La clause principale est: 'Que te soit (notifié) de sa part l'acte de divorce et de répudiation'"; Milik, "Le travail," 21.

108. Greenfield's lecture views were described by Ilan in "Notes and Observations on a Newly Published Divorce Bill from the Judaean Desert," *HTR* 89 (1996): 197. Ilan's title referenced the thin booklet that Yardeni, while assisting Greenfield, published in 1995: תעודות נחל צאלים (Jerusalem: Israel Exploration Society and the Ben Gurion University in the Negev Press, 1995).

109. A. Yardeni and J. C. Greenfield, "נחל צאלים 13: שובר של כתובה," in היהודים בעולם ההלניסטי והרומי: מחקרים לזכרו של מנחם שטרן (ed. I. Gafni, A. Oppenheimer, and D. R. Schwartz; Jerusalem: Merkaz Zalman Shazar, 1996), 197–208.

110. DJD 27, 65–70 and Plates 8–9. Yardeni cautiously allowed, however, that the document might in fact be a גט; if so, however, certain forms (discussed below) defied explanation.

111. Thus Ilan, "Notes and Observations," 198: "In my view, however, there are no linguistic switches inside the text that justify such an elaborate interpretation, and I find it farfetched." Her own method proceeded from a phrase-by-phrase comparison with the Masada גט, *Mur* 19, and was generally convincing. Ilan argued that Milik was correct, that *P.Hever* 13 was a letter of divorce given by a woman. Her treatment of the difficult phrases was less convincing.

112. Published by Cotton in DJD 27, 250–74 and Plates 45–46. Cotton herself argued that "the use of crossing diagonal strokes does not, in itself, invalidate the document thus crossed. It is merely a visual representation of the fact that the document is no longer in force, so that it will no longer be used. *Presumably* there was also a deed of divorce *or* a receipt for the return of the dowry" (250, emphasis mine). Note that even on her presumption one would not need both a גט and a שובר. Consequently, provided that the common documents—*ketubbah* and גט—could be produced, the *ketubbah* could simply be lined out, and assuming coherence between logic and the meager surviving evidence, a שובר would never be needed.
113. Lewis, *Documents: Greek Papyri,* 83.
114. Ibid., 86.
115. G. Horrocks, *Greek: A History of the Language and Its Speakers* (London/New York: Longman, 1997), 103–4.
116. Thus line 9, עלה = עלי.
117. It is proposed to restore ד[נה] in 6b rather than Yardeni's suggested ד[י], for reasons of smoother grammar. Note also that the form לך, which she found a bit problematic morphologically (expected for a female is לכי), no longer requires special explanation, since it is the expected masculine form.
118. Ilan, "Notes and Observations." She also drew attention to other such evidence, including the much earlier Jewish materials from Elephantine, the Marcan passage on divorce implying that both men and women could initiate the process (Mark 10:11–12), and Josephus's report on Salome, Herod's sister, who sent her husband a bill of divorce (*A.J.* 15.259–60).
119. Cf. the remarks of H. Cotton, "The Rabbis and the Documents," in *Jews in a Graeco-Roman World* (ed. M. Goodman; Oxford: Oxford University Press, 1998), 167–79.
120. The relation may have been intended as explicit in the document. Line 3, part of the portion establishing the boundaries of the property being sold, reads, למדנחה ירתה מתת בר אבי, "to the west, the heirs of Mattat . . ." Yardeni took בר אבי as a hypocoristic for בר אביה, "b. Abbaye," though commenting, "The name אבי is rare, and does not appear in other documents from this period known to me" (23). Ilan, *Lexicon,* 357, understood אבי as a hypocoristic of the name אבא, Abba; but apart from the present possible instance, that form occurs just once in the materials her lexicon analyzes. A better alternative may be to see a scribal error here. Mattat intended to reference himself as Hazak's father but carelessly failed to inscribe his patronym. Restoring that missing name would eliminate the need to explain a troublesome form and dissolve the strange "coincidence" of a rare patronym belonging to a person with the same personal name as the scribe—itself uncommon as a hypocoristic. One would have למדנחה ירתה מתת בר <שמעון> אבי, "to the west, the heirs of Mattat b. Simon, my father." The proposed correction fits the subjective formulation of

the contract, in which Hazak speaks in the first person. The statement would mean that two or more of Mattat's family members owned the parcel to the east in partnership, a common situation in the Judaean texts.

121. Yardeni, DJD 27, 19–25 and Plate 1; Cotton, ibid., 158–65.

122. Given Mattat's orthography in *P.Hever* 13, perhaps it would be better to restore the toponym as עינגדה], but nothing is at stake for our purposes. The expression כפר עין גדי is a bit odd, and its prospect may have contributed to Yardeni's and Cotton's hesitancy in assigning this text to the Komaise materials. Ordinarily one would expect merely עין גדי if that village were the place of composition. In fact the expression we (may) get sounds like the product of a scribe more accustomed to composing documents in Greek, where the use of the equivalent for כפר, κώμη, was common in denoting En Gedi and perhaps was the default (cf. *P.Yadin* 16:16 and 18:36, κώμη Αἰνγαδῶν). Additional reason for thinking that Mattat may have produced more Greek than Semitic documents, especially when he lived in Mahoza, is the expression he used in designating Shelamzion b. Joseph as illiterate in *P.Hever* 13; it resonates with the typical Greek expression. He wrote, שלמצין ברת יהוסף על נפשה שאלה כתב מתת ב[ר] שמעון ממרא, "Shelamzion b. Joseph hereby (witnesses) concerning herself; she having asked (him), Mattat b. Simon wrote at her dictation" (lines 11–12). The use of the verb שאל, "to ask," is otherwise unknown in such formulae in Semitic contracts produced by Judaeans, though it is not entirely unknown elsewhere (Greenfield, "Because She Did Not Know Letters," 41). Here it sounds like an effort to create a rough equivalent to the usual Greek expression designating a *hypographeus,* as known for example from *P.Yadin* 15:34, Ἐλεάζαρος Ἐλεάζαρου ἔγραψα ὑπὲρ αὐτῆς ἐρωτηθείς.

123. So Yardeni, DJD 27, 70 and Plate 10.

124. E. Stern, *En-Gedi Excavations I. Conducted by B. Mazar and I. Dunayevsky. Final Report (1961–1965)* (Jerusalem: Israel Exploration Society, Institute of Archaeology, and Hebrew University of Jerusalem, 2007); Y. Hirschfeld, *En-Gedi Excavations II. Final Report (1996–2002)* (Jerusalem: Israel Exploration Society, Institute of Archaeology, and Hebrew University of Jerusalem, 2007). Much of the following description of the site derives from these reports.

125. For an intriguing proposed topography of the site in the period between the revolts, see Eshel, *Ein Gedi,* 55–58.

126. See Hirschfeld, *En-Gedi Excavations II,* Plate IV, for an example. For En Gedi as a harbor, see the discussion by G. Hadas, "Where Was the Harbor of En-Gedi Situated?," *IEJ* 43 (1993): 45–49.

127. *Nat.* 13.45, "sicciores ex hoc genere Nicolai, sed amplitudinis praecipuae: quaterni cubitorum longitudinem efficiunt." For a brief but useful discussion of Pliny's description of the Judaean date palms, see Stern, *Greek and Latin Authors,* 1:490–95.

128. Aramaic text cited from M. Tadmor, ed., כתובות מספרות (Jerusalem: Israel Museum, 1972), 186.

129. B. Rosen and S. Ben-Yehoshua, "The Agriculture of Roman-Byzantine En-Gedi and the Enigmatic 'Secret of the Village,'" in Hirschfeld, *En-Gedi Excavations II*, 630. For an interesting discussion of aspects of the horticulture, see J. Patrich, "Agricultural Development in Antiquity: Improvements in the Cultivation and Production of Balsam," in *Qumran—The Site of the Dead Sea Scrolls: Archaeological Interpretations and Debates* (ed. K. Galor, J.-B. Humbert, and J. Zangenberg; Leiden: Brill, 2006), 141–48.
130. Y. Hirschfeld, *The Palestinian Dwelling in the Roman-Byzantine Period* (Jerusalem: Franciscan Printing Press and Israel Exploration Society, 1995), 22. Pages 57–83 of this book go on to elaborate in good detail what is known of this type of house on the basis of excavations conducted throughout ancient Palestine.
131. On the southern synagogue, see Lewis's comments in *Greek Papyri, ad* 19:13.
132. *P.Hever* 64:34.
133. H. Cotton, "Land Tenure in the Documents from the Nabataean Kingdom and the Roman Provinces of Arabia," *ZPE* 119 (1998): 1–11. Various lines of evidence converge to suggest that balsam was cultivated in Mahoza as in En Gedi. First, cultivation of the tree at nearby Zoar is explicit in sources of the fourth century, Eusebius and Jerome (Rosen and Ben-Yehoshua, "Secret of the Village," 636). Nothing requires the assumption that the first mention in the sources be equated with the inception of cultivation; better method would usually assume the opposite. Thus, balsam had probably been cultivated for some time at Zoar before the fact happened to be mentioned by any surviving source. Second, it appears that the value of the products connected to balsam was so great that the plant was cultivated wherever conditions and know-how could be brought together; see J. Zangenberg, "Opening Up Our View: Khirbet Qumran in a Regional Perspective," in *Religion and Society in Roman Palestine: Old Questions, New Approaches* (D. R. Edwards, ed.; New York/London: Routledge, 2004), 172, and F. N. Hepper and J. E. Taylor, "Date Palms and Opobalsam in the Madaba Mosaic Map," *PEQ* 136 (2004): 35–44. And third, it seems that the Nabataean kings—who owned plantations in Mahoza adjoining Babatha's according to our texts—decided to get in on the action in the early first century and produce unguents from balsam at En Boqeq, another oasis near the Dead Sea, thirty kilometers south of En Gedi. For the scientific evidence of such, see M. Fischer, M. Gichon, and O. Tal, *'En Boqeq: Excavations in an Oasis on the Dead Sea, Vol. II, The Officina. An Early Roman Building on the Dead Sea Shore* (Mainz: Verlag Philip von Zabern, 2000). These authors connect En Boqeq to En Gedi and portray it as a Jewish operation, but Andrea Berlin has convincingly argued for the connection to the Nabataean kingdom (although it does seem that Jews may have been employed there, judging by the impurity-proof stone pottery in evidence). See Berlin, "Business at the Bottom of the World," *JRA* 15 (2002): 646–50. If the royal house was engaged at En Boqeq, it seems reasonable to infer that they would have taken advantage of the possibilities at Mahoza no less.

134. *P.Yadin* 16:17–24. This argument belongs to Cotton and Greenfield, e.g., "Babatha's *Patria,*" 126–34, esp. 131–32.
135. E. A. Knauf, "P.Yadin 1: Notes on Moabite Toponymy and Topography," *Scripta Classica Israelica* 22 (2003): 181–87, quotation from p. 184.
136. K. Politis, "The Discovery and Examination of the Khirbet Qazone Cemetery and Its Significance Relative to Qumran," in Galor, Humbert, and Zangenberg, *Interpretations and Debates,* 213–19, esp. 218, and Politis, "Death at the Dead Sea," *BAR* 38 (2012): 42–53, 67–68; cf. K. D. Politis and H. Granger-Taylor, "Nabataeans on the Dead Sea Littoral," in *Petra Rediscovered: Lost City of the Nabataean Kingdom* (ed. G. Markoe: New York: Harry N. Abrams in association with the Cincinnati Art Museum, 2003), 110–12.
137. But note that Yardeni's publications in DJD 27 do connect additional documents to the site, though not always explicitly.
138. G. W. Bowersock has aptly observed that the reconstruction of the name with two *alphas* is "hardly necessary" and that "it could just as well be [B]arou." Thus his "Hadrianic Documents," 658. For further details on the precise possibilities for the name based on Eusebius and Jerome, cf. his note 4 on that page.
139. Josephus, *B.J.* 7.180–89 (LCL, Thackeray).
140. On this point, cf. J. Naveh, "On Formal and Informal Spelling of Unpronounced Gutterals," *Scripta Classica Israelica* 15 (1996): 263–67, and further detail in Chapter 4.
141. *Onomast.* 205; cf. M. Avi-Yonah, *Gazetteer of Roman Palestine* (Jerusalem: Hebrew University and Carta, 1976), s.v. Baaras (p. 34). Broshi and Qimron, "House Sale Deed," 207, give the map reference as 207 113.
142. For a convenient map of twenty-seven cave locations, see H. Eshel and D. Amit, מערות המפלט מתקופת בר-כוכבא (Tel Aviv: Israel Exploration Society, College of Judea and Samaria, and C. G. Foundation, 1998), 15. Additional details may be found in H. Eshel, "Bar Kokhba Caves," *DEJ* 417–18. Besides caves, hiding complexes of various kinds are also associated with the Second Revolt. Several types have been connected with family units: the "family storage complex," the "hideout and family storage complex," and the "hideout and family storage complex with cistern." See Kloner and Zissu, "Hiding Complexes," 183–84.
143. For the three names, see the respective entries in Ilan, *Lexicon,* 392–93, 298, and 81–82.
144. The connection with the First Revolt destruction was suggested by Cotton in her "Ein Gedi," 139–54.
145. See above, note 133.
146. The family's predominant male names were, it seems, Judah, Eleazar, Joseph, and Jesus. Recognition of their recurrence aids in reconstruction of the genealogy.
147. The suggestion that Jesus b. Jesus was Babatha's cousin on her mother's side is based upon the following considerations. First, Salome Komaise almost certainly married a cousin (see below). Second, Jesus b. Jesus had a grandfather

named Joseph (nicknamed Zaboud; Ilan, *Lexicon*, 89, prefers to classify this appellation as a second name, not a nickname. It derived from זבדיה). Babatha likewise; her mother Miriam's father was Joseph b. Menashe. Third, Jesus b. Jesus had a brother Joseph, who is one of the objects of complaints Babatha makes in *P.Yadin* 13, as supplying her orphan son Jesus, the man's own nephew, insufficient support from the family lands and commercial operations (cf. Lewis, *Documents: Greek Papyri, ad* 13:17). This was certainly a family dispute on at least one level. The suggestion here is that Babatha saw Joseph as failing in his family obligations both as an uncle to her son and as a cousin to herself. Fourth, and perhaps most telling, is that her husband Jesus b. Jesus evidently had a brother, Jacob, who served as Babatha's guardian (אדון) for the purposes of the dowry deposit recorded in *P.Yadin* 17. He is referenced in the subscription as being in that role, and he signed the document in second position, immediately below Judah b. Eleazar Khthousion, recipient of the dowry. (Reading line 2 of the verso as [יעקב ב]ר̇ יש̇̇[וע שהד]; Yardeni in Lewis, *Documents: Greek Papyri,* 73, offered no reading; in her *Textbook,* 1:139, she offered] °°° [.) As discussed in Chapter 1, in the Roman East the role of legal guardian for a woman was normally filled by male relatives, often according to a hierarchy of relation, and only in the situation where she had no male relatives would an outsider act for her (Taubenschlag, *Law of Greco-Roman Egypt,* 171 nn. 6–7; Youtie, "ΥΠΟΓΡΑΦΕΥΣ," 213). Thus the presumption would be that Jacob b. Jesus was a relative, and not merely a former in-law who happened to be available. *P.Yadin* 17 dates to 128 C.E., four years after the death of Babatha's first husband, and she had been remarried for three years. Two other men who either were relatives of Babatha or soon would be signed as witnesses to the action recorded, Tomah b. Simon, her brother, and Joseph b. Hananiah, a future in-law (two months later). One would not expect Jacob to act here, so far removed in time from the end of his brother's marriage to Babatha, rather than those men, unless he were himself also related to Babatha by blood. Hence, the suggestion that he was; if so, then Jesus also. The marriages mentioned accord with priestly views, which maintained the propriety of marriage between first cousins. The Pharisees, and later the rabbinic halakhah, favored instead a variant endogamous practice, that of a man marrying his niece. If the facts are correctly interpreted in this study, then a version of that second option also appears in the history of Babatha's families, in that Salome Grapte, Babatha's agnate aunt, chose for her second marriage her own nephew, Babatha's brother Joseph. Thus it appears that among our families as a whole neither view was followed as a matter of strict ideology. These issues are central to some of the sectarian texts among the Dead Sea Scrolls (e.g., CD 5:7–11). Texts arguing by implication for the rabbinic position include *m. Ned.* 8:7 and 9:10. For an excellent, thought-provoking recent discussion, see Aharon Shemesh, *Halakhah in the Making* (Berkeley: University of California Press, 2009), 80–95.

148. For discussion, see Greenfield and Cotton, "Babatha's Property and the Law of Succession."
149. Oudshoorn, *Roman and Local Law,* assumed throughout her study that Babatha was an only child (e.g., 295). Her reasoning was apparently based on *P.Yadin* 7, the deed in which Babatha's father Simon gifts her mother with all of his property (while granting himself usufruct) and further stipulates that Babatha might live in a small shed he owned should she lack a husband at any point after his death. He mentions no siblings and makes no further provisions. But we simply cannot know what lands and properties Simon may already have distributed before creating this document in 120 C.E., when he was evidently contemplating his own mortality and may have been either aged or in poor health, or both. Therefore, most earlier scholars have held the view expressed by, e.g., Ranon Katzoff: "We do not know if she had siblings" ("Babatha," *EDSS* 1:73). The reasoning and approach by which the present study arrives at different conclusions have been explained.
150. Yadin, *Bar-Kokhba,* 202–5. On pp. 202–3 are color photographs of the glassware.
151. Lewis, *Documents: Greek Papyri,* 22–24.
152. R. Katzoff, "Polygamy in P.Yadin?," *ZPE* 109 (1995): 128–32. The statement quoted appears on p. 132.
153. Lewis, "Judah's Bigamy," *ZPE* 116 (1997): 152.
154. *P.Hever* 7:3, and cf. the discussion above for reasons justifying this reading of the line.
155. Yadin et al., eds., *Hebrew, Aramaic and Nabatean-Aramaic Papyri,* 148. The term occurs in a lacunose phrase that the editors read as]תך חורתא ופיא חפירא. They suggested that חפירא is an adjective meaning "dug, excavated," and this is a possible understanding. In that case the phrase might be translated as they proposed, "(*land*), white, complete, excavated" (144). But the term or its cognates occur elsewhere and seem then to reference a named landmark or subsection of a garden plot: e.g., *P.Yadin* 44:11, המקום שנקרה החפיר, "the place called He-Haphir," and *P.Hever* 62 frgs. c–m 15–16, μέρος ἥ[μισυ κ]ήπου φοινικῶνος ἐν ὁρίοις Μαωζων τῆς αὐτῆς λεγομένου Χαφφουρ[α] (=חפורה). If taken with this understanding, *P.Hever* 42 might better be translated, "(*land*), white (*and*) complete, *The Haphir*" (Aramaic is frequently asyndetic). Note, by the way, the irony that the Hebrew *P.Yadin* 44 uses an Aramaic form for its plot's name, while *P.Hever* 62, written in Greek and generally reflecting an Aramaic and Nabataean speech environment, uses a Hebrew one. The latter fact suggests that—if the name was not entirely ad hoc for the purposes of composing the document—some places in Mahoza bore Hebrew names, pointing to the use of vernacular Hebrew among the Judaeans living there.
156. It is of course also possible that the Aramaic spoken by both Judaeans and Nabataeans in the region of the Dead Sea used Arabisms by reason of the

contact the two peoples had with each other. Thus the suggestion above is tentative. For further discussion of the Arabisms, see Chapter 5.

157. *P.Hever* 65:10–12. The question of whether he already owned the property depends on the reconstruction of a lacuna; see Cotton's note, DJD 27, 235 *ad* 65:11. Note that according to the Madeba Map, Livias was yet another site connected with the balsam industry (Hepper and Taylor, "Madaba Mosaic Map").
158. Note the Hebraism here; the text is composed in Aramaic.
159. Yadin et al., eds., *Hebrew, Aramaic and Nabatean-Aramaic Papyri,* 257–67 and Plate 55.
160. Bar Tousha may have been the writer of the document. Yardeni points out several notable peculiarities of the hand, and the nib of the pen was held virtually parallel to the line when writing, a stance not usually characteristic of professional scribes (DJD 27, 60–61). Several of the scribes of theNaḥal Ḥever archive of Bar Kokhba letters held the pen at the same awkward angle, and their amateur status as writers is manifest. See Chapter 4 for details.
161. The possible vocalization and identification of תשה with Baba Levi hinge on *P.Hever* 63 line 1, which is damaged and so of uncertain reading and interpretation. It is possible to read there a description of Salome as follows: Σαλ]ωμη Ληουει Του[(as noted by Cotton, DJD 27, 199) and then to align the broken third element with the תשה of *P.Hever* 12 (a suggestion that Cotton does not make). For the association of תשה with an Aramaic root for "weak," see Ilan, *Lexicon,* 417. She noted that the forms תשא and תשי are known from Egypt as female names and suggests a hypothetical vocalization, "Tasha." If the connection between the Greek and Aramaic texts here suggested is correct, then of course Baba Levi was Tousha. Otherwise, the Semitic vocalization remains unknown and the theory of an earlier marriage is preferable. A third option, that "brother" in *P.Hever* 12 is not a literal term, is possible but much less attractive.
162. Christopher Jones, "Salome Also Called Grapte," *Scripta Classica Israelica* 21 (2002): 165–68, suggests "pretty as a picture" (168).
163. Ilan, *Lexicon,* 217–18.
164. See Cotton's full discussion in DJD 27, 224–37.
165. G. W. Bowersock, "The Tel Shalem Arch and P. Naḥal Ḥever/Seiyal 8," in Schäfer, ed., *Bar Kokhba War Reconsidered,* 171–80, esp. 177–78.
166. Yadin et al., eds., *Hebrew, Aramaic and Nabatean-Aramaic Papyri,* 317.
167. The notion that the mere appellation Bar Hita could reference Eleazar b. Eleazar b. Hita—in other words, that he might be known simply by his grandfather's handle—is consistent with what we observe with the treatment of the similar situation involving references to Judah b. Eleazar Khthousion. More than twenty references to Judah survive in our documents: he is variously Judah b. Eleazar Khthousion (e.g., *P.Yadin* 14, 17, 18, 19, and 26); Judah b. Eleazar (e.g., *P.Yadin* 16, 17, 18); Judah b. Khthousion, which is not far from the use of Bar Hita,

since it references only the grandfather, skipping the patronym (e.g., *P.Yadin* 14, 15, and 21–22); and, once, Bar Khthousion (as an appositional phrase to the expression "Judah, my husband" in the subscription to *P.Yadin* 22). Incidentally, no difference of usage is apparent between Judah's self-descriptions and those of him by others, whether in Greek or in Aramaic, nor are differences evident between the bodies of the contracts and the subscriptions.

168. Yadin et al., eds., *Hebrew, Aramaic and Nabatean-Aramaic Papyri,* 287–92. The final editors suggested that this Eleazar may be the son but that the matter "is uncertain" (287). In the prosopography on pp. 387–90 they made no assignment at all. Yadin himself regarded the Eleazars of *P.Yadin* 50 and 56 as the son in both cases (*Bar-Kokhba,* 128, 175–80).
169. *Hypographeus: P.Yadin* 44; witness: *P.Yadin* 45, *P.Hever* 13; scribe: *P.Yadin* 42–43, *P.Hever* 49; addressed: *P.Yadin* 49–50, 52, 54–56, 58, 63; subject: *P.Yadin* 57.
170. Ilan, *Lexicon,* 391–92.
171. μετὰ τούτους ἱερεύς τις Ἀνανίας υἱὸς Μασβάλου [*v.l.* Μασαμβάλου, A. Schalit, *Namenwörterbuch zu Flavius Josephus* (Leiden: Brill, 1968), 83] τῶν ἐπιστήμων καὶ ὁ γραμματεὺς τῆς βουλῆς Ἀριστεύς, γένος ἐξ Ἀμμαοῦς, καὶ σὺν τούτοις πεντεκαίδεκα τῶν ἀπὸ τοῦ δήμου λαμπρῶν ἀναιροῦνται.
172. *Vit.* 1.1, "Εμοὶ δὲ γένος ἐστὶν οὐκ ἄσημος, ἀλλ᾽ ἐξ ἱερέων ἄνωθεν καταβεβηκός."
173. Yadin noted this possible connection in his "Expedition D," 43 n. 11: "Mr. A. Mevorakh, of Haifa, who called my attention to [the passage in Josephus], assumes that the Masabala mentioned in the letters may also have been a noted priest." In *Bar-Kokhba,* Yadin made the idea more explicitly his own: "Masabala is a rather rare name; Josephus mentions one Masabala, father of the priest Hanan, who was killed by Shimeon bar Giora in the First Revolt. . . . Our Masabala could well have belonged to the same family" (125). Yadin lacked the great resource of Ilan's *Lexicon,* of course, and so could not know precisely how rare the name actually was.
174. E.g., Peter Schäfer, "Bar Kokhba and the Rabbis," in *Bar Kokhba War Reconsidered,* 19–20.
175. Anthony J. Saldarini, *Pharisees, Scribes and Sadducees in Palestinian Society* (Wilmington, Del.: Michael Glazier, 1988; repr., Grand Rapids, Mich.: Eerdmans, 2001), 241–76.
176. Johnson, *Bookrolls and Scribes,* 159.
177. "In the sources . . . there is no allusion to a Jewish library as a public institution." Thus Y. Shavit, "The 'Qumran Library' in the Light of the Attitude Towards Books and Libraries in the Second Temple Period," in *Methods of Investigation of the Dead Sea Scrolls and the Khirbet Qumran Site* (ed. M. O. Wise et al.; New York: New York Academy of Sciences, 1994), 306.
178. Aharoni, "Expedition B—The Cave of Horror," 196.
179. Yardeni, *Textbook,* 1:199, 2:72.
180. Beyer, *Aramäischen Texte,* 2:289.

181. Aharoni always spoke of "at least 40 people" (e.g., "Expedition B—The Cave of Horror," 198), but scientifically all that forensic analysis could affirm was that the number was "a minimum of twenty-one individuals." Thus Patricia Smith, "Skeletal Remains," *EDSS* 2:881.
182. Aharoni, "Exhibition B—The Cave of Horror," 199. Note also his words on p. 195: "The only remnants of writing found in the front part of the cave were three small fragments of papyrus. . . . These documents, unlike those found in the inner depths of the cave, had not been touched by the bedouin and must therefore have been torn up and dropped at this spot in antiquity. In one fragment the letters בית (house) can be clearly deciphered." This is all that survived of any archive of the sons of Simon that may have been held by the Cave of Horrors.
183. *B.J.* 7.335: "πρότερον δὲ καὶ τὰ χρήματα καὶ τὸ φρούριον πυρὶ διαφθείρωμεν· λυπηθήσονται γὰρ Ῥωμαῖοι, σαφῶς οἶδα, μήτε τῶν ἡμετέρων σωμάτων κρατήσαντες καὶ τοῦ κέρδους ἁμαρτόντες."

Chapter 4. Epistolary Culture in Roman Judaea

1. Some are exceedingly fragmentary, hence their classification as letters is uncertain.
2. Pardee et al., *Handbook,* 2.
3. Notable contributions since the *Handbook* include new editions of numerous Aramaic letters in B. Porten and A. Yardeni, *Letters.* Vol. 1 of *Textbook of Aramaic Documents from Ancient Egypt* (Winona Lake, Ind.: Eisenbrauns, 1986), and Porten and Yardeni, *Ostraca and Assorted Inscriptions.* Vol. 4 of *Textbook of Aramaic Documents from Ancient Egypt* (Winona Lake, Ind.: Eisenbrauns, 1999), and of many Hebrew letters in J. Renz, *Die althebräischen Inschriften. Part 1: Text und Kommentar; Part 2: Zusammenfassende Erörterungen. Paläographie und Glossar* (Darmstadt: Wissenschaftliche Buchgesellschaft, 1995). Fundamental grammars are T. Muraoka and B. Porten, *A Grammar of Egyptian Aramaic* (Leiden: Brill, 1998), and S. Gogel, *A Grammar of Epigraphic Hebrew* (Atlanta: Scholars Press, 1998). Note also the recent overview, analysis, and translation of Hebrew letters by Dennis Pardee, "Hebrew Letters," in *Archival Documents from the Biblical World* (*The Context of Scripture,* 3 vols.; ed. W. W. Hallo and K. Lawson Younger, Jr., Leiden: Brill, 2002) 3:77–86. A very handy collection of seventy-nine Aramaic and Hebrew letters from the biblical period (virtually everything that survives more or less intact), with original language texts and translations and much original scholarship, is J. M. Lindenberger, *Ancient Aramaic and Hebrew Letters* (2nd ed.; Atlanta: Society of Biblical Literature, 2003). A. Lemaire and A. Yardeni published eight new, mostly fragmentary Hebrew letters, probably originating near Khirbet el-Kom, in "New Hebrew Ostraca from the Shephelah," in *Biblical Hebrew in Its Northwest Semitic Setting* (ed. S. Fassberg and A. Hurvitz; Jerusalem: Magnes, 2006), 197–210.

4. It was the discovery of thousands of nonliterary papyri in Egypt in the latter part of the nineteenth century that gave birth to scholarly analysis of the formal features of Greek letters—and, since Latin letters borrowed and adapted those of the Greek, by extension, of Latin letters as well. For the discoveries, see H. Cuvigny, "The Finds of Papyri: The Archaeology of Papyrology," in Bagnall, ed., *Papyrology,* 30–58; Turner, *Greek Papyri,* 21–24, remains a useful, succinct account. Important studies of formal features given impetus and substance by the excavation of the papyri include G. A. Gerhard, "Untersuchungen zur Geschichte des griechischen Briefes I," *Philologus* 64 (1905): 27–65; F. X. J. Exler, *The Form of the Ancient Greek Letter* (Washington, D.C.: Catholic University of America, 1923); E. Bickermann, "Beiträge zur antiken Urkundengeschichte, III. Ἔντευξις und ὑπόμνημα," *APF* 9 (1930): 155–82; H. Koskenniemi, *Studien zur Idee und Phraseologie des griechischen Briefes bis 400 n. Chr.* (Helsinki: Akateeminen Kirjakauppa, 1956); Chan-Hie Kim, *Form and Structure of the Familiar Greek Letter of Recommendation* (Missoula, Mont.: Society of Biblical Literature, 1972); Kim, "The Papyrus Invitation," *JBL* 94 (1975): 391–402; and J. L. White, *The Form and Structure of the Official Petition: A Study in Greek Epistolography* (Missoula, Mont.: Society of Biblical Literature, 1972).
5. R. de Vaux, "Les grottes de Murabbaʿat et leurs documents," *RB* 60 (1953): 245–67; de Vaux, "Quelques textes hébreux de Murabbaʿat," *RB* 60 (1953): 268–75; and J. T. Milik, "Une lettre de Siméon bar Kokhba," *RB* 60 (1953): 276–94.
6. These numbers are according to the bibliography in Pardee et al., *Handbook,* 128–29. They are perhaps not exhaustively comprehensive, but very little escaped these authors' notice.
7. *P.Yadin* 49 (black and white photograph, three lines out of fifteen), *P.Yadin* 50 (color, five lines of a total of fifteen), *P.Yadin* 52 (black and white, entire), *P.Yadin* 53 (color, entire), *P.Yadin* 57 (black and white, entire), and *P.Yadin* 59 (black and white, entire). *P.Yadin* 52 and 59 are the Greek letters. See Yadin, *Bar-Kokhba,* 127–33. Scholars were able to cull a number of additional words and phrases appearing in the letters from Yadin, "Expedition D," 40–50, but this report provided no additional color or high-contrast photographs.
8. F. Millar, *The Roman Near East 31 BC–AD 337* (Cambridge, Mass.: Harvard University Press, 1993), 545–46.
9. Virtually the only substantive review was that by Newman, "Old and New." As a measure of the desuetude into which study of the letters had now fallen, one may consider a putative "standard" translation into Italian. The translator, C. Martone, relied entirely upon Milik's editions in DJD 2 for the Murabbaʿat letters, either ignoring or unaware of Yardeni's great improvements on those editions in her *Textbook.* Thus Martone, "Le lettere di Bar Kokhba provenienti dal Deserto di Giuda: testo e traduzione," in *Loquentes linguis: studi linguistici e orientali in onore di Fabrizio A. Pennacchietti* (ed. P. G. Borbone, A. Mengozzi, and M. Tosco; Wiesbaden: Harassowitz, 2006), 469–74.

10. D. Schwiderski, *Handbuch des nordwestsemitischen Briefformulars* (Berlin: Walter de Gruyter, 2000). Note that this treatment preceded both Yardeni's *Textbook* and the *editio princeps* of the letters in John b. Ba'yah's archive.
11. Joseph Fitzmyer, "Some Notes on Aramaic Epistolography," *JBL* 93 (1974): 201–25, reprinted in Fitzmyer, *Wandering Aramean,* 183–204, cited here.
12. D. Pardee, "An Overview of Ancient Hebrew Letters," *JBL* 97 (1978): 321–46 (with the collaboration of J. David Whitehead and Paul-E. Dion), and Paul-E. Dion, "Les types épistolaires hébréo-araméens jusqu'au temps de Bar-Kokhbah," *RB* 86 (1979): 544–79 (with the collaboration of Pardee and Whitehead). Dion's article did not extend to the Bar Kokhba letters, despite the title; a second article was promised that would (554), but it never appeared—a casualty, it seems, of the extreme delay in publication of the texts. Another study inspired by Fitzmyer, intended as a corrective to certain aspects of his method, was P. S. Alexander, "Remarks on Aramaic Epistolography in the Persian Period," *JSS* 23 (1978): 155–70.
13. The normal expression in the Arsames materials is "From X to (על) Y," whereas the Aramaic Bar Kokhba texts say "From X to (ל) Y." For the Arsames evidence, see G. R. Driver, *Aramaic Documents of the Fifth Century B.C.* (Osnabrück: Otto Zeller, 1968), Arsham 1 (10), Arsham 2 (12), Arsham 3 (13), etc.
14. Indeed, the subtitle of Schwiderski's book was *Ein Beitrag zur Echtheitsfrage der aramäischen Briefe des Esrabuches,* and he drew sharp attention to much later Second Temple elements in Ezra's letters.
15. Fitzmyer, "Some Notes," 191–93.
16. Quotation ibid., 194.
17. Pardee et al., *Handbook,* 156.
18. Ibid., 162.
19. E.g., "Dion suggests that the choice of the one-word greeting formula [שלום] was conditioned by contemporary Greek usage [χαίρειν]" (126), and "For the possible influence of Greek [ἔρρωσο] in the development of the greeting formula [*sic*] which consists of a form of *hwh* + *slm,* see Dion" (127, followed by a reference to Dion, "A Tentative Classification of Aramaic Letter Types," SBLSP 11 [1977]: 434–35).
20. One other nod in the direction of Greek letters should be noted as appearing in the interim (1984). P. S. Alexander opined in his "Epistolary Literature," in CRINT 2.2:592: "It is not unlikely that in the narrow circle of the followers of Bar Kokhba a common letter-form would have emerged which would have been employed whatever the language of communication. . . . If this is so, then it would appear that the convergence of letter-forms was towards Greek practice."
21. "Die Bar-Kosiba-Texte zeigen, daß die Korrespondenz zur Zeit des zweiten jüdischen Aufstandes auch innerhalb einer Gruppe nicht auf eine Sprache fixiert blieb, sondern Hebräisch, Aramäisch und Griechisch nebeneinander Verwendung fanden. Dieser synchrone Gebrauch läßt zahlreiche Gemeinsamkeiten auf der formalen Ebene erwarten"; Schwiderski, *Handbuch,* 245.

22. The situation with the Hebrew letters is a bit more complex than with the Aramaic. Most of these letters use the formula "*from* X to Y," which suggests a kind of elliptical header, "(A letter) from X to Y," rather than a greeting, since insertion of a verb such as אמר makes no sense when "from" is added. The word שלום would then have to be taken as the beginning of actual address. Some variation is expected, of course, and is found within the other ancient epistolary traditions being compared as well.
23. Greek formulae were more various than Schwiderski had practical reason to observe. For fuller treatment, see Exler, *Form,* 23–77, and J. White, *Light from Ancient Letters* (Philadelphia: Fortress, 1986), 198–202.
24. Although Schwiderski did not deal with Latin, it is useful for our later discussion to note the substantial correspondence of that language's usage with the formulae in this paragraph. Typical for the *praescriptio* is *aliquis aliqui salutem dicit* (usually abbreviated as *s.d., salutem,* or *s.*). For the final salutation one often finds *vale* or *cura ut valeas.* On these formulae and their variants, see P. Cugusi, *Evoluzione e forme dell' epistolografia latina nella tarda Repubblica e nei primi due secoli dell' Impero* (Rome: Herder, 1983), 47–67, and S. Corbinelli, *Amicorum colloquia absentium: La scrittura epistolare a Roma tra comunicazione quotidiana e genere letterario* (Naples: M. D'Auria, 2008), 36–56, 89–125.
25. "Man [muß] von einer substantiellen Beeinflussung des hebräischen und aramäischen Briefformulars durch den griechischen Briefstil ausgehen"; Schwiderski, *Handbuch,* 318.
26. Yadin and Naveh, *Masada I,* 51.
27. Schwiderski, *Handbuch,* 322. Since Schwiderski wrote, an Aramaic letter inscribed on an ostracon and found during the Jewish Quarter excavations has been published. The original editor was Esther Eshel, but the more recent edition by Ada Yardeni and Jonathan Price in *CIIP* 626–27 (no. 621) improves the readings and interpretation and is conveniently consulted. Dating to the first century B.C.E. or first century C.E., the letter concludes elliptically שלם לשלם, literally, "peace, to peace," but perhaps meaning, "(Be) well, now and in the future." This is an apparent reflex of the common Greek variation on ἔρρωσο, ἔρρωσο πολλοῖς χρόνοις (cf. Exler, *Form,* 75–76). The letter solidifies Schwiderski's epigraphic argument for the *terminus ante quem* of Greek influence on Semitic epistolography in Judaea.
28. 4Q550 frg. 1:6. Schwiderski wrote before the publication of the *editio princeps,* basing himself upon several preliminary treatments. The quotation here and identification of the portion follow the *editio princeps,* Émile Puech, *Textes araméens deuxième partie (4Q550–575a, 4Q580–4Q587): Qumrân grotte 4.XXVII.* (DJD 37; Oxford: Clarendon, 2009), 12.
29. Schwiderski, *Handbuch,* 338, following Beyer, *Aramäischen Texte,* 1994, 1:113 (mistakenly cited as 133 in the *Handbuch,* 338 n. 63).
30. See Puech's discussion of dating in DJD 37, 7–9, and esp. 7 n. 19.

31. "Offen blieb . . . die genaue Entstehungszeit der Formel, die aufgrund der epigraphischen Quellen zwischen dem ausgehenden 4. Jh. v. Chr. . . . und der frühesten epigraphischen Bezeugung von שלם als Eingangsgruß wie auch הוה שלם als Schlußgruß im 1. Jh. v. Chr. anzusetzen war. Mit dem vorliegenden literarischen Text (ca. 200 v. Chr.) läßt sich die Verwendung bis ins 3. Jh. v. Chr. bestimmen"; Schwiderski, *Handbuch*, 341.
32. See conveniently the discussion by Alexander, "Epistolary Literature," 579–88.
33. Schwiderski, *Handbuch*, 322.
34. Qimron and Strugnell, DJD 10. The six copies are 4Q394–399. On the dating, see Michael O. Wise, "The Origins and History of the Teacher's Movement," in *The Oxford Handbook of the Dead Sea Scrolls* (ed. T. H. Lim and J. J. Collins; Oxford: Oxford University Press, 2010), 92–122, esp. 107–9. For further discussion of the text's genre and language, see note 199 below.
35. Note the words of Peter Parsons, for many years head of the Oxyrhynchus Papyri Project: "Large numbers of letters survive among the papyri, enough to indicate how frequent the practice was" (Peter Parsons, *City of the Sharp-Nosed Fish* [London: Weidenfeld and Nicolson, 2007], 123). Roger Bagnall recently observed that of 5,063 surviving Ptolemaic-period documents in Greek, more than 20 percent are letters. For one subperiod during those years, the percentage is closer to 60 percent. See Bagnall, *Everyday Writing*, 33–35.
36. Cf. the words of Exler in *Form*, 126–27: "It is remarkable how . . . well most [Egyptian] letters were written. . . . One of the reasons for this remarkable correctness of expression and spelling may be the employment of professional scribes. Not a few papyri have been found which were written in the same hand yet addressed by and to entirely different persons."
37. C. Bradford Welles, *Royal Correspondence in the Hellenistic Period* (London, 1934; repr., Chicago: Ares, n.d.), xxxix.
38. G. J. Bahr, "The Subscriptions in the Pauline Letters," *JBL* 87 (1968): 27–41.
39. Apul. *Apol.* 69. The spelling of *subscribtio* is unique.
40. Cicero said that his ordinary practice was to write to his friend Atticus and his brother Quintus with his own hand. But if he could not find time to write the entire letter, he sought to add at least a few words at the bottom because he knew that the esteem this practice betokened was not lost on them. See particularly *Att.* 2.23.1, *Q Fr.* 2.2.1, and *Att.* 16.15.1 and the discussion in Peter White, *Cicero in Letters* (Oxford: Oxford University Press, 2010), 65.
41. Note for discussion Alan Bowman, *Life and Letters on the Roman Frontier* (London: British Museum, 1994), 88. See below for fuller references on the Vindolandan discoveries.
42. Table 4.1 does not include *Mur* 50, which is questionable on the grounds of the words that can be read (although Milik included it among his category of possible letters), and *P.Hever* 36, which is so fragmentary that classification as a letter is precarious.

43. "Celui-ci prend l'affaire à coeur et réagit énergiquement: lettre 'manu propria,' formule solennelle de serment, menace des fers aux pieds, rappel d'un cas analogue d'un certain Ben Aphlul [referenced in the missive]"; Milik, DJD 2, 159.
44. Ibid., 160.
45. Yadin, "Expedition D," 45.
46. Pardee et al., *Handbook,* 131.
47. Yadin et al., *Hebrew, Aramaic and Nabatean-Aramaic Papyri,* Plate 83 (bottom), over against DJD 2, Plate 46 (top).
48. Lindenberger, *Ancient Aramaic and Hebrew Letters,* 6. For a very full discussion of techniques, see B. Porten, "Aramaic Papyri and Parchments: A New Look," *BA* 42 (1979): 74–104.
49. White, *Cicero,* 197 n. 5, notes that surviving examples were rolled, and that Sen. *Epist.* 45.13, "sed ne epistulae modum excedam, quae non debet sinistram manum legentis inplere," implies that a letter would be read like a scroll, unrolling into the reader's left hand.
50. Milik, DJD 2, 155.
51. Thus are *P.Yadin* 57, 58, and 61. *P.Hever* 30, although a standard portion of papyrus, was also folded horizontally to create four folds.
52. E. Randolph Richards, *Paul and First-Century Letter Writing* (Downers Grove, Ill.: Intervarsity, 2004), 76 and n. 16, 86.
53. For *P.Yadin* 52, see Cotton's comments in Yadin et al., *Hebrew, Aramaic and Nabatean-Aramaic Papyri,* 353.
54. Yadin, "Expedition D," 41.
55. A. K. Bowman and J. D. Thomas, *Vindolanda: The Latin Writing-Tablets* (London: Society for the Promotion of Roman Studies, 1983), 37. The Vindolandan materials have a complex history of edition and reedition brought about by continuous discoveries at the site and consequent improved understanding, not only of the new materials, but also of the old, which have then required reassessment. Thus the materials of this first volume were all reedited along with new finds in Bowman and Thomas's second volume, *The Vindolanda Writing-Tablets (Tabulae Vindolandenses II)* (London: British Museum, 1994). The reediting did not stop there, however, and the definitive editions of the finds published in these first two volumes are now the online versions found at Vindolanda Tablets Online, http://vindolanda.csad.ox.ac.uk, hosted by the Centre for the Study of Ancient Documents. Then there are the further discoveries made at the site in the early 1990s; for now, these do not exist in online versions but appeared in Bowman and Thomas's third volume, *The Vindolanda Writing-Tablets (Tabulae Vindolandenses III)* (London: British Museum, 2003). Recent publications helpful for context and the history of excavation include A. Birley, *Garrison Life at Vindolanda* (Tempus, 2002; repr., Gloucestershire: History Press, 2010), and R. Birley, *Vindolanda: A Roman Frontier Fort on Hadrian's Wall* (Gloucestershire: Amberley, 2009).

56. In their first volume, pp. 33–37, Bowman and Thomas discuss the numerous Roman sites where wooden writing tablets have been discovered. Only about half a dozen sites instance leaf-tablets, as opposed to the far more easily preserved, much thicker "stylus" type. In volume two, they remark regarding leaf-tablets, "Their use must have been very widespread . . . this medium was the counterpart of papyrus at least in the north-western provinces of the empire" (40).
57. Bowman and Thomas, *Tabulae Vindolandenses II,* 41.
58. The leaves were known in Latin as *tiliae* after the lime tree from which they first derived; Bowman and Thomas, *Tabulae Vindolandenses III,* 13.
59. One additional wooden leaf is known from Judaea. Inscribed in Greek in a documentary hand, it is too fragmentary to judge further confidently. Perhaps it was a letter; it contains a word that the editors suggest restoring as Ἰου]δαικοί. See Cotton and Geiger, *Masada II,* 90 and Plate 9.
60. Bowman and Thomas, *Tabulae Vindolandenses II,* 40, and *Tabulae Vindolandenses III,* 13.
61. E. Randolph Richards, *The Secretary in the Letters of Paul* (Tübingen: J. C. B. Mohr, 1991), and Richards, *Paul and First-Century Letter Writing.*
62. Richards, *Paul and First-Century Letter Writing,* 64 (italics added). For full discussion of these roles see Richards, *Secretary,* 23–53, and *Paul and First-Century Letter Writing,* 59–80.
63. A. Mentz, *Die Tironische Noten: eine Geschichte der römischen Kurzschrift* (Berlin: de Gruyter, 1944), and A. Stein, "Die Stenographie im römischen Senat," *Archiv für Stenographie* 56 (1905): 177–86.
64. Sen. *Epist.* 40.25.
65. F. W. G. Foat, "On Old Greek Tachygraphy," *JHS* 21 (1901): 238–67 (Greek was first); H. Boge, *Griechische Tachygraphie und Tironische Noten: Ein Handbuch der antiken und mittelalterlichen Schnellschrift* (Berlin: Akademie Verlag, 1973) (Latin was first).
66. Benoit, DJD 2, 275–77, and Plates 103–5.
67. Cf. Driver, *Aramaic Documents,* 2, and Plates 24a–24b.
68. "Non seulement on y discerne des lettres grecques comme δ, θ ou φ . . . mais encore on y reconnaît bien des tracés qui s'apparentent au système tachygraphique grec déjà connu. . . . Une comparaison révèle de nombreuses analogies de formes, en même temps que des différences. Il se pourrait que nous ayons ici une variété assez personnelle"; Benoit, DJD 2, 276–77.
69. Only the Letter of Abaskantos and *P.Hever* 67 were certainly letters; the others are all extremely fragmentary and so more dubious. For Mas741, see Cotton and Geiger, *Masada II,* 85–88; and for Mas745–746, see ibid., 91–93. For *P.Hever* 67, see Cotton, DJD 27, 244–47. For *P.Har Yishai* 2, see Cohen, "New Greek Papyri," 92–95; it "shows some features of a private letter" (93). For *P.8Hever* 4, see Lifshitz, "Greek Documents from the Cave of Horror," 206–7, and Cotton,

DJD 38, 171–72. Lifshitz was more sanguine about its possible epistolary character than Cotton evidently was, as she did not mention the option, being perhaps overcautious. He, on the other hand, spoke more confidently than the remains warrant: "The cursive character of the writing justifies the assumption that before us is a fragment of a letter" (206). One person writes addressing another (συ) in an otherwise vanished context. For *P.Jericho* 19, see DJD 38, 103–5. Its editor, Nahum Cohen, refrained from assigning the exiguous portions a genre; but one may, as he noted, reasonably read/restore the word "letter" in frg. a line 3 (ἐπισ[τολή), and there is mention of "sending" (διέστειλεν), with two names in the dative case in the immediate context (frg. b lines 2–3).

70. For the isolation of these letters, see Alexander, "Epistolary Literature," 580 n. 5. On the problem of determining their authenticity, see his further discussion on pp. 585–88.

71. "Sed, quaeso, epistula mea ad Varronem valdene tibi placuit? Male mi sit si umquam quicquam tam enitar. Ergo ne Tironi quidem dictavi, qui totas περιοχὰς persequi solet, sed Spintharo syllabatim"; Cic. *Att.* 13.25.3, referring to *Fam.* 9.8. See G. J. Bahr's comments in "Paul and Letter Writing in the First Century," *CBQ* 28 (1966): 470, where he adduced Seneca regarding this type of dictation. Alluding to a certain man who stammered, Vinicius, Seneca advised Lucilius on the proper manner of speech—speak well, rather than at length—telling him: "Aliquis tam insulsus intervenerit quam qui illi singula verba vellenti, tamquam dictaret, non diceret, ait, 'Dic, numquid dicas?'" (*Epis.* 40.10). Dictation one syllable at a time was as stilted as a stammer.

72. For some of the practical implications of the difficulty and hence rarity of *syllabatim* dictation, cf. O. Roller, *Das Formular der paulinischen Briefe: Ein Beitrag zur Lehre vom antiken Briefe* (Stuttgart: W. Kohlhammer, 1933), 333.

73. Of course, not all rough drafts prove that a secretary was involved. Authors might produce both draft and final copy.

74. White, *Light from Ancient Letters,* provides several Greek examples on pp. 28 (*PCair Zen* I 59015), 81 (*PTebtI* 12), 83 (*PTebtI* 26), and 88–89 (*PTebtI* 34). Preserved among the Vindolandan materials are many rough drafts. The largest group occurs among the extensive correspondence of Flavius Cerialis, who was a near contemporary of Simon b. Kosiba. See conveniently Bowman and Thomas, *Tabulae Vindolandenses II,* 200–213 (nos. 225–41). Drafts can be recognized by the absence of opening and closing formulae in particular, and in some instances by comparison with a fair copy that also survives and displays modified phrasing. For an extensive discussion of a draft from Vindolanda, illustrated with photographs, see Alan K. Bowman, *The Roman Writing Tablets from Vindolanda* (London: British Museum, 1983), 41–44.

75. See the discussion of Bowman and Thomas, *Tabulae Vindolandenses II,* 42.

76. Nep. *Att.* 16.3.

77. See, e.g., White, *Cicero,* 183 n. 24 for further discussion.
78. Milik, DJD 2, 167–68; cf. Pardee et al., *Handbook,* 139: "The restorations are all quite hazardous . . . and the formulae quite unattested." Yardeni's edition is in her *Textbook* 1:163.
79. Pardee et al., *Handbook,* 139.
80. Quite apart from the issue of the reading, Milik's male recipient of a letter from Simon b. Kosiba bore a name that is elsewhere female, as shown by Ilan, *Lexicon,* 421 (where she adopted his reading, evidently unaware of Yardeni's correction).
81. Yardeni reads/restores]°שמ שלום י°[[2] ן°[ ]מחנים [[1].
82. Yardeni's reading in line 4 was]מלח, which also allows a possible reconstruction of מלח]מה, "war."
83. Cf. F. Millar, "Empire, Community and Culture in the Roman Near East," *JJS* 38 (1987): 147: "The two great Jewish revolts, of 66 and 132, were religious and nationalist movements of a strikingly modern kind; they were also almost unique instances of state-formation within the Roman Empire." For full discussion of the terms "nationalist/nationalism" and their meanings in this ancient context, see D. Mendels, *The Rise and Fall of Jewish Nationalism* (New York: Doubleday, 1992), 1–54, and D. Goodblatt, *Elements of Ancient Jewish Nationalism* (Cambridge: Cambridge University Press, 2006), 1–27.
84. Milik, DJD 2, 167.
85. Ibid.
86. Cic. *Att.* 3.15.8. Cf. the letters to Atticus written a decade later, during other times of difficulty for the orator, *Att.* 11.2.4, 11.5.3, and 11.7.7. Here, too, Cicero requests that Atticus substitute for him in corresponding with others, writing in Cicero's name. Cicero could not afford to absent himself from the agonistic letter writing that was political correspondence among the elite, "much of whose epistolary effort was devoted to repairing, protecting, or improving their position vis-à-vis their peers" (White, *Cicero,* 10).
87. "Statius mihi narravit, scriptas ad te solere afferi, ab se legi, et, si iniquae sint, fieri te certiorem; antequam vero ipse ad te venisset, nullum delectum litterarum fuisse; ex eo esse volumnia selectarum epistularum, quae reprehendi solerent"; Cic. *Q Fr.* 1.2.8.
88. Cic. *Fam.* 12.12.1 and *Att.* 10.18.1, respectively. "Corycean" was proverbial for "spy." A related security method known from Cicero finds echoes in the Bar Kokhba correspondence. This was the suppression of proper names so as to guard critical information from unwanted readers. Cicero applied this method on numerous occasions (e.g., *Att.* 2.19.4; 6.4.3; 6.5.1). An analog from Judaea is *Mur* 44, where b. Kosiba tells Jesus b. Galgula to requisition grain from a certain person, but suppresses the individual's name: ופקדתי תמי שיתן לד תחטין, "And I have given orders concerning the man who will give you the wheat" (lines 8–9). On the Ciceronian letters referenced, see John Nicholson, "The Delivery and Confidentiality of Cicero's Letters," *CJ* 90 (1994): 49, 54–55.

89. "Frequently the letter carrier is named," wrote Eldon Jay Epp, and supplied numerous examples in "New Testament Papyrus Manuscripts and Letter Carrying in Greco-Roman Times," in *The Future of Early Christianity* (ed. Birger A. Pearson; Minneapolis: Fortress, 1991), 35–56; quotation on p. 46.
90. "The scribe was sometimes hired to deliver the letter as well as to write it. The messenger would have been somewhat more trustworthy in these cases—both as interpreter of the letter's contents and as letter carrier—than messengers who merely happened to be traveling toward the letter's destination": thus White, *Light from Ancient Letters,* 216. Cicero was sometimes so eager to hear from Atticus that he sent Tiro to his friend, not only to pick up the missive, but presumably also to take it down from dictation on the spot (Cic., *Att.* 15.8.1). Regardless of issues of pseudonymity, a possible example of secretary-carrier from the New Testament is Silvanus or Silas, referenced in 1 Pet 5:12. See, e.g., J. N. D. Kelly, *The Epistles of Peter and of Jude* (London: Adam & Charles Black, 1969), 214–16 for discussion.
91. Note the comments of Nicholson, "Delivery and Confidentiality," 42–44.
92. Yardeni, *Textbook* 1:165, noted the descender of a *lamed* beneath the last line of the letter but suggested no reading or restoration. It seems clear that one should read/restore a form of the typical farewell formula, e.g., [הוו ש]ל̊[ום], "Be well!" The *ductus* and shape of the stroke correspond to other *lamed*'s in the body, tentatively indicating it was the secretary who wrote the words.
93. Milik, DJD 2, 163, observed what he took as a close similarity but finally concluded that the hands were not the same. But Yardeni's letter-by-letter charts and stroke-by-stroke analysis in *Textbook,* 1:158 and 1:160, demonstrate that every surviving letter of one missive is "within the range" offered by the other. This seems to be one scribe.
94. *Mur* 44:2–3 read according to Yardeni, *Textbook,* 1:159, שתשלח תבי חמשת כורין ח[טי]ן [ש]אש לביתי אצלך, "You are to send me—have brought—five *kors* of wheat held in my storehouse there with you." Her reading was new and a great improvement over earlier attempts that impeded an accurate understanding of Kosiba's request; cf. Pardee et al., *Handbook,* 133. *Mur* 45 is badly broken but reads in line 1 ביתי and in line 2 דגן, "grain," suggesting the proposed interpretation. For the biblical בית אוצר note, e.g., Mal 3:10, Neh 10:39, Dan 1:2. In early rabbinic literature אוצר can also reference an official government storehouse of grain collecting taxes paid in kind. *t. Demai* 1:13 speaks of one such at Yabneh (Jamnia) that was used to supply rations to Roman soldiers serving in the area, an exercise of the *annona* tax.
95. Epp, "New Testament Papyrus Manuscripts," 43.
96. Charpin, *Reading and Writing in Babylon,* 136–37.
97. Hdt. 8.98.
98. F. Preisigke, "Die Ptolemaische Staatspost," *Klio* 8 (1907): 241–77.
99. See the comments of B. Isaac, "Infrastructure," in *Oxford Handbook of Jewish Daily Life,* 146, and for details A. Kolb, *Transport und Nachrichtentransfer im Römischen Reich* (Berlin: Akademie Verlag, 2000).

100. Epp, "New Testament Papyrus Manuscripts," 47, discusses the case of a soldier in Bostra complaining that his father in Karanis does not reply to his many letters. The papyrus containing the soldier's remonstrance with his father dates to 107 C.E.
101. Milik, DJD 2, 157. Note that Milik did mention on p. 158 Ginsberg's suggested rendering, "celui qui consigne l'attestation des témoins," which is essentially the way Pardee and co-authors understood the term.
102. Pardee et al., *Handbook*, 126.
103. I.e., this is an internal *Hiphil.* This use is attested in the Hebrew Bible, e.g., Isa 48:6, Job 29:11, Mal 2:14. Yardeni's rendering of מעיד was similar in its import, "testifying" (*Textbook* 2:64). See also above Chapter 1 note 8 on the phrase על נפשה/על נפשו.
104. On the carriers in earlier times, note, e.g., Samuel A. Meier, *The Messenger in the Ancient Semitic World* (Atlanta: Scholars Press, 1988).
105. Plin. *Ep.* 10.17B, 10.18.
106. R. K. Sherk, *Roman Documents from the Greek East* (Baltimore: Johns Hopkins University Press, 1969), no. 34:8–9. The Romans modeled their diplomatic methods and epistolary vocabulary after those of the Greeks, as Sherk observed: "Whatever the nature of earlier official Roman correspondence may have been, it now acquired and forever retained the general form and style of the Hellenistic models" (189). For discussion of those models, see Welles, *Royal Correspondence,* xxxvii–xxxviii, and the notes attending the numerous official letters contained in his volume.
107. The two principles of these paragraphs are discussed in detail by Margaret Mitchell in her classic essay "New Testament Envoys in the Context of Greco-Roman Diplomatic and Epistolary Conventions: The Example of Timothy and Titus," *JBL* 111 (1992): 641–62, esp. 647–51.
108. E.g., White, *Light from Ancient Letters,* 10:15–16, Welles, *Royal Correspondence,* no. 52:68–72.
109. Yardeni, *Textbook* 1:182, read, °[ ]די אמ °[. Her treatment in the *editio princeps* was identical (Yadin et al., *Hebrew, Aramaic and Nabatean-Aramaic Papyri,* 346), her only comment being, "the expected greeting at the end of the letter may be restored with certainty, but the two preceding words [those in question here] are unintelligible" (348). As often, the participle here expresses the future.
110. M. Luther Stirewalt, *Paul, the Letter Writer* (Grand Rapids, Mich.: Eerdmans, 2003), 1–25.
111. "Τοῦ δ' ἐπιγιγνομένου χειμῶνος ἥκοντες ἐς τὰς Ἀθήνας οἱ παρὰ τοῦ Νικίου ὅσα τε ἀπὸ γλώσσης εἴρητο αὐτοῖς εἶπον, καὶ εἴ τίς τι ἐπηρώτα ἀεκρίνοντο, καὶ τὴν ἐπιστολὴν ἀπέδοσαν. ὁ δὲ γραμματεὺς ὁ τῆς πόλεως παρελθὼν ἀνέγνω τοῖς Ἀθηναίοις δηλοῦσαν τοιάδε" (the letter follows); Thuc. 7.10.
112. "Οἱ μὲν οὖν ἀπολυθέντες κατῆλθον εἰς Ἀντιόχειαν, καὶ συναγαγόντες τὸ πλῆθος ἐπέδωκαν τὴν ἐπιστολήν. ἀναγνόντες δὲ ἐχάρησαν ἐπὶ τῇ παρακλήσει. Ἰούδας

τε καὶ Σιλᾶς καὶ αὐτοὶ προφῆται ὄντες διὰ λόγου πολλοῦ παρεκάλεσαν τοὺς ἀδελφοὺς καὶ επεστήριξαν"; Acts 15:30–32.

113. Stirewalt, *Paul,* 8.
114. White, *Light from Ancient Letters,* 189.
115. A. Malherbe, *Ancient Epistolary Theorists* (Atlanta: Scholars Press, 1988), 6.
116. E.g., Yadin, *Bar Kokhba,* 181; Cotton, "Languages," 227.
117. For the coins, see conveniently Y. Meshorer, *A Treasury of Jewish Coins* (Jerusalem: Yad Ben-Zvi Press, 2001), 23–59 and 115–65. Herod and his dynasty pointedly chose Greek for their issues. Note that the *sicarii* at Masada used the paleo-Hebrew script even for nametags: Yadin and Naveh, *Masada I,* esp. 16. Of course, during these years the script was not always and only a propaganda device; see J. Naveh, *Early History of the Alphabet* (Leiden: Brill, 1982), 119–22.
118. Included here among those not conforming is *Mur* 48. We have argued above, however, that it was a file copy and thus, unlike fair copies, would not be expected to employ the bookhand. If this understanding is correct, then the portion of Hebrew letters that should have followed the script protocol, and did, becomes 73 percent.
119. The two Greek Bar Kokhba letters are also in cursive script.
120. The nonconforming letters manifest the pattern that our postulate, an epistolary culture in which laypeople learned to write letters, would predict. Since in the Mediterranean the bookhand was a part of scribal training, but not of ordinary training for literacy, only occasionally would laypeople be able to produce a bookhand.
121. See Dio Cass. 69.12 for a description of the guerrilla methods, which utilized anfractuous tunnels and hideouts hollowed out beneath the villages. For a brief synopsis of the archaeology of the hideouts, cf. H. Eshel, "Bar Kokhba Caves," *DEJ* 417–18, and for an excellent popular and well-illustrated treatment of one of these hideouts, beneath the village of Horvat Ethri some twenty-five kilometers to the southwest of Jerusalem, see Boaz Zissu, "Village Razed, Rebel Beheaded," *BAR* 33 (2007): 32–41.
122. For helpful discussion of the chanceries and *ab epistulis* in the Mediterranean world, see Welles, *Royal Correspondence,* xxxvii–xxxix, and F. Millar, "Emperors at Work," *JRS* 57 (1967): 9–19. Millar later amplified and recast some of his views in *The Emperor in the Roman World* (Ithaca, N.Y.: Cornell University Press, 1977), 213–28.
123. Cotton's edition appeared in Yadin et al., *Hebrew, Aramaic and Nabatean-Aramaic Papyri,* 351–62. Lifshitz's article was B. Lifshitz, "Papyrus grecs du désert de Juda," *Aeg* 42 (1962): 240–56.
124. Cotton, in Yadin et al., *Hebrew, Aramaic and Nabatean-Aramaic Papyri,* 354.
125. This idea became important for her argument elsewhere that Nabataeans and, reasonably, other non-Judaeans joined the revolt against Rome under Bar

Kokhba. Note here especially "Nabataean Participation in the Revolt (*P.Yadin* 52)," in Schäfer, *Bar Kokhba War Reconsidered,* 133–52.

126. The fullest discussion of this point in the literature is Luc Devillers, "La lettre de Soumïos et les Ioudaioi Johanniques," *RB* 105 (1998): 556–81, esp. 572–79.
127. H. Lapin, "Palm Fronds and Citrons: Notes on Two Letters from Bar Kosiba's Administration," *HUCA* 64 (1993): 122.
128. Cotton, *Hebrew, Aramaic and Nabatean-Aramaic Papyri,* 359.
129. Ibid., 361.
130. These are Wanah b. Ishmael of *P.Yadin* 18, who signed with a level 1 hand, and PN b. Zaidu of *P.Yadin* 2 (level 2 hand).
131. Thus Lewis, *Documents: Greek Papyri,* 48.
132. It is possible that Yohana b. Makhuta, the scribe of *P.Yadin* 5 and 9, was Jewish, the product of intermarriage. He was the scribe of *P.Yadin* 8 as well, composed in Judaean Aramaic and in the Jewish script. In that text he referred to himself not as Yohana, but as Yohanan, using the Judaean form of the name.
133. The data derive from *P.Yadin* 12, 15, 16, 18, 19, 20, 22 and *P.Hever* 62, 64. The three signatories producing Greek were the witnesses to *P.Yadin* 12 and *P.Hever* 62 already mentioned, and Σ]ουμαῖος Κα[.]αβαῖου of *P.Yadin* 19. Ilan, *Lexicon,* 216, regarded this last as a Jew.
134. The data derive from the texts cited above: *P.Yadin* 1, 2, 3, 4, 5, and 9.
135. Ilan, *Lexicon,* 215–17.
136. As one would expect if Soumaios does indeed derive from Samuel, the formal name is also attested among Nabataeans: Avraham Negev, *Personal Names in the Nabatean Realm* (Jerusalem: Hebrew University, 1991), 147.
137. Edition in Yadin et al., *Hebrew, Aramaic and Nabatean-Aramaic Papyri,* 322–28.
138. *P.Yadin* 57:3, 4, *P.Yadin* 58:2. The word מחנה is the one used in the Pentateuch for the collective of the Israelite holy warriors as they converge on Canaan. Note that the word occurs in Old Aramaic and thereafter disappears from the Aramaic dialects, only to reappear in the Bar Kokhba letters (*DISO*^{2} [1995], 613–14). It was not known in other dialects of the time. Presumably, its reemergence among the Judaeans was no rebirth but an adoption by bilinguals. A more typical Aramaic equivalent for מחנה is known from the Judaean literary texts of the time, משריתא (plural at the *Genesis Apocryphon* [1QapGen] 21:1).
139. Cotton's translation of θύρσους as "wands" in *P.Yadin* 52 is overspecific. Here the Greek term exemplifies its frequent equivalence with κλάδος, strictly just "branch," not palm branch. The greater specification is inherent in Aramaic ללבין, and in any case all concerned will have known what sort of branch was involved.
140. "Camp of the Judaeans" is of course equally possible as a meaning.
141. E.g., LSJ s.v., esp. V.2.
142. Ilan does not discuss the point, but it is likely that the Hebrew "Samuel" (š^{ə}mûēl) was pronounced by some Judaeans "Sumuel" (i.e., š^{u}mûēl). The hypocoristic

"Shummai" reflects this formal alternative. This suggestion depends upon two observations made by earlier scholars. First, as evidenced by both Hebrew and Aramaic Qumran texts, the pattern קטול (qᵉtol) was apparently pronounced qᵒtol, being spelled indifferently קטול or קוטל, even for the same word; thus Elisa Qimron, *The Hebrew of the Dead Sea Scrolls* (Atlanta: Scholars Press, 1986), 37 n. 45. This was a type of assimilation. The construct form זובל, "glory" (Masoretic זְבוּל) that appears in *P.Hever* 6 frg. 3:2 seems to show that a similar assimilation occurred in related noun patterns; זְבוּל was originally *zubūl or *zabūl (Hans Bauer and Pontus Leander, *Historische Grammatik der Hebräischen Sprache des Alten Testaments* [Hildesheim: Georg Olms, 1965], 473). Second, short and super-short /u/ often comes across in Septuagintal transcriptions of Hebrew names as [o]; and this same shift is evident also in some manuscripts containing Mishnaic Hebrew. See Kutscher, *History of the Hebrew Language,* §§ 175, 200, and literature cited. Samuel is rendered Σομόηλος by the Letter of Aristeas (*Let. Aris.* 47–48). According to most scholars, the letter probably originated in Judaea, not in Egypt, and probably in the first century B.C.E., not the ostensible third.

143. We have no reason to believe that anyone would have apologized for *not* writing in Aramaic, although technically the term Ἑβραεστὶ could embrace that possibility, if some scholars are correct in their interpretation of the word. The correct understanding remains a debate, however, within which the present usage is not unimportant. For further consideration, see, e.g., Ott, "Muttersprache"; Lapide, "Insights"; and Rajak, *Josephus,* 230–32.

144. *Mur* 42 indicates that the Roman forces were in the vicinity of Herodium at the time the letter was written, very close to Beth-Mashiko, itself certainly near Herodium. *Mur* 45 reports to Jesus b. Galgula a battle, evidently important to Jesus strategically, in which the Romans had killed many of "the brothers." One has the impression of a tightening noose. *Mur* 47 mentions Tekoa explicitly in a broken context. The town would have been within the jurisdiction of Herodium as its topographic capital, and so its affairs under Jesus's authority. This connection between the affairs of Tekoa and Herodium finds further corroboration in *Mur* 174, written at Herodium, as it seems, by the same scribe who penned *Mur* 7. The former document involves a principal, said to be from Tekoa (line 5), whose name does not survive. He borrows money from one Simon b. Judah. This document was eventually deposited in the archive at Herodium. Thus Herodium was the military and bureaucratic center under whose authority Tekoa and its citizens lay. Yet in the Naḥal Ḥever correspondence is evidence that an appreciable number of its citizen soldiers had fled to En Gedi. It is reasonable—though of course hypothetical—to suspect that their town had been struck by Roman forces, who would then shortly have assaulted nearby Herodium as well. *P.Yadin* 55 commands John b. Baʿyah and Masabala to send to Bar Kokhba any man

from Tekoa there in En Gedi. Greater tension becomes evident in *P.Yadin* 54, where Simon, writing through Samuel b. Ammi, tells the two commanders of En Gedi, "As for any Tekoan man found there with you—the houses in which they dwell are to be burned down, and I will punish you (that they are still there)" (lines 11–13). Last, *P.Yadin* 61 is directly addressed to the "men of Tekoa" but was sent to En Gedi and so wound up in John's archive. Unfortunately, it is too damaged to extract meaningful information.

145. On the monumental arch, see Werner Eck and Gideon Foerster, "Ein Trimphbogen für Hadrian im Tal von Beth Shean bei Tel Shalem," *JRA* 12 (1999): 294–313; Eck, "Hadrian, the Bar Kokhba Revolt, and the Epigraphic Transmission," in Schäfer, ed., *Bar Kokhba War Reconsidered,* 153–70; and Bowersock, "The Tel Shalem Arch and P. Naḥal Ḥever/Seiyal 8," in ibid., 170–80.

146. In Yadin et al., *Hebrew, Aramaic and Nabatean-Aramaic Papyri,* 280.

147. Ibid., 312.

148. Ibid., 324.

149. Ibid., 329.

150. Thus Yardeni, ibid., 337.

151. White, *Light from Ancient Letters,* 190.

152. Ibid., 189; Malherbe, *Ancient Epistolary Theorists,* 6; and Stanley K. Stowers, *Letter Writing in Greco-Roman Antiquity* (Philadelphia: Westminster, 1986), 32.

153. *P.Paris* 63, dating to 164/163 B.C.E., embraces four such letters, edited by U. Wilcken in *Urkunden der Ptolemäerzeit (Ältere Funde)* I (Berlin/Leipzig: W. de Gruyter, 1927), as nos. 110–11 and 144–45; see further on them in Koskenniemi, *Studien,* 57–59. Parsons, *City of the Sharp-Nosed Fish,* 129–30, described a model letter of consolation surviving in *P.Hamb* 4.254 (second century C.E.), copied out by a modestly skilled writer, with a number of misspellings and poor syntax. Clearly not yet a literary literate, the person left blanks for the names. Cribiore, *Writing, Teachers and Students,* 208 (no. 147) contains a βραδέως γράφων practicing the beginning of a letter to a brother. "Native" (i.e., Coptic-speaking) Egyptian schools during this period routinely had beginning students copy out the formulaic frames of letters; see Monika R. M. Hasitzka, *Neue Texte und Dokumentation zum Koptisch-Unterricht* (Vienna: Hollinek, 1990), nos. 120, 124, 128, and 134 (181 and 183 are teachers' models). For further general comments, see Cribiore, *Gymnastics,* 215–19.

154. O. Montevecchi, ed., *Papyri Bononienses (P. Bon.) I (1–50)* (Milan: Vitae a Pensiero, 1953).

155. See most conveniently Malherbe, *Ancient Epistolary Theorists,* 30–41. Malherbe includes the Greek text, an English translation, and generic analysis and contextualization.

156. Thus, e.g., Cic. *Fam.* 2.4.1, 12.30.1; Demetr. *Eloc.* 223.

157. Cic. *Fam.* 9.21.1.

158. Sen. *Epist.* 75.1.

159. Plin. *Ep.* 7.9.8.
160. See the rather late and obscure authorities listed in Malherbe, *Ancient Epistolary Theorists,* 13.
161. Cic. *Fam.* 1.26.
162. L. R. Palmer, *The Latin Language* (London: Faber and Faber, 1954), 151, and cf. 74–94 for colloquial Latin as a comparison. For an overview of scholarship since Palmer wrote, note Hilla Halla-aho, "Epistolary Latin," in *A Companion to the Latin Language* (ed. J. Clarkson; West Sussex: Wiley-Blackwell, 2011), 426–44, esp. 430–34. Her summary statements of current consensus are noteworthy: "Cicero's letters to Atticus are . . . the best evidence of a colloquial style during the Classical period and, together with the plays of Plautus and Terence, form our best evidence of spoken Latin" (428), and "It is usually taken as granted that if a feature is found in the non-literary material, and especially if it coincides with a feature in the literary corpus, it can without further considerations be placed in the colloquial bag" (431–32).
163. "La thèse de savants comme Segal, Ben Iehuda et Klausner, d'après lesquels l'hébreu mishnique a été une langue parlée par la population de la Judée aux époques perse et gréco-romaine, n'est plus une hypothèse, elle est un fait établi. . . . On a l'impression que Ben Kosba s'efforce d'imposer le dialecte parlé par lui-même et par ses combattants comme le seul moyen d'expression officiel et littéraire. Yehudah ha-Nasi et ses successeurs ne feront que mener ce premier essai à son terme en élevant le mishnique au rang de langue religieuse et juridique"; Milik, DJD 2, 70.
164. E. Y. Kutscher, "לשונן של האיגרות העבריות והארמיות של בר כוסבה ובני דורו." The study originally appeared as two parts, divided by language, in *Leshonenu* 25 (1960–1961): 117–33 and *Leshonenu* 26 (1961–1962): 7–23. The study was then reprinted as part of Kutscher's collected works: E. Kutscher, מחקרים בעברית ובארמית (ed. Z. Ben Hayyim et al.; Jerusalem: Magnes/Hebrew University, 1977), 54.
165. "האיגרות העבריות," 60 ("עדיין לשון חיה"). Beyond Kutscher's study of the two groups of letters, helpful recent analyses consulted for the present sketch of Hebrew and Aramaic include G. W. Nebe, "Die Hebräische Sprache der Naḥal Ḥever Dokumente 5/6 Ḥev 44–46," in *The Hebrew of the Dead Sea Scrolls and Ben Sira* (ed. T. Muraoka and J. F. Elwolde; Leiden: Brill, 1997), 150–57; the overview of grammar in Yadin et al., *Hebrew, Aramaic and Nabatean-Aramaic Papyri,* 14–26; Ursula Schattner-Rieser, *Textes araméens de la Mer Morte* (Brussels: Éditions Safran, 2005), 129–33 (on *P.Yadin* 50, 54, 57); and Healey, *Aramaic Inscriptions,* 123–29 (*P.Yadin* 50 and 54).
166. A very useful recent survey of introductory matters such as these is Miguel Pérez Fernández, *An Introductory Grammar of Rabbinic Hebrew* (trans. J. Elwolde; Leiden: Brill, 1999), 1–15. Further details can be discovered in, e.g., M. Bar-Asher, "Mishnaic Hebrew: An Introductory Survey," in *CHJ* 4:369–403.

167. This statement is a slight but standard simplification. Some speakers of BH probably possessed twenty-five consonantal phonemes. The fuller reality will be discussed in Chapter 5.
168. For details of BH as shown in Table 4.2, see, e.g., R. Steiner, "Ancient Hebrew," in *The Semitic Languages* (ed. R. Hetzron; London/New York: Routledge, 1997), 145–73, esp. 147–48, and P. Kyle McCarter, "Hebrew," in *The Cambridge Encyclopedia of the World's Ancient Languages* (ed. R. Woodard; Cambridge: Cambridge University Press, 2004), 319–64, esp. 324–25.
169. See R. Woodard, "Attic Greek," in *Cambridge Encyclopedia of the World's Ancient Languages,* 614–49, esp. 616, and Philomen Probert, "Phonology," in *A Companion to the Ancient Greek Language* (ed. E. J. Bakker; Chichester: Wiley-Blackwell, 2010), 85–103, esp. 85–96.
170. Horrocks, *Greek,* 113.
171. Accordingly, Table 4.4 is only one possible presentation of the data, but space prohibits full argument and discussion. That will have to await another occasion.
172. A very useful supplement to this discussion is Martin G. Abegg, Jr., "Linguistic Profile of the Isaiah Scrolls," in Eugene Ulrich and Peter Flint, *Qumran Cave 1. II: The Isaiah Scrolls. Part 2: Introductions, Commentary, and Textual Variations* (DJD 32; Oxford: Clarendon, 2010), 25–41.
173. Naveh, "Formal and Informal Spelling," 263. Even the Masoretic grammar of BH recognizes the weak pronunciation of these letters and *resh* by disallowing their doubling (*dagesh*).
174. Cf. Ilan, *Lexicon,* 218–35.
175. Thus *P.Hever* 49 (partially reconstructed) and *P.Yadin* 6, 14–15, 17–18, 21–22, and *P.Hever* 64. In point of fact, as Naveh noted, biblical יוסף contains no theophorous element. The Second Temple spelling represented a metanalysis.
176. Yadin and Naveh, *Masada I,* 36.
177. Naveh, "Formal and Informal Spelling," 266; Yardeni, *Textbook,* 1:159.
178. Charles Krahmalkov, *A Phoenician-Punic Grammar* (Leiden: Brill, 2001), 20–27.
179. Z. Ben-Hayyim, *A Grammar of Samaritan Hebrew* (Winona Lake, Ind.: Eisenbrauns, 2000), 35–37.
180. Kutscher, "האיגרות הארמיות," 120–21; Healey, *Aramaic Inscriptions,* 127.
181. Ilan, *Lexicon,* 266–67.
182. M. Bar-Asher, "על הלשון בשטר מבית—עמר," *Cathedra* 132 (2009): 28–29: "נראה ששני התעתיקים . . . מלמדים שהסופר היה נתון להשפעת ההגייה היוונית." The suggestion here is, of course, not precisely that of Bar-Asher, who spoke of a *scribe* under influence. We are positing Greek influence on the *speakers of the region* where the contract was composed: the vicinity of Beth ʿAmar, whence the scribe most likely originated.
183. Scholars frequently speak of such nunation in the Hebrew of this period as an Aramaizing phenomenon, but it actually presents a phonological, not morphological, issue and one not peculiar to Aramaic. Clearly, for example, one cannot

distinguish on orthographic grounds "Hebrew" plurals from "Aramaic." So it is not precisely true that Hebrew has become more like Aramaic in these regards. It is rather that the earlier differences between them have ceased to exist, and the languages have converged—a subtle, but critical distinction.

184. An exception is יתהום, written by Judah b. Eleazar in the subscription to *P.Yadin* 17 (line 41). The editors comment, "Similar archaic forms are found in other Babatha texts, but in the Bar Kokheba [*sic*] letters יתהן is found" (Lewis, *Documents: Greek Papyri,* 141). But this is an illusory archaism, a mere matter of coincidence. The two forms compared are just different possible spellings of an identical pronunciation.

185. R. Steiner, "Why Bishlam (Ezra 4:7) Cannot Rest 'In Peace': On the Aramaic and Hebrew Sound Changes That Conspired to Blot Out the Remembrance of Bel-Shalam the Archivist," *JBL* 126 (2007): 392–401, esp. 397–99.

186. Qimron, *Hebrew,* 26–27.

187. For a different explanation, see J. Naveh, "בשולי השטרות מכפר ברו," in שי לחיים רבין, 232 and literature cited.

188. The form שיהיוו that appears in *P.Yadin* 44:16 is arguably another example of dealing with a succession of two vowels by inserting a glide and so is not, *pace* the editors, a scribal error (Yadin et al., *Hebrew, Aramaic and Nabatean-Aramaic Papyri,* 17). We rather gain important insight into how Hebrew actually sounded as spoken in En Gedi.

189. Thus, for example, התזמנתון* becomes in Biblical Aramaic הזדמנתון, and התצדק* becomes in BH הצטדק. See in general the standard grammars, e.g., P. Joüon and T. Muraoka, *A Grammar of Biblical Hebrew* (2 vols.; Rome: Pontificio Istituto Biblico 2005), 1:74 and 1:158.

190. For Samaritan Hebrew, note the comments of Ben-Hayyim in *Grammar of Samaritan Hebrew,* 118, 223, and Stefan Schorch, "Spoken Hebrew of the Late Second Temple Period According to Oral and Written Samaritan Tradition," in *Conservatism and Innovation in the Hebrew Language of the Hellenistic Period* (ed. J. Joosten and J. Sébastien Rey; Leiden: Brill, 2008), 187–89. For Jewish Palestinian Aramaic, see D. Golomb, *A Grammar of Targum Neofiti* (Chico, Calif.: Scholars Press, 1985), 134, and for Samaritan Aramaic, R. Macuch, *Grammatik des Samaritanischen Aramäisch* (Berlin: Walter de Gruyter, 1982), 64, 152–54. The situation in the coeval Christian Palestinian Aramaic is unclear. Several forms that suggest the assimilation process here discussed, and listed by F. Schulthess, *Grammatik des Christlich-Palästinischen Aramäisch* (1924; repr., Hildesheim: Georg Olms, 1982), 22, are ignored in the more recent treatment of the dialect by C. Müller-Kessler, *Grammatik des Christlich-Palästinisch-Aramäischen. Teil 1. Schriftlehre, Lautlehre, Formenlehre* (Zürich: Georg Olms, 1991), 55, 163, and 171. Thus the matter requires a separate investigation.

191. S. A. Kaufman, "On Methodology in the Study of the Targums and Their Chronology," *JSNT* 23 (1985): 123.

192. The literature on the issue is extensive. As an entrée, see, e.g., J. A. Emerton, "*Maranatha* and *Ephphatha*," *JTS* 18 (1967): 427–31, and Sh. Morag, "ἐφφαθά (Mark VII. 34): Certainly Hebrew, not Aramaic?," *JSS* 17 (1972): 198–202.
193. Slips appear in both Hebrew and Aramaic texts. As to Hebrew, note the numerous forms and helpful remarks of Kutscher, *Language and Linguistic Background,* 345–46, and Qimron, *Hebrew,* 55–56. As to Aramaic, the suggested assimilation may explain the *Ketib* of Dan 2:9, הזמנתון, from original התזמנתון. Presumably, the vernacular process infected a Judaean scribe who copied this portion in Second Temple times. The Masoretic *Qere* reflects the early literary Aramaic norms, הזדמנתון. Cf. H. Bauer and P. Leander, *Grammatik des Biblisch-Aramäischen* (1927; repr., New York: Hildesheim, 1981), 111. Unfortunately, it is not possible to compare the MT here with an earlier Aramaic text-form, as this word does not survive in 4Q212 (4QDan[a]). Only a few letters of Dan 2:9 are extant in that manuscript. See E. Ulrich et al., *Qumran Cave 4. XI: Psalms to Chronicles* (DJD 16; Oxford: Clarendon, 2000), 243.
194. J. Cantineau, *Le Nabatéen* (1930; repr. Osnabrück: Otto Zeller, 1978), 72–73.
195. Readings according to Yardeni, *Textbook,* 1:159 and 1:165, respectively.
196. Broshi and Qimron, "Hebrew I.O.U.," 293–94. Note also a similar process in late Punic, whereby initial [yi] > [i]; Krahmalkov, *Phoenician-Punic,* 23.
197. Examples in Ilan, *Lexicon,* 112–25.
198. -זה ש does not occur in Tannaitic Hebrew (sometimes termed MH[1]), but only in Amoraic (MH[2]). By that time, the early fourth century, many scholars believe Hebrew was no longer a living language among the rabbis.
199. -בשל ש seems to be a calque of Aramaic -בדיל ד, and is otherwise known only in the earlier form בשל אשר (Qoh 8:17) and from the Qumranic "Halakhic Letter," 4QMMT. The latter text is important as a forerunner to the Bar Kokhba texts' use of a register close to speech for epistolary purposes. The editors of 4QMMT argued that its language was closer to MH than to BH, especially lexically, but that in certain grammatical aspects it was more akin to BH. They finally concluded, "Its similarity to MH results from the fact that both MMT and MH reflect spoken forms of Hebrew current in the Second Temple period" (Qimron and Strugnell, DJD 10, 108). For further analysis of the language of 4QMMT, see Sh. Morag, "סגנון לשון במגילת מקצת מעשה התורה–האם כתב 'מורה הצדק' איגרת זאת?" *Tarbiz* 65 (1996): 209–23.
200. That is, Tannaitic texts of the West. Babylonian texts use the form more frequently.
201. המך represents an isogloss with eastern MH.
202. Reading with Yardeni in Yadin et al., *Hebrew, Aramaic and Nabatean-Aramaic Papyri,* 296, except that she did not add the editorial correction <Gedi>, nor restore the suggested first word in line 2, [שלום].
203. Cotton et al., *CIIP* 432–36 (nos. 410–12). Note that the attachment of the definite article to the *nomen regens* is attested in the Hebrew Bible, likely due to

contamination of the text by copyists who spoke our vernacular: e.g., היום הוסדה in Exod 9:18. See the comments by G. R. Driver, "Colloquialisms in the Old Testament," in *Mélanges Marcel Cohen* (ed. D. Cohen; The Hague: Mouton, 1970), 235.

204. Lewis Glinert, *Modern Hebrew: An Essential Grammar* (3rd ed.; New York/London: Routledge, 2005), 32. He noted that the usage is frowned upon in writing.

205. B. Waltke and M. O'Connor, *An Introduction to Biblical Hebrew Syntax* (Winona Lake, Ind.: Eisenbrauns, 1990), 177–83.

206. Two spellings of the particle in the Beth ʿAmar text might be seen as problematic for this equation. The scribe writes, "I have received everything" as תיכול התקבלת (line 7) and תיכל התקבלת (line 8). Bar-Asher's explanation for this orthography is that the [a] of /ta-/ has attenuated to an [i] in the closed, unaccented syllable formed by its attachment to the nominal form; so his "על הלשון," 28. This is a reasonable, indeed probable conclusion; but one wonders, given the original vowel of the "mother form" אֵת, whether a more complex process may be involved. This is particularly the case since historically the vowel of that mother form was /a/, which secondarily became [e] in certain morphosyntactic situations. But when did that happen in the development of the literary and vernacular forms of Hebrew? In other words, could the *yodh* here represent an [e] associated with את rather than the /a/ associated with the definite article?

207. Yardeni, *Textbook,* 2:15–16, 146–47.

208. Krahmalkov, *Phoenician-Punic,* 281.

209. The envoy bearing it is Eleazar b. Eleazar, an official in that town, as discussed in Chapter 3.

210. *P.Hever* 30:8, following Yardeni's reading in the *editio princeps,* DJD 27, 104.

211. מִבֵּין preceding a substantive occurs in *Demai* 7:4, *Ma'as.* 1:7, *'Erub.* 10:15, and *Qinnim* 2:3. This is actually a biblical construction. מִבֵּינְתַיִים meaning "among them" occurs in *Sukkah* 1:7 (*ter*), *Kelim* 13:4, and *Kelim* 13:8. The form בינותים appears without מן in *P.Yadin* 44:2, where context favors the understanding "among them" (not "between them," as translated in the *editio princeps,* since four men are involved).

212. Nebe, "Hebräische Sprache," 150–57.

213. For helpful comments, see Abba Ben-David, לשון מקרא ולשון חכמים (2 vols.; Tel-Aviv: Dvir, 1967–1971), 2:100–101.

214. In particular, he used code-switching, sprinkling his letters with Greek; but he did so freely only with Atticus. See Simon Swain, "Bilingualism in Cicero? The Evidence of Code-Switching," in *Bilingualism in Ancient Society* (ed. J. N. Adams, M. Janse, and S. Swain; Oxford: Oxford University Press, 2002), 128–67.

215. Moreshet, לקסיקון הפועל שנתחדש בלשון התנאים. That they are present in both Aramaic and early MH is undeniable. Whether derivation is always the proper explanation is another matter. Can one say that a given MH word is

derived from Aramaic simply because it does not appear in BH, has origins hidden from view, and looks like Aramaic? Given our ignorance of dialects of Hebrew, beginning in the biblical period and on down to Roman times, the procedure is questionable. Also, it is just not that easy to tell Hebrew and Aramaic apart. Usually, scholars rely on vocalization patterns and consonantal correspondences vis-à-vis the original Semitic stock of consonants to make these judgments. "Standard" Hebrew is then relatively easy to distinguish from "standard" Aramaic: for Proto-Semitic /d̲/, for example, Hebrew yields ז, Aramaic ד. Half a dozen such differences exist. But both poetic BH and dialectal Hebrew of the biblical period sometimes show "Aramaic" correspondence. Furthermore, our knowledge of vocalization is highly fragmentary. Until recently, scholars had not taken these methodological problems very seriously, but that has begun to change. See, e.g., D. L. Penney, "Towards a Prehistory of Biblical Hebrew Roots: Phoneme Constraint and Polymorphism" (Ph.D. diss., University of Chicago, 1993), passim; A. Hurvitz, "Hebrew and Aramaic in the Biblical Period: The Problem of 'Aramaisms' in Linguistic Research on the Hebrew Bible," in *Biblical Hebrew: Studies in Chronology and Typology* (ed. I. Young; London/New York: T&T Clark, 2003), 24–37; and I. Young, R. Rezetko, and M. Ehrensvärd, *Linguistic Dating of Biblical Texts* (2 vols.; London: Equinox, 2008), 1:201–22 and 2:73–74.

216. Ilse Lehiste, *Lectures on Language Contact* (Cambridge, Mass.: MIT Press, 1988), 19–27.

217. In DJD 27, 104 Yardeni offered ידוע יהיה לך שׂ°°°°°°°הגאי/ו°[?] שה°° [ ], translating, "Let it be known to you that . . . from . . ." Yardeni, *Textbook,* 1:183 and 2:69 presented the same understandings.

218. *HALOT* s.v. This lexicon also observed that the word never occurs in Tannaitic Hebrew, being attested only in MH².

219. Yardeni, DJD 27, 104 read, שנטרפו אח°[ ]ן[ ]°[ ], "that brothers(?) were . . . [. . .]."

220. *DCH,* s.v.

221. Kutscher, "האיגרות העבריות," 59. Of his own view he noted simply, "קשה להלום." Of Milik's suggestion, "que cela soit connu de toi" (DJD 2, 162), he wrote again simply, "אין להלום פירוש זה."

222. Yardeni, *Textbook,* 2:64. It was only Yardeni's improved reading of the phrase, it should be noted, that made possible the understanding suggested here.

223. Note also *P.Yadin* 54:5, speaking of wheat (חנטין): ותתנון יתהן באספליא, "you are to keep it under guard." Here again, sending is involved, as Simon b. Kosiba orders the wheat transported to him.

224. Cf., e.g., Hdt. 2.121, Isoc. *Evagoras* 9.30, and Xen. *Hier.* 2.10.

225. See BDAG s.v. and literature cited.

226. Ch. Rabin, "The Beginnings of Classical Arabic," *Studia Islamica* 4 (1955): 19–37, esp. 21.

227. No grammar devoted exclusively to these texts exists. Instead, existing grammars include these texts within broader selections of material, a defensible approach but one that inevitably obscures the unique aspects of the letters and subscriptions. Thus Beyer's *Aramäischen Texte* embraces a very broad group of Aramaic materials and is open to trenchant criticism regarding classification, the very point we must engage in seeking a mirror that may reflect the vernacular (on Beyer's classification, cf. the review of his work by S. F. Bennett in *Maarav* 4 [1987]: 243–60, esp. 245–49). Schattner-Reiser, *L'araméen des manuscrits de la mer Morte I. Grammaire* (Lausanne: Éditions du Zèbre, 2004), suffers to a lesser degree from the same problem, as does T. Muraoka, *A Grammar of Qumran Aramaic* (Leuven/Paris/Walpole, Mass.: Peeters, 2011). The only dictionary dedicated to the materials, Sokoloff's *Dictionary of Judaean Aramaic*, is "important" but not "indispensable," precisely for similar issues of inclusion and exclusion; thus Edward Cook's review in *Maarav* 11 (2004): 95–101 (the contrasting adjectives are his, 101).
228. Cf. e.g., M. Sokoloff, "Qumran Aramaic in Relation to the Aramaic Dialects," in *Dead Sea Scrolls Fifty Years After*, 746–67.
229. Kutscher, "האיגרות הארמיות," 38 (my translation).
230. The subscriptions were legal acknowledgments of a person's obligations under a given contract. More than any other element of a contract, they were of the essence, since they represented the agreements of the principals. Given the constitutive nature of those acknowledgments, Judaeans seem often to have tried to represent the oral statements involved quite closely. We saw an example in Chapter 3 with Judah Cimber's subscription to *P.Yadin* 18, written for him by a *hypographeus* who wrote Greek fluently, but Aramaic poorly. He chose to sign for Cimber in the latter, arguably so as to represent his actual spoken words. Another example appears in the Beth ʿAmar text. Although the writ is composed in Aramaic, at the point that the widow Miriam b. Jacob is represented as stating her acknowledgment (מודה אני, lines 4–5), the scribe shifted into Hebrew. When she was finished, he shifted back into Aramaic (line 12). Thus it seems that acknowledgments, in particular, often reflected speech relatively closely. But this judgment must be balanced against the understanding that what was said by the person in question was probably coached by the scribe, since untrained ordinary people would not spontaneously produce the required legal expressions.
231. It was principally Greenfield and Yardeni who edited for final publication the subscriptions analyzed in Lewis, *Documents: Greek Papyri*, 135–49, although Yadin (through surviving notes) and Naveh also contributed to the readings and discussions.
232. Yadin et al., *Hebrew, Aramaic and Nabatean-Aramaic Papyri*, 23. The subscription form referenced received the following comment in Lewis, *Documents: Greek Papyri*, 142: "הקחת. 'I have given in marriage.' The use of the *haphel* is unusual

in this period, but it occurs elsewhere in our texts ([*P.Yadin*] 15). It may be seen as an attempt to write in the archaic language typical of legal texts. It is not found in *P.Yadin* 7, where the *aphel* is used. The writer, or the court official who dictated the declaration to him, may have been influenced by Nabatean usage, where the *haphel* is found alongside the *aphel*."

233. A most helpful concise overview is Edward Cook, "The Aramaic of the Dead Sea Scrolls," in *The Dead Sea Scrolls After Fifty Years: A Comprehensive Assessment* (ed. Peter W. Flint and James C. VanderKam; 2 vols.; Leiden: Brill, 1998–1999), 2:359–78. Cook also provided a guide to other important studies.
234. *P.Yadin* 27:11.
235. Cf. אגרת in *P.Yadin* 53:1.
236. E.g., the nonprofessional writer of *Mur* 19 used *status absolutus* אנת, meaning "a wife" in the upper text (19:6), but in the parallel lower text, in the identical syntactic situation, opted for the *status emphaticus* אנתא (19:18).
237. For תעבד[ון] לה[, Yardeni reads, תעבד[ו] ל[(*Textbook* 1:182), but the size of the lacuna and the use of לא rather than אל favors the longer imperfect. Regarding the jussive, note also the loss of the functionally equivalent old precative, להוה. Thus *P.Yadin* 55:6–7 ידיע יהוה, "let it be known," over against BA ידיע להוא, Ezra 4:12.
238. Kutscher, "האיגרות הארמיות," 48–51.
239. Ibid., 42–43.
240. So *HALOT* s.v. One occurrence is uncertain (Qoh 11:3).
241. Driver, *Aramaic Documents,* 9:3, spelled באפריע. Driver was, however, unaware of the connection to later Jewish literature. For that, see Sokoloff, *Jewish Palestinian Aramaic,* s.v.
242. The term סיפה, "sword," occurs in *P.Yadin* 54, and it is equivalent to another military term, Greek ξίφος. But ξίφος lacks a Greek etymology, and the evidence from Mycenaean points to a borrowing from a pre-Greek language, possibly Egyptian. See Robert Beekes, *Etymological Dictionary of Greek* (Leiden: Brill, 2010), s.v., and note e.g., Heinrich Lewy, *Die semitischen Fremdwörter im Griechischen* (Berlin: Gaertner, 1895), 176–77, and *DISO*[2] (1995), 784.
243. Notice, however, that in colloquial speech הן and אם would frequently have been pronounced identically.
244. Yardeni's reading here was]קצת היך בישׁ[ ]ב (DJD 27, 104).
245. See *HALOT* s.v.
246. Yaron Matras, *Language Contact* (Cambridge: Cambridge University Press, 2009), 212–16; Donald Winford, *An Introduction to Contact Linguistics* (Oxford: Blackwell, 2003), 63: "Importation of inflections appears to be generally rare in situations of language maintenance, though it does occur if there is sufficient congruence between the inflections involved."
247. Eshel, "Survey of the Refuge Caves," 109.

Chapter 5. Language and Literacy in Roman Judaea

1. For the lingua franca model, note especially the influential study by J. Fitzmyer, "The Phases of the Aramaic Language," in *Wandering Aramean,* 61–62 and 71–74. The languages-in-contact model was argued in Wise, "Accidents and Accidence," in *Thunder in Gemini,* 111–19, although this study did not use the phrase to label its approach. The helpful nomenclature derives from Goodblatt, *Elements,* 57–59, where he argued for this model.
2. For the Assyrian period, see e.g., H. Tadmor, "The Aramaization of Assyria: Aspects of Western Impact," in *Mesopotamien und seine Nachbarn* (ed. H.-J. Nissen and J. Renger; Berlin: Dietrich Reimer Verlag, 1982), 49–70. For the later periods, see e.g., J. Greenfield, "Aramaic in the Achaemenian Empire," in *The Cambridge History of Iran. Vol. 2: The Median and Achaemenian Periods* (ed. I. Gershevitch; Cambridge: Cambridge University Press, 1985), 698–713 and 918–22.
3. M. Folmer, *The Aramaic Language in the Achaemenid Period: A Study in Linguistic Variation* (Leuven: Peeters, 1995), documents the significant degree of standardization alongside local variations.
4. For the Moṣa stamp impressions, see J. Zorn, J. Yellin, and J. Hayes, "The *m(w) ṣh* Stamp Impressions and the Neo-Babylonian Period," in *IEJ* 44 (1994): 161–83; for the Samaria Papyri, Gropp et al., DJD 28, 3–116; for *P.Jericho* 1, Eshel and Misgav, DJD 38, 21–30; for the Khirbet el-Qom documents, I. Ephal and J. Naveh, *Aramaic Ostraca of the Fourth Century BC from Idumaea* (Jerusalem: Magnes and the Israel Exploration Society, 1996), and A. Lemaire, *Nouvelles inscriptions araméennes d'Idumeé au Musée d'Israël* (Paris: Gabalda, 1996).
5. Frank H. Polak, "Sociolinguistics and the Judean Speech Community in the Achaemenid Empire," in *Judah and the Judeans in the Persian Period* (ed. O. Lipschits and M. Oeming; Winona Lake, Ind.: Eisenbrauns, 2006), 589–628; quotation on p. 592.
6. Note Fitzmyer's declaration in his "Methodology in the Study of the Aramaic Substratum of Jesus' Sayings in the New Testament," in *Jésus aux origines de la christologie* (ed. J. Dupont; Louvain: Leuven University, 1975), 86: "I remain very skeptical about the alleged differences between the literary and spoken forms of Aramaic of this period." Cf. his statement in "Languages of Palestine," 39, and his review of M. Black, *An Aramaic Approach to the Gospels and Acts,* in *CBQ* 30 (1968): 417–28.
7. 2 Kgs 10:32–33; 12:17–18; 13:3–7.
8. 1 Chr 2:23 and 7:14.
9. B. Oded, *Mass Deportations and Deportees in the Neo-Assyrian Empire* (Wiesbaden: Dr. Ludwig Reichert Verlag, 1979), 27–29, 44 n. 20, 49, 51–52, 63, 65–67, and 96.
10. J. Hoftijzer and G. van der Kooij, *Aramaic Texts from Deir Alla* (Leiden: Brill, 1976); J. Hackett, *The Balaam Text from Deir Alla* (Chico, Calif.: Scholars Press, 1984).

11. Neh 13:23–24. Josephus speaks of intermarriage between members of the ruling classes of Samaria and Jerusalem continuing into the Hellenistic period at least, *A.J.* 11.306–312.
12. J. Greenfield, "Standard Literary Aramaic," in *Actes du premier congrès international de linguistique sémitique et chamito-sémitique, Paris 16–19 juillet 1969* (ed. A. Caquot and D. Cohen; The Hague: Mouton, 1974), 280–89; reprinted in *'Al Kanfei Yonah: Collected Studies of Jonas C. Greenfield on Semitic Philology* (ed. Shalom M. Paul, Michael Stone, and Avital Pinnick; 2 vols.; Leiden: Brill, 2001) 1:111–20 (cited here).
13. "[Standard Literary Aramaic] is NOT Palestinian Aramaic unless one means by this term only the written language used in the country, and it seems to me to be a cardinal error for anyone to assume that it approximates the spoken Palestinian Aramaic of its period." So Greenfield, ibid., 117 (emphasis his).
14. Actually, some Aramaists have argued that Imperial Aramaic continued. What Greenfield called Standard Literary Aramaic, they suggested, was just a form of that dialect that lived on after the decline of Persia because of its familiarity to scribes. In favor of this view: (1) no major dialect differences exist between Imperial Aramaic and SLA; and (2) Greenfield's position requires the scenario of a very rapid overthrow of one standard dialect in favor of another, essentially identical form. See Edward M. Cook, "A New Perspective on the Language of Onqelos and Jonathan," in *The Aramaic Bible: Targums in Their Historical Context* (ed. D. R. G. Beattie and M. J. McNamara; Sheffield: JSOT, 1994), 142–56, esp. 145–46. In either view, Judaean Aramaic as spoken would be very distinct from the literary language.
15. See Klaus Beyer, "Der reichsaramäische Einschlag in der ältesten syrischen Literatur," *ZDMG* 116 (1966): 242–54. Greenfield comments on Beyer's argument, "For the 'Old Syriac Gospels' I would assume that the 'Einschlag' was that of Standard Literary Aramaic rather than Reichsaramäisch" ("Standard Literary Aramaic," 120). On the inscriptions, note the comment of Drijvers and Healey, "The features which separate Classical Syriac from Old Syriac . . . are features which Old Syriac shares with Achaemenid and immediately post-Achaemenid Aramaic" (H. J. W. Drijvers and J. F. Healey, *The Old Syriac Inscriptions of Edessa and Osrhoene* [Leiden: Brill, 1999], 21–22).
16. Hillers and Cussini, *Palmyrene Aramaic Texts,* 57–63. Note Beyer's comments on the text in *Aramäischen Texte,* 1:42–43.
17. Wasserstein, "Non-Hellenized Jews," 111.
18. This consensus found expression in a vast literature. Representative were Kutscher, *History of the Hebrew Language,* and Sáenz-Badillos, *History of the Hebrew Language.*
19. The studies where one may find the discussion reflected in this paragraph are numerous. Among the most useful are T. Muraoka and J. F. Elwode, eds., *The Hebrew of the Dead Sea Scrolls and Ben Sira* (Leiden: Brill, 1997); T. Muraoka and

J. F. Elwode, eds., *Diggers at the Well* (Leiden: Brill, 2000); I. Young, ed., *Biblical Hebrew: Studies in Chronology and Typology* (London: T&T Clark, 2003); A. Berleujung and P. van Hecke, eds., *The Language of Qohelet in Its Context* (Leuven: Peeters, 2007); J. Joosten and J.-S. Rey, eds., *Conservatism and Innovation in the Hebrew Language of the Hellenistic Period* (Leiden: Brill, 2008); Young, Rezetko, and Ehrensvärd, *Linguistic Dating;* J. Joosten, "Hebrew, Aramaic and Greek in the Qumran Scrolls," in Lim and Collins, eds., *Oxford Handbook of the Dead Sea Scrolls,* 351–74; and W. Smelik, "The Languages of Roman Palestine," in *Oxford Handbook of Jewish Daily Life,* 122–41.

20. Most of their two volumes is dedicated to laying out the details of their approach, but the synthetic statement is Young, Rezetko, and Ehrensvärd, *Linguistic Dating,* 2:72–105.

21. The concept of multiple variant literary editions of the books of Hebrew scripture is relatively new and owes most to the work of Eugene Ulrich. Note especially his *Dead Sea Scrolls and the Origins of the Bible,* 34–120. For a concise view of the current state of thinking regarding the interaction between textual and literary criticism, book by book, see E. Tov, *Textual Criticism of the Hebrew Bible* (3rd ed.; Minneapolis: Fortress, 2012), 283–326.

22. The authors recognized the potential corroboration that the surviving preexilic Hebrew inscriptions might provide their synchronic model. These materials could theoretically help them to whet their tool somewhat, because they were not passed down by scribal transmission; they treated them in *Linguistic Dating,* 1:143–72. They were able to find some evidence for LBH phenomena but unable to produce the required *significant accumulation* of traits. This inability, as they viewed it, owed largely to the paucity of what survives, and to its limited generic parallelism with the scriptural materials. This is, of course, a possible interpretation of their data, but it is also possible that a greater mass of material might have yielded little additional accumulation. We simply cannot know. In the event, they were forced to a critical admission: "We can see that the Hebrew inscriptions are not to be classified as LBH. Even though we identified an accumulation of nine LBH linguistic elements in the Arad Ostraca, this is little higher than the degree of accumulation of LBH features usually found in core EBH books" (1:170). This result might lead one to conclude that the inscriptions are then SBH/EBH. But the inscriptional material is not precisely like that of SBH/EBH either. It is a *tertium quid.* But where it differs from SBH, it tends to be typologically earlier, as the authors acknowledge. Thus, once again, the data are fully compatible with the broad outlines of the consensus, wherein earlier materials—perhaps once more like the inscriptions than they presently seem to be—were passed down and modified by later scribes.

23. Jan Joosten, "The Disappearance of Iterative WEQATAL in the Biblical Hebrew Verbal System," in Fassberg and Hurvitz, eds., *Biblical Hebrew,* 135–47.

24. Jan Joosten, "Pseudo-Classicisms in Late Biblical Hebrew, in Ben Sira, and in Qumran Hebrew," in *Sirach, Scrolls, and Sages* (ed. T. Muraoka and J. Elwolde; Leiden: Brill, 1999), 146–59.
25. Young, Rezetko, and Ehrensvärd, *Linguistic Dating,* 1:250–79.
26. Ibid., 1:275. The authors reference Carr's point that the core LBH books of Chronicles, Esther, Ezra, and Nehemiah were peripheral to education, at least to judge from the Judaean Desert finds as a whole (Carr, *Writing,* 155).
27. Qimron has penned a number of articles urging QH as a vernacular; a useful summary of his views is his "The Nature of DSS Hebrew and Its Relation to BH and MH," in *Diggers at the Well,* 232–44. He was formerly a supporter of the consensus view linking QH directly to LBH; thus his *Hebrew of the Dead Sea Scrolls,* 116.
28. Joshua Blau, "A Conservative View of the Language of the Dead Sea Scrolls," in *Diggers at the Well,* 20–22 (emphasis his).
29. Steven E. Fassberg, "The Infinitive Absolute as Finite Verb and Standard Literary Hebrew of the Second Temple Period," in *Hebrew Language of the Hellenistic Period,* 47–60. He observed on pp. 59–60, "The standard literary language is a web, not always seamless, but a web, nonetheless, of First Temple and Second Temple elements. It differed considerably from the colloquial speech of the time (cf. the Bar Kokhba letters)."
30. One cannot rule out that some groups may have attempted to speak a variety of the literary tongue, whether these be sectarians or simply priestly cohorts of various sorts. For such, however, we have no definite evidence.
31. Hengel, *Judaism and Hellenism,* particularly 1:58–65; Victor Tcherikover, *Hellenistic Civilization and the Jews* (Jewish Publication Society of America, 1959; repr., New York: Atheneum, 1982), 1–151. Note also the following classic studies: Morton Smith, *Palestinian Parties and Politics That Shaped the Old Testament* (New York: Columbia University Press, 1971), 57–81, 227–37; Arnaldo Momigliano, *Alien Wisdom: The Limits of Hellenization* (Cambridge: Cambridge University Press, 1975), 74–96; and Martin Hengel, *Jews, Greeks and Barbarians* (J. Bowden, trans.; Philadelphia: Fortress, 1980), 110–26, 170–74.
32. Hengel, *Judaism and Hellenism,* 58.
33. The relevant Zeno papyri are still most conveniently consulted in *CPJ* 1:115–30.
34. Tcherikover's famous analysis of the Tobiads, scattered throughout the pages of his *Hellenistic Civilization,* may conveniently be accessed as a continuous narrative in his "The Tobiads in Light of the Zenon Papyri," in *Emerging Judaism* (ed. Michael E. Stone and David Satran; Minneapolis: Fortress, 1989), 77–99.
35. Hengel, *Judaism and Hellenism,* 63.
36. Tal Ilan, "The Greek Names of the Hasmoneans," *JQR* 78 (1987–1988): 1–20.
37. On these points, see Ilan, *Lexicon,* 1:53–57. For female names, see further her "Notes on the Distribution of Women's Names in Palestine in the Second Temple and Mishnaic Period," *JJS* 40 (1989): 186–200.
38. Lewis, *Documents: Greek Papyri,* 13.

39. Yardeni restored here Aramaic [בר], but it is possible under high magnification to make out a bit of the descending stroke of the final *nun* of Hebrew בן. Also, for the first witness to the contract, PN b. Simon (presumably Jesus's brother), Yardeni did not read the final *nun,* but a portion of the letter is visible (cf. Yadin et al., *Hebrew, Aramaic and Nabatean-Aramaic Papyri,* 66).
40. DJD 27, Plate 27.
41. For *Mur* 22 and *Mur* 30, see Yardeni's editions in her *Textbook,* 1:47–48 and 1:51–52, respectively.
42. See the edition of the initial lines of the text in Chapter 2.
43. The category "other" is abstracted from the forty-two instances in evidence.
44. For further detail, see the discussions of these situations in Chapters 3 and 4, respectively.
45. A reasonable estimate is that there were ten thousand to twenty thousand priests in Judaea in our years. Josephus gives the number as twenty thousand in *Ag. Ap.* 2.108, and in contrast to many of his numbers, scholars take this one seriously. Priests seem to have constituted about 10 percent of the population at the time of the return from Babylon, but that percentage continuously declined all during the Second Temple period. Thus Menahem Stern, "Aspects of Jewish Society: The Priesthood and Other Classes," CRINT 1.2:595–96. Not all scribes were priests, of course—scribes were the larger category—but there was considerable overlap, as argued earlier.
46. Charles Ferguson, "Diglossia," *Word* 15 (1959): 325–40. The article is reprinted (along with other significant studies on the topic) in *Sociolinguistics: The Essential Readings* (ed. C. B. Paulston and G. R. Tucker; Oxford: Blackwell, 2003), 345–58, here cited. The connection of diglossia to the situation of ancient Hebrew is of course not new. Gary Rendsburg, for example, has made the issue a particular focus of his research over many years. Cf. his *Diglossia in Ancient Hebrew* (New Haven, Conn.: American Oriental Society, 1990), which concerned the biblical period. A helpful recent overview (though with conclusions quite different from the present study) is Jonathan M. Watt, "The Current Landscape of Diglossia Studies: The Diglossic Continuum in First-Century Palestine," in *Diglossia and Other Topics in New Testament Linguistics* (ed. Stanley Porter; Sheffield: Sheffield Academic Press, 2000), 18–36.
47. Ferguson, "Diglossia," 354.
48. Joshua Fishman, "Bilingualism With and Without Diglossia; Diglossia With and Without Bilingualism," in *Sociolinguistics,* 359–66. Cf. L. Timm, "Bilingualism, Diglossia and Language Shift in Brittany," *International Journal of the Sociology of Language* 25 (1980): 29–41.
49. Note the comments of the editors, *Sociolinguistics,* 343–44.
50. Thus, e.g., Kees Versteegh, "Dead or Alive? The Status of the Standard Language," in *Bilingualism in Ancient Society* (ed. J. N. Adams, M. Janse, and S. Swain; Oxford: Oxford University Press, 2002), 52–74.

51. Yadin, "Expedition D," 40, and "Expedition D—The Cave of the Letters," 229.
52. Roger Bagnall has observed in the case of the Egyptian discoveries that "the literature possessed at home as adults also reflected the authors read in school" (*Early Christian Books in Egypt* [Princeton, N.J.: Princeton University Press, 2009], 21). Cornelia Roemer has concurred: "The texts read in school determined the tastes and reading habits of adults" ("The Papyrus Roll in Egypt, Greece and Rome," in *A Companion to the History of the Book* [ed. S. Eliot and J. Rose; West Sussex: Wiley-Blackwell, 2009], 92). The Judaean findings fit the same pattern if Carr and others are correct that their education focused on the scriptural books, with the Torah at the center, as Homer was elsewhere.
53. S. Talmon, "Hebrew Fragments from Masada," in *Masada VI, The Yigael Yadin Excavations 1963–1965, Final Reports* (ed. S. Talmon and Y. Yadin; Jerusalem: Israel Exploration Society, 1999), 1–149.
54. The copy of Ben Sira would divide Christians, as some consider it canonical and others outside the canon.
55. The editors offered the implausible suggestion that the work was "written in a combination of both languages," i.e., Aramaic and Hebrew (*Masada VI,* 137). The term מקרה, meaning "incident" or "case," is unequivocally Hebrew. The sole evidence for Aramaic is אלכן, by the editors' own admission only "apparently [an] Aramaic vocable (137)," and they did not suggest what it means. It is better understood as the common Hebrew term אל with a nunating possessive suffix, explicable in terms of neutralization of final nasals, as discussed in the previous chapter. It means "your (pl.) God."
56. See Chapter 3, note 27.
57. Millar, "Empire, Community and Culture," 147 (emphasis added). Note that the Judaeans themselves were well aware of the ethnic identity destruction that accompanied the spread of Greco-Roman culture. Discussing the changes of ancient toponyms to create names more intelligible to the dominant culture, Josephus wrote: "Ἕλληνες δ' εἰσὶν οἱ τούτου καταστάντες αἴτιοι· ἰσχύσαντες γὰρ ἐν τοῖς ὕστερον ἰδίαν ἐποιήσαντο καὶ τὴν πάλαι δόξαν, καλλωπίσαντες τὰ ἔθνη τοῖς ὀνόμασι πρὸς τὸ συνετὸν αὐτοις καὶ κόσμον θέμενοι πολιτείας ὡς ἀφ' αὐτῶν γεγονόσιν" (*A.J.* 1.121).
58. William Johnson, *Readers and Reading Culture in the High Roman Empire* (Oxford: Oxford University Press, 2010), passim, but esp. 17–31.
59. Ibid., 20.
60. For information on such issues regarding the Judaean Desert texts, see Tov, *Scribal Practices,* esp. 57–129.
61. Described by Peter Flint in DJD 38, 142.
62. Tov, *Scribal Practices,* 128–29.
63. Johnson, *Readers,* 22. Concerning the book as status symbol, Johnson continued, "We see this evident in iconography, in which hundreds of reliefs, statues, paintings and mosaics bear witness to the bookroll's importance as an emblem of high culture."

64. With one possible exception, all known Second Temple synagogues lack architectural provision for the storage of book rolls (Lee I. Levine, "The First Century Synagogue," in *Religion and Society in Roman Palestine,* 87–88). (The one exception is the Masada synagogue, where the closed-off corner room in the synagogue may have been used to store books. Even if so, however, the situation was so unusual that we cannot safely deduce customary practice.) Normally, books must have been brought in and then removed again each week. This fact seems to question the notion of community ownership of the texts. For if the community owned them, where would they be stored, if not in the community building? More likely, the owners were wealthy members of the community who kept the scrolls at their homes in the interim. Thus, providing the books for synagogue use in Roman Judaea might be seen as a kind of liturgy.
65. Rex Winsbury, *The Roman Book* (London: Duckworth, 2009), 119–21.
66. Reported by Quintilian, *Inst.* 1.8.2.
67. Winsbury, *Roman Book,* 119–21; quotation on p. 121.
68. Ibid., 122.
69. Johnson, *Readers,* 31.
70. Even today, educated native speakers of Israeli Hebrew cannot read that language as rapidly as do native speakers of English their own language. Supplying the vowels and so solving the writing system's serial mini-puzzles just takes time, even with modern texts that use more distinct letterforms, fuller orthography, current grammar, and quotidian vocabulary. Ancient Judaean readers had things considerably worse. They had to make do with a much less efficient writing system encoding a language differing no less from their vernacular than Latin does from standard Italian. See Joseph Shimron and Tamar Sivan, "Reading Proficiency and Orthography: Evidence from Hebrew and English," *Language Learning* 44 (1994): 5–27, and Joseph Shimron, *Reading Hebrew* (New York/London: Routledge, 2005), passim.
71. Cf. Chapter 4, Tables 4.2 and 4.4.
72. Richard Steiner, "On the Dating of Hebrew Sound Changes (*Ḫ > Ḥ and Ġ > ʿ) and Greek Translations (2 Esdras and Judith)," *JBL* 124 (2005): 229–67, building particularly upon Joshua Blau, *On Polyphony in Biblical Hebrew* (Jerusalem: Israel Academy of Sciences and Humanities, 1962), passim. Note Blau's recent concise summary in his *Phonology and Morphology of Biblical Hebrew* (Winona Lake, Ind.: Eisenbrauns, 2010), 75–76.
73. Blau, *Polyphony,* dated the merger of /ġ/ with /ʿ/ in spoken Hebrew to the later third century B.C.E. but suggested that "ġ disappeared from the spoken language, yet was still, it seems, retained in literary solemn language, as in the public reading of the Bible in the synagogues" (39–40). Steiner argued for the suggested date regarding /ḫ/ and /ḥ/ ("On the Dating of Hebrew Sound Changes," 248–51).
74. Note Josephus's attempt to represent what were apparently a formal (Νῶχος) and an informal spoken pronunciation of the name of Noah (Νῶε) at *A.J.* 1.129, as discussed by Steiner, "On the Dating of Hebrew Sound Changes," 240–41.

75. The matter is highly complex, but we have at least some knowledge of three Masoretic traditions (Babylonian, Palestinian, and Tiberian), a Samaritan tradition, the reading traditions behind the Hebrew transcriptions in Jerome's writings and Origen's *Hexapla,* and two or more traditions lying behind the Old Greek renderings. Because our data are so often incomplete, we cannot always be certain whether we are dealing with *actual* differences of tradition or merely differences in *representing* this or that point of tradition.
76. Ben-Hayyim, *Grammar of Samaritan Hebrew,* 1–13.
77. The Samaritan vocalization follows Mark Shoulson, *The Torah: Jewish and Samaritan Versions Compared* (Mhaigh Eo, Ireland: Evertype, 2008), 596.
78. Much of the critical data regarding the "non-Massoretic" Hebrew grammar found in the Old Greek, Jerome, and the *Hexapla* was collected by Alexander Sperber, "Hebrew Based upon Greek and Latin Transliterations," *HUCA* 12–13 (1937–1938): 103–275. His analysis was not that of a modern linguist. For some insightful comments regarding Sperber's data by just such a person, see Joel M. Hoffman, *In the Beginning: A Short History of the Hebrew Language* (New York/London: New York University Press, 2004), 90–117.
79. E.g., Emanuel Tov, "Did the Septuagint Translators Always Understand Their Hebrew Text?," in his *The Greek and Hebrew Bible: Collected Essays on the Septuagint* (Leiden: Brill, 1999), 203–18.
80. Edward Cook, "Aramaic," *DEJ* 360–62.
81. Jan Joosten, "The Knowledge and Use of Hebrew in the Hellenistic Period: Qumran and the Septuagint," in *Diggers at the Well,* 115–30.
82. Lawrence Schiffman, *The Eschatological Community of the Dead Sea Scrolls* (Atlanta: Scholars Press, 1989), 14. The translation is mine but incorporates aspects of Schiffman's commentary. In particular, note his widely accepted suggestion that ספר ההגי is to be equated with the Torah (15).
83. Ibid., 15.
84. Cf. Martin S. Jaffe, *Torah in the Mouth* (Oxford: Oxford University Press, 2001), esp. 15–38.
85. *m. Avot* 5:21.
86. Alan K. Bowman and Greg Woolf, eds., *Literacy and Power in the Ancient World* (Cambridge: Cambridge University Press, 1994). Substantive reviews include Robin Osborne, *CR* 45 (1995): 46–47; Michael Maas, *JRS* 85 (1995): 264; Rosamond McKitterick, *History Today* 46 (1996): 55–56; and Eric Robinson, *Notes and Queries* 43 (1996): 64–65.
87. Martin Goodman, "Texts, Scribes and Power in Roman Judaea," in *Literacy and Power,* 99–108.
88. Luke 12:16–21; 15:11–32; 16:1–8, 19; 20:9–16; Mark 12:1–9; Matt 20:1–16; 21:33–41.
89. Women are abstracted as virtually always illiterate. See below for details.
90. Moses Finley, *The Ancient Economy* (Berkeley: University of California Press, 1973).

91. Gerhard Lenski, *Power and Privilege: A Theory of Social Stratification* (New York: McGraw-Hill, 1966).
92. Saldarini, *Pharisees, Scribes and Sadducees,* 35–49.
93. Fabian Udoh, "Economics in Palestine," *DEJ* 557–61.
94. For the economic effect of the Temple, note especially Marty E. Stevens, *Temples, Tithes, and Taxes* (Peabody, Mass.: Hendrickson, 2006).
95. Plin. *Nat.* 5.70, *Hierosolyma, longe clarissima urbium Orientis non Iudaeae modo;* Tac. *Hist.* 5.2, *famosa urbs.*
96. Udoh, "Economics," 557.
97. Neville Morley, "The Poor in the City of Rome," in *Poverty in the Roman World* (ed. Margaret Atkins and Robin Osborne; Cambridge: Cambridge University Press, 2006), 21–39; Walter Scheidel, "Stratification, Deprivation, and Quality of Life," in ibid., 40–59.
98. See Figures 3.6 and 3.7 for the relations and Appendix B for the literate behaviors of these men.
99. Lewis, *Documents: Greek Papyri,* 26 (emphasis added).
100. The tables in this chapter tabulate the facts: for Hebrew texts, eleven of twelve who could not sign in Hebrew signed in Aramaic; for Greek, seventy of seventy; for Nabataean, thirteen of thirteen.
101. Cf. e.g., Joseph Fitzmyer's more recent comments in his *The Genesis Apocryphon of Qumran Cave 1 (1Q20): A Commentary* (3rd ed.; Rome: Pontifical Biblical Institute, 2004), 28.
102. See the discussion in Rendsburg, *Diglossia,* 35–67.
103. For the imperfect, note e.g., *Mur* 20 line 3, תהוא for תהוין and line 7, תהך for תהכין; *Mur* 21, line 10, יהון for יהוין and line 15, תהון for תהוין; and *P.Yadin* 10, line 2, תצבא for תצבין. Note also the use of masculine forms for feminine of the pronominal suffixes, e.g., *Mur* 20 line 17, ירתיך for ירתיכי and *Mur* 21, line 10, כתבתיכ [*sic*] for כתבתיכי and line 19, לותך for לותכי. *Mur* 21 also uses אנת for אנתי throughout (e.g., lines 11, 12, and 16), and *P.Yadin* 10 everywhere writes the feminine singular pronominal suffix as ך-.
104. Note *Mur* 25 line 15, ולמזבנה for ולזבנה, "and to sell" (*Pael*) (mirrored at *P.Hever* 21 line 8); *P.Hever* 9 line 8, למשפיה ולמקימה for לשפיה ולקימה, "to clear (of debt) and establish" (*Paels*). "Syriac" forms include *P.Yadin* 7 line 17, למזבנו, "to sell" for standard לזבנה (*Pael*), (mirrored at *P.Yadin* 42 line 9); *P.Yadin* 7 line 17 למורתו, "to give as inheritance" for לירתה (*Pael*); and *P.Yadin* 7 line 26, למנעלו, "to bring in" for לאנעלה (*Aphel*). For analysis note particularly Greenfield, "לצורת המקור."
105. See the comments in Yigael Yadin, Jonas C. Greenfield, and Ada Yardeni, "Babatha's Ketubba," *IEJ* 44 (1994): 89–90.
106. See the editors' discussion in Yadin et al., *Hebrew, Aramaic and Nabatean-Aramaic Papyri,* 134.
107. Ibid., 103.

108. Ibid., 90–107. Note also two studies by Greenfield, “Some Arabic Loanwords in the Aramaic and Nabatean Texts from Naḥal Ḥever,” in *'Al Kanfei Yonah: Collected Studies of Jonas C. Greenfield on Semitic Philology* (ed. Shalom M. Paul, Michael E. Stone, and Avital Pinnock; 2 vols.; Leiden: Brill, 2001), 1:497–508, and “*Kullu nafsin bima kasabat rahina:* The Use of *rhn* in Aramaic and Arabic,” in ibid., 1:453–59.

109. This is particularly so in view of Hezser's strongly worded conclusions: “In practically all areas in which writing was commonly used in antiquity there is much less evidence for Jewish than for Roman society” (*Jewish Literacy,* 500). The statement is true on its face: there is less evidence. But this may mean only that less evidence has survived. Our real task is to reconstruct what once was. Hezser recognized virtually no lay production of texts, whereas this study has argued for a notable amount. Extrapolations therefore end up in significantly different places.

110. We discussed in Chapter 2 reasons to believe that *Mur* 8 was the product of individuals drawing rations from the national grain stores at Herodium, each man or group signing for what was received. No scribe was involved. *Mur* 19 was the writ of divorce that Miriam b. Jonathan received at Masada in 71 C.E. The writer *may* have been her former husband, Joseph b. Naqsan. Milik noted the irregularity of the lines and the great variation in letterforms and sizes, all signs of a nonprofessional writer. He characterized the hand as “peu habile” (DJD 2, 104). Naveh also remarked on the writing, “כתב קורסיבי וולגארי רשלני למדי” (“על חרס וגומא” 89). We discussed the nonprofessional character of *Mur* 21 in Chapter 2 at some length; see the further comment immediately below. The writer was the father of the bride, Lazar b. Joseph, and he wrote only at level 2. Milik observed of the writer of *Mur* 27 that his product was “écriture cursive très irrégulière, d'un *ductus* peu habile et hésitant” (DJD 2, 138): evidently, this was a lay writer. Similarly, he wrote of the “interligne irrégulier” and “lettres maladroitement formées” of *Mur* 34 (DJD 2, 151). As for the remaining texts in the list, we know that the authors wrote concerning their own affairs and were not scribes: John b. Eli of Kephar-Baru, Jacob b. Simon b. Diqna of Yakim, and Judah b. Eleazar Khthousion, late of Mahoza, born in En Gedi.

111. A. Biscardi, “Nuove testimonianze di un papiro arabo-giudaico per la storia del processo provinciale romano,” in *Studi in Onore di Gaetano Scherillo* (ed. A. Biscardi; Milan: Cisalpino-La Goliardica, 1972), 111–52, esp. 140–51.

112. The editors suggested that Judah was mixing up singular forms with plurals, and that is strictly true, judging by the graphic results. But the *reason* for those mistakes is that the words sounded more or less the same because of nasalization.

113. Note Broshi and Qimron, “House Sale Deed” (*P.Hever* 8a), and especially Healey, *Aramaic Inscriptions,* 129–36 (*P.Hever* 8).

114. E.g., at line 6 Jacob wrote דשר, as Yardeni noted (DJD 27, 48), when the word required was רשי, "entitled." The graphic form is meaningless.
115. E.g., at line 10, Lazar produced the form ואתבנכ] (reading with Yardeni, *Textbook,* 1:55), evidently a graphic error for ואהבנכ]. Note, incidentally, that this would be an imperfect of יהב, for which, in the imperfect, formal Judaean Aramaic regularly substituted the verb נתן (suppletion).
116. E.g., Alison Cornish, *Vernacular Translation in Dante's Italy: Illiterate Literature* (Cambridge: Cambridge University Press, 2011), passim.
117. Schürer, *The History* (ed. G. Vermes et al.), 2:26 and 2:28, respectively. Some scholars locate the rise of the Targumim in the period before the Second Revolt. See the discussion in Paul M. Flesher and Bruce Chilton, *The Targums: A Critical Introduction* (Waco, Tex.: Baylor University Press, 2011), 273–74.
118. Daniel Stökl Ben Ezra, "Old Caves and Young Caves: A Statistical Reevaluation of a Qumran Consensus," *DSD* 14 (2007): 315. On pp. 320–21, Ben Ezra concluded that the probability that all these scrolls came from the same collection of manuscripts is less than 1 percent.
119. Pfann, "Reassessing the Judaean Desert Caves," 160.
120. Ibid., 167.
121. Joseph Patrich, "Khirbet Qumran in Light of New Archaeological Explorations in the Qumran Caves," in *Methods of Investigation of the Dead Sea Scrolls and the Khirbet Qumran Site* (ed. Michael O. Wise et al.; New York: New York Academy of Sciences, 1994), 73–95; quotation on p. 77.
122. Pfann, "Reassessing the Judaean Desert Caves," 161.
123. For the publication and description of the phylacteries, see G. Lankester Harding, "Minor Finds," in D. Barthélemy and J. T. Milik, *Qumran Cave 1* (DJD 1; Oxford: Clarendon, 1955), 7; R. de Vaux and J. T. Milik, *Qumran grotte 4.II* (DJD 6; Oxford: Clarendon, 1982), 48–79; M. Baillet, J. T. Milik, and R. de Vaux, *Les "petites grottes" de Qumran* (DJD 3; Oxford: Clarendon, 1962), 149–59 and 174; and Yigael Yadin, *Tefillin from Qumran (X Q Phyl 1–4)* (Jerusalem: Israel Exploration Society and the Shrine of the Book, 1969). Yadin suspected that the phylacteries he published, obtained from the bedouin via an anonymous antiquities dealer, originated in Cave 4; but being uncertain, he designated them as deriving from a Cave X (Yadin, *Tefillin,* 8). Note that the phylactery from Cave 5 was perhaps not such, although Milik argued it was; it contained Psalm 119.
124. David Rothstein, "From Bible to Murabbaʿat: Studies in the Literary, Textual and Scribal Features of Phylacteries and Mezuzot in Ancient Israel and Early Judaism" (Ph.D. diss., University of California–Los Angeles, 1992), 181. See also the comments by Norman Golb, *Who Wrote the Dead Sea Scrolls?* (New York: Touchstone, 1996), 102–4, 351.
125. The numbers in the table derive from Tov, DJD 39, and Tov, *Revised Lists.* The total for Cave 4 is difficult to know precisely, and one might construe Tov's

listings in more than one way; for purposes of comparison, it seemed useful to adopt the figure Ben Ezra gave. The median age listed under paleography is taken from Ben Ezra, "Old Caves and Young Caves," 317.

126. One might perhaps defend the idea that some of these deposits derived from communal institutions, e.g., synagogue collections. Yet, as we saw above, the architecture of Second Temple synagogues argues that no collections were held there. Further, it seems strange to think that many synagogues would hold materials in the various languages and scripts one finds in the majority of the Qumran cave deposits, when presumably many of the members, as ordinary Judaeans, could scarcely comprehend SBH.
127. Nick Veldhuis, "Levels of Literacy," in *The Oxford Handbook of Cuneiform Culture* (ed. Karen Radner and Eleanor Robson; Oxford: Oxford University Press, 2011), 68–89; quotation on p. 82.
128. Elias J. Bickerman, *The Jews in the Greek Age* (Cambridge, Mass.: Harvard University Press, 1988), 51.
129. Wasserstein, "Non-Hellenized Jews," 124. An appendix listed and analyzed many examples of the loanwords Wasserstein had in mind (132–35).
130. Unfortunately, because of the damaged condition of most of the texts in question, this point is difficult to test. If many people were able to sign in Greek, then we would expect that most of the witnesses and *hypographeis* would be related to the principals in the contracts, for reasons explained earlier. If few were related, that would imply that people often had to search outside the family to find Greek writers, meaning that such were relatively scarce. Damage to the contracts makes it impossible to pursue the matter with any confidence; one can say, however, that the surviving data do not support the notion that Greek writers were easy to find in many families. Where lines of relation can be traced, the signers are not usually related to the principals. See the appendices for full accounting of the facts.
131. Tov, DJD 8, 131–42. Technically, the scroll is thought to belong to the *kaige*-Th group.
132. W. F. Smelik, "Language, Locus, and Translation Between the Talmudim," *Journal for the Aramaic Bible* 3 (2001): 199–224, esp. 212–21.
133. *Gen. Rab.* 36:8.
134. *m. Meg.* 1:8. It is possible that the Tanna in question was instead the identically named grandson of our figure. In that case, he belonged to the third generation and was the father of Judah the Prince and so could boast at least equal prestige. The third generation of the Tannaim was the time of Hadrian.
135. See now conveniently Cotton et al., *CIIP,* 53–56.
136. Peter J. Parsons, "The Scripts and Their Date," in Tov, DJD 8, 19–26, and Parsons, "The Palaeography and Date of the Greek Manuscripts," in P. W. Skehan, E. Ulrich, and J. E. Sanderson, eds., *Qumran Cave 4.IV: Palaeo-Hebrew and Greek Biblical Manuscripts* (DJD 9; Oxford: Clarendon, 1992), 7–13.

137. Acts 6:9.
138. A. Salvesen, *Symmachus in the Pentateuch* (Manchester: University of Manchester Press, 1991), passim.
139. *t. Meg.* 3:13 (Zuckermandel). The text is slightly corrupt by haplography. Where it reads near the end אין להם מי שיקרא אחד, 3:12 guides the correction to אין להם מי שיקרא אלא אחד (thus translated).
140. Cf. Plates 1–20 for the Minor Prophets scroll in Tov, DJD 8, and Plates 38–43, 46–47 for the Qumran materials in Skehan, Ulrich, and Sanderson, DJD 9.
141. L. Rahmani, *Catalogue of Jewish Ossuaries,* 13.
142. Lewis, *Documents: Greek Papyri,* 88.
143. Ibid., 83. Cf. Chapter 3.
144. Stanley E. Porter, "The Functional Distribution of Koine Greek in First-Century Palestine," in *Diglossia and Other Topics,* 61. Porter referenced Horrocks, *Greek,* but only very generally, with "*passim.*" In point of fact, his summary of Horrocks's statements did not represent very accurately what that author actually said about historical-grammatical developments; cf. pp. 49, 58–59, 66, 121–22, 124–26, 216–17, 265, and 301.
145. E.g., respectively, line 12, αὐτῷ for αὐτοῦ; line 14–15, ἥμισυ οἰκοιμάτων καὶ . . . ἐνοῦσι for ἥμισυ οἰκοιμάτων καὶ . . . ἐνόντων; line 14, χωρὶς αὐλῆς μικκῆς παλεὰν for χωρὶς αὐλῆς μικκῆς παλαιὰς; lines 22–23, μετὰ τε τελευτῆσαι τοῦ αυτοῦ Ἰουδα for μετὰ τε τελευτῆσαι τὸν αὐτὸν Ἰουδα; and for correct use of the dative, lines 19–20, σὺν εἰσόδοις καὶ ἐξόδοις, etc.
146. Cotton, DJD 27, 206. On p. 207, she translated the text back into Aramaic, proving her point.
147. Thus, ἐν Μαωζὰς, line 3; Σαλώμη . . . Κομαΐση θυγατρὸς . . . χέρειν, lines 3–6; σὺν ὕδατος αὐτῆς for σὺν ὕδατι αὐτοῦ (sc. κῆπος), line 8.
148. τὰ ὑπάρχοντά μοι ἐν Μαωζας, line 8.
149. For the nominative, ἧς γείτωνες ἀνατολῶν κῆπον κυριακὸν καλούμενον Γανναθ Αββαιδαια, lines 9–10; for the genitive, ἥμισυ ἀυλῆς ἀνοιῳγμένον εἰς νότον, line 13; and for the dative, σὺν οἰκοίματα δύο, line 13.
150. Perhaps the most egregious issue with lexicon occurs in *P.Hever* 64:6–7. The scribe was trying to express that the gifting the writ describes was to last in perpetuity, normally expressed in Aramaic by מן יומא דנה ולעלם. Idiomatic Greek, as Cotton showed using Egyptian parallels, would require something like ἀπό τοῦ νῦν εἰς τὸν ἀεὶ χρόνον. Instead, this scribe produced ἀπὸ τῆς σήμερον δόσιν αἰωνίου, essentially a calque on the Aramaic.
151. Lewis, *Documents: Greek Papyri,* 54.
152. On this point, see especially Martin Goodman's comments in his review article, "Babatha's Story."
153. *P.Yadin* 6 is a tenancy agreement composed in Nabataean and dating to the year 119C.E. *P.Yadin* 9 is a Nabataean writ that, though severely damaged, appears to be a waiver. It dates to Year 17 of Provincia Arabia. The continued use of

the native legal language alongside the Roman-sponsored Greek parallels the situation in Judaea, where Aramaic and, to a much lesser degree (apparently), Hebrew continued in legal use long after Rome annexed the province in 6 C.E.

154. Plainly, Germanus was trained in Judaean Aramaic as well as (and before?) in Greek; he translated into Greek the Aramaic subscription that Babeli b. Menahem wrote for Babatha in *P.Yadin* 27. One assumes that his graphic production, so much better than his linguistic, owed much to years of Semitic writing. Also working in two distinct linguistic and script traditions were a certain PN b. Simon (of unknown relationship to the homonymous scribe of *P.Yadin* 19; perhaps the same man?), who composed *P.Yadin* 7 in Judaean Aramaic, and Yohana b. Makhuta, who scribed *P.Yadin* 8 in the Judaean dialect but otherwise wrote in Nabataean. PN b. Simon, according to Yardeni, "was trained in the Nabatean scribal tradition" (Yardeni in Yadin et al., *Hebrew, Aramaic and Nabatean-Aramaic Papyri,* 74). Yet he was Judaean by name and presumably by birth. It is striking that when Yohana b. Makhuta wrote in Judaean Aramaic, he referred to himself using the Judaean equivalent of his Nabataean name, thus "Yohanan" (*P.Yadin* 8:10). Because of the obvious economic advantage attaching to the ability to cater to an all-embracing client pool, the scribes of Mahoza plied their trade as extensively as each one's ability to handle languages and scripts would permit. Hence it appears likely that, as suggested, some of them would move quickly after annexation to acquire Greek as best they could. Judging from their self-styling as *librarii,* at least two of them, Tehinah b. Simon and Germanus, were rewarded with work for local Roman forces.

155. See the studies by Mark Patkowski, "The Sensitive Period for the Acquisition of Syntax in a Second Language," *Language Learning* 30 (1980): 449–72; Jacqueline Johnson and Elissa Newport, "Critical Period Effects in Second Language Learning: The Influence of Maturational State on the Acquisition of English as a Second Language," *Cognitive Psychology* 21 (1989): 60–99; and R. M. DeKeyser, "Beyond Focus on Form: Cognitive Perspectives on Learning and Practicing Second Language Grammar," in *Focus on Form in Classroom Second Language Acquisition* (ed. C. J. Doughty and J. Williams; Cambridge: Cambridge University Press, 1998), 42–63. An excellent summary of the issues is Patsy M. Lightbown and Nina Spada, *How Languages Are Learned* (3rd ed.; Oxford: Oxford University Press, 2006), 67–75.

156. *P.Hever* 6 was originally published with the title "Eschatological Hymn." The scholar responsible for that *editio princeps,* Matthew Morgenstern, explained in a footnote that additional study and input from other scholars had persuaded him that a more proper title would be "Petition for Reconstruction of the Temple." This would certainly be a very appropriate book for Eleazar to be reading in the context of the Second Revolt, the principal aim of which was to rebuild the Temple in Jerusalem. Since the initial publication, significant progress has been made in understanding the text's structure. It is a prayer

consisting of three blessings, the third of which describes the reception of the Law at Sinai and then focuses on the commandment to rebuild the Temple. See DJD 38, 193–200, and in particular Menahem Kister, "נוסחי ברכה ותפילה לאור קטעים ליטורגיים ממדבר יהודה," *Tarbiz* 77 (2008): 331–55.

157. Because the Egyptian epistolary papyri often use the term "brother" as no more than an honorific, we cannot be certain that Hanan was John's biological brother. But the level of informality in the format of *P.Yadin* 57 encourages the possibility.

158. Josephus, *A.J.* 20.263–65 (LCL, trans. Louis H. Feldman, modified).

159. A recent full analysis of the phenomenon of the *recitatio* is E. Valette-Cagnac, *La Lecture à Rome* (Paris: Belin, 1997), passim. Winsbury's chapter on the topic in *Roman Book,* 95–110, also contains many helpful insights. Josephus and his involvement in Roman literary life have recently been a focus of scholarly interest, and two books in particular should be noted as containing numerous important studies: Jonathan Edmondson, Steve Mason, and James Rives, eds., *Flavius Josephus and Flavian Rome* (Oxford: Oxford University Press, 2005), and Joseph Sievers and Gaia Lembi, eds., *Josephus and Jewish History in Flavian Rome and Beyond* (Leiden: Brill, 2005). Specifically helpful for Roman literary life, books, and readers in the period between Vespasian and Trajan is Elaine Fantham, *Roman Literary Culture* (Baltimore: Johns Hopkins University Press, 1996), 183–221.

160. See the comments by Simon Swain, *Hellenism and Empire* (Oxford: Clarendon, 1996), 44–51, 298–329. In general, evidence for provincial pronunciation of Greek and Latin in these years is scant. Note especially the comments of Millar in "Local Cultures in the Roman Empire," 250–52.

161. William A. Johnson, "Introduction," in *Ancient Literacies,* 3.

162. Millar, "Empire, Community and Culture," 147.

163. Yardeni in Yadin et al., *Hebrew, Aramaic and Nabatean-Aramaic Papyri,* 324.

164. Sharp-eyed readers may have noticed that the number of witnesses included in this category is only 156, not the 157 obtained by subtracting the 24 scribes from the total pool of 181. The reason is that one witness was female and so is not counted in considering *male* householders. She was Julia Crispina, who subscribed *P.Yadin* 20 in Greek in a level 3 hand. Tal Ilan has fully investigated this figure and persuasively suggested that she was "the last Herodian princess in Palestine." See her "Julia Crispina, Daughter of Berenicianus, a Herodian Princess in the Babatha Archive: A Case Study in Historical Identification," *JQR* 82 (1992): 361–81 (quotation from p. 370). Ilan further suggested that Julia was involved with life in En Gedi because of the known Herodian ownership of balsam groves there.

165. On this point, see the discussion of *Mur* 8 and *Mur* 24 in Chapter 2.

166. For the prolegomena to such a fact, see Catherine Hezser, *Jewish Slavery in Antiquity* (Oxford: Oxford University Press, 2005), 87.

167. Cressy, "Levels of Illiteracy," 105–24, esp. 107–8.

168. Hanson, "Ancient Illiteracy," 167.
169. Only with the advent of the nineteenth century did female illiteracy cease to be the norm in the West. Thus Martyn Lyons, "New Readers in the Nineteenth Century: Women, Children, Workers," in *A History of Reading in the West* (ed. Guglielmo Cavallo and Roger Chartier; Boston: University of Massachusetts Press, 1999), 313–44.
170. Hanson, "Ancient Illiteracy," 164.
171. Mary Carruthers, *The Book of Memory: A Study of Memory in Medieval Culture* (2nd ed.; Cambridge: Cambridge University Press, 2008), 9–10.
172. Ibid., 12.
173. In addition to Carruthers's book, Jocelyn Small's *Wax Tablets of the Mind: Cognitive Studies of Memory and Literacy in Classical Antiquity* (New York/London: Routledge, 1997) is full of fascinating and helpful analysis and anecdotes regarding memorial culture. Specific to Judaea are Jaffee, *Torah in the Mouth;* Jacob Neusner, *The Memorized Torah* (Chico, Calif.: Scholars Press, 1985); and Birger Gerhardsson, *Memory & Manuscript: Oral Tradition and Written Transmission in Rabbinic Judaism and Early Christianity* (1961; repr., Grand Rapids, Mich.: Eerdmans, 1998). Gerhardsson's work went through a period when it was either ignored or severely criticized for its method, but it has lately been rehabilitated and recognized as profound by some of the very critics who earlier were most severe. See the foreword by Jacob Neusner in the edition cited, pp. xxv–xlvi.
174. Even in modern times this intensive reading has been the experience of many. Abraham Lincoln, to take one famous example, grew up on about a dozen books that stood on his single shelf. He read them so often that a great many of the phrases they contained stayed with him the rest of his life, influencing his thought and shaping the cadences of some of his best-known speeches and writings. See Fred Kaplan, *Lincoln: The Biography of a Reader* (New York: HarperCollins, 2008), 3–29.
175. Sen. *Ep.* 2.3–4.
176. Thus, one does not find in ancient Judaea much in the way of information management systems to assist readers in the retrieval of particular facts or quotations, etc. Even such things as detailed tables of contents were largely unknown, although Pliny's *Historia Naturalis* and Josephus's *Antiquities* were exceptions in this regard. Compilation and summarization were essentially the only devices needed. Accordingly, for example, 4Q339 provides a list of false prophets culled from the scriptures, and 4Q174 similarly a group of passages relating to messianic expectations. 4Q38 contains excerpts from Deut 5, 11, and 32. With expanding literacy and book production later in the history of the West, management systems became necessary; cf. e.g., Roger Chartier, *The Order of Books* (Stanford, Calif.: Stanford University Press, 1994), and Ann M. Blair, *Too Much to Know: Managing Scholarly Information Before the Modern Age* (New Haven, Conn.: Yale University Press, 2010).

177. *Ag. Ap.* 1.38.
178. The most direct insight into this issue may be vouchsafed by the famous letter *P.Oxy.* XVIII 292, describing the efforts of illustrious Alexandrian scholars in the second century C.E. to obtain books known to exist but outside their personal experience. On this papyrus, see most recently Rosalia Hatzilambrou, "*P. Oxy.* XVIII 2192 Revisited," in *Oxyrhynchus: A City and Its Texts,* 282–6.
179. See, e.g., the still useful article by Joseph Fitzmyer, "The Use of Explicit Old Testament Quotations in Qumran Literature and in the New Testament," in *Essays on the Semitic Background of the New Testament* (Missoula, Mont.: Scholars Press, 1971), 3–58.
180. *t. Meg.* 2:5. Tannaitic texts stress as much the written character of scripture as the orality of its nonwritten accompaniment, e.g., *not* reciting Targum from a written text. On the relation of orality to text in rabbinic pedagogy, see Shlomo Naeh, "אומנות הזיכרון מבנים של זיכרון ותבניות של טכסט בספרות חזל," in *Mehqerei Talmud III: Talmudic Studies Dedicated to the Memory of Professor Ephraim E. Urbach* (ed. Yaakov Sussmann and David Rosenthal; Jerusalem: Magnes, 2005), 543–89, and Steven D. Fraade, "Literary Composition and Oral Performance in Early Midrashim," *Oral Tradition* 14 (1999): 33–51; Fraade, "Language Mix and Multilingualism in Ancient Palestine: Literary and Inscriptional Evidence," *Jewish Studies* 48 (2012): 1*–40*.
181. Oral reading predominated even in the medieval scriptorium and particularly in northern Europe was practiced at least until the thirteenth century. Only with vernacular writers in the fourteenth century did authors compose for readers, not listeners. In Britain and France, literate elite audiences continued to prefer public reading to private through the late fifteenth century, in this regard being not unlike the classical elites of the Greco-Roman world, who, as Pliny the Elder, often assigned others to read rather than labor with the text themselves. The literature here is immense; see among many, e.g., Jacqueline Hamesse, "The Scholastic Model of Reading," in *Reading in the West,* 103–19; Paul Saenger, "Reading in the Later Middle Ages," in ibid., 120–48; D. H. Green, *Medieval Listening and Reading: The Primary Reception of German Literature, 800–1300* (Cambridge: Cambridge University Press, 1994); Mark Chinca and Christopher Young, eds., *Orality and Literacy in the Middle Ages* (Turnhout, Belgium: Brepols, 2005); and Joyce Coleman, *Public Reading and the Reading Public in Late Medieval England and France* (Cambridge: Cambridge University Press, 1996).
182. *Ag. Ap.* 1.42.
183. The complexity of language usage uncovered in this study does not easily find expression in terms of models of complementary distribution. Thus such attempts as Watt, "Current Landscape"; Spolsky, "Triglossia and Literacy"; and Michael O. Wise, "Languages of Palestine," in *Dictionary of Jesus and the Gospels* (ed. Joel B. Green and Scott McKnight; Downers Grove, Ill.; InterVarsity, 1992), 434–44, while not without some value, oversimplify the situation.

Index of Subjects

Index of Modern Authors

Index of Ancient Sources

DEAD SEA SCROLLS AND MASADA TEXTS

CLASSICAL TEXTS

BIBLICAL TEXTS

HEBREW BIBLE

NEW TESTAMENT

APOCRYPHA

PSEUDEPIGRAPHIC TEXTS

RABBINIC TEXTS

BAR KOKHBA TEXTS, OTHER PAPYRI, AND OSTRACA